WORD WORKERS
TEACHER RESOURCE BOOK

HUNTER CALDER

ISBN 1 74020 066 7

Pascal Press
PO Box 250
Glebe NSW 2037
(02) 9557 4844
www.pascalpress.com.au

Edited by Fiona Sim
Illustrations by Greg Anderson-Clift
Graphic design and cover design by Sue Hunter
Cover illustration by Luke Jurevicius
Typeset by Modern Art Production Group, Melbourne
Printed in Australia by McPherson's Printing Group

Contents

Preface: A note from Hunter Calder **1**

Introduction **2**
About the author 2
Purpose and approach 2
Before you start 2
Word Workers and the Reading Freedom 2000 program 3
Glossary of terms 4

Chapter 1: What is Word Workers? **7**
A series overview 7
Skills and rules taught in Word Workers: an overview 8
Using Word Workers in the classroom 9
How to use the Word Workers Teacher Resource Book 10
Before using Word Workers 10

Chapter 2: Skills for successful teaching **12**
Phonemic awareness 12
Blending 14
Correcting reading errors 17
Basic sight vocabulary 17
Double letter sounds (consonant digraphs) 19
Long vowel rules 20
The soft 'c' and 'g' 22
Complex double letter sounds (diphthongs) 23
Vowels before 'r' 24
Irregular word patterns 24
Silent letters 24
Compound words 25
Dividing words into syllables 26
Pronouncing long words 30
Structural analysis 30
Pronouncing words with the prefix – base word – suffix pattern 31
Teaching spelling 31
Common prefixes and their meanings 33
Learning tricky suffixes 33
Reading Freedom brain busters 34

Chapter 3: Working with parents 35
What should parents expect? 35
Simplify the subject 35
Getting the environment right 36
Skills parents can teach 36
Common impediments to reading acquisition 37
Correcting reading mistakes 37
Teaching parents to blend words 38
The Neurological Impress Method 39

Chapter 4: Teacher resource materials 41
Using the 'bed' page 41
Using the Word Workers auditory discrimination exercises 41
Using the Word Workers blending chart 41
Using the Word Workers silent 'gh' sound chart 42
Using the suffix sound chart 42
Word Workers charts and exercises 43
Checklists of general and specific symptoms of reading problems 49
Progress charts: Books 1–7 51
Reading Freedom basic sight vocabulary record sheet 58
Word Workers Achievement Test record sheet 59
Word Workers merit certificate 60

Chapter 5: Teaching notes and answer pages 61
The Word Workers Teachers Checklist 62
Book 1 64
Book 2 96
Book 3 156
Book 4 212
Book 5 274
Book 6 334
Book 7 370
Achievement Tests 406

A note from Hunter Calder

The *Reading Freedom 2000 Word Workers* program is written for the teacher who wants to use his or her time and ability effectively when teaching basic reading skills. The students this teacher works with may be six years old or sixty, they may have widely different backgrounds and widely different abilities, but, for this teacher, the goal remains the same: to produce self-reliant readers.

This teacher is a busy professional who has little tim‿ to wade through academic and educational jargon and simply wants a clear, precise and practical program to use in a wide range of professional and classroom settings. Additionally, this teacher wants to be able to enlist the support of parents to ensure that these skills are reinforced in the home environment.

Should these goals and requirements play a big part in your teaching ambitions, then *Word Workers* is the program for you. I wish you well in your work.

Introduction

About the author

Hunter Calder has extensive experience as a reading teacher, consultant, teacher trainer, and lecturer both in Australia and North America. He has a Master of Arts from the University of Sydney and a Master of Education from the University of New South Wales. His many publications include the acclaimed *Reading Freedom* program, as well as numerous articles in professional journals and magazines. Hunter received the International Literacy Year Medal of Merit for the *Reading Freedom* books. He is director of his own private diagnostic learning centre — The Lorn Learning Centre, in Maitland, New South Wales.

Purpose and approach

Word Workers is a carefully structured program specifically designed for early to intermediate level readers. It takes students sequentially through the hierarchy of phonic skills. It is based on contemporary research on the ways students best learn to read.

Phonics teaches students the regularities in letter–sound relationships by exposing them to phonic rules and generalisations that conform to a well-defined hierarchy of skills. Each activity book and each unit of work in *Word Workers* is built upon words or skills students have encountered previously. Students gain confidence in their word attack skills because they are expected to apply their phonic knowledge only to words that are accessible to them. Once students master the regularities and simple generalisations inherent in phonics instruction they are introduced to irregularities and more complex word structures.

Before you start

Teaching someone to read is a big responsibility. The *Word Workers Teacher Resource Book* is designed to make that responsibility much easier for you. Follow the simple procedures and principles outlined here and you will be surprised at how rewarding the experience will be for your students, and how successful you will be in your teaching. Read through this manual carefully before you start.

Students who are acquiring basic reading skills thrive on reliability and consistency. They are the most important factors in teaching anyone to learn to read. Reliability and consistency are exactly what students receive in *Word Workers.* Remind yourself before you start that you are teaching a set of simple skills and, like any skill, reading improves significantly with regular practice. Be sure to explain this to your students.

Now it is time to use *Word Workers.* Teaching students to read is not difficult. Anyone can learn to read, and anyone who can read can teach someone else to read. This means that the phonics method is an ideal vehicle to enable parents and teachers to work together to improve reading.

Word Workers and the Reading Freedom 2000 Program

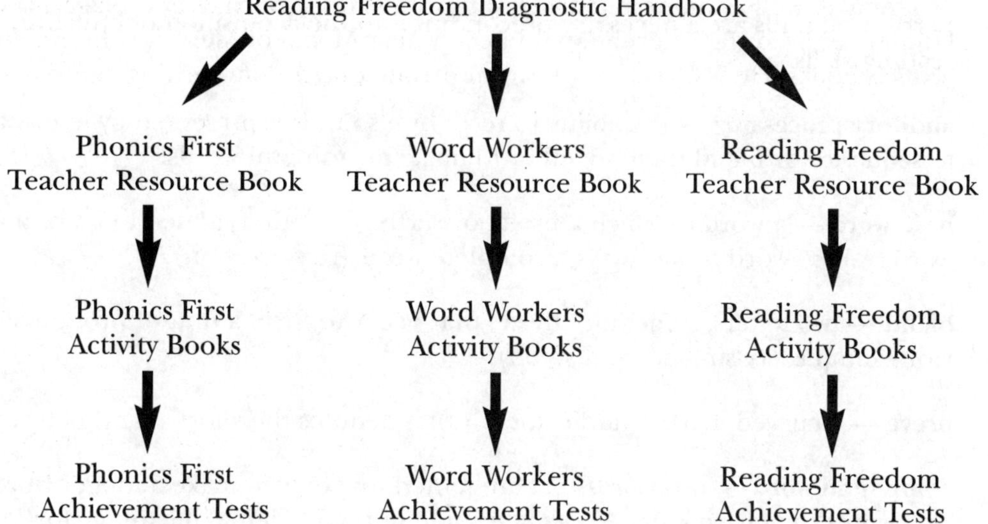

Glossary of terms

attention deficit disorder (ADD or ADHD) — a medically identifiable condition whereby part of the brain is not fully developed. This immaturity can be treated by stimulant medication. Symptoms vary from hyperactive behaviour to disruptive, impulsive behaviour through to quiet inattentiveness. Inability to concentrate effectively can lead to reading difficulties and failure at school.

auditory perception — the ability to hear and distinguish the sound being analysed as distinct from other sounds. A developmental skill that enables children to discriminate individual sounds in spoken words. Good auditory perception skills are a necessary precondition to the acquisition of effective reading skills.

auditory processing — the ability to recognise sounds represented by letters and to sequence or blend them together to make meaningful words.

base word — a word to which a prefix or suffix, or both, is added to make a new word. A base word is *not* always a complete word (re - *cep* - tion).

blend — two letters, sometimes three, that occur to form a unit of pronunciation (for example, st-, str-, -nd, and so on).

breve — a curved mark or indicator (˘) that denotes the short sound of a vowel.

compound word — two words that are joined together to make a longer word. The words that are combined contain some of their original meaning (for example, surfboard, football).

consonants — a group of letters that represent obstructed speech sounds. Although, when the letter 'y' says a long vowel sound, it acts as a vowel (for example, in the word 'happy', the letter 'y' says the long 'e' sound).

consonant digraphs — two consonants that are combined together to represent a single speech sound (for example, sh-, -ng).

contraction — a word that is made when two words are joined together to make a shorter word. An apostrophe (') takes the pleace of the letter or letters left out (for example, let us — let's).

digraphs — a combination of two letters that represents a sound that is not the same sound the letters make when they occur by themselves. Two letters that come together to make a single sound. (See also *vowel* and *consonant.*)

diphthong — two vowel sounds that are joined together to form a compound sound which comes within a single syllable (for example, oi, ow, and so on).

initial position — a letter or letters positioned at the beginning of a word.

macron — a short, straight horizontal mark (¯) placed over a vowel to indicate that it says the long sound.

medial position — a letter or letters positioned in the middle of a word.

multidisciplinary approach — an approach that recognises the need for professional assessment in areas related to reading difficulties, in addition to the purely educational.

phoneme — a single speech sound which is the smallest unit of sound that distinguishes one spoken unit from another (for example, can, man).

phonemic awareness — the understanding that speech is composed of a sequence of individual sounds and the ability to perceive spoken words as such. The ability to analyse and manipulate individual sounds in spoken words is an essential precondition for the acquisition of effective reading skills.

phonetics — a scientific discipline that deals with sound. Alphabetical letters represent the sounds of spoken language in writing. Some letters or combinations of letters may represent several different speech sounds. In a precise phonetic transcription, each symbol represents only one speech sound. The symbols in dictionaries that indicate pronunciation function like phonetic symbols.

phonics — the method of teaching reading that enables students to analyse the association of letters in printed words with the sounds of letters in the spoken words they represent. It is a term that applies to teaching the forty-four speech sounds and the letters represented by them. It develops the skills of recognising sound–symbol relationships and using them to derive meaning from the written word.

polysyllable (multi-syllable) — a word containing two or more syllables.

prefix — a letter or group of letters that is added to the beginning of a base word to form a new word and often changes its meaning (for example, un-happy).

sight vocabulary — a core of words that students must be able to recognise instantly. Basic sight vocabulary words make up approximately two-thirds of all vocabulary in beginning reading books, and one-half of all adult level reading material. The Dolch list is the most widely-known and used list. Reliable knowledge of these words is an essential part of effective reading skills.

structural analysis — a skill that is taught to enable readers to analyse words on the basis of their structure, especially through the recognition of prefixes, base words and suffixes (for instance, un-accept-able).

suffix — a letter or group of letters that are added to the end of a base word to form a new word (for example, happi-ness).

syllable — the smallest part of a word that contains a vowel. Syllables can be an individual word (for example, I, a) or part of a word (for example, hap-pen).

syllabification (syllabication) — a skill that is taught to enable readers to analyse words on the basis of their syllabic structure, using the two word patterns — VCCV and VCV (for example, pro-fes-sor).

terminal position — a letter group of letters positioned at the end of a word.

visual perception — the ability to understand what is seen. A developmental skill that enables children to analyse, organise and interpret what is seen. Good visual perception skills are an essential precondition for the acquisition of reading skills.

vowel digraph — a combination of two vowels that represent a single speech sound (for example, ai, ee, oa, and so on).

vowels — a group of letters that represent unobstructed and free-flowing speech sounds.

whole language — a method of teaching reading that advocates the *holistic* approach. Students learn to recognise words as *wholes,* rely on context, and guess at unknown words. Reading instruction should be indirect and unsystematic so that children learn *naturally.* Direct, systematic and structured teaching of phonics is discouraged.

CHAPTER 1

What is Word Workers?

A series overview

Word Workers is the intermediate level in the *Reading Freedom 2000* program. It is supported and complemented by the *Reading Freedom Diagnostic Handbook* and the *Word Workers Achievement Tests. Word Workers* is intended for beginning readers as well as for primary to early secondary students. It can be used in a school setting or by parents at home.

Word Workers adopts a phonic approach to learning to read. Students learn how to ascribe sounds to letters, and how to apply the regularities in letter–sound relationships by following generalised rules.

Each activity book teaches a specific set of skills. Within the activity books, each successive unit of work focuses on a particular skill or set of letter–sound relationships. The *Teacher Resource Book* provides lesson plans for each book, with suggestions for small group work, numbers of activity pages to be completed, and particular skills to be taught or reinforced. On completing each activity book, student progress can be demonstrated and assessed using the complementary test in the *Word Workers Achievement Tests* book.

The skills taught in each book of *Word Workers* are:

Book 1: Phonemic awareness

Phonemic awareness is the essential precondition for successful reading acquisition. In this book students are taught to discriminate vowel and consonant sounds in words. They are also introduced to the basic sight words needed to work with *Word Workers* Book 2. Simple blending techniques are introduced once students master vowel and consonant sounds. Students expand their phonemic awareness skills to include transitional elements to prepare them for the next stage in their reading acquisition. They are expected to recognise letter–sound relationships and write letters for the sounds they hear. Students are also expected to demonstrate alphabet knowledge as well as to continue to add to their knowledge of basic sight vocabulary. Blending skills are consolidated and refined.

Book 2: Single letter–sound correspondences

Students learn to apply phonemic awareness skills to read simple three-sound words — 'bat', 'hen', 'lock'. Simple and regularly occurring consonant digraphs — 'ck', 'll', 'ss' — are introduced. The activity pages in each unit consolidate the acquisition of these basic reading skills. Blending skills are consolidated and refined as each vowel sound is introduced.

Book 3: Initial and terminal blends

Students learn to read words containing initial and terminal blends — 'nd', 'st', 'cr', and so on. The activity pages consolidate the acquisition of these skills. Initial and terminal blending skills are introduced and practised.

Book 4: Consonant digraphs, long vowel rules, irregular long vowels, soft 'c' and 'g'

Students learn to read words containing these sounds and phonic generalisations. The activity pages consolidate the acquisition of these skills. Blending techniques are used to apply to new skills as they are introduced.

Book 5: Digraphs, diphthongs, vowels before 'r', silent letters

Students learn to read words containing these sounds and phonic generalisations. Blending techniques are used to apply to new skills as they are introduced.

Book 6: Compound words and syllabification

Students learn to read and spell compound words and those with the basic syllabification patterns (VCCV and VCV). They also read multisyllable words.

Book 7: Structural analysis and contractions

Students learn to read and spell words containing common prefixes and suffixes. They also learn to recognise commonly occurring contractions.

Once students complete the *Word Workers* books, they then proceed to *Reading Freedom* which is the senior level. Students who experience difficulty or require consolidation at a particular unit should complete the complementary unit in *Phonics First*.

Skills and rules taught in Word Workers: an overview

A quick overview of the skills and phonic generalisations taught in *Word Workers* and the activity book in which each is to be found is contained below.

Skill	*Activity Book*
Phonemic awareness	Book 1
Basic sight vocabulary	Books 1 and 2
Blending	Predominantly in Books 1–4 (if necessary — all books)
Initial and terminal blends	Book 3
Consonant digraphs	Book 4

Long vowel rules	Book 4
Soft ‘c’ and ‘g’	Book 4
Diphthongs	Book 5
Vowels before ‘r’	Book 5
Irregular word patterns	Book 5
Silent letters	Book 5
Compound words	Book 6
Syllabification	Book 6
Structural analysis	Book 7
Contractions	Book 7

Using Word Workers in the classroom

The *Word Workers Teacher Resource Book* provides a background in the basic teaching skills and techniques necessary to start beginning readers on the path to literacy acquisition. Lesson plans for each activity book are provided in Chapter 5. If you are unfamiliar with any of the teaching techniques in this book, practise before teaching them.

Carefully consider aspects of your classroom management. There is no need to march an entire class uniformly through the program. You may find it helpful to group students on the basis of ability. Students who acquire reading skills easily can work at more advanced stages then those who need reinforcement at a particular stage. This is where professional judgment plays a vital part. Observe students carefully. After a week or two of instruction, those students who can work independently at a higher skill level and those who need more intensive work will be apparent. Teachers can then form reading groups and assign work in the activity books to suit individual abilities. Use the *Reading Freedom Diagnostic Handbook* to assess students having difficulty mastering basic phonics skills. You can then structure lessons to cater for different ability levels.

Teachers will want to consider carefully different aspects of their classroom management — whether to work with a whole class or to group students on the basis of individual ability. The decision is entirely dependent on the professional discretion of the teacher. Some students are ready to read the minute they get to school, others need considerable preliminary work before they acquire their basic reading skills. Teachers can begin a lesson with the whole class by saying the *Reading Freedom* sound charts chorally. The teaching of blending skills is another task that can be demonstrated to the whole class, although students needing intensive help require individual attention or work within the confines of a small group. The teacher can then set activities for small groups based on individual needs. Once these are completed, the lesson can be concluded by reading for pleasure to the whole class from a book selected by the teacher or provided by a student.

The golden rule for teaching phonics successfully is to provide students with lots of opportunities for practice and reinforcement. At all stages in your teaching, be sure to reinforce skills that have been learned until students reliably master the full complement of phonics skills. Lots of praise and a consistent system of reward works wonders, as does enthusiastic and skilful teaching. If these principles and attributes are present in your teaching, you will find the structure and systematic organisation of *Word Workers* a great benefit to the students for whom you are responsible.

How to use the Word Workers Teacher Resource Book

The *Word Workers Teacher Resource Book* has two main purposes. It is a guide for the successful use of the *Word Workers* activity books. It is also a ready resource for teachers who require a concise explanation of the basic techniques of phonics instruction. In view of these objectives, the *Teacher Resource Book* contains two main sections. The first gives a detailed description of the teaching methods in the phonic hierarchy of skills. Also included in this section are hints for working with parents and suggestions on how parents can help their children at home.

The second section provides teaching aids to be applied to classroom work. This section includes page miniatures with answers so teachers can follow student responses and monitor progress on a daily basis. It also contains record sheets for monitoring progress, a chart to record performance within each activity book, blending charts and individual sound charts, as well as a checklist of the symptoms of reading problems.

A thorough reading of the *Teacher Resource Book* will pay long-term instructional dividends. As well as providing an overview of the techniques of effective phonics instruction, it also provides practical suggestions for teaching the units within each book, as well as for the activities contained within each unit. A basic lesson plan format is provided for each book. Before starting a new book or unit, consult the *Teacher Resource Book* for a ready reference on how to present the skills or phonic generalisations that are included. All suggestions and teaching techniques have a proven record of success in the long history of phonics instruction.

Before using Word Workers

Word Workers is a highly versatile series. It is intended principally for students in an infants or primary school setting, but can be used equally effectively with older students who experience difficulty learning to read. The activity books can be used with a whole class or by teachers who want to work with small groups. The fact that each activity book sequentially develops phonic skills and generalisations means teachers can cater for a wide range of ability levels within the confines of a single classroom. Teachers can start lessons with a whole class and then send different groups to work in different books and on different phonic skills. Use the *Teacher Resource Book* to supervise progress.

Teachers who use *Word Workers* as a beginning reading program should adhere to the following guidelines before they start and while they are using it. Careful preparation and knowledge of the subject matter lead to effective instruction and successful students.

Read the *Teacher Resource Book*. Prepare by becoming familiar with the material to be taught and the techniques for teaching it. The *Word Workers Teacher Resource Book* is a comprehensive guide to beginning reading instruction.

Look at the individual activity books to see the skills taught in each book. An important part of the familiarisation process is to look at each book and to learn beforehand what is expected of students and the skills you will teach.

Refresh your knowledge if necessary. Before starting a new book, be sure to refresh your memory on the skills to be taught. If necessary, practise teaching the skills before presenting them to the class or small group.

Use the *Reading Freedom* Sound Charts. Put the *Reading Freedom* Sound Charts in a prominent place in the classroom (use the single and double letter charts as well as the common blend chart). They are an indispensable teaching tool and should be used at the start of every lesson.

Consult the *Reading Freedom Diagnostic Handbook*. If you are aware of students with literacy problems, consult the *Reading Freedom Diagnostic Handbook* for accurate and reliable placement in the most appropriate *Word Workers* activity book.

Become familiar with the *Word Workers Achievement Tests Book*. The achievement tests complement each activity book and are to be used as the books are completed. If you are familiar with the structure and degree of difficulty in each test, you will be able to provide appropriate instruction accordingly.

Look at suggested lesson plans. The *Teacher Resource Book* contains a suggested lesson plan for each activity book. Use the plans as a guideline to your teaching and alter them to suit your style as you become more familiar with the *Word Workers* methods and techniques.

Have attainable expectations of the work to be accomplished in each lesson. Limit work on activity pages to that which is possible in a lesson of approximately twenty minutes. Two or three pages is usually enough. The amount of work and duration of the lesson is subject to the teacher's professional judgment and the ability of the students.

Use the record sheets and progress charts. When activity books or units of work are completed be sure to complete the appropriate record sheet. This gives teachers a quick and reliable overview of class, group, and individual progress.

A word of caution when using *Word Workers*. Students learn when they are ready to learn and no sooner. Do not push them too hard. If you ask them to do something they are not ready for, you will only frustrate them and yourself. Some beginning readers find reading difficult and unpleasant until they learn some basic skills. Keep your lessons short. Twenty minutes to half an hour is plenty to begin with. As students progress, you can extend lesson length if necessary. Be positive and full of praise. Even when your students have a bad day, find something they did well and compliment them on it. Small rewards like gold stars and stickers work wonders and provide the motivation to go on to learn something new.

CHAPTER 2

Skills for successful teaching

Phonemic awareness

Do students know the sounds of the letters?

A major problem for students who have not learned effectively is poor or undeveloped phonemic awareness — the knowledge of the sounds of the letters of the alphabet and how to manipulate them to make words. The single letter–sound relationships are taught first. Beginning readers need these sounds before they can start reading. These sounds are introduced in *Word Workers* Book 1.

Vowels and consonants

Tell students that there are two types of sounds — *vowels* and *consonants.* Write the words 'vowel' and 'consonant' on the board. Point to the words and say, 'this long word says "vowel"'. Have students say the word. Then say, 'this long word says "consonant"', and have them say the word. Then write the vowel letters beside the word 'vowel':

vowels — **a e i o u**
consonants

A major reason for teaching the two types of sounds — 'vowels' and 'consonants' — is to enable students to locate mistakes in words and correct them when they occur. Anomalies like the letter 'y' saying a vowel sound are included later, once students master the regularities of phonics.

Now show students the *Reading Freedom* single letter–sound wall charts or the single letter sounds on pages 1–3 of *Word Workers* Books 1 and 2. Say the sounds of the letters. Have the students repeat the sounds after you, then have them say the sounds together. Then ask each student to say a column or row of sounds until each student has done this. Make choral recitation of the sound charts a habit at the beginning of every lesson. The sounds you are teaching at this stage are *beginning* sounds, except for one — the letter 'x' which says the sound 'ks'. The letter 'x' rarely comes as a beginning sound. For that reason it is taught as an *ending* sound — 'x' as in 'box'.

Students need to be able to do more than learn beginning sounds. They need to learn to discriminate the location of individual sounds in words. For instance, they need to know where the 'b', 'a' and 't' are located in the word 'bat'. There are a number of activities that develop this skill. The easiest and by far the most pleasant way is to play word games. Beginning and ending consonants can be taught and then reinforced using 'I spy'. To make things simple, indicate what you want the students to 'spy' by holding the object in your hand. Pick up a pen and say, 'I spy something that begins with the sound "p"'. Choose a different object and do this with each student until he or she knows the beginning sound reliably. Once beginning sounds are mastered, students work with ending consonants. Pick up a book and say, 'I spy something that ends with the sound "k"'. Once they can identify beginning and ending sounds, alternate between them.

A similar although more formal activity to this is found on page 44 of the *Word Workers Teacher Resource Book.* These activities consolidate knowledge of beginning and ending consonant sounds as well as where to locate vowel sounds. The vowel sounds come at the beginning and middle of the words. Be sure to explain this to your students. Use this page along with 'I spy', and continue it to the end of Book 1. If you practise this regularly, students rapidly gain competence in their knowledge of where sounds are located in words.

The 'bed'

Many students have problems with the letters 'b', 'd' and 'p'. They make reversals (for example 'b' for 'd') and rotations ('p' for 'b'). Sometimes they reverse entire words (for example, 'was' for 'saw', 'no' for 'on'). One way of helping students overcome reversals and rotations is to have them make a 'bed' and keep it handy when they read. A 'bed' page is provided on page 43 of the *Word Workers Teacher Resource Book.* It should also be placed prominently around the classroom so students can refer to it when necessary.

When a student reverses or rotates a letter, say, 'Look at your bed'. The student looks at the 'bed', then looks back at the word and usually makes the appropriate correction. If a student misreads the word 'bed' as 'dad', say, 'Look at the first letter in your bed. What does it say?' The student responds with the sound 'b'. Then say, 'Look at the word. Tell me what the first sound in the word is.' The student will read the word correctly. If after two or three attempts the student remains unable to say the word, read it and have the student repeat it. Never leave a mistake uncorrected.

Photocopy the 'bed' below for students, cut it out, and encourage them to use it while seated at their desks. It is a useful supplement to the 'bed' page provided on page 43.

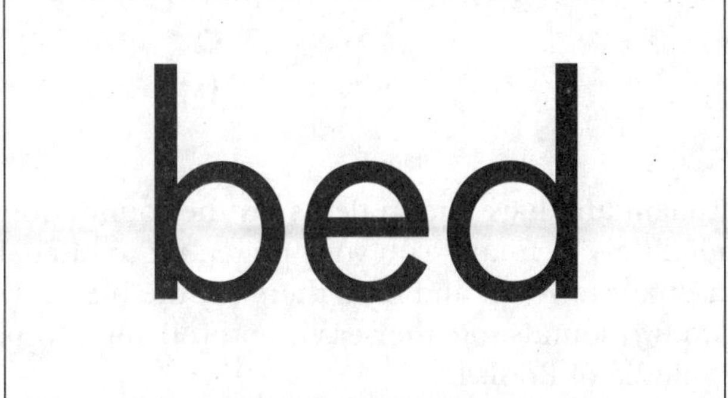

Blending

Of all the skills that prepare a student for learning to read, blending is the most important. Blending is nothing more than putting sounds together to make words — the sounds 'b' - 'a' - 't' combine to make 'bat'. Blending depends on good phonemic awareness — knowledge of beginning, middle and ending sounds. Teaching students to blend sounds into words bridges the gap between getting them ready to learn and actually reading. Students who are quick to learn how to isolate sounds in words should start blending as soon as possible in Book 1. This makes the task of learning to read much easier when they start *Word Workers* Book 2.

It is important to realise from the outset that blending is nothing more than a tool to enable students to develop fluent and accurate word recognition. Once students start reading single letter–sound words in Book 2, they are to *read* the words and not rely solely on *blending* them together. This is a natural progression that develops from the blending techniques students learn as they work through Book 1. In Book 2 blending becomes a device to correct mistakes when they occur, as well as a technique to ensure accurate and fluent reading. The key is to encourage students to read without relying too heavily on blending. With time and regular practice, the transition from blending to reading is achieved smoothly.

Blending skills in Word Workers Book 1: consonant–vowel blends

The first blending skill students learn goes from beginning consonant to the vowel sounds. Start teaching this skill as soon as possible. Most students are ready when they have shown proficiency with 'I spy' and the auditory discrimination exercises on page 44.

Write the vowels on the board in vertical order. Then write a consonant beside them. Demonstrate how blending works. If you are working with a group of students, have them do it with you and in chorus after that. Then go from student to student and make sure each can blend efficiently. A simple way of ensuring success is to ask the student for the beginning sound of his or her first name or surname (if it begins with a consonant) and blend it with the vowels. A blending chart for use in the classroom or for parents to use at home is provided on page 45 of this *Teacher Resource Book*. Practise this skill regularly. Teach it like this:

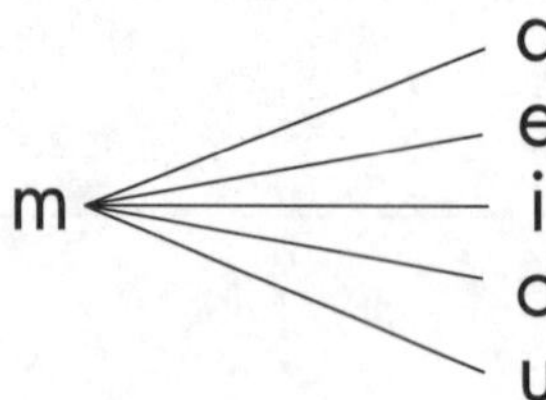

Point to the consonant and have the students say the sound; point to the vowel and have the students say it; finally, run your finger, piece of chalk, or whiteboard marker from consonant to vowel and have them say the blend. Do this until students can blend two sounds together easily and reliably. Most students are able to do this by the middle of Book 1.

In order to enable students to work comfortably with word patterns or word families, they need to blend from vowel to consonant. Write the vowel sounds on the board in vertical order. Then write a consonant beside them on the right-hand side. Demonstrate how this type of blending works.

If you are working with a group of students, have them do it in chorus after demonstrating the technique. Then go from student to student and make sure each of them can blend efficiently.

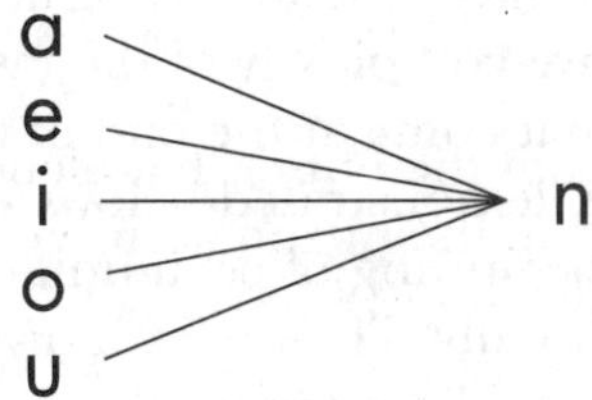

Point to the vowel and have the students say the sound; point to the consonant and have the students say it; finally, run your finger, piece of chalk, or whiteboard marker from vowel to consonant and have them say the blend. Do this until the students blend two sounds together easily and reliably. Once students are proficient at this blending skill (typically toward the end of *Word Workers* Book 1), move on to the next level of blending.

Blending skills in Word Workers Book 2: consonant–word pattern blends

A slightly more complex blending skill must be taught before starting *Word Workers* Book 2. Instead of blending single letter–sounds, students now blend initial consonants with word patterns or word families. The teaching technique is the same, but the skill to be mastered is a little more complex.

Write a common word pattern from Unit 1 in Book 2, for instance, the word pattern 'an'. Beside the word pattern write the consonants that blend with the pattern to make a word. Do this as follows:

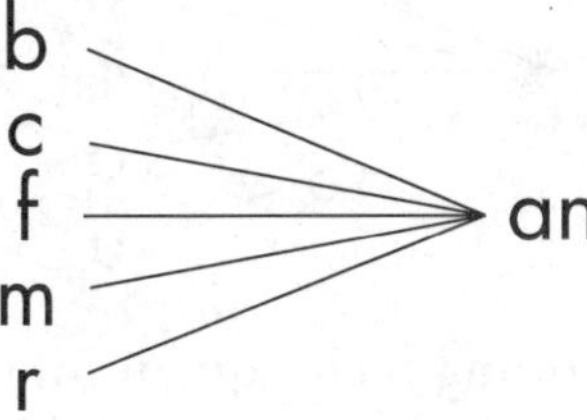

Using the vowel to consonant technique, have the students blend the word pattern 'an'. Now demonstrate the process, going from consonant to word pattern. Next have the students blend the words chorally. Then have individual students blend the words. When starting a new unit, use the most common word patterns to demonstrate the consonant–word pattern blending process. Continue drilling with blending activities until the skill becomes automatic by the end of Book 2.

Blending skills in Word Workers Book 3: initial and terminal blends

Some students may have not fully developed blending skills by the end of *Word Workers* Book 2. The initial and terminal blends they learn in Book 3 can be difficult for them to master. Students practise blending with the new word patterns using the techniques learned earlier.

Teach these blending skills the same way as earlier in the program. The difference at this stage is in the relative complexity of the task. Students learn words with terminal blends (blends that come at the end of a word, for instance, 'nd', 'mp', 'sk'). Using the technique demonstrated below, teach the blends presented on the introductory page at the beginning of each unit of work. Say each blend and make students repeat it chorally. Then have individual students say them. Do this until the blends are recognised automatically.

Write the vowels on the board and then write a terminal blend beside them.

For example:

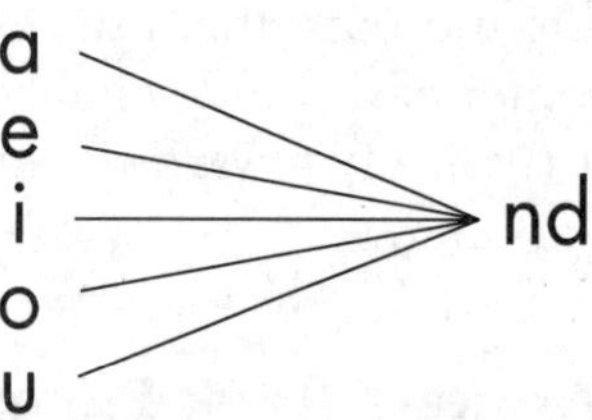

Make sure students can pronounce the blend and then demonstrate the blending process. Have them blend the sounds chorally. Then give each student a different blend to work with. To emphasise the linking process run your finger, piece of chalk, or whiteboard marker from the vowel to the blend. The student says the vowel first, then the blend, and then puts them both together.

Once students learn the terminal blends, they learn initial blends. Teach these the same way as terminal blends. Write an initial blend on the board beside the vowels.

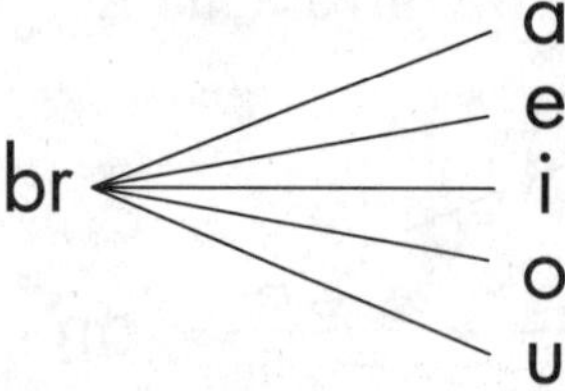

Have students practise the blending technique until you are satisfied each student is proficient at the skill. The development of good blending skills is essential if students are to become effective and competent readers.

Students blend words only when they are learning a new word pattern or when they make a mistake.

Using the Reading Freedom Common Blends Chart

Before starting a unit of work, teach the blends students are to learn carefully and methodically. The introductory page of each unit presents the blends to be learned. Ensure that students are able to repeat them. Say the blend then have students repeat it chorally and then have individual students say each blend. Once they have been learned on the introductory page, students say the blends at the beginning of each lesson using the *Reading Freedom* Common Blends Chart. Continue with this until students complete Book 3.

Correcting reading errors

Take particular care when students make reading mistakes. Be positive about any errors and accept them for what they are. Students do not deliberately set out to misread words. You can turn each mistake into a positive experience if you approach it in the right way.

Because students know the names of the two types of letters — 'vowels' and 'consonants' — it is easy to indicate the place in the word errors occur. For instance, when a student misreads a word like 'truck' as 'track', you can say: 'What is the vowel sound in that word?' The student will look at the vowel and say 'u'. You then say, 'What is that word with a "u" in it?' The student then says 'truck'. Use this technique when students make mistakes with vowels.

When a student adds a letter to a word, for instance, reading 'stand' as 'strand', ask: 'Can you see an "r" sound in that word?' The student looks again and will read it correctly. If students make the same mistake again, have them blend the word. If, after three attempts, the student still misreads the word, say the word and have the student repeat it. Never leave a mistake uncorrected.

You do students no favours by saying 'no', or 'that's not right' when a mistake is made. Students need to know *exactly* where the mistake occurred so it can be corrected. Do this consistently and you will be pleased at how quickly their reading improves. On the other hand, if you do not point out the exact place the mistake occurred, the student is none the wiser. Be calm and patient when mistakes are made, and be sure to praise students after they read the word correctly.

The key to correcting reading errors is to show students the exact place in the words they occur.

Basic sight vocabulary

If vowels are the cement that holds words together, then basic sight words are the cement that holds what we read together. Basic sight words make up one-half of everything literate adults read, and approximately two-thirds of the material beginning readers encounter. If students learn to recognise basic sight words automatically they have more time to work on words that require the use of phonics skills.

There are two sets of basic sight word lists included in *Word Workers.* The first set on page 4 of Book 1 contains the sight words students need to work successfully with Book 2. Have them learn these thoroughly while you teach the phonemic awareness activities in Book 1. The second set of sight words is the *Reading Freedom* basic sight vocabulary lists on pages 5–9 of Book 2. Once students master the earlier lists of sight vocabulary they should be taught the longer *Reading Freedom* lists.

How to teach sight vocabulary

Show students the sight vocabulary lists on page 4 in Book 1. They are to read the words going *down* the lists. Tell them to learn the words by sight, and not to sound them out. Students at this level often take some time mastering the basic sight vocabulary.

As they learn the words list by list, some students are unable to remember more than two or three words at a time. Acknowledge this and reward any signs of progress. Reward them with a gold star for each list or part list learned, and with an extra special sticker when they are all mastered.

Students who have difficulty learning all the words in a list can learn them in groups of three or four words at a time. Occasionally parents and teachers, through misplaced enthusiasm, try to push students through the lists too quickly. Sometimes students are asked to read too many lists at one time. The golden rule is never ask a student to read more than two lists in one lesson. Younger students should read only one list per night.

Students enjoy sight word games. Two that are helpful and motivational when learning basic sight words are 'Snap' and 'Concentration'. Print the words from each list on cardboard cards and away they go! For 'Snap' you need two cards for each word. Students play in pairs and the one who recognises the matching word first says 'Snap' and adds the cards to his or her pile. When all the words are read, the student with the most cards is the winner. 'Concentration' also requires two cards for each word. Students place the cards face down on a table and turn two cards over until the same two words are paired together. The game continues until all the words are paired. The student with the most cards is the winner. Parents find these games enjoyable to play with students at home.

When students make mistakes reading sight vocabulary, correct them gently by saying the word. Make sure students repeat it before continuing. Never leave a mistake uncorrected. Uncorrected reading errors become bad reading habits. Some students have difficulty with certain words. When this happens, make a 'hard word' list on a separate sheet of paper. Include it with the sight words and, after they read a list, have them read their 'hard word' list.

Once the *Word Workers* sight vocabulary is learned, the student can learn List 1 of the *Reading Freedom* basic sight vocabulary on page 5 of Book 2. Continue with the lists until each list is learned. Once you are satisfied students have learned the words, have them read going up the page.

As students move through the lists, there is a tendency to assume the earlier lists are no longer important. The students have learned them, and it is time to move on. *Not true!* When your students move on to a new sight word list, always have them read a list learned previously. This enables students to keep the words current and should be continued until they 'over-learn' the words.

Double letter sounds (consonant digraphs)

In Unit 1 of *Word Workers* Book 4 students learn consonant digraphs. A digraph is two letters that go together to make one sound. The consonant digraphs covered in *Word Workers* are the sounds 'sh' as in 'ship', 'th' as in 'three', 'ch' as in 'chick', 'wh' as in 'wheel', 'qu' as in 'queen' , and 'ng' as in 'king'. Practise saying these sounds before showing students how to say them.

Demonstrate the sounds using the *Reading Freedom* Double Letter Sound Chart or the introductory page for Unit 1, Book 4. Demonstrate the sounds, then students say them together, then each student says the sounds individually.

At this level students often think they are learning something 'harder' and are intimidated by it. A bit of reassurance is needed. Even though the double letter sounds may look difficult, they aren't. Tell the students this is just another skill they need to become good readers. Write the word 'ship' on the board.

ship

Blend through the word and demonstrate that the new sound 'sh' blends together with the other sounds just as they learned earlier.

<u>sh</u>ip

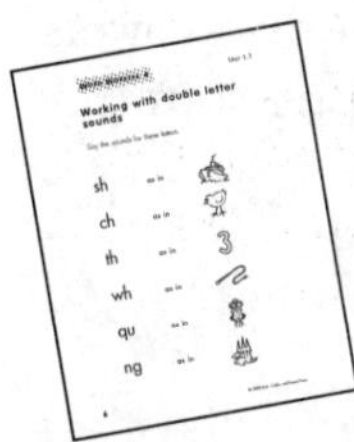

Explain that even though 'ship' has four letters it has only *three* sounds. Dispel any anxiety by explaining that once they know the consonant digraph sounds, words with these sounds are as easy to read as words they know already. Have students blend with consonant digraphs until the unit is completed.

It often helps to photocopy the introductory page of this unit and give it to students to refer to as they read. Follow this practice whenever students learn a new phonics skill. In time, and with regular practice, they are able to say new sounds effortlessly. Add the consonant digraphs to your *Reading Freedom* sound chart drill at the beginning of each lesson. Do this as each new phonic skill is learned so students regularly practise their entire repertoire. This keeps everything fresh and up to date. Remember, you are teaching a set of simple skills which makes reading easy and rewarding. Like any skill, it improves only with regular and consistent practice.

Long vowel rules

Teach these rules well, and you open an important door into reading acquisition. Vowel sounds cause all sorts of problems for students who are learning to read, and they are a serious problem for students with reading difficulties. The reason is that vowels don't always say what they look like they should say. Teach students the long vowel rules and you go a long way to making sense out of something that confuses them.

In Units 2 and 3 of Book 4, the long vowel rules are taught as phonic generalisations so students can expand their word attack skills. Many words containing long vowel sounds do not conform to these generalisations; in *Word Workers* students never encounter irregularities until they master these simple rules. The vocabulary in each unit is carefully controlled so students gradually build their accuracy and confidence. Irregular long vowel words are introduced only when students are skilful readers of words containing regular and consistent phonic generalisations.

Before teaching the rules you must introduce the *long* vowel sounds. Long vowels are the *names* of the letters. Short vowels are those which students learned in Books 1 to 3. Point to the vowels on the *Reading Freedom* Single Letter Sound Chart. Have them tell you the short sound and then the long sound. Do this chorally and then make sure individual students know both the long and short sounds of the vowels. Reinforce this by asking students for the long and short vowel sounds in your drill at the start of each lesson. Tell them that knowing the long sounds of the vowels will help them read many more words than they do now.

The double-vowel rule: 'When two vowels go walking...'

In Unit 2 students learn the 'double vowel rule' — 'when two vowels go walking, the first one does the talking and it says its long sound'. Write these words on the board:

rain
feet
tie
coat
cue

Tell students to listen carefully to the vowel sounds in the words as you read them. Read the words twice. When you finish, ask whether the words have a long or short vowel sound. The students will reply 'long sound'.

Explain that there is a rule to help them read words like these:

When two vowels go walking, the first one does the talking.

Read the words again and draw a horizontal stroke (or macron: ¯) over the first vowel and an oblique stroke through the second as you read them. Emphasise the long sound.

rāi̸n
fēe̸t
tīe̸
cōa̸t
cūe̸

Do this with each word to ensure students understand the rule. Stress the long sound of the vowel as you read the words. Make sure students learn the rule using the rhyme and that they understand it as well as repeat it. Have them recite it at the beginning of each lesson.

Phonic generalisations like 'when two vowels go walking...' and the 'bossy "e" rule' increase the confidence and competence of students while they improve their knowledge of the written word. The structure of *Word Workers* is carefully controlled so students develop accuracy and fluency at each stage of the phonic hierarchy. Students are never asked to read unfamiliar words or those containing word patterns and rules they have not been previously taught. Only later, and after demonstrating mastery of these rules, are students introduced to the irregularities in the language.

Vowel–consonant–final 'e' rule: 'When the bossy "e" comes around...'

The second long vowel rule is the vowel–consonant–final 'e' rule — 'When the bossy "e" comes around the vowel says its long sound'. This is taught in Unit 3. Write these words on the board:

cap
Pet
rip
hop
cub

Tell students to listen to the words as you read them and tell you whether the vowels in the words say their long or short sounds. Read each word twice, carefully and clearly. The students will say they hear a 'short' vowel sound. Now write the letter 'e' beside the words:

cape
Pete
ripe
hope
cube

Read these words twice, carefully and clearly. Ask the students if the vowels in these words say their long sounds or short sounds. They respond by saying 'long sounds'. Tell them there is another rule to tell them when the vowels say their long sounds:

When the bossy 'e' comes around, the vowel says its long sound.

Demonstrate the rule by placing your hand over the final 'e'. Say '"cap" becomes...', take your hand off the 'e' and encourage the students to say...'cape'. Do this with each word until the students learn the rule. Make them memorise the rhyme and repeat it at the beginning of each lesson.

The soft 'c' and 'g'

Explain this rule carefully and it will help students overcome their uncertainty with the sounds made by the letters 'c' and 'g'. Many readers are confused when the letter 'c' says the sound 'k' in words like 'cup' and 'cat', and yet says the sound 's' in words like 'cent' and 'city'. They are equally confused with the letter 'g' in words like 'gulp' and 'game' only to encounter it as the sound 'j' in words like 'gem' and 'gym'.

A simple way to overcome this uncertainty is to develop the following grid for students:

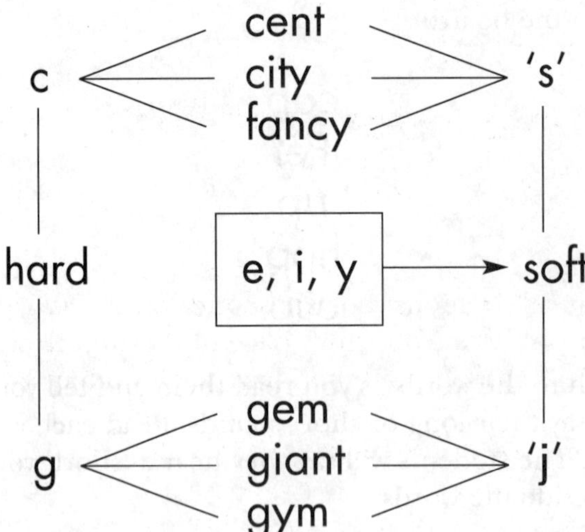

Write the letter 'c' on the board. Ask the student what sound it says. They respond by saying 'c' as in 'cat'. Tell them this is true for many words, but sometimes the letter 'c' says a different sound. Write the words 'cent', 'city' and 'fancy' beside the 'c'. Read the words clearly and carefully, stressing the 's' sound, and ask what sound the 'c' says in these words. The students respond by saying 's'. Now write the letter 's' beside the words. Draw three lines from the 'c' to the words and another three lines from the words to the 's'.

Now write the letter 'g' on the board. Ask the students what sound it says. They respond saying 'g' as in 'goat'. Tell them this is true for most words, but sometimes the letter 'g' says a different sound. Write the words 'gem', 'giant' and 'gym' beside the 'g'. Read the words clearly and carefully, stressing the 'j' sound, and ask what sound the 'g' says in these words. The students respond by saying 'j'. Now write the letter 'j' beside the words. Draw three lines from the 'g' to the words and another three lines from the words to the 'j'.

Tell students the sounds 'c' as in 'cat' and 'g' as in 'goat' are the hard sounds for the letters. When the letters say 's' as in 'cent' and 'j' as in 'gem' they are the soft sounds. Now write the letters 'e', 'i' and 'y' in a box in the middle of the grid. Explain that the 'c' says its soft sound 's' and the 'g' says its soft sound 'j' when they are followed by an 'e', 'i' or 'y'.

Point to the 'c' and 'g' on the *Reading Freedom* wall chart. Ask students for the hard and soft sounds. They respond chorally. Make sure individual students can say both sounds. Then ask when the 'c' and 'g' say their soft sounds. Students respond saying, 'When they are followed by an "e", "i" or a "y". Include this rule with the long vowel rules during the phonics drill at the beginning of each lesson. Careful teaching and lots of practice with words containing the soft 'c' and 'g' sounds will make this relatively easy for your students to learn.

The letters 'c' and 'g' say their soft sounds when they are followed by an 'e', 'i' or 'y'.

Complex double letter sounds (diphthongs)

In Unit 1 of Book 5 students learn the diphthongs 'oo' as in 'book' and 'oo' as in 'moon'; 'ow' as in 'owl' and 'ou' as in 'house'; 'ow' as in 'bowl'; 'oi' as in 'boil' and 'oy' as in 'boy'; 'aw' as in 'saw' and 'au' as in 'sauce'. Demonstrate the sounds on the *Reading Freedom* wall chart or on the introductory page of this unit. Have the students say the sounds chorally and then have each student say them.

Photocopy the introductory page for students to refer to as they read. You may find it necessary to go over the sounds several times before students become comfortable with them. Explain that some different word patterns say the *same* sound (for instance, 'ow' as in 'cow' and 'ou' as in 'house'), while others with the same spelling say *different* sounds (for instance, 'ow' as in 'cow' and 'ow' as in 'snow'). Explain that from now on they must concentrate on their spelling because there are often different word patterns for the same sound. Lots of practice and drill is needed with these sounds if students are to learn them effectively. Incorporate the diphthong sounds into the phonics drill at the start of each lesson.

Vowels before 'r'

In Unit 2 students learn the digraph sounds of the vowels before 'r'. Teach these as you do any other new sounds. Demonstrate the sounds on the wall chart or on the introductory page. Say them yourself, have the students say the sounds chorally, and then individually. Explain that there are only *three* basic sounds to learn ('ar' as in 'star', 'or' as in 'fork', are different, while 'er' as in 'fern', 'ir' as in 'bird', and 'ur' as in 'church' share the same sound), but there are *five* spelling patterns for the sounds. As with the diphthongs, students must concentrate on their spelling because there can be different spelling patterns for the same sound.

Photocopy the introductory page with these sounds for students to refer to as they read. Lots of practice and drill is needed with these sounds if students are to learn them effectively. You may find it necessary to go over the sounds several times before students become comfortable reading them. Incorporate the vowels before 'r' into the phonics drill at the start of each lesson.

Irregular word patterns

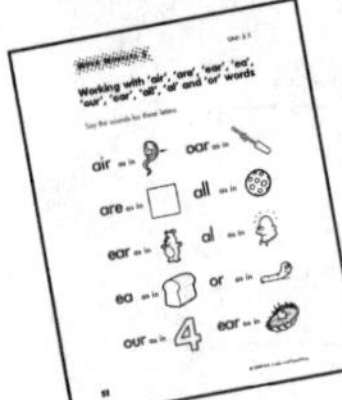

Students encounter these sounds in Unit 3. Teach them as you do any other sounds. Demonstrate them on the sound charts or on the introductory page. Have the students say the sounds chorally and then individually. Photocopy the introductory page with the sounds for students to refer to as they read.

Lots of practice and drill is needed with these sounds if students are to learn them effectively. You may find it necessary to go over the sounds several times before students become comfortable reading them. Incorporate the irregular word patterns into the phonics drill at the start of each lesson.

Silent letters

Prior to Unit 4 every skill students learned taught them a new skill or set of sounds to master. Now students learn that words often contain silent letters. Show students the silent letters on the introductory page. Ask them if they can hear the sounds in the words as you say them. Explain that, while the letters may be included in the spelling pattern of the words, they are not pronounced when we say them. Most of the word patterns are easy to learn.

Write the following words on the board:

bomb
comb
tomb

Say the words for the students. Show them how the same word pattern can say three different sounds: short 'o' in 'bomb', long 'o' in 'comb' and 'oo' as in 'moon' and in 'tomb'. Tell students that you can teach them to recognise silent letters in words, but it is their responsibility to remember how to pronounce individual words once they learn to read them. In practice, as students attain this stage in the phonic hierarchy they often make a distinction in pronunciation using context clues within sentences.

A silent letter pattern that needs attention is 'gh'. An effective way of teaching this is to present the most common word patterns in which the silent 'gh' occurs. Write the following word patterns on the board:

igh — long 'i' sound
eigh — long 'a' sound
ough — 'aw' sound

Tell students the 'igh' pattern in 'high' says the long 'i' sound; the 'eigh' pattern in 'eight' says the long 'a' sound; and the 'ough' pattern in 'brought' says the 'aw' sound. The 'ough' pattern may be pronounced differently by some students. It is not uncommon to hear it pronounced as the 'or' sound or the short 'o' sound. Whatever the pronunciation, students need to learn to apply it to these word patterns. If they bring up irregularities for the 'ough' sound (for example, 'cough' and 'through'), explain that in this unit they are learning regularities and not exceptions to the rule. With regular practice and drill, students are able to master words containing silent letters comfortably.

The wall chart on page 46 of the *Word Workers Teacher Resource Book* is provided for this purpose. Tell students when they are unsure of the correct sound to look at the wall chart and say it. Display the chart prominently in the classroom.

Compound words

At this stage, students are taught to read and spell *compound words.* This is an easy skill to master and an easy skill to teach. Tell them *a compound word is a word made from two smaller words* (for example, 'football', 'inside', 'rainfall'). If students know the meaning of the smaller words, they usually understand the larger word.

Demonstrate the technique for dividing compound words as follows:

1 Write 'Compound Words' on the board and tell students that learning how to divide this kind of word is easy.

2 Now write 'football' on the board and say it, then say it again emphasising the two words that make it a compound word.

football

3 Write the two words that are combined like this:

foot – ball

Ask the students for compound words they know. Write their contributions on the board and demonstrate how they are divided.

Dividing words into syllables

Of all the skills that develop independent readers, this is the most important. The technical term is *syllabification.* It is a simple skill to learn if it is well taught, although it requires lots of practice and reinforcement. The sequence of skills is as follows:

Dividing VCCV words

Here students learn the first of the basic word patterns (vowel-consonant-consonant-vowel) which enables them to divide simple two-syllable words. There are five simple rules to learn.

1 Write the word 'syllable' on the board. Tell students *a syllable is the smallest part of a word that has a vowel in it.* Explain that, when they are dividing words into syllables, they have to look for the *first* vowel.

2 Now write the word 'winter' on the board. Explain that since a syllable is the smallest part of a word that has a vowel in it, they have to look for the first vowel in 'winter'. Ask a student where the first vowel is and write 'v' above the letter 'i'. Then ask another student *what is the next letter, a vowel or a consonant?* Write the letter 'c' above the letter 'n'. Ask another student if the next letter is a vowel or a consonant and write the letter 'c' above the letter 't'. Ask another student the same question for the next letter and then write the letter 'v' above the 'e'. The students do not have to consider the letter 'r' because it is not followed by a vowel. What you have written on the board will look like this:

```
 V C C V
wi n t e r
```

Tell students *words that have the VCCV pattern are divided between the two consonants.* Write it on the board like this:

VC | CV

Ask students *between which two letters should the word be divided?* (obtain the letter *names*), and write it on the board like this:

```
 VC | CV
win | ter
```

3 Next, write the word 'happy' on the board.

Ask a student where the first vowel is and then go through the word until you reach the letter 'y'. Tell students to look at the letter 'y' and ask if it says a *vowel* or a *consonant* sound. Emphasise the long 'e' sound when you say the word. Once they understand that the letter 'y' says the long 'e' sound, tell them *when the letter 'y' says a vowel sound it counts as a vowel.*

Divide it like this:

VC | CV
hap | py

4 Next, write 'umpire' on the board. Tell students that a word cannot have more syllables than it has vowel sounds. Go from student to student placing 'v' or 'c' above the vowels and consonants. Say the word again and ask them if they can hear the final 'e' in 'umpire'. Tell them *when a word ends with a silent final 'e' it does not count as a vowel.* Show them it is divided like this:

VC | CV
um | pire

5 Write the word 'merchant' on the board. Go from student to student and write the letters 'v' or 'c' above the vowels and consonants. When you get to the double letter sound 'ch', pause and ask if the 'c' and 'h' come together to say *one* or *two* sounds. Obtain the answer 'one' and tell them *when two letters come together to say one sound, they are counted as one letter.* Divide it like this:

VC | C V
mer | chant

When dividing words, students use dashes (–) between the two syllables rather than vertical or oblique lines (/). These can look like letters and cause confusion when the words are read. Students divide the words like this:

ap – pear

Dividing VCV words

At this stage students learn the second basic word pattern (vowel-consonant-vowel) for dividing two-syllable words. The same rules apply here as they do for VCCV words.

1 Remind students that *a syllable is the smallest part of a word that contains a vowel.* Remind them also that a VCCV word is divided between the two consonants and write the pattern on the board. Now tell students they are going to learn a new pattern for dividing words into syllables.

2 Write the word 'oval' on the board. Ask a student to find the first vowel and then go through the word writing 'v' or 'c' above the vowels and consonants. What you have written on the board will look like this:

V C V
o v a l

Tell them words *that have the VCV pattern are divided between the first vowel and the consonant.* Write it like this:

V – CV

Ask a student which two letters the word should be divided between (obtain the letter names) and write it like this:

V | CV
o | val

3 Next write the word 'navy' on the board. Ask a student where the first vowel is and then go through the word until you reach the letter 'y'. Say the word and ask whether the letter 'y' says a *vowel* or *consonant* sound. Emphasise the long 'e' sound when you say the word. Once students understand that the letter 'y' says the long 'e' sound, tell them *when the letter 'y' says a vowel sound it counts as a vowel.* Divide it as follows:

V | CV
na | vy

4 Next, write 'polite' on the board. Explain that a word cannot have more syllables than it has vowel *sounds.* Go through the word placing 'v' or 'c' above the vowels and consonants. Say the word again and ask if they can hear the final 'e' in 'polite'. Tell students *when a word ends with a silent final 'e' it does not sound as a vowel.* Divide it like this:

V | C V
po | l i t e

5 Now write the word 'siphon' on the board. Go through the word and write the letters 'v' and 'c' over the vowels and consonants. When you get to the 'ph', pause and ask if the letters 'ph' say one or two sounds. Obtain the answer 'one', and tell students *when two letters come together to say one sound, they are counted as one letter.* Divide it like this:

si | phon

A hint for pronouncing VCV words is to tell the students that the first vowel in words with this pattern often says its long sound. When dividing words, students use dashes. Students divide the words like this:

si | lent

Dividing 'le' ending words

At this stage, students learn another commonly occurring word pattern: words that end in 'le'. The same rules apply here as they did earlier.

1 Write the word 'stumble' on the board. Tell them words that have 'le' endings are divided by joining the consonant to the 'le' to make the second syllable. Divide it as follows:

stum | ble

Explain that the 'le' ending is pronounced using the sound the letter 'l' says in 'lamp'.

2 Write the word 'table' on the board. Tell students when the first syllable ends with a vowel, the vowel usually says its long sound:

ta | ble

3 Write the words 'eagle' and 'chuckle' on the board. Tell students *when two letters go together to say one sound they are counted as one letter.* Show them the words are divided as follows:

ea | gle
chu | ckle

4 Write the word 'whistle' on the board. Tell students when *the 'le' ending has a silent letter before it, divide the word the same way as other 'le' ending words.*

whis | tle

Reinforce the syllabification rules by having students repeat them when they go through the *Reading Freedom* sound charts at the beginning of each lesson.

Dividing long words

Students now combine all the syllabification skills to read and spell words containing three syllables. Explain that while the words may look difficult, they are easy if the students use the rules they have learned.

1 Write the two syllabification patterns on the board — VCCV and VCV — and go over the basic rules. Tell students when dividing long words they use the two patterns and remember the rules.

2 Write the word 'professor' on the board. Ask them to look for the first vowel. Go through the word writing 'v' or 'c' over the vowels and consonants. What you write on the board will look like this:

V C V C C V
p r o f e s s o r

Ask the students how 'professor' should be divided. What they tell you will look like this:

pro – fes – sor

The key to understanding the technique of dividing long words is that the *last* vowel of the first word pattern becomes the *first* vowel of the next word pattern. Give further examples on the board until students can confidently divide long words.

For example:

V C C V C V
h i s t o r y

becomes

his – to – ry

Another example:

V C V C V
e d u c a t e

becomes

e – du – cate

A helpful hint when teaching this is to have students divide several words and show them to you. That way you can be sure each student is applying the skills properly before he or she finds they have done an entire page incorrectly.

Pronouncing long words

Many students divide words perfectly, but are unable to pronounce them. At this stage in their reading development, many students read and use words without pronouncing them correctly. Be positive when this happens. It is not a *reading* error, it is a *pronunciation* error. Students often need to be taught a word's customary pronunciation. If they read a word correctly, but mispronounce it, reassure them and say 'You have *read* that word correctly, but this is how it is usually *pronounced*'. Make sure the students say each word after you tell them its correct pronunciation. Encourage students to use a dictionary or ask teachers or parents if they are unsure of a word's correct pronunciation.

Structural analysis

At this stage the students learn another, and often simpler, way of reading long words. This method asks students to analyse a word's structure and divide it into its *prefix – base word – suffix* pattern. Tell students *a prefix is a part of the word that comes at the beginning to change the word's meaning. A suffix is the part of a word that comes at the end to change the way a word works in a sentence.* Write the word 'unripeness' on the board:

unripeness

Draw a single line under the prefix 'un'. Show the students how it changes the meaning of the word from 'ripeness' to 'unripeness'. Next draw two lines under the suffix.

unripeness

Tell students that the part of the word that is not underlined is called the *base word.* Explain that prefixes and suffixes are pronounced the same way in most words and, if they know how to pronounce them, all they have to do is concentrate on sounding out the base word.

Some students have difficulty with the idea of a base word because in many words the base word is not a complete word. If students are to master the skill of structural analysis and divide long words competently, they must understand the base word is not always a complete word. Write the following words on the board:

unfitness — unfitness
exception — exception

Explain that, in 'unfitness', the base word is a complete word by itself. Then show students that, in the word 'exception', the base word 'cep' is not a complete word. Tell them *a base word is not always a complete word.*

Many students balk at unknown words because of their length. A practical hint when this happens is to encourage them to place a thumb or finger over the prefix and the suffix and sound out the base word. They then add on the prefix and suffix and read the word correctly. This technique is especially helpful when students encounter words with which they are unfamiliar. It is not used with every word.

Pronouncing words with the prefix – base word – suffix pattern

Students who are able to recognise prefixes and suffixes and understand how they function in words are able, with practice, to read long and complex words without difficulty. While many students divide words perfectly, they cannot pronounce them. Many of the words they encounter are completely unknown to them. Be positive when this happens. It is not a *reading* error, it is a *pronunciation* error. Students often need to be taught a word's customary pronunciation. If they read a word correctly but mispronounce it, reassure them and say, 'You have *read* that word correctly, but this is how it is usually *pronounced*'. Encourage them to use a dictionary or ask teachers or parents if they are unsure of a word's correct pronunciation.

Teaching spelling

The development of effective spelling skills is a cornerstone of the *Reading Freedom 2000* program. Remember to *teach* spelling rather than simply test it. The ability to spell words depends on the ability to read them accurately. Spelling accuracy usually lags behind reading development, but is no less dependent on learning basic phonics skills. The key to teaching students to spell is *never* to ask anything of them that is beyond their reading ability. If students can read words using a particular skill, they can learn to spell them. A simple rule of thumb is to expect students to spell words at their present stage of phonics knowledge but no more.

Good spellers are made and not born. Teaching spelling develops with regular practice and reinforcement. Give lots of spelling practice as students learn new skills. Make the process as positive as possible. Poor spellers need patient and careful teaching if they are to succeed. Teach them to do the little things well — like learning basic phonic skills — until they can do the big things well — like read and spell long and complex words.

Be regular and consistent in spelling practice, and be systematic in its application. Make the process as easy as possible. When asking students to spell a word like 'difficult', say it *three* times. Twice by itself and once in context — '*difficult*' ... 'Learning to spell is not *difficult*' ... '*difficult*'. Encourage students to say the word syllable-by-syllable — *dif - fi - cult.* In time they do this by themselves. But while they are still learning to *spell* — *teach* them, don't test them!

Spelling games

A way of reinforcing the acquisition of spelling skills is through enjoyable activities. A time-honoured way of improving spelling ability is the 'spelling bee'. Divide the group or class into teams; the number of teams depends on the size of the group or class. A student from each team spells a word. Keep track of the 'score'. The team with the most words spelled correctly is the winner.

One variation is to give 'bonus points'. When a student spells a word incorrectly, a student on the other team has the opportunity to spell the word as a bonus point, and then spells another word. Never allow a spelling mistake to go uncorrected. Played in good spirit, spelling bees are an enjoyable and educationally profitable way of developing accurate spelling habits in students. If used properly, spelling bees ensure that students enjoy what they are doing and respond to the challenge positively.

The improvement of spelling skills does not have to end with the phonic skill being taught. It is important to promote the spelling of basic sight vocabulary words. Sight words like those in *Reading Freedom* sight vocabulary should be used to improve a student's spelling of commonly used words. Once students are capable of spelling words containing the skills they have learned and are competent with basic sight words, you can expand the horizon gently. You may want to incorporate the spelling of local place names, states and major cities. Be selective in the words you ask some students to spell. Give inefficient spellers easier words than other students. The key to the improvement of spelling is worth repeating again — *teach it, don't test it!*

Common prefixes and their meanings

In *Word Workers* Book 7 students learn to recognise the most common prefixes. They learn the basic rule that a prefix is a part of the word that comes at the beginning to change the word's meaning. Here is a list of the prefixes taught in Book 7 and their meanings.

Prefix	Meaning	Example
ex	out, from	export
un	not, opposite	unlike
re	back, again	return
de	down, from, away	depress
com	with, together	combine
en	in, into, make	enclose
in	not, out	insane
con	with, together	connect
be	about, around, all over	beside
pre	before	prefix
pro	for, onward	propose
di	twice, double	divide
ad	direction, tendency, addition	advance
dis	opposite	dislike

Learning tricky suffixes

Teaching structural analysis skills is a simple procedure, but there is a way of making it even simpler. The suffix 'tion' often causes difficulty. Explain that the suffix 'tion' is pronounced 'shun' and, when it has an 'a' with it, pronounce it 'ashun' (emphasise the long 'a'); when it has an 'i' with it, pronounce it 'ishun' (emphasise the short 'i'); and when it has a 'u' with it, pronounce it 'ushun' (emphasise the long 'u'). Another suffix that can prove difficult is the 'ous' suffix. Explain that it is pronounced just like the word 'us'. This simple approach can help students overcome their confusion with these suffixes and make your teaching much more effective.

Use the suffix wall chart provided on page 47 of the *Word Workers Teacher Resource Book* and incorporate it when you go through the sound charts and the phonic rules. Display the suffix chart prominently on the wall so students can refer to it when reading words that contain the 'ation', 'ition', 'ution' and 'ous' suffixes.

-tion – shun
-ation – āshun
-ition – ishun
-ution – ūshun
-ous – us

Reading Freedom brain busters

Once you teach your students a skill, it is important to keep it current by regular drill. The *Reading Freedom* brain busters (on page 48 of this book) are designed to do just this. The questions should be introduced as they are learned. Add to them as each new skill is taught. Use this simple quiz at the beginning of your lessons as you move through the upper levels of the phonic hierarchy.

CHAPTER 3

Working with parents

Apart from their own dedication and professional expertise, the greatest asset teachers of reading have is the parents of students. A committed parent is an invaluable teaching aid, although they need careful guidance to become effective. This section of the *Word Workers Teacher Resource Book* offers suggestions about how parents can help at home.

Many parents are not sure what children should achieve as they progress through the stages of reading acquisition. They want them to read of course, but when should they show signs of progress? For that matter, what are the signs of progress? One of the key responsibilities of the reading teacher is to explain to parents what they can realistically expect of children in the beginning school years.

What should parents expect?

Explain carefully to parents your expectations of their child's reading acquisition. For successful reading acquisition to occur, there are a set number of criteria to expect of students halfway through Kindergarten or early Year 1. The rule of thumb is this: students should know the names of the letters of the alphabet, the sounds they make, and some simple sight words. They should have some idea of phonemic awareness skills and possibly be attempting to blend sounds together to read simple words. If your students cannot do these things halfway through Kindergarten, you have good reason to be concerned.

Parents of older students with reading problems expect them to receive special treatment to overcome the difficulty. Typically, these students will have some reading skills that are not sufficient to enable them to read independently. The *Reading Freedom Diagnostic Handbook* enables teachers to assess precisely a student's reading difficulty. The teacher's task is to diagnose areas of weakness in students, prescribe a program of correction and explain to parents how they can help at home. Parents who are concerned about their children should have the problems identified and be given practical suggestions about working at home to assist in correcting the problem.

Simplify the subject

Parents tend to regard learning to read as a mystery that is best left to professionals. You cannot emphasise enough that reading is a skill to be learnt like any other. Explain that there is no mystery in learning to read or in teaching it. For many parents there is often little system discernible in the process of reading instruction.

Reassure parents that some students learn more quickly than others, and that some students are ready to learn to read earlier than others. Parents expect to see their children steadily acquiring reading skills. The job of the professional educator is to explain that reading acquisition is a developmental process which relies upon a series of interrelated factors. Communicate any concerns when students do not progress satisfactorily. They need to know the factors that impede a student's progress. If they know what to look for, they can help you nip reading problems in the bud. The checklists of general and specific symptoms of reading problems on pages 49 and 50 of the *Word Workers Teacher Resource Book* should be completed by teachers as well as parents of students with reading difficulties.

Getting the environment right

A well established home environment is critical to success. Tell parents about the importance of establishing a routine and list some basic study skills. The place used for working with children must be well lit and well heated or cooled, depending on the season. Keep distractions to an absolute minimum — no televisions, telephones, stereos or video games within earshot. Keep brothers or sisters out of the way for the duration of the lesson. It is hard enough to get children to sit down and read without the added burden of unnecessary interruptions. Do not prolong the experience. Home lessons should not exceed thirty minutes, in fact twenty minutes is about enough. Encourage parents to conduct reading sessions in a warm and positive atmosphere. If their child has done something during the day that requires immediate punishment, delay it until the lesson is over. It is almost impossible to work constructively with a child who suffers from bruised feelings.

Skills parents can teach

Once learning to read is demystified, parents can help teachers develop the preconditions beginning readers need. The first precondition is to develop good phonemic awareness skills. Students must be taught the sounds letters make and be shown how to isolate them in words — to be able to tell where the 'b', 'a' and 't' come in 'bat'. Students must also be taught to manipulate or sequence sounds together to make words.

Parents can reinforce phonemic awareness at home by playing the game 'I spy' with children. Explain that they are to hold the object to be 'spied' in their hand; for instance, a book or a pen. Tell parents to start with beginning sounds — 'I spy something beginning with...'. Once students can discriminate beginning sounds reliably, parents can ask the student for ending sounds — 'I spy something ending with....'. Rhyming activities are also helpful to improve knowledge of how sounds work in words. Tell parents to give students pairs of words and ask whether or not they rhyme — 'Do "big" and "dig" rhyme?' 'Do "run" and "dog" rhyme?'

Book 1 of *Word Workers* is devoted exclusively to the development of phonemic awareness skills. Used positively, and in conjunction with the auditory perception exercises and blending chart on pages 44 and 45 of this *Teacher Resource Book*, students gradually develop phonemic awareness skills. Some, of course, take longer than others. Explain this to parents and encourage them to help their child by using these simple techniques at home.

Parents can also help children acquire basic sight vocabulary. Tell them that knowledge of basic sight vocabulary is an essential building block in the acquisition of reading skills. Words like 'and', 'are', 'can', 'come', and so on, occur over and over in the books young readers encounter. So much so, that nearly two-thirds of the material read by beginning readers is made up of basic sight vocabulary. Parents can help to teach the *Word Workers* sight vocabulary and the *Reading Freedom* basic sight vocabulary at home using games like 'Snap' and 'Concentration'. Show them how to use the sight vocabulary teaching techniques explained on pages 18 and 19 and encourage them to incorporate the techniques in their children's homework.

Common impediments to reading acquisition

Many students have poor visual perception skills. They have difficulty organising what they see effectively. Many students reverse letters, numbers, or whole words — reading 'b' for 'd' or 'was' for 'saw'. This can persist well into the primary years. Students who are unsure of the letters or words they see on a page, or who strain to see clearly, may have difficulties developing accurate reading skills. Tell parents when you suspect that a student has a vision problem, and recommend they have their child assessed by an eye-care practitioner.

Many students are unable to concentrate long enough to benefit from reading instruction. These students may suffer from attention deficit disorder. This medically identifiable condition affects a significant number of children. If you suspect a student suffers from one of the forms of ADD, contact the parents and recommend that their family doctor refers them to a pediatrician or pediatric neurologist. The *Reading Freedom Diagnostic Handbook* has checklists of the symptoms of vision problems and attention deficit disorder. Ask parents to help by filling these in.

Correcting reading mistakes

One of the keys to developing reading skills is to correct reading mistakes constructively and positively. Few parents know how to do this effectively. Indeed, for many, helping children to read at home often becomes an ordeal. There is no need for children to feel inadequate if they make mistakes when parents 'help' them read; not if parents are shown the techniques to use at home while listening to their children read.

Some students do not acquire reading skills as readily as their peers. Explain to parents that their children are normal children, just like the others at their school. Even the brightest of children regularly make mistakes when they read. It is not that their child lacks intelligence. It is not that they don't try. Many students with reading problems are intelligent and try desperately hard to read. It's just that no matter what they do, the acquisition of simple reading skills escapes them. Tell parents that, when helping, the first thing they have to do is take a step back and look carefully at the way they are trying to help.

Parents need to be shown productive ways of helping. The first thing to work on is any negative attitudes to reading mistakes. Explain that exasperation shown when mistakes occur is counterproductive and often exacerbates the problem. Tell them to confront reading errors systematically and logically. Assure parents that knowing *how* to correct reading errors allows them to be calm and effective when helping their children. If they communicate a positive approach, home reading sessions will be smooth and productive.

Be sure parents and students know the two types of letters — *vowels* (a, e, i, o and u) and *consonants.* They need to know this to work efficiently with sounds in words. Show them an effective technique to use when students make mistakes. If the child misreads a vowel sound, for instance, 'bad' as 'bud', say 'What is the vowel in that word?' The child looks at the vowel and says 'a'. Then say 'Now put the "a" in the word.' The student then says 'bad'. When the child adds a letter (for instance, reading 'stand' as 'strand') ask, 'Is there an "r" sound in that word?' If a letter is omitted (for instance, reading 'strand' as 'stand') ask your child if there is an 'r' in the word. The child will look again and read it correctly. If the child still has trouble, *blend* the word. If it is still incorrect after three attempts, say the word and have the child repeat it. Never leave a mistake uncorrected.

Children are so anxious to please they will use any device to gain the approval of the listener. They guess words by their shape or within the context of the sentence. This technique may be useful for more advanced readers but is not useful at the earliest stage of reading acquisition. Whatever the cause of the mistake, emphasise to parents that their response to reading errors is critical to their child's continued progress and self-confidence.

Tell parents that the key to correcting a reading error is to isolate the *exact* place in the word it occurs. They do children no favours by saying 'no', or 'that's not right', or 'try again' when they make mistakes. They need to know *where* mistakes are made if they are to correct them. If parents fail to point out the exact place in a word where the mistake occurred, children are none the wiser and cannot make the appropriate correction.

Although showing parents how to correct reading mistakes takes a few minutes, the rewards are worth the time: a consistent and supportive home environment is invaluable to productive lessons at school.

Teaching parents to blend words

Sounding out words, or *blending,* is a difficult task for some children — much more difficult than it appears to literate adults. Very few parents have any idea how to make blending simple and productive for their children. Teachers can show parents the blending techniques described on pages 14–17, then show them how to develop this skill at home by using the blending chart on page 45. Two or three minutes work on the skill each night is adequate.

Show parents that blending techniques have two uses: they develop reading accuracy and fluency and they are an effective way of correcting reading errors. When a mistake occurs, tell parents to isolate the mistake in the word. If, after two or three attempts, the child is still unable to read the word correctly, tell them to have the child blend the word. If the student is still unable to read the word correctly, the parent reads the word and has the student repeat it. Be sure parents understand that blending, like any other skill, is learned and perfected with lots of practice. This simple skill makes reading easier for children when they make mistakes, and it allows parents to be positive and constructive at home.

The Neurological Impress Method

Parents can improve a child's accuracy and fluency by using an effective technique called the *Neurological Impress Method.* The Neurological Impress Method or NIM, is an imposing name for a simple teaching technique to improve reading skills. The NIM is a multisensory approach involving a student's sight, hearing and speech. It is best carried out on a one-to-one basis, and, for this reason, it is a useful tool in the home. The procedure is straightforward. Parent and child read aloud together at home ten minutes a day, five or six times a week. Once they reach a total of four hours, a significant improvement in reading should be apparent. Learning to use the NIM is relatively painless and involves no special training. Parents need patience and tolerance, and a mutual commitment between themselves and their children to persist with the method for at least four hours and, preferably, for eight to twelve hours.

Starting up

If possible, demonstrate the technique to parents before they attempt it at home. Sit the student beside you at your right, three to six inches in front so your voice is close to the student's ear — almost speaking into it. Then, together, you read aloud from the book while your finger points *exactly* to the words as they read. Move your finger simultaneously with your voice, so the child's eyes follow each word as they see, hear, and speak it. The child's reading will follow the pattern of what is read, so read slowly and clearly, and with rhythm and emphasis. Do not correct mistakes as they occur.

To start with, children may read as much as a word behind the parent's voice. With practice, they should soon keep up. If a child cannot keep up, tell parents to slow their rate of reading, and encourage the child to keep going and to forget about mistakes. The aim is to promote fluency of reading and train the eyes to move freely across the page. The NIM is not a comprehension exercise so parents do not question the child about what has been read.

Helpful hints

Successful use of the NIM depends upon the conditions being right. Keep distractions to an absolute minimum. Regular work habits are essential, as is the need to conduct each ten minute session in a pleasant, non-threatening manner. The method demands a high degree of concentration on the part of the child so parents should never extend the session beyond ten minutes.

Parents should not be afraid of exposing children to difficult words in the passage. In any ten minute session, it is possible for the child to encounter upwards of 1500 words. Too little exposure to difficult words is worse than too much. As far as possible parents should match what they are reading to their child's level of reading ability, or slightly below it. An easy way is to let the child choose the material. A glance through the pages should give parents an idea of the complexity of its vocabulary. If they are uncertain, encourage them to ask your professional opinion.

Be sure to emphasise to parents that, helpful as it is, the NIM is not a substitute for direct reading instruction. Caution them that they are not to expect too much; students with reading difficulties require systematic teaching of basic reading skills, and the *Neurological Impress Method* is a useful way of complementing the systematic phonics instruction students receive in *Word Workers.*

Using the NIM

- Regular ten minute sessions.
- Select suitable reading material.
- Sit the child to parent's right, three to six inches in front of him or her.
- Parent's finger synchronises with word and voice.
- Practise before starting.
- Use the NIM for eight to twelve hours.
- Maintain a positive attitude.
- Have realistic expectations.

CHAPTER 4

Teacher resource materials

The material in this section can be photocopied for use with your class.

Using the 'bed' page

Make a copy of this page (see page 43 of this book) and display it prominently in the classroom. Students can overcome reversal and rotation problems with letters by referring to the wall chart during the lesson. When a student makes a mistake; for instance, reading 'dab' as 'bad' say, 'Look at the bed'.

Using the Word Workers auditory discrimination exercises

Auditory perception, auditory discrimination, and phonemic awareness are terms that are often used interchangeably. They have the same objective: they teach students to locate individual sounds in words. The development of this simple skill is critical if beginning readers are to acquire basic reading skills effectively. The exercises on the following page are designed to develop auditory perception skills. Be sure to include this activity as part of each lesson when teaching Book 1.

The first set of words teaches beginning and ending consonants. Tell students they are listening for consonant sounds. Then explain that they are listening for beginning consonants. For example, say the consonant sound 'b'. Ask students whether they hear 'b' at the beginning or the ending of the word 'bat'. Use the same procedure for ending consonants once students reliably recognise beginning consonants. Say the consonant sound 'p'. Ask students whether they hear the 'p' at the beginning or the end of 'cap'. Go around the room until each student is given two or three examples. Some students will recognise the position of the sound immediately, while others may need the sound emphasised until they can reliably locate its position in the word. Use the same procedure for the vowel sounds. The difference is that the students are to listen for the vowel sounds at the beginning and middle of words.

Using the Word Workers blending chart

Once students are competent at locating the position of sounds in words, they can be taught the skill of blending. Start blending consonants to vowels early in Book 1. Once this is learned, the vowel to consonant technique is introduced later in the book.

Use the chart provided on page 45. Write a consonant to the *left* of the vertical array of vowels. Point to the consonant and say the sound, then point to the vowel and say it, then say them together. Demonstrate the technique, have the students say the blends with you, and then have them blend individually.

For blending vowels to consonants, write the consonant to the *right* of the array of vowels. Then, using the same procedure, have students blend from vowel to consonant. This skill allows students to form the word patterns they will encounter when they start Book 2.

A complete explanation of blending skills is provided on pages 14–17 of this *Teacher Resource Book*. Read it carefully before using the blending chart.

Enlist the services of parents to reinforce blending techniques. Give them copies of the blending chart and encourage them to use it with their child at home.

Using the silent 'gh' sound chart

This word pattern requires careful teaching in Unit 4 of Book 5. Tell the students that the 'ough' pattern in 'bought' says the 'aw' sound; the 'eigh' pattern in 'eight' says the long 'a' sound; and the 'igh' pattern in 'high' says the long 'i' sound.

The 'ough' pattern may be pronounced differently by some students. It is not uncommon to hear the word pronounced as the 'or' sound or the short 'o' sound. Whatever the pronunciation, students need to learn to apply it in words containing the spelling pattern. Place the chart prominently in the classroom and have students refer to it if they have difficulty with silent 'gh' words.

Using the suffix sound chart

The word patterns on this chart should be taught carefully to simplify reading words containing these suffixes. Explain that the suffix 'tion' says 'shun' and, when it has an 'a' before it, it says 'ashun'; when there is an 'i' in front of it, it says 'ishun'; and when there is a 'u' with it, it says 'ushun'. Explain that the suffix 'ous' says 'us'.

Reading Freedom 2000

Word Workers 'bed' page

Reading Freedom 2000

Auditory discrimination exercises

Consonant sounds

Beginning

b	bat, ball, bus, book, boy
c	cat, cap, car, cool, clown
d	dog, dab, dig, duck, drop
f	fish, fun, fly, five, fire
g	gun, girl, ghost, got, get
h	hat, hen, head, help, high
j	jug, jump, jet, junk, just
k	kite, king, Ken, kit, kettle
l	lamp, lunch, live, long, let
m	moon, man, mud, my, make
n	nest, net, nice, never, not
p	pig, pear, pull, play, pot
r	ring, run, rock, rope, rabbit
s	snake, sun, sing, sell, stop
t	ten, tip, two, tall, time
v	van, vase, vote, voice, vest
w	watch, well, wind, wish, will
y	yacht, yes, yell, year, you
z	zebra, zip, zero, zap, zone

Ending

b	rob, cab, club, grab, job
d	rod, hid, red, said, bad
f	off, cliff, laugh, leaf, sniff
g	dog, big, pig, bag, rag
k	rock, back, tick, luck, neck
l	ball, yell, bill, dull, doll
m	ram, some, him, home, time
n	moon, run, tin, fan, hen
p	cap, rip, stop, cup, nap
r	car, stir, her, fur, for
s	yes, guess, mess, gas, fuss
t	cat, bet, pot, cut, bit
v	wave, five, leave, cave, wove
x	six, fox, wax, box, fix
z	fizz, buzz, jazz, fuzz, tizz

Vowel sounds

Beginning

a	act, apple, ant, at, an
e	elf, edge, end, Ed, Eskimo
i	it, is, if, igloo, imp
o	off, on, odd, often, ox
u	up, us, under, ugly, uncle

Middle

a	bat, can, bag, wax, cap
e	red, ten, peg, wet, bell
i	bit, pick, miss, fizz, Tim
o	pot, tom, gone, boss, dog
u	tub, sun, cut, fuss, mud

Reading Freedom 2000

Word Workers blending chart

a

e

i

o

u

Reading Freedom 2000

Word Workers sound chart

igh = ī

eigh = ā

ough = aw

Reading Freedom 2000

Word Workers suffix chart

tion = shun

ation = āshun

ition = ĭshun

ution = ūshun

ous = us

Reading Freedom brain busters

Q. What is a compound word?
A. A compound word is two small words that go together to make a big word.

Q. What is a syllable?
A. A syllable is the smallest part of a word that has a vowel in it.

Q. Where do you divide VCCV words?
A. Between the two consonants.

Q. Where do you divide VCV words?
A. Between the first vowel and consonant.

Q. When the letter 'y' says a vowel sound, do you count it as a vowel?
A. Yes.

Q. When a word has a silent final 'e', does that final 'e' count as a vowel?
A. No.

Q. When two letters go together to make one sound, do they count as one or two letters?
A. One.

Q. When dividing words with 'le' endings, do you join the consonant to the 'le' ending?
A. Yes.

Q. What is a prefix?
A. A part of a word that comes at the beginning to change its meaning.

Q. What is a suffix?
A. A suffix comes at the end of a word and changes the way the word works in a sentence.

Q. Take away the prefix, take away the suffix, and what do you have left?
A. The base word.

Q. Is a base word always a complete word?
A. No.

Checklist of general symptoms of reading problems

If the student displays four or more of these symptoms, he or she should obtain an assessment from a specialist reading instructor.

- ☐ Bright and mentally alert, lots of interests and hobbies but performs below potential at school.
- ☐ Poor self-image and self-confidence with school-related tasks, is anxious and insecure about them.
- ☐ Negative attitude to school, unhappy and unwilling to attend.
- ☐ Reading ability does not reflect generally good spoken vocabulary.
- ☐ Negative attitude to reading, reluctant to read, does so only when asked, makes excuses to avoid having to read.
- ☐ Difficulty organising homework, slow to finish, assignments often incomplete.
- ☐ Poor concentration, easily distracted, hyperactive, impulsive and fidgety, tendency to daydream.
- ☐ Difficulty with physical activities, poor co-ordination, dislikes sport and games.
- ☐ Poor understanding of simple instructions and requests.
- ☐ Chooses small books and leafs through them quickly, looks mostly at the pictures.
- ☐ Shows good recall of events and comprehension of stories when they are read aloud but not when the child reads silently.
- ☐ Signs of visual discomfort when reading, rubs eyes, poor posture, squints or frowns, complains of headaches, book held too close or too far away, points at words with finger.

Checklist of specific symptoms of reading problems

If the student displays four or more of these symptoms, he or she should obtain an assessment from a specialist reading instructor.

- ☐ Has difficulty recognising basic sight words ('and', 'are', 'can', 'come' and so on).
- ☐ Does not know sounds of letters ('a' as in 'apple', 'ow' as in 'cow' and so on).
- ☐ Guesses at unknown words.
- ☐ Has difficulty blending sounds together to make words (cannot blend 'b' - 'a' - 't' to make 'bat').
- ☐ Unable to read words of two or more syllables.
- ☐ Rate of reading is slow and laborious fl delays of 3 to 5 seconds, very hesitant, refusals are common.
- ☐ Regularly subvocalises (moves lips) when reading.
- ☐ Unable to isolate and sequence sounds in words (does not know where the sound 't' comes in 'bat').
- ☐ Repeats words and phrases, includes words.
- ☐ Often skips or omits words or loses place.
- ☐ Substitutes one word for another ('kitten' becomes 'cat', 'stamp' becomes 'stump' and so on).
- ☐ Ignores punctuation, words run together.
- ☐ Reverses and rotates letters in words ('dab' becomes 'dad', 'cab' becomes 'cap' and so on).
- ☐ Reverses whole words ('no' becomes 'on', 'was' becomes 'saw' and so on).
- ☐ Partial pronunciation of words ('expectation' becomes 'exception').

Reading Freedom 2000

Word Workers Book 1

Progress chart

Page	Skill	Date started	Date mastered	Comments
1–3	Vowel and consonant sounds			
4	Sight vocabulary			
5–8 (Unit 1)	Rhyming words			
9–12 (Unit 2)	Initial consonants			
13–16 (Unit 3)	Terminal consonants			
17–20 (Unit 4)	Medial vowels			
21–24 (Unit 5)	Initial consonants			
25–28 (Unit 6)	Terminal consonants			
29–32 (Unit 7)	Silent letters			
33–36 (Unit 8)	Initial consonants			
37–40 (Unit 9)	Terminal consonants			
41–44 (Unit 10)	Medial vowels			
45–48 (Unit 11)	Consonants			
49–55 (Unit 12)	Alphabet revision			
56–60 (Unit 13)	Medial vowels			

Name of student/group .... Class ....

Reading Freedom 2000

Word Workers Book 2

Progress chart

Page	Skill	Date started	Date mastered	Comments
1–3	Vowel and consonant sounds			
4	*Word Workers* sight vocabulary			
5–9	*Reading Freedom* sight vocabulary			
10–26 (Unit 1)	Short 'a' sound			
27–43 (Unit 2)	Short 'e' sound			
44–60 (Unit 3)	Short 'i' sound			
61–78 (Unit 4)	Short 'o' sound			
79–96 (Unit 5)	Short 'u' sound			
97–116 (Unit 6)	Medial vowels			

Name of student/group .... Class ....

Reading Freedom 2000

Word Workers Book 3

Progress chart

Page	Skill	Date started	Date mastered	Comments
1	*Word Workers* sight vocabulary			
2–6	*Reading Freedom* sight vocabulary			
7–26 (Unit 1)	Terminal blends			
27–46 (Unit 2)	Initial blends			
47–66 (Unit 3)	Initial blends			
67–87 (Unit 4)	Initial and terminal blends			
88–108 (Unit 5)	Initial and terminal blends			

Name of student/group.. Class..........................

Reading Freedom 2000

Word Workers Book 4

Progress chart

Page	Skill	Date started	Date mastered	Comments
1–5	*Reading Freedom* sight vocabulary			
6–26 (Unit 1)	Consonant digraphs			
27–50 (Unit 2)	Long vowel sounds			
51–72 (Unit 3)	Bossy 'e' rule			
73–95 (Unit 4)	Soft 'c' and 'g'			
96–120 (Unit 5)	Revision			

Name of student/group .... Class ....

Word Workers Book 5

Progress chart

Page	Skill	Date started	Date mastered	Comments
1–5	*Reading Freedom* sight vocabulary			
6–29 (Unit 1)	Diphthongs (oo, oi, oy, ou, ow, aw, au)			
30–51 (Unit 2)	Vowels before 'r'			
52–73 (Unit 3)	Digraphs (air, are, ear, ea, our, oar, all, al, or)			
74–95 (Unit 4)	Silent letters			
96–116 (Unit 5)	Revision unit			

Name of student/group .... Class ....

Reading Freedom 2000

Word Workers Book 6

Progress chart

Page	Skill	Date started	Date mastered	Comments
1–11 (Unit 1)	Compound words			
12–22 (Unit 2)	Syllabification (VCCV words)			
23–33 (Unit 3)	Syllabification (VCV words)			
34–45 (Unit 4)	Syllabification (VCCV and VCV words)			
46–56 (Unit 5)	Syllabification ('le' words)			
57–67 (Unit 6)	Syllabification (long words)			

Name of student/group .... Class ....

Reading Freedom 2000

Word Workers Book 7

Progress chart

Page	Skill	Date started	Date mastered	Comments
1–12 (Unit 1)	Structural analysis (un, re, ex, ness, ful, ance)			
13–24 (Unit 2)	Structural analysis (com, en, de, ition, ment, ous)			
25–36 (Unit 3)	Structural analysis (be, con, in, able, ent, al)			
37–48 (Unit 4)	Structural analysis (dis, pro, ad, ive, ure, age)			
49–62 (Unit 5)	Structural analysis revision			
63–68 (Unit 6)	Contractions			

Name of student/group .... Class ....

Reading Freedom
Basic sight vocabulary record sheet

Name	List 1	List 2	List 3	List 4	List 5	List 6	List 7	List 8	List 9	List 10
	/24	/24	/24	/24	/24	/24	/24	/24	/24	/24
	/24	/24	/24	/24	/24	/24	/24	/24	/24	/24
	/24	/24	/24	/24	/24	/24	/24	/24	/24	/24
	/24	/24	/24	/24	/24	/24	/24	/24	/24	/24
	/24	/24	/24	/24	/24	/24	/24	/24	/24	/24
	/24	/24	/24	/24	/24	/24	/24	/24	/24	/24
	/24	/24	/24	/24	/24	/24	/24	/24	/24	/24
	/24	/24	/24	/24	/24	/24	/24	/24	/24	/24
	/24	/24	/24	/24	/24	/24	/24	/24	/24	/24
	/24	/24	/24	/24	/24	/24	/24	/24	/24	/24
	/24	/24	/24	/24	/24	/24	/24	/24	/24	/24
	/24	/24	/24	/24	/24	/24	/24	/24	/24	/24
	/24	/24	/24	/24	/24	/24	/24	/24	/24	/24
	/24	/24	/24	/24	/24	/24	/24	/24	/24	/24
	/24	/24	/24	/24	/24	/24	/24	/24	/24	/24
	/24	/24	/24	/24	/24	/24	/24	/24	/24	/24
	/24	/24	/24	/24	/24	/24	/24	/24	/24	/24
	/24	/24	/24	/24	/24	/24	/24	/24	/24	/24
	/24	/24	/24	/24	/24	/24	/24	/24	/24	/24
	/24	/24	/24	/24	/24	/24	/24	/24	/24	/24
	/24	/24	/24	/24	/24	/24	/24	/24	/24	/24
	/24	/24	/24	/24	/24	/24	/24	/24	/24	/24
	/24	/24	/24	/24	/24	/24	/24	/24	/24	/24
	/24	/24	/24	/24	/24	/24	/24	/24	/24	/24
	/24	/24	/24	/24	/24	/24	/24	/24	/24	/24

Word Workers Achievement Test record sheet

Name	Test 1 Date /	Test 2 Date /	Test 3 Date /	Test 4 Date /	Test 5 Date /	Test 6 Date /	Test 7 Date /	Test 8 Date /	Test 9 Date /
	/100	/100	/100	/100	/100	/100	/100	/100	/100
	/100	/100	/100	/100	/100	/100	/100	/100	/100
	/100	/100	/100	/100	/100	/100	/100	/100	/100
	/100	/100	/100	/100	/100	/100	/100	/100	/100
	/100	/100	/100	/100	/100	/100	/100	/100	/100
	/100	/100	/100	/100	/100	/100	/100	/100	/100
	/100	/100	/100	/100	/100	/100	/100	/100	/100
	/100	/100	/100	/100	/100	/100	/100	/100	/100
	/100	/100	/100	/100	/100	/100	/100	/100	/100
	/100	/100	/100	/100	/100	/100	/100	/100	/100
	/100	/100	/100	/100	/100	/100	/100	/100	/100
	/100	/100	/100	/100	/100	/100	/100	/100	/100
	/100	/100	/100	/100	/100	/100	/100	/100	/100
	/100	/100	/100	/100	/100	/100	/100	/100	/100
	/100	/100	/100	/100	/100	/100	/100	/100	/100
	/100	/100	/100	/100	/100	/100	/100	/100	/100
	/100	/100	/100	/100	/100	/100	/100	/100	/100
	/100	/100	/100	/100	/100	/100	/100	/100	/100
	/100	/100	/100	/100	/100	/100	/100	/100	/100
	/100	/100	/100	/100	/100	/100	/100	/100	/100
	/100	/100	/100	/100	/100	/100	/100	/100	/100
	/100	/100	/100	/100	/100	/100	/100	/100	/100
	/100	/100	/100	/100	/100	/100	/100	/100	/100
	/100	/100	/100	/100	/100	/100	/100	/100	/100

Word Workers

Merit certificate

Awarded to

____

upon the successful completion of

Word Workers Book _____

Teacher ____________________

Date _______________

CHAPTER 5

Teaching notes

For intermediate readers (ages 7–11)
WORD WORKERS
BOOK 4
HUNTER CALDER
Consonant digraphs, long vowel rules, soft 'c' and 'g'

For intermediate readers (ages 7–11)
WORD WORKERS
BOOK 5
HUNTER CALDER
Digraphs and diphthongs, vowels before 'r', silent letters

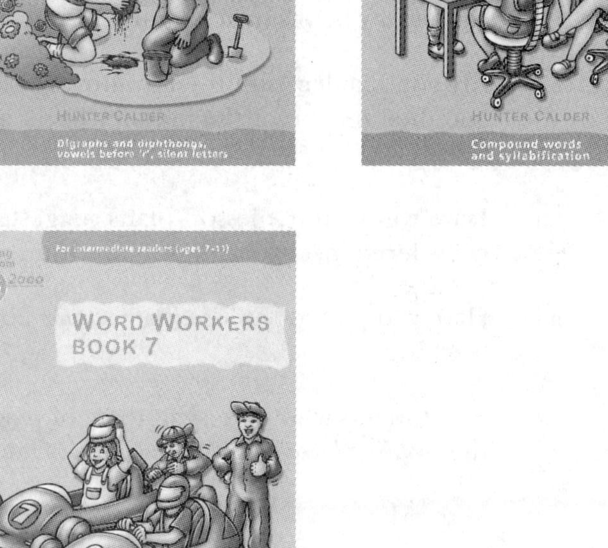

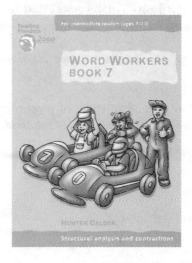

The Word Workers teacher's checklist

Here is a checklist of some of the basics that underlie the *Word Workers* approach. The purpose of the checklist is to ensure the delivery of quality reading instruction to students and provide the best possible advice to their parents. Every issue in the checklist is covered in detail in the earlier chapters in this book. Go through this checklist carefully and research answers for those questions you are unsure of. Use it as an organisational tool when starting new students with the *Word Workers* program.

The phonics method of instruction

☐ Are you familiar with the basic rationale that directs the phonics method of reading instruction?

☐ Are you familiar with the phonic hierarchy of skills?

☐ Can you explain to parents the need for a systematic and structured approach to reading instruction?

☐ Can you explain why phonemic awareness skills are an essential precondition for beginning readers?

☐ Can you locate each phonic skill within the framework of the *Word Workers* activity books?

Before teaching Word Workers

☐ Are you aware of the function and level of *Word Workers* within the *Reading Freedom 2000* program?

☐ Have you read the *Word Workers Teacher Resource Book* and examined each of the activity books to acquaint yourself with the skills they teach?

☐ Are you familiar with the monitoring procedure that is part of *Word Workers* and the function of the mastery pages and the *Word Workers* achievement tests?

☐ Have you read the lesson plans suggested for each activity book and considered incorporating them within your instructional framework?

☐ Have you placed the *Reading Freedom 2000* wall charts prominently in your teaching area?

☐ For students who have symptoms of reading problems, have you consulted the *Reading Freedom 2000 Diagnostic Handbook* to assess difficulties?

Classroom management

- ☐ Have you mastered the instructional techniques and approaches that will make your lessons successful?
- ☐ Do you know the essential criteria for correcting a student's reading errors?
- ☐ Are you effective at correcting reading errors?
- ☐ Do you know how to build upon the progressive attainment of phonic rules and generalisation and incorporate this knowledge at the beginning of each lesson in conjunction with the *Reading Freedom 2000* wall charts or the sound charts contained within the books?
- ☐ Do you explain new concepts and rules carefully to parent and student alike?
- ☐ When teaching something new, do you make sure the students have a good grasp of the information by making them demonstrate it for you?
- ☐ Are you prepared to enlist parental support to help students master basic reading skills at home?

Teaching the phonic hierarchy

- ☐ Are you familiar with and confident in teaching the different skills that develop phonemic awareness in its earliest stages?
- ☐ Are you aware of the techniques required to teach sight vocabulary effectively?
- ☐ Can you explain to parents why teaching sight vocabulary is an essential part of effective reading skills, and ways of making learning it as easy as possible for parent and student alike?
- ☐ Do you have a good grasp of syllabification skills, and are you able to teach them effectively?
- ☐ Can you teach structural analysis skills effectively?
- ☐ Are you aware of the limitations of the concept of base words?
- ☐ Can you teach the 'tion' suffix and its variants effectively?
- ☐ Are you clear about why is there so much emphasis placed on the idea that *Reading Freedom* teachers must *teach* spelling and not test it?

Using Book 1

Word Workers Book 1 teaches students the phonemic awareness skills necessary for successful reading acquisition. Below are some suggestions on how to use the book effectively. More detailed information on the teaching processes can be found in Chapter 2: 'Skills for successful teaching'. An activity-by-activity guide is provided with the answers.

- Read the section in the *Teacher Resource Book* that gives instructions on teaching the different phonemic awareness and blending activities.
- Become familiar with the suggested lesson plan for Book 1 on the next page.

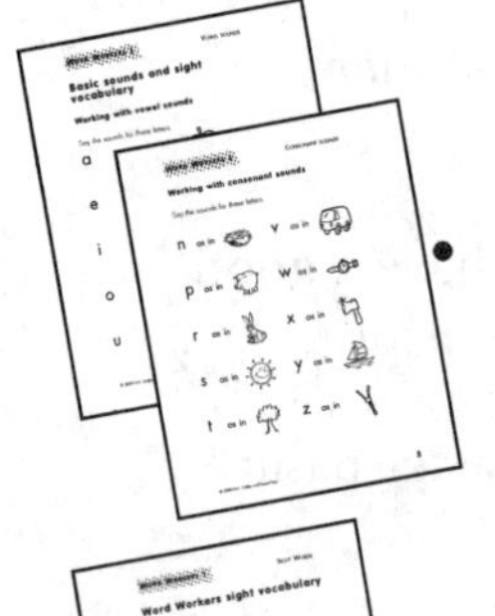

- Teach the initial vowel and consonant sounds from the *Reading Freedom 2000* single letter–sound wall chart or from pages 1–3 in Book 1. Teach the 'x' sound carefully. It is the only terminal sound on the chart.

- Teach students the *Word Workers* sight vocabulary. Once they learn these words they can begin learning the *Reading Freedom* basic sight vocabulary lists from Book 2.
- Teach phonemic awareness using 'I spy' and the auditory discrimination exercises on page 44 of the *Teacher Resource Book.*

- Show students how to use the 'bed' to overcome reversals and rotations.
- The first unit of Book 1 asks students to discriminate rhyming words. If they are to work successfully with the unit, students need to know the sight words 'yes' and 'no'. Be sure they can read these words before assigning the activity.
- Gradually introduce the blending activities. Start with the consonant-vowel pattern, then introduce the vowel-consonant pattern and, before starting Book 2, give the students practice with the consonant-word pattern blending activity. This skill can be introduced early in Book 1.
- Enlist parent support whenever possible. Parents are particularly helpful teaching sight vocabulary and reinforcing blending activities at home.
- When Book 1 is completed, record students' progress using *Word Workers* Achievement Test 1.

Book 1: Suggested lesson plan

Based on a lesson of approximately 30 minutes.

1 Students say a row of sounds from the *Reading Freedom 2000* single letter–sound wall chart or from pages 1–3 in Book 1. For small groups, each student can say a row or column of sounds. If your class is large, select students to say a row or column until all the sounds have been repeated. Be sure different students say the sounds each lesson.

2 When teaching with small groups each student reads a column of *Word Workers* sight vocabulary (once this is mastered they read a column of *Reading Freedom* basic sight vocabulary). When teaching the whole class, select students to read a column of sight words. Five or six columns is enough to start your lesson with. Be sure different students read the sight words each lesson.

3 Explain and demonstrate the skill to be learned. Ensure that students understand the concept involved and know what is required of them.

4 Assign activity pages to be completed (the number of pages depends on the teacher's professional judgment as well as the ability and enthusiasm of the student).

5 Play 'I spy' for two or three minutes. Then use the auditory discrimination exercises from page 44 in a game-like atmosphere. Keep score of the student who gets the most correct responses. Limit this activity to two or three minutes also. Make sure each student has the opportunity to make at least one response.

6 Early in Book 1, introduce consonant-vowel blending skills. Incorporate this in the lesson plan. It can substitute for 'I spy' and the auditory discrimination exercises. Some students require more work with blending techniques than others. Form a group of these students and give them extra practice while other students work on activity pages.

7 Reward students for achievement in phonemic awareness skills or in learning sight vocabulary with stamps, stickers or gold stars. When they complete the activity book and finish the complementary achievement test (found in *Word Workers Achievement Tests*) they receive a *Word Workers* Merit Certificate.

8 Assign any homework after demonstrating the activities. Ensure students understand the concept and what is to be done.

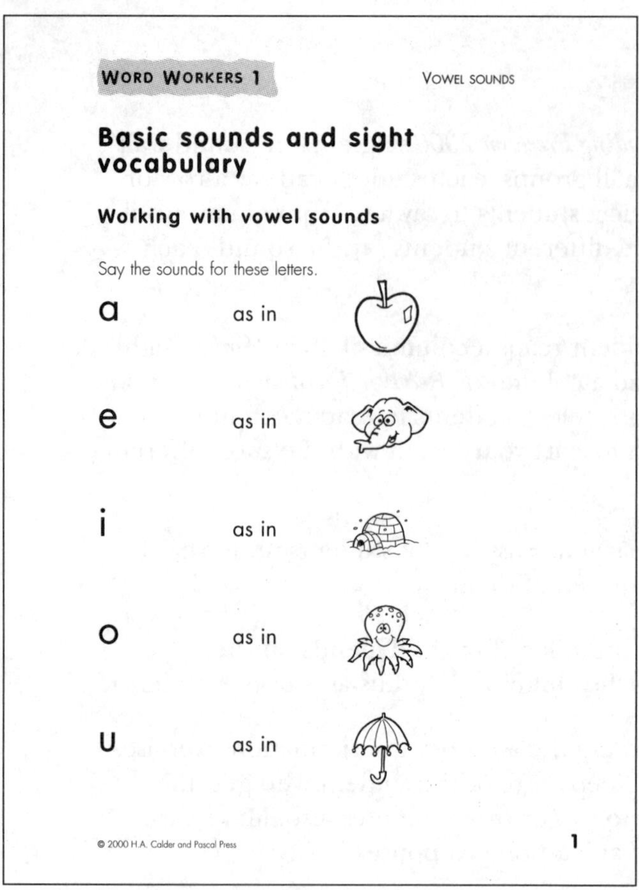
WORD WORKERS 1 VOWEL SOUNDS

Basic sounds and sight vocabulary

Working with vowel sounds

Say the sounds for these letters.

a as in

e as in

i as in

o as in

u as in

© 2000 H.A. Calder and Pascal Press 1

For the following pages:

Teach students the sounds for these letters. All letters except for 'x' are taught as beginning or initial sounds. In a medial or terminal position in words, the sound for the letter 'x' is a combination of the sounds 'k' and 's', to make the sound 'ks'.

Students say the vowel sounds.

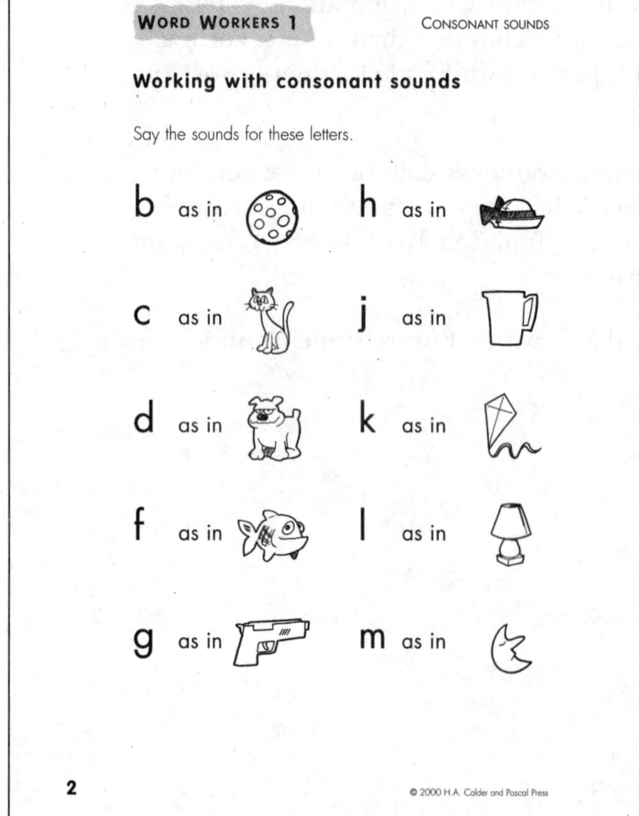
WORD WORKERS 1 CONSONANT SOUNDS

Working with consonant sounds

Say the sounds for these letters.

b as in h as in

c as in j as in

d as in k as in

f as in l as in

g as in m as in

2 © 2000 H.A. Calder and Pascal Press

Students say the consonant sounds.

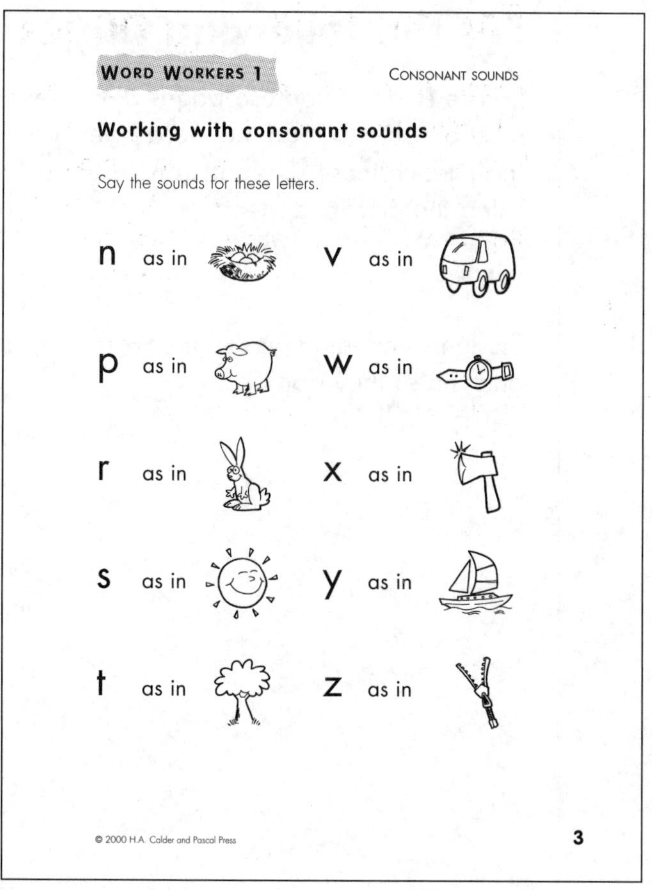
WORD WORKERS 1 CONSONANT SOUNDS

Working with consonant sounds

Say the sounds for these letters.

n as in | v as in
p as in | w as in
r as in | x as in
s as in | y as in
t as in | z as in

© 2000 H.A. Calder and Pascal Press 3

Students say the consonant sounds.

WORD WORKERS 1 SIGHT WORDS

Word Workers sight vocabulary

Learn these sight words.

a	no	are	out	come
as	oh	and	put	little
by	on	all	see	look
he	so	but	saw	said
I	to	her	the	them
in	up	his	too	then
is	we	Mrs	was	they
		not	you	there
		now		with

4 © 2000 H.A. Calder and Pascal Press

These lists contain the basic sight words students need to work successfully with *Word Workers*. Teach these words list by list until they are mastered. Practise them regularly and reward students for progress.

WORD WORKERS 1 UNIT 1.1

Name .... Date ....

Working with rhyming words

Underline 'yes' if the words rhyme and 'no' if they don't.

1. yes/no
2. yes/no
3. yes/no
4. yes/no
5. yes/no
6. yes/no
7. yes/no
8. yes/no
9. yes/no
10. yes/no
11. yes/no
12. yes/no

© 2000 H.A. Calder and Pascal Press 5

WORD WORKERS 1 UNIT 1.2

Name .... Date ....

Underline 'yes' if the words rhyme and 'no' if they don't.

1. yes/no
2. yes/no
3. yes/no
4. yes/no
5. yes/no
6. yes/no
7. yes/no
8. yes/no
9. yes/no
10. yes/no
11. yes/no
12. yes/no

6 © 2000 H.A. Calder and Pascal Press

For the following pages:

Before students can use pages 5–8, they must be able to read the words 'yes' and 'no'. Teach these as sight words before using the activity pages.

Students underline 'yes' if the words rhyme and 'no' if they don't.

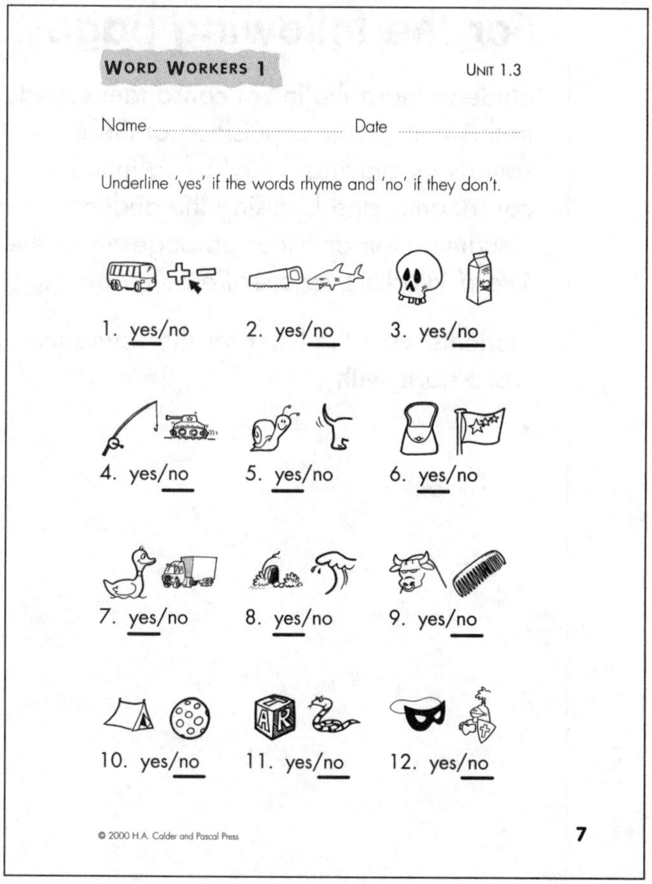
WORD WORKERS 1 UNIT 1.3

Name .... Date ....

Underline 'yes' if the words rhyme and 'no' if they don't.

1. yes/no 2. yes/no 3. yes/no

4. yes/no 5. yes/no 6. yes/no

7. yes/no 8. yes/no 9. yes/no

10. yes/no 11. yes/no 12. yes/no

© 2000 H.A. Calder and Pascal Press 7

Students underline 'yes' if the words rhyme and 'no' if they don't.

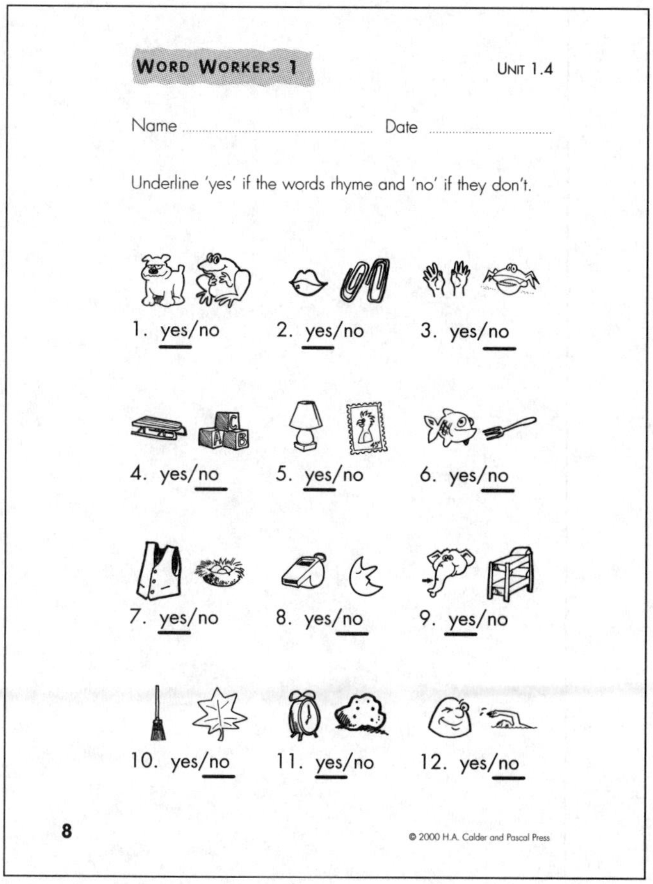
WORD WORKERS 1 UNIT 1.4

Name .... Date ....

Underline 'yes' if the words rhyme and 'no' if they don't.

1. yes/no 2. yes/no 3. yes/no

4. yes/no 5. yes/no 6. yes/no

7. yes/no 8. yes/no 9. yes/no

10. yes/no 11. yes/no 12. yes/no

8 © 2000 H.A. Calder and Pascal Press

Word Workers 1 Unit 2.1

Name .... Date ....

Working with beginning sounds

Write the letter that the word *starts* with.

1. starts with b
2. starts with g
3. starts with l
4. starts with c
5. starts with h
6. starts with m
7. starts with d
8. starts with j
9. starts with n
10. starts with f
11. starts with k
12. starts with p

© 2000 H.A. Calder and Pascal Press 9

For the following pages:

Students learn the initial consonant sounds in this unit. Assist acquisition of these sounds by playing 'I spy' using initial consonants, and by using the auditory discrimination activities on page 44 of the *Word Workers Teacher Resource Book.*

Students write the letter for the sound the word starts with.

Word Workers 1 Unit 2.2

Name .... Date ....

Write the letter that the word *starts* with.

1. starts with r
2. starts with w
3. starts with c
4. starts with s
5. starts with g
6. starts with d
7. starts with t
8. starts with z
9. starts with f
10. starts with v
11. starts with b
12. starts with h

10 © 2000 H.A. Calder and Pascal Press

WORD WORKERS 1 UNIT 2.3

Name .... Date ....

Write the letter that the word *starts* with.

1. starts with y
2. starts with l
3. starts with f
4. starts with h
5. starts with m
6. starts with s
7. starts with c
8. starts with n
9. starts with t
10. starts with d
11. starts with p
12. starts with v

 11

WORD WORKERS 1 UNIT 2.4

Name .... Date ....

Write the letter that the word *starts* with.

1. starts with w
2. starts with c
3. starts with p
4. starts with t
5. starts with d
6. starts with h
7. starts with r
8. starts with f
9. starts with n
10. starts with b
11. starts with g
12. starts with l

12

Students write the letter for the sound the word starts with.

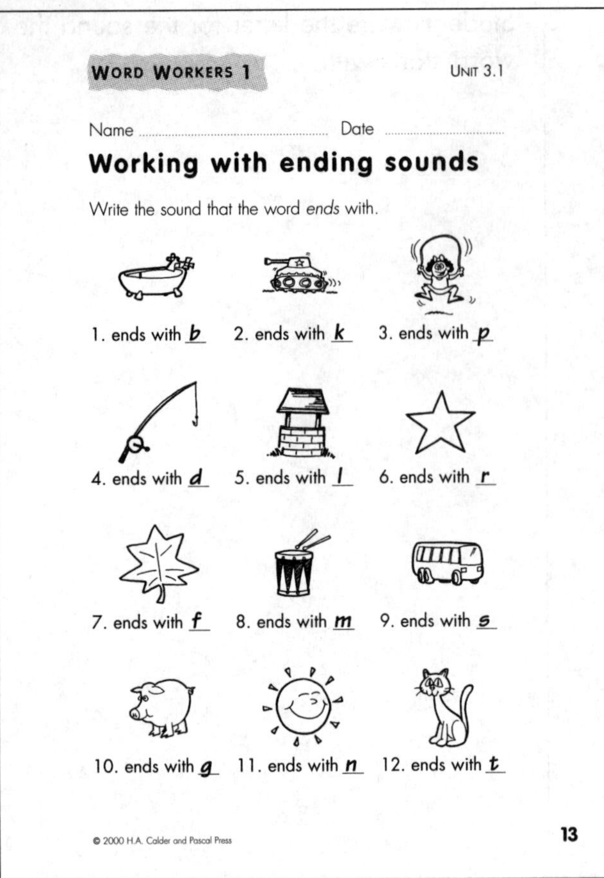

Word Workers 1 Unit 3.1

Name .... Date ....

Working with ending sounds

Write the sound that the word *ends* with.

1. ends with b
2. ends with k
3. ends with p
4. ends with d
5. ends with l
6. ends with r
7. ends with f
8. ends with m
9. ends with s
10. ends with g
11. ends with n
12. ends with t

© 2000 H.A. Calder and Pascal Press 13

For the following pages:

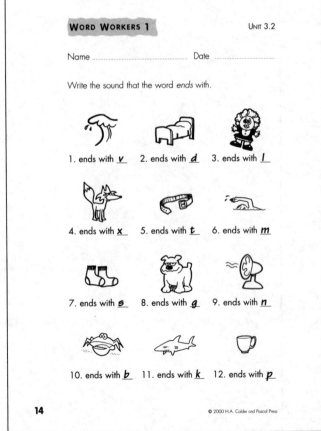

Students learn the terminal consonant sounds in this unit. Assist acquisition of these sounds by playing 'I spy' using initial consonants, and by using the auditory discrimination activities on page 44 of the *Word Workers Teacher Resource Book*.

Students write the letter for the sound the word ends with.

Word Workers 1 Unit 3.2

Name .... Date ....

Write the sound that the word *ends* with.

1. ends with v
2. ends with d
3. ends with l
4. ends with x
5. ends with t
6. ends with m
7. ends with s
8. ends with g
9. ends with n
10. ends with b
11. ends with k
12. ends with p

14 © 2000 H.A. Calder and Pascal Press

WORD WORKERS 1 UNIT 3.3

Name .... Date ....

Write the sound that the word *ends* with.

1. ends with r
2. ends with x
3. ends with b
4. ends with s
5. ends with p
6. ends with g
7. ends with t
8. ends with b
9. ends with k
10. ends with n
11. ends with d
12. ends with l

 15

WORD WORKERS 1 UNIT 3.4

Name .... Date ....

Write the sound that the word *ends* with.

1. ends with k
2. ends with s
3. ends with l
4. ends with n
5. ends with t
6. ends with v
7. ends with p
8. ends with m
9. ends with f
10. ends with g
11. ends with x
12. ends with s

16

Students write the letter for the sound the word ends with.

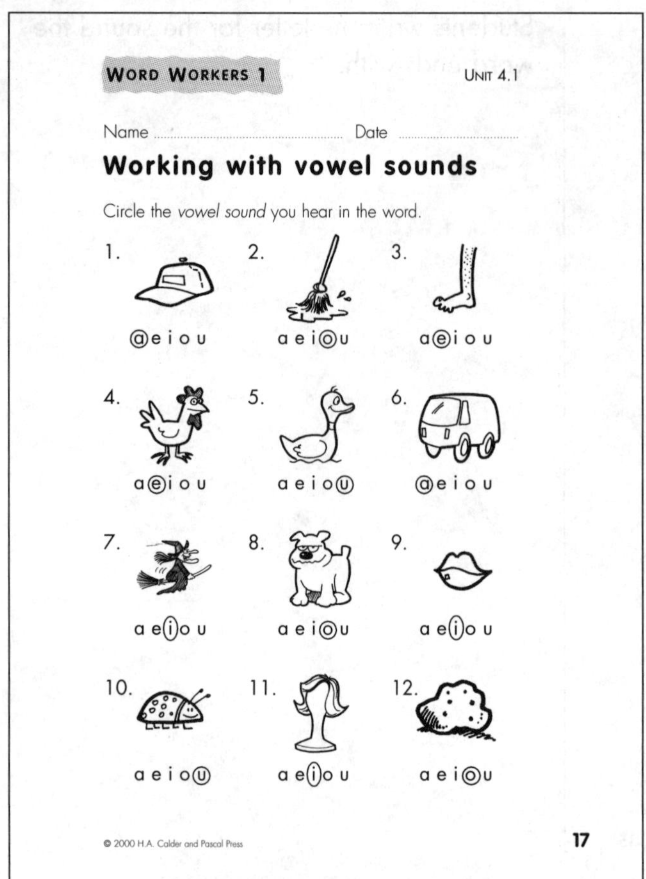

WORD WORKERS 1 UNIT 4.1

Name .... Date ....

Working with vowel sounds

Circle the *vowel sound* you hear in the word.

1. **a** e i o u
2. a e i **o** u
3. a **e** i o u
4. a **e** i o u
5. a e i o **u**
6. **a** e i o u
7. a e **i** o u
8. a e i **o** u
9. a e **i** o u
10. a e i o **u**
11. a e **i** o u
12. a e i **o** u

© 2000 H.A. Calder and Pascal Press 17

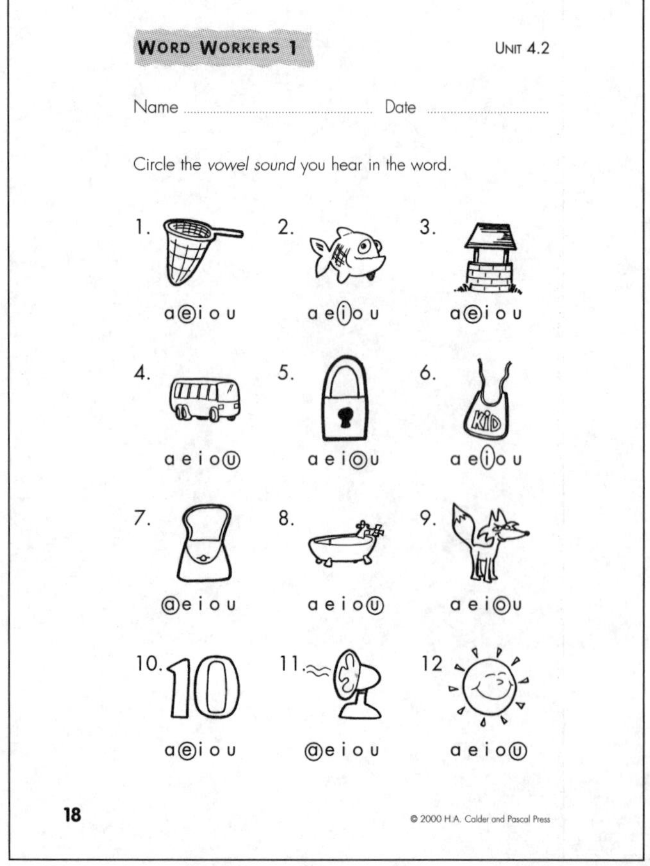

WORD WORKERS 1 UNIT 4.2

Name .... Date ....

Circle the *vowel sound* you hear in the word.

1. a **e** i o u
2. a e **i** o u
3. a **e** i o u
4. a e i o **u**
5. a e i **o** u
6. a e **i** o u
7. **a** e i o u
8. a e i o **u**
9. a e i **o** u
10. a **e** i o u
11. **a** e i o u
12. a e i o **u**

18 © 2000 H.A. Calder and Pascal Press

For the following pages:

Students learn medial vowels in this unit. Assist acquisition of these sounds by using the initial and medial vowel auditory discrimination exercises on page 44 of the *Word Workers Teacher Resource Book.*

At this stage, start blending activities using the consonant–vowel blending technique. This technique is described on pages 14–17 of the *Word Workers Teacher Resource Book.*

Students circle the vowel sound they hear in the word.

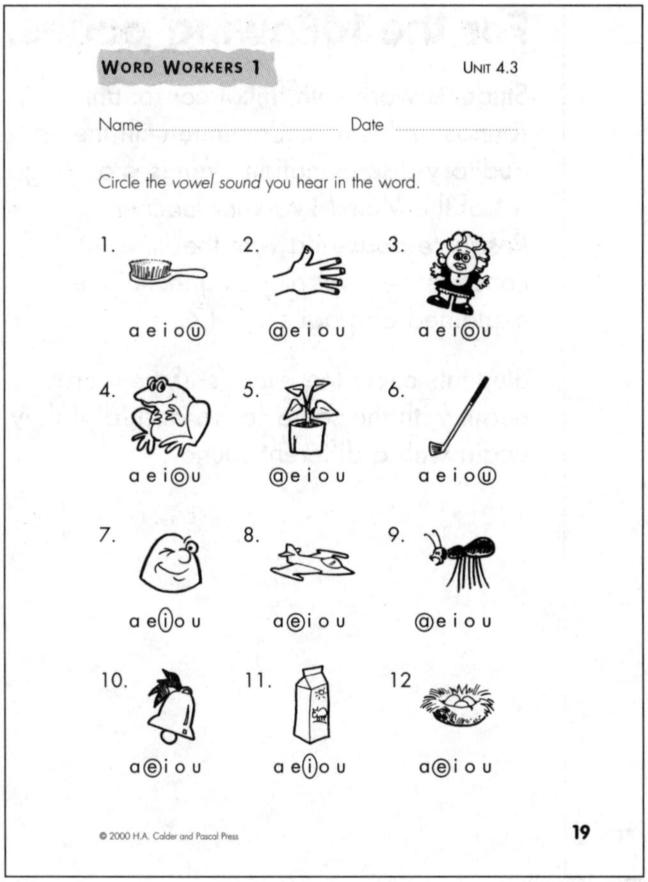
WORD WORKERS 1 UNIT 4.3

Name .... Date ....

Circle the *vowel sound* you hear in the word.

1. a e i o (u)
2. (a) e i o u
3. a e i (o) u
4. a e i (o) u
5. (a) e i o u
6. a e i o (u)
7. a e (i) o u
8. a (e) i o u
9. (a) e i o u
10. a (e) i o u
11. a e (i) o u
12. a (e) i o u

© 2000 H.A. Calder and Pascal Press 19

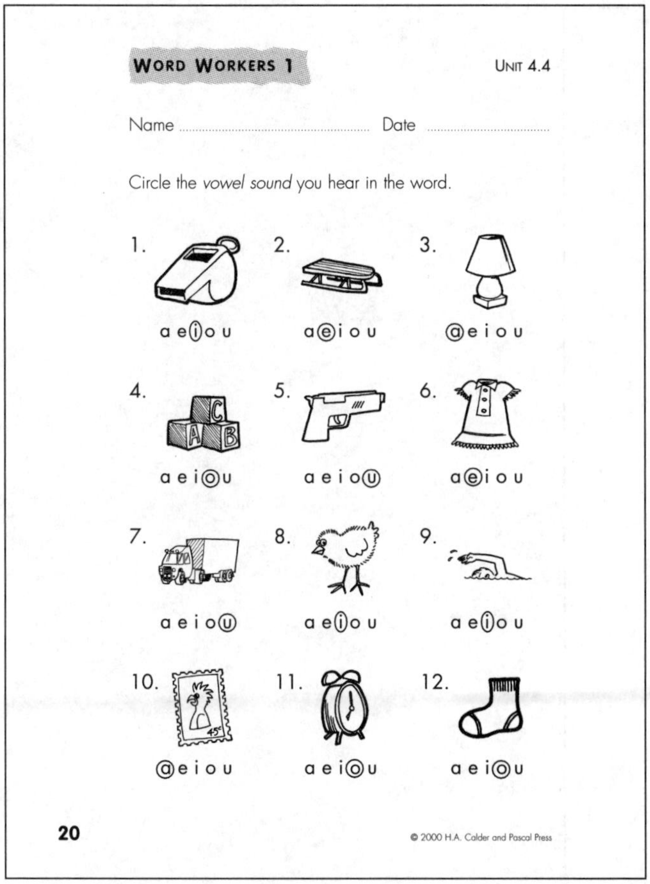
WORD WORKERS 1 UNIT 4.4

Name .... Date ....

Circle the *vowel sound* you hear in the word.

1. a e (i) o u
2. a (e) i o u
3. (a) e i o u
4. a e i (o) u
5. a e i o (u)
6. a (e) i o u
7. a e i o (u)
8. a e (i) o u
9. a e (i) o u
10. (a) e i o u
11. a e i (o) u
12. a e i (o) u

20 © 2000 H.A. Calder and Pascal Press

Students circle the vowel sound they hear in the word.

WORD WORKERS 1 UNIT 5.1

Name .... Date ....

More beginning sounds

Circle 's' if the words *begin* with the *same* sound or 'd' if the words begin with a *different* sound.

1. s/d 2. s/d 3. s/d

4. s/d 5. s/d 6. s/d

7. s/d 8. s/d 9. s/d

10. s/d 11. s/d 12. s/d

© 2000 H.A. Calder and Pascal Press 21

WORD WORKERS 1 UNIT 5.2

Name .... Date ....

Circle 's' if the words *begin* with the *same* sound or 'd' if the words begin with a *different* sound.

1. s/d 2. s/d 3. s/d

4. s/d 5. s/d 6. s/d

7. s/d 8. s/d 9. s/d

10. s/d 11. s/d 12. s/d

22 © 2000 H.A. Calder and Pascal Press

For the following pages:

Students work with initial consonant sounds in this unit. Continue with the auditory discrimination exercises on page 44 of the *Word Workers Teacher Resource Book* and with the consonant–vowel blending technique explained on pages 14–17.

Students circle the letter 's' if the words begin with the same sound and 'd' if they begin with a different sound.

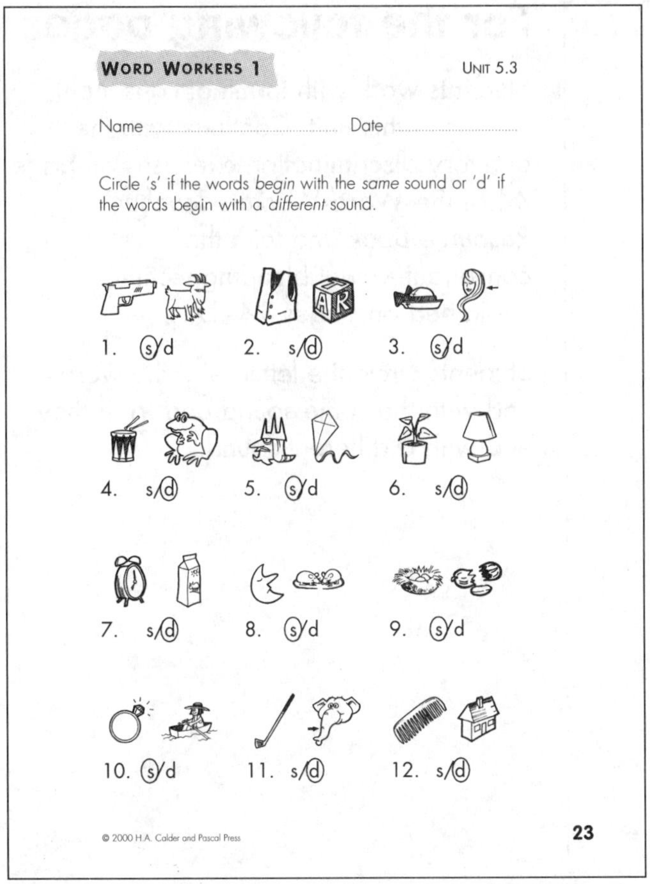

WORD WORKERS 1 UNIT 5.3

Name .... Date ....

Circle 's' if the words *begin* with the *same* sound or 'd' if the words begin with a *different* sound.

1. **s**/d 2. s/**d** 3. **s**/d

4. s/**d** 5. **s**/d 6. s/**d**

7. s/**d** 8. **s**/d 9. **s**/d

10. **s**/d 11. s/**d** 12. s/**d**

© 2000 H.A. Calder and Pascal Press 23

Students circle the letter 's' if the words begin with the same sound and 'd' if they begin with a different sound.

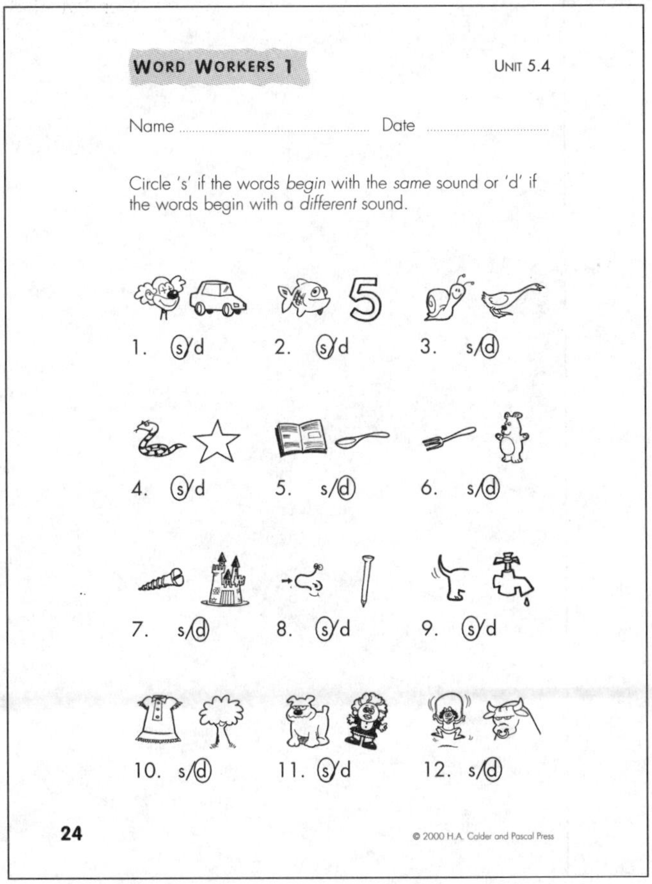

WORD WORKERS 1 UNIT 5.4

Name .... Date ....

Circle 's' if the words *begin* with the *same* sound or 'd' if the words begin with a *different* sound.

1. **s**/d 2. **s**/d 3. s/**d**

4. **s**/d 5. s/**d** 6. s/**d**

7. s/**d** 8. **s**/d 9. **s**/d

10. s/**d** 11. **s**/d 12. s/**d**

24 © 2000 H.A. Calder and Pascal Press

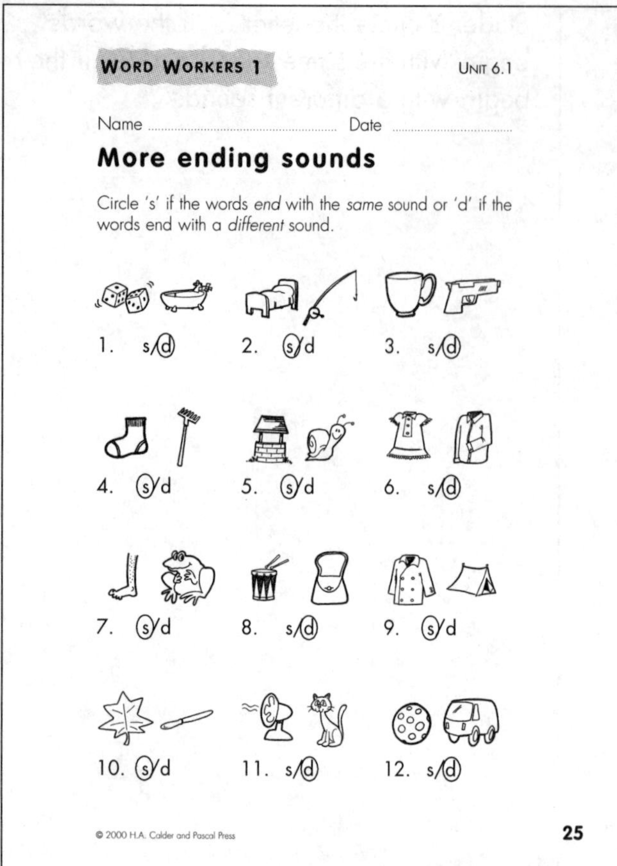

WORD WORKERS 1 UNIT 6.1

Name .... Date ....

More ending sounds

Circle 's' if the words *end* with the *same* sound or 'd' if the words end with a *different* sound.

1. s/d 2. s/d 3. s/d

4. s/d 5. s/d 6. s/d

7. s/d 8. s/d 9. s/d

10. s/d 11. s/d 12. s/d

© 2000 H.A. Calder and Pascal Press 25

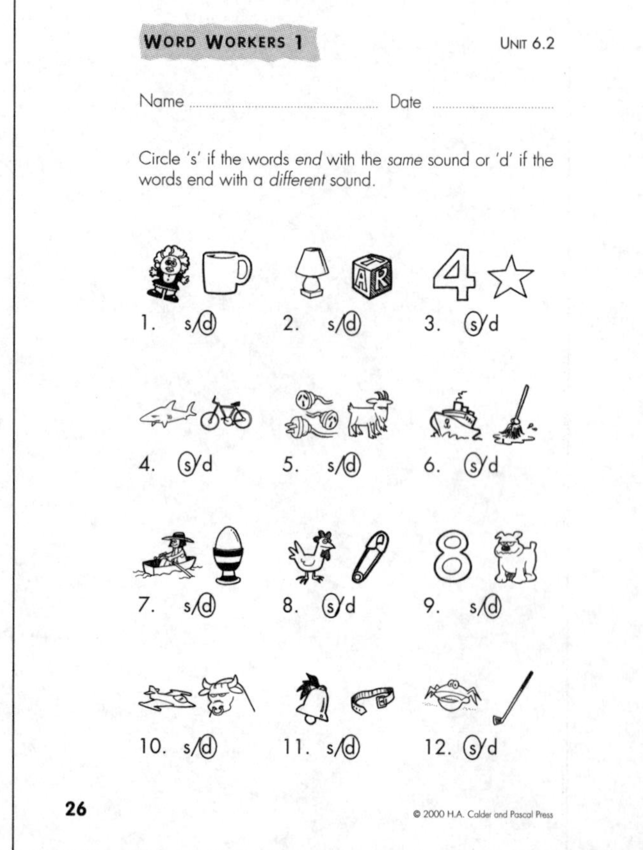

WORD WORKERS 1 UNIT 6.2

Name .... Date ....

Circle 's' if the words *end* with the *same* sound or 'd' if the words end with a *different* sound.

1. s/d 2. s/d 3. s/d

4. s/d 5. s/d 6. s/d

7. s/d 8. s/d 9. s/d

10. s/d 11. s/d 12. s/d

26 © 2000 H.A. Calder and Pascal Press

For the following pages:

Students work with terminal consonant sounds in this unit. Continue with the auditory discrimination exercises on page 44 of the *Word Workers Teacher Resource Book* and with the consonant–vowel blending technique explained on pages 14–17.

Students circle the letter 's' if the words end with the same sound and 'd' if they end with a different sound.

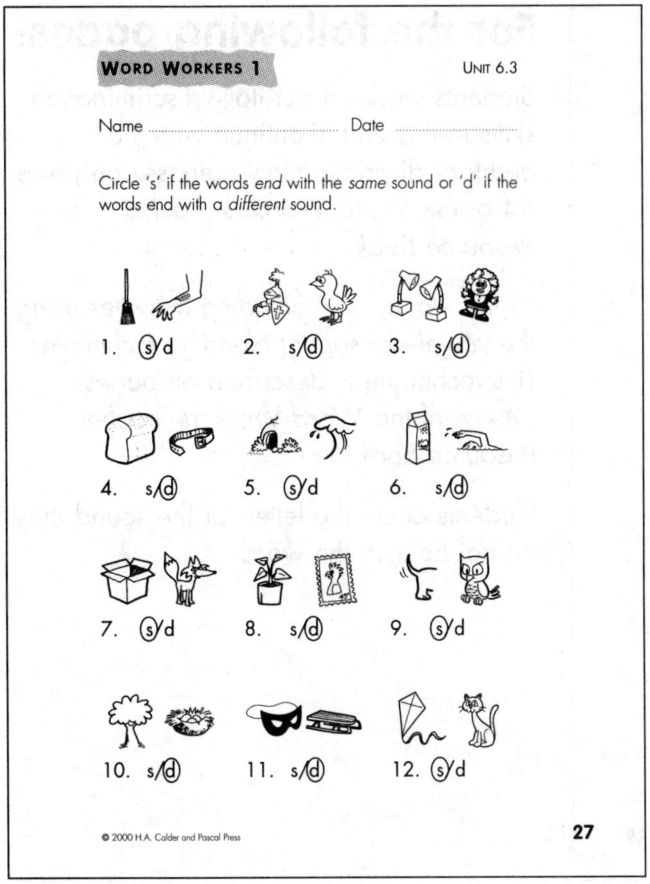

WORD WORKERS 1 UNIT 6.3

Name .... Date ....

Circle 's' if the words *end* with the *same* sound or 'd' if the words end with a *different* sound.

1. (s)/d 2. s/(d) 3. s/(d)

4. s/(d) 5. (s)/d 6. s/(d)

7. (s)/d 8. s/(d) 9. (s)/d

10. s/(d) 11. s/(d) 12. (s)/d

© 2000 H.A. Calder and Pascal Press 27

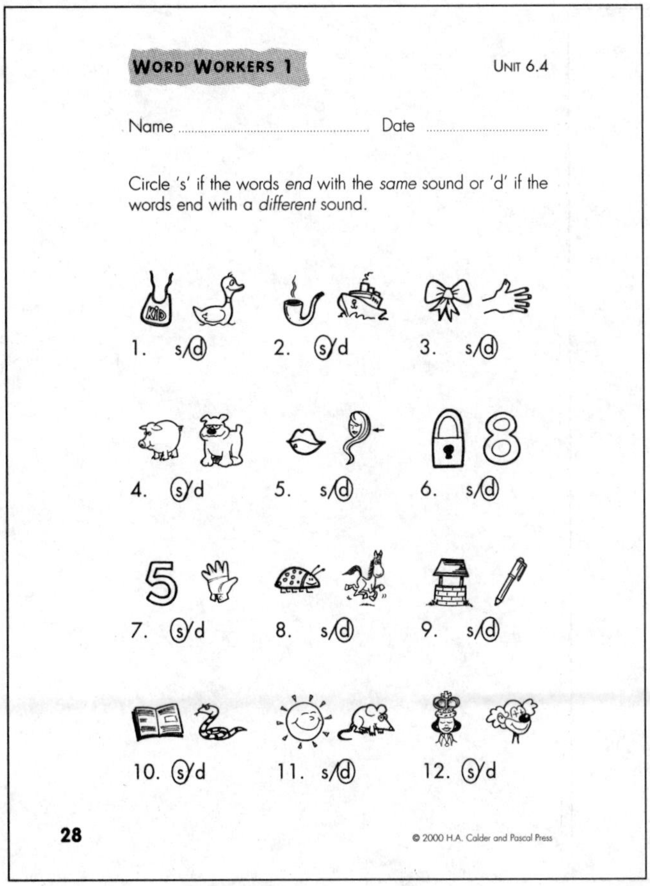

WORD WORKERS 1 UNIT 6.4

Name .... Date ....

Circle 's' if the words *end* with the *same* sound or 'd' if the words end with a *different* sound.

1. s/(d) 2. (s)/d 3. s/(d)

4. (s)/d 5. s/(d) 6. s/(d)

7. (s)/d 8. s/(d) 9. s/(d)

10. (s)/d 11. s/(d) 12. (s)/d

28 © 2000 H.A. Calder and Pascal Press

Students circle the letter 's' if the words end with the same sound and 'd' if they end with a different sound.

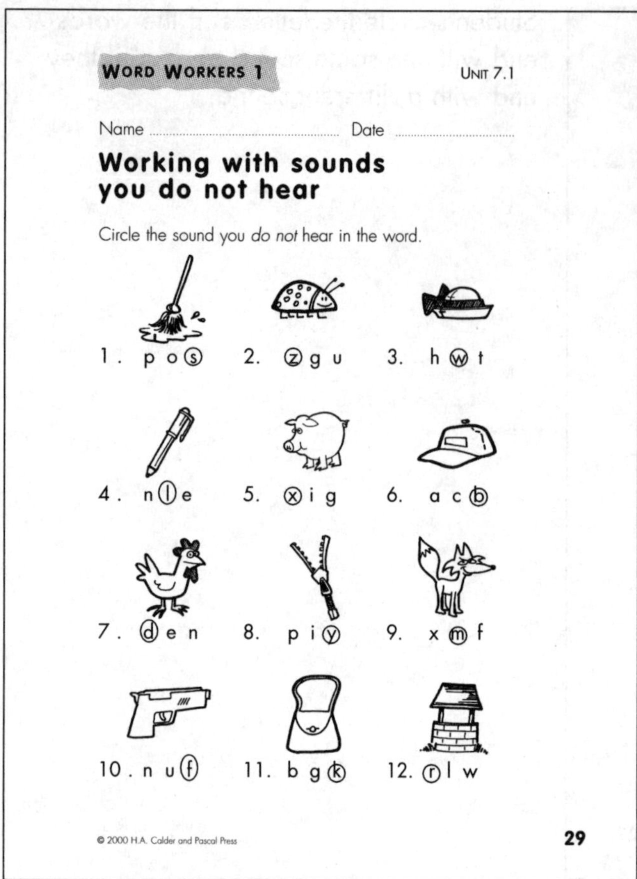
WORD WORKERS 1

UNIT 7.1

Name .... Date ....

Working with sounds you do not hear

Circle the sound you *do not* hear in the word.

1. p o s 2. z g u 3. h w t

4. n l e 5. x i g 6. a c b

7. d e n 8. p i y 9. x m f

10. n u f 11. b g k 12. r l w

© 2000 H.A. Calder and Pascal Press 29

WORD WORKERS 1

UNIT 7.2

Name .... Date ....

Circle the sound you *do not* hear in the word.

1. h i l 2. d o p 3. r u n

4. s u t 5. v k o 6. i f w

7. t e x 8. a n z 9. y u b

10. a d o 11. w e g 12. i t j

30 © 2000 H.A. Calder and Pascal Press

For the following pages:

Students work on auditory discrimination skills in this unit. Continue with the auditory discrimination exercises on page 44 of the *Word Workers Teacher Resource Book*.

At this stage, start blending activities using the vowel–consonant blending technique. This technique is described on pages 14–17 of the *Word Workers Teacher Resource Book*.

Students circle the letter for the sound they do not hear in the word.

WORD WORKERS 1 UNIT 7.3

Name .... Date ....

Circle the sound you *do not* hear in the word.

1. m (i) r 2. (t) r f 3. l b (y)

4. (l) t s 5. n (u) k 6. s i (z)

7. s e (w) 8. l (v) c 9. (o) h n

10. l b (a) 11. m a (x) 12. d r (a)

© 2000 H.A. Calder and Pascal Press 31

WORD WORKERS 1 UNIT 7.4

Name .... Date ....

Circle the sound you *do not* hear in the word.

1. g (b) t 2. p (l) m 3. p (s) t

4. (c) l t 5. (b) o l 6. n (o) t

7. k (m) r 8. r (a) a 9. s (j) p

10. i (w) k 11. l m (o) 12. a (k) f

32 © 2000 H.A. Calder and Pascal Press

Students circle the letter for the sound they do not hear in the word.

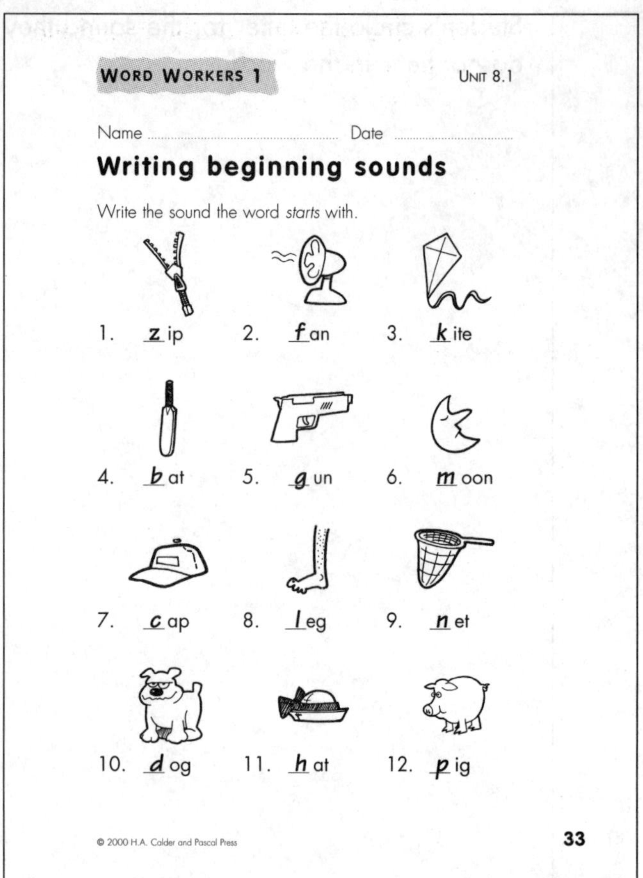

WORD WORKERS 1 UNIT 8.1

Name .... Date ....

Writing beginning sounds

Write the sound the word *starts* with.

1. z ip 2. f an 3. k ite

4. b at 5. g un 6. m oon

7. c ap 8. l eg 9. n et

10. d og 11. h at 12. p ig

 33

For the following pages:

Students work with initial consonant sounds in this unit. Continue with the auditory discrimination exercises on page 44 of the *Word Workers Teacher Resource Book* and with the vowel–consonant blending technique explained on pages 14–17.

Students write the letter for the sound the word starts with.

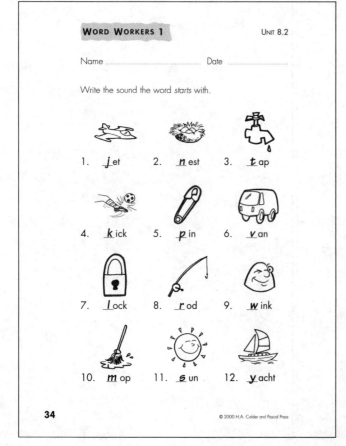

WORD WORKERS 1 UNIT 8.2

Name .... Date ....

Write the sound the word *starts* with.

1. j et 2. n est 3. t ap

4. k ick 5. p in 6. v an

7. l ock 8. r od 9. w ink

10. m op 11. s un 12. y acht

34

WORD WORKERS 1 UNIT 8.3

Name .... Date ....

Write the sound the word *starts* with.

1. s ock 2. m ug 3. d uck

4. t ank 5. l eaf 6. f rog

7. v est 8. b ug 9. g oose

10. w ell 11. c lap 12. h and

 35

Students write the letter for the sound the word starts with.

WORD WORKERS 1 UNIT 8.4

Name .... Date ....

Write the sound the word *starts* with.

1. b ell 2. g oat 3. m ask

4. c at 5. h ill 6. n ut

7. d oll 8. s kip 9. p en

10. f ish 11. l amp 12. r ing

36

WORD WORKERS 1 UNIT 9.1

Name .... Date ....

Writing ending sounds

Write the sound the word *ends* with.

1. tu b 2. bow l 3. ca r
4. mil k 5. dru m 6. bu s
7. be d 8. su n 9. ha t
10. do g 11. ta p 12. bo x

© 2000 H.A. Calder and Pascal Press 37

For the following pages:

Students work with terminal consonant sounds in this unit. Continue with the auditory discrimination exercises on page 44 of the *Word Workers Teacher Resource Book* and with the consonant–vowel blending technique explained on pages 14–17.

Students write the letter for the sound the word ends with.

WORD WORKERS 1 UNIT 9.2

Name .... Date ....

Write the sound the word *ends* with.

1. ca v e 2. bu g 3. cli p
4. bi b 5. stoo l 6. sta r
7. win k 8. swi m 9. sock s
10. ro d 11. gu n 12. ca t

38 © 2000 H.A. Calder and Pascal Press

Name .... Date ....

Write the sound the word *ends* with.

1. fo x 2. fro g 3. stam p

4. cra b 5. fi v e 6. fou r

7. shar k 8. broo m 9. hor s e

10. sle d 11. pe n 12. je t

Name .... Date ....

Write the sound the word *ends* with.

1. clu b 2. coo k 3. han d

5. pi g 5. wa v e 6. ar m

7. fa n 8. cu p 9. si x

10. lamp s 11. nes t 12. lea f

Students write the letter for the sound the word ends with.

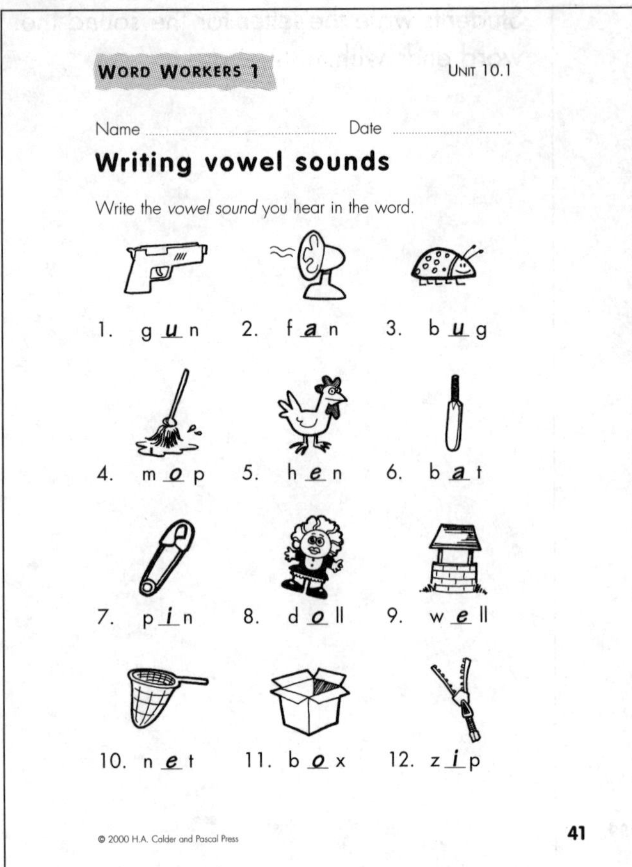

WORD WORKERS 1 UNIT 10.1

Name .... Date ....

Writing vowel sounds

Write the *vowel sound* you hear in the word.

1. g u n 2. f a n 3. b u g

4. m o p 5. h e n 6. b a t

7. p i n 8. d o ll 9. w e ll

10. n e t 11. b o x 12. z i p

© 2000 H.A. Calder and Pascal Press 41

For the following pages:

Students learn medial vowels in this unit. Assist acquisition of these sounds by using the initial and medial vowel auditory discrimination exercises on page 44 of the *Word Workers Teacher Resource Book*.

At this stage, start blending activities using the consonant–word pattern blending technique. This technique is described on pages 14–17 of the *Word Workers Teacher Resource Book*.

Students write the letter for the vowel sound they hear in the word.

WORD WORKERS 1 UNIT 10.2

Name .... Date ....

Write the *vowel sound* you hear in the word.

1. fr o g 2. tr u nk 3. a nt

4. n e st 5. m i lk 6. bl o ck

7. h a t 8. tr u ck 9. v e st

10. w i nk 11. r o d 12. t u b

42 © 2000 H.A. Calder and Pascal Press

Students write the letter for the vowel sound they hear in the word.

WORD WORKERS 1 UNIT 10.3

Name .... Date ....

Write the *vowel sound* you hear in the word.

1. n u t 2. d o g 3. h i ll

4. b e ll 5. cr a b 6. p e n

7. v a n 8. w i g 9. f o x

10. b u s 11. c a p 12. t e n

© 2000 H.A. Calder and Pascal Press 43

WORD WORKERS 1 UNIT 10.4

Name .... Date ....

Write the *vowel sound* you hear in the word.

1. s i x 2. st o p 3. d u ck

4. b a g 5. t e nt 6. s o ck

7. dr u m 8. l i ps 9. fl a g

10. n e st 11. p i g 12. r o ck

44 © 2000 H.A. Calder and Pascal Press

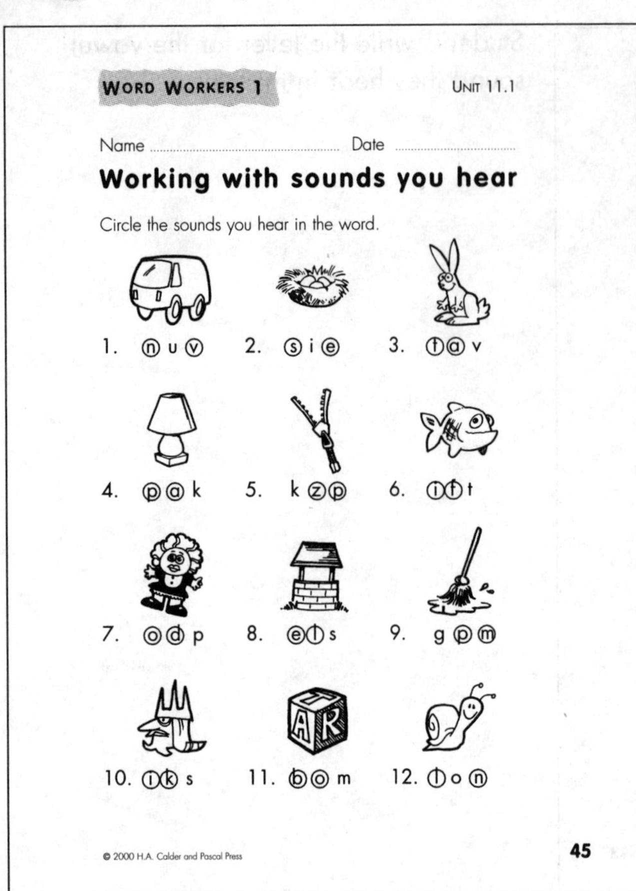
WORD WORKERS 1 UNIT 11.1

Name .... Date ....

Working with sounds you hear

Circle the sounds you hear in the word.

1. n u v 2. s i e 3. t a v

4. p a k 5. k z p 6. i f t

7. o d p 8. e l s 9. g p m

10. i k s 11. b o m 12. l o n

© 2000 H.A. Calder and Pascal Press 45

WORD WORKERS 1 UNIT 11.2

Name .... Date ....

Circle the sounds you hear in the word.

1. n s i 2. a j t 3. v u m

4. g o w 5. i r m 6. b i k

7. u t n 8. x l o 9. h a p

10. e f h 11. x l o 12. u d r

46 © 2000 H.A. Calder and Pascal Press

For the following pages:

Students work on auditory discrimination skills in this unit. Continue with the consonant–word pattern blending technique described on pages 14–17 of the *Word Workers Teacher Resource Book*.

Students circle the letters for the sounds they do hear in the word.

Students circle the letters for the sounds they do hear in the word.

WORD WORKERS 1 UNIT 11.3

Name .... Date ....

Circle the sounds you hear in the word.

1. y ⓓⓡ 2. ⓚⓡ w 3. j ⓕⓛ

4. d ⓘⓢ 5. ⓐ b ⓣ 6. k ⓡⓢ

7. u ⓔⓓ 8. ⓡⓕ e 9. ⓧ t ⓑ

10. ⓢⓛ h 11. ⓦⓘ p 12. y ⓞⓢ

 47

WORD WORKERS 1 UNIT 11.4

Name .... Date ....

Circle the sounds you hear in the word.

1. i ⓥⓒ 2. ⓗ m ⓡ 3. ⓖⓐ z

4. ⓝⓟ u 5. f ⓧⓢ 6. ⓜ b ⓛ

7. r ⓦⓖ 8. ⓐⓟ l 9. ⓡ k ⓔ

10. o ⓛⓑ 11. ⓡⓤ y 12. l ⓒⓜ

48

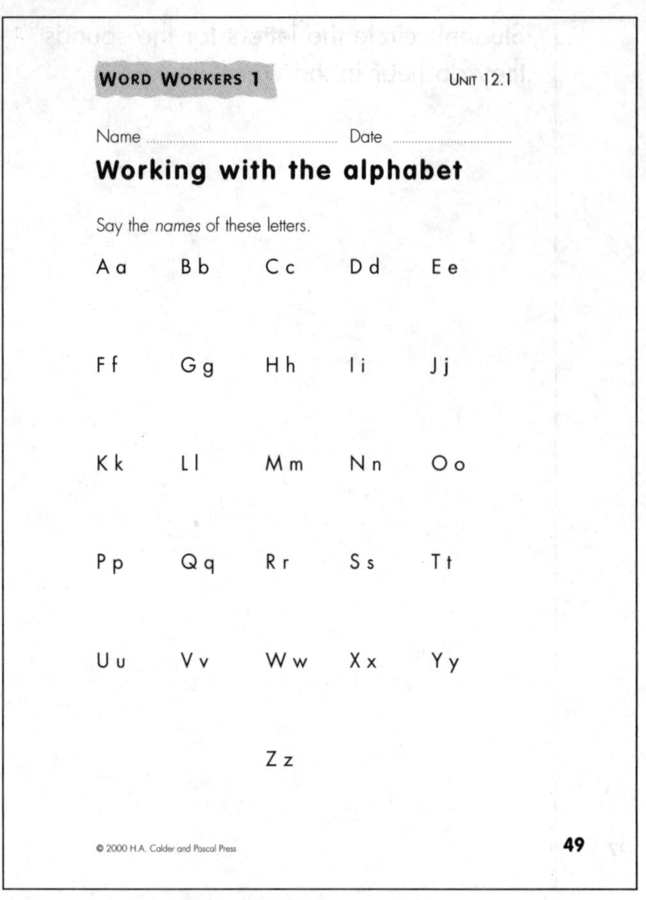

WORD WORKERS 1 UNIT 12.1

Name .... Date ....

Working with the alphabet

Say the *names* of these letters.

A a B b C c D d E e

F f G g H h I i J j

K k L l M m N n O o

P p Q q R r S s T t

U u V v W w X x Y y

Z z

© 2000 H.A. Calder and Pascal Press 49

For the following pages:

Practise alphabet knowledge at a different stage of the lesson than the reinforcement of single letter sounds.

Students say the names for the letters. Ask them to say the name for both the upper case and lower case letter.

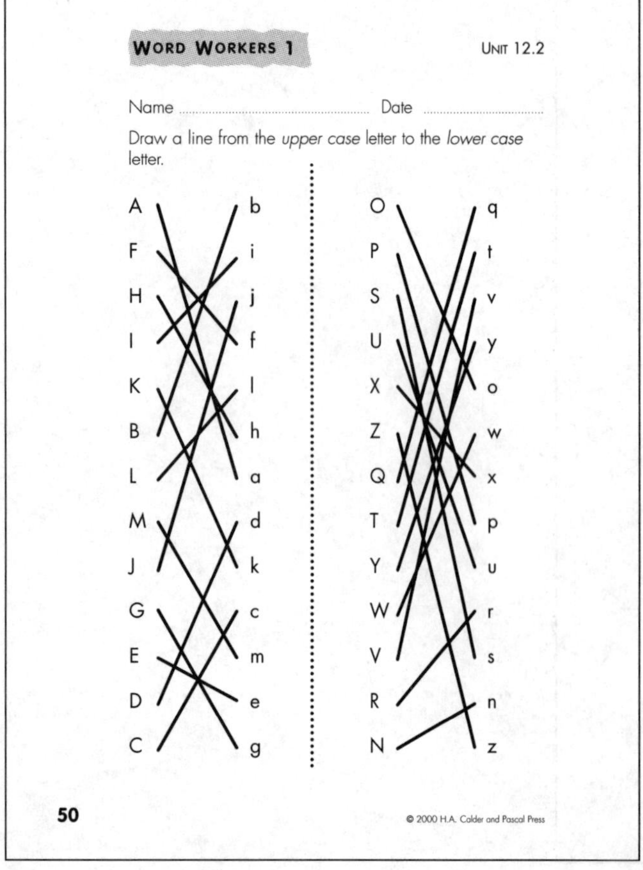

WORD WORKERS 1 UNIT 12.2

Name .... Date ....

Draw a line from the *upper case* letter to the *lower case* letter.

A	b	O	q
F	i	P	t
H	j	S	v
I	f	U	y
K	l	X	o
B	h	Z	w
L	a	Q	x
M	d	T	p
J	k	Y	u
G	c	W	r
E	m	V	s
D	e	R	n
C	g	N	z

50 © 2000 H.A. Calder and Pascal Press

Students draw a line from the upper case letter to the lower case letter in the opposite column.

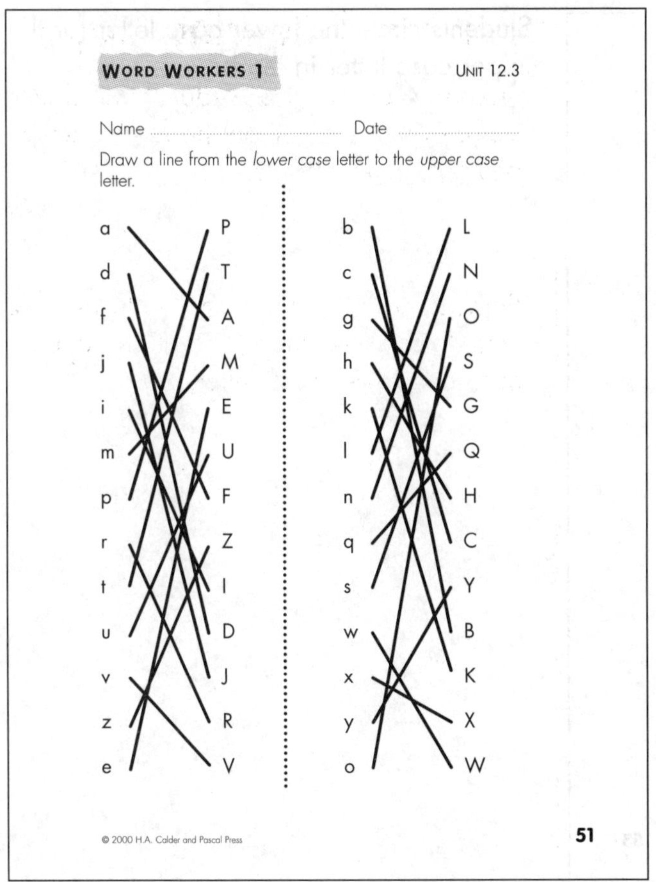
WORD WORKERS 1 UNIT 12.3

Name .... Date ....

Draw a line from the *lower case* letter to the *upper case* letter.

a	P	b	L
d	T	c	N
f	A	g	O
j	M	h	S
i	E	k	G
m	U	l	Q
p	F	n	H
r	Z	q	C
t	I	s	Y
u	D	w	B
v	J	x	K
z	R	y	X
e	V	o	W

© 2000 H.A. Calder and Pascal Press 51

Students draw a line from the lower case letter to the upper case letter in the opposite column.

WORD WORKERS 1 UNIT 12.4

Name .... Date ....

Circle the *lower case* letter for the *upper case* letter in the box.

B	a	c	e	(b)	z
X	d	b	c	(x)	a
D	f	(d)	c	z	y
E	(e)	y	d	x	a
F	l	(f)	w	e	x
I	(i)	v	g	w	f
L	u	(l)	v	h	g
K	t	u	(k)	h	i
N	t	s	i	j	(n)
O	r	j	(o)	k	s
R	k	n	l	q	(r)
T	l	m	o	(t)	p
U	(u)	o	n	p	m

52 © 2000 H.A. Calder and Pascal Press

Students circle the lower case letter for the upper case letter in the box.

WORD WORKERS 1 UNIT 12.5

Name .... Date ....

Circle the *lower case* letter for the *upper case* letter in the box.

A	x	z	y	w	(a)
W	y	(w)	l	b	z
C	a	(c)	v	z	u
G	d	v	(g)	u	a
H	(h)	e	s	b	t
J	t	c	f	s	(j)
M	d	g	r	b	(m)
P	r	e	q	(p)	h
Q	p	(q)	f	i	o
S	(s)	o	j	g	p
V	m	k	(v)	n	h
Z	l	n	(z)	i	m
Y	d	k	j	(y)	l

© 2000 H.A. Calder and Pascal Press 53

Students circle the lower case letter for the upper case letter in the box.

WORD WORKERS 1 UNIT 12.6

Name .... Date ....

Circle the *upper case* letter for the *lower case* letter in the box.

a	Z	(A)	C	Y	X
j	A	Y	B	(J)	W
q	B	C	(Q)	X	V
s	D	W	(S)	U	C
d	T	E	V	A	(D)
i	F	E	S	U	(I)
l	R	(L)	T	G	F
f	G	S	(F)	H	Q
n	R	H	I	(N)	P
t	(T)	J	Q	I	O
w	K	N	J	P	(W)
z	L	K	(Z)	O	M
e	Z	M	(E)	N	L

54 © 2000 H.A. Calder and Pascal Press

Students circle the upper case letter for the lower case letter in the box.

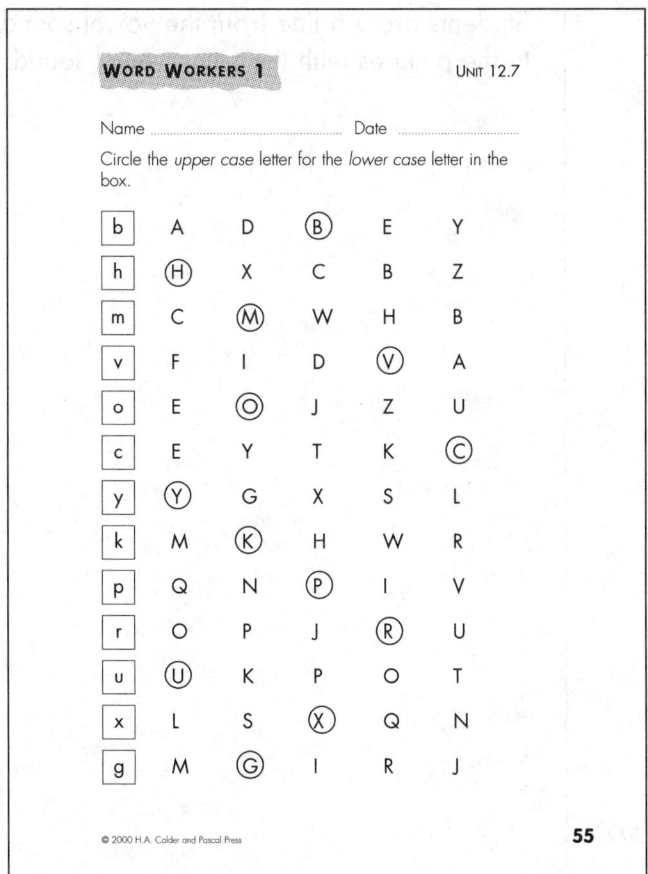

WORD WORKERS 1 UNIT 12.7

Name .... Date ....

Circle the *upper case* letter for the *lower case* letter in the box.

b	A	D	**B**	E	Y
h	**H**	X	C	B	Z
m	C	**M**	W	H	B
v	F	I	D	**V**	A
o	E	**O**	J	Z	U
c	E	Y	T	K	**C**
y	**Y**	G	X	S	L
k	M	**K**	H	W	R
p	Q	N	**P**	I	V
r	O	P	J	**R**	U
u	**U**	K	P	O	T
x	L	S	**X**	Q	N
g	M	**G**	I	R	J

© 2000 H.A. Calder and Pascal Press 55

Students circle the upper case letter for the lower case letter in the box.

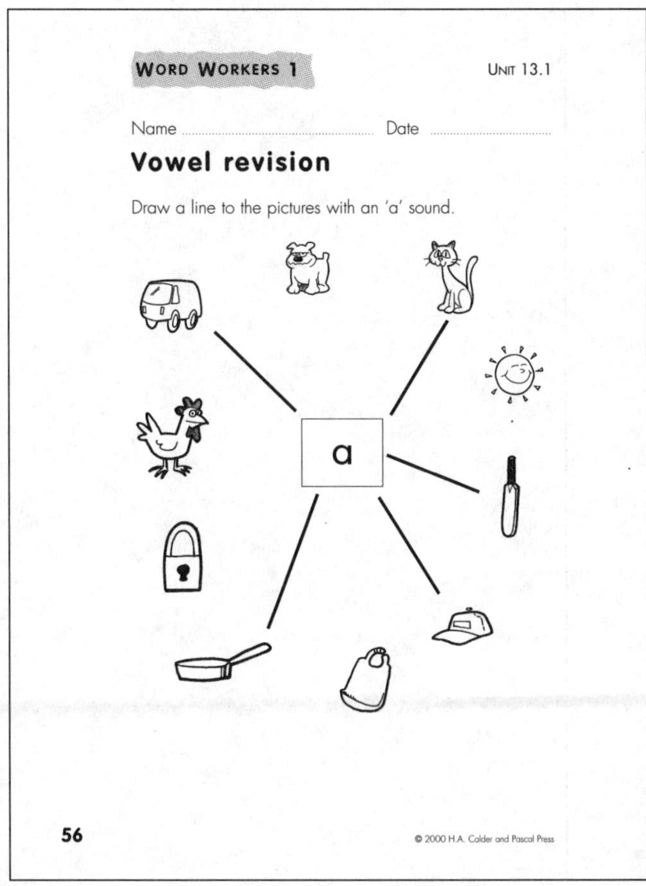

WORD WORKERS 1 UNIT 13.1

Name .... Date ....

Vowel revision

Draw a line to the pictures with an 'a' sound.

56 © 2000 H.A. Calder and Pascal Press

For the following pages:

Students learn medial vowels in this unit. Assist acquisition of these sounds by using the initial and medial vowel auditory discrimination exercises on page 44 of the *Word Workers Teacher Resource Book*.

Students draw a line from the vowel sound to the pictures with the same vowel sound.

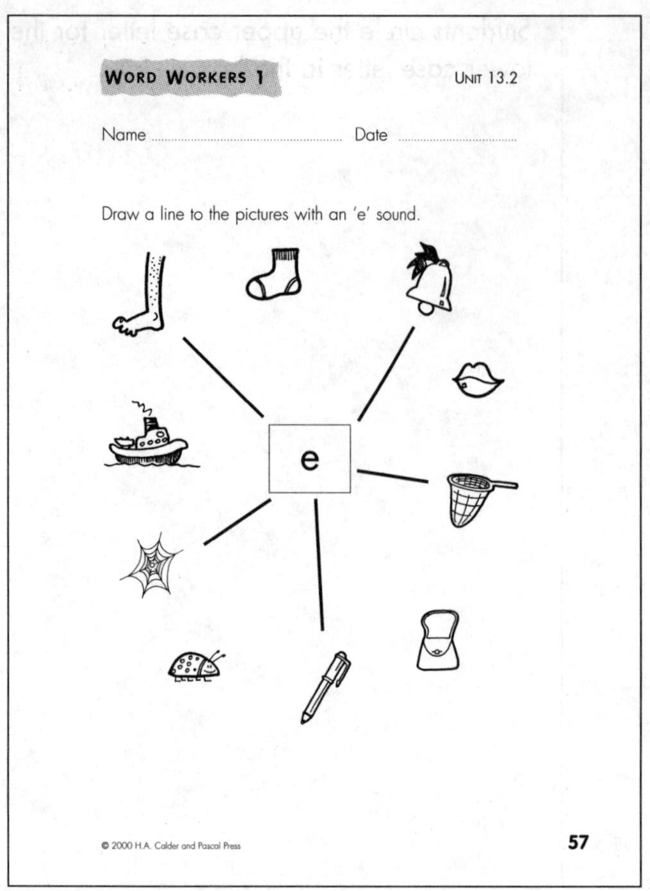

Students draw a line from the vowel sound to the pictures with the same vowel sound.

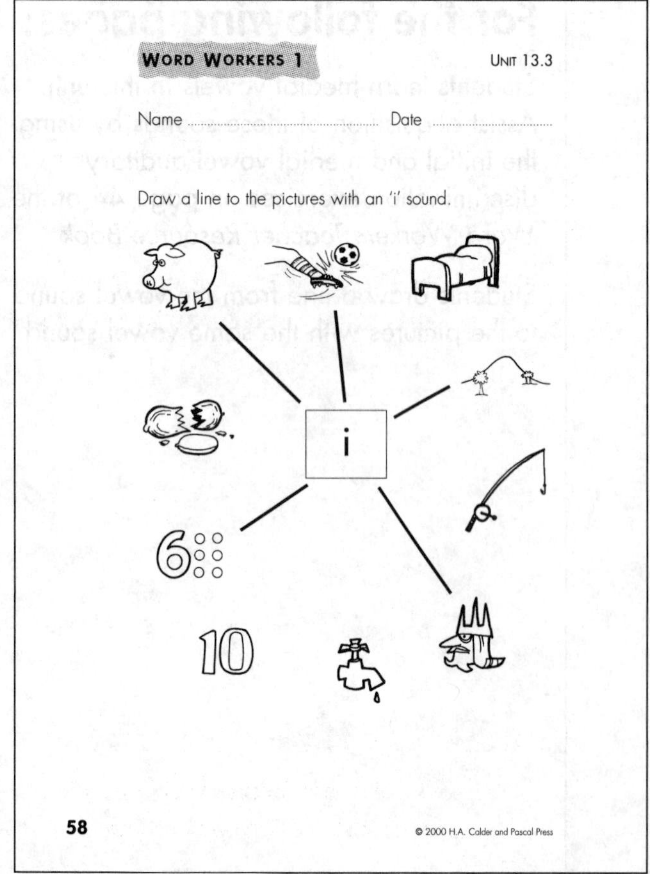

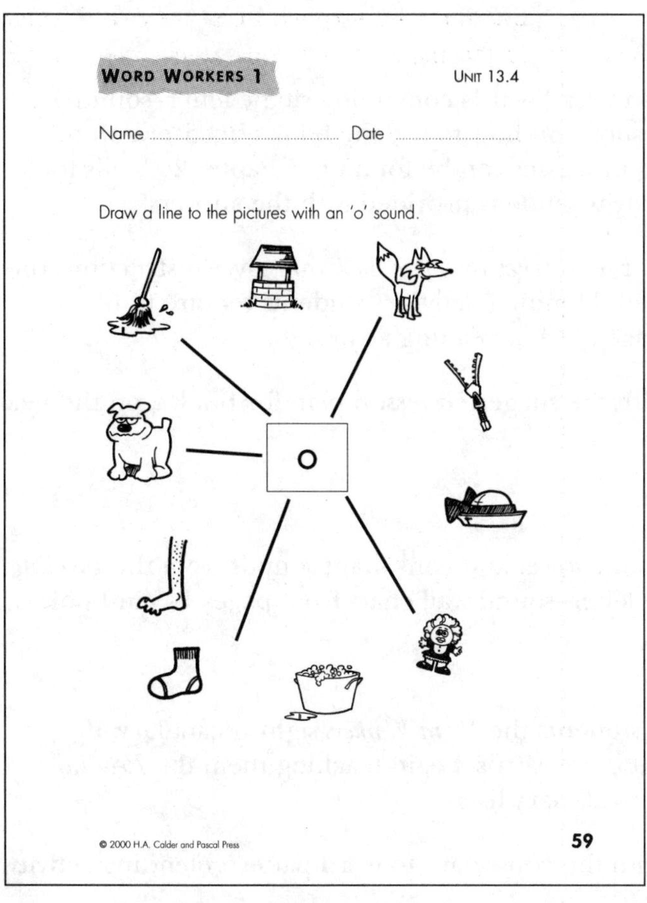

WORD WORKERS 1 UNIT 13.4

Name .... Date ....

Draw a line to the pictures with an 'o' sound.

o

59

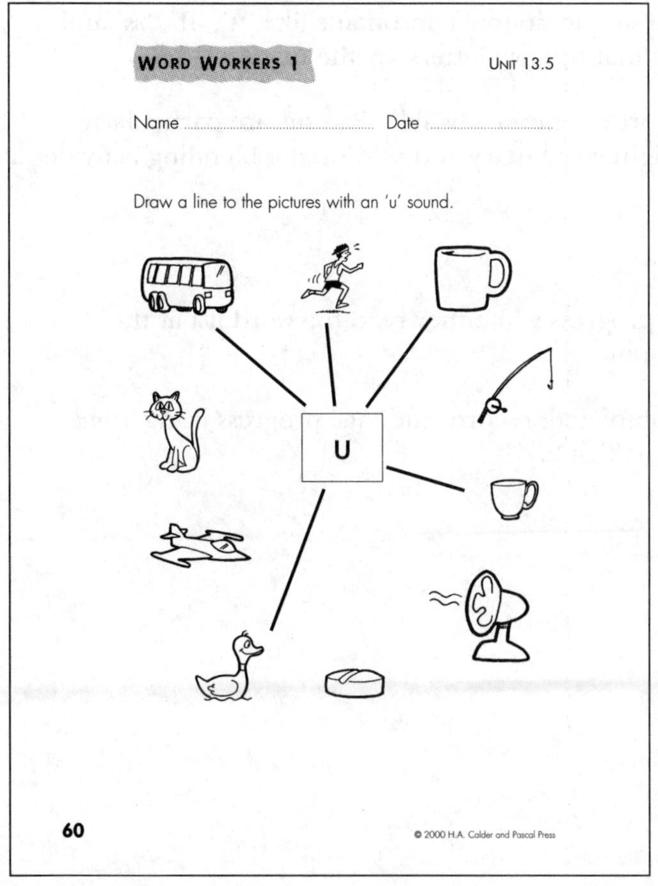

WORD WORKERS 1 UNIT 13.5

Name .... Date ....

Draw a line to the pictures with an 'u' sound.

u

60

Students draw a line from the vowel sound to the pictures with the same vowel sound.

* Students complete *Word Workers Achievement Test 1* after completing this unit.

Using Book 2

Word Workers Book 2 teaches students to read words containing single letter–sound combinations. Below are some suggestions on how to use the book effectively. More detailed information on the teaching processes can be found in Chapter 2: 'Skills for successful teaching'. An activity-by-activity guide is provided with the answers.

- Read the section in the *Teacher Resource Book* that gives instructions on teaching the different blending activities students require to be successful at this stage of their reading acquisition.
- Become familiar with the suggested lesson plan for Book 2 on the next page.

- Continue the drill with vowel and consonant sounds from the *Reading Freedom 2000* single letter–sound wall chart from pages 1–3 in Book 2.
- Continue teaching students the *Word Workers* sight vocabulary. If students have learnt these words, begin teaching them the *Reading Freedom* basic sight vocabulary lists.
- Continue to drill with the consonant to word pattern blending activity.
- Teach students the simple double consonants like 'tt', 'ff', 'ss' and 'ck'. Remind them that the two letters say the first sound.
- Enlist parent support whenever possible. Parents are particularly helpful teaching sight vocabulary and reinforcing blending activities at home.

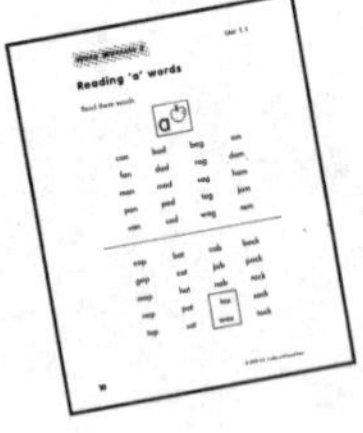

- Monitor students' progress while they read the word list at the beginning of each unit.
- When Book 2 is completed, record students' progress using *Word Workers* Achievement Test 2.

Book 2: Suggested lesson plan

Based on a lesson of approximately 30 minutes.

1 Students say a row of sounds from the *Reading Freedom 2000* single letter–sound wall chart or from pages 1–3 in Book 2. For small groups, each student can say a row or column of sounds. If your class is large, select students to say a row or column until all the sounds have been repeated. Be sure different students say the sounds each lesson.

2 In small group lessons, each student reads a column of *Reading Freedom* basic sight vocabulary (assuming *Word Workers* sight vocabulary has been mastered; if not, continue with it until it has been learned). When teaching the whole class, select students to read a column of sight words. Five or six columns is enough to start your lesson with. Be sure different students read the sight words each lesson.

3 Explain and demonstrate the vowel sound to be learned (see Chapter 2: 'Skills for successful teaching' if any guidance is necessary). Carefully explain the activities on the page or pages to be completed. Ensure that students understand the concepts involved and know what is required of them.

4 Assign activity pages to be completed (the number of pages depends on the teacher's professional judgment as well as the ability and enthusiasm of the student).

5 In Book 2, continue practising consonant-word pattern blending skills. Continue with this until the book is completed, learning new word patterns containing the vowel sounds as they are introduced sequentially. Some students require more work with blending techniques than others. Form a group of these students and give them extra practice while other students work on activity pages.

7 Reward students for achievement on the activity pages or in learning sight vocabulary with stamps, stickers or gold stars. When they complete the activity book and finish the complementary achievement test (found in *Word Workers Achievement Tests*) they receive a *Word Workers* Merit Certificate.

8 Assign any homework after demonstrating the activities. Ensure students understand the concept and what is to be done.

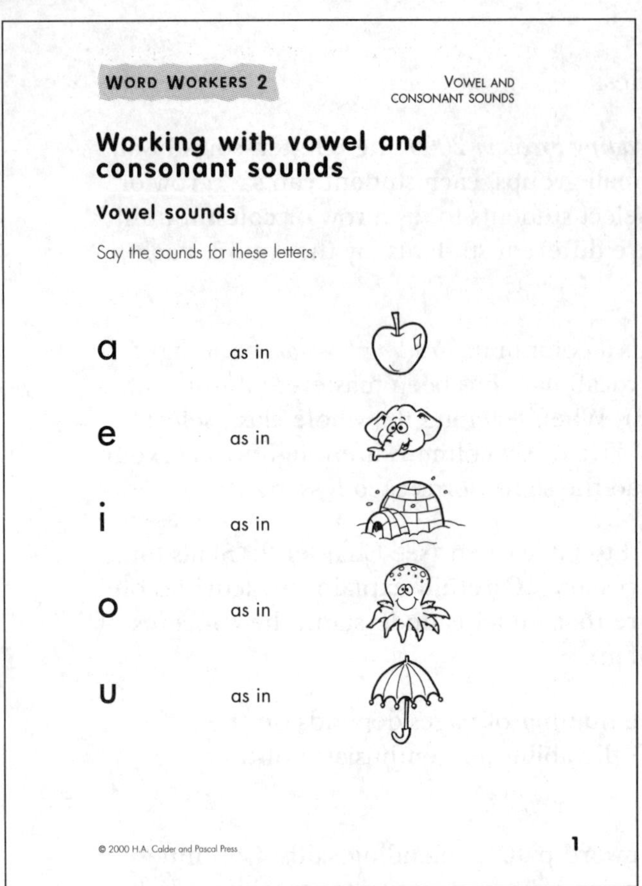
WORD WORKERS 2
VOWEL AND CONSONANT SOUNDS

Working with vowel and consonant sounds

Vowel sounds

Say the sounds for these letters.

a as in

e as in

i as in

o as in

u as in

© 2000 H.A. Calder and Pascal Press

1

For the following pages:

Teach students the sounds for these letters. All letters except for 'x' are taught as beginning or initial sounds. In a medial or terminal position in words, the sound for the letter 'x' is a combination of the sounds 'k' and 's', to make the sound 'ks'.

Students say the vowel sounds.

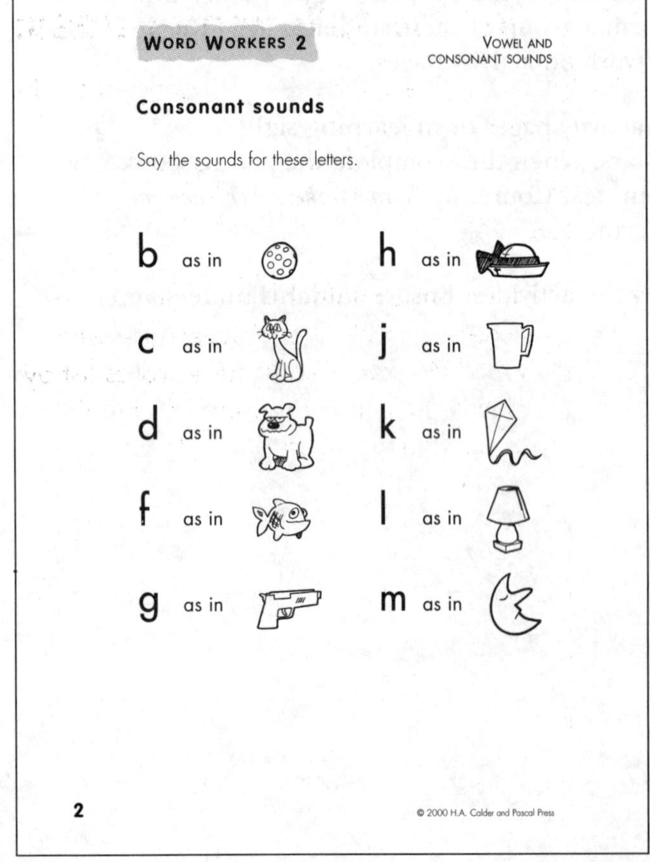
WORD WORKERS 2
VOWEL AND CONSONANT SOUNDS

Consonant sounds

Say the sounds for these letters.

b as in

c as in

d as in

f as in

g as in

h as in

j as in

k as in

l as in

m as in

2

© 2000 H.A. Calder and Pascal Press

Students say the consonant sounds.

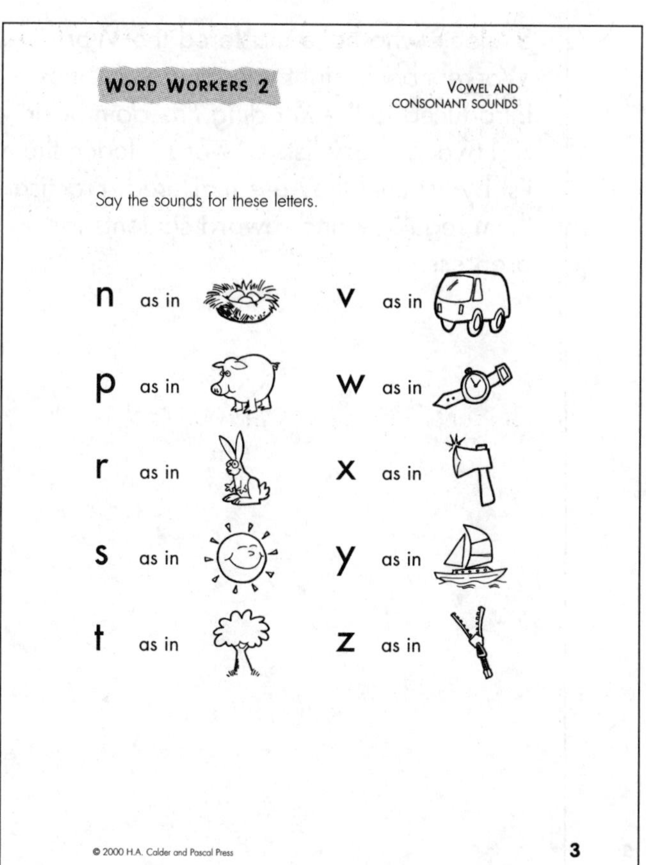

WORD WORKERS 2 VOWEL AND CONSONANT SOUNDS

Say the sounds for these letters.

n as in
v as in
p as in
w as in
r as in
x as in
s as in
y as in
t as in
z as in

© 2000 H.A. Calder and Pascal Press 3

Students say the consonant sounds.

WORD WORKERS 2 SIGHT VOCABULARY

Word Workers sight vocabulary

Learn these sight words.

a	no	are	out	come
as	oh	and	put	little
by	on	all	see	look
he	so	but	saw	said
I	to	her	the	them
in	up	his	too	then
is	we	Mrs	was	they
		not	you	there
		now		with

4 © 2000 H.A. Calder and Pascal Press

For the following pages:

Students learn these sight words list by list. Reward successful acquisition of sight vocabulary with stars and stickers.

These lists contain the basic sight words students need to work successfully with *Word Workers*. Teach these words list by list until they are mastered. Practise them regularly and reward students for progress.

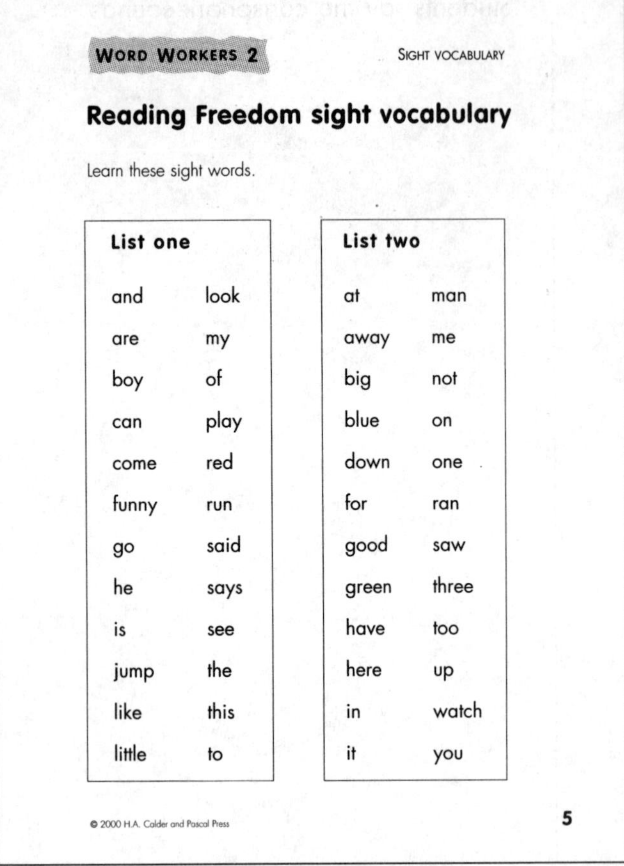

WORD WORKERS 2 SIGHT VOCABULARY

Reading Freedom sight vocabulary

Learn these sight words.

List one		List two	
and	look	at	man
are	my	away	me
boy	of	big	not
can	play	blue	on
come	red	down	one
funny	run	for	ran
go	said	good	saw
he	says	green	three
is	see	have	too
jump	the	here	up
like	this	in	watch
little	to	it	you

© 2000 H.A. Calder and Pascal Press 5

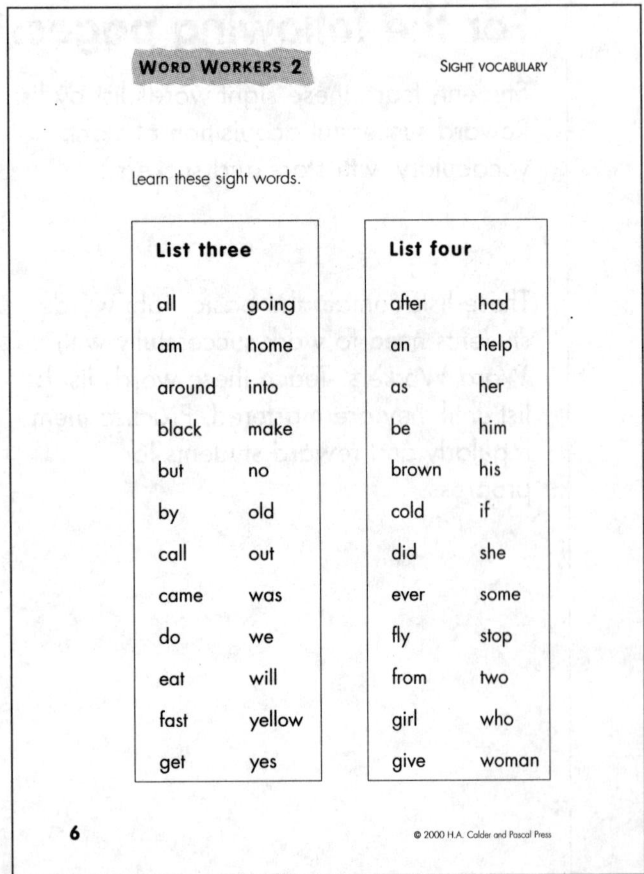

WORD WORKERS 2 SIGHT VOCABULARY

Learn these sight words.

List three		List four	
all	going	after	had
am	home	an	help
around	into	as	her
black	make	be	him
but	no	brown	his
by	old	cold	if
call	out	did	she
came	was	ever	some
do	we	fly	stop
eat	will	from	two
fast	yellow	girl	who
get	yes	give	woman

6 © 2000 H.A. Calder and Pascal Press

Students who have mastered the *Word Workers* basic sight vocabulary are now introduced to the *Reading Freedom* basic sight vocabulary lists of words. Teach them list by list until they are mastered. Practise them regularly and reward students for progress.

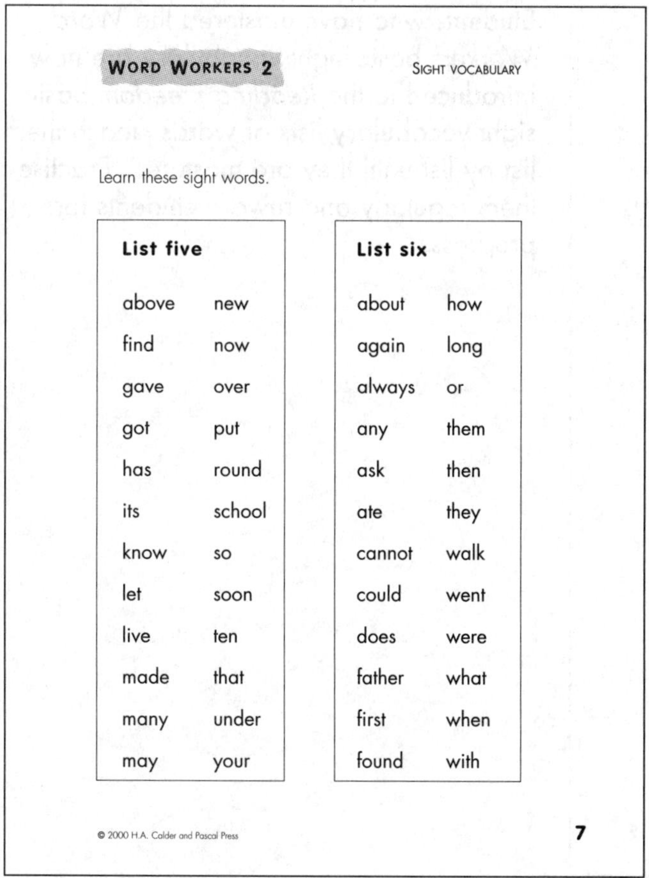

Word Workers 2 Sight vocabulary

Learn these sight words.

List five	
above	new
find	now
gave	over
got	put
has	round
its	school
know	so
let	soon
live	ten
made	that
many	under
may	your

List six	
about	how
again	long
always	or
any	them
ask	then
ate	they
cannot	walk
could	went
does	were
father	what
first	when
found	with

© 2000 H.A. Calder and Pascal Press 7

Students who have mastered the *Word Workers* basic sight vocabulary are now introduced to the *Reading Freedom* basic sight vocabulary lists of words. Teach them list by list until they are mastered. Practise them regularly and reward students for progress.

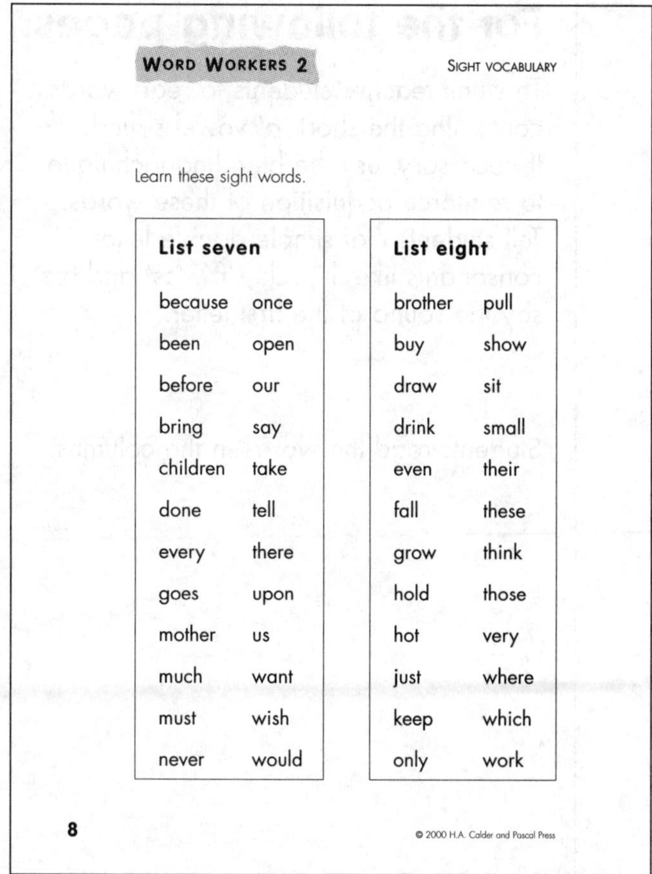

Word Workers 2 Sight vocabulary

Learn these sight words.

List seven	
because	once
been	open
before	our
bring	say
children	take
done	tell
every	there
goes	upon
mother	us
much	want
must	wish
never	would

List eight	
brother	pull
buy	show
draw	sit
drink	small
even	their
fall	these
grow	think
hold	those
hot	very
just	where
keep	which
only	work

8 © 2000 H.A. Calder and Pascal Press

WORD WORKERS 2 — SIGHT VOCABULARY

Learn these sight words.

List nine		List ten	
best	pick	baby	sing
better	please	daughter	sister
both	pretty	far	sleep
clean	read	house	something
cut	shall	hurt	son
eight	six	kind	start
five	today	laugh	thank
four	try	Mr	together
full	use	Mrs	warm
light	well	own	wash
myself	why	right	water
off	write	seven	white

© 2000 H.A. Calder and Pascal Press 9

Students who have mastered the *Word Workers* basic sight vocabulary are now introduced to the *Reading Freedom* basic sight vocabulary lists of words. Teach them list by list until they are mastered. Practise them regularly and reward students for progress.

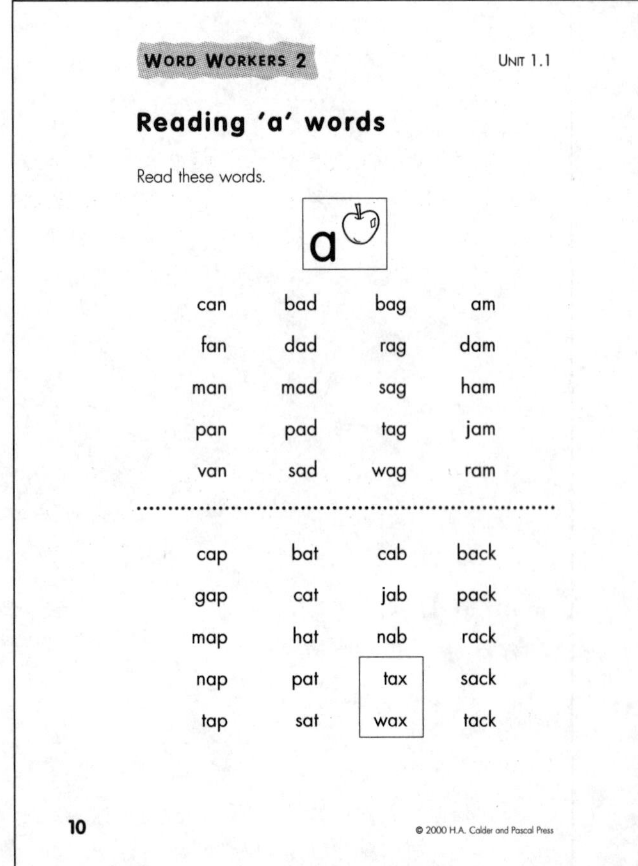

WORD WORKERS 2 — UNIT 1.1

Reading 'a' words

Read these words.

a

can	bad	bag	am
fan	dad	rag	dam
man	mad	sag	ham
pan	pad	tag	jam
van	sad	wag	ram

cap	bat	cab	back
gap	cat	jab	pack
map	hat	nab	rack
nap	pat	tax	sack
tap	sat	wax	tack

10 © 2000 H.A. Calder and Pascal Press

For the following pages:

This unit teaches students to read words containing the short 'a' vowel sound. If necessary, use the blending technique to reinforce acquisition of these words. Tell students that simple double letter consonants like 'll', 'ck', 'ff', 'ss' and 'zz' say the sound of the first letter.

Students read the words in the columns.

WORD WORKERS 2 UNIT 1.2

Name .... Date ....

Write the words for the pictures.

1. tap 2. pan 3. hat

4. fan 5. cap 6. bag

7. bat 8. van 9. cat

 11

Students write the words for the pictures. If necessary, they refer to the word lists to find the correct spelling.

WORD WORKERS 2 UNIT 1.3

Name .... Date ....

Complete the words by writing the vowel sound.

a	a	a
v a n	t a x	P a m
b a n	M a x	j a m
D a n	w a x	r a m

Underline the word with the different letter pattern.

1. mad rag sad pad dad
2. ram jam Sam ham ran
3. wag nab sag nag bag
4. hat had sat pat fat
5. back tack rack tag sack

12

Activity 1: Students complete the words by writing in the letter printed above each column.

Activity 2: Students read the words going across the page. They underline the one word that is different from the others.

WORD WORKERS 2 UNIT 1.4

Name .... Date ....

Read these words.

cap caps	bags bag	hat hats	pads pad
packs pack	tap taps	pans pan	jab jabs

Write the word for the picture.

1. caps 2. cat 3. tacks

4. tap 5. pans 6. van

© 2000 H.A. Calder and Pascal Press 13

Activity 1: Students read the words in the boxes. Tell them to add the endings to the smallest word or base word.

Activity 2: Students write the words for the pictures. Tell them to add the letter 's' if there is more than one. If necessary, they refer to the word lists to find the correct spelling.

WORD WORKERS 2 UNIT 1.5

Name .... Date ....

Underline the word for the picture.

pat	gap	fan	packs
bat	nap	pan	<u>tacks</u>
sat	<u>tap</u>	<u>van</u>	racks
<u>hat</u>	map	man	sacks

Underline the word from each column that fits the word shape box.

tap	ham	bad	cap	tack
pan	tax	nap	wax	cat
sad	tap	sack	am	man
back	ran	jab	sag	tan
pan	tap	jab	wax	tack

14 © 2000 H.A. Calder and Pascal Press

Activity 1: Students look at the columns of words. They underline the word in each column that matches the picture above it.

Activity 2: Students look at the columns of words. Tell them to put the word from each column that fits into the 'word shape' box below it.

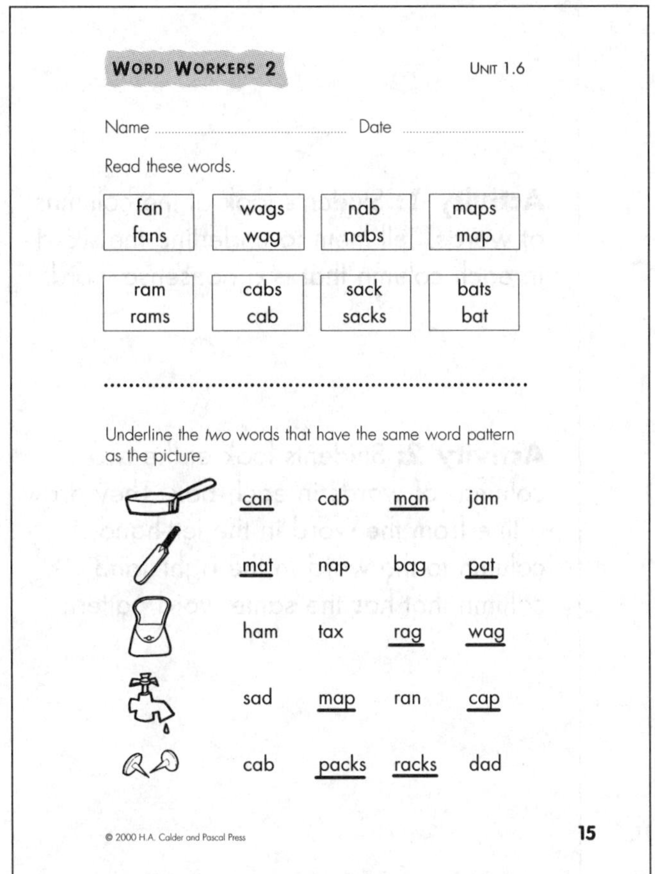
WORD WORKERS 2 UNIT 1.6

Name .... Date ....

Read these words.

fan fans	wags wag	nab nabs	maps map
ram rams	cabs cab	sack sacks	bats bat

Underline the *two* words that have the same word pattern as the picture.

can cab man jam

mat nap bag pat

ham tax rag wag

sad map ran cap

cab packs racks dad

© 2000 H.A. Calder and Pascal Press 15

Activity 1: Students read the words in the boxes. Tell them to add the endings to the smallest word or base word.

Activity 2: Students look at the pictures and the words on the lines beside them. They underline the two words in each line that have the same word pattern as the picture.

WORD WORKERS 2 UNIT 1.7

Name .... Date ....

Complete the words with the word pattern from the picture.

f at	t an	g ap	b acks
v at	b an	m ap	s acks
m at	m an	n ap	p acks

Put each column in alphabetical order.

a		a		a	
dad	bag	hat	hat	wag	ram
bag	cab	nap	jam	wax	sack
fan	dad	pack	mad	sack	tag
cab	fan	mad	nap	ram	wag
gap	gap	jam	pack	tag	wax

16 © 2000 H.A. Calder and Pascal Press

Activity 1: Students look at the pictures above the columns. They use the word pattern from each picture to complete the words in the column below.

Activity 2: Students place the words in each column in alphabetical order.

WORD WORKERS 2 UNIT 1.8

Name .... Date ....

Underline the nonsense word.

1. bad	2. vack	3. dam	4. bag	5. bat
mad	back	zam	map	rag
nad	sack	ham	fap	wag
sad	pack	Sam	sap	pag

Draw a line to the word with the same word pattern.

can	sack	jam	wag	fan	tack
rack	mad	cab	ham	nap	ram
tap	ran	sat	nab	back	gap
sad	map	tag	pat	am	pan

© 2000 H.A. Calder and Pascal Press 17

Activity 1: Students look at the columns of words. Tell them to underline the word in each column that is a nonsense word.

Activity 2: Students look at the two columns of words in each box. They draw a line from the word in the left-hand column to the word in the right-hand column that has the same word pattern.

WORD WORKERS 2 UNIT 1.9

Name .... Date ....

Read these words.

cans can | rag rags | mat mats | tacks tack

sad sadder | fatter fat | mad madder

Underline the word that completes the sentence.

1. The cat sat on Max's (hat/pat).
2. The fat (man/tan) had a sack.
3. Jan's (bags/wags) are in the van.
4. Dad had Jack's (fat/bat).
5. Ann sat in the (back/rack) of the cab.

18 © 2000 H.A. Calder and Pascal Press

Activity 1: Students read the words in the boxes. Tell them to add the endings to the smallest word or base word.

Activity 2: Students read the sentences. They underline the word in brackets that best completes the sentence.

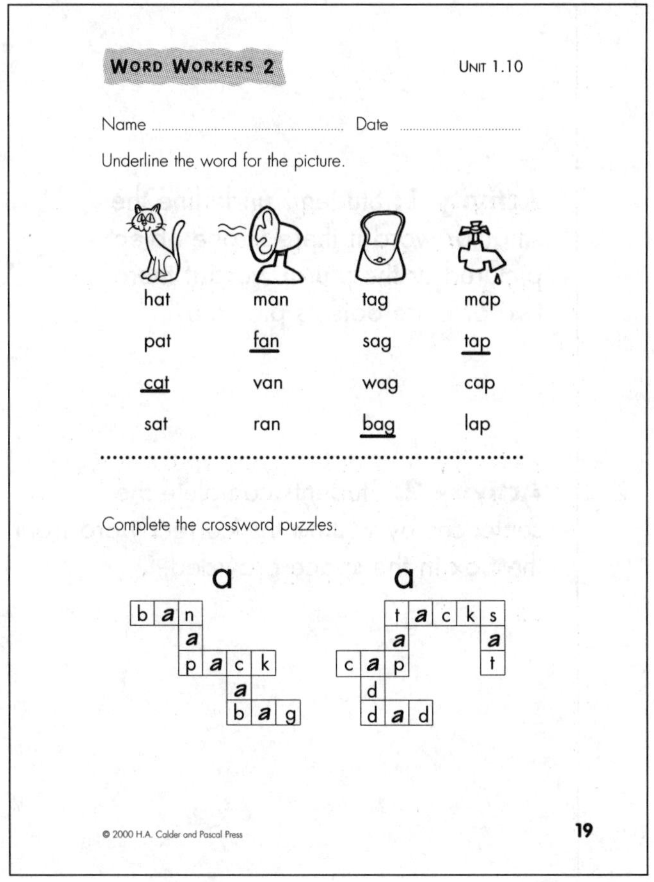
WORD WORKERS 2 UNIT 1.10

Name .... Date ....

Underline the word for the picture.

hat	man	tag	map
pat	fan	sag	tap
cat	van	wag	cap
sat	ran	bag	lap

Complete the crossword puzzles.

a a

b a n / a / p a c k / a / b a g

t a c k s / a / a / c a p / t / d / d a d

© 2000 H.A. Calder and Pascal Press 19

Activity 1: Students look at the columns of words. They underline the word in each column that matches the picture above it.

Activity 2: Students complete the crossword puzzles. They write the letter(s) indicated in the blank spaces to make words that can be read going down or across the page.

WORD WORKERS 2 UNIT 1.11

Name .... Date ....

Write the word with the correct spelling.

1.	sac	sack	sak	*sack*
2.	cat	catt	kat	*cat*
3.	tapp	tapz	taps	*taps*
4.	tax	taks	taz	*tax*
5.	mapp	mab	map	*map*

Fill in the missing letters to complete the word.

1. *b* at *s*
2. *p* ac *k*
3. *j* a *m*
4. *t* ack *s*
5. *v* an *s*

pack
tacks
bats
vans
jam

20

Activity 1: Students read the words going across the page, then write the word that is spelt correctly.

Activity 2: Students read the words in the box, then write the missing letters to complete the column of words on the left.

Word Workers 2 Unit 1.12

Name .... Date ....

Underline the word for the picture.

pan <u>pans</u> <u>fan</u> fans tack <u>tacks</u>

hat <u>hats</u> <u>van</u> vans <u>bag</u> bags

Complete the sentences with the words in the box.

sack fat van hat ham

1. Max had a nap in the back of his *van*.
2. Mrs Jack had a can of *ham*.
3. The man ran at the *fat* cat.
4. Jan's *hat* was on her lap.
5. Sam had his bat in a *sack*.

© 2000 H.A. Calder and Pascal Press 21

Activity 1: Students underline the singular word if there is one object pictured or the plural word if there are two or more objects pictured.

Activity 2: Students complete the sentences by writing the correct word from the box in the space provided.

Word Workers 2 Unit 1.13

Name .... Date ....

Draw a line from the picture to the matching word.

tack rack sack — rap map lap — fat sat rat — tan pan ban

Number the words in the box in alphabetical order, then answer the questions.

4 rack	*5* sad	*3* jam
6 wag	*2* jab	*1* hat

1. Which word comes *before* 'wag'? *sad*
2. Which word comes *after* 'jab'? *jam*
3. Which word comes *after* 'hat'? *jab*
4 Which word comes *before* 'sad'? *rack*
5. Which word comes *before* 'jab'? *hat*
6. Which word comes *after* 'sad'? *wag*

22 © 2000 H.A. Calder and Pascal Press

Activity 1: Students say the word for the picture and then draw a line from the picture to the correct word beside it.

Activity 2: Students number the words in the box in alphabetical order, then use this information to answer the questions below.

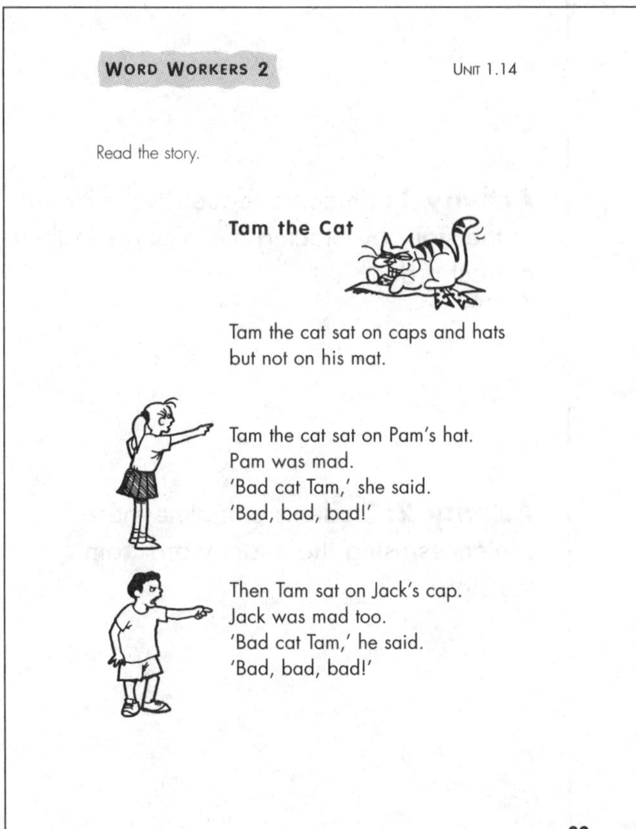

Word Workers 2 Unit 1.14

Read the story.

Tam the Cat

Tam the cat sat on caps and hats
but not on his mat.

Tam the cat sat on Pam's hat.
Pam was mad.
'Bad cat Tam,' she said.
'Bad, bad, bad!'

Then Tam sat on Jack's cap.
Jack was mad too.
'Bad cat Tam,' he said.
'Bad, bad, bad!'

© 2000 H.A. Calder and Pascal Press 23

Word Workers 2 Unit 1.15

Jack and Pam said to the cat,
'You rat Tam.
You sat on the hats.
You sat on the caps.
But not on the mat.
Bad, bad, bad!'

But Tam the cat sat and sat.
Then he said to Jack and Pam.
'I sat on the hat.
I sat on the cap.
But I am not a rat.
I am a cat.
Cat, cat, cat!'

24 © 2000 H.A. Calder and Pascal Press

For the following pages:

This story is designed to reinforce the skills learned in this and previous units of work. At no stage do students encounter unfamiliar words or skills. Students read the story and answer the questions silently. Correct the work by having them read the story and answer the questions orally.

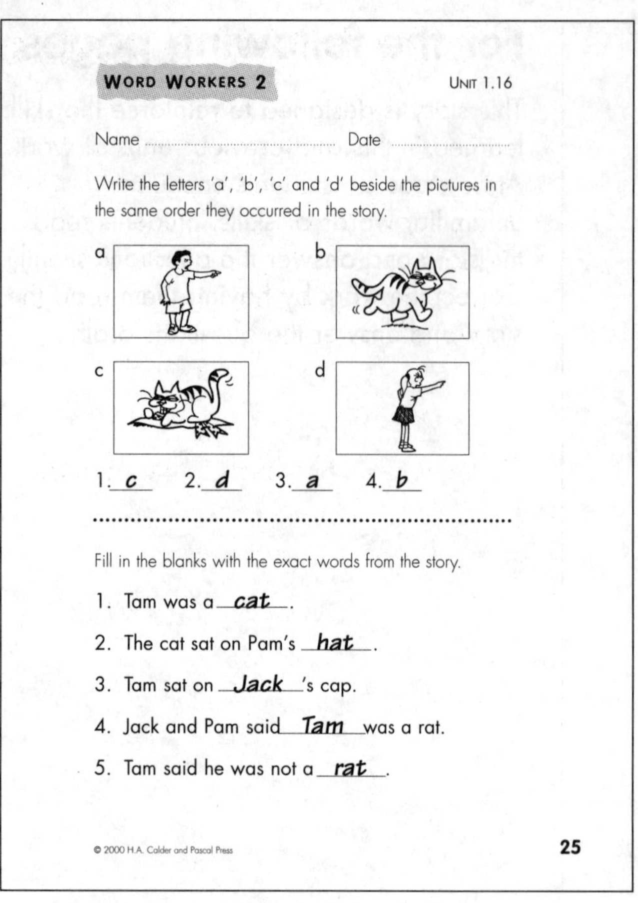

WORD WORKERS 2 UNIT 1.16

Name .... Date ....

Write the letters 'a', 'b', 'c' and 'd' beside the pictures in the same order they occurred in the story.

a b

c d

1. *c* 2. *d* 3. *a* 4. *b*

Fill in the blanks with the exact words from the story.

1. Tam was a *cat*.
2. The cat sat on Pam's *hat*.
3. Tam sat on *Jack*'s cap.
4. Jack and Pam said *Tam* was a rat.
5. Tam said he was not a *rat*.

 25

Activity 1: Students sequence the events in the story by placing the pictures in their correct order.

Activity 2: Students complete these sentences using the exact word from the story.

WORD WORKERS 2 UNIT 1.17

Name .... Date ....

Complete the sentences with the words in the box.

Jack and *Pam* said to the cat,

'You *rat* Tam.

You sat on the *hats*.

You *sat* on the caps.

But not on the *mat*.

Bad, bad, bad!'

rat hats Pam sat mat

Write the letters 'a', 'b', 'c' and 'd' beside the sentences in the same order they occurred in the story.

1. Tam the cat sat and sat. *d*
2. Pam was mad. *b*
3. Tam sat on caps and hats. *a*
4. Jack was mad too. *c*

26

Activity 1: Students complete this cloze exercise using the words from the box.

Activity 2: Students sequence the events in the story by placing them in their correct order.

For the following pages:

This unit teaches students to read words containing the short 'e' vowel sound. If necessary, use the blending technique to reinforce acquisition of these words. Tell students that simple double letter consonants like 'll', 'ck', 'ff', 'ss' and 'zz' say the sound of the first letter.

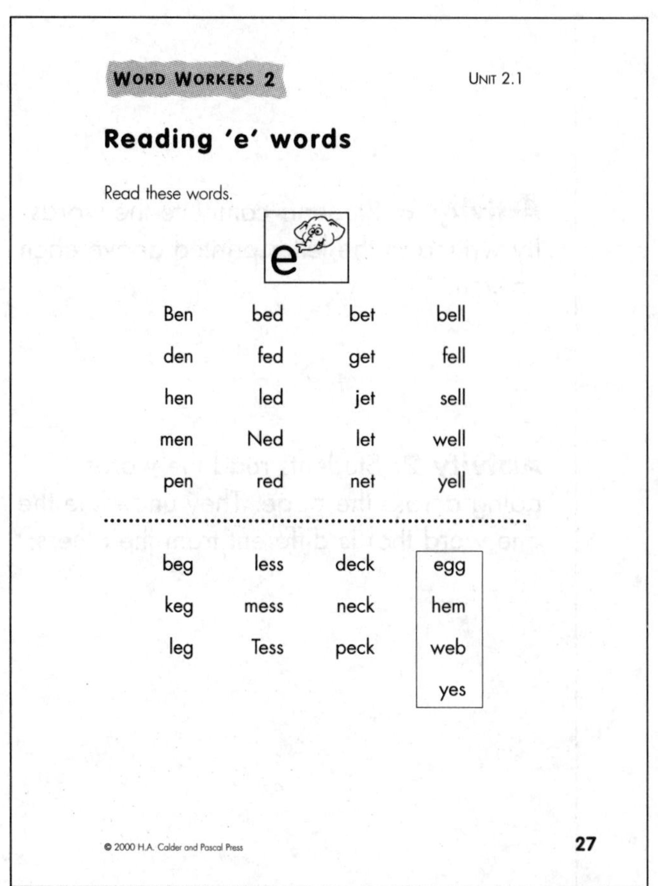

WORD WORKERS 2 — UNIT 2.1

Reading 'e' words

Read these words.

e

Ben	bed	bet	bell
den	fed	get	fell
hen	led	jet	sell
men	Ned	let	well
pen	red	net	yell

beg	less	deck	egg
keg	mess	neck	hem
leg	Tess	peck	web
			yes

© 2000 H.A. Calder and Pascal Press — 27

Students read the words in the columns.

WORD WORKERS 2 — UNIT 2.2

Name .... Date ....

Write the words for the pictures.

1. *ten* 2. *jet* 3. *bell*

4. *bed* 5. *egg* 6. *pen*

7. *leg* 8. *hen* 9. *net*

28 — © 2000 H.A. Calder and Pascal Press

Students write the words for the pictures. If necessary, they refer to the word lists to find the correct spelling.

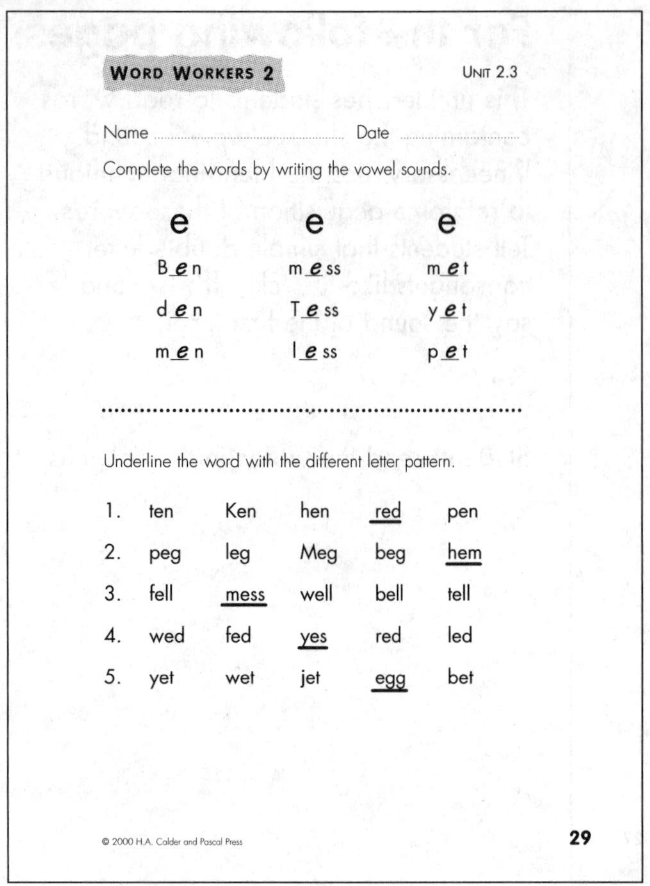

WORD WORKERS 2 UNIT 2.3

Name .... Date ....

Complete the words by writing the vowel sounds.

e	e	e
B*e*n	m*e*ss	m*e*t
d*e*n	T*e*ss	y*e*t
m*e*n	l*e*ss	p*e*t

Underline the word with the different letter pattern.

1. ten Ken hen <u>red</u> pen
2. peg leg Meg beg <u>hem</u>
3. fell <u>mess</u> well bell tell
4. wed fed <u>yes</u> red led
5. yet wet jet <u>egg</u> bet

© 2000 H.A. Calder and Pascal Press 29

Activity 1: Students complete the words by writing in the letter printed above each column.

Activity 2: Students read the words going across the page. They underline the one word that is different from the others.

WORD WORKERS 2 UNIT 2.4

Name .... Date ....

Read these words.

beds bed	leg legs	yell yells	gets get
peck pecks	sells sell	hen hens	eggs egg

Write the word for the pictures.

1. *bells* 2. *bed* 3. *egg*

4. *web* 5. *pens* 6. *well*

30 © 2000 H.A. Calder and Pascal Press

Activity 1: Students read the words in the boxes. Tell them to add the endings to the smallest word or base word.

Activity 2: Students write the words for the pictures. Tell them to add the letter 's' if there is more than one. If necessary, they refer to the word lists to find the correct spelling.

WORD WORKERS 2 UNIT 2.5

Name .... Date ....

Underline the word for the picture.

wet	bell	beg	ten
net	fell	keg	men
pet	well	leg	hen
bet	tell	peg	den

Write the word from each column that fits the word shape box.

less	egg	net	Ben	ten
yell	yes	jell	mess	pet
red	den	fed	jet	neck
pet	deck	keg	led	bed
yell	egg	keg	mess	bed

 31

Activity 1: Students look at the columns of words. They underline the word in each column that matches the picture above it.

Activity 2: Students look at the columns of words. Tell them to put the word from each column that fits into the 'word shape' box below it.

WORD WORKERS 2 UNIT 2.6

Name .... Date ....

Read these words.

pen pens	begs beg	deck decks	bets bet
bells bell	jet jets	keg kegs	tells tell

Underline the *two* words that have the same word pattern as the picture.

men	hem	wed	Ken
Tess	fell	neck	yell
yes	yet	get	mess
beg	deck	peg	web
deck	wet	den	hen

32

Activity 1: Students read the words in the boxes. Tell them to add the endings to the smallest word or base word.

Activity 2: Students look at the pictures and the words on the lines beside them. They underline the two words in each line that have the same word pattern as the picture.

WORD WORKERS 2 UNIT 2.7

Name .... Date ....

Complete these words using the word pattern from the picture.

m en	r ed	l et	j ell
B en	f ed	w et	f ell
d en	w ed	p et	t ell

Put each column in alphabetical order.

e		e		e	
egg	beg	peck	get	yell	mess
beg	deck	jell	hem	mess	red
jet	egg	hem	jell	set	set
deck	fell	get	led	red	wet
fell	jet	led	peck	wet	yell

 33

Activity 1: Students look at the pictures above the columns. They use the word pattern from each picture to complete the words in the column below.

Activity 2: Students place the words in each column in alphabetical order.

WORD WORKERS 2 UNIT 2.8

Name .... Date ....

Underline the nonsense word.

1. Ben	2. deck	3. ress	4. get	5. yed
nen	neck	less	net	fed
hen	meck	Tess	jet	red
ten	peck	mess	ket	bed

Draw a line to the word with the same word pattern.

beg	bed	bet	yell	neck	red
ten	keg	jell	fed	tell	leg
led	pet	mess	jet	Ted	peck
net	men	wed	less	peg	fell

34

Activity 1: Students look at the columns of words. Tell them to underline the word in each column that is a nonsense word.

Activity 2: Students look at the two columns of words in each box. They draw a line from the word in the left-hand column to the word in the right-hand column that has the same word pattern.

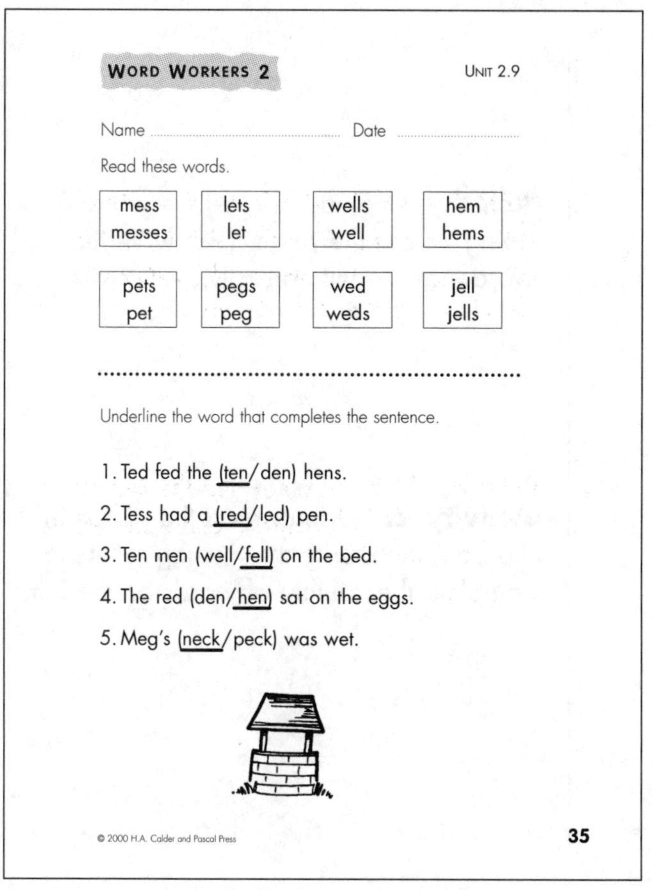

WORD WORKERS 2 UNIT 2.9

Name .... Date ....

Read these words.

mess messes	lets let	wells well	hem hems
pets pet	pegs peg	wed weds	jell jells

Underline the word that completes the sentence.

1. Ted fed the (ten/den) hens.
2. Tess had a (red/led) pen.
3. Ten men (well/fell) on the bed.
4. The red (den/hen) sat on the eggs.
5. Meg's (neck/peck) was wet.

© 2000 H.A. Calder and Pascal Press 35

Activity 1: Students read the words in the boxes. Tell them to add the endings to the smallest word or base word.

Activity 2: Students read the sentences. They underline the word in brackets that best completes the sentence.

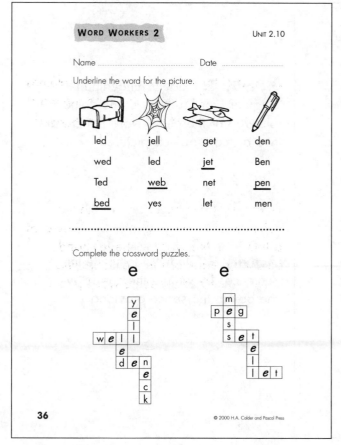

WORD WORKERS 2 UNIT 2.10

Name .... Date ....

Underline the word for the picture.

led	jell	get	den
wed	led	jet	Ben
Ted	web	net	pen
bed	yes	let	men

Complete the crossword puzzles.

e e

y e l l; w e l l; e; d e n; e c k

m; p e g; s; s e t; e; l; l e t

36 © 2000 H.A. Calder and Pascal Press

Activity 1: Students look at the columns of words. They underline the word in each column that matches the picture above it.

Activity 2: Students complete the crossword puzzles. They write the letter indicated in the blank spaces to make words that can be read going down or across the page.

WORD WORKERS 2 UNIT 2.11

Name .... Date ....

Write the word with the correct spelling.

1. egs eggs eggz *eggs*
2. deck dec dek *deck*
3. hhen hen henn *hen*
4. mez mes mess *mess*
5. red redd reb *red*

Fill in the missing letters to create the word.

1. *l* es *s*
2. *h* en *s*
3. *y* ell *s*
4. *b* e *t*
5. *n* ec *k*

yells
bet
hens
neck
less

© 2000 H.A. Calder and Pascal Press 37

Activity 1: Students read the words going across the page, then write the word that is spelt correctly.

Activity 2: Students read the words in the box, then write the missing letters to complete the column of words on the left.

WORD WORKERS 2 UNIT 2.12

Name .... Date ....

Underline the word for the picture.

egg eggs hen hens net nets

well wells web webs bell bells

Complete the sentences with the words in the box.

ten	well	neck	eggs	hens

1. Jed fed the *hens* in the pen.
2. The back of Ben's *neck* was red.
3. Jess let Meg get the *eggs*.
4. The men met at the *well*.
5. Tess had *ten* red pens.

38 © 2000 H.A. Calder and Pascal Press

Activity 1: Students underline the singular word if there is one object pictured or the plural word if there are two or more objects pictured.

Activity 2: Students complete the sentences by writing the correct word from the box in the space provided.

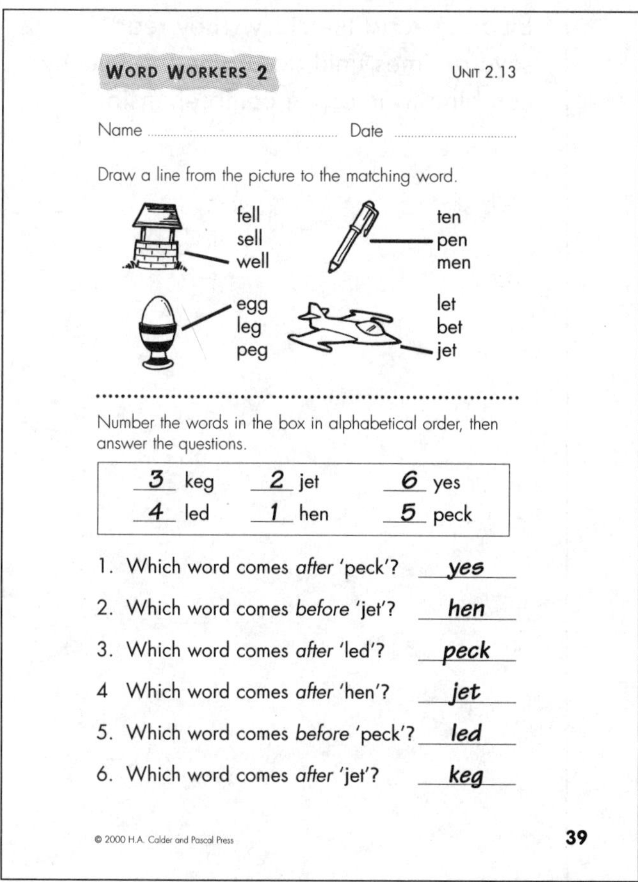

WORD WORKERS 2 UNIT 2.13

Name .... Date ....

Draw a line from the picture to the matching word.

fell
sell
well

ten
pen
men

egg
leg
peg

let
bet
jet

Number the words in the box in alphabetical order, then answer the questions.

3 keg	2 jet	6 yes
4 led	1 hen	5 peck

1. Which word comes *after* 'peck'? yes
2. Which word comes *before* 'jet'? hen
3. Which word comes *after* 'led'? peck
4 Which word comes *after* 'hen'? jet
5. Which word comes *before* 'peck'? led
6. Which word comes *after* 'jet'? keg

© 2000 H.A. Calder and Pascal Press 39

Activity 1: Students say the word for the picture and then draw a line from the picture to the correct word beside it.

Activity 2: Students number the words in the box in alphabetical order, then use this information to answer the questions below.

WORD WORKERS 2 UNIT 2.14

Read the story.

The Little Red Hen Gets Wet

Tess and Jeff had ten red hens.
Peck, peck . . . peck, peck.

Tess fed them in the pen.
Jeff had to get the eggs.
Ten red hens in the pen.
Peck, peck . . . peck, peck.

Tess saw a little red hen get out of the pen.
'Jeff,' said Tess. 'Look at the hen.
It is on the well.'
Peck, peck . . . peck, peck.

40 © 2000 H.A. Calder and Pascal Press

For the following pages:

This story is designed to reinforce the skills learned in this and previous units of work. At no stage do students encounter unfamiliar words or skills. Students read the story and answer the questions silently. Correct the work by having them read the story and answer the questions orally.

WORD WORKERS 2 UNIT 2.15

The red hen fell in the well.
'Get the net Jeff,' said Tess.
In the well, the little red hen was wet.
'Get the hen with the net, Jeff,' said Tess.

Jeff said to the little red hen,
'Get in the net and get out of the well.'
Then Jeff had the hen in the net.
He led the wet red hen back to the pen.
Now there are ten red hens in the pen.
Peck, peck . . . peck, peck.

© 2000 H.A. Calder and Pascal Press 41

Students read the story. They read it several times until accuracy and fluency combine to improve comprehension.

WORD WORKERS 2 UNIT 2.16

Name .... Date ....

Write the letters 'a', 'b', 'c', and 'd' beside the pictures in the same order they occurred in the story.

a b

c d

1. *b* 2. *d* 3. *a* 4. *c*

Answer the questions with the exact word from the story.

1. Tess and Jeff had *ten* red hens.
2. Tess saw the little red hen get out of the *pen*.
3. The hen *fell* in the well.
4. Jeff had to get the hen in the *net*.
5. Jeff led the *wet red hen* back to the pen.

42 © 2000 H.A. Calder and Pascal Press

Activity 1: Students sequence the events in the story by placing the pictures in their correct order.

Activity 2: Students complete these sentences using the exact word from the story.

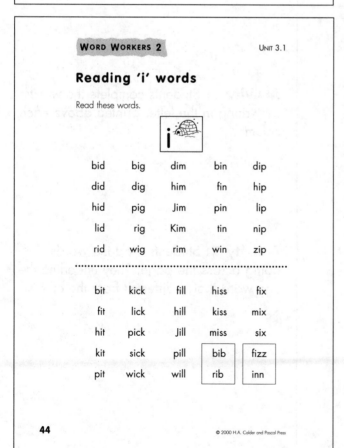

WORD WORKERS 2 UNIT 2.17

Name .... Date ....

Complete the sentences with the words in the box.

Jeff said to the little *red* hen.

'Get in the net and *get* out of the well.'

Then Jeff had the hen in the *net* .

He *led* the wet red hen back to the pen.

Now there are *ten* red hens in the pen.

Peck, peck . . . peck, peck.

get	red	net	ten	led

Write the letters 'a', 'b', 'c' and 'd' beside the sentences in the same order they occurred in the story.

1. Tess saw the little red hen get out the pen. *b*
2. The little red hen was wet. *d*
3. The red hen fell in the well. *c*
4. Jeff had to get the eggs. *a*

© 2000 H.A. Calder and Pascal Press 43

Activity 1: Students complete this cloze exercise using the words from the box.

Activity 2: Students sequence the events in the story by placing them in their correct order.

WORD WORKERS 2 UNIT 3.1

Reading 'i' words

Read these words.

i

bid	big	dim	bin	dip
did	dig	him	fin	hip
hid	pig	Jim	pin	lip
lid	rig	Kim	tin	nip
rid	wig	rim	win	zip

bit	kick	fill	hiss	fix
fit	lick	hill	kiss	mix
hit	pick	Jill	miss	six
kit	sick	pill	bib	fizz
pit	wick	will	rib	inn

44 © 2000 H.A. Calder and Pascal Press

For the following pages:

This unit teaches students to read words containing the short 'i' vowel sound.
If necessary, use the blending technique to reinforce acquisition of these words.
Tell students that simple double letter consonants like 'll', 'ck', 'ff', 'ss' and 'zz' say the sound of the first letter.

Students read the words in the columns.

WORD WORKERS 2

UNIT 3.2

Name .... Date ....

Write the words for the pictures.

1. zip 2. wig 3. hill

4. pig 5. six 6. lips

7. pin 8. bib 9. kick

45

Students write the words for the pictures. If necessary, they refer to the word lists to find the correct spelling.

WORD WORKERS 2

UNIT 3.3

Name .... Date ....

Complete the words by writing the vowel sound.

i	i	i
f_i_n	r_i_b	k_i_ss
t_i_n	b_i_b	m_i_ss
w_i_n	f_i_b	h_i_ss

Underline the word with the different letter pattern.

1.	sit	pit	kit	hit	kid
2.	hip	rip	nip	rig	zip
3.	lick	pick	bit	tick	sick
4.	win	mix	bin	pin	tin
5.	mill	pill	till	fizz	hill

46

Activity 1: Students complete the words by writing in the letter printed above each column.

Activity 2: Students read the words going across the page. They underline the one word that is different from the others.

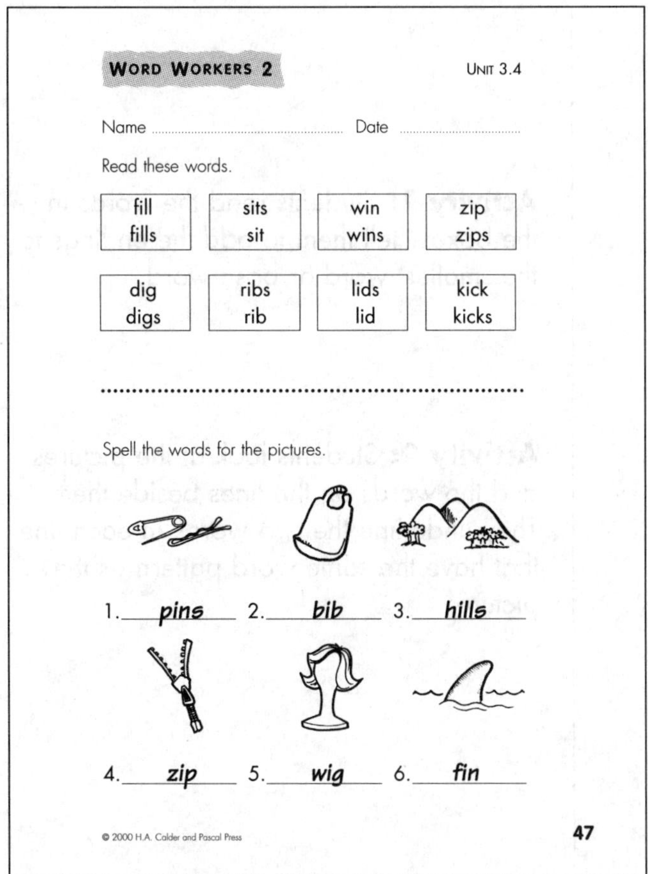

WORD WORKERS 2 UNIT 3.4

Name .... Date ....

Read these words.

fill fills	sits sit	win wins	zip zips
dig digs	ribs rib	lids lid	kick kicks

Spell the words for the pictures.

1. *pins* 2. *bib* 3. *hills*

4. *zip* 5. *wig* 6. *fin*

© 2000 H.A. Calder and Pascal Press 47

Activity 1: Students read the words in the boxes. Tell them to add the endings to the smallest word or base word.

Activity 2: Students write the words for the pictures. Tell them to add the letter 's' if there is more than one. If necessary, they refer to the word lists to find the correct spelling.

WORD WORKERS 2 UNIT 3.5

Name .... Date ....

Underline the word for the picture.

pill	hip	<u>kick</u>	tin
<u>hill</u>	dip	pick	bin
will	<u>zip</u>	sick	win
Jill	nip	wick	<u>fin</u>

Write the word from each column that fits the word shape box.

pig	will	mix	bit
big	fill	fizz	fit
wig	hill	miss	hit
dig	pill	inn	pit
wig	*pill*	*fizz*	*pit*

48 © 2000 H.A. Calder and Pascal Press

Activity 1: Students look at the columns of words. They underline the word in each column that matches the picture above it.

Activity 2: Students look at the columns of words. Tell them to put the word from each column that fits into the 'word shape' box below it.

WORD WORKERS 2 — UNIT 3.6

Name .... Date ....

Read these words.

bids bid	wigs wig	hit hits	miss misses
tin tins	pills pill	pick picks	lips lip

Underline the *two* words that have the same word pattern as the picture.

fizz sick mix fix

tin lid win hip

rig bib pig kit

fit fill will Kim

fib rib inn bid

 49

Activity 1: Students read the words in the boxes. Tell them to add the endings to the smallest word or base word.

Activity 2: Students look at the pictures and the words on the lines beside them. They underline the two words in each line that have the same word pattern as the picture.

WORD WORKERS 2 — UNIT 3.7

Name .... Date ....

Complete these the words using the word pattern from the picture.

m ill	r ig	w in	t ip
J ill	b ig	k in	l ip
B ill	f ig	t in	n ip

Put each column in alphabetical order.

i		i		i	
him	big	kick	Jill	sick	rid
fill	did	Jill	kick	zip	sick
did	fill	lid	lid	will	tip
big	fizz	mix	mix	tip	will
fizz	him	rim	rim	rid	zip

50

Activity 1: Students look at the pictures above the columns. They use the word pattern from each picture to complete the words in the column below.

Activity 2: Students place the words in each column in alphabetical order.

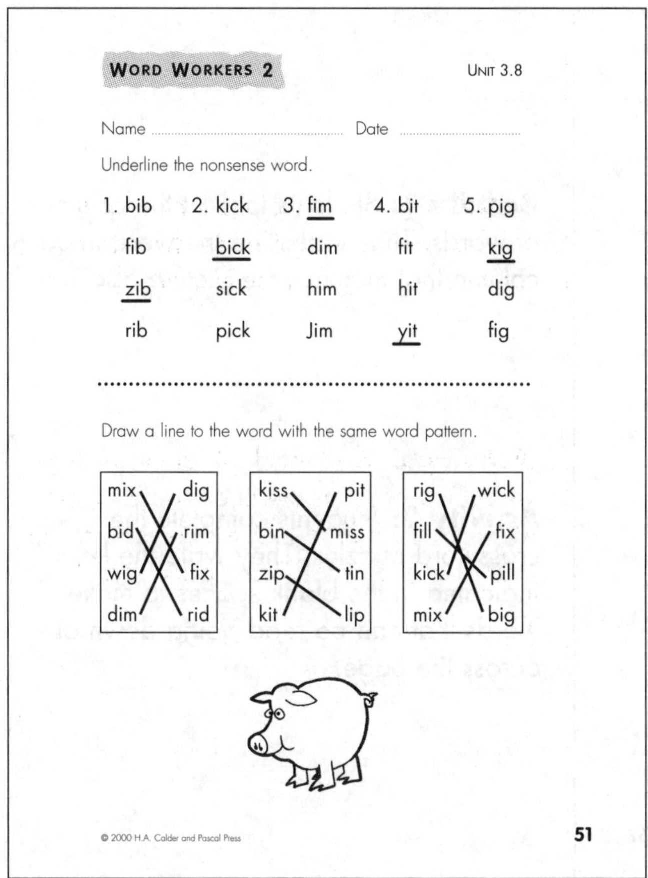

WORD WORKERS 2 UNIT 3.8

Name .... Date ....

Underline the nonsense word.

1. bib	2. kick	3. fim	4. bit	5. pig
fib	bick	dim	fit	kig
zib	sick	him	hit	dig
rib	pick	Jim	yit	fig

Draw a line to the word with the same word pattern.

mix	dig	kiss	pit	rig	wick
bid	rim	bin	miss	fill	fix
wig	fix	zip	tin	kick	pill
dim	rid	kit	lip	mix	big

© 2000 H.A. Calder and Pascal Press 51

Activity 1: Students look at the columns of words. Tell them to underline the word in each column that is a nonsense word.

Activity 2: Students look at the two columns of words in each box. They draw a line from the word in the left-hand column to the word in the right-hand column that has the same word pattern.

WORD WORKERS 2 UNIT 3.9

Name .... Date ....

Read these words.

dip dips	fills fill	lick licks	hits hit
bigger big	fit fitter	dim dimmer	sicker sick

Underline the word that completes the sentence.

1. The lid did not (bit/fit) the bin.
2. Did Tim (dig/wig) the big pit?
3. Six little pigs (lid/hid) in the hills.
4. The kid had a (rip/nip) in his bib.
5. Jill had to (kick/pick) up the big bin.

52 © 2000 H.A. Calder and Pascal Press

Activity 1: Students read the words in the boxes. Tell them to add the endings to the smallest word or base word.

Activity 2: Students read the sentences. They underline the word in brackets that best completes the sentence.

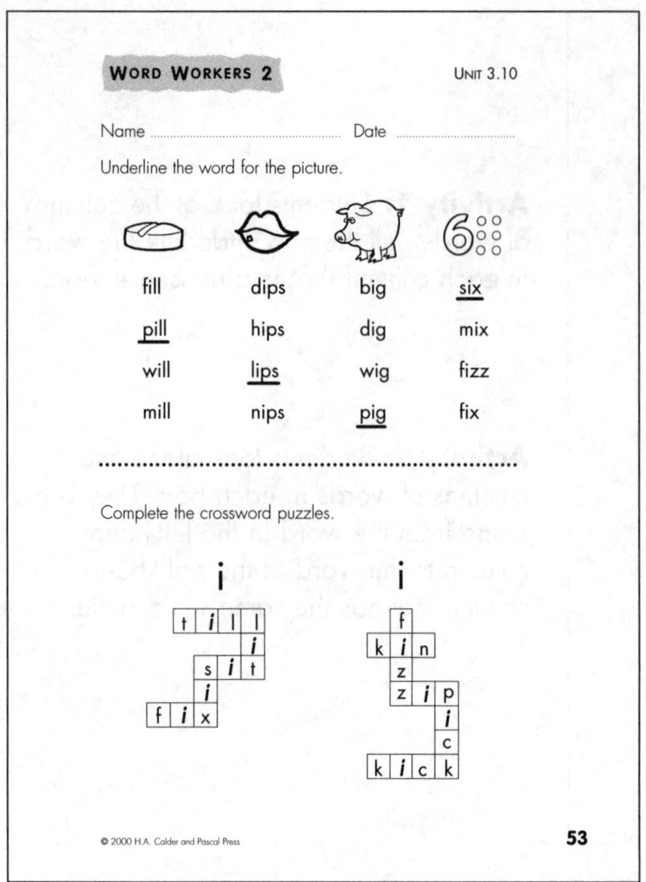

WORD WORKERS 2 UNIT 3.10

Name .... Date ....

Underline the word for the picture.

fill	dips	big	<u>six</u>
<u>pill</u>	hips	dig	mix
will	<u>lips</u>	wig	fizz
mill	nips	<u>pig</u>	fix

Complete the crossword puzzles.

i

t i l l, i, s i t, i, f i x

i

f, k i n, z, z i p, i, c, k i c k

© 2000 H.A. Calder and Pascal Press 53

Activity 1: Students look at the columns of words. They underline the word in each column that matches the picture above it.

Activity 2: Students complete the crossword puzzles. They write the letter indicated in the blank spaces to make words that can be read going down or across the page.

WORD WORKERS 2 UNIT 3.11

Name .... Date ....

Write the word with the correct spelling.

1. fiss fiz fizz ___*fizz*___
2. sick sik sic ___*sick*___
3. zipp zip zib ___*zip*___
4. kiss kis kiz ___*kiss*___
5. ribb wib rib ___*rib*___

Fill in the missing letters to complete the word.

1. *p* ick *s*
2. *r* i *d*
3. *f* il *l*
4. *d* ig *s*
5. *m* is *s*

fill
miss
picks
rid
digs

54 © 2000 H.A. Calder and Pascal Press

Activity 1: Students read the words going across the page, then write the word that is spelt correctly.

Activity 2: Students read the words in the box, then write the missing letters to complete the column of words on the left.

WORD WORKERS 2 UNIT 3.12

Name .... Date ....

Underline the word for the picture.

zip zips pin pins bib bibs

pig pigs wig wigs hill hills

Complete the sentences with the words in the box.

dig	sick	pig	pick	bib

1. Did Jill sit on the big *pig* ?
2. Jim had to *dig* a bigger pit.
3. The kid's *bib* was too big for him.
4. Miss Hill was too *sick* to sit up in bed.
5. Tim had to *pick* up the bin's lid.

© 2000 H.A. Calder and Pascal Press 55

Activity 1: Students underline the singular word if there is one object pictured or the plural word if there are two or more objects pictured.

Activity 2: Students complete the sentences by writing the correct word from the box in the space provided.

WORD WORKERS 2 UNIT 3.13

Name .... Date ....

Draw a line from the picture to the matching word.

will
fill
pill

tips
lips
hips

bib
fib
rib

tin
win
fin

Number the words in the box in alphabetical order, then answer the questions.

4 fizz	*2* dig	*5* hid
1 bid	*6* lip	*3* fix

1. Which word comes *after* 'hid'? *lip*
2. Which word comes *after* 'bid'? *dig*
3. Which word comes *before* 'lip'? *hid*
4 Which word comes *before* 'fizz'? *fix*
5. Which word comes *before* 'dig'? *bid*
6. Which word comes *after* 'fix'? *fizz*

56 © 2000 H.A. Calder and Pascal Press

Activity 1: Students say the word for the picture and then draw a line from the picture to the correct word beside it.

Activity 2: Students number the words in the box in alphabetical order, then use this information to answer the questions below.

WORD WORKERS 2 UNIT 3.14

Read the story.

Tim Finn's Bin

Tim Finn's mill was in the hills.
His bin was by the mill.

Zig-zig the pig hid in the hills.
He was not a little pig.
Zig-zig was a big pig
and he had a big dinner.
He had it in Tim Finn's bin.

Tim was in a tizz.
'The pig will tip the bin,' he said.
'He will get his bib.
And sit on the lid.
And lick the bin,
and all the little bits on his lips.'

© 2000 H.A. Calder and Pascal Press 57

WORD WORKERS 2 UNIT 3.15

'I will fix that pig,' Tim Finn said.
'I will get rid of Zig-zig.'
And Tim Finn did.
He hid in his mill.
'Zig-zig will come with his bib,' he said.
'But the bin will not tip.'

And Tim Finn's bin did not tip.
Zig-zig hit it with his hip.
He hit the lid with a kick.
But the bin did not tip.
Zig-zig did not see the zip on the lid.

So Tim Finn's bin will not tip
now the lid has a zip.
And Zig-zig, the big pig, misses his dinners.

58 © 2000 H.A. Calder and Pascal Press

For the following pages:

This story is designed to reinforce the skills learned in this and previous units of work. At no stage do students encounter unfamiliar words or skills. Students read the story and answer the questions silently. Correct the work by having them read the story and answer the questions orally.

WORD WORKERS 2 UNIT 3.16

Name .... Date ....

Write the letters 'a', 'b', 'c' and 'd' beside the pictures in the same order they occurred in the story.

a b

c d

1. *d* 2. *a* 3. *b* 4. *c*

Fill in the blanks with the exact words from the story.

1. Tim Finn's *mill* was in the hills.
2. Zig-zig had a big *dinner* .
3. Tim was in a *tizz* .
4. Tim Finn's bin did not *tip* .
5. Zig-zig did not see the *zip* on the lid.

 59

Activity 1: Students sequence the events in the story by placing the pictures in their correct order.

Activity 2: Students complete these sentences using the exact word from the story.

WORD WORKERS 2 UNIT 3.17

Name .... Date ....

Complete the sentences with the words in the box.

Tim was in a *tizz* .

'The pig will *tip* the bin,' he said.

'He will get his bib.

And sit on the *lid* .

And *lick* the bin.

And all the little *bits* on his lips.'

tip	bits	lid	lick	tizz

Write the letters 'a', 'b', 'c' and 'd' beside the sentences in the same order they occurred in the story.

1. Tim Finn hid in his mill. *b*
2. Zig-zig misses his dinners. *d*
3. Tim was in a tizz. *a*
4. Zig-zig hit the bin with his hip. *c*

60

Activity 1: Students complete this cloze exercise using the words from the box.

Activity 2: Students sequence the events in the story by placing them in their correct order.

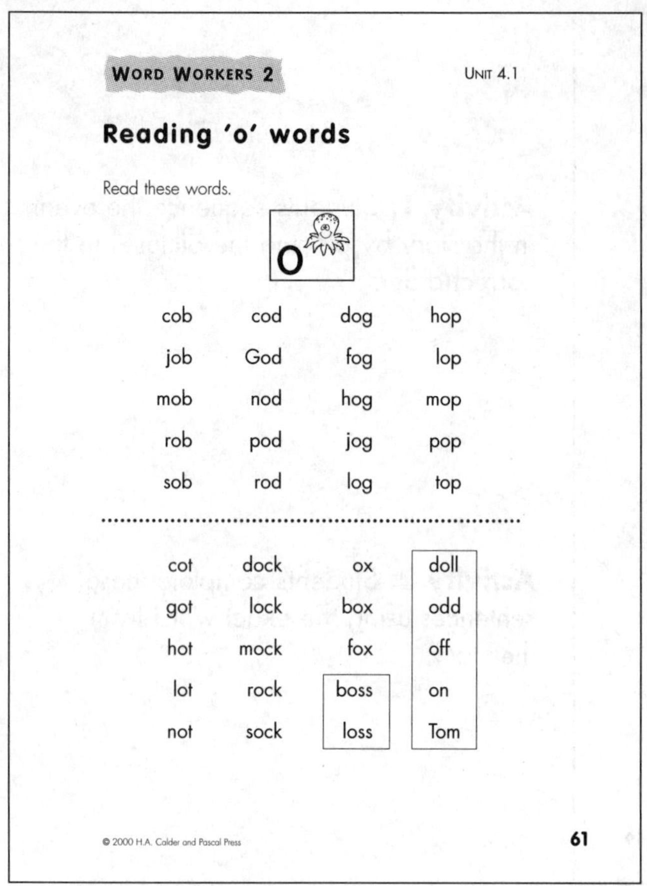

WORD WORKERS 2 UNIT 4.1

Reading 'o' words

Read these words.

o

cob	cod	dog	hop
job	God	fog	lop
mob	nod	hog	mop
rob	pod	jog	pop
sob	rod	log	top

cot	dock	ox	doll
got	lock	box	odd
hot	mock	fox	off
lot	rock	boss	on
not	sock	loss	Tom

© 2000 H.A. Calder and Pascal Press 61

For the following pages:

This unit teaches students to read words containing the short 'o' vowel sound.
If necessary, use the blending technique to reinforce acquisition of these words.
Tell students that simple double letter consonants like 'll', 'ck', 'ff', 'ss' and 'zz' say the sound of the first letter.

Students read the words in the columns.

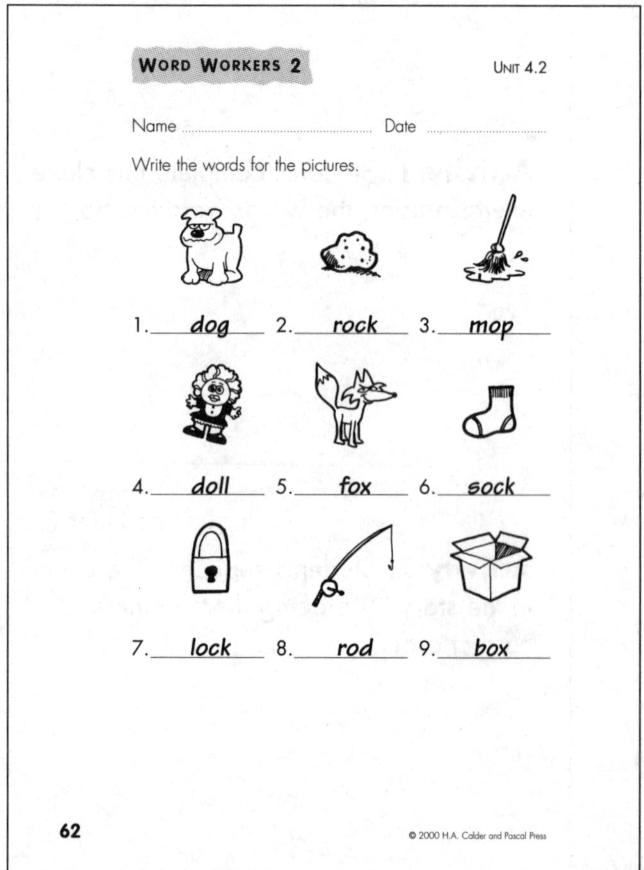

WORD WORKERS 2 UNIT 4.2

Name .... Date ....

Write the words for the pictures.

1. *dog* 2. *rock* 3. *mop*

4. *doll* 5. *fox* 6. *sock*

7. *lock* 8. *rod* 9. *box*

62 © 2000 H.A. Calder and Pascal Press

Students write the words for the pictures.
If necessary, they refer to the word lists to find the correct spelling.

WORD WORKERS 2 UNIT 4.3

Name .... Date ....

Complete the words by writing the vowel sound.

o	o	o
l_o_p	d_o_ck	m_o_b
t_o_p	m_o_ck	c_o_b
m_o_p	r_o_ck	r_o_b

Underline the word with the different letter pattern.

1. tot rot jot box dot
2. cog job dog hog fog
3. dock sock doll mock lock
4. off pop top hop mop
5. job lob rob mob sod

© 2000 H.A. Calder and Pascal Press 63

Activity 1: Students complete the words by writing in the letter(s) printed above each column.

Activity 2: Students read the words going across the page. They underline the one word that is different from the others.

WORD WORKERS 2 UNIT 4.4

Name .... Date ....

Read these words.

nod nods	dogs dog	hops hop	sobs sob
doll dolls	locks lock	log logs	cots cot

Write the words for the pictures.

1. socks 2. fox 3. rod

4. dog 5. dolls 6. mop

64 © 2000 H.A. Calder and Pascal Press

Activity 1: Students read the words in the boxes. Tell them to add the endings to the smallest word or base word.

Activity 2: Students write the words for the pictures. Tell them to add the letter 's' if there is more than one. If necessary, they refer to the word lists to find the correct spelling.

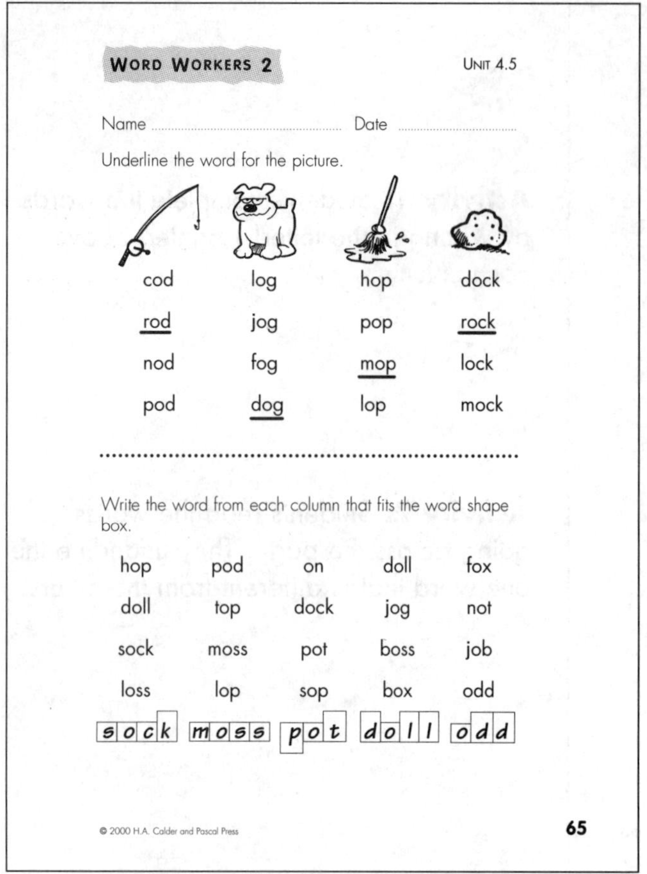

WORD WORKERS 2 UNIT 4.5

Name .... Date ....

Underline the word for the picture.

cod	log	hop	dock
rod	jog	pop	rock
nod	fog	mop	lock
pod	dog	lop	mock

Write the word from each column that fits the word shape box.

hop	pod	on	doll	fox
doll	top	dock	jog	not
sock	moss	pot	boss	job
loss	lop	sop	box	odd
sock	moss	pot	doll	odd

© 2000 H.A. Calder and Pascal Press 65

Activity 1: Students look at the columns of words. They underline the word in each column that matches the picture above it.

Activity 2: Students look at the columns of words. Tell them to put the word from each column that fits into the 'word shape' box below it.

WORD WORKERS 2 UNIT 4.6

Name .... Date ....

Read these words.

boxes box	pot pots	rock rocks	rob robs
jog jogs	bosses boss	mops mop	rod rods

Underline the *two* words that have the same word pattern as the picture.

mock	doll	dock	boss
tot	top	pod	hop
box	hog	off	pox
on	sob	God	nod
log	jog	jot	lop

66 © 2000 H.A. Calder and Pascal Press

Activity 1: Students read the words in the boxes. Tell them to add the endings to the smallest word or base word.

Activity 2: Students look at the pictures and the words on the lines beside them. They underline the two words in each line that have the same word pattern as the picture.

WORD WORKERS 2 UNIT 4.7

Name .... Date ....

Complete these words using the word pattern from the picture.

m ock	n od	t op	j ot
d ock	G od	l op	h ot
l ock	p od	h op	l ot

Put each column in alphabetical order.

o		o		o	
dog	boss	loss	job	Tom	moss
cod	cod	mop	loss	pop	pop
boss	dog	odd	mop	rod	rod
got	fox	nod	nod	moss	sob
fox	got	job	odd	sob	Tom

 67

Activity 1: Students look at the pictures above the columns. They use the word pattern from each picture to complete the words in the column below.

Activity 2: Students place the words in each column in alphabetical order.

WORD WORKERS 2 UNIT 4.8

Name .... Date ....

Underline the nonsense word.

1. cob	2. hot	3. nox	4. loss	5. hog
vob	got	ox	moss	rog
mob	lot	fox	poss	jog
rob	wot	box	boss	fog

Draw a line to the word with the same word pattern.

rod	mob	toss	rob	cot	sock
hop	nod	dog	moss	dock	pop
sob	loss	job	fox	top	hog
boss	top	box	jog	fog	got

68

Activity 1: Students look at the columns of words. Tell them to underline the word in each column that is a nonsense word.

Activity 2: Students look at the two columns of words in each box. They draw a line from the word in the left-hand column to the word in the right-hand column that has the same word pattern.

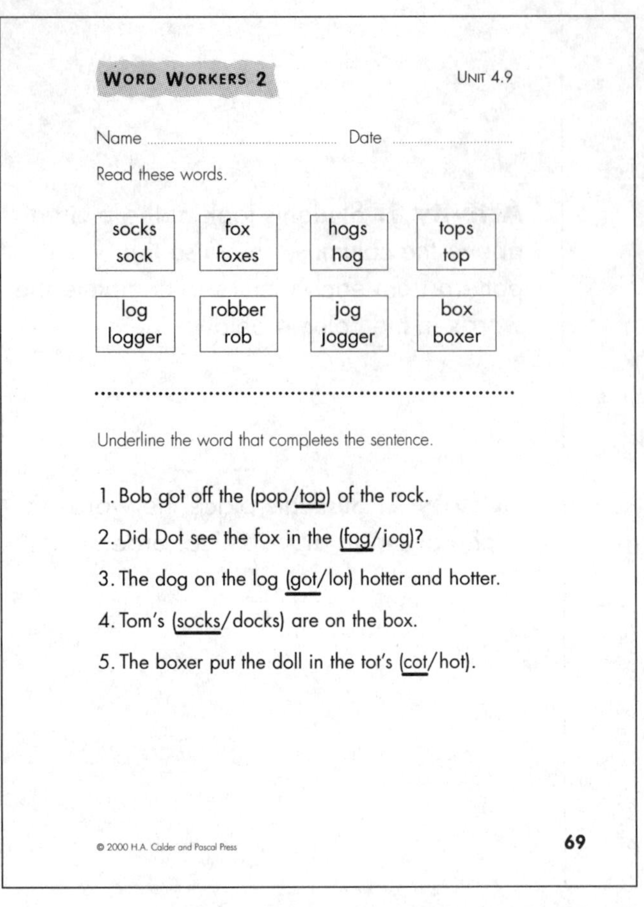

WORD WORKERS 2 — UNIT 4.9

Name .... Date ....

Read these words.

socks sock	fox foxes	hogs hog	tops top
log logger	robber rob	jog jogger	box boxer

Underline the word that completes the sentence.

1. Bob got off the (pop/top) of the rock.
2. Did Dot see the fox in the (fog/jog)?
3. The dog on the log (got/lot) hotter and hotter.
4. Tom's (socks/docks) are on the box.
5. The boxer put the doll in the tot's (cot/hot).

© 2000 H.A. Calder and Pascal Press 69

Activity 1: Students read the words in the boxes. Tell them to add the endings to the smallest word or base word.

Activity 2: Students read the sentences. They underline the word in brackets that best completes the sentence.

WORD WORKERS 2 — UNIT 4.10

Name .... Date ....

Underline the word for the picture.

rock	box	got	doll
pock	fox	cot	dock
lock	ox	pot	dog
sock	pox	not	dot

Complete the crossword puzzles.

70 © 2000 H.A. Calder and Pascal Press

Activity 1: Students look at the columns of words. They underline the word in each column that matches the picture above it.

Activity 2: Students complete the crossword puzzles. They write the letter indicated in the blank spaces to make words that can be read going down or across the page.

WORD WORKERS 2 UNIT 4.11

Name .... Date ....

Write the word with the correct spelling.

1. dol doll boll *doll*
2. sock sok soc *sock*
3. hobbs hopps hops *hops*
4. boz boss bos *boss*
5. loks losk locks *locks*

Fill in the missing letters to complete the word.

1.	*j* og *s*	loss
2.	*o* d *d*	dock
3.	*l* os *s*	odd
4.	*o* f *f*	jogs
5.	*d* oc *k*	off

© 2000 H.A. Calder and Pascal Press 71

Activity 1: Students read the words going across the page, then write the word that is spelt correctly.

Activity 2: Students read the words in the box, then write the missing letters to complete the column of words on the left.

WORD WORKERS 2 UNIT 4.12

Name .... Date ....

Underline the word for the picture.

doll dolls rock rocks mop mops

sock socks box boxes lock locks

Complete the sentences with the words in the box.

hop	cot	socks	rock	top

1. The fox sat on *top* of the log.
2. The dog will *hop* on the rock.
3. Tom's *socks* are in the big box.
4. The dolls are in the *cot* .
5. Mrs Moss will toss the *rock* off the dock.

72 © 2000 H.A. Calder and Pascal Press

Activity 1: Students underline the singular word if there is one object pictured or the plural word if there are two or more objects pictured.

Activity 2: Students complete the sentences by writing the correct word from the box in the space provided.

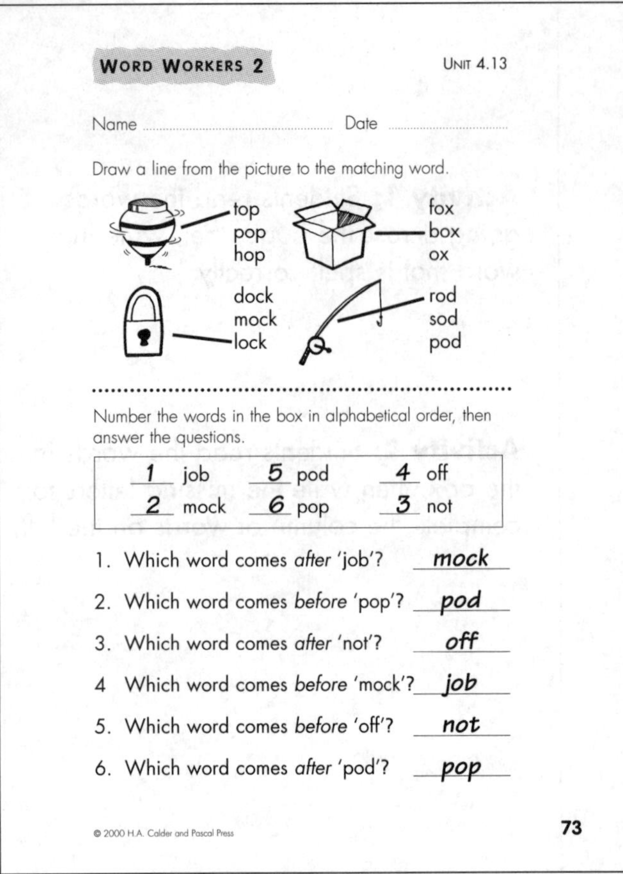

WORD WORKERS 2 UNIT 4.13

Name .... Date ....

Draw a line from the picture to the matching word.

top
pop
hop

fox
box
ox

dock
mock
lock

rod
sod
pod

Number the words in the box in alphabetical order, then answer the questions.

1 job	5 pod	4 off
2 mock	6 pop	3 not

1. Which word comes *after* 'job'? *mock*
2. Which word comes *before* 'pop'? *pod*
3. Which word comes *after* 'not'? *off*
4 Which word comes *before* 'mock'? *job*
5. Which word comes *before* 'off'? *not*
6. Which word comes *after* 'pod'? *pop*

© 2000 H.A. Calder and Pascal Press 73

Activity 1: Students say the word for the picture and then draw a line from the picture to the correct word beside it.

Activity 2: Students number the words in the box in alphabetical order, then use this information to answer the questions below.

WORD WORKERS 2 UNIT 4.14

Read the story.

Boz the Dog

Boz, the dog, and a fox and a hog sat on top of a box.

'There is a mob on this box and it is too hot,' said Boz to the fox. 'Hop off the box and hop on the log.
'I will not hop off the box,' said the fox to the dog.

74 © 2000 H.A. Calder and Pascal Press

For the following pages:

This story is designed to reinforce the skills learned in this and previous units of work. At no stage do students encounter unfamiliar words or skills. Students read the story and answer the questions silently. Correct the work by having them read the story and answer the questions orally.

So Boz said to the hog, 'There is a mob on this box and it is too hot. Hop off the box and hop on the rock.'
'I will not hop off the box,' said the hog to the dog.

Then the fox and the hog said to Boz, 'We will not hop off the box and hop on the log and the rock. *You* hop off the box. You are not the boss!'

So Boz, the dog, and the fox and the hog sat on the box. It got hotter and hotter.

Then Boz said to the fox and the hog,
'You will not hop off the box?'
'Not I,' said the fox.
'Not I,' said the hog.
So Boz said, 'I will hop off the box.'

And Boz did. He got off the box, but he did not hop on the log. He did not hop on the rock. He got *in* the log by the rock. Boz was not hot in the log.

But the fox and the hog did not hop off the box.
'You are not the boss,' said the fox to the hog.
'And you are not the boss,' said the hog to the fox.

So the fox and the hog sat on top of the box.
It got hotter and hotter. But Boz, the dog, was not hot in his log.

Students read the story. They read it several times until accuracy and fluency combine to improve comprehension.

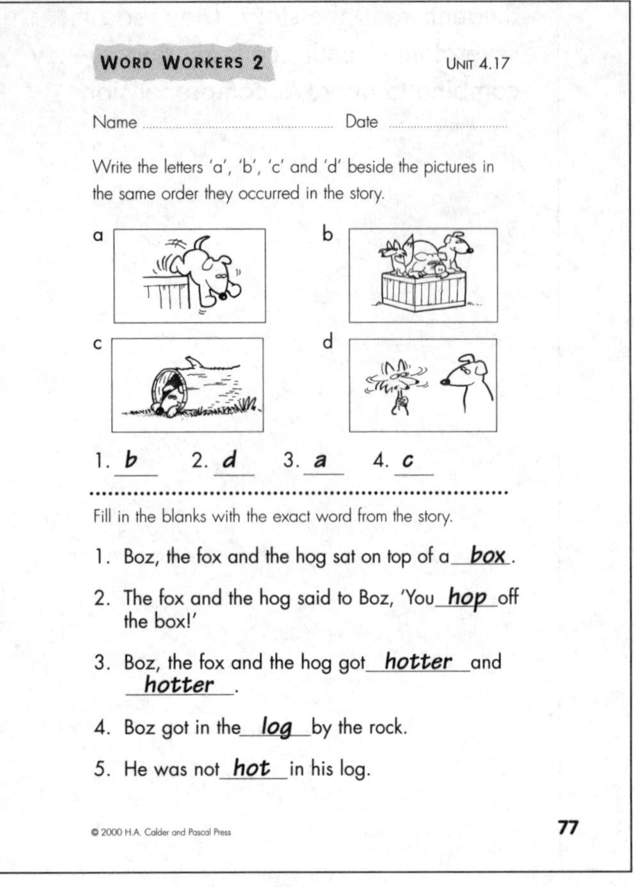

WORD WORKERS 2 UNIT 4.17

Name .... Date ....

Write the letters 'a', 'b', 'c' and 'd' beside the pictures in the same order they occurred in the story.

a b c d

1. *b* 2. *d* 3. *a* 4. *c*

Fill in the blanks with the exact word from the story.

1. Boz, the fox and the hog sat on top of a *box*.
2. The fox and the hog said to Boz, 'You *hop* off the box!'
3. Boz, the fox and the hog got *hotter* and *hotter*.
4. Boz got in the *log* by the rock.
5. He was not *hot* in his log.

© 2000 H.A. Calder and Pascal Press 77

Activity 1: Students sequence the events in the story by placing the pictures in their correct order.

Activity 2: Students complete these sentences using the exact word from the story.

WORD WORKERS 2 UNIT 4.18

Name .... Date ....

Complete the sentences with the words in the box.

Then the fox and the *hog* said to Boz,

'We will not hop off the *box* and hop on the

log and the rock. You are not the *boss*.

So Boz, the dog, and the *fox* and the hog sat

on the box. It got hotter and hotter.

fox	hog	boss	box	log

Write the letters 'a', 'b', 'c', and 'd' beside the sentences in the same order they occurred in the story.

1. Boz said, 'I will hop off the box.' *b*
2. 'I will not hop off the box,' said the fox to the dog. *a*
3. Boz, the dog, was not hot in his log. *d*
4. Boz got in the log. *c*

78 © 2000 H.A. Calder and Pascal Press

Activity 1: Students complete this cloze exercise using the words from the box.

Activity 2: Students sequence the events in the story by placing them in their correct order.

For the following pages:

This unit teaches students to read words containing the short 'u' vowel sound. If necessary, use the blending technique to reinforce acquisition of these words. Tell students that simple double letter consonants like 'll', 'ck', 'ff', 'ss' and 'zz' say the sound of the first letter.

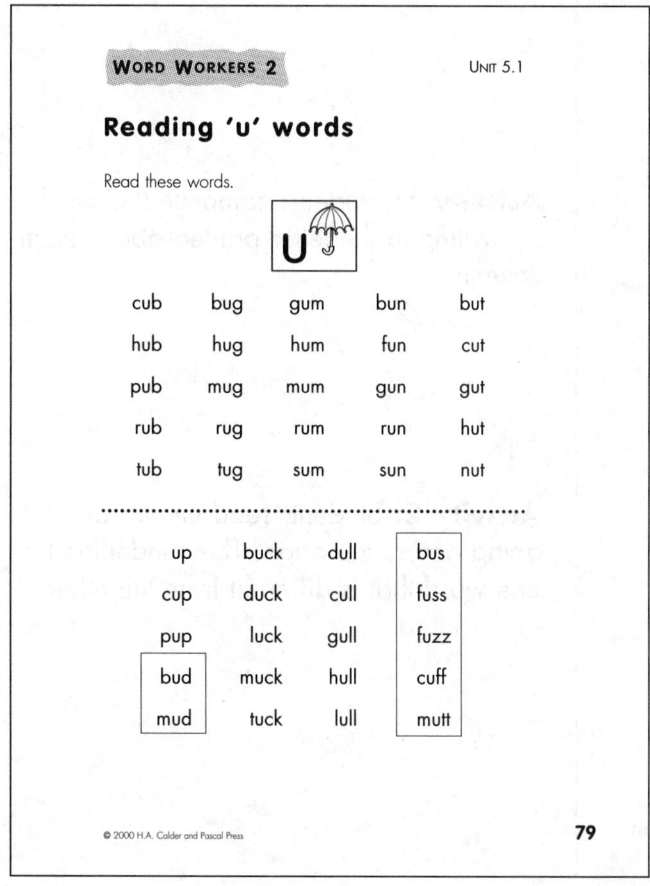

WORD WORKERS 2 UNIT 5.1

Reading 'u' words

Read these words.

u

cub	bug	gum	bun	but
hub	hug	hum	fun	cut
pub	mug	mum	gun	gut
rub	rug	rum	run	hut
tub	tug	sum	sun	nut

up	buck	dull	bus
cup	duck	cull	fuss
pup	luck	gull	fuzz
bud	muck	hull	cuff
mud	tuck	lull	mutt

© 2000 H.A. Calder and Pascal Press 79

Students read the words in the columns.

WORD WORKERS 2 UNIT 5.2

Name .... Date ....

Write the words for the pictures.

1. *mug* 2. *gun* 3. *run*

4. *sun* 5. *nut* 6. *cup*

7. *bus* 8. *duck* 9. *tub*

80 © 2000 H.A. Calder and Pascal Press

Students write the words for the pictures. If necessary, they refer to the word lists to find the correct spelling.

WORD WORKERS 2 UNIT 5.3

Name .... Date ....

Complete the words by writing the vowel sound.

U	U	U
f_u_n	d_u_ll	r_u_g
b_u_n	h_u_ll	h_u_g
s_u_n	c_u_ll	d_u_g

Underline the word with the different letter pattern.

1. cub hub mud tub rub
2. bug cuff rug tug mug
3. but hut cut bus gut
4. duck mutt luck tuck muck
5. fuss gum rum sum mum

© 2000 H.A. Calder and Pascal Press 81

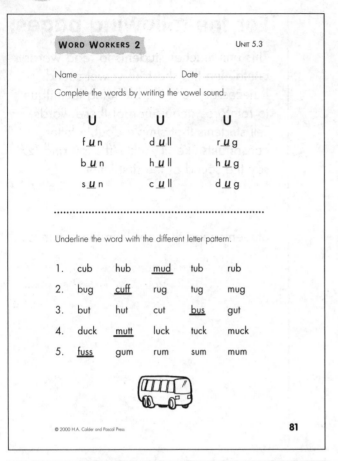

Activity 1: Students complete the words by writing in the letter printed above each column.

Activity 2: Students read the words going across the page. They underline the one word that is different from the others.

WORD WORKERS 2 UNIT 5.4

Name .... Date ....

Read these words.

cut cuts	runs run	puffs puff	rub rubs
gulls gull	bud buds	hugs hug	hum hums

Write the words for the pictures.

1. *sun* 2. *cups* 3. *bug*

4. *ducks* 5. *bus* 6. *mugs*

82 © 2000 H.A. Calder and Pascal Press

Activity 1: Students read the words in the boxes. Tell them to add the endings to the smallest word or base word.

Activity 2: Students write the words for the pictures. Tell them to add the letter 's' if there is more than one. If necessary, they refer to the word lists to find the correct spelling.

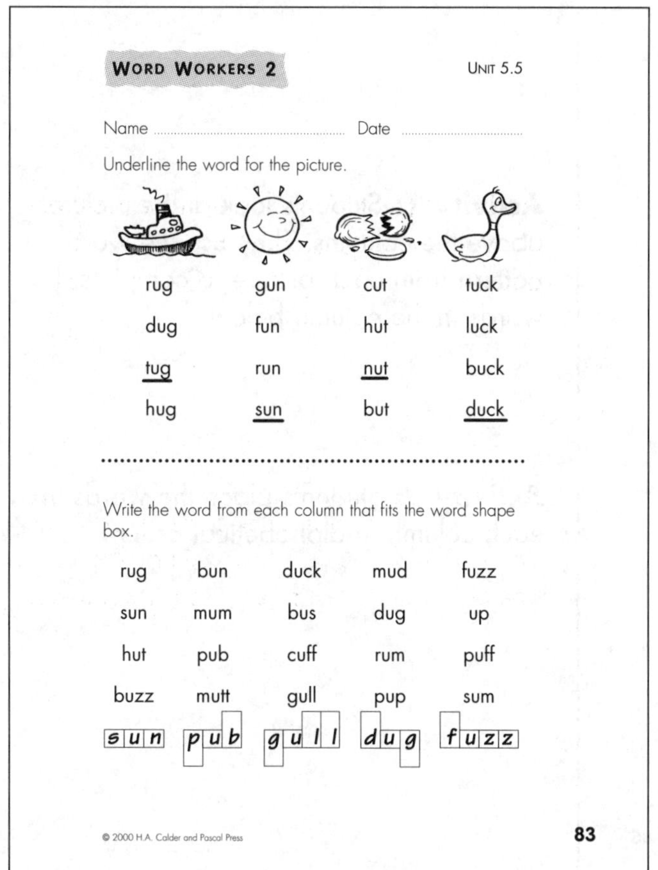
WORD WORKERS 2 UNIT 5.5

Name .... Date ....

Underline the word for the picture.

rug	gun	cut	tuck
dug	fun	hut	luck
tug	run	nut	buck
hug	sun	but	duck

Write the word from each column that fits the word shape box.

rug	bun	duck	mud	fuzz
sun	mum	bus	dug	up
hut	pub	cuff	rum	puff
buzz	mutt	gull	pup	sum
sun	pub	gull	dug	fuzz

© 2000 H.A. Calder and Pascal Press 83

Activity 1: Students look at the columns of words. They underline the word in each column that matches the picture above it.

Activity 2: Students look at the columns of words. Tell them to put the word from each column that fits into the 'word shape' box below it.

WORD WORKERS 2 UNIT 5.6

Name .... Date ....

Read these words.

guns gun	cup cups	bug bugs	tubs tub
fusses fuss	mug mugs	huts hut	cuff cuffs

Underline the *two* words that have the same word pattern as the picture.

mug	bud	dug	cub
hut	luck	tuck	rug
fun	bun	hull	sum
us	fuzz	tub	Gus
cup	hug	fuss	lug

84 © 2000 H.A. Calder and Pascal Press

Activity 1: Students read the words in the boxes. Tell them to add the endings to the smallest word or base word.

Activity 2: Students look at the pictures and the words on the lines beside them. They underline the two words in each line that have the same word pattern as the picture.

WORD WORKERS 2 UNIT 5.7

Name .... Date ....

Complete these words using the word pattern from the picture.

h ub	n un	l uck	r ug
c ub	f un	b uck	t ug
p ub	s un	t uck	h ug

Put each column in alphabetical order.

U		U		U	
gum	buck	mum	fuzz	tuck	mutt
dug	cuff	hub	hub	mutt	pup
buck	dug	nut	lull	rug	rug
cuff	fun	fuzz	mum	sub	sub
fun	gum	lull	nut	pup	tuck

 85

Activity 1: Students look at the pictures above the columns. They use the word pattern from each picture to complete the words in the column below.

Activity 2: Students place the words in each column in alphabetical order.

WORD WORKERS 2 UNIT 5.8

Name .... Date ....

Underline the nonsense word.

1. bug	2. fuss	3. wup	4. hum	5. gull
rug	cuff	pup	lum	dull
cug	fuzz	cup	mum	vull
mug	fuff	up	sum	hull

Draw a line to the word with the same word pattern.

fun	duck	dug	buzz	puff	mud
luck	pup	hum	Gus	hut	hull
hub	sun	bus	rug	bud	cuff
cup	rub	fuzz	sum	dull	nut

86

Activity 1: Students look at the columns of words. Tell them to underline the word in each column that is a nonsense word.

Activity 2: Students look at the two columns of words in each box. They draw a line from the word in the left-hand column to the word in the right-hand column that has the same word pattern.

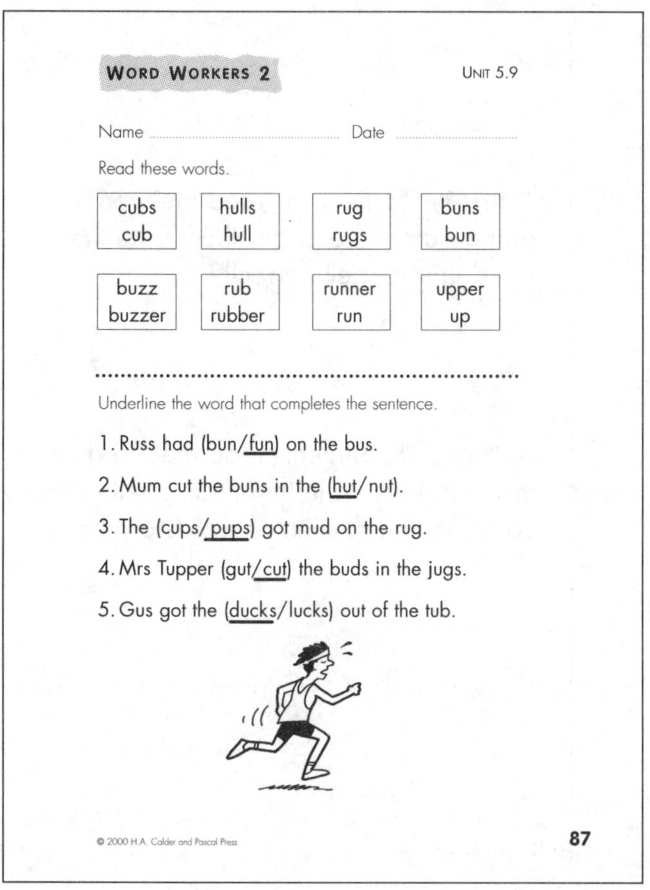

WORD WORKERS 2 UNIT 5.9

Name .... Date ....

Read these words.

cubs cub	hulls hull	rug rugs	buns bun
buzz buzzer	rub rubber	runner run	upper up

Underline the word that completes the sentence.

1. Russ had (bun/fun) on the bus.
2. Mum cut the buns in the (hut/nut).
3. The (cups/pups) got mud on the rug.
4. Mrs Tupper (gut/cut) the buds in the jugs.
5. Gus got the (ducks/lucks) out of the tub.

© 2000 H.A. Calder and Pascal Press 87

Activity 1: Students read the words in the boxes. Tell them to add the endings to the smallest word or base word.

Activity 2: Students read the sentences. They underline the word in brackets that best completes the sentence.

WORD WORKERS 2 UNIT 5.10

Name .... Date ....

Underline the word for the picture.

run	tug	cup	rub
fun	hug	up	tub
gun	bug	pup	hub
nun	mug	puff	cub

Complete the crossword puzzles.

U: c, b u z z, f, f u n, u, t u g

U: f, g u l l, s, b u s, u, g u n

88 © 2000 H.A. Calder and Pascal Press

Activity 1: Students look at the columns of words. They underline the word in each column that matches the picture above it.

Activity 2: Students complete the crossword puzzles. They write the letter indicated in the blank spaces to make words that can be read going down or across the page.

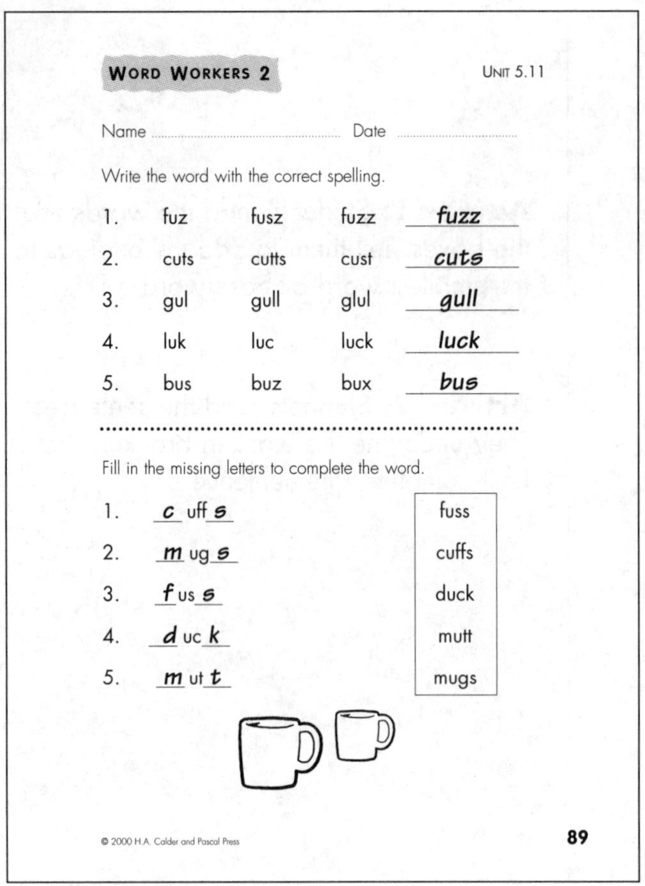

WORD WORKERS 2 UNIT 5.11

Name .... Date ....

Write the word with the correct spelling.

1.	fuz	fusz	fuzz	*fuzz*
2.	cuts	cutts	cust	*cuts*
3.	gul	gull	glul	*gull*
4.	luk	luc	luck	*luck*
5.	bus	buz	bux	*bus*

Fill in the missing letters to complete the word.

1. *c* uff *s*
2. *m* ug *s*
3. *f* us *s*
4. *d* uc *k*
5. *m* ut *t*

fuss
cuffs
duck
mutt
mugs

© 2000 H.A. Calder and Pascal Press 89

Activity 1: Students read the words going across the page, then write the word that is spelt correctly.

Activity 2: Students read the words in the box, then write the missing letters to complete the column of words on the left.

WORD WORKERS 2 UNIT 5.12

Name .... Date ....

Underline the word for the picture.

<u>sun</u> suns duck <u>ducks</u> <u>tub</u> tubs

cup <u>cups</u> bug <u>bugs</u> <u>gun</u> guns

Complete the sentences with the words in the box.

jug	run	buns	nuts	mud

1. Mutt, the dog, got *mud* on mum's rug.
2. The buds are in the *jug*.
3. Russ had a *run* in the hot sun.
4. The *nuts* are in the mug.
5. Mrs Huff had butter on the *buns*.

90 © 2000 H.A. Calder and Pascal Press

Activity 1: Students underline the singular word if there is one object pictured or the plural word if there are two or more objects pictured.

Activity 2: Students complete the sentences by writing the correct word from the box in the space provided.

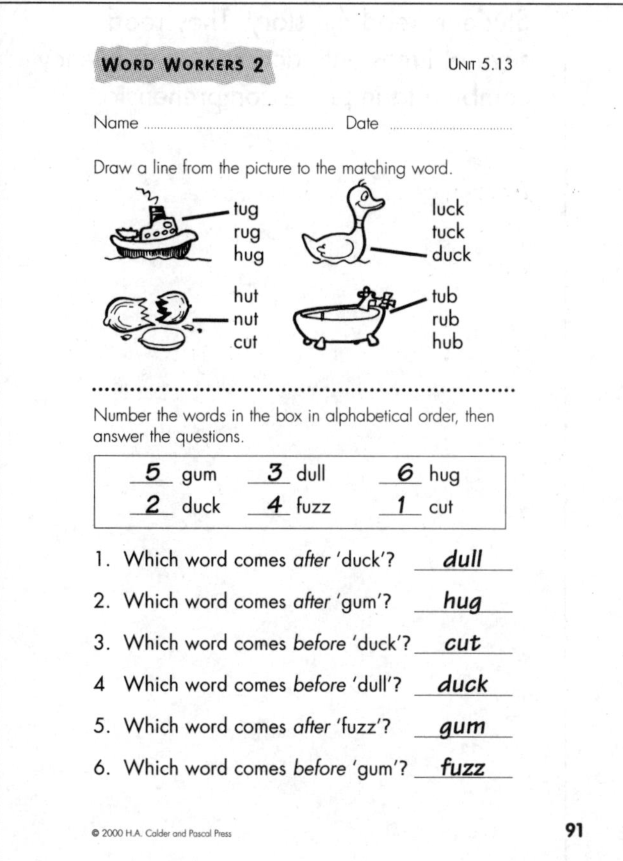

WORD WORKERS 2 UNIT 5.13

Name .... Date ....

Draw a line from the picture to the matching word.

tug
rug
hug

luck
tuck
duck

hut
nut
cut

tub
rub
hub

Number the words in the box in alphabetical order, then answer the questions.

5 gum	3 dull	6 hug
2 duck	4 fuzz	1 cut

1. Which word comes *after* 'duck'? dull
2. Which word comes *after* 'gum'? hug
3. Which word comes *before* 'duck'? cut
4 Which word comes *before* 'dull'? duck
5. Which word comes *after* 'fuzz'? gum
6. Which word comes *before* 'gum'? fuzz

© 2000 H.A. Calder and Pascal Press 91

Activity 1: Students say the word for the picture and then draw a line from the picture to the correct word beside it.

Activity 2: Students number the words in the box in alphabetical order, then use this information to answer the questions below.

WORD WORKERS 2 UNIT 5.14

Read the story.

The Mud on Mrs Hull's Rug

Russ Hull dug in the mud and the muck.
Muff, the pup, dug with him.
Russ and Muff had fun.
They dug and dug in the mud and the muck.

Russ and Muff saw a bug buzz by.
'Hummm . . . buzzz.'

Mrs Hull had butter on a bun.
'Run up with the pup,' she said to Russ.
'O.K. mum,' Russ said.

92 © 2000 H.A. Calder and Pascal Press

For the following pages:

This story is designed to reinforce the skills learned in this and previous units of work. At no stage do students encounter unfamiliar words or skills. Students read the story and answer the questions silently. Correct the work by having them read the story and answer the questions orally.

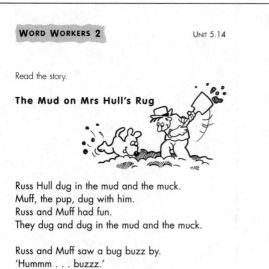

WORD WORKERS 2 UNIT 5.15

Russ and Muff got out of the mud.
'Come on Muff', Russ said.
'We will run and see mum and get butter on a bun.'

But Russ and Muff, the pup, got mud on the rug.
'Oh yuck,' said Mrs Hull. 'Look at Muff. Look at you.
Look at the mud and the muck on my rug.
Yuck. Yuck. Yuck!'

© 2000 H.A. Calder and Pascal Press 93

WORD WORKERS 2 UNIT 5.16

'No butter on a bun till you get in the tub.'
Russ and Muff, the pup, got in the tub.
'The muck and the mud will come off if I rub and rub,' said Mrs Hull.
'Get in the tub with the pup.'

Back in the mud, the bug said, 'Hummm . . . hummm.'
Back in the tub, Mrs Hull had to rub and rub.
'Yuck. Yuck. Yuck!' she said.

94

Students read the story. They read it several times until accuracy and fluency combine to improve comprehension.

WORD WORKERS 2 UNIT 5.17

Name .... Date ....

Write the letters 'a', 'b', 'c' and 'd' beside the pictures in the same order they occurred in the story.

a b

c d

1. *a* 2. *c* 3. *d* 4. *b*

Fill in the blanks with the exact words from the story.

1. Russ and Muff dug in the *mud* and the *muck*.
2. Mrs Hull had *butter* on a bun.
3. Russ and Muff got *mud* on the rug.
4. Mrs Hull said '*Oh* *yuck*!'
5. Back in the mud, the *bug* said 'Hummm.'

© 2000 H.A. Calder and Pascal Press 95

Activity 1: Students sequence the events in the story by placing the pictures in their correct order.

Activity 2: Students complete these sentences using the exact word from the story.

WORD WORKERS 2 UNIT 5.18

Name .... Date ....

Complete the sentences with the words in the box.

No butter on a *bun* till you get in the tub.

Russ and *Muff*, the pup, got in the *tub*.

'The muck and the *mud* will come off if I rub and rub,' said Mrs Hull.

'Get in the tub with the *pup*.'

Muff	tub	mud	pup	bun

Write the letters 'a', 'b', 'c' and 'd' beside the sentences in the same order they occurred in the story.

1. Russ and Muff, the pup, got mud on the rug. *c*
2. Back in the tub Mrs Hull had to rub and rub. *d*
3. Russ and Muff saw a bug buzz by. *b*
4. Russ and Muff dug in the mud and the muck. *a*

96 © 2000 H.A. Calder and Pascal Press

Activity 1: Students complete this cloze exercise using the words from the box.

Activity 2: Students sequence the events in the story by placing them in their correct order.

WORD WORKERS 2 UNIT 6.1

Reading 'a', 'e', 'i', 'o', 'u' words

Read these words.

1.	can	ten	rid	sum
2.	dug	mad	led	pig
3.	cut	hop	wag	get
4.	dim	hub	nod	jam
5.	fell	gap	tin	mum
6.	jog	mess	zip	dull
7.	lot	cab	neck	kit
8.	pup	mop	tax	egg
9.	wick	mud	cob	bus
10.	rig	rock	fuss	fill

 97

WORD WORKERS 2 UNIT 6.2

Read these words.

1.	hem	box	dad	den
2.	mix	pet	tag	gum
3.	doll	mug	odd	ham
4.	rod	hat	sell	fizz
5.	tap	leg	miss	nut
6.	hot	bat	hid	less
7.	fuzz	loss	jab	deck
8.	lip	tub	pack	job
9.	yes	bib	gull	off
10.	man	yell	lit	fox

98

For the following pages:

This unit provides revision in short vowel sounds. Students who have particular difficulty acquiring this skill may need the reinforcement of the phonemic awareness activities contained in *Word Workers Book 1*.

Students read the words in the columns.

WORD WORKERS 2 UNIT 6.3

Name .... Date ....

Write the words for the pictures.

1. bug 2. doll 3. pig
4. well 5. six 6. tub
7. fox 8. bib 9. net
10. bag 11. rod 12. bat
13. pen 14. tap 15. nut

 99

Students write the words for the pictures. If necessary, they refer to the word lists to find the correct spelling.

WORD WORKERS 2 UNIT 6.4

Name .... Date ....

Read these words.

fill fills	can cans	hops hop	eggs egg	gull gulls
cuts cut	legs leg	zip zips	tag tags	rocks rock
hat hats	dolls doll	mugs mug	dips dip	get gets

Complete these words by writing the vowel sound.

a	e	i	o	u
c_a_n	m_e_ss	p_i_g	_o_ff	m_u_m
j_a_b	t_e_n	f_i_zz	h_o_t	d_u_ll
h_a_m	s_e_ll	k_i_t	f_o_x	r_u_n
r_a_ck	l_e_d	t_i_n	p_o_p	b_u_zz
m_a_t	p_e_g	h_i_d	m_o_ss	c_u_p

100

Activity 1: Students read the words in the boxes. Tell them to add the endings to the smallest word or base word.

Activity 2: Students complete the words by writing in the letter printed above each column.

WORD WORKERS 2 UNIT 6.5

Name .... Date ....

Underline the nonsense word.

1. nut	2. mad	3. pill	4. leg	5. loss
cut	yad	bill	heg	moss
lut	pad	till	peg	voss
hut	lad	zill	Meg	boss

Write the words for the pictures.

1. *cup* 2. *hats* 3. *dolls*

4. *van* 5. *hen* 6. *socks*

7. *mugs* 8. *bell* 9. *hills*

© 2000 H.A. Calder and Pascal Press 101

Activity 1: Students look at the columns of words. Tell them to underline the word in each column that is a nonsense word.

Activity 2: Students write the words for the pictures. Tell them to add the letter 's' if there is more than one. If necessary, they refer to the word lists to find the correct spelling.

WORD WORKERS 2 UNIT 6.6

Name .... Date ....

Complete these words using the word pattern from the picture.

r *ag*	g *et*	r *ip*	l *ock*	f *un*
t *ag*	w *et*	t *ip*	d *ock*	r *un*
w *ag*	p *et*	h *ip*	m *ock*	g *un*

Underline the word that completes the sentence.

1. Six fat pups sat in the (not/hot) sun.
2. Meg and Jan hid in the (back/rack) of the hut.
3. Ross had to (run/sun) to get on the bus.
4. Mum (wed/fed) the hens in the pen.
5. Pam had to (hop/top) off the wet rocks.

102 © 2000 H.A. Calder and Pascal Press

Activity 1: Students look at the pictures above the columns. They use the word pattern from each picture to complete the words in the column below.

Activity 2: Students read the sentences. They underline the word in brackets that best completes the sentence.

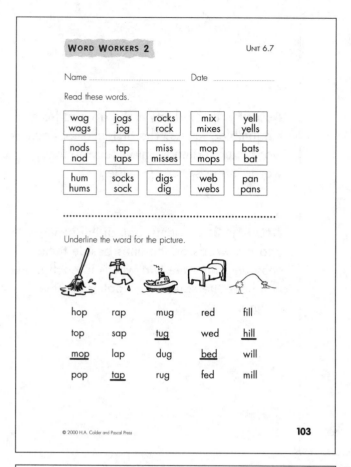

WORD WORKERS 2

UNIT 6.7

Name .... Date ....

Read these words.

wag wags	jogs jog	rocks rock	mix mixes	yell yells
nods nod	tap taps	miss misses	mop mops	bats bat
hum hums	socks sock	digs dig	web webs	pan pans

Underline the word for the picture.

hop	rap	mug	red	fill
top	sap	tug	wed	hill
mop	lap	dug	bed	will
pop	tap	rug	fed	mill

© 2000 H.A. Calder and Pascal Press 103

Activity 1: Students read the words in the boxes. Tell them to add the endings to the smallest word or base word.

Activity 2: Students look at the columns of words. They underline the word in each column that matches the picture above it.

WORD WORKERS 2

UNIT 6.8

Name .... Date ....

Draw a line to the word with the same word pattern.

lip	ram	peg	tan	deck	lad
box	well	miss	leg	dad	peck
yell	zip	rod	kiss	hop	will
mud	fox	man	mug	gun	pop
jam	bud	dug	sod	fill	sun

Complete the sentences with the words for the pictures.

1. His dad's ___hat___ fell in the tub.
2. Ann sat on the rock in the hot ___sun___.
3. The fat ___cat___ sat on mum's lap.
4. ___Ten___ men got in the back of the van.
5. Meg got a bug in the ___net___.

104 © 2000 H.A. Calder and Pascal Press

Activity 1: Students look at the two columns of words in each box. They draw a line from the word in the left-hand column to the word in the right-hand column that has the same word pattern.

Activity 2: Students look at the pictures and then complete the sentences below by writing the correct word for the picture in the space provided.

Word Workers 2 Unit 6.9

Name .... Date ....

Write the word for these jumbled letters. The first letter is underlined.

llif	*fill*	ufss	*fuss*	fof	*off*
olt	*lot*	nam	*man*	tah	*hat*
geg	*egg*	fxo	*fox*	dcke	*deck*
mah	*ham*	ssim	*miss*	tuc	*cut*

Underline the *two* words that have the same word pattern as the picture.

hat	red	bud	mat
fit	peg	had	beg
tin	bin	fox	sun
fill	mess	lock	rock
sun	buzz	fun	tan

© 2000 H.A. Calder and Pascal Press 105

Activity 1: Students make a word from the jumbled letters. The first letter of each word is underlined. Students write the words in the spaces provided.

Activity 2: Students look at the pictures and the words on the lines beside them. They underline the two words in each line that have the same word pattern as the picture.

Word Workers 2 Unit 6.10

Name .... Date ....

Read these words.

mess messes	pack packs	lips lip	guns gun	fizzes fizz
hot hotter	fatter fat	redder red	dull duller	sicker sick
jog jogger	boxer box	batter bat	runner run	zip zipper

Underline the word for the picture.

sick	bun	red	lock	fat
pick	run	hem	dock	rat
lick	fun	web	mock	hat
kick	gun	fed	rock	mat

106 © 2000 H.A. Calder and Pascal Press

Activity 1: Students read the words in the boxes. Tell them to add the endings to the smallest word or base word.

Activity 2: Students look at the columns of words. They underline the word in each column that matches the picture above it.

WORD WORKERS 2 UNIT 6.11

Name .... Date ....

Write the word from each column that fits the word shape box.

wag	well	bin	hot	gun
rag	yell	pin	pot	run
tag	bell	fin	not	sun
sag	fell	win	rot	bun
tag	*well*	*win*	*pot*	*bun*

....

Underline the word that completes the sentence.

1. Sam (pat/sat) on top of the dock.
2. Pat got the eggs out of the (van/ran).
3. Can Tim fix the (tip/rip) in his sock?
4. Mum was mad; there was mud on the (rug/mug).
5. Did the dog nip the (pick/sick) man's leg?

© 2000 H.A. Calder and Pascal Press 107

Activity 1: Students look at the columns of words. Tell them to put the word from each column that fits into the 'word shape' box below it.

Activity 2: Students read the sentences. They underline the word in brackets that best completes the sentence.

WORD WORKERS 2 UNIT 6.12

Name .... Date............

Put each column in alphabetical order.

a		e		i	
lad	*back*	egg	*egg*	sick	*fizz*
back	*lad*	yes	*jell*	inn	*inn*
mad	*mad*	pen	*keg*	nip	*nip*
sat	*sat*	keg	*pen*	rid	*rid*
tap	*tap*	jell	*yes*	fizz	*sick*

o		u	
dog	*dog*	lull	*bus*
ox	*got*	bus	*lull*
hop	*hop*	sun	*rut*
pod	*ox*	tuck	*sun*
got	*pod*	rut	*tuck*

108 © 2000 H.A. Calder and Pascal Press

Students place the words in each column in alphabetical order.

WORD WORKERS 2 UNIT 6.13

Name .... Date ....

Write the word with the correct spelling.

1. locks lox loks *locks*
2. les lless less *less*
3. obb odd od *odd*
4. tags taggs tagz *tags*
5. mudd mub mud *mud*

Fill in the missing letters to complete the word.

1.	*p* ac *k*	mess
2.	*m* es *s*	buzz
3.	*f* i *x*	pack
4.	*b* uz *z*	dolls
5.	*d* oll *s*	fix

 109

Activity 1: Students read the words going across the page, then write the word that is spelt correctly.

Activity 2: Students read the words in the box, then write the missing letters to complete the column of words on the left.

WORD WORKERS 2 UNIT 6.14

Name .... Date ....

Underline the word for the picture.

mug <u>mugs</u> <u>net</u> nets hat <u>hats</u>

<u>wig</u> wigs <u>fox</u> foxes hen <u>hens</u>

Complete the sentences with the words in the box.

lock	bugs	bed	bit	pack

1. Six socks are on the *bed*.
2. Mrs Mills had a *lock* on the box.
3. The *bugs* are at the back of the hut.
4. The cat *bit* the rat on the leg.
5. The man's *pack* fell off his back.

110

Activity 1: Students underline the singular word if there is one object pictured or the plural word if there are two or more objects pictured.

Activity 2: Students complete the sentences by writing the correct word from the box in the space provided.

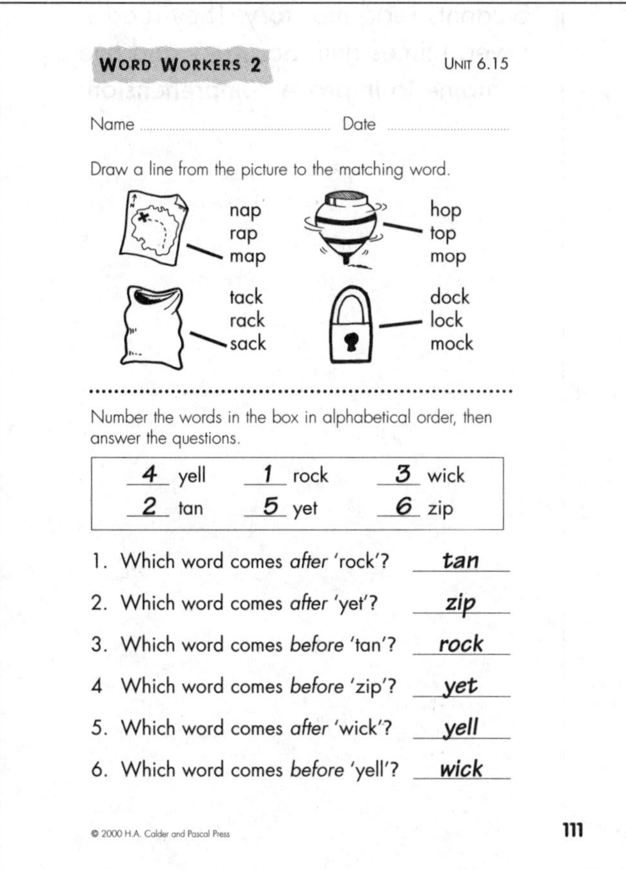

WORD WORKERS 2 UNIT 6.15

Name .... Date ....

Draw a line from the picture to the matching word.

nap
rap
map

hop
top
mop

tack
rack
sack

dock
lock
mock

Number the words in the box in alphabetical order, then answer the questions.

4 yell	1 rock	3 wick
2 tan	5 yet	6 zip

1. Which word comes *after* 'rock'? tan
2. Which word comes *after* 'yet'? zip
3. Which word comes *before* 'tan'? rock
4 Which word comes *before* 'zip'? yet
5. Which word comes *after* 'wick'? yell
6. Which word comes *before* 'yell'? wick

 111

Activity 1: Students say the word for the picture and then draw a line from the picture to the correct word beside it.

Activity 2: Students number the words in the box in alphabetical order, then use this information to answer the questions below.

WORD WORKERS 2 UNIT 6.16

Read the story.

The Mess in Ned's Pen

A fox got in Ned's pen. It got a fat red hen by the neck. Ned's dog, his pigs and his six ducks saw the fox get the hen. 'Yap, yap!' said his dog. 'Nog, nog!' said his pigs. 'Wack, wack!' said his ducks.

The dog, the pigs and the ducks ran at the fox. So the fox set off with the hen. It ran into the mud in Ned's pen. So did the dog, the pigs and the ducks. They fell in the mud too. All of them — the fox, the hen, the dog, the pigs and the ducks! It was a big mess.

112

For the following pages:

These exercises following the story consolidate knowledge of single letter–sound correspondences. They reinforce these skills with a simple comprehension story and activities based on the sounds and sight vocabulary acquired in *Word Workers Book 1*. Encourage multiple readings of the story to promote confidence and enhance fluency.

Students read the story. They read it several times until accuracy and fluency combine to improve comprehension.

WORD WORKERS 2 UNIT 6.17

Then Ned ran out of his hut with his gun. He saw the mess in his pen. There in the mud was the fox with his hen, his dog, his pigs and his ducks. Ned ran into the pen to get the fox. Then *he* fell in the mud! Now it was a big, big mess.

Ned's dog had a nip at the fox and bit it on the leg. The fox let the hen go and ran out of the pen. It ran and ran up the hill. Ned got out of the mud. He gave the dog a pat on the back. Then Ned fed the hen, the pigs and the ducks.

 113

WORD WORKERS 2 UNIT 6.18

Now Ned sits by his hut with his dog and his gun. He looks up at the hill to see if the fox will come back. But the fox will not come back. Not to the mess in Ned's pen.

114

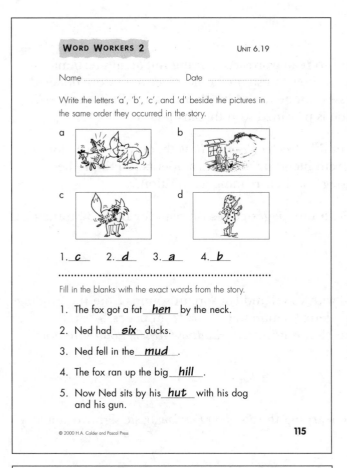

WORD WORKERS 2 UNIT 6.19

Name .... Date ....

Write the letters 'a', 'b', 'c', and 'd' beside the pictures in the same order they occurred in the story.

a

b

c

d

1. *c* 2. *d* 3. *a* 4. *b*

Fill in the blanks with the exact words from the story.

1. The fox got a fat *hen* by the neck.
2. Ned had *six* ducks.
3. Ned fell in the *mud*.
4. The fox ran up the big *hill*.
5. Now Ned sits by his *hut* with his dog and his gun.

 115

Activity 1: Students sequence the events in the story by placing the pictures in their correct order.

Activity 2: Students complete these sentences using the exact word from the story.

WORD WORKERS 2 UNIT 6.20

Name .... Date ....

Complete the sentences with the words in the box.

Then Ned ran out of his *hut* with his gun. He saw the mess in his *pen*. There in the mud was the *fox* with his hen, his dog, his pigs and his ducks. Ned *ran* into the pen to get the fox. The *he* fell in the *mud*! Now it was a big, big mess.

fox	hut	pen	mud	ran

Write the letters 'a', 'b', 'c' and 'd' beside the sentences in the same order they occurred in the story.

1. The fox set off with the hen. *b*
2. Ned ran out of his hut with his gun. *c*
3. Now Ned sits by his hut with his dog and his gun. *d*
4. The fox got a fat red hen by the neck. *a*

116

Activity 1: Students complete this cloze exercise using the words from the box.

Activity 2: Students sequence the events in the story by placing them in their correct order.

* Students complete *Word Workers Achievement Test 2* after completing this unit.

Using Book 3

Word Workers Book 3 teaches students to read words containing initial and terminal blends. Below are some suggestions on how to use the book effectively. More detailed information on the teaching processes can be found in Chapter 2: 'Skills for successful teaching'. An activity-by-activity guide is provided with the answers.

- Read the section in the *Teacher Resource Book* that gives instructions on teaching the different blending activities students require to be successful at this stage of their reading acquisition.
- Become familiar with the suggested lesson plan for Book 3 on the next page.

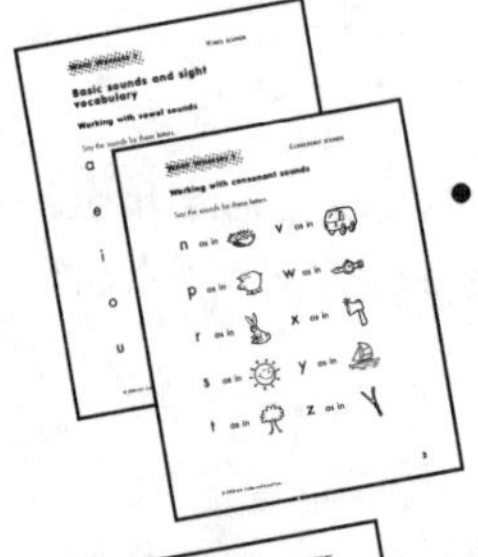

- Continue the drill with vowel and consonant sounds from the *Reading Freedom 2000* single letter–sound wall chart from pages 1–3 in Book 2. Also introduce the blends using the *Reading Freedom 2000* common blends wall chart.

- Students continue learning the *Reading Freedom* basic sight vocabulary lists.

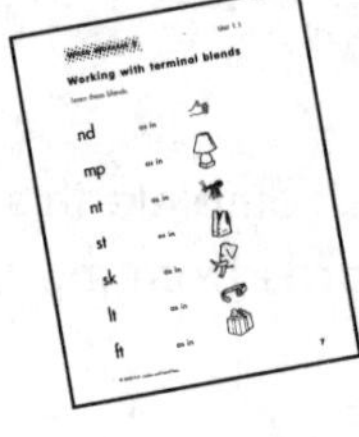

- Introduce the initial and terminal blends as students encounter them in each successive unit.

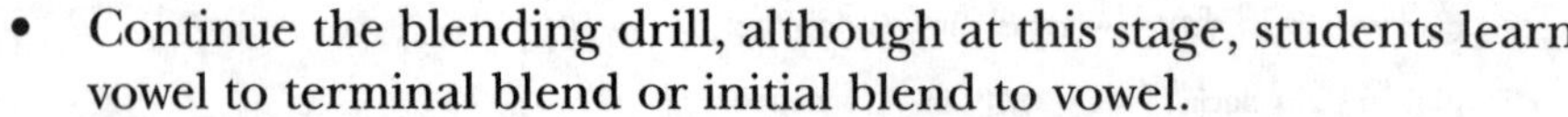

- Continue the blending drill, although at this stage, students learn vowel to terminal blend or initial blend to vowel.

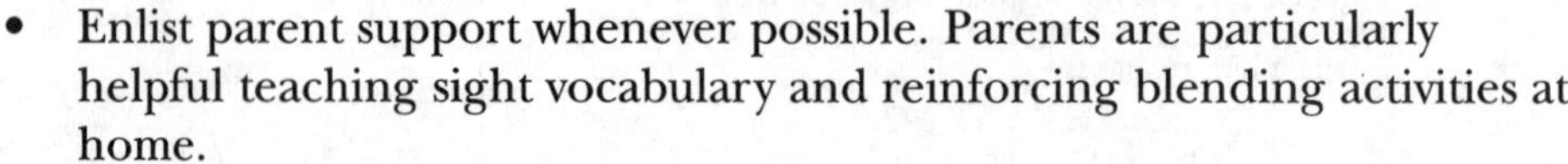

- Enlist parent support whenever possible. Parents are particularly helpful teaching sight vocabulary and reinforcing blending activities at home.

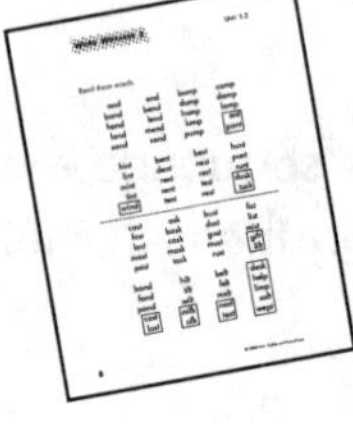

- Monitor students' progress while they read the word list at the beginning of each unit.
- When Book 3 is completed, record students' progress using *Word Workers* Achievement Test 3.

Book 3: Suggested lesson plan

Based on a lesson of approximately 30 minutes.

1 Students say a row of sounds from the *Reading Freedom 2000* single letter–sound and common blends wall chart. For small groups, each student can say a row or column of sounds. If your class is large, select students to say a row or column until all the sounds have been repeated. Be sure different students say the sounds each lesson.

2 In small group lessons, each student reads a column of *Reading Freedom* basic sight vocabulary. When teaching the whole class, select students to read a column of sight words. Five or six columns is enough to start your lesson with. Be sure different students read the sight words each lesson.

3 Explain and demonstrate the vowel sound to be learned (see Chapter 2: 'Skills for successful teaching' if any guidance is required). Carefully explain the activities on the page or pages to be completed. Ensure that students understand the concepts involved and know what is required of them.

4 Assign activity pages to be completed (the number of pages depends on the teacher's professional judgment as well as the ability and enthusiasm of the student).

5 In Book 3, demonstrate and practise the vowel–terminal blend blending technique first. Then, from Unit 2 on, demonstrate and practise the initial blend–vowel blending technique. Continue with this until the book is completed, learning new initial and terminal blends as they are introduced. Some students require more work with blending techniques than others. Form a group of these students and give them extra practice while other students work on activity pages.

6 Reward students for achievement on the activity pages or in learning sight vocabulary with stamps, stickers or gold stars. When they complete the activity book and finish the complementary achievement test (found in *Word Workers Achievement Tests*) they receive a *Word Workers* Merit Certificate.

7 Assign any homework after demonstrating the activities. Ensure students understand the concept and what is to be done.

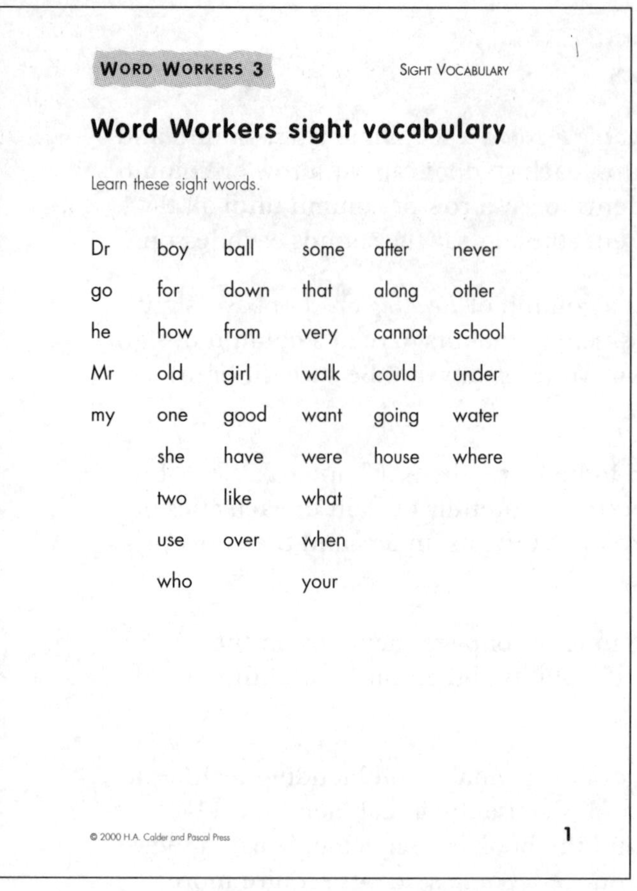

WORD WORKERS 3 — SIGHT VOCABULARY

Word Workers sight vocabulary

Learn these sight words.

Dr	boy	ball	some	after	never
go	for	down	that	along	other
he	how	from	very	cannot	school
Mr	old	girl	walk	could	under
my	one	good	want	going	water
	she	have	were	house	where
	two	like	what		
	use	over	when		
	who		your		

© 2000 H.A. Calder and Pascal Press — 1

For the following pages:

Students learn these sight words list by list. Reward successful acquisition of sight vocabulary with stars and stickers.

These lists contain the basic sight words students need to work successfully with *Word Workers*. Teach these words list by list until they are mastered. Practise them regularly and reward students for progress.

WORD WORKERS 3 — SIGHT VOCABULARY

Reading Freedom sight vocabulary

Learn these sight words.

List one		List two	
and	look	at	man
are	my	away	me
boy	of	big	not
can	play	blue	on
come	red	down	one
funny	run	for	ran
go	said	good	saw
he	says	green	three
is	see	have	too
jump	the	here	up
like	this	in	watch
little	to	it	you

2 — © 2000 H.A. Calder and Pascal Press

Students who have mastered the *Word Workers* basic sight vocabulary are now introduced to the *Reading Freedom* basic sight vocabulary lists of words. Teach them list by list until they are mastered. Practise them regularly and reward students for progress.

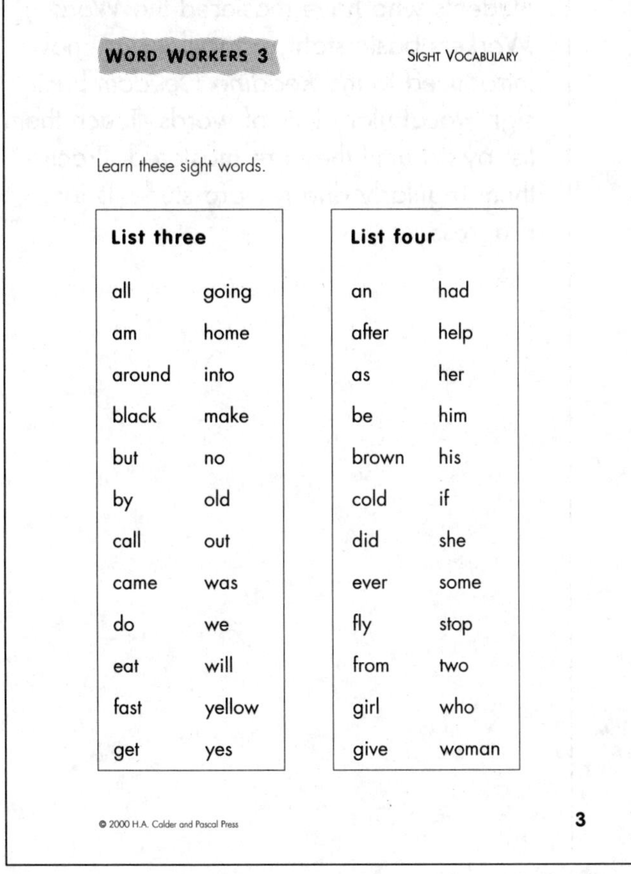

WORD WORKERS 3 SIGHT VOCABULARY

Learn these sight words.

List three	
all	going
am	home
around	into
black	make
but	no
by	old
call	out
came	was
do	we
eat	will
fast	yellow
get	yes

List four	
an	had
after	help
as	her
be	him
brown	his
cold	if
did	she
ever	some
fly	stop
from	two
girl	who
give	woman

© 2000 H.A. Calder and Pascal Press 3

Students who have mastered the *Word Workers* basic sight vocabulary are now introduced to the *Reading Freedom* basic sight vocabulary lists of words. Teach them list by list until they are mastered. Practise them regularly and reward students for progress.

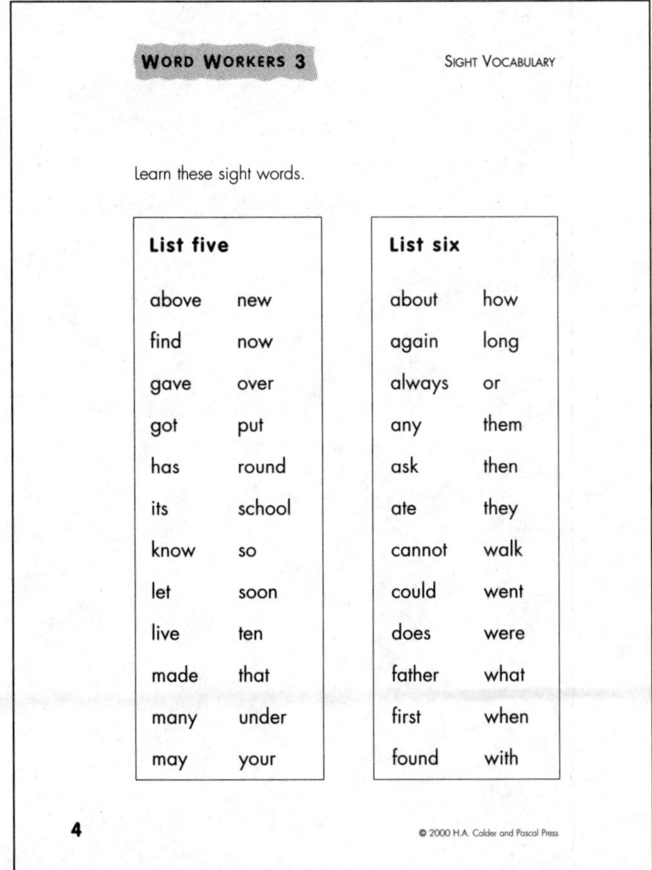

WORD WORKERS 3 SIGHT VOCABULARY

Learn these sight words.

List five	
above	new
find	now
gave	over
got	put
has	round
its	school
know	so
let	soon
live	ten
made	that
many	under
may	your

List six	
about	how
again	long
always	or
any	them
ask	then
ate	they
cannot	walk
could	went
does	were
father	what
first	when
found	with

4 © 2000 H.A. Calder and Pascal Press

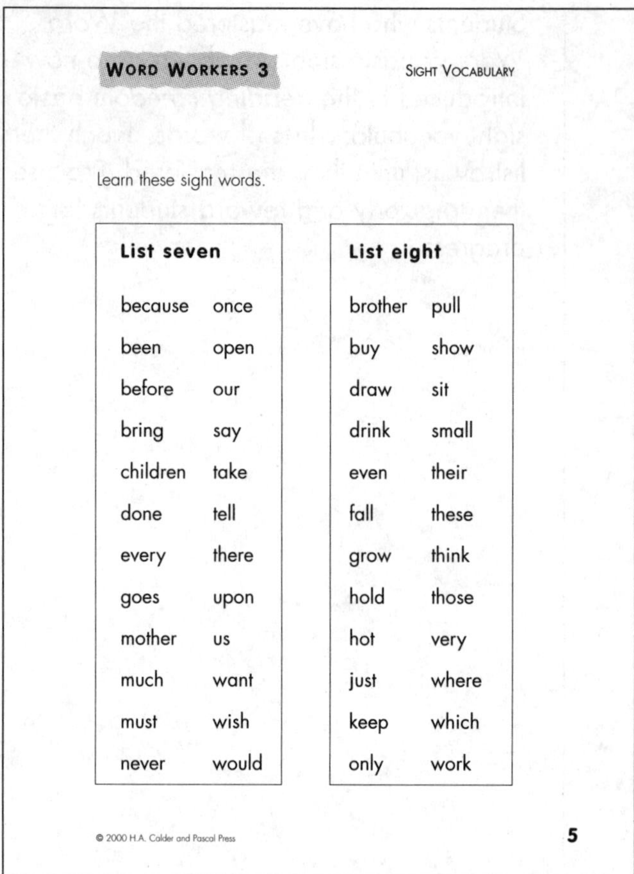

WORD WORKERS 3 — SIGHT VOCABULARY

Learn these sight words.

List seven

because	once
been	open
before	our
bring	say
children	take
done	tell
every	there
goes	upon
mother	us
much	want
must	wish
never	would

List eight

brother	pull
buy	show
draw	sit
drink	small
even	their
fall	these
grow	think
hold	those
hot	very
just	where
keep	which
only	work

© 2000 H.A. Calder and Pascal Press 5

Students who have mastered the *Word Workers* basic sight vocabulary are now introduced to the *Reading Freedom* basic sight vocabulary lists of words. Teach them list by list until they are mastered. Practise them regularly and reward students for progress.

WORD WORKERS 3 — SIGHT VOCABULARY

Learn these sight words.

List nine

best	pick
better	please
both	pretty
clean	read
cut	shall
eight	six
five	today
four	try
full	use
light	well
myself	why
off	write

List ten

baby	sing
daughter	sister
far	sleep
house	something
hurt	son
kind	start
laugh	thank
Mr	together
Mrs	warm
own	wash
right	water
seven	white

6 © 2000 H.A. Calder and Pascal Press

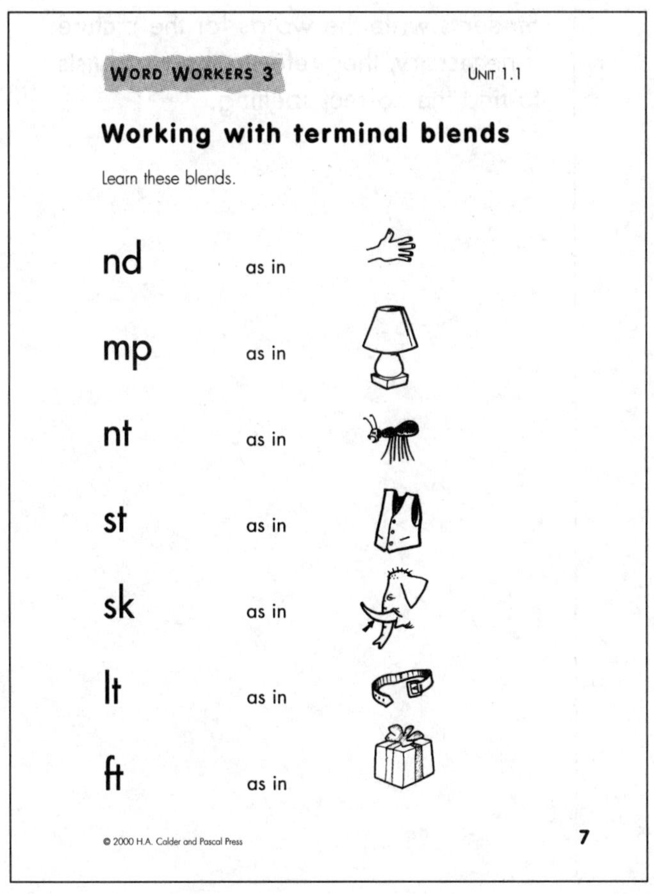
WORD WORKERS 3 UNIT 1.1

Working with terminal blends

Learn these blends.

nd as in

mp as in

nt as in

st as in

sk as in

lt as in

ft as in

© 2000 H.A. Calder and Pascal Press 7

For the following pages:

Teach these terminal blends carefully. Make sure each student knows them. To reinforce knowledge of these blends and to promote reading acquisition, use the vowel to terminal blend blending technique.

From now on, incorporate knowledge of these blends using the Reading Freedom *Common Blends Wall Chart.*

WORD WORKERS 3 UNIT 1.2

Read these words.

and	end	bump	camp
band	bend	dump	damp
hand	lend	hump	lamp
land	mend	lump	ant
sand	send	pump	pant
hint	bent	best	hunt
lint	dent	nest	punt
mint	rent	rest	runt
tint	sent	test	dusk
wind	tent	vest	tusk

cast	ask	bust	fist
fast	bask	dust	list
last	cask	gust	mist
mast	mask	must	gift
past	task	rust	lift
bond	hilt	belt	desk
fond	tilt	felt	help
pond	wilt	melt	limp
cost	milk	next	soft
lost	silk	text	wept

8 © 2000 H.A. Calder and Pascal Press

Students read the words in the columns.

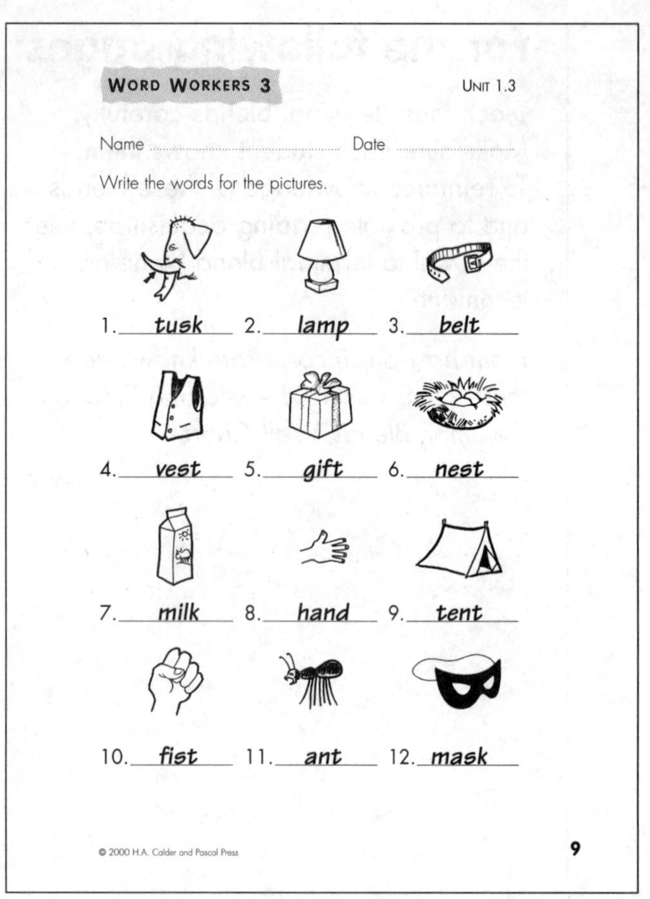
WORD WORKERS 3 UNIT 1.3

Name .... Date ....

Write the words for the pictures.

1. *tusk* 2. *lamp* 3. *belt*

4. *vest* 5. *gift* 6. *nest*

7. *milk* 8. *hand* 9. *tent*

10. *fist* 11. *ant* 12. *mask*

© 2000 H.A. Calder and Pascal Press 9

Students write the words for the pictures. If necessary, they refer to the word lists to find the correct spelling.

WORD WORKERS 3 UNIT 1.4

Name .... Date ....

Read these words.

land lands landed	pumps pumped pump	lasted last lasts	melt melted melts
hinted hints hint	helps helped help	mend mended mends	rests rest rested

Underline the word for the picture.

damp	test	<u>tusk</u>	felt	task
ramp	pest	dusk	<u>belt</u>	cask
camp	<u>vest</u>	husk	pelt	<u>mask</u>
<u>lamp</u>	zest	musk	welt	ask

10 © 2000 H.A. Calder and Pascal Press

Activity 1: Students read the words in the boxes. Tell them to add the endings to the smallest word or base word.

Activity 2: Students look at the columns of words. They underline the word in each column that matches the picture above it.

WORD WORKERS 3 UNIT 1.5

Name .... Date ....

Underline the nonsense word.

1. cast	2. hilt	3. hamp	4. mint	5. lump
last	filt	damp	tint	yump
past	wilt	ramp	zint	dump
rast	tilt	camp	hint	hump

Write the words for the pictures.

1. hands 2. belt 3. tusk

4. mask 5. gift 6. lamps

7. milk 8. tents 9. vest

© 2000 H.A. Calder and Pascal Press 11

Activity 1: Students look at the columns of words. Tell them to underline the word in each column that is a nonsense word.

Activity 2: Students write the words for the pictures. Tell them to add the letter 's' if there is more than one. If necessary, they refer to the word lists to find the correct spelling.

WORD WORKERS 3 UNIT 1.6

Name .... Date ....

Complete these words with the word pattern from the picture.

s and	v ent	m usk	z est	f elt
b and	r ent	d usk	w est	p elt
l and	w ent	h usk	t est	w elt

Underline the correct word to complete the sentence.

1. Mrs Hill lifted the (sifts/gifts) off the desk.
2. Jeff and Rod camped in the (tent/went).
3. The duck sat in the (rest/nest) at the pond.
4. The jet landed with a (bump/hump).
5. The man lost the (melt/belt) for his pants.

12 © 2000 H.A. Calder and Pascal Press

Activity 1: Students look at the pictures above the columns. They use the word pattern from each picture to complete the words in the column below.

Activity 2: Students read the sentences. They underline the word in brackets that best completes the sentence.

WORD WORKERS 3

UNIT 1.7

Name .... Date ....

Read these words.

pant	tests	tended	asks
pants	tested	tend	asked
panted	test	tends	ask

listed	wilt	bumped	handed
lists	wilted	bump	hand
list	wilts	bumps	hands

Complete the words by writing the vowel sounds.

a	e	i	o	u
s a nd	n e st	t i nt	b o nd	p u mp
p a nt	d e sk	w i nd	s o ft	h u nt
c a mp	b e nt	m i lk	l o st	t u sk
h a nd	s e nd	l i mp	p o nd	l u mp
l a mp	m e lt	g i ft	c o st	d u st

13

Activity 1: Students read the words in the boxes. Tell them to add the endings to the smallest word or base word.

Activity 2: Students complete the words by writing in the letter printed above each column.

WORD WORKERS 3

UNIT 1.8

Name .... Date ....

Draw a line to the word with the same word pattern.

gift	pant	next	weld	milk	task
ant	lost	imp	band	bond	pump
help	lift	held	gust	lump	mend
cost	punt	sand	text	bend	pond
bunt	yelp	dust	limp	cask	silk

Complete these sentences by writing the words for the pictures.

1. Mum asked Tim to hand her the *lamp* .
2. The cat jumped off the top of the *desk* .
3. Bill hunted for the duck's *nest* at the pond.
4. The *tent* next to Tess fell in the wind.
5. Mrs Ross held the milk in her left *hand* .

14

Activity 1: Students look at the two columns of words in each box. They draw a line from the word in the left-hand column to the word in the right-hand column that has the same word pattern.

Activity 2: Students look at the pictures and then complete the sentences below by writing the correct word for the picture in the space provided.

WORD WORKERS 3 UNIT 1.9

Name .... Date ....

Write the word for these jumbled letters.
The first letter is underlined.

skam	mask	danb	band	antp	pant
filt	lift	lsit	list	mupb	bump
tepw	wept	skut	tusk	tnit	tint
xent	next	dnob	bond	telf	felt

Underline the *two* words with the same word pattern as the picture.

felt	melt	help	tilt
fast	sand	pump	land
lost	lift	mint	sift
husk	dust	wind	dusk
bent	held	dent	desk

© 2000 H.A. Calder and Pascal Press 15

Activity 1: Students make a word from the jumbled letters. The first letter of each word is underlined. Students write the words in the spaces provided.

Activity 2: Students look at the pictures and the words on the lines beside them. They underline the two words in each line that have the same word pattern as the picture.

WORD WORKERS 3 UNIT 1.10

Name .... Date ....

Read these words.

rest rests rested	limp limped limps	lifted lifts lift	rents rent rented
faster fastest fast	soft softest softer	dampest damp damper	

Underline the word for the picture.

test	land	tent	damp	mist
rest	sand	went	and	fist
nest	band	bent	ant	list
west	hand	sent	pant	lift

16 © 2000 H.A. Calder and Pascal Press

Activity 1: Students read the words in the boxes. Tell them to add the endings to the smallest word or base word.

Activity 2: Students look at the columns of words. They underline the word in each column that matches the picture above it.

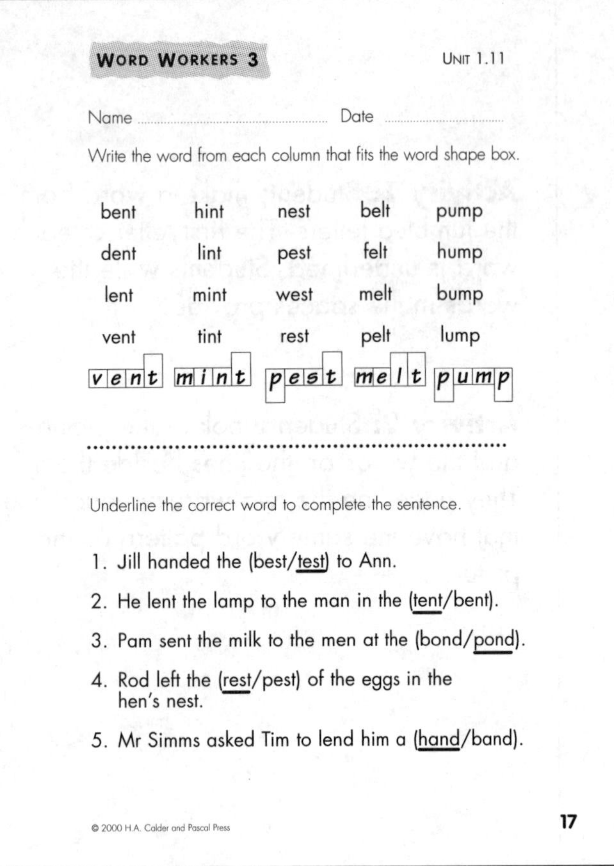

Word Workers 3 Unit 1.11

Name .... Date ....

Write the word from each column that fits the word shape box.

bent	hint	nest	belt	pump
dent	lint	pest	felt	hump
lent	mint	west	melt	bump
vent	tint	rest	pelt	lump
vent	mint	pest	melt	pump

Underline the correct word to complete the sentence.

1. Jill handed the (best/test) to Ann.
2. He lent the lamp to the man in the (tent/bent).
3. Pam sent the milk to the men at the (bond/pond).
4. Rod left the (rest/pest) of the eggs in the hen's nest.
5. Mr Simms asked Tim to lend him a (hand/band).

© 2000 H.A. Calder and Pascal Press 17

Activity 1: Students look at the columns of words. Tell them to put the word from each column that fits into the 'word shape' box below it.

Activity 2: Students read the sentences. They underline the word in brackets that best completes the sentence.

Word Workers 3 Unit 1.12

Name .... Date ....

Put each column in alphabetical order.

a		e		i	
past	band	welt	sent	hint	fist
band	lamp	yelp	vest	silk	gift
lamp	mask	zest	welt	limp	hint
pant	pant	vest	yelp	fist	limp
mask	past	sent	zest	gift	silk

o		u	
lost	bond	punt	fund
pond	cost	tusk	gust
cost	fond	pump	pump
bond	lost	fund	punt
fond	pond	gust	tusk

18 © 2000 H.A. Calder and Pascal Press

Students place the words in each column in alphabetical order.

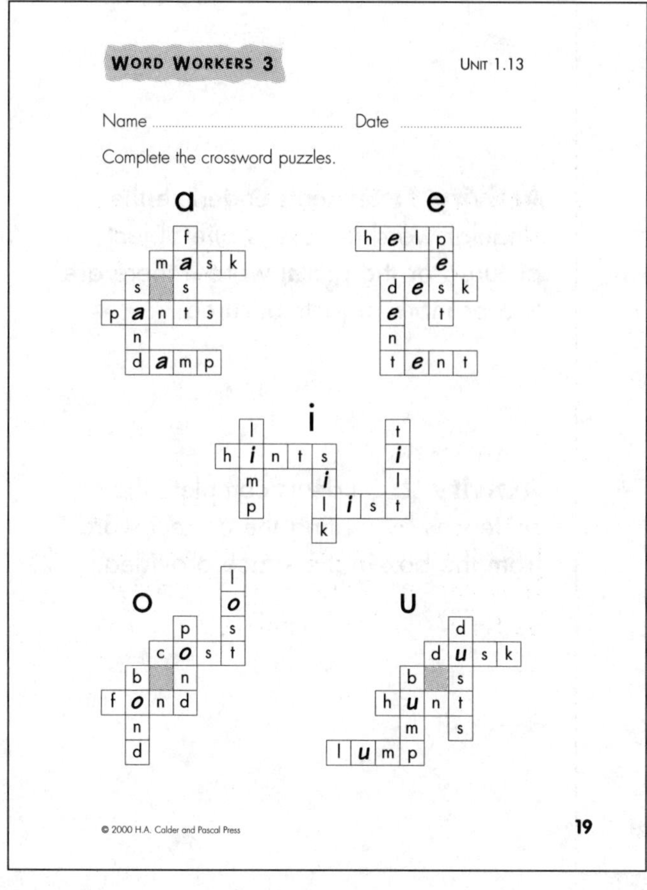
WORD WORKERS 3 UNIT 1.13

Name .... Date ....

Complete the crossword puzzles.

a e i o u

© 2000 H.A. Calder and Pascal Press 19

Students complete the crossword puzzles. They write the letter indicated in the blank spaces to make words that can be read going down or across the page.

WORD WORKERS 3 UNIT 1.14

Name .... Date ....

Write the word with the correct spelling.

1.	test	testt	tist	*test*
2.	nekst	nex	next	*next*
3.	mlik	milk	milck	*milk*
4.	kamp	capm	camp	*camp*
5.	fasst	fast	fust	*fast*

Fill in the missing letters to complete the word.

1. *b* ump *s*
2. *t* en *t*
3. *l* and *s*
4. *s* of *t*
5. *l* ifte *d*

tent
soft
bumps
lifted
lands

20 © 2000 H.A. Calder and Pascal Press

Activity 1: Students read the words going across the page, then write the word that is spelt correctly.

Activity 2: Students read the words in the box, then write the missing letters to complete the column of words on the left.

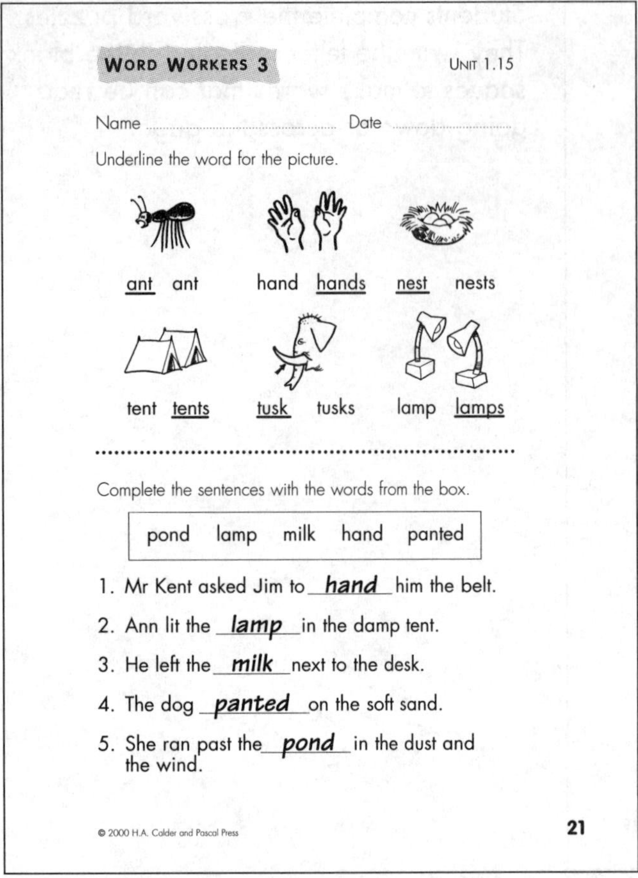

Word Workers 3 Unit 1.15

Name .... Date ....

Underline the word for the picture.

ant ant	hand hands	nest nests
tent tents	tusk tusks	lamp lamps

Complete the sentences with the words from the box.

pond	lamp	milk	hand	panted

1. Mr Kent asked Jim to *hand* him the belt.
2. Ann lit the *lamp* in the damp tent.
3. He left the *milk* next to the desk.
4. The dog *panted* on the soft sand.
5. She ran past the *pond* in the dust and the wind.

© 2000 H.A. Calder and Pascal Press 21

Activity 1: Students underline the singular word if there is one object pictured or the plural word if there are two or more objects pictured.

Activity 2: Students complete the sentences by writing the correct word from the box in the space provided.

Word Workers 3 Unit 1.16

Name .... Date ....

Draw a line from the picture to the matching word.

desk tusk silk	sift lift gift
pant sent ant	sand hand land

Number the words in the box in alphabetical order, then answer the questions.

3 cost	*6* hilt	*1* band
4 desk	*2* camp	*5* dust

1. Which word comes *before* 'camp'? *band*
2. Which word comes *after* 'dust'? *hilt*
3. Which word comes *before* 'cost'? *camp*
4. Which word comes *after* 'desk'? *dust*
5. Which word comes *after* 'camp'? *cost*
6. Which word comes *before* 'dust'? *desk*

22 © 2000 H.A. Calder and Pascal Press

Activity 1: Students say the word for the picture and then draw a line from the picture to the correct word beside it.

Activity 2: Students number the words in the box in alphabetical order, then use this information to answer the questions below.

WORD WORKERS 3 UNIT 1.17

Read the story.

The Tent by the Pond

Mr Mott set up his tent by the pond. Then he sat on the soft sand. 'At last I can rest,' he said. Mr Mott felt a gust of wind on the back of his neck. He went in the tent and set up his bed.

Mr and Mrs Duck's nest was next to the tent. Mr Mott did not see it. Mrs Duck sat on six eggs in her nest. 'Wack, wack!' she said. Mrs Duck was mad at Mr Mott. If the tent fell it would land on the nest. She sent Mr Duck to get rid of the tent.

Mr Duck went up to Mr Mott's tent. Ten pegs held it up. Mr Duck lifted the pegs out of the soft sand. Then he left with the pegs in his bill. Mr Mott rested on the bed in his tent.

 23

WORD WORKERS 3 UNIT 1.18

Just then a lot of ants went in the tent. They got up on the end of Mr Mott's bed. The ants bit him on the leg. 'There are ants in my pants!' he yelled.

Mr Mott jumped up. He bumped the top of the tent. Mr Duck had the pegs that held it up. The tent fell on top of Mr Mott. Mr Mott fell back on the bed. The ants ran out of the tent. The tent just missed Mrs Duck and her six eggs.

Mr Mott limped out of the tent and felt his leg. His camp was a mess. He had lost the pegs that held up the tent. Mr Mott packed up his tent by the pond. He left the wind, the sand and the ants to Mr and Mrs Duck, and to the nest with six eggs.

24

For the following pages:

This story is designed to reinforce the skills learned in this and previous units of work. At no stage do students encounter unfamiliar words or skills. Students read the story and answer the questions silently. Correct the work by having them read the story and answer the questions orally.

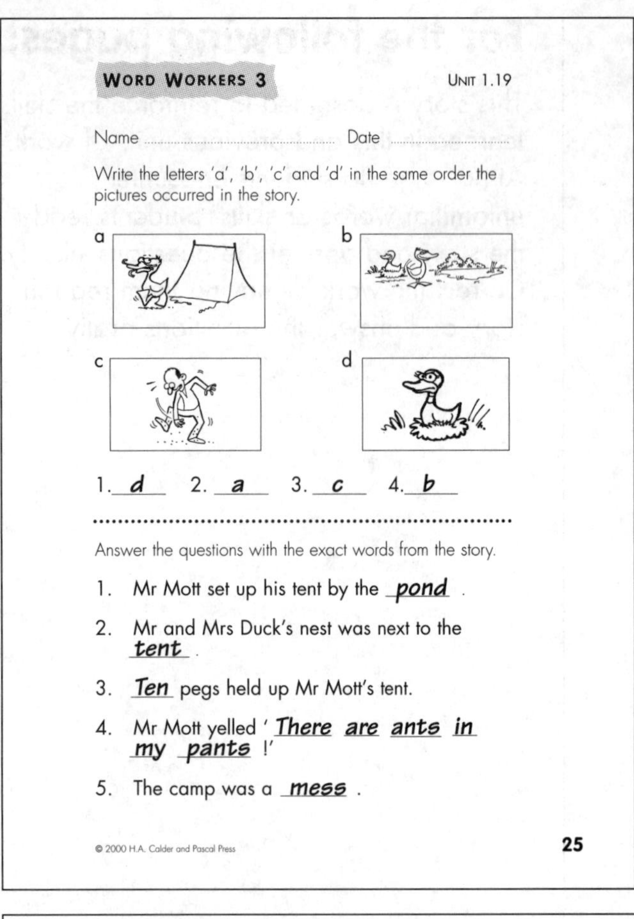

WORD WORKERS 3 UNIT 1.19

Name .... Date ....

Write the letters 'a', 'b', 'c' and 'd' in the same order the pictures occurred in the story.

a b c d

1. *d* 2. *a* 3. *c* 4. *b*

Answer the questions with the exact words from the story.

1. Mr Mott set up his tent by the *pond* .
2. Mr and Mrs Duck's nest was next to the *tent* .
3. *Ten* pegs held up Mr Mott's tent.
4. Mr Mott yelled '*There are ants in my pants* !'
5. The camp was a *mess* .

© 2000 H.A. Calder and Pascal Press 25

Activity 1: Students sequence the events in the story by placing the pictures in their correct order.

Activity 2: Students complete these sentences using the exact word from the story.

WORD WORKERS 3 UNIT 1.20

Name .... Date ....

Fill in the blanks with the correct word from the box.

Mr and Mrs Duck's *nest* was next to the tent. Mr Mott did not see it. Mrs Duck sat on six *eggs* in her nest. 'Wack,Wack!' she said. Mrs Duck was *mad* at Mr Mott. If the tent fell it would *land* on the nest. She sent Mr Duck to get rid of the *tent* .

land	mad	eggs	tent	nest

Write the letters 'a', 'b', 'c' and 'd' beside the sentences in the same order they occurred in the story.

1. 'There are ants in my pants!' *c*
2. Mr Mott limped out of the tent. *d*
3. Mr Mott felt a gust of wind on the back of his neck. *a*
4. Mr Duck lifted the pegs out of the soft sand. *b*

26 © 2000 H.A. Calder and Pascal Press

Activity 1: Students complete this cloze exercise using the words from the box.

Activity 2: Students sequence the events in the story by placing them in their correct order.

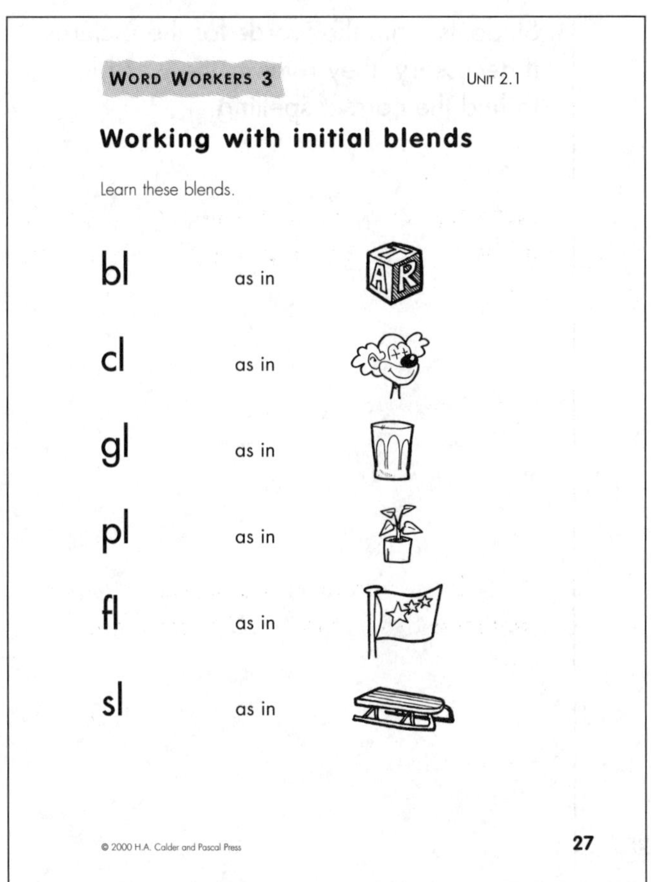

WORD WORKERS 3 UNIT 2.1

Working with initial blends

Learn these blends.

bl as in

cl as in

gl as in

pl as in

fl as in

sl as in

© 2000 H.A. Calder and Pascal Press 27

For the following pages:

Teach these initial blends carefully. Make sure each student knows them. To reinforce knowledge of these blends and to promote reading acquisition, use the vowel to initial blend technique.

From now on, incorporate knowledge of these blends using the Reading Freedom *Common Blends Wall Chart.*

WORD WORKERS 3 UNIT 2.2

Read these words.

black	clam	clod	glad
bled	clan	clog	gland
blend	clap	clop	Glen
bless	clamp	clot	glint
blimp	clip	clock	glum
bliss	click	clomp	gloss
block	class	club	glass
blond		cluck	
blunt		clump	
blast			

flab	flip	plan	slab	slid
flag	flit	plant	slam	slim
flap	flint	plug	slap	slip
flat	flick	plum	slat	slit
flax	flop	plus	slack	slick
flack	flock	pluck	slant	slop
flask	floss	plump	sled	slot
			slept	slug
				slump

28 © 2000 H.A. Calder and Pascal Press

Students read the words in the columns.

WORD WORKERS 3 UNIT 2.3

Name .... Date ....

Write the words for the pictures.

1. *plug* 2. *clock* 3. *blimp*

4. *clap* 5. *plus* 6. *flag*

7. *block* 8. *glass* 9. *sled*

10. *club* 11. *plant* 12. *clip*

 29

Students write the words for the pictures. If necessary, they refer to the word lists to find the correct spelling.

WORD WORKERS 3 UNIT 2.4

Name .... Date ....

Read these words.

plan plans planned	claps clapped clap	plugged plug plugs	blasts blast blasted
flipped flips flip	block blocked blocks	plants plant planted	slammed slam slams

Underline the word for the picture.

clan	blimp	slab	plump	club
cluck	bled	slip	plus	clip
clog	blunt	slump	plug	clamp
clap	block	slept	plant	clock

30

Activity 1: Students read the words in the boxes. Tell them to add the endings to the smallest word or base word.

Activity 2: Students look at the columns of words. They underline the word in each column that matches the picture above it.

WORD WORKERS 3 UNIT 2.5

Name .... Date ....

Underline the nonsense word.

1. plant	2. sled	3. pliff	4. flop	5. slump
blat	bless	clip	clock	glum
clap	flemp	slim	slop	fluzz
glad	bled	flick	clond	plump

Write the words for the pictures.

1. *blimp* 2. *plugs* 3. *plant*

4. *clubs* 5. *clock* 6. *clips*

7. *glass* 8. *blocks* 9. *sled*

 31

Activity 1: Students look at the columns of words. Tell them to underline the word in each column that is a nonsense word.

Activity 2: Students write the words for the pictures. Tell them to add the letter 's' if there is more than one. If necessary, they refer to the word lists to find the correct spelling.

WORD WORKERS 3 UNIT 2.6

Complete the words with the word pattern from the picture.

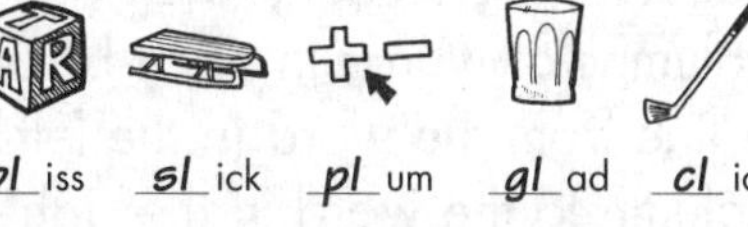

bl iss	*sl* ick	*pl* um	*gl* ad	*cl* ick
bl ond	*sl* ab	*pl* ug	*gl* int	*cl* amp
bl ed	*sl* ept	*pl* an	*gl* and	*cl* ot
bl ack	*sl* ot	*pl* ant	*gl* oss	*cl* an

Underline the correct word to complete the sentence.

1. The pigs flopped in the (slop/slap) in the pen.
2. Jill held the (flag/flat) as it flapped in the wind.
3. Glen slept next to the (clop/clock).
4. Mrs Blunt asked the (glass/class) to add ten plus ten.
5. The plump hen clucked as it pecked at the (plants/slants).

32

Activity 1: Students look at the pictures above the columns. They use the word pattern from each picture to complete the words in the column below.

Activity 2: Students read the sentences. They underline the word in brackets that best completes the sentence.

WORD WORKERS 3 UNIT 2.7

Name .... Date ....

Read these words.

glint glints glinted	slapped slap slaps	slumps slumped slump	clamped clamps clamp
click clicked clicks	blends blended blend	flaps flap flapped	clipped clip clips

Complete these words.

a	e	i	o	u
sl_a_b	bl_e_d	cl_i_p	bl_o_nd	pl_u_mp
bl_a_ck	sl_e_pt	bl_i_mp	pl_o_t	gl_u_m
cl_a_mp	sl_e_d	sl_i_ck	cl_o_mp	bl_u_nt
gl_a_d	Gl_e_n	gl_i_nt	sl_o_p	cl_u_b
pl_a_nt	fl_e_d	fl_i_p	fl_o_ck	pl_u_s

© 2000 H.A. Calder and Pascal Press 33

Activity 1: Students read the words in the boxes. Tell them to add the endings to the smallest word or base word.

Activity 2: Students complete the words by writing in the letter printed above each column.

WORD WORKERS 3 UNIT 2.8

Name .... Date ....

Draw a line to the word with the same word pattern.

clap	class	glint	flick	clip	blot
flit	clock	slick	plump	slant	flip
glass	slit	plum	flint	slot	plant
slop	flap	slump	cluck	bled	flat
block	flop	pluck	glum	slat	fled

Complete the sentences by writing the words for the pictures.

1. The _flag_ on the blimp flapped in the wind.
2. Ross slipped off the back of the _sled_.
3. Mr Till's black _clock_ ticked at the back of the class.
4. She slid the last _plant_ into the van.
5. Miss Bliss handed the _glass_ of milk to Glen.

34 © 2000 H.A. Calder and Pascal Press

Activity 1: Students look at the two columns of words in each box. They draw a line from the word in the left-hand column to the word in the right-hand column that has the same word pattern.

Activity 2: Students look at the pictures and then complete the sentences below by writing the correct word for the picture in the space provided.

WORD WORKERS 3 UNIT 2.9

Name .... Date ....

Write the word for these jumbled letters.
The first letter is underlined.

lops	slop	fintl	flint	slup	plus
mlup	plum	locck	clock	tlaf	flat
sslib	bliss	sdil	slid	scals	class
lafg	flag	plof	flop	bimpl	blimp

Underline the *two* words with the same word pattern as the picture.

clot	slump	flop	clog
flat	blast	flask	glad
glum	plus	plump	slump
class	slam	clam	blond
gland	slim	flat	slick

© 2000 H.A. Calder and Pascal Press 35

Activity 1: Students make a word from the jumbled letters. The first letter of each word is underlined. Students write the words in the spaces provided.

Activity 2: Students look at the pictures and the words on the lines beside them. They underline the two words in each line that have the same word pattern as the picture.

WORD WORKERS 3 UNIT 2.10

Name .... Date ....

Read these words.

slip slips slipped	flicked flick flicks	clucks clucked cluck	slant slanted slants
blond blonder blondest	slimmer slimmest slim	flat flattest flatter	slickest slick slicker

Underline the word for the picture.

plug	glum	plant	black	flag
pluck	glass	pluck	bless	flock
plus	gland	plum	blast	flask
plan	glint	plug	block	flint

36 © 2000 H.A. Calder and Pascal Press

Activity 1: Students read the words in the boxes. Tell them to add the endings to the smallest word or base word.

Activity 2: Students look at the columns of words. They underline the word in each column that matches the picture above it.

WORD WORKERS 3 UNIT 2.11

Name .... Date ....

Write the word from each column that fits the word shape box.

plum	glad	flask	clap
plus	gland	flop	class
plant	glass	flit	clan
plump	glint	flint	click
plump	glass	flit	clap

Underline the correct word to complete the sentence.

1. Ann left six plump (glums/plums) on top of the desk.
2. Tim had not planned to lift the (blocks/flocks).
3. Jill (clipped/slipped) and fell flat on her back.
4. The man was (glad/gland) Tom had plugged in the lamp.
5. Mrs Moss slipped the (flips/clips) into the flat box.

 37

Activity 1: Students look at the columns of words. Tell them to put the word from each column that fits into the 'word shape' box below it.

Activity 2: Students read the sentences. They underline the word in brackets that best completes the sentence.

WORD WORKERS 3 UNIT 2.12

Name .... Date ....

Put each column in alphabetical order.

a		e		i	
flag	black	bled	bled	click	blimp
black	blast	flex	fled	glint	click
glad	clap	slept	flex	blimp	clip
blast	flag	fled	Glen	clip	flint
clap	glad	Glen	slept	flint	glint

o		u	
clot	block	plum	blunt
blond	blond	slump	glum
flop	clot	plump	plum
block	flop	glum	plump
slop	slop	blunt	slump

38

Students place the words in each column in alphabetical order.

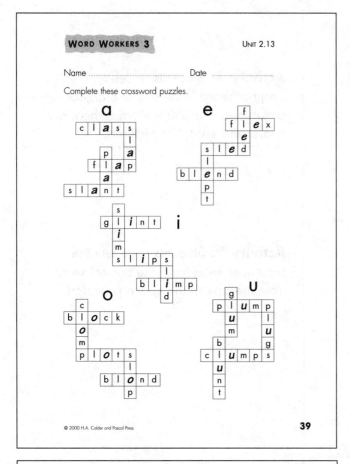

WORD WORKERS 3 UNIT 2.13

Name .... Date ....

Complete these crossword puzzles.

a: class, flap, slant, slap

e: flex, sled, blend, fled, slept

i: glint, slips, blimp, slim, slid

o: block, plots, blond, slop

u: plump, clumps, glum, plugs, blunt

 39

Students complete the crossword puzzles. They write the letter indicated in the blank spaces to make words that can be read going down or across the page.

WORD WORKERS 3 UNIT 2.14

Name .... Date ....

Write the word with the correct spelling.

1.	clamd	clamp	klamp	*clamp*
2.	gless	glas	glass	*glass*
3.	flaps	flasps	flapps	*flaps*
4.	slipped	slipt	sliped	*slipped*
5.	plugg	pluj	plug	*plug*

Fill in the missing letters to complete the word.

1.	*p* lante *d*	slap
2.	*f* loc *k*	slept
3.	*s* la *p*	slimmer
4.	*s* lep *t*	flock
5.	*s* limme *r*	planted

40

Activity 1: Students read the words going across the page, then write the word that is spelt correctly.

Activity 2: Students read the words in the box, then write the missing letters to complete the column of words on the left.

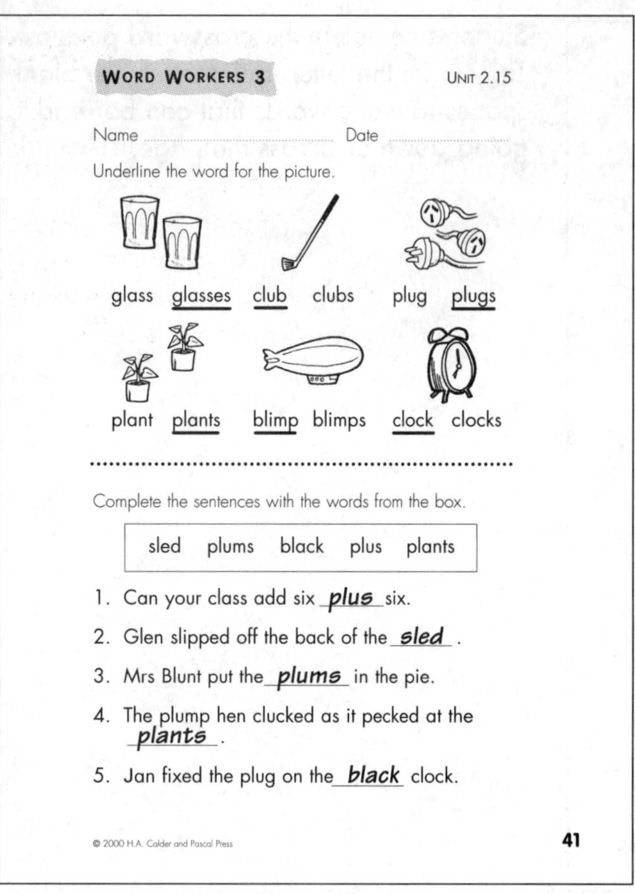

WORD WORKERS 3 UNIT 2.15

Name .... Date ....

Underline the word for the picture.

glass <u>glasses</u> <u>club</u> clubs plug <u>plugs</u>

plant <u>plants</u> <u>blimp</u> blimps <u>clock</u> clocks

Complete the sentences with the words from the box.

sled	plums	black	plus	plants

1. Can your class add six *plus* six.
2. Glen slipped off the back of the *sled* .
3. Mrs Blunt put the *plums* in the pie.
4. The plump hen clucked as it pecked at the *plants* .
5. Jan fixed the plug on the *black* clock.

 41

Activity 1: Students underline the singular word if there is one object pictured or the plural word if there are two or more objects pictured.

Activity 2: Students complete the sentences by writing the correct word from the box in the space provided.

WORD WORKERS 3 UNIT 2.16

Name .... Date ....

Draw a line from the picture to the matching word.

bled
fled
sled

slip
slop
slack

clot
club
cluck

plot
plan
plus

Number the words in the box in alphabetical order, then answer the questions.

1	blend	*4*	click	*2*	blunt
6	glad	*5*	flat	*3*	clam

1. Which word comes *before* 'blunt'? *blend*
2. Which word comes *after* 'flat'? *glad*
3. Which word comes *before* 'click'? *clam*
4. Which word comes *before* 'glad'? *flat*
5. Which word comes *after* 'clam'? *click*
6. Which word comes *after* 'blend'? *blunt*

42

Activity 1: Students say the word for the picture and then draw a line from the picture to the correct word beside it.

Activity 2: Students number the words in the box in alphabetical order, then use this information to answer the questions below.

WORD WORKERS 3 UNIT 2.17

Read the story.

Glen's Glass of Milk

Glen Mills slept in his bed.

'Up you get, Glen,' Mrs Mills said. 'You must get to school.'

'Tick, tock. Tick, tock. Tick, tock.' Glen's clock ticked as he slept in his soft bed. 'BZZZZ! BZZZZ!' Glen slapped at the clock. He missed it and hit the glass of milk. The glass fell off his desk. The milk went on the rug. What a mess!

'Up you get, Glen,' Mrs Mills said. 'You must not miss your bus.'

Then Mrs Mills went in and saw the mess. She saw the glass Glen hit and the milk on the rug. Mrs Mills looked glum. Then she looked mad. 'Glen, get out of bed!' she yelled.

 43

WORD WORKERS 3 UNIT 2.18

Glen jumped up. He slipped on the rug and fell in the milk. Then he slid in the milk and slammed into the desk. Glen fell flat on his back. The clock fell too and landed in his lap.

Mrs Mills was very mad. She looked at the glass. She looked at the milk on the rug. Then she looked at Glen. He was very wet. He held the clock in his hand. It went, 'tick, tock, tick, tock, tick, tock.'

Glen left his mum and the mess on the rug. Off to school he went. He was very glad to get on the bus and get to class.

44

For the following pages:

This story is designed to reinforce the skills learned in this and previous units of work. At no stage do students encounter unfamiliar words or skills. Students read the story and answer the questions silently. Correct the work by having them read the story and answer the questions orally.

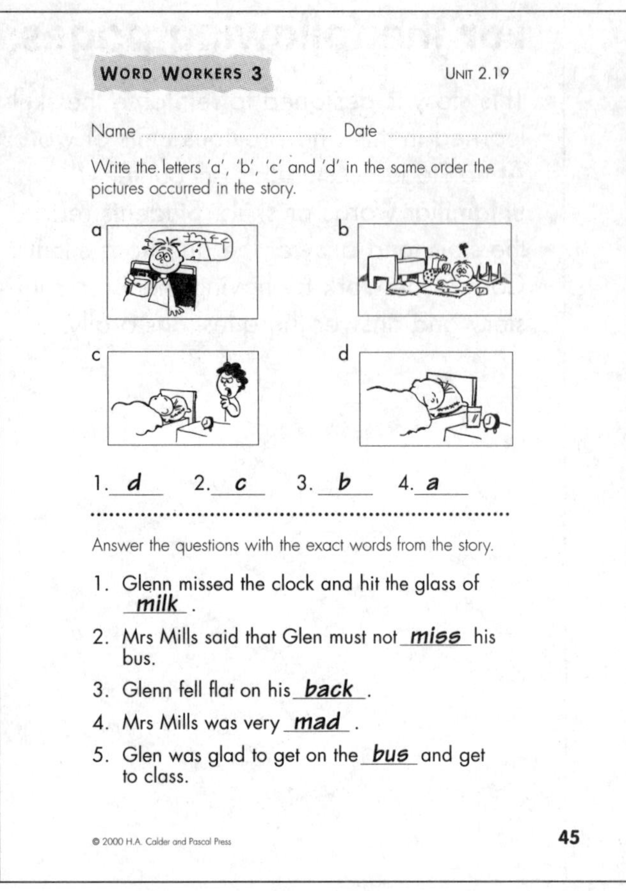

WORD WORKERS 3 UNIT 2.19

Name .... Date ....

Write the letters 'a', 'b', 'c' and 'd' in the same order the pictures occurred in the story.

a b c d

1. *d* 2. *c* 3. *b* 4. *a*

Answer the questions with the exact words from the story.

1. Glenn missed the clock and hit the glass of *milk* .
2. Mrs Mills said that Glen must not *miss* his bus.
3. Glenn fell flat on his *back* .
4. Mrs Mills was very *mad* .
5. Glen was glad to get on the *bus* and get to class.

© 2000 H.A. Calder and Pascal Press 45

Activity 1: Students sequence the events in the story by placing the pictures in their correct order.

Activity 2: Students complete these sentences using the exact word from the story.

WORD WORKERS 3 UNIT 2.20

Name .... Date ....

Fill in the blanks with the correct word from the box.

Then Mrs Mills went in and saw the mess. She saw the *glass* Glen hit and the milk on the rug. Mrs Mills looked *glum* . Then she looked mad. 'Glen, get out of bed!' she yelled.

Glen jumped up. He *slipped* on the rug and fell in the milk. Then he *slid* in the milk and slammed into the desk. Glen fell flat on his back. The *clock* fell too and landed in his lap.

glum slipped glass clock slid

Write the letters 'a', 'b', 'c' and 'd' beside the sentences in the same order they occurred in the story.

1. Glen left his mum and the mess on the rug. *d*
2. Mrs Mills looked glum. *c*
3. Glen's clock ticked as he slept in his soft bed. *a*
4. The milk went on the rug. *b*

46 © 2000 H.A. Calder and Pascal Press

Activity 1: Students complete this cloze exercise using the words from the box.

Activity 2: Students sequence the events in the story by placing them in their correct order.

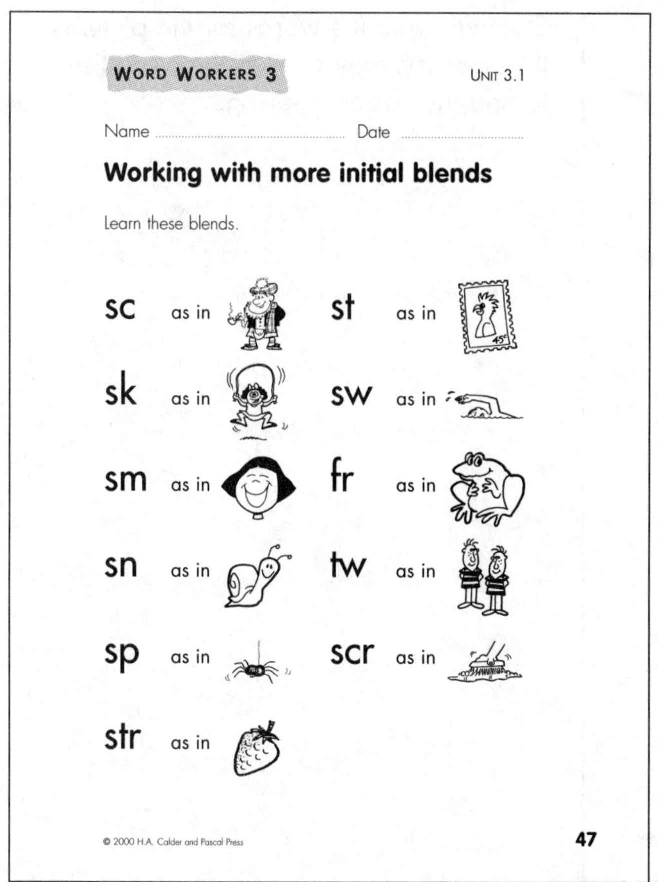

WORD WORKERS 3 UNIT 3.1

Name .... Date ....

Working with more initial blends

Learn these blends.

sc as in

st as in

sk as in

sw as in

sm as in

fr as in

sn as in

tw as in

sp as in

scr as in

str as in

© 2000 H.A. Calder and Pascal Press 47

For the following pages:

Teach these initial blends carefully. Make sure each student knows them. To reinforce knowledge of these blends and to promote reading acquisition, use the vowel to initial blend technique.

From now on, incorporate knowledge of these blends using the Reading Freedom *Common Blends Wall Chart.*

WORD WORKERS 3 UNIT 3.2

Read these words.

scab	skid	smog	snack	span
scan	skim	smug	snag	spat
scat	skin	smack	snap	speck
scalp	skip	smell	snip	spell
scamp	skit	smock	sniff	spend
scant	skiff		snob	spent
	skill		snub	spin
	skull		snuff	spit
			snug	spill
				spot
				spun

....

stab	stop	swag	fret	scrap
stack	stock	swam	frill	script
stand	stomp	swell	frog	scrub
stamp	stub	swept	frock	scruff
stem	stun	swig	frost	strap
step	stuck	swift	twig	strand
stiff	stuff	swim	twin	strip
still	stump	swum	twist	sprint
stick	stunt			
stink				

48 © 2000 H.A. Calder and Pascal Press

Students read the words in the columns.

WORD WORKERS 3 UNIT 3.3

Name .... Date ....

Write the words for the pictures.

1. stamp 2. stem 3. skip

4. swim 5. stop 6. skull

7. steps 8. frog 9. stump

© 2000 H.A. Calder and Pascal Press 49

Students write the words for the pictures. If necessary, they refer to the word lists to find the correct spelling.

WORD WORKERS 3 UNIT 3.4

Name .... Date ....

Read these words.

stop stops stopped	skipped skip skips	sniffs sniffed sniff	spill spilled spills
stacked stacks stack	strap straps strapped	twists twisted twist	stamped stamp stamps

Underline the word for the picture.

swig	<u>stump</u>	skill	scab	stamp
swell	stub	<u>skip</u>	scrub	still
<u>swim</u>	strip	skim	<u>skull</u>	stand
swift	stock	skit	skin	<u>steps</u>

50 © 2000 H.A. Calder and Pascal Press

Activity 1: Students read the words in the boxes. Tell them to add the endings to the smallest word or base word.

Activity 2: Students look at the columns of words. They underline the word in each column that matches the picture above it.

WORD WORKERS 3 UNIT 3.5

Name .... Date ....

Underline the nonsense word.

1. scamp	2. snep	3. twist	4. frog	5. scruff
scan	snap	spin	spot	stuck
scod	snug	swull	stock	strup
script	sniff	swift	stob	swum

Write the words for the pictures.

1. *skulls* 2. *frog* 3. *stamps*

4. *stem* 5. *stumps* 6. *swim*

7. *steps* 8. *stop* 9. *skip*

 51

Activity 1: Students look at the columns of words. Tell them to underline the word in each column that is a nonsense word.

Activity 2: Students write the words for the pictures. Tell them to add the letter 's' if there is more than one. If necessary, they refer to the word lists to find the correct spelling.

WORD WORKERS 3 UNIT 3.6

Complete the words with the word pattern from the picture.

st ill	*sw* ift	*fr* ock	*sk* id	*st* omp
st ack	*sw* ept	*fr* ost	*sk* ill	*st* uck
st and	*sw* ig	*fr* et	*sk* it	*st* unt
st ock	*sw* ell	*fr* ill	*sk* in	*st* ick

Underline the correct word to complete the sentence.

1. Stan's van skidded to a (stop/stump).
2. The frog jumped off the (stunt/stump).
3. Fran slipped on the (stocks/steps) and twisted her leg.
4. The (twins/twigs) went for a swim in the pond.
5. Sam's mum (swept/swift) up the mess when he spilled the milk.

52

Activity 1: Students look at the pictures above the columns. They use the word pattern from each picture to complete the words in the column below.

Activity 2: Students read the sentences. They underline the word in brackets that best completes the sentence.

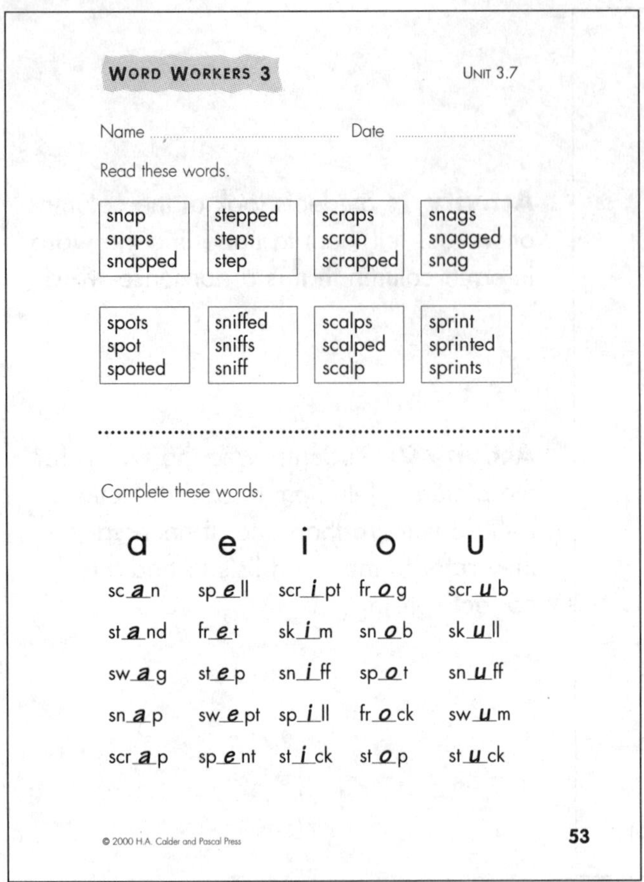

WORD WORKERS 3 UNIT 3.7

Name .... Date ....

Read these words.

snap snaps snapped	stepped steps step	scraps scrap scrapped	snags snagged snag
spots spot spotted	sniffed sniffs sniff	scalps scalped scalp	sprint sprinted sprints

Complete these words.

a	e	i	o	u
sc_a_n	sp_e_ll	scr_i_pt	fr_o_g	scr_u_b
st_a_nd	fr_e_t	sk_i_m	sn_o_b	sk_u_ll
sw_a_g	st_e_p	sn_i_ff	sp_o_t	sn_u_ff
sn_a_p	sw_e_pt	sp_i_ll	fr_o_ck	sw_u_m
scr_a_p	sp_e_nt	st_i_ck	st_o_p	st_u_ck

© 2000 H.A. Calder and Pascal Press 53

Activity 1: Students read the words in the boxes. Tell them to add the endings to the smallest word or base word.

Activity 2: Students complete the words by writing in the letter printed above each column.

WORD WORKERS 3 UNIT 3.8

Name .... Date ....

Draw a line to the word with the same word pattern.

scab	spill	strap	frock	spell	snag
skin	stamp	scrub	snap	swim	spin
frill	spin	stock	skip	skiff	swell
spit	stab	stuff	snub	swag	sniff
scamp	skit	snip	snuff	twin	skim

Complete the sentences by writing the words for the pictures.

STOP

1. Fran had to _swim_ to the end of the pond.
2. Dr Frost left the _skull_ on top of the desk.
3. Ann slipped on the _steps_ and twisted her leg.
4. The twins ran and skipped till Mrs Scott yelled '_stop_!'
5. Jim cut up the _stump_ and stacked the logs next to the hut.

54 © 2000 H.A. Calder and Pascal Press

Activity 1: Students look at the two columns of words in each box. They draw a line from the word in the left-hand column to the word in the right-hand column that has the same word pattern.

Activity 2: Students look at the pictures and then complete the sentences below by writing the correct word for the picture in the space provided.

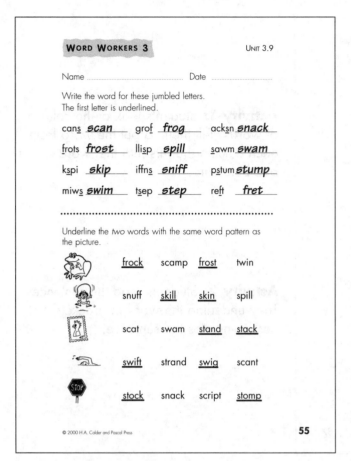

WORD WORKERS 3 UNIT 3.9

Name .... Date ....

Write the word for these jumbled letters.
The first letter is underlined.

cans scan grof frog acksn snack
frots frost llisp spill sawm swam
kspi skip iffns sniff pstum stump
miws swim tsep step reft fret

Underline the *two* words with the same word pattern as the picture.

frock scamp frost twin
snuff skill skin spill
scat swam stand stack
swift strand swig scant
stock snack script stomp

© 2000 H.A. Calder and Pascal Press 55

Activity 1: Students make a word from the jumbled letters. The first letter of each word is underlined. Students write the words in the spaces provided.

Activity 2: Students look at the pictures and the words on the lines beside them. They underline the two words in each line that have the same word pattern as the picture.

WORD WORKERS 3 UNIT 3.10

Name .... Date ....

Read these words.

skin skins skinned	spills spilled spill	snipped snip snips	strands stranded strand

swift swifter swiftest	slimmest slim slimmer	stiff stiffest stiffer

Underline the word for the picture.

speck	frost	stick	stem	skiff
spin	frog	stab	step	skin
spot	frock	stand	steps	skim
span	fret	stamp	still	skid

56 © 2000 H.A. Calder and Pascal Press

Activity 1: Students read the words in the boxes. Tell them to add the endings to the smallest word or base word.

Activity 2: Students look at the columns of words. They underline the word in each column that matches the picture above it.

WORD WORKERS 3 UNIT 3.11

Name .... Date ....

Write the word from each column that fits the word shape box.

fret	swag	spot	stomp
frog	swell	speck	stunt
frock	swept	spell	stub
frost	swim	spin	strap
frog	*swept*	*spell*	*stunt*

Underline the correct word to complete the sentence.

1. Sam left a stack of (stamps/stumps) on his desk.
2. Meg (skipped/skinned) up to the top of the steps.
3. Spot sniffed the frog as it hopped off the (stump/stunt).
4. Jill slipped in the frost and (skilled/spilled) the milk.
5. Mum sat (still/skill) as the twins swam past.

 57

Activity 1: Students look at the columns of words. Tell them to put the word from each column that fits into the 'word shape' box below it.

Activity 2: Students read the sentences. They underline the word in brackets that best completes the sentence.

WORD WORKERS 3 UNIT 3.12

Name .... Date ....

Put each column in alphabetical order.

a		e		i	
scrap	*scant*	step	*speck*	stick	*script*
stand	*scrap*	swept	*spend*	script	*skit*
swag	*stamp*	swell	*step*	swift	*snip*
scant	*stand*	spend	*swell*	skit	*stick*
stamp	*swag*	speck	*swept*	snip	*swift*

o		u	
stop	*snob*	stump	*scruff*
snob	*spot*	scruff	*snuff*
stock	*stock*	swum	*stub*
spot	*stomp*	stub	*stump*
stomp	*stop*	snuff	*swum*

58

Students place the words in each column in alphabetical order.

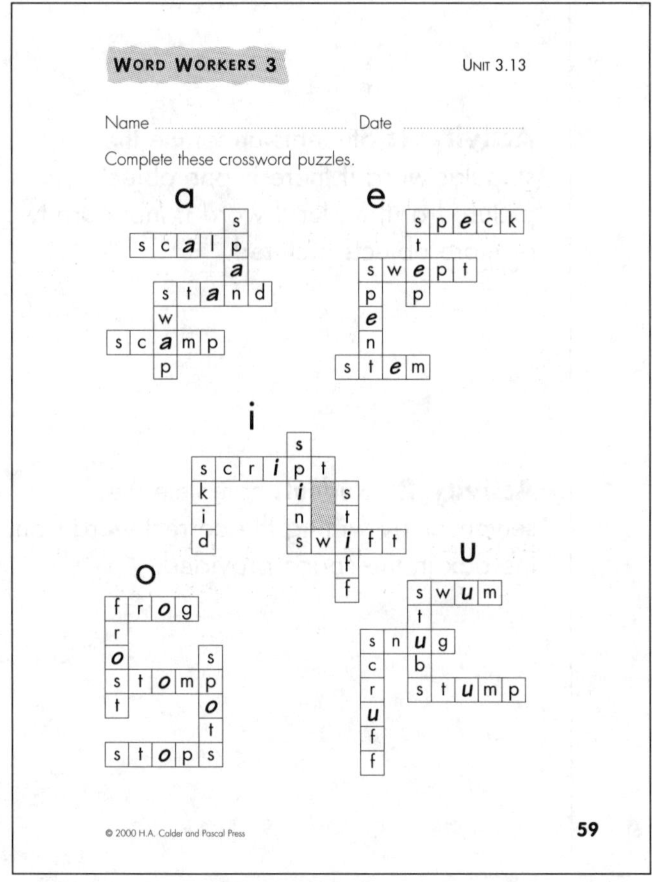
WORD WORKERS 3 UNIT 3.13

Name .... Date ....

Complete these crossword puzzles.

 59

Students complete the crossword puzzles. They write the letter indicated in the blank spaces to make words that can be read going down or across the page.

WORD WORKERS 3 UNIT 3.14

Name .... Date ....

Write the word with the correct spelling.

1.	sclap	scalp	splac	*scalp*
2.	twists	twinst	twissts	*twists*
3.	scrapt	scapped	scrapped	*scrapped*
4.	spell	spel	spall	*spell*
5.	stosp	stops	stopz	*stops*

Fill in the missing letters to complete the word.

1. *s* crub *s*
2. *t* wiste *d*
3. *s* nac *k*
4. *s* pen *d*
5. *s* cam *p*

snack
spend
scrubs
scamp
twisted

60

Activity 1: Students read the words going across the page, then write the word that is spelt correctly.

Activity 2: Students read the words in the box, then write the missing letters to complete the column of words on the left.

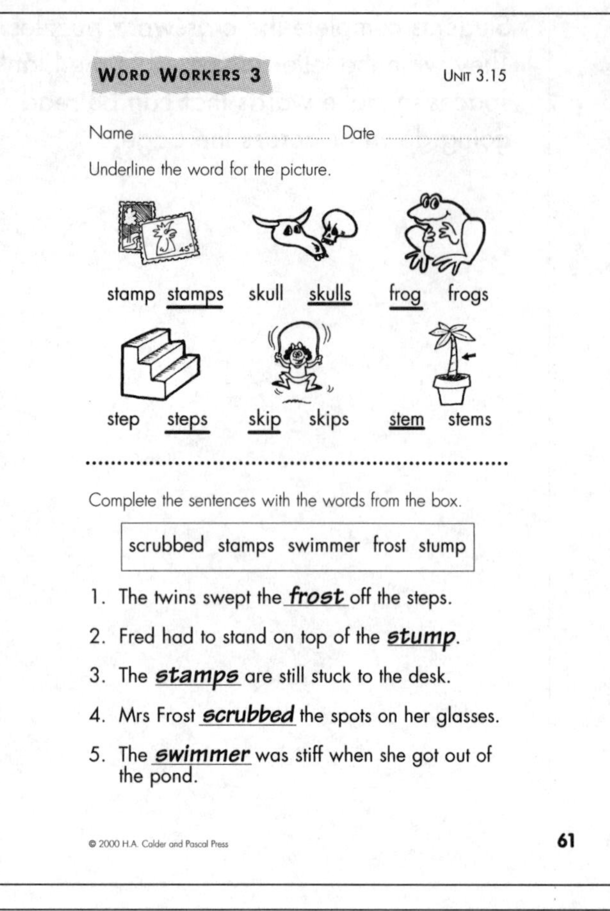

WORD WORKERS 3 UNIT 3.15

Name .... Date ....

Underline the word for the picture.

stamp <u>stamps</u> skull <u>skulls</u> <u>frog</u> frogs

step <u>steps</u> <u>skip</u> skips <u>stem</u> stems

Complete the sentences with the words from the box.

scrubbed stamps swimmer frost stump

1. The twins swept the ***frost*** off the steps.
2. Fred had to stand on top of the ***stump***.
3. The ***stamps*** are still stuck to the desk.
4. Mrs Frost ***scrubbed*** the spots on her glasses.
5. The ***swimmer*** was stiff when she got out of the pond.

© 2000 H.A. Calder and Pascal Press 61

Activity 1: Students underline the singular word if there is one object pictured or the plural word if there are two or more objects pictured.

Activity 2: Students complete the sentences by writing the correct word from the box in the space provided.

WORD WORKERS 3 UNIT 3.16

Name .... Date ....

Draw a line from the picture to the matching word.

stop / spit / spot — stump / stomp / stuff

stamp / stack / stand — skit / skid / skill

Number the words in the box in alphabetical order, then answer the questions.

6	twig	*5*	swift	*2*	scrub
1	scan	*4*	stuck	*3*	smell

1. Which word comes *before* 'twig'? ***swift***
2. Which word comes *before* 'stuck'? ***smell***
3. Which word comes *after* 'scan'? ***scrub***
4. Which word comes *after* 'swift'? ***twig***
5. Which word comes *after* 'smell'? ***stuck***
6. Which word comes *before* 'scrub'? ***scan***

62 © 2000 H.A. Calder and Pascal Press

Activity 1: Students say the word for the picture and then draw a line from the picture to the correct word beside it.

Activity 2: Students number the words in the box in alphabetical order, then use this information to answer the questions below.

WORD WORKERS 3 UNIT 3.17

Read the story.

Fran's Big Swim

Scamp was a little black dog. He sat on the steps and panted in the hot sun. Fran sat next to him. She was hot too. She was *too* hot. She just had to go for a swim in the pond.

Fran's mum said, 'No swim. Not till the steps are swept. Not till they are scrubbed.' Fran said it was too hot for that. So Fran and her little black dog sat on the steps in the hot sun.

As they sat, a big frog hopped past. It stopped at the steps. Scamp got up. He yapped at the frog. 'Ruff! Ruff! Ruff!' Off he went after the frog. 'Stop Scamp!' Fran yelled at the little black dog. Then she sprinted after Scamp and the frog.

 63

WORD WORKERS 3 UNIT 3.18

The big frog hopped very fast. It landed on a stump by the pond. Scamp jumped at it but he missed. Then the frog hopped onto the dock. Scamp ran after it but the frog hopped off the end of the dock. It landed in the pond with a soft 'Plop!'

Scamp skidded to a stop at the end of the dock. He slipped on a wet spot and fell in the pond. Just then Fran sprinted up. She slipped on the wet spot too. In the pond she went. Fran and Scamp landed in the pond with a big 'Spat!'

Fran swam back to the dock. She lifted Scamp out. They puffed and panted as they ran back to the steps. Fran swept them as fast as she could. Then she scrubbed them. Then she sat down for a rest. Scamp sat next to her and panted in the hot sun.

64

For the following pages:

This story is designed to reinforce the skills learned in this and previous units of work. At no stage do students encounter unfamiliar words or skills. Students read the story and answer the questions silently. Correct the work by having them read the story and answer the questions orally.

WORD WORKERS 3 UNIT 3.19

Name .... Date ....

Write the letters 'a', 'b', 'c' and 'd' in the same order the pictures occurred in the story.

a b c d

1. *d* 2. *c* 3. *a* 4. *b*

Answer the questions with the exact words from the story.

1. Fran and her dog, *Scamp*, sat on the steps.
2. Fran's mum said '*No* *swim*'.
3. The big frog hopped off the end of the *dock*.
4. Scamp and Fran landed in the *pond* with a 'Splat!'
5. They did not go back to the pond for a *swim*.

© 2000 H.A. Calder and Pascal Press 65

Activity 1: Students sequence the events in the story by placing the pictures in their correct order.

Activity 2: Students complete these sentences using the exact word from the story.

WORD WORKERS 3 UNIT 3.20

Name .... Date ....

Fill in the blanks with the correct word from the box.

The big *frog* hopped very fast. It landed on a *stump* by the pond. Scamp jumped at it but he *missed*. Then the frog hopped onto the *dock*. Scamp ran after it but the frog hopped off the end of the dock. It landed in the *pond* with a soft 'Plop!'

pond	missed	dock	frog	stump

Write the letters 'a', 'b', 'c' and 'd' beside the sentences in the same order they occurred in the story.

1. Fran's mum said, 'No swim'. *b*
2. Fran and Scamp landed in the pond with a big 'Splat!' *c*
3. Fran swept the steps as fast as she could. *d*
4. Fran just had to go for a swim in the pond. *a*

66 © 2000 H.A. Calder and Pascal Press

Activity 1: Students complete this cloze exercise using the words from the box.

Activity 2: Students sequence the events in the story by placing them in their correct order.

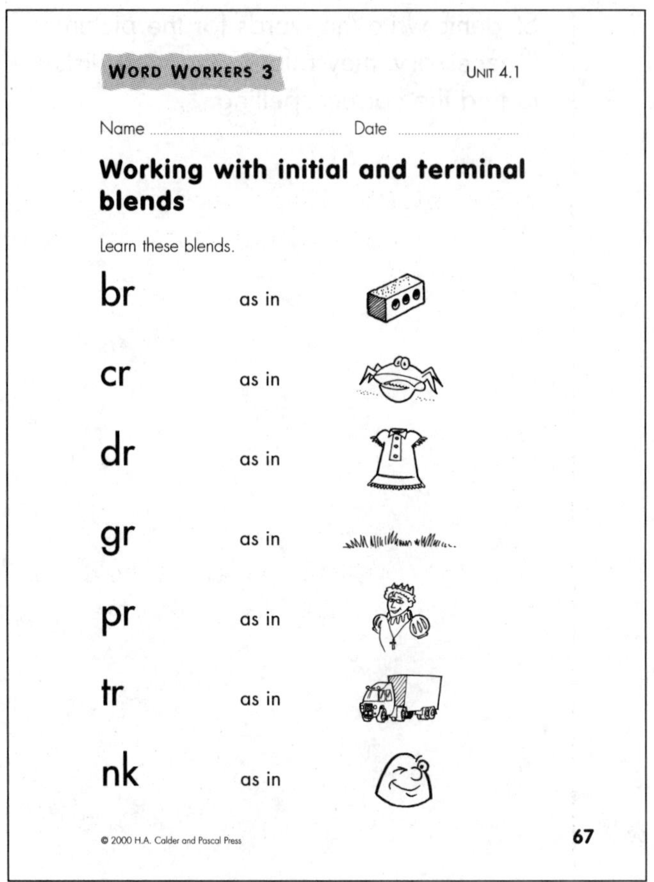

WORD WORKERS 3 UNIT 4.1

Name .... Date ....

Working with initial and terminal blends

Learn these blends.

br as in

cr as in

dr as in

gr as in

pr as in

tr as in

nk as in

© 2000 H.A. Calder and Pascal Press 67

For the following pages:

Teach these initial and terminal blends carefully. Make sure each student knows them. To reinforce knowledge of these blends and to promote reading acquisition, use both the initial blend to vowel and vowel to terminal blend technique.

From now on, incorporate knowledge of these blends using the Reading Freedom *Common Blends Wall Chart.*

WORD WORKERS 3 UNIT 4.2

Read these words.

brag	crab	drab	grab	pram	trap
bran	crag	drag	grand	press	track
brand	cram	dress	grant	prim	tramp
brat	crack	drip	Greg	prod	trend
brig	cramp	drift	grim	prop	trim
brick	crept	drop	grin	prompt	trip
brisk	crib	drug	grip		trick
brass	crop	drum	grit		trot
	cross	draft	grub		truck
	crust		gruff		trust
	craft		grunt		trump
			grass		

bank	blank	ink	blink	bunk	clunk
rank	clank	link	clink	dunk	plunk
sank	flank	mink	slink	hunk	slunk
tank	plank	pink	brink	junk	drunk
yank	crank	sink	drink	punk	trunk
	drank	wink		sunk	
	Frank				
	prank				
	spank				

68 © 2000 H.A. Calder and Pascal Press

Students read the words in the columns.

WORD WORKERS 3 UNIT 4.3

Name .... Date ....

Write the words for the pictures.

1. *crab* 2. *dress* 3. *drip/drop*

4. *truck* 5. *drum* 6. *trunk*

7. *tank* 8. *wink* 9. *bunk*

© 2000 H.A. Calder and Pascal Press 69

Students write the words for the pictures. If necessary, they refer to the word lists to find the correct spelling.

WORD WORKERS 3 UNIT 4.4

Name .... Date ....

Read these words.

prod prods prodded	blinked blink blinks	tricks tricked trick	traps trapped trap	grabbed grabs grab
rank ranked ranks	dresses dressed dress	cracked crack cracks	trusted trust trusts	grins grinned grin

Underline the word for the picture.

brisk	spank	<u>crab</u>	trust	blank
brass	<u>tank</u>	crept	trend	junk
<u>brick</u>	Frank	crack	<u>truck</u>	bunk
brag	drink	cramp	trump	<u>trunk</u>

70 © 2000 H.A. Calder and Pascal Press

Activity 1: Students read the words in the boxes. Tell them to add the endings to the smallest word or base word.

Activity 2: Students look at the columns of words. They underline the word in each column that matches the picture above it.

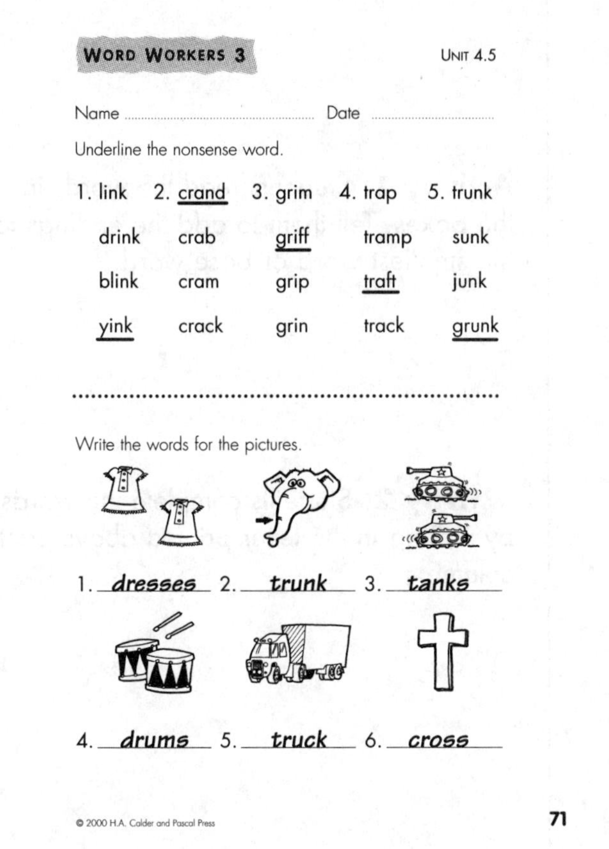

WORD WORKERS 3 UNIT 4.5

Name .... Date ....

Underline the nonsense word.

1. link	2. crand	3. grim	4. trap	5. trunk
drink	crab	griff	tramp	sunk
blink	cram	grip	traft	junk
yink	crack	grin	track	grunk

Write the words for the pictures.

1. dresses 2. trunk 3. tanks

4. drums 5. truck 6. cross

© 2000 H.A. Calder and Pascal Press 71

Activity 1: Students look at the columns of words. Tell them to underline the word in each column that is a nonsense word.

Activity 2: Students write the words for the pictures. Tell them to add the letter 's' if there is more than one. If necessary, they refer to the word lists to find the correct spelling.

WORD WORKERS 3 UNIT 4.6

Complete the words with the word pattern from the picture.

bl ink	cr amp	dr um	pl unk	tr ack
s ink	cr ept	dr ess	s unk	tr ump
dr ink	cr op	dr aft	cl unk	tr im
p ink	cr ust	dr ag	h unk	tr amp

Underline the correct word to complete the sentence.

1. Frank dragged the (trunks/clunks) off the back of the truck.
2. Jan tripped in the (grand/grass) and ripped her best dress.
3. Mrs Grant (grinned/gritted) at the tot in the pram.
4. Gran left the drink on the rack next to the (blink/sink).
5. The men lifted the (bricks/ticks) off the wet grass.

72 © 2000 H.A. Calder and Pascal Press

Activity 1: Students look at the pictures above the columns. They use the word pattern from each picture to complete the words in the column below.

Activity 2: Students read the sentences. They underline the word in brackets that best completes the sentence.

WORD WORKERS 3

UNIT 4.7

Name .... Date ....

Read these words.

tramp tramps tramped	yanked yank yanks	brands branded brand	gripped grip grips
dropped drop drops	tracks tracked track	crank cranked cranks	drafted drafts draft

Complete these words.

a	e	i	o	u
gr_a_b	pr_e_ss	sl_i_nk	tr_o_t	tr_u_ck
tr_a_mp	cr_e_pt	gr_i_n	dr_o_p	gr_u_ff
b_a_nk	dr_e_ss	br_i_sk	pr_o_p	tr_u_st
gr_a_ss	Gr_e_g	cr_i_b	pr_o_d	cl_u_nk
br_a_g	tr_e_nd	tr_i_m	cr_o_ss	cr_u_st

Activity 1: Students read the words in the boxes. Tell them to add the endings to the smallest word or base word.

Activity 2: Students complete the words by writing in the letter printed above each column.

WORD WORKERS 3

UNIT 4.8

Name .... Date ....

Draw a line to the word with the same word pattern.

brag	junk	cramp	trust	brink	trick
trip	grass	blink	yank	prop	pink
trunk	drag	crust	sink	brick	dunk
brass	flank	grab	tramp	grim	crop
blank	grip	sank	crab	slunk	prim

Complete the sentences by writing the words for the pictures.

1. Stan grinned as he dumped the junk into the _truck_.
2. The _crab_ left its tracks when it crept over the sand.
3. The man blinked as the _tank_ clanked past the bank.
4. Ann dropped the drink on her pink _dress_.
5. Mum crept past as the twins slept in the _bunk_.

Activity 1: Students look at the two columns of words in each box. They draw a line from the word in the left-hand column to the word in the right-hand column that has the same word pattern.

Activity 2: Students look at the pictures and then complete the sentences below by writing the correct word for the picture in the space provided.

WORD WORKERS 3 UNIT 4.9

Name .... Date ....

Write the word for these jumbled letters.
The first letter is underlined.

dnrag	grand	ribsk	brisk	nuks	sunk
rudm	drum	ppro	prop	trab	brat
ttrus	trust	trusc	crust	nkwi	wink
naks	sank	sreds	dress	frugf	gruff

Underline the *two* words with the same word pattern as the picture.

drag	grand	prod	drop
brass	brisk	trap	crust
prompt	blank	trust	trump
sink	grub	prim	drink
clamp	crank	cramp	plank

© 2000 H.A. Calder and Pascal Press 75

Activity 1: Students make a word from the jumbled letters. The first letter of each word is underlined. Students write the words in the spaces provided.

Activity 2: Students look at the pictures and the words on the lines beside them. They underline the two words in each line that have the same word pattern as the picture.

WORD WORKERS 3 UNIT 4.10

Name .... Date ....

Read these words.

link links linked	crams crammed cram	dripped drips drip	clunked clunk clunks
brisk brisker briskest	grander grandest grand	grim grimmer grimmest	gruffer gruffest gruff

Underline the word for the picture.

sink	drag	plunk	dress	grass
clink	drop	sunk	drug	gruff
wink	drink	clunk	drift	grit
slink	draft	bunk	drip	grunt

76 © 2000 H.A. Calder and Pascal Press

Activity 1: Students read the words in the boxes. Tell them to add the endings to the smallest word or base word.

Activity 2: Students look at the columns of words. They underline the word in each column that matches the picture above it.

WORD WORKERS 3

UNIT 4.11

Name .... Date ....

Write the word from each column that fits the word shape box.

pram	tramp	ink	crop
prod	trend	blink	cram
prompt	truck	sink	crept
press	trim	clink	crib
press	tramp	blink	crept

Underline the correct word to complete the sentence.

1. Tom crept after the fox and (trimmed/trapped) it in the pen.
2. Nan (crammed/cracked) the eggs when she dropped them in the sink.
3. The runner (tricked/tripped) when he got a cramp in his leg.
4. Tess left the (dress/draft) she pressed on top of her bed.
5. The drummer in the brass band (clinked/winked) at Greg.

 77

Activity 1: Students look at the columns of words. Tell them to put the word from each column that fits into the 'word shape' box below it.

Activity 2: Students read the sentences. They underline the word in brackets that best completes the sentence.

WORD WORKERS 3

UNIT 4.12

Name .... Date ....

Put each column in alphabetical order.

a		e		i	
cram	blank	dress	crept	wink	sink
blank	brand	press	dress	trick	slink
brand	crack	crept	Greg	sink	trick
drag	cram	trend	press	trim	trim
crack	drag	Greg	trend	slink	wink

o		u	
trot	crop	trust	drum
prod	drop	sunk	gruff
crop	prod	gruff	sunk
drop	prop	drum	trunk
prop	trot	trunk	trust

78

Students place the words in each column in alphabetical order.

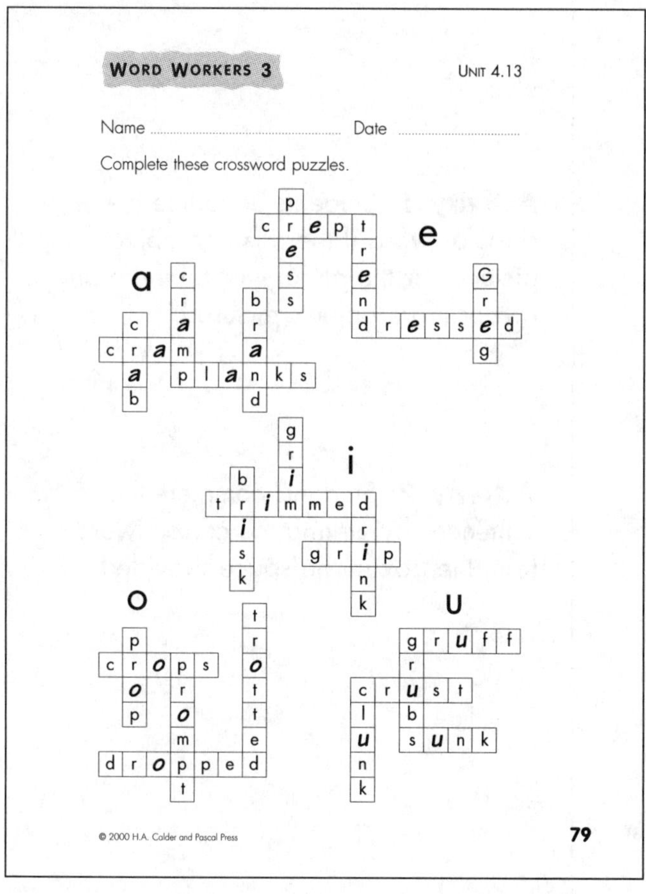
WORD WORKERS 3 UNIT 4.13

Name .... Date ....

Complete these crossword puzzles.

 79

Students complete the crossword puzzles. They write the letter indicated in the blank spaces to make words that can be read going down or across the page.

WORD WORKERS 3 UNIT 4.14

Name .... Date ....

Write the word with the correct spelling.

1.	dressd	dresst	dressed	*dressed*
2.	bank	banck	bnak	*bank*
3.	brist	brisk	brisck	*brisk*
4.	blinx	blinsk	blinks	*blinks*
5.	trusded	trusted	trustd	*trusted*

Fill in the missing letters to complete the word.

1. *p* romp *t* — cramp
2. *w* inke *d* — clanks
3. *c* ram *p* — prompt
4. *p* resse *d* — winked
5. *c* lank *s* — pressed

80

Activity 1: Students read the words going across the page, then write the word that is spelt correctly.

Activity 2: Students read the words in the box, then write the missing letters to complete the column of words on the left.

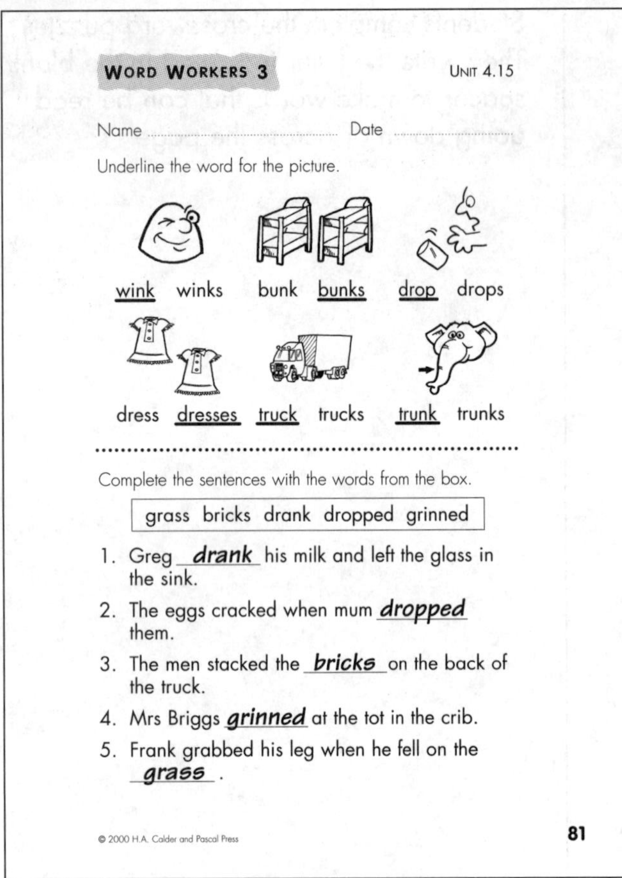

WORD WORKERS 3 UNIT 4.15

Name .... Date ....

Underline the word for the picture.

<u>wink</u> winks bunk <u>bunks</u> <u>drop</u> drops

dress <u>dresses</u> <u>truck</u> trucks <u>trunk</u> trunks

Complete the sentences with the words from the box.

grass bricks drank dropped grinned

1. Greg ***drank*** his milk and left the glass in the sink.
2. The eggs cracked when mum ***dropped*** them.
3. The men stacked the ***bricks*** on the back of the truck.
4. Mrs Briggs ***grinned*** at the tot in the crib.
5. Frank grabbed his leg when he fell on the ***grass*** .

© 2000 H.A. Calder and Pascal Press 81

Activity 1: Students underline the singular word if there is one object pictured or the plural word if there are two or more objects pictured.

Activity 2: Students complete the sentences by writing the correct word from the box in the space provided.

WORD WORKERS 3 UNIT 4.16

Name .... Date ....

Draw a line from the picture to the matching word.

grab
grass
grub

trip
trust
trunk

cross
crib
crust

brag
brass
brick

Number the words in the box in alphabetical order, then answer the questions.

2	brisk	***6***	grim	***5***	drip
3	crop	***4***	drink	***1***	blink

1. Which word comes *before* 'crop'? ***brisk***
2. Which word comes *before* 'drink'? ***crop***
3. Which word comes *before* 'brisk'? ***blink***
4. Which word comes *after* 'crop'? ***drink***
5. Which word comes *after* 'drip'? ***grim***
6. Which word comes *after* 'drink'? ***drip***

82 © 2000 H.A. Calder and Pascal Press

Activity 1: Students say the word for the picture and then draw a line from the picture to the correct word beside it.

Activity 2: Students number the words in the box in alphabetical order, then use this information to answer the questions below.

For the following pages:

This story is designed to reinforce the skills learned in this and previous units of work. At no stage do students encounter unfamiliar words or skills. Students read the story and answer the questions silently. Correct the work by having them read the story and answer the questions orally.

Read the story.

The Junkman

Mr Tinker was a junkman. He dumped the junk into the back of his truck. The Bragg twins, Greg and Frank, saw Mr Tinker stop his truck and jump out.

The twins ran up to see what was in the truck. The junkman let them have a look. In the truck were cracked cups and mugs. There were bits of rag and an old pink dress. There were ten bricks and a pack of brass tacks.

'What do you do with the junk?' Greg asked. 'I fix it and mend it, and then I sell it,' said Mr Tinker. 'Can we help you get your junk?' Frank asked.

Mr Tinker said he would be glad of the help. So Greg and Frank got lots of junk — an old sink they dragged out of the pond, a rat-trap that was next to a stump, a black pram and a big trunk — lots and lots of junk for Mr Tinker.

Greg and Frank's mum saw the twins with the junk. 'What is that for?' Mrs Bragg asked?

'It is for Mr Tinker. He said we could help him.'

'OK,' said Mrs Bragg. 'You can help, but no junk in the house.'

Greg winked at Frank. 'We can put the junk under our bunks until Mr Tinker comes back,' he said.

When Mrs Bragg went out, the twins put the junk under their bunk beds. 'What did you do with the junk?' Mrs Bragg asked when she got back. Then she saw a clump of dust on the rug. She bent down to pick it up. Then she saw the junk.

Mrs Bragg blinked. Then she looked at the twins. Her neck got red when she was mad. It was *very* red just then.

WORD WORKERS 3 UNIT 4.19

'Get that mess out of my house.' she yelled.

Greg and Frank dragged the junk out fast — very fast. Just then Mr Tinker went past. He helped the twins lift the junk into the back of his truck.

'That is a lot of good junk,' he said. 'Now I have a gift for you. It was left at the dump. Have fun with it.' Mr Tinker lifted a drum kit off the truck. Greg and Frank grabbed the sticks. 'Rat-a-tat-tat... bam, blam!' Off to their house they ran.

Mrs Bragg saw them with the drum kit. 'Oh, no!' was all she said.

'Rat-a-tat-tat... rat-a-tat-tat... bam, blam!' went the drums.

Mr Tinker grinned as he got back in his truck. The junk in the back went clink and clunk as he set off.

 85

Students read the story. They read it several times until accuracy and fluency combine to improve comprehension.

WORD WORKERS 3 UNIT 4.20

Name .... Date ....

Write the letters 'a', 'b', 'c' and 'd' in the same order the pictures occurred in the story.

a b c d

1. *c* 2. *d* 3. *a* 4. *b*

Answer the questions with the exact words from the story.

1. Mr Tinker was a *junkman*.
2. Greg and Frank dragged an old *sink* out of the pond.
3. Mrs Bragg said, 'No *junk* in the house.'
4. The twins hid the junk under the *bunk beds*.
5. Mrs Bragg's neck got *red* when she was mad.

86

Activity 1: Students sequence the events in the story by placing the pictures in their correct order.

Activity 2: Students complete these sentences using the exact word from the story.

WORD WORKERS 3 UNIT 4.21

Name .... Date ....

Fill in the blanks with the correct word from the box.

'What do you do with the *junk*?' Greg asked. 'I fix it and mend it, and then I sell it,' said Mr *Tinker*. 'Can we help you get your junk?' Frank asked. Mr Tinker said he would be *glad* of the help. So Greg and Frank got lots of junk — an old sink they dragged out of the pond, a rat-trap that was next to a *stump*, a black pram and a big trunk — lots and lots of junk for Mr Tinker. Greg and Frank's mum saw the *twins* with the junk.

Tinker	junk	stump	twins	glad

Write the letters 'a', 'b', 'c' and 'd' beside the sentences in the same order they occurred in the story.

1. Mr Tinker lifted a drum kit off the truck. *d*
2. Greg and Frank ran up to see what was in the truck. *a*
3. Greg and Frank's mum saw the twins with the junk. *b*
4. The twins put the junk under their bunk beds. *c*

 87

Activity 1: Students complete this cloze exercise using the words from the box.

Activity 2: Students sequence the events in the story by placing them in their correct order.

WORD WORKERS 3 UNIT 5.1

More work with blends

Read these words.

1. cramp	spend	slid	fond
2. dust	plump	frost	wink
3. step	plant	belt	grass
4. twin	clock	punt	tank
5. swept	blimp	cost	truck
6. stamp	blend	limp	drop
7. scrub	flag	text	blink
8. frog	cluck	mask	fret
9. glint	trot	dump	flat
10. desk	brick	stock	blunt

88

Students read the words in the columns.

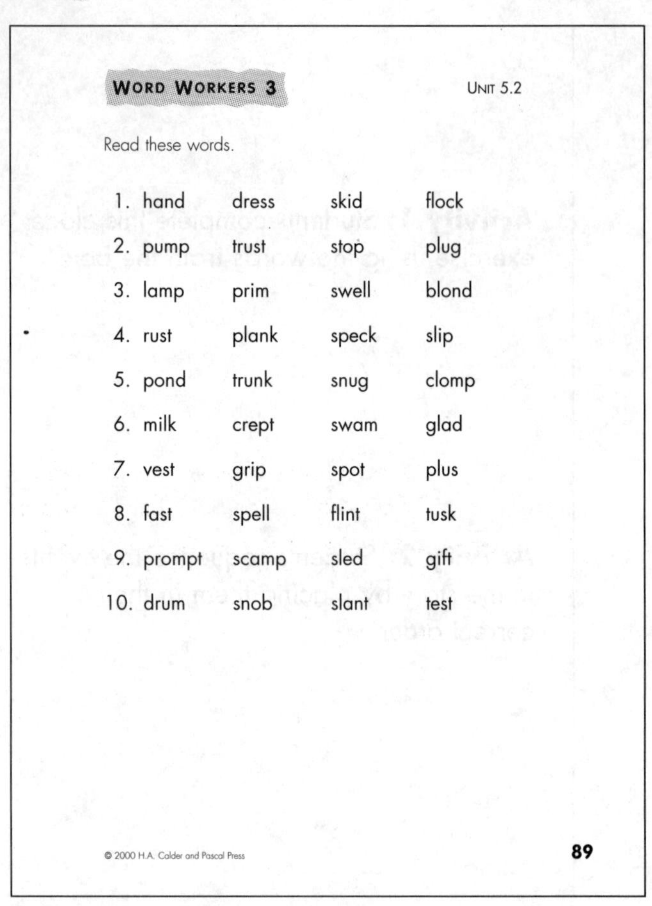

WORD WORKERS 3 UNIT 5.2

Read these words.

1. hand	dress	skid	flock
2. pump	trust	stop	plug
3. lamp	prim	swell	blond
4. rust	plank	speck	slip
5. pond	trunk	snug	clomp
6. milk	crept	swam	glad
7. vest	grip	spot	plus
8. fast	spell	flint	tusk
9. prompt	scamp	sled	gift
10. drum	snob	slant	test

© 2000 H.A. Calder and Pascal Press 89

Students read the words in the columns.

WORD WORKERS 3 UNIT 5.3

Name .... Date ....

Write the words for the pictures.

1. *tank* 2. *steps* 3. *blimp*

4. *gift* 5. *crab* 6. *skull*

7. *plant* 8. *nest* 9. *hand*

10. *stamp* 11. *sled* 12. *plus*

13. *clock* 14. *dress* 15. *swim*

90 © 2000 H.A. Calder and Pascal Press

Students write the words for the pictures. If necessary, they refer to the word lists to find the correct spelling.

WORD WORKERS 3 UNIT 5.4

Name .... Date ....

Read these words.

stop stops stopped	cracked crack cracks	flips flipped flip	scrubbed scrubs scrub	melt melted melts
pumps pumped pump	prod prods prodded	slapped slap slaps	twists twist twisted	mend mended mends

Underline the word for the picture.

slick	plugs	felt	stunt	clam
slip	plums	melt	stump	class
slid	plump	belt	stuck	clap
slink	plus	pelt	stub	clamp

 91

Activity 1: Students read the words in the boxes. Tell them to add the endings to the smallest word or base word.

Activity 2: Students look at the columns of words. They underline the word in each column that matches the picture above it.

WORD WORKERS 3 UNIT 5.5

Name .... Date ....

Underline the nonsense word.

1. lend	2. clab	3. frog	4. blank	5. stuck
mend	clap	frop	drank	stump
send	class	frock	kank	stuzz
kend	clam	frost	sank	stub

Write the words for the pictures.

1. hands 2. drum 3. blocks

4. clips 5. tents 6. frog

7. stem 8. truck 9. lamps

92

Activity 1: Students look at the columns of words. Tell them to underline the word in each column that is a nonsense word.

Activity 2: Students write the words for the pictures. Tell them to add the letter 's' if there is more than one. If necessary, they refer to the word lists to find the correct spelling.

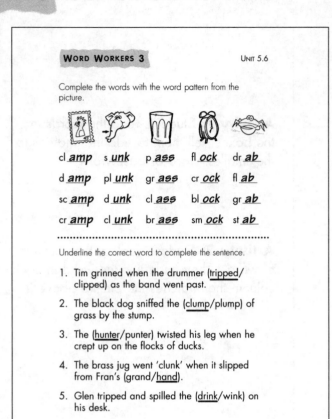

WORD WORKERS 3 UNIT 5.6

Complete the words with the word pattern from the picture.

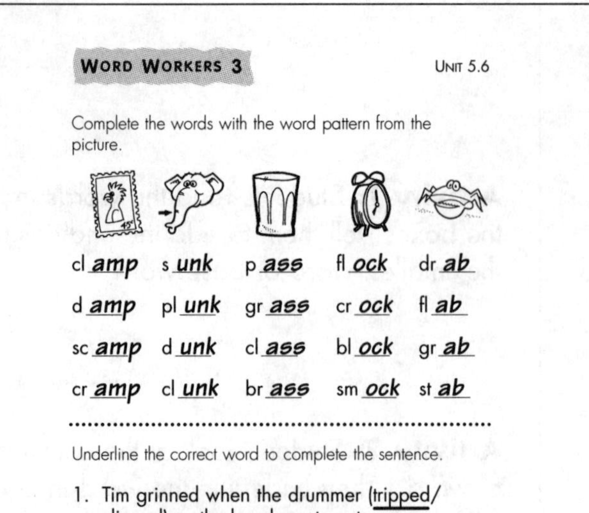

cl amp	s unk	p ass	fl ock	dr ab
d amp	pl unk	gr ass	cr ock	fl ab
sc amp	d unk	cl ass	bl ock	gr ab
cr amp	cl unk	br ass	sm ock	st ab

Underline the correct word to complete the sentence.

1. Tim grinned when the drummer (tripped/clipped) as the band went past.
2. The black dog sniffed the (clump/plump) of grass by the stump.
3. The (hunter/punter) twisted his leg when he crept up on the flocks of ducks.
4. The brass jug went 'clunk' when it slipped from Fran's (grand/hand).
5. Glen tripped and spilled the (drink/wink) on his desk.

 93

Activity 1: Students look at the pictures above the columns. They use the word pattern from each picture to complete the words in the column below.

Activity 2: Students read the sentences. They underline the word in brackets that best completes the sentence.

WORD WORKERS 3 UNIT 5.7

Name .... Date ....

Read these words.

plump plumper plumpest	blondest blond blonder	softest softer soft	swift swiftest swifter	slicker slick slickest
flattest flatter flat	fast fastest faster	stiff stiffer stiffest	slimmer slim slimmest	dampest damper damp

Complete these words.

a	e	i	o	u
gr a nt	bl e d	sk i ff	fl o p	l u mp
tr a mp	Gl e n	spr i nt	bl o nd	g u st
b a nk	sl e d	st i ll	cl o t	d u sk
br a nd	sl e pt	scr i pt	sl o p	h u nt
pr a m	fl e d	tw i g	fl o ck	m u st

94

Activity 1: Students read the words in the boxes. Tell them to add the endings to the smallest word or base word.

Activity 2: Students complete the words by writing in the letter(s) printed above each column.

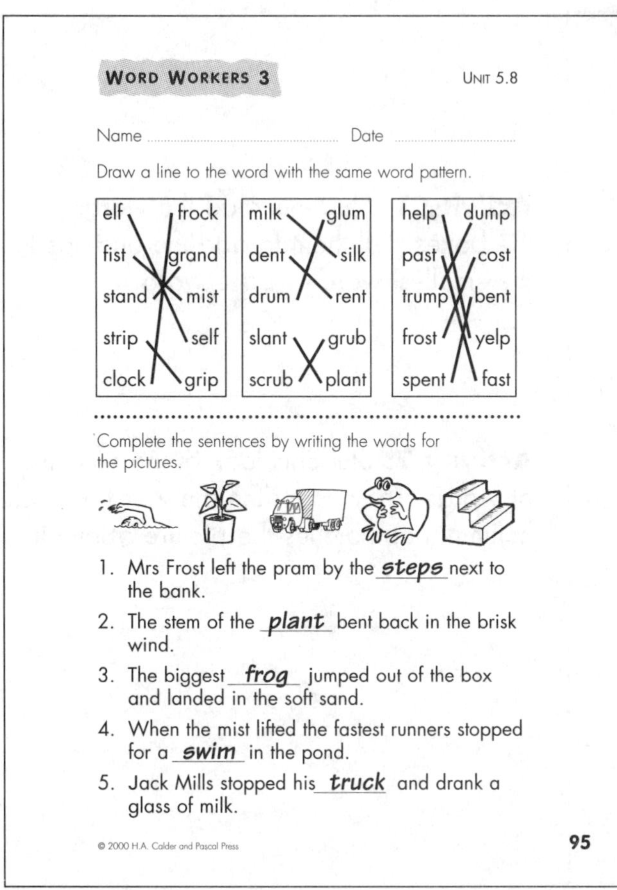

WORD WORKERS 3 UNIT 5.8

Name .... Date ....

Draw a line to the word with the same word pattern.

elf	frock
fist	grand
stand	mist
strip	self
clock	grip

milk	glum
dent	silk
drum	rent
slant	grub
scrub	plant

help	dump
past	cost
trump	bent
frost	yelp
spent	fast

Complete the sentences by writing the words for the pictures.

1. Mrs Frost left the pram by the *steps* next to the bank.
2. The stem of the *plant* bent back in the brisk wind.
3. The biggest *frog* jumped out of the box and landed in the soft sand.
4. When the mist lifted the fastest runners stopped for a *swim* in the pond.
5. Jack Mills stopped his *truck* and drank a glass of milk.

© 2000 H.A. Calder and Pascal Press 95

Activity 1: Students look at the two columns of words in each box. They draw a line from the word in the left-hand column to the word in the right-hand column that has the same word pattern.

Activity 2: Students look at the pictures and then complete the sentences below by writing the correct word for the picture in the space provided.

WORD WORKERS 3 UNIT 5.9

Name .... Date ....

Write the word for these jumbled letters.
The first letter is underlined.

figt	*gift*	knub	*bunk*	piks	*skip*
plim	*limp*	trucs	*crust*	nitw	*twin*
skam	*mask*	ppro	*prop*	smiw	*swim*
hnit	*hint*	inkls	*slink*	entsp	*spent*

Underline the *two* words with the same word pattern as the picture.

crank	rest	test	tent
task	sand	pant	land
stock	swift	stomp	slump
frock	gruff	flank	flap
drank	draft	pram	plank

96 © 2000 H.A. Calder and Pascal Press

Activity 1: Students make a word from the jumbled letters. The first letter of each word is underlined. Students write the words in the spaces provided.

Activity 2: Students look at the pictures and the words on the lines beside them. They underline the two words in each line that have the same word pattern as the picture.

WORD WORKERS 3 UNIT 5.10

Name .... Date ....

Read these words.

trot trots trotted	limped limps limp	skids skid skidded	rusted rusts rust	stamp stamped stamps
blinked blink blinks	drops dropped drop	dump dumped dumps	grips grip gripped	stopped stops stop

Underline the word for the picture.

spell	blink	sink	gust	bless
span	bless	<u>wink</u>	zest	<u>dress</u>
<u>spot</u>	blast	drink	mist	mess
spun	<u>blimp</u>	pink	<u>fist</u>	less

© 2000 H.A. Calder and Pascal Press 97

Activity 1: Students read the words in the boxes. Tell them to add the endings to the smallest word or base word.

Activity 2: Students look at the columns of words. They underline the word in each column that matches the picture above it.

WORD WORKERS 3 UNIT 5.11

Name .... Date ....

Write the word from each column that fits the word shape box.

spend	pelt	scrap	flick
spell	felt	stamp	plum
spin	next	swift	flask
snug	wept	twist	class
snug	next	scrap	plum

Underline the correct word to complete the sentence.

1. The drink Ann spilled (<u>landed</u>/handed) on her best dress.
2. Fred and Jim slept snug as a bug in the (clunks/<u>bunks</u>).
3. Spot, the black dog, (lumped/<u>limped</u>) past the biggest cat.
4. The (<u>class</u>/grass) sat still when Miss Black slapped the desk.
5. Jan (<u>clapped</u>/strapped) her hands as the fastest swimmer swam past.

98 © 2000 H.A. Calder and Pascal Press

Activity 1: Students look at the columns of words. Tell them to put the word from each column that fits into the 'word shape' box below it.

Activity 2: Students read the sentences. They underline the word in brackets that best completes the sentence.

WORD WORKERS 3 UNIT 5.12

Name .... Date ....

Put each column in alphabetical order.

a		e		i	
crab	*brag*	desk	*belt*	skill	*script*
brag	*brat*	belt	*bend*	script	*skill*
brat	*crab*	mend	*desk*	sniff	*sniff*
craft	*craft*	next	*mend*	snip	*snip*
drag	*drag*	bend	*next*	sprint	*sprint*

o		u	
clomp	*blond*	trust	*slunk*
flock	*clod*	sunk	*sunk*
clod	*clomp*	truck	*truck*
blond	*flock*	slunk	*trump*
flop	*flop*	trump	*trust*

 99

Students place the words in each column in alphabetical order.

WORD WORKERS 3 UNIT 5.13

Name .... Date ....

Complete these crossword puzzles.

a: flag, clamp, blast, cast, glass, rank

e: speck, spent, crept, rent, rend

i: milk, clip, swift, spin, wind

o: plod, prom, crop, stop, trots

u: slump, dust, blunt, plunk, stuck

100

Students complete the crossword puzzles. They write the letter indicated in the blank spaces to make words that can be read going down or across the page.

WORD WORKERS 3 UNIT 5.14

Name .... Date ....

Write the word with the correct spelling.

1. bulnt blunt bluntt *blunt*
2. skids scids skidz *skids*
3. stwep swipt swept *swept*
4. blimp bilmp blimt *blimp*
5. dropt dropped dropd *dropped*

Fill in the missing letters to complete the word.

1.	*g* ras *s*	sniffed
2.	*b* lock *s*	grass
3.	*s* niffe *d*	drummer
4.	*d* rumme *r*	spent
5.	*s* pen *t*	blocks

 101

Activity 1: Students read the words going across the page, then write the word that is spelt correctly.

Activity 2: Students read the words in the box, then write the missing letters to complete the column of words on the left.

WORD WORKERS 3 UNIT 5.15

Name .... Date ....

Underline the word for the picture.

cross crosses sled sleds clip clips

twin twins desk desks flag flags

Complete the sentences with the words from the box.

drink	black	slept	junk	dress

1. The fastest sprinter stopped for a *drink*.
2. The *black* cat jumped up on the bunk bed.
3. The man dumped the *junk* in the big trunk.
4. Mrs Grant spilled milk on her best *dress*.
5. The dog *slept* on the back steps.

102

Activity 1: Students underline the singular word if there is one object pictured or the plural word if there are two or more objects pictured.

Activity 2: Students complete the sentences by writing the correct word from the box in the space provided.

WORD WORKERS 3 UNIT 5.16

Name .... Date ....

Draw a line from the picture to the matching word.

lift belt sift	class glass brass
clip drip slip	sand hand stand

Number the words in the box in alphabetical order, then answer the questions.

2 milk	6 plump	3 nest
4 plan	1 mast	5 plug

1. Which word comes *after* 'nest'? plan
2. Which word comes *before* 'plump'? plug
3. Which word comes *after* 'mast'? milk
4. Which word comes *before* 'plan'? nest
5. Which word comes *after* 'plug'? plump
6. Which word comes *before* 'milk'? mast

 103

Activity 1: Students say the word for the picture and then draw a line from the picture to the correct word beside it.

Activity 2: Students number the words in the box in alphabetical order, then use this information to answer the questions below.

WORD WORKERS 3 UNIT 5.17

Read the story.

Fred Frost's Dog

Fred Frost stacked big boxes of plums on his truck. His dog, Tramp, helped him. 'Gruff! Gruff!' Tramp yapped as Fred lifted the boxes.

The truck next to Fred's was Bill Black's. Bill was Fred's best pal. He said that his truck was a lot faster than Fred's. But Fred grinned and said, 'Not your old bus — my rig is the fastest truck in the west!'

When the boxes of plums were stacked, the men set off. Tramp, the big black dog, jumped in and sat next to Fred. He panted and puffed as Fred's truck bumped along. Bill Black's truck bumped after them.

104

For the following pages:

This story is designed to reinforce the skills learned in this and previous units of work. At no stage do students encounter unfamiliar words or skills. Students read the story and answer the questions silently. Correct the work by having them read the story and answer the questions orally.

WORD WORKERS 3 UNIT 5.18

As they went past a bank, a man in a mask ran out. It was a robber. He held a gun in his hand. 'Crack! Crack!' The robber's gun went off. Fred and Bill slammed their trucks to a stop.

Tramp jumped out of Fred's truck. 'Gruff! Gruff!' The big black dog went after the man in the mask. He jumped on him and bit his leg. The robber kicked and yelled but Tramp would not let go.

Fred and Bill ran up to help Tramp. They jumped on the robber and grabbed the gun. Now the man in the mask did not kick. He did not yell. The gun dropped out of his hand. Fred and Bill held on to the robber. Tramp sat down and panted and puffed.

Then the cops grabbed the robber and tossed him in their van. Off went his mask and off sped the cops with a glum robber in the back of the van.

 105

WORD WORKERS 3 UNIT 5.19

Fred got back in his truck. Tramp hopped in next to him. 'Good dog, Tramp,' Fred said as he patted him. Bill patted Tramp too. Then Fred Frost grinned at Bill Black. 'Get back in that old rig of yours, Bill,' he said. '*My* truck is the fastest in the west!'

So Bill jumped in his truck. 'Vrummm! Vrummm!' Off went the men in their big trucks. Tramp panted and puffed as he sat next to Fred. 'Gruff! Gruff!' he yapped. The trucks with their boxes of plums bumped along — Fred Frost and Bill Black in the fastest trucks in the west. And Tramp too — the dog who stopped the bank robber.

106

Students read the story. They read it several times until accuracy and fluency combine to improve comprehension.

WORD WORKERS 3 UNIT 5.20

Name .... Date ....

Write the letters 'a', 'b', 'c' and 'd' in the same order the pictures occurred in the story.

a b c d

1. b 2. c 3. a 4. d

Fill in the blanks with the exact words from the story.

1. Fred Frost lifted big boxes of *plums* onto his truck.
2. Bill Black said his truck was a lot *faster* than Fred's.
3. A man in a *mask* ran out of the bank.
4. Tramp bit the robber's *leg* .
5. Fred and Bill *held* on to the robber.

 107

Activity 1: Students sequence the events in the story by placing the pictures in their correct order.

Activity 2: Students complete these sentences using the exact word from the story.

WORD WORKERS 3 UNIT 5.21

Name .... Date ....

Fill in the blanks with the correct word from the box.

Fred got back in his *truck* . Tramp hopped in next to him. 'Good dog *Tramp* ,' Fred said as he patted him. Bill patted Tramp too. Then Fred Frost *grinned* at Bill Black. 'Get back in that old *rig* of yours, Bill,' he said. 'My truck is the *fastest* in the west!'

Tramp	truck	fastest	grinned	rig

Write the letters 'a', 'b', 'c' and 'd' beside the sentences in the same order they occurred in the story.

1. The robber kicked and yelled but Tramp did not let go. *c*
2. The cops grabbed the robber and tossed him in their van. *d*
3. Bill said his truck was a lot faster than Fred's. *a*
4. As they went past a bank, a man in a mask ran out. *b*

108

Activity 1: Students complete this cloze exercise using the words from the box.

Activity 2: Students sequence the events in the story by placing them in their correct order.

* Students complete *Word Workers Achievement Test 3* after completing this unit.

Using Book 4

Word Workers Book 4 teaches students to read words containing consonant digraphs, long vowel rules, soft 'c' and 'g', and irregular long vowel rules. Below are some suggestions on how to use the book effectively. More detailed information on the teaching processes can be found in Chapter 2: 'Skills for successful teaching'. An activity-by-activity guide is provided with the answers.

- Read the section in the *Teacher Resource Book* that gives instructions on teaching the different rules and generalisations students need to know to be successful at this stage of their reading acquisition. 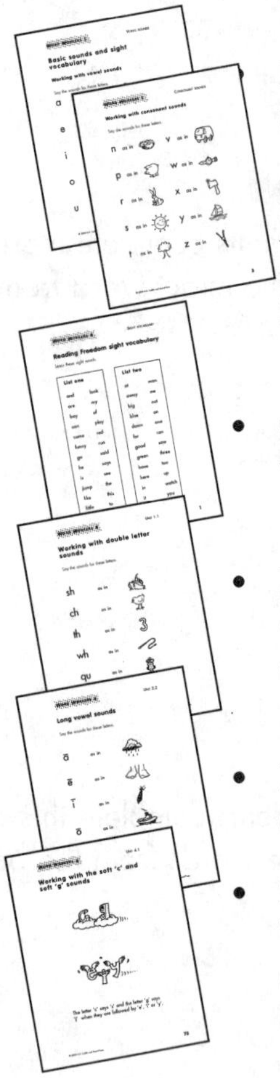
- Become familiar with the suggested lesson plan for Book 4 on the next page.
- Continue the drill with vowel and consonant sounds from the *Reading Freedom 2000* single letter–sound and common blends wall charts. As new phonics rules and generalisations are introduced, they can be incorporated into the drill at the beginning of each lesson.
- Students continue learning the *Reading Freedom* basic sight vocabulary lists.
- Introduce the consonant digraphs before beginning Unit 1. Begin drilling at the start of the lesson, using the *Reading Freedom 2000* wall charts or page 6 in Book 4.
- Introduce students to the long vowel rules before beginning Units 2 and 3.
- Introduce students to the soft 'c' and 'g' and irregular long vowels before beginning Unit 4. Explain to students that the letter 'y' can also say a vowel sound. In words like 'cry', it says the long 'i' sound. Also show how in words like 'chief' the 'ie' pattern says the long 'e' sound.
- Continue the blending drill, especially focussing on consonant digraphs. Book 4 incorporates initial consonant digraph to vowel blending as well as vowel to terminal consonant digraph blending.
- Enlist parent support whenever possible. Parents are particularly helpful teaching sight vocabulary and reinforcing blending activities at home. 
- Monitor students' progress while they read the word list at the beginning of each unit.
- When Units 1 and 2 of Book 4 are completed, record students' progress using *Word Workers* Achievement Test 4 and when Units 3 and 4 are completed, record students' progress using Test 5.

Book 4: Suggested lesson plan

Based on a lesson of approximately 30 minutes.

1 Students say a row of sounds from the *Reading Freedom 2000* single letter–sound and common blends wall charts. For small groups, each student can say a row or column of sounds. If your class is large, select students to say a row or column until all the sounds have been repeated. As new sounds, rules and phonic generalisations are encountered in Book 4, incorporate them at the start of each lesson. For instance, when students reach Unit 3, ask them to repeat the 'bossy "e" rule' after the single letter–sound chart is completed. This applies only to students who have been taught the skill or generalisation. Be sure different students say the sounds each lesson.

2 When teaching with small groups, each student reads a column of *Reading Freedom* basic sight vocabulary. When teaching the whole class, select students to read a column of sight words. Five or six columns is enough to start your lesson with. Be sure different students read the sight words each lesson.

3 Explain and demonstrate the sounds or phonic generalisations to be learned. Carefully explain the activities on the page or pages to be completed. Ensure that students understand the concepts involved and know what is required of them. Ask students to repeat the rules to you once they have been taught.

4 Assign activity pages to be completed (the number of pages depends on the teacher's professional judgment as well as the ability and enthusiasm of the student).

5 In Book 4, demonstrate and practise blending with each of the sounds and rules taught. Continue with this until the book is completed, using new sounds and rules as they are introduced. At this stage of instruction, blending skills are often firmly in place. The teacher's professional judgment and the ability of the student determines the need to continue with it.

6 Reward students for achievement on the activity pages or in learning sight vocabulary with stamps, stickers or gold stars. When they complete the activity book and finish the complementary Achievement Tests (found in *Word Workers Achievement Tests*) they receive a *Word Workers* Merit Certificate.

7 Assign any homework after demonstrating the activities. Ensure students understand the concept and what is to be done.

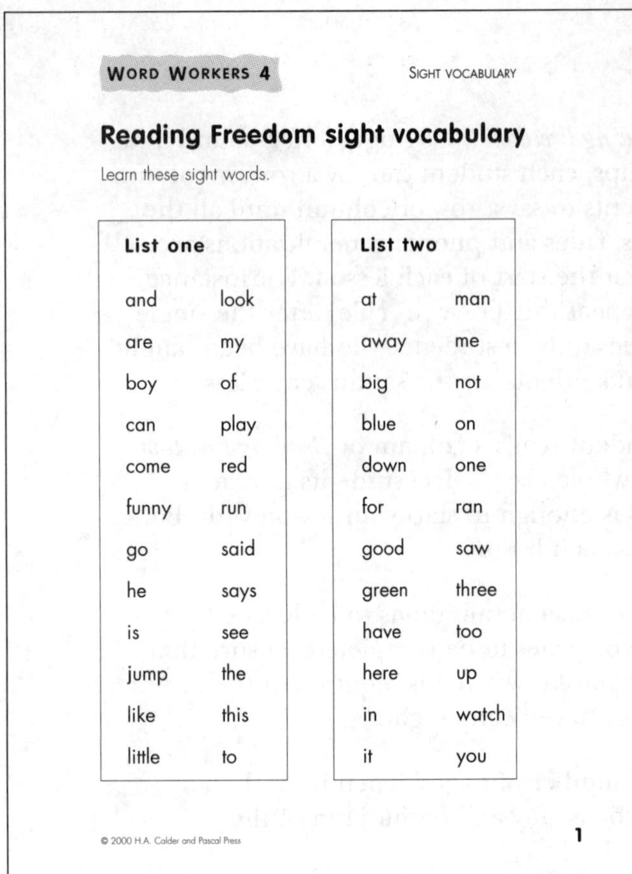

WORD WORKERS 4 SIGHT VOCABULARY

Reading Freedom sight vocabulary

Learn these sight words.

List one	
and	look
are	my
boy	of
can	play
come	red
funny	run
go	said
he	says
is	see
jump	the
like	this
little	to

List two	
at	man
away	me
big	not
blue	on
down	one
for	ran
good	saw
green	three
have	too
here	up
in	watch
it	you

© 2000 H.A. Calder and Pascal Press 1

WORD WORKERS 4 SIGHT VOCABULARY

Learn these sight words.

List three	
all	going
am	home
around	into
black	make
but	no
by	old
call	out
came	was
do	we
eat	will
fast	yellow
get	yes

List four	
an	had
after	help
as	her
be	him
brown	his
cold	if
did	she
ever	some
fly	stop
from	two
girl	who
give	woman

2 © 2000 H.A. Calder and Pascal Press

For the following pages:

Students learn these sight words list by list. Reward successful acquisition of sight vocabulary with stars and stickers.

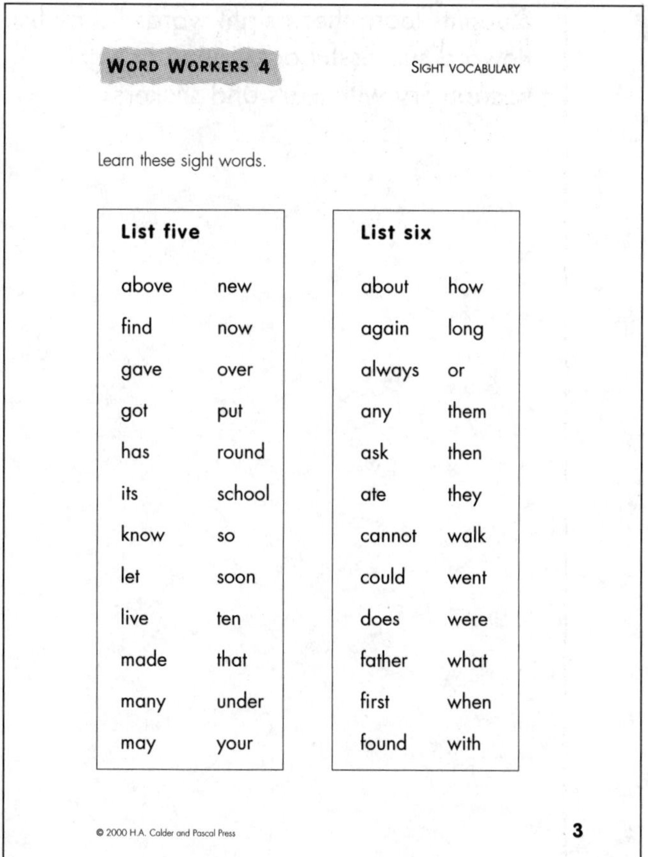
WORD WORKERS 4 SIGHT VOCABULARY

Learn these sight words.

List five	
above	new
find	now
gave	over
got	put
has	round
its	school
know	so
let	soon
live	ten
made	that
many	under
may	your

List six	
about	how
again	long
always	or
any	them
ask	then
ate	they
cannot	walk
could	went
does	were
father	what
first	when
found	with

© 2000 H.A. Calder and Pascal Press 3

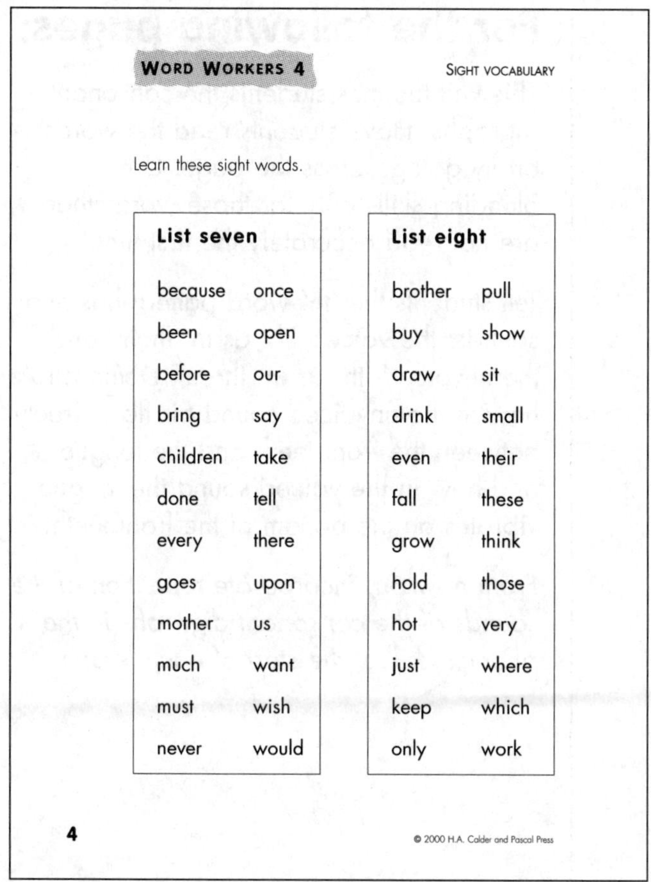
WORD WORKERS 4 SIGHT VOCABULARY

Learn these sight words.

List seven	
because	once
been	open
before	our
bring	say
children	take
done	tell
every	there
goes	upon
mother	us
much	want
must	wish
never	would

List eight	
brother	pull
buy	show
draw	sit
drink	small
even	their
fall	these
grow	think
hold	those
hot	very
just	where
keep	which
only	work

4 © 2000 H.A. Calder and Pascal Press

Students learn these sight words list by list. Reward successful acquisition of sight vocabulary with stars and stickers.

WORD WORKERS 4 — SIGHT VOCABULARY

Learn these sight words.

List nine		List ten	
best	pick	baby	sing
better	please	daughter	sister
both	pretty	far	sleep
clean	read	house	something
cut	shall	hurt	son
eight	six	kind	start
five	today	laugh	thank
four	try	Mr	together
full	use	Mrs	warm
light	well	own	wash
myself	why	right	water
off	write	seven	white

© 2000 H.A. Calder and Pascal Press — 5

Students learn these sight words list by list. Reward successful acquisition of sight vocabulary with stars and stickers.

WORD WORKERS 4 — UNIT 1.1

Working with double letter sounds

Say the sounds for these letters.

sh as in

ch as in

th as in

wh as in

qu as in

ng as in

6 — © 2000 H.A. Calder and Pascal Press

For the following pages:

This unit teaches students the consonant digraphs. Have students read the words orally going across the page. Use blending skills only for those words that are not read accurately the first time.

Tell students the 'th' word pattern has two sounds: the voiced 'th' as in 'them' and the unvoiced 'th' as in 'three'. Demonstrate how in the unvoiced sound air flows freely between the front teeth and the tongue, and how in the voiced sound the tongue vibrates on the bottom of the front teeth.

From now on, incorporate repetition of the sounds of the consonant digraphs in the phonics drill at the start of each lesson.

Students read the words in the columns.

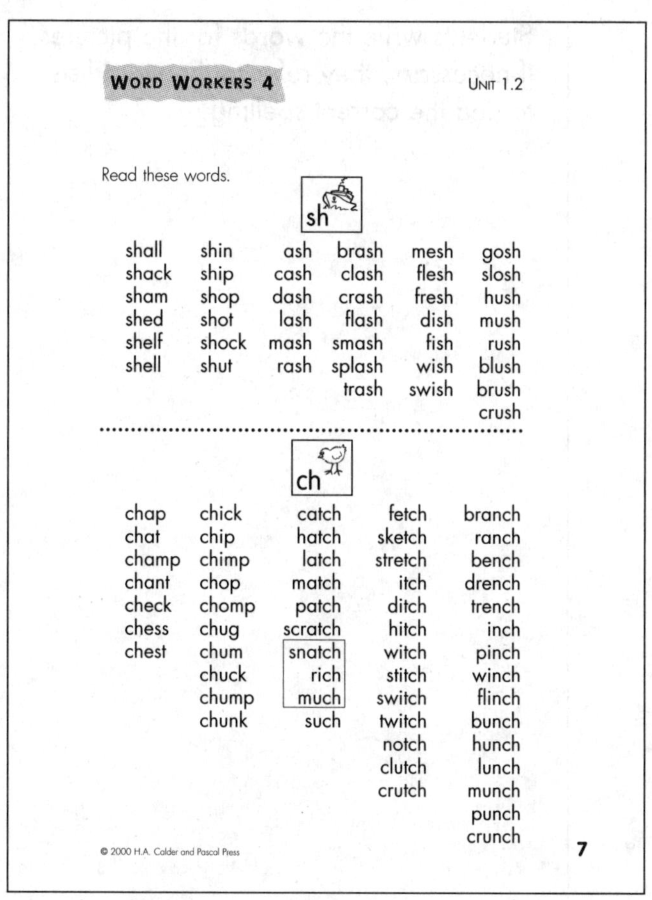
WORD WORKERS 4 UNIT 1.2

Read these words.

sh

shall	shin	ash	brash	mesh	gosh
shack	ship	cash	clash	flesh	slosh
sham	shop	dash	crash	fresh	hush
shed	shot	lash	flash	dish	mush
shelf	shock	mash	smash	fish	rush
shell	shut	rash	splash	wish	blush
			trash	swish	brush
					crush

ch

chap	chick	catch	fetch	branch
chat	chip	hatch	sketch	ranch
champ	chimp	latch	stretch	bench
chant	chop	match	itch	drench
check	chomp	patch	ditch	trench
chess	chug	scratch	hitch	inch
chest	chum	snatch	witch	pinch
	chuck	rich	stitch	winch
	chump	much	switch	flinch
	chunk	such	twitch	bunch
			notch	hunch
			clutch	lunch
			crutch	munch
				punch
				crunch

© 2000 H.A. Calder and Pascal Press 7

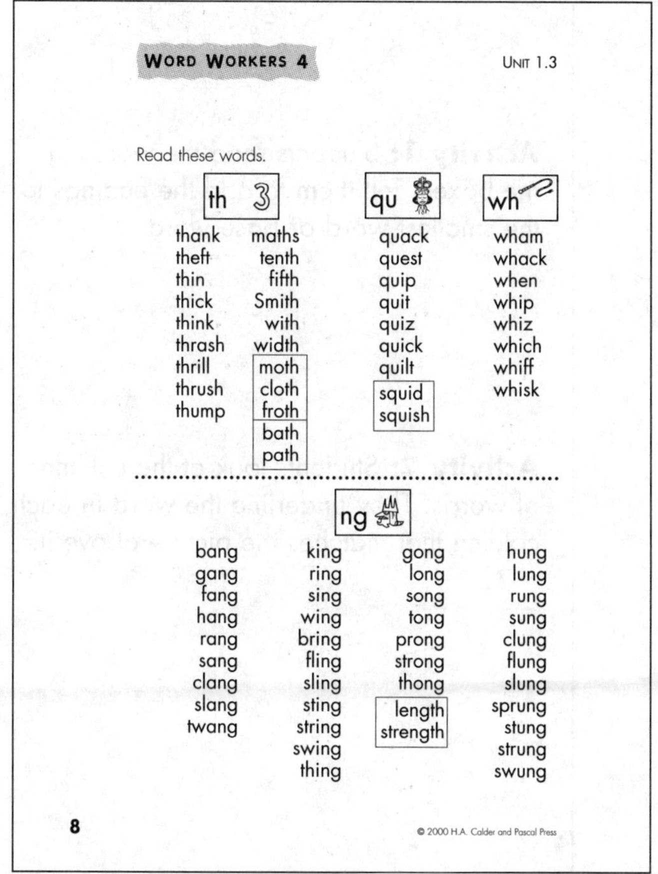
WORD WORKERS 4 UNIT 1.3

Read these words.

th qu wh

thank	maths	quack	wham
theft	tenth	quest	whack
thin	fifth	quip	when
thick	Smith	quit	whip
think	with	quiz	whiz
thrash	width	quick	which
thrill	moth	quilt	whiff
thrush	cloth	squid	whisk
thump	froth	squish	
	bath		
	path		

ng

bang	king	gong	hung
gang	ring	long	lung
fang	sing	song	rung
hang	wing	tong	sung
rang	bring	prong	clung
sang	fling	strong	flung
clang	sling	thong	slung
slang	sting	length	sprung
twang	string	strength	stung
	swing		strung
	thing		swung

8 © 2000 H.A. Calder and Pascal Press

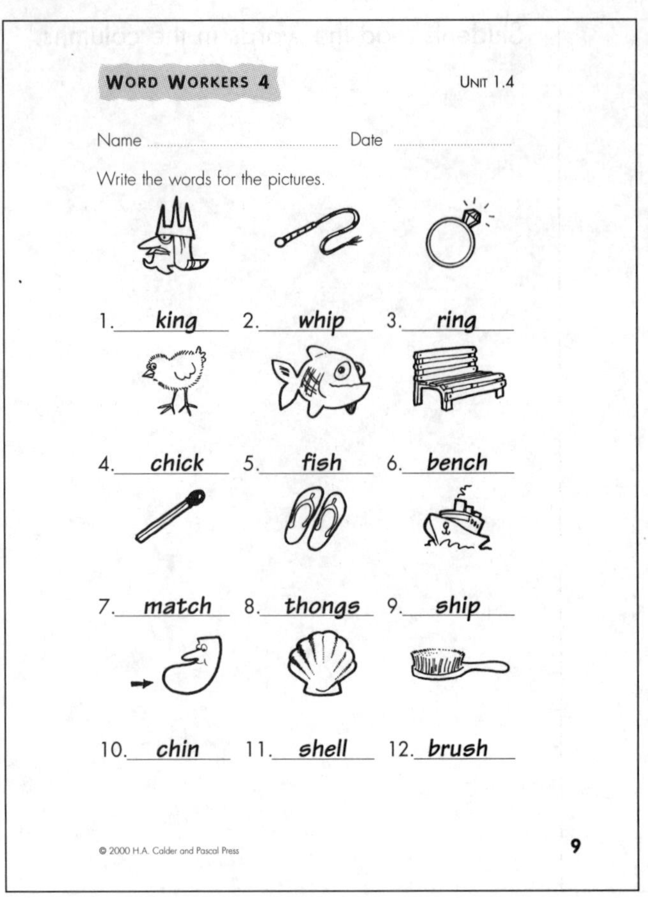

WORD WORKERS 4 UNIT 1.4

Name .... Date ....

Write the words for the pictures.

1. king 2. whip 3. ring

4. chick 5. fish 6. bench

7. match 8. thongs 9. ship

10. chin 11. shell 12. brush

© 2000 H.A. Calder and Pascal Press 9

Students write the words for the pictures. If necessary, they refer to the word lists to find the correct spelling.

WORD WORKERS 4 UNIT 1.5

Name .... Date ....

Read these words.

shop shops shopped shopping	thanked thanking thanks thank	quizzing quiz quizzes quizzed	chops chop chopped chopping
crashing crashed crashes crash	scratches scratched scratch scratching	punch punched punching punches	pinch pinched pinches pinching

Underline the word for the picture.

chill	fling	shell	quit	path
champ	swing	shelf	quiz	with
chick	string	shock	quilt	width
chug	ring	shin	quick	bath

10 © 2000 H.A. Calder and Pascal Press

Activity 1: Students read the words in the boxes. Tell them to add the endings to the smallest word or base word.

Activity 2: Students look at the columns of words. They underline the word in each column that matches the picture above it.

WORD WORKERS 4 UNIT 1.6

Name .... Date ....

Underline the nonsense word.

1. think	2. sing	3. quit	4. chonk	5. whip
theft	strong	quim	chill	which
thin	fong	quack	chess	when
thamp	hung	quest	chap	whick

Write the words for the pictures.

1. crutches 2. ship 3. ring

4. thongs 5. shells 6. witch

7. chips 8. fish 9. matches

 11

Activity 1: Students look at the columns of words. Tell them to underline the word in each column that is a nonsense word.

Activity 2: Students write the words for the pictures. Tell them to add the letter 's' if there is more than one. If necessary, they refer to the word lists to find the correct spelling.

WORD WORKERS 4 UNIT 1.7

Name .... Date ....

Complete these words with the word pattern from the picture.

lun ch	ch amp	wh ich	stro ng	di sh
flin ch	ch um	wh en	ha ng	ca sh
ran ch	ch est	wh iz	thi ng	sma sh
tren ch	ch ant	wh isk	stu ng	fre sh

Underline the correct word to complete the sentence.

1. Mrs Long stacked the dishes on the (shelf/self).
2. Tom chopped up the thick branch that fell on the (path/bath).
3. The (thing/king) hid the fifth ring in the chest.
4. The tenth singer (rang/sang) the longest song.
5. When the wind shifted he (shut/shot) the ship's hatch.

12

Activity 1: Students look at the pictures above the columns. They use the word pattern from each picture to complete the words in the column below.

Activity 2: Students read the sentences. They underline the word in brackets that best completes the sentence.

WORD WORKERS 4 UNIT 1.8

Name .... Date ....

Read these words.

stretch stretches stretched stretching	punched punching punches punch	shocking shocks shock shocked	chilling chill chilled chills
thin thinner thinnest	strongest stronger strong	richer rich richest	quickest quick quicker

Complete the words by writing the vowel sounds.

a	e	i	o	u
sh *a* ll	fl *e* sh	th *i* n	g *o* sh	ch *u* nk
qu *a* ck	sh *e* lf	w *i* sh	ch *o* mp	sh *u* t
ch *a* nt	sk *e* tch	qu *i* z	th *o* ng	th *u* mp
r *a* nch	qu *e* st	p *i* nch	n *o* tch	fl *u* ng
th *a* nk	ch *e* ck	sw *i* sh	sh *o* t	cl *u* tch

 13

Activity 1: Students read the words in the boxes. Tell them to add the endings to the smallest word or base word.

Activity 2: Students complete the words by writing in the letter printed above each column.

WORD WORKERS 4 UNIT 1.9

Name .... Date ....

Draw a line to the word with the same word pattern.

bang	path	punch	thong	lunch	smash
much	dash	strong	cling	crash	flesh
bath	hang	length	blush	flung	hunch
cash	crush	string	munch	scratch	clung
rush	such	hush	strength	fresh	patch

Complete these sentences by writing the words for the pictures.

1. Mrs Smith sat on a *bench* and had her lunch.
2. Tess said, 'I wish I could catch a *fish* .'
3. The sixth *chick* flapped its wings when it hatched from its shell.
4. Dad sang and splashed as he sat in the *bath* .
5. Tim hid under the *quilt* when the thunder crashed.

14

Activity 1: Students look at the two columns of words in each box. They draw a line from the word in the left-hand column to the word in the right-hand column that has the same word pattern.

Activity 2: Students look at the pictures and then complete the sentences below by writing the correct word for the picture in the space provided.

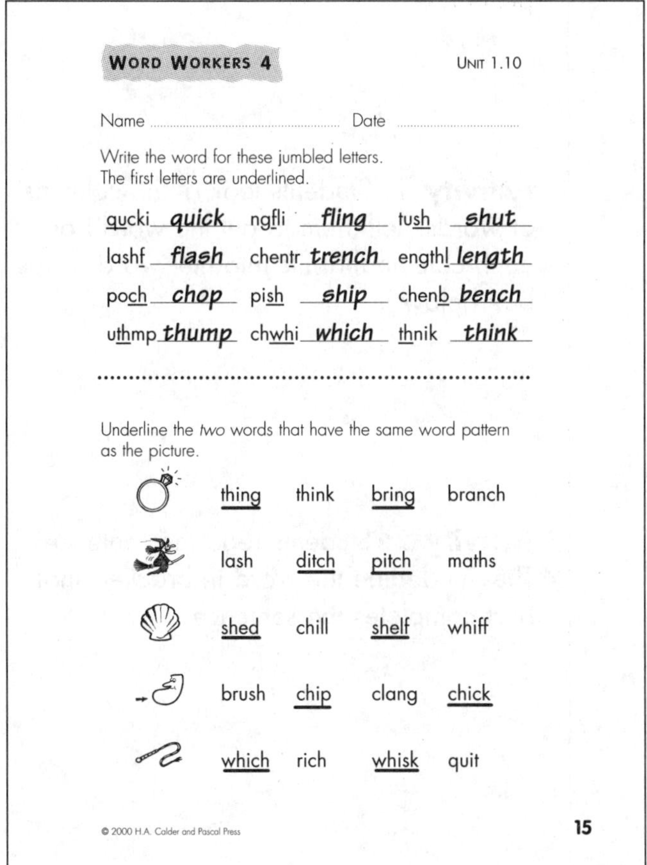

WORD WORKERS 4 UNIT 1.10

Name .... Date ....

Write the word for these jumbled letters.
The first letters are underlined.

qucki	quick	ngfli	fling	tush	shut
lashf	flash	chentr	trench	engthl	length
poch	chop	pish	ship	chenb	bench
uthmp	thump	chwhi	which	thnik	think

Underline the *two* words that have the same word pattern as the picture.

thing think bring branch

lash ditch pitch maths

shed chill shelf whiff

brush chip clang chick

which rich whisk quit

© 2000 H.A. Calder and Pascal Press 15

Activity 1: Students make a word from the jumbled letters. The first letter of each word is underlined. Students write the words in the spaces provided.

Activity 2: Students look at the pictures and the words on the lines beside them. They underline the two words in each line that have the same word pattern as the picture.

WORD WORKERS 4 UNIT 1.11

Name .... Date ....

Read these words.

match matches matched matching	smashed smashing smash smashes	shipping ships shipped ship	thumps thumped thump thumping
thick thicken	quick quicken	lengthen length	freshen fresh

Underline the word for the picture.

snatch	wish	theft	lunch	ship	sting
notch	fish	thin	pinch	shock	king
match	thrash	thump	bench	shall	sing
clutch	blush	thongs	branch	shut	bring

16 © 2000 H.A. Calder and Pascal Press

Activity 1: Students read the words in the boxes. Tell them to add the endings to the smallest word or base word.

Activity 2: Students look at the columns of words. They underline the word in each column that matches the picture above it.

WORD WORKERS 4 UNIT 1.12

Name .... Date ....

Write the word from each column that fits the word shape box.

theft	which	quick	shop	chest
thin	whisk	quell	shack	chill
thump	when	quit	shelf	champ
thank	whiff	quip	shin	chat

thin when quit shin chat

Underline the correct word to complete the sentence.

1. Beth (smashed/dashed) up the path to get to the swings.
2. Mr King checked to see if the (chills/chests) were in the shed.
3. Mrs Strong thanked Sam for (bringing/stinging) her lunch from the shop.
4. Jan said, 'Gosh, I did not think I had that much (crash/cash).'
5. Patch, the dog, scratched and itched when Ted (brushed/blushed) him.

 17

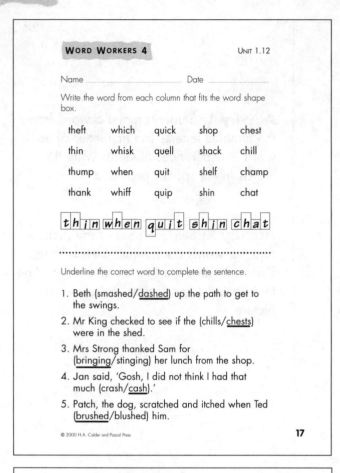

Activity 1: Students look at the columns of words. Tell them to put the word from each column that fits into the 'word shape' box below it.

Activity 2: Students read the sentences. They underline the word in brackets that best completes the sentence.

WORD WORKERS 4 UNIT 1.13

Name .... Date ....

Put each column in alphabetical order.

ch		sh		th	
check	*bench*	shelf	*flash*	path	*fifth*
bench	*bunch*	plush	*mash*	fifth	*path*
drench	*check*	shift	*plush*	thrill	*sixth*
bunch	*drench*	mash	*shelf*	with	*thrill*
hatch	*hatch*	flash	*shift*	sixth	*with*

wh		ng		qu	
which	*whack*	long	*clang*	quiz	*quack*
whack	*when*	sting	*long*	quack	*quest*
whiff	*which*	thong	*sting*	quit	*quilt*
whiz	*whiff*	clang	*strong*	quest	*quit*
when	*whiz*	strong	*thong*	quilt	*quiz*

18

Students place the words in each column in alphabetical order.

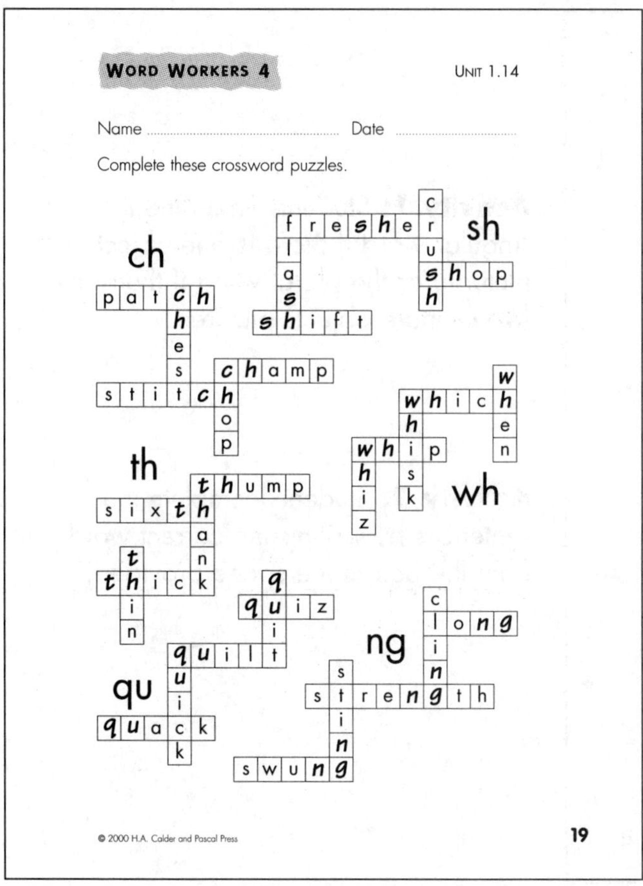

WORD WORKERS 4 UNIT 1.14

Name .... Date ....

Complete these crossword puzzles.

 19

Students complete the crossword puzzles. They write the letter(s) indicated in the blank spaces to make words that can be read going down or across the page.

WORD WORKERS 4 UNIT 1.15

Name .... Date ....

Write the word with the correct spelling.

1. branck	branch	banch	*branch*
2. whip	whimp	whipp	*whip*
3. lengf	length	lengt	*length*
4. strumg	strug	strung	*strung*
5. quick	qwick	quik	*quick*

Fill in the missing letters to complete the word.

1. *s* hi *p*	shopping
2. *s* cratche *d*	thanked
3. *s* hoppin *g*	ship
4. *t* hanke *d*	wishes
5. *w* ishe *s*	scratched

20

Activity 1: Students read the words going across the page, then write the word that is spelt correctly.

Activity 2: Students read the words in the box, then write the missing letters to complete the column of words on the left.

WORD WORKERS 4 UNIT 1.16

Name .... Date ....

Underline the word for the picture.

thong thongs bench benches ring rings

match matches ship ships chick chicks

Complete the sentences with the words from the box.

ring	think	song	fish	chopped

1. Mrs Smith left the fish in the dish.
2. The singers sang the tenth song.
3. The strongest man chopped the thick branch.
4. The king's ring was in the chest.
5. Josh did not think he was much good at maths.

© 2000 H.A. Calder and Pascal Press 21

Activity 1: Students underline the singular word if there is one object pictured or the plural word if there are two or more objects pictured.

Activity 2: Students complete the sentences by writing the correct word from the box in the space provided.

WORD WORKERS 4 UNIT 1.17

Name .... Date ....

Draw a line from the picture to the matching word.

quick quilt quiz

rush brush crush

trench drench bench

chin chill chimp

Number the words in the box in alphabetical order, then answer the questions.

6 quit	4 mesh	2 lung
3 match	5 pitch	1 king

1. Which word comes *after* 'king'? lung
2. Which word comes *before* 'mesh'? match
3. Which word comes *before* 'lung'? king
4. Which word comes *after* 'match'? mesh
5. Which word comes *after* 'pitch'? quit
6. Which word comes *after* 'mesh'? pitch

22 © 2000 H.A. Calder and Pascal Press

Activity 1: Students say the word for the picture and then draw a line from the picture to the correct word beside it.

Activity 2: Students number the words in the box in alphabetical order, then use this information to answer the questions below.

WORD WORKERS 4 UNIT 1.18

Read the story.

Fish and Chips for Dinner

Sam Smith and his dog, Patch, went to the pond to catch a fish. Sam held his fishing rod. Patch sniffed in the thick grass next to the path. 'When I catch a fish,' Sam said, 'we will have fish and chips for dinner.' So Sam fished and fished, but he did not catch a thing. 'I wish I could catch a fish,' he said. But he did not catch a fish, no matter how much he wished.

'Bad luck Patch,' Sam Smith said. 'Come on, we will have some lunch.' Sam sat on a bench and munched his lunch... Chomp, chomp, chomp. Patch scratched an itch on his chin. Just then a fish jumped in the pond with a splash. 'Look at the fish!' Sam yelled. Quick as a flash he shot off the bench. 'Now I will catch a fish,' he said as he ran down the path. Patch went 'Yap, yap, yap!' as he ran after him.

 23

WORD WORKERS 4 UNIT 1.19

But Sam had left his lunch on the bench. A gull saw the lunch and snatched it. Patch saw the gull. 'Yap, yap, yap!' He rushed back up the path. The gull flapped its wings and hopped off the bench. It still had Sam's lunch. Now Patch had to run back *down* the path after the gull... back to where Sam was catching a fish.

Patch looked at the gull as he ran. He did not see Sam. 'Thump! Bang! Crash!' Sam got a shock when Patch ran into him. Sam fell in the pond with a big splash. He dropped his fishing rod. He lost the fish. He sloshed and splashed in the pond. Patch jumped in to help him. At last Sam and Patch got out of the pond.

'Squish, squish, squish,' went Sam as he walked back to the bench. But there was no lunch left. 'Oh no,' he said to Patch. 'I lost my fishing rod. I lost the fish. And now I have lost my lunch!' So Sam and Patch left the pond. They did not have fish and chips for dinner. After they left, the fish jumped and splashed and the gull munched on the rest of Sam Smith's lunch.

24

For the following pages:

Students read the story. They read it several times until accuracy and fluency combine to improve comprehension.

WORD WORKERS 4 UNIT 1.20

Name .... Date ....

Write the letters 'a', 'b', 'c' and 'd' in the same order the pictures occurred in the story.

a b

c d

1. *b* 2. *a* 3. *d* 4. *c*

Fill in the blank with the exact word from the story.

1. Sam Smith said, 'I wish I could *catch* a fish.'
2. A *fish* jumped in the pond with a splash.
3. A gull saw Sam's lunch and *snatched* it.
4. There was a big *splash* when Sam fell in the pond.
5. Sam and Patch did not have *fish* and *chips* for dinner.

© 2000 H.A. Calder and Pascal Press 25

Activity 1: Students sequence the events in the story by placing the pictures in their correct order.

Activity 2: Students complete these sentences using the exact word from the story.

WORD WORKERS 4 UNIT 1.21

Name .... Date ....

Fill in the blanks with the correct word from the box.

'Bad luck Patch,' Sam Smith said. 'Come on, we will have some *lunch*.' Sam sat on a bench and munched his lunch... Chomp, chomp, chomp. Patch *scratched* an itch on his chin. Just then a fish jumped in the pond with a *splash*. 'Look at the fish!' Sam yelled. Quick as a flash he shot off the bench. 'Now I will *catch* a fish,' he said as he ran down the path. *Patch* went 'Yap, yap, yap!' as he ran after him.

Patch splash catch scratched lunch

Write the letters 'a', 'b', 'c' and 'd' beside the sentences in the same order they occurred in the story.

1. A gull saw the lunch and snatched it. *b*
2. Sam fell in the pond with a big splash. *c*
3. They did not have fish and chips for dinner. *d*
4. Patch sniffed in the thick grass next to the path. *a*

26 © 2000 H.A. Calder and Pascal Press

Activity 1: Students complete this cloze exercise using the words from the box.

Activity 2: Students sequence the events in the story by placing them in their correct order.

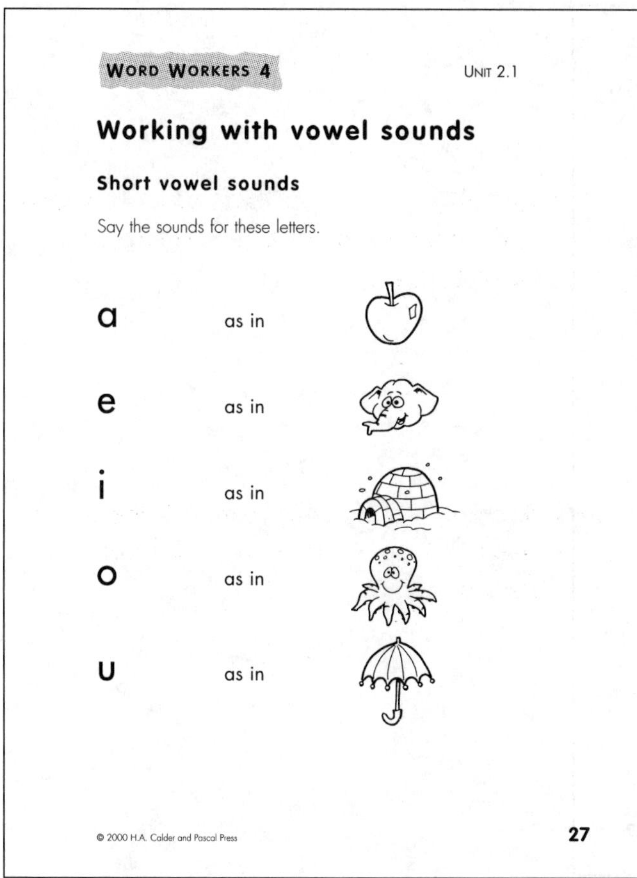

WORD WORKERS 4 UNIT 2.1

Working with vowel sounds

Short vowel sounds

Say the sounds for these letters.

a as in

e as in

i as in

o as in

u as in

© 2000 H.A. Calder and Pascal Press 27

WORD WORKERS 4 UNIT 2.2

Long vowel sounds

Say the sounds for these letters.

ā as in

ē as in

ī as in

ō as in

ū as in

28 © 2000 H.A. Calder and Pascal Press

For the following pages:

This unit teaches students the double vowel rule. Have students repeat the rule until it is learned satisfactorily.

From now on, incorporate repetition of the long and short sounds of the vowels and the double vowel rule in the phonics drill at the start of each lesson.

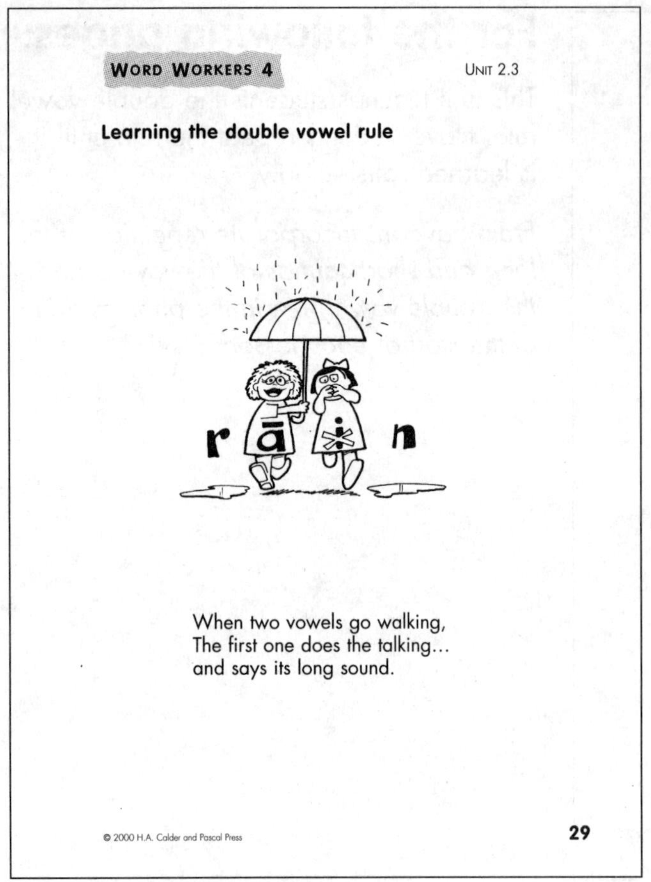
WORD WORKERS 4 UNIT 2.3

Learning the double vowel rule

When two vowels go walking,
The first one does the talking…
and says its long sound.

© 2000 H.A. Calder and Pascal Press 29

WORD WORKERS 4 UNIT 2.4

Read these words.

bee	feed	peek	feel
fee	need	seek	heel
see	seed	week	peel
free	weed	cheek	reel
tree	bleed	creek	steel
three	speed	beef	wheel
seen	deep	beer	feet
green	creep	peer	meet
queen	sheep	cheer	fleet
screen	sleep	queer	greet
seem	steep	steer	sheet
	sweep		street
			sweet

beak	deal	beam	ear	eat	each
leak	meal	seam	dear	beat	beach
peak	real	team	hear	heat	peach
weak	seal	cream	near	meat	reach
creak	squeal	scream	rear	neat	teach
sneak	steal	steam	tear	seat	bleach
speak	heap	stream	year	cheat	preach
squeak	leap	bean	clear	wheat	east
streak	cheap	lean	spear	bead	beast
leaf		mean		lead	feast
				read	least

30 © 2000 H.A. Calder and Pascal Press

Students read the words in the columns.

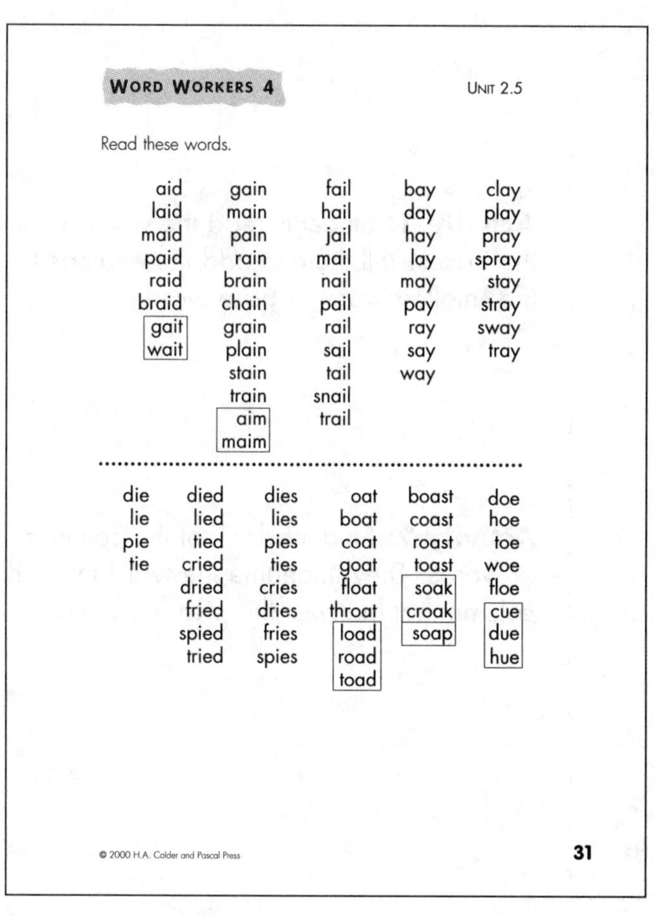

WORD WORKERS 4 UNIT 2.5

Read these words.

aid	gain	fail	bay	clay
laid	main	hail	day	play
maid	pain	jail	hay	pray
paid	rain	mail	lay	spray
raid	brain	nail	may	stay
braid	chain	pail	pay	stray
gait	grain	rail	ray	sway
wait	plain	sail	say	tray
	stain	tail	way	
	train	snail		
	aim	trail		
	maim			

die	died	dies	oat	boast	doe
lie	lied	lies	boat	coast	hoe
pie	tied	pies	coat	roast	toe
tie	cried	ties	goat	toast	woe
	dried	cries	float	soak	floe
	fried	dries	throat	croak	cue
	spied	fries	load	soap	due
	tried	spies	road		hue
			toad		

© 2000 H.A. Calder and Pascal Press 31

Students read the words in the columns.

WORD WORKERS 4 UNIT 2.6

Name .... Date ....

Write the words for the pictures.

1. *goat* 2. *tree* 3. *tie*

4. *tail* 5. *toast* 6. *queen*

7. *sheep* 8. *snail* 9. *feet*

10. *boat* 11. *leaf* 12. *chain*

32 © 2000 H.A. Calder and Pascal Press

Students write the words for the pictures. If necessary, they refer to the word lists to find the correct spelling.

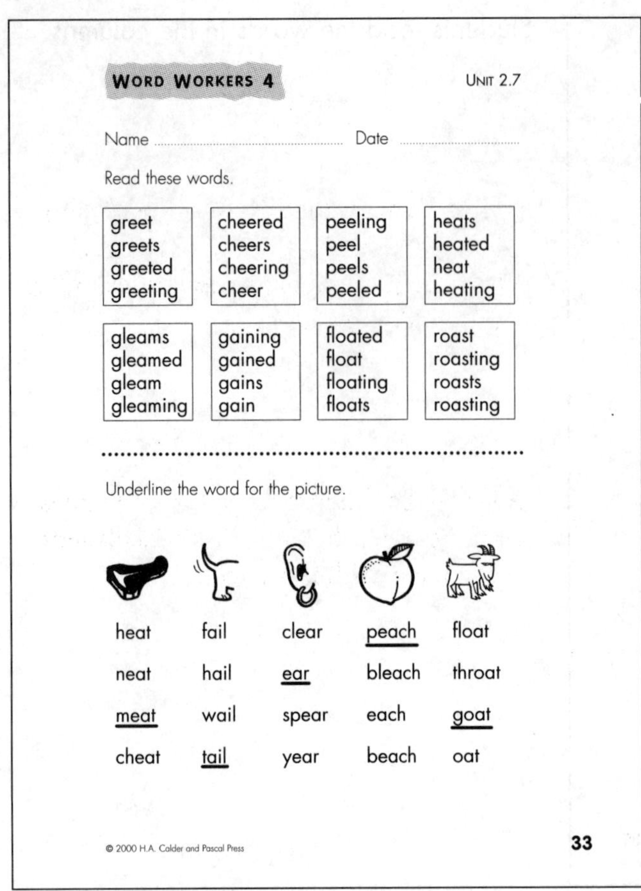

Word Workers 4 Unit 2.7

Name .... Date ....

Read these words.

greet greets greeted greeting	cheered cheers cheering cheer	peeling peel peels peeled	heats heated heat heating
gleams gleamed gleam gleaming	gaining gained gains gain	floated float floating floats	roast roasting roasts roasting

Underline the word for the picture.

heat	fail	clear	<u>peach</u>	float
neat	hail	<u>ear</u>	bleach	throat
<u>meat</u>	wail	spear	each	<u>goat</u>
cheat	<u>tail</u>	year	beach	oat

© 2000 H.A. Calder and Pascal Press 33

Activity 1: Students read the words in the boxes. Tell them to add the endings to the smallest word or base word.

Activity 2: Students look at the columns of words. They underline the word in each column that matches the picture above it.

Word Workers 4 Unit 2.8

Name .... Date ....

Underline the nonsense word.

1. float	2. snail	3. cheek	4. pie	5. beak
toad	stain	<u>leem</u>	<u>chie</u>	heat
<u>groast</u>	paid	speed	lies	<u>treach</u>
boast	<u>kail</u>	sweep	tied	beam

Write the words for the pictures.

1. *trees* 2. *tie* 3. *chain*

4. *nails* 5. *boat* 6. *leaf*

7. *bees* 8. *tail* 9. *coats*

34 © 2000 H.A. Calder and Pascal Press

Activity 1: Students look at the columns of words. Tell them to underline the word in each column that is a nonsense word.

Activity 2: Students write the words for the pictures. Tell them to add the letter 's' if there is more than one. If necessary, they refer to the word lists to find the correct spelling.

WORD WORKERS 4 UNIT 2.9

Name .... Date ....

Complete these words with the word pattern from the picture.

p *ail*	h *ear*	br *ain*	tr *ee*	thr *oat*
tr *ail*	sp *ear*	dr *ain*	s *ee*	b *oat*
s *ail*	y *ear*	m *ain*	f *ee*	fl *oat*
j *ail*	r *ear*	str *ain*	fr *ee*	g *oat*

Underline the correct word to complete the sentence.

1. Each day that (week/creek) the maid left the toast on the tray.
2. Next May Mr and Mrs Green will (pail/sail) down the east coast.
3. The coach did not mean to (scream/dream) at the team.
4. Mr Steel will (meat/eat) lean roast beef for his meal.
5. The class (strained/drained) to hear what the teacher was saying.

 35

Activity 1: Students look at the pictures above the columns. They use the word pattern from each picture to complete the words in the column below.

Activity 2: Students read the sentences. They underline the word in brackets that best completes the sentence.

WORD WORKERS 4 UNIT 2.10

Name .... Date ....

Read these words.

seem seems seemed seeming	reached reaches reaching reach	screaming screams scream screamed	toasts toast toasted toasting
green greener greenest	nearest nearer near	weaker weak weakest	plain plainest plainer
beat beaten	cheapen cheap	sweeten sweet	weak weaken

Complete the words by writing the vowel sounds.

ai	ay	ea	ee	ie	oa
h *ai* l	w *ay*	s *ea* t	fr *ee*	t *ie* s	r *oa* d
ai m	pl *ay*	f *ea* st	st *ee* p	p *ie*	c *oa* st
g *ai* n	str *ay*	p *ea* ch	sh *ee* t	l *ie*	thr *oa* t
p *ai* d	m *ay*	w *ea* k	sw *ee* p	d *ie*	t *oa* st
pl *ai* n	sw *ay*	dr *ea* m	qu *ee* n	tr *ie* d	c *oa* t

36

Activity 1: Students read the words in the boxes. Tell them to add the endings to the smallest word or base word.

Activity 2: Students complete the words by writing in the letters printed above each column.

WORD WORKERS 4 — UNIT 2.11

Name .... Date ....

Draw a line to the word with the same word pattern.

feet	deer	lie	cue	paid	toad
stay	sweet	need	die	float	bleach
toast	pray	due	wail	mean	maid
bead	coast	tail	green	road	throat
queer	lead	seen	speed	reach	bean

Complete these sentences by writing the words for the pictures.

1. Jean tied the **goat** to the tree with a chain.
2. Gail was too weak to speak to the **queen** .
3. They had seen the deer in the **trees** near the creek.
4. 'It may **rain** ,' Dean said. 'So I think I will bring my coat.'
5. A **snail** is eating the green leaf.

© 2000 H.A. Calder and Pascal Press 37

Activity 1: Students look at the two columns of words in each box. They draw a line from the word in the left-hand column to the word in the right-hand column that has the same word pattern.

Activity 2: Students look at the pictures and then complete the sentences below by writing the correct word for the picture in the space provided.

WORD WORKERS 4 — UNIT 2.12

Name .... Date ....

Write the word for these jumbled letters.
The first letters are underlined.

nees	**seen**	eapl	**leap**	peesh	**sheep**
drea	**dear**	ude	**due**	iel	**lie**
rayst	**stray**	dmai	**maid**	troath	**throat**
aibrn	**brain**	neescr	**screen**	psear	**spear**

Underline the *two* words that have the same word pattern as the picture.

cream	tree	see	least
coast	raid	reach	roast
cue	pie	toe	lie
drain	stray	strain	aim
near	peep	squeak	creep

38 © 2000 H.A. Calder and Pascal Press

Activity 1: Students make a word from the jumbled letters. The first letter of each word is underlined. Students write the words in the spaces provided.

Activity 2: Students look at the pictures and the words on the lines beside them. They underline the two words in each line that have the same word pattern as the picture.

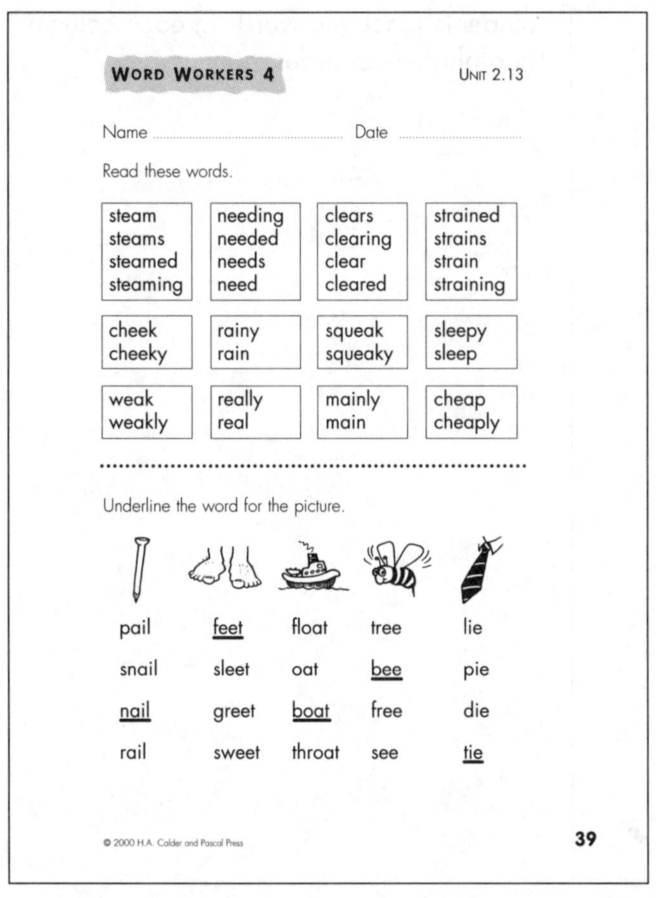

WORD WORKERS 4 UNIT 2.13

Name .... Date ....

Read these words.

steam steams steamed steaming	needing needed needs need	clears clearing clear cleared	strained strains strain straining
cheek cheeky	rainy rain	squeak squeaky	sleepy sleep
weak weakly	really real	mainly main	cheap cheaply

Underline the word for the picture.

pail	feet	float	tree	lie
snail	sleet	oat	bee	pie
nail	greet	boat	free	die
rail	sweet	throat	see	tie

© 2000 H.A. Calder and Pascal Press 39

Activity 1: Students now have to read words learned in this unit containing the 'y' ending. In these words, the letter 'y' says the long 'e' sound.

Students also have to read words learned in this unit containing the 'ly' ending. In these words, the letter 'y' says the long 'e' sound.

Activity 2: Students look at the columns of words. They underline the word in each column that matches the picture above it.

WORD WORKERS 4 UNIT 2.14

Name .... Date ....

Write the word from each column that fits the word shape box.

seem	cheap	toad	maid
feed	steal	coast	day
cheer	least	road	pray
deep	sneak	boast	gain
deep	least	road	pray

Underline the correct word to complete the sentence.

1. The boat floated in the (bay/stay) just off the coast of Spain.
2. Lee cleared her throat but she still could not (sneak/speak).
3. Mrs Weeks said, 'This (flea/tea) is too sweet.'
4. The sheep had a sleep under the (free/tree) next to the creek.
5. Mr Reed did not eat the (peach/bleach) pie.

40 © 2000 H.A. Calder and Pascal Press

Activity 1: Students look at the columns of words. Tell them to put the word from each column that fits into the 'word shape' box below it.

Activity 2: Students read the sentences. They underline the word in brackets that best completes the sentence.

Word Workers 4 Unit 2.15

Name .... Date ....

Put each column in alphabetical order.

ai		ay		ea	
main	*laid*	way	*play*	deal	*beach*
laid	*main*	stray	*pray*	beach	*beak*
plain	*paid*	play	*ray*	fear	*cheap*
rail	*plain*	ray	*stray*	beak	*deal*
paid	*rail*	pray	*way*	cheap	*fear*

ee		oa	
heel	*fleet*	throat	*croak*
fleet	*free*	soap	*goat*
keep	*green*	toast	*soap*
green	*heel*	croak	*throat*
free	*keep*	goat	*toast*

 41

Students place the words in each column in alphabetical order.

Word Workers 4 Unit 2.16

Name .... Date ....

Complete these crossword puzzles.

ai: train, pail, strain, nail, snail

ay: play, sway, pay, clay, stray

ea: yea, cheat, scream, seal, year, steals

oa: toast, croaks, road, soa(s), coast, throat

ee: cheers, seet, peel, peed, deep

42

Students complete the crossword puzzles. They write the letters indicated in the blank spaces to make words that can be read going down or across the page.

WORD WORKERS 4 UNIT 2.17

Name .... Date ....

Write the word with the correct spelling.

1. wheal wheel whell *wheel*
2. roest rost roast *roast*
3. stray srayt straiy *stray*
4. sope soap stoap *soap*
5. peach pech peech *peach*

Fill in the missing letters to complete the word.

1. *c* ree *k*	cried
2. *c* haine *d*	cheering
3. *c* heerin *g*	chained
4. *c* rie *d*	played
5. *p* laye *d*	creek

 43

Activity 1: Students read the words going across the page, then write the word that is spelt correctly.

Activity 2: Students read the words in the box, then write the missing letters to complete the column of words on the left.

WORD WORKERS 4 UNIT 2.18

Name .... Date ....

Underline the word for the picture.

goat goats queen queens tree trees

chain chains nail nails bee bees

Complete the sentences with the words from the box.

jeans	trees	beach	boat	teacher

1. The class will say the *teacher* is straining their brains.
2. They went sailing in the *boat* for six weeks.
3. Dean's *jeans* got soaked in the rain.
4. Gail had a meal near the three *trees* .
5. Mr and Mrs Steel will go to the *beach* this year.

44

Activity 1: Students underline the singular word if there is one object pictured or the plural word if there are two or more objects pictured.

Activity 2: Students complete the sentences by writing the correct word from the box in the space provided.

WORD WORKERS 4 UNIT 2.19

Name .... Date ....

Draw a line from the picture to the matching word.

meat / treat / beat — reach / bleach / peach

meet / feet / greet — spear / tear / ear

Number the words in the box in alphabetical order, then answer the questions.

6 eat	2 bleed	3 chain
4 cheer	5 dear	1 beak

1. Which word comes *before* 'bleed'? **beak**
2. Which word comes *after* 'dear'? **eat**
3. Which word comes *before* 'cheer'? **chain**
4. Which word comes *after* 'beak'? **bleed**
5. Which word comes *before* 'eat'? **dear**
6. Which word comes *after* 'chain'? **cheer**

 45

Activity 1: Students say the word for the picture and then draw a line from the picture to the correct word beside it.

Activity 2: Students number the words in the box in alphabetical order, then use this information to answer the questions below.

WORD WORKERS 4 UNIT 2.20

Read the story.

The Boat at the Creek

'I do not feel like getting up,' Lee Reed said. 'I do not feel like going to school. I will tell mum that I do not feel well. She will tell me to stay in bed all day. But I do not feel like staying in bed. That is no fun. So, when mum goes out, I will sneak down to the creek and play.'

Lee's mum said, 'O.K. Lee, you do not have to go to school, but you must stay in bed all day!' So Lee stayed in bed, reading and playing with her dolls. She waited for Mrs Reed to go out.

It was a clear day. The hot sun beat down. At the creek the bees were buzzing. The toads were croaking. The sheep were eating green grass. Mr Weeks was fishing in his little boat. He tied it to a tree with a chain and went to have a cup of tea.

46

For the following pages:

Students read the story. They read it several times until accuracy and fluency combine to improve comprehension.

At last Mrs Reed went out. 'I am going to get some meat for dinner,' she said to Lee. 'You must sleep till I get back.' When she left, Lee ran down the path to the creek. No-one saw her sneak out of the house. Not the buzzing bees. Not the croaking toads. Not the sheep eating grass. Not Mr Weeks who was drinking his cup of tea.

Down at the creek the little boat floated in the stream. Lee got in it and slipped the chain off the tree. The boat floated down the creek. It went faster and faster. Lee did not like that at all. It was going way too fast. 'Help' she screamed. 'Help! Help!' Then Lee tried to jump out of the boat. She hit her toe and tripped. Splash! Into the creek she went. 'Help!' she cried weakly as she splashed in the stream.

Mr Weeks put his hand to his ear. 'I hear a scream,' he said. He dropped his cup of tea and ran down to the creek. There was Lee Reed. She was getting weaker and weaker. Mr Weeks reached out with a long branch. Lee grabbed it.

Then Mr Weeks dragged her out of the creek.

Lee was soaking wet. Now she really did feel sick. 'I feel like I drank all the creek,' she said. Mr Weeks helped her back up the trail to her house. Mrs Reed was on the steps looking for Lee. Then she saw her with Mr Weeks. She waited for them to get up to the house.

'Well Lee,' she said. 'I see you had a swim. Look at you. You are soaked! Thank you Mr Weeks for bringing Lee back. Now I will put her in bed — after she has a long bath.' And Mrs Reed did just that. But then Lee really did get sick. She had to stay in bed all week. When she got better, she did not play in the creek... not without her mum and her dad.

Students read the story. They read it several times until accuracy and fluency combine to improve comprehension.

WORD WORKERS 4 UNIT 2.23

Name .... Date ....

Write the letters 'a', 'b', 'c' and 'd' in the same order the pictures occurred in the story.

a b c d

1. *d* 2. *b* 3. *a* 4. *c*

Fill in the blank with the exact word from the story.

1. Lee Reed did not *feel* like going to school.
2. Mrs Reed went out to get some *meat* for dinner.
3. No-one saw Lee *sneak* out of the house.
4. Mr Weeks reached Lee with a long *branch*.
5. Then Lee really did get sick; she had to stay in bed all *week*.

© 2000 H.A. Calder and Pascal Press 49

Activity 1: Students sequence the events in the story by placing the pictures in their correct order.

Activity 2: Students complete these sentences using the exact word from the story.

WORD WORKERS 4 UNIT 2.24

Name .... Date ....

Fill in the blanks with the correct word from the box.

Mr Weeks put his hand to his *ear*. 'I hear a scream,' he said. He dropped his cup of tea and ran down to the *creek*. There was Lee Reed. She was *getting* weaker and weaker. Mr Weeks *reached* out with a long branch. Lee grabbed it. Then Mr Weeks *dragged* her out of the creek.

creek ear reached dragged getting

Write the letters 'a', 'b', 'c' and 'd' beside the sentences in the same order they occurred in the story.

1. Lee tried to jump out of the boat. *c*
2. Mr Weeks reached out with a long branch. *d*
3. Lee stayed in bed, reading and playing with her dolls. *a*
4. Mr Weeks was fishing in his little boat. *b*

50 © 2000 H.A. Calder and Pascal Press

Activity 1: Students complete this cloze exercise using the words from the box.

Activity 2: Students sequence the events in the story by placing them in their correct order.

* Students complete *Word Workers Achievement Test 4* after completing this unit.

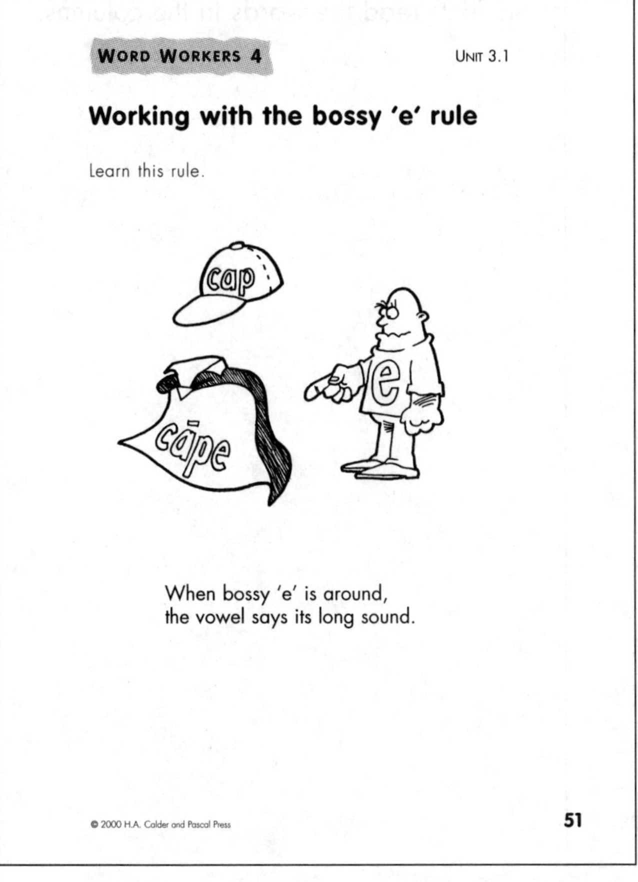

WORD WORKERS 4 UNIT 3.1

Working with the bossy 'e' rule

Learn this rule.

When bossy 'e' is around,
the vowel says its long sound.

© 2000 H.A. Calder and Pascal Press 51

For the following pages:

Teach the vowel–consonant–final 'e' rule carefully and have students repeat it until it is learned satisfactorily.

From now on, incorporate repetition of the vowel–consonant–final 'e' rule in the phonics drill at the start of each lesson.

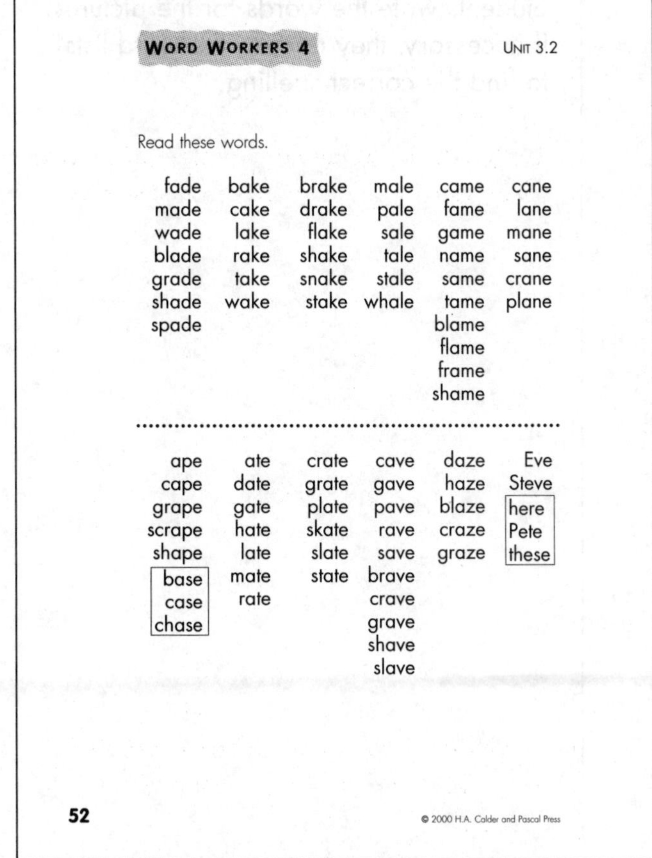

WORD WORKERS 4 UNIT 3.2

Read these words.

fade	bake	brake	male	came	cane
made	cake	drake	pale	fame	lane
wade	lake	flake	sale	game	mane
blade	rake	shake	tale	name	sane
grade	take	snake	stale	same	crane
shade	wake	stake	whale	tame	plane
spade				blame	
				flame	
				frame	
				shame	

ape	ate	crate	cave	daze	Eve
cape	date	grate	gave	haze	Steve
grape	gate	plate	pave	blaze	here
scrape	hate	skate	rave	craze	Pete
shape	late	slate	save	graze	these
base	mate	state	brave		
case	rate		crave		
chase			grave		
			shave		
			slave		

52 © 2000 H.A. Calder and Pascal Press

Students read the words in the columns.

WORD WORKERS 4 UNIT 3.3

Read these words.

ride	life	bike	file	lime	fine
side	wife	hike	pile	time	nine
tide	strife	like	tile	crime	pine
wide		spike	smile	grime	shine
bride		strike	while	prime	twine
pride				slime	whine

pipe	fire	rise	bite	dive
ripe	hire	wise	kite	five
wipe	tire	size	spite	live
snipe	wire		white	drive
swipe	spire			strive
stripe				

joke	hole	bone	hope	nose	cove
poke	pole	cone	mope	hose	wove
woke	role	lone	rope	rose	drove
choke	sole	tone	scope	chose	stove
smoke	stole	prone	slope	close	doze
spoke	code	stone		those	froze
stroke	rode	home		note	

cube	dune	cure	cute	duke
tube	tune	pure	mute	fume
				fuse
				mule

 53

Students read the words in the columns.

WORD WORKERS 4 UNIT 3.4

Name .... Date ....

Write the words for the pictures.

1. *cake* 2. *bone* 3. *pipe*

4. *bike* 5. *five* 6. *snake*

7. *nose* 8. *whale* 9. *kite*

10. *nine* 11. *spade* 12. *rake*

54

Students write the words for the pictures. If necessary, they refer to the word lists to find the correct spelling.

WORD WORKERS 4 UNIT 3.5

Name .... Date ....

Read these words.

bake bakes baked baking	flames flamed flaming flame	joking joked joke jokes	saved saves save saving
likes liking like liked	whining whine whined whines	blames blame blaming blamed	wiped wipe wiping wipes

Underline the word for the picture.

hike	base	rode	skate	pine
pipe	lake	pole	wave	drive
wise	chase	nose	blaze	bite
five	gate	scope	rave	strife

 55

Activity 1: Students read the words in the boxes. Tell them to add the endings to the smallest word or base word.

Activity 2: Students look at the columns of words. They underline the word in each column that matches the picture above it.

WORD WORKERS 4 UNIT 3.6

Name .... Date ....

Underline the nonsense word.

1. bake	2. white	3. joke	4. pave	5. frame
flake	kite	ploke	drave	game
wake	pite	choke	shave	chame
crake	bite	spoke	brave	name

Write the words for the pictures.

1. *bones* 2. *wave* 3. *pipes*

4. *bike* 5. *whale* 6. *roses*

7. *kite* 8. *spades* 9. *cave*

56

Activity 1: Students look at the columns of words. Tell them to underline the word in each column that is a nonsense word.

Activity 2: Students write the words for the pictures. Tell them to add the letter 's' if there is more than one. If necessary, they refer to the word lists to find the correct spelling.

WORD WORKERS 4 UNIT 3.7

Name .... Date ....

Complete these words with the word pattern from the picture.

p ave	n ose	m ake	wh ine	st one
sh ave	h ose	sh ake	v ine	l one
g ave	ch ose	fl ake	sh ine	t one
br ave	p ose	w ake	f ine	c one

Underline the correct word to complete the sentence.

1. Dave ate the (rake/cake) Mrs Jones baked.
2. After the (game/name) Jane rode home on her bike.
3. Mr James and his wife (drove/stove) past the lake.
4. The man broke his (chose/nose) when he fell in the hole.
5. Mrs Lane left the grapes on top of the (crate/state).

© 2000 H.A. Calder and Pascal Press 57

Activity 1: Students look at the pictures above the columns. They use the word pattern from each picture to complete the words in the column below.

Activity 2: Students read the sentences. They underline the word in brackets that best completes the sentence.

WORD WORKERS 4 UNIT 3.8

Name .... Date ....

Read these words.

blaze blazes blazed blazing	cure cures curing cured	hopes hoping hope hoped	tired tires tiring tire
cuter cute cutest	palest pale paler	white whitest whiter	stalest staler stale
ripe ripen	froze frozen	taken take	stolen stole

Complete the words by writing the vowel sounds.

a	e	i	o	u
sh a ve	P e te	p i ne	w o ve	c u te
c a se	E ve	sp i ke	ch o ke	m u te
gr a de	St e ve	wh i te	l o ne	d u ne
sh a ke	th e se	sh i ne	n o te	d u ke
wh a le	h e re	d i ve	h o me	t u ne

58 © 2000 H.A. Calder and Pascal Press

Activity 1: Students read the words in the boxes. Tell them to add the endings to the smallest word or base word.

Activity 2: Students complete the words by writing in the letter printed above each column.

WORD WORKERS 4 UNIT 3.9

Name .... Date ....

Draw a line to the word with the same word pattern.

fade	stone	crime	shave	rode	wise
side	blade	stale	choke	rise	code
slope	white	joke	state	tame	shake
kite	hope	gave	lime	flake	cape
lone	bride	rate	pale	shape	frame

Complete these sentences by writing the words for the pictures.

1. Mr Blake left his ***spade*** next to the gate.
2. The bride scraped the ***cake*** off her plate.
3. Mrs White chased the ***snake*** with a rake.
4. Steve rode his bike into the ***cave*** .
5. Mike's dog put the ***bone*** into the hole it dug.

 59

Activity 1: Students look at the two columns of words in each box. They draw a line from the word in the left-hand column to the word in the right-hand column that has the same word pattern.

Activity 2: Students look at the pictures and then complete the sentences below by writing the correct word for the picture in the space provided.

WORD WORKERS 4 UNIT 3.10

Name .... Date ....

Write the word for these jumbled letters.
The first letters are underlined.

sohe	***hose***	diwe	***wide***	tibe	***bite***
etad	***date***	tmae	***tame***	satte	***state***
driep	***pride***	seno	***nose***	reka	***rake***
veas	***save***	chesa	***chase***	edam	***made***

Underline the *two* words that have the same word pattern as the picture.

strike	pine	wise	hike
grade	save	fame	gave
mate	chase	slate	lane
smile	ripe	swipe	pride
blaze	came	pale	stale

60

Activity 1: Students make a word from the jumbled letters. The first letter of each word is underlined. Students write the words in the spaces provided.

Activity 2: Students look at the pictures and the words on the lines beside them. They underline the two words in each line that have the same word pattern as the picture.

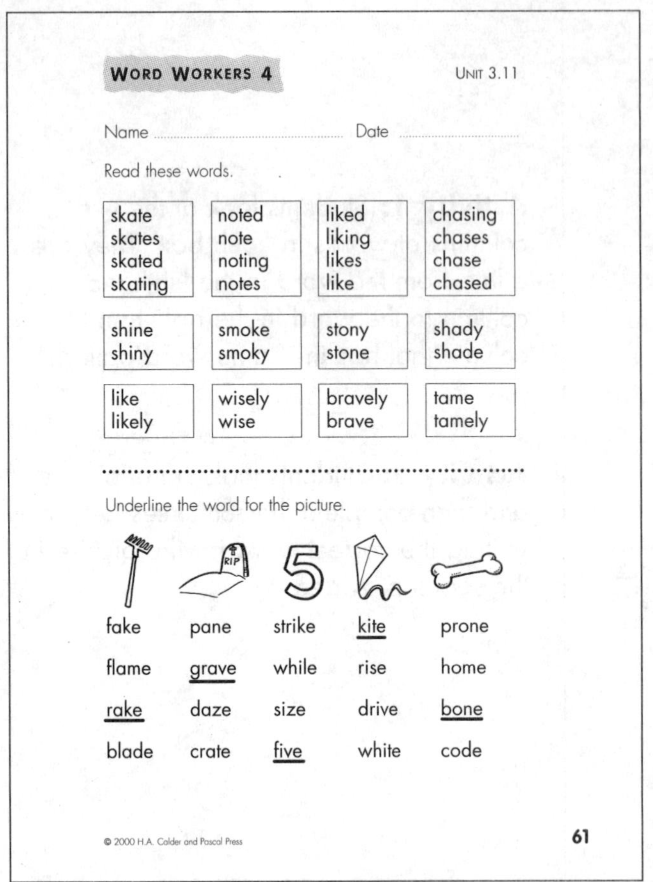

WORD WORKERS 4 UNIT 3.11

Name .... Date ....

Read these words.

skate skates skated skating	noted note noting notes	liked liking likes like	chasing chases chase chased
shine shiny	smoke smoky	stony stone	shady shade
like likely	wisely wise	bravely brave	tame tamely

Underline the word for the picture.

fake	pane	strike	kite	prone
flame	grave	while	rise	home
rake	daze	size	drive	bone
blade	crate	five	white	code

© 2000 H.A. Calder and Pascal Press 61

Activity 1: Students read the words in the boxes. Tell them to add the endings to the smallest word or base word.

Activity 2: Students look at the columns of words. They underline the word in each column that matches the picture above it.

WORD WORKERS 4 UNIT 3.12

Name .... Date ....

Write the word from each column that fits the word shape box.

stake	fine	grate	poke
cake	whine	plate	broke
flake	nine	gate	woke
bake	twine	crate	smoke

flake whine crate poke

Underline the correct word to complete the sentence.

1. 'I hope I am not too (plate/late),' Mrs Stone said.
2. Mr Baker (cave/gave) his wife a bunch of roses.
3. Kate sat in the shade under the (pine/line) tree.
4. The dog whined while it sat by the (tide/side) gate.
5. Jake blamed Pete when the rake was (spoken/broken).

62 © 2000 H.A. Calder and Pascal Press

Activity 1: Students look at the columns of words. Tell them to put the word from each column that fits into the 'word shape' box below it.

Activity 2: Students read the sentences. They underline the word in brackets that best completes the sentence.

WORD WORKERS 4 UNIT 3.13

Name .... Date ....

Put each column in alphabetical order.

a		e		i	
crane	*brave*	Pete	*Eve*	wire	*rise*
brave	*crane*	Eve	*here*	strive	*spike*
game	*date*	these	*Pete*	twine	*strive*
date	*game*	Steve	*Steve*	spike	*twine*
grade	*grade*	here	*these*	rise	*wire*

o		u	
scope	*home*	tube	*cure*
rose	*prone*	cure	*cute*
prone	*rose*	dune	*duke*
stove	*scope*	cute	*dune*
home	*stove*	duke	*tube*

 63

Students place the words in each column in alphabetical order.

WORD WORKERS 4 UNIT 3.14

Name .... Date ....

Complete these crossword puzzles.

a: blames, plate, shave, lead, scale

e: these, Pete, Steve, eve, here

i: wise, shine, whine, line, bride

o: notes, drove, slope, spoke, slope

u: cube, mute, dune, duke, tune

64

Students complete the crossword puzzles. They write the letter indicated in the blank spaces to make words that can be read going down or across the page.

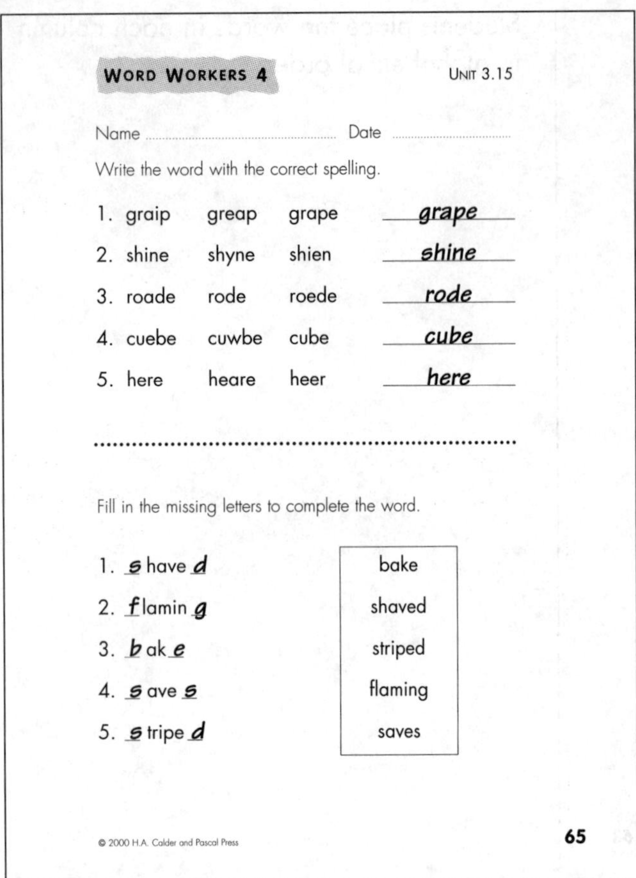

WORD WORKERS 4 UNIT 3.15

Name .... Date ....

Write the word with the correct spelling.

1. graip greap grape ___grape___
2. shine shyne shien ___shine___
3. roade rode roede ___rode___
4. cuebe cuwbe cube ___cube___
5. here heare heer ___here___

....

Fill in the missing letters to complete the word.

1. _s_ have _d_	bake
2. _f_ lamin _g_	shaved
3. _b_ ak _e_	striped
4. _s_ ave _s_	flaming
5. _s_ tripe _d_	saves

© 2000 H.A. Calder and Pascal Press 65

Activity 1: Students read the words going across the page, then write the word that is spelt correctly.

Activity 2: Students read the words in the box, then write the missing letters to complete the column of words on the left.

WORD WORKERS 4 UNIT 3.16

Name .... Date ....

Underline the word for the picture.

whale whales spade spades rose roses

bike bikes wave waves bone bones

....

Complete the sentences with the words from the box.

white	gave	grapes	rode	grade

1. Steve ___gave___ his skates to Pete.
2. Mrs Jones chose the ___white___ rose.
3. We ate the ___grapes___ in the boat at the lake.
4. Next year Jake will be in the sixth ___grade___.
5. Dale smiled while she ___rode___ her bike home.

66 © 2000 H.A. Calder and Pascal Press

Activity 1: Students underline the singular word if there is one object pictured or the plural word if there are two or more objects pictured.

Activity 2: Students complete the sentences by writing the correct word from the box in the space provided.

WORD WORKERS 4 UNIT 3.17

Name .... Date ....

Draw a line from the picture to the matching word.

	rave pave grave		chose rose hose
	bike spike hike		vine spine nine

Number the words in the box in alphabetical order, then answer the questions.

2 prime	5 stone	3 ripe
4 shake	6 time	1 plane

1. Which word comes *after* 'stone'? time
2. Which word comes *after* 'ripe'? shake
3. Which word comes *before* 'prime'? plane
4. Which word comes *after* 'shake'? stone
5. Which word comes *after* 'plane'? prime
6. Which word comes *before* 'shake'? ripe

 67

Activity 1: Students say the word for the picture and then draw a line from the picture to the correct word beside it.

Activity 2: Students number the words in the box in alphabetical order, then use this information to answer the questions below.

WORD WORKERS 4 UNIT 3.18

Read the story.

No way, Jane Graves!

When she was just five years old Jane Graves said she would be a baseball player. But the boys said, 'No way, Jane Graves!' Now that she is nine, Jane still wants to play baseball. But the boys say to her, 'No way, Jane Graves. Girls do not play baseball!'

This made Jane mad. 'I can play the game. I can hit and catch better than you!' she would tell them. But the boys just smiled and said 'No way, Jane Graves, no way!' So Jane had to look on while the boys played.

Then, on a fine spring day, a boy came up and spoke to Jane. His name was Pete White. He was the best player on the team. 'Hi Jane,' Pete said, 'would you like to play in the game today?' Jane nearly choked. 'Me?' she said. 'You want me to play in a game?' 'Yes,' Pete said, 'if you play well you can play with us all the time.' Jane smiled at Pete. 'O.K.,' she said. 'I will play. At last I get to play in a real game!'

68

For the following pages:

Students read the story. They read it several times until accuracy and fluency combine to improve comprehension.

When the other team saw Jane, they said, 'Look — a girl. They are going to use a girl in the game. No way a girl can play. No way!' Pete White gave her a pat on the back. 'Come on Jane Graves,' he said. 'You can do it.'

After a while it was time for Jane to bat. She came up to home plate and tried to smile as the other team yelled at her. All she could hear was, 'No way, Jane Graves. No way!'

And there *was* no way. Not this time. It was three strikes and out. Jane's chin was on her chest when she came back to the bench. Pete White smiled and said, 'Bad luck Jane, you will do it next time.'

The game went on and on, and then it was Jane's last time at bat. The other team was leading by three runs. Jane had a lump in her throat when she came up to the plate. She tried not to let her hands shake.

'No way, Jane Graves. No way!' came the yell. Jane gritted her teeth. 'This time I *will* do it,' she said. Three of her team mates were on base. Jane had to drive them in with a home run to win the game. The pitch came in — strike one! The next pitch came in — strike two! 'No way, Jane Graves. No way!'

Then the next pitch came in. Jane swung at it — CRACK! The ball shot off her bat. It rose and rose in the sky. Jane had hit a home run. While she ran past each base her team mates cheered and cheered. Jane's home run let them win the game.

Pete White waited for Jane at home plate. He gave her a pat on the back. 'You did it this time Jane Graves. You really did,' he said. 'You made the team. You can really play the game.' Jane just smiled at him and said, 'See you next week Pete.' And she did. Jane played in lots of games. But after her big home run no-one on the other teams yelled, 'No way, Jane Graves. Girls do not play baseball!'

Students read the story. They read it several times until accuracy and fluency combine to improve comprehension.

WORD WORKERS 4 UNIT 3.21

Name .... Date ....

Write the letters 'a', 'b', 'c' and 'd' in the same order the pictures occurred in the story.

a b

c d

1. *b* 2. *a* 3. *c* 4. *d*

Fill in the blanks with the exact words from the story.

1. When she was just *five* years old Jane Graves wanted to be a baseball player.
2. *Pete White* asked Jane if she would like to play in a game.
3. The other team was leading by *three* runs.
4. The ball *shot* off Jane's bat.
5. Jane had hit a *home run* to win the game.

 71

Activity 1: Students sequence the events in the story by placing the pictures in their correct order.

Activity 2: Students complete these sentences using the exact word from the story.

WORD WORKERS 4 UNIT 3.22

Name .... Date ....

Fill in the blanks with the correct word from the box.

Then, on a *fine* spring day, a boy came up and spoke to Jane. His *name* was Pete White. He was the best player on the team. 'Hi Jane,' Pete said, 'would you like to play in the game today?' Jane nearly *choked*. 'Me?' she said. 'You want me to play in a game?' 'Yes,' Pete said, 'if you play well you can play with us all the *time*.' Jane smiled at Pete. 'O.K.,' she said. 'I will play. At last I get to play in a real *game*!'

name	fine	time	game	choked

Write the letters 'a', 'b', 'c' and 'd' beside the sentences in the same order they occurred in the story.

1. The other team was leading by three runs. *c*
2. Jane's chin was on her chest when she came back to the bench. *b*
3. Jane had hit a home run. *d*
4. Jane had to look on while the boys played. *a*

72

Activity 1: Students complete this cloze exercise using the words from the box.

Activity 2: Students sequence the events in the story by placing them in their correct order.

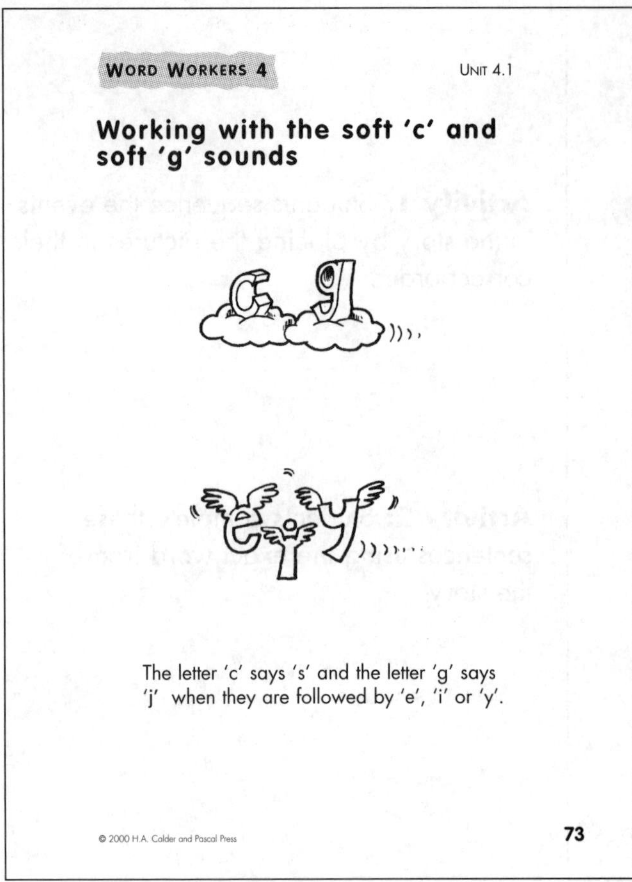

For the following pages:

Teach the soft 'c' and soft 'g' sounds by developing the grid as shown on page 22 of the *Word Workers Teacher Resource Book*.

From now on, incorporate knowledge of the soft 'c' and 'g' sounds in the phonics drill at the start of each lesson.

Tell students that some words they are to learn in this unit contain long vowel rules but do not conform to any of the rules they have learned. Explain that the letter 'y' in these words says the long 'i' sound and the words containing the 'ie' pattern say the long 'e' sound. Before starting the activity pages, give students practice reading the words.

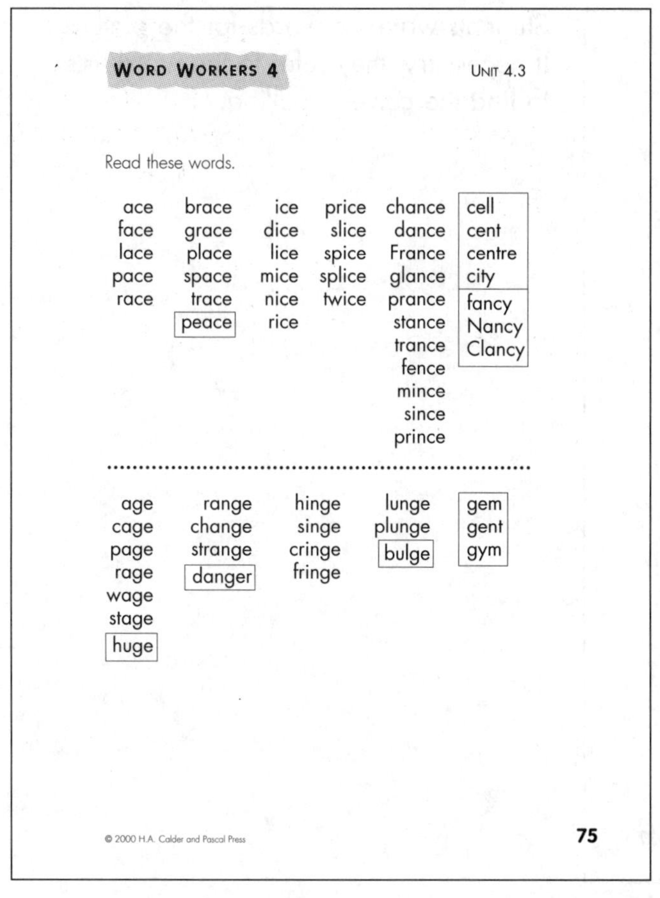

WORD WORKERS 4 UNIT 4.3

Read these words.

ace	brace	ice	price	chance	cell
face	grace	dice	slice	dance	cent
lace	place	lice	spice	France	centre
pace	space	mice	splice	glance	city
race	trace	nice	twice	prance	fancy
	peace	rice		stance	Nancy
				trance	Clancy
				fence	
				mince	
				since	
				prince	

age	range	hinge	lunge	gem
cage	change	singe	plunge	gent
page	strange	cringe	bulge	gym
rage	danger	fringe		
wage				
stage				
huge				

© 2000 H.A. Calder and Pascal Press 75

Students read the words in the columns.

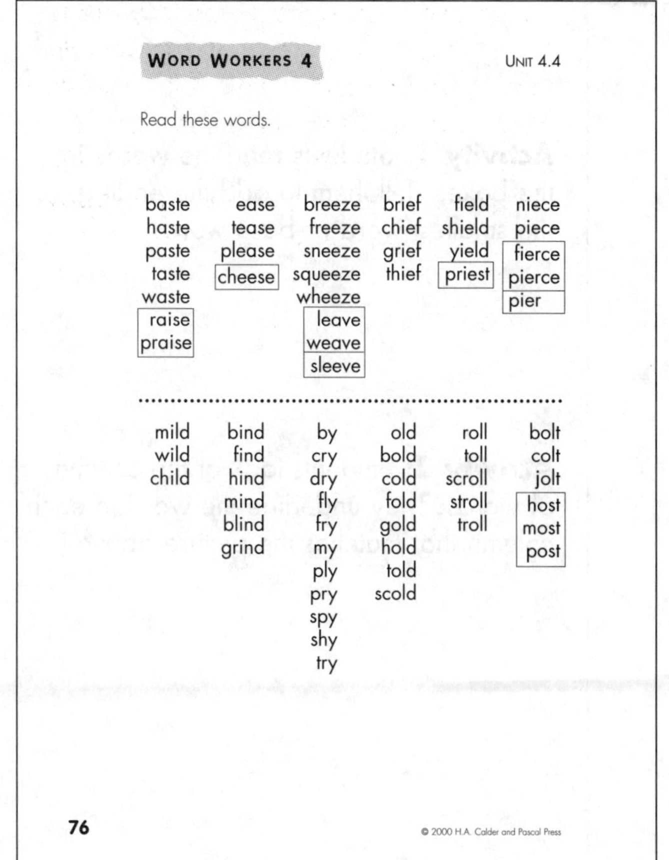

WORD WORKERS 4 UNIT 4.4

Read these words.

baste	ease	breeze	brief	field	niece
haste	tease	freeze	chief	shield	piece
paste	please	sneeze	grief	yield	fierce
taste	cheese	squeeze	thief	priest	pierce
waste		wheeze			pier
raise		leave			
praise		weave			
		sleeve			

mild	bind	by	old	roll	bolt
wild	find	cry	bold	toll	colt
child	hind	dry	cold	scroll	jolt
	mind	fly	fold	stroll	host
	blind	fry	gold	troll	most
	grind	my	hold		post
		ply	told		
		pry	scold		
		spy			
		shy			
		try			

76 © 2000 H.A. Calder and Pascal Press

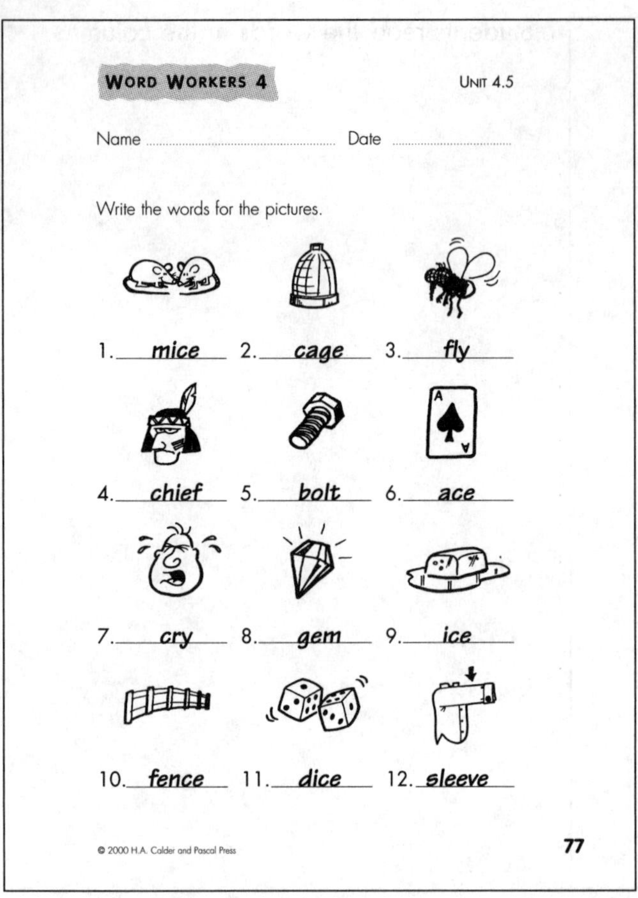

WORD WORKERS 4 UNIT 4.5

Name .... Date ....

Write the words for the pictures.

1. mice 2. cage 3. fly

4. chief 5. bolt 6. ace

7. cry 8. gem 9. ice

10. fence 11. dice 12. sleeve

© 2000 H.A. Calder and Pascal Press 77

Students write the words for the pictures. If necessary, they refer to the word lists to find the correct spelling.

WORD WORKERS 4 UNIT 4.6

Name .... Date ....

Read these words.

race races raced racing	teased teases teasing tease	bolts bolt bolting bolted	sneezed sneezing sneezes sneeze
danced dancing dance dances	change changed changes changing	rolling roll rolls rolled	minded mind minding minds

Underline the word for the picture.

please	chance	twice	<u>stage</u>	thief
sneeze	<u>dance</u>	spice	rage	grief
tease	stance	<u>dice</u>	cage	<u>chief</u>
<u>cheese</u>	glance	rice	wage	brief

78 © 2000 H.A. Calder and Pascal Press

Activity 1: Students read the words in the boxes. Tell them to add the endings to the smallest word or base word.

Activity 2: Students look at the columns of words. They underline the word in each column that matches the picture above it.

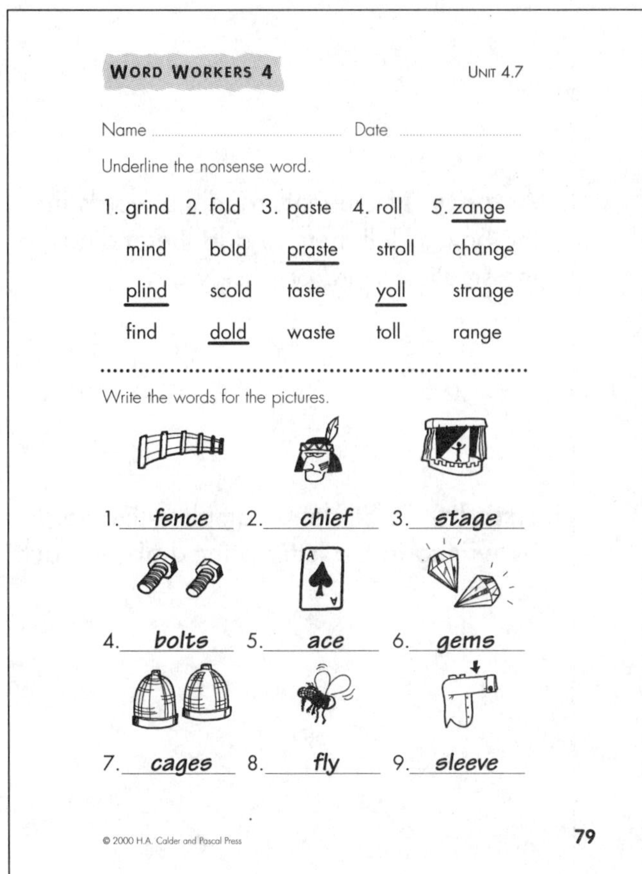

WORD WORKERS 4 UNIT 4.7

Name .... Date ....

Underline the nonsense word.

1. grind	2. fold	3. paste	4. roll	5. zange
mind	bold	praste	stroll	change
plind	scold	taste	yoll	strange
find	dold	waste	toll	range

Write the words for the pictures.

1. fence 2. chief 3. stage

4. bolts 5. ace 6. gems

7. cages 8. fly 9. sleeve

© 2000 H.A. Calder and Pascal Press 79

Activity 1: Students look at the columns of words. Tell them to underline the word in each column that is a nonsense word.

Activity 2: Students write the words for the pictures. Tell them to add the letter 's' if there is more than one. If necessary, they refer to the word lists to find the correct spelling.

WORD WORKERS 4 UNIT 4.8

Name .... Date ....

Complete these words with the word pattern from the picture.

pr ice	cr y	st age	pl ace	d ice
tw ice	sp y	c age	f ace	sp ice
n ice	b y	r age	br ace	r ice
sl ice	wh y	w age	sp ace	spl ice

Underline the correct word to complete the sentence.

1. The stranger was told twice that his change was ten (cents/gents).
2. Mr Page sneezed and wheezed when he had a bad (fold/cold).
3. The ranger had to hold the broken fence (post/host).
4. The little (mild/child) sat in the cold breeze.
5. The thief could not find the (face/place) where the gold was hidden.

80 © 2000 H.A. Calder and Pascal Press

Activity 1: Students look at the pictures above the columns. They use the word pattern from each picture to complete the words in the column below.

Activity 2: Students read the sentences. They underline the word in brackets that best completes the sentence.

WORD WORKERS 4 UNIT 4.9

Name .... Date ....

Read these words.

please pleases pleased pleasing	try tried trying tries	squeezes squeezed squeezing squeeze	tasting taste tastes tasted
fierce fiercer fiercest	wilder wildest wild	strangest strange stranger	nicer nice nicest
	old olden	golden gold	

Complete the words by writing the vowel sounds.

a	e	i	o	u
r *a* ise	ch *e* ese	m *i* ld	m *o* st	h *u* ge
f *a* ce	f *e* nce	r *i* ce	j *o* lt	l *u* nge
w *a* ge	g *e* nt	h *i* nge	sc *o* ld	b *u* lge
p *a* ste	l *e* ave	gr *i* nd	str *o* ll	pl *u* nge
ch *a* nge	c *e* ll	tw *i* ce	f *o* ld	

 81

Activity 1: Students read the words in the boxes. Tell them to add the endings to the smallest word or base word.

Activity 2: Students complete the words by writing in the letter printed above each column.

WORD WORKERS 4 UNIT 4.10

Name .... Date ....

Draw a line to the word with the same word pattern.

field	change	fierce	find	niece	scroll
raise	brace	thief	pierce	paste	wage
mild	shield	hind	grief	roll	slice
range	praise	lunge	glance	page	piece
lace	child	dance	plunge	rice	waste

Complete these sentences by writing the words for the pictures.

1. Nancy was too shy to dance on the *stage*.
2. Mr Rice made a face when he tasted the *cheese*.
3. Mrs Grace asked her niece to find the last *page* of the paper.
4. Most of the *ice* in the freezer had melted.
5. Clancy rolled the *dice* twice.

82

Activity 1: Students look at the two columns of words in each box. They draw a line from the word in the left-hand column to the word in the right-hand column that has the same word pattern.

Activity 2: Students look at the pictures and then complete the sentences below by writing the correct word for the picture in the space provided.

WORD WORKERS 4 UNIT 4.11

Name .... Date ....

Write the word for these jumbled letters.
The first letters are underlined.

grae	rage	testa	taste	llor	roll
dolt	told	ldich	child	dinf	find
nceda	dance	lyf	fly	cela	lace
cenie	niece	mots	most	brife	brief

Underline the *two* words that have the same word pattern as the picture.

sneeze grief roll thief

age lace fancy rage

spy mild why grind

host jolt colt hold

fence pierce stance glance

 83

Activity 1: Students make a word from the jumbled letters. The first letter of each word is underlined. Students write the words in the spaces provided.

Activity 2: Students look at the pictures and the words on the lines beside them. They underline the two words in each line that have the same word pattern as the picture.

WORD WORKERS 4 UNIT 4.12

Name .... Date ....

Read these words.

field fields fielded fielding	pasted pasting pastes paste	folds fold folding folded	fried frying fries fry
taste tasty	ice icy	breezy breeze	easy ease
nice nicely	blindly blind	briefly brief	wild wildly

Underline the word for the picture.

place	stage	weave	prince	fry
space	page	tease	fence	ply
face	age	sleeve	mince	spy
race	wage	leave	trance	fly

84

Activity 1: Students read the words in the boxes. Tell them to add the endings to the smallest word or base word.

Activity 2: Students look at the columns of words. They underline the word in each column that matches the picture above it.

WORD WORKERS 4 UNIT 4.13

Name .... Date ....

Write the word from each column that fits the word shape box.

brief	cell	huge	breeze
chief	centre	stage	sneeze
thief	city	wage	squeeze
grief	cent	page	wheeze

grief city huge squeeze

Underline the correct word to complete the sentence.

1. Nancy sliced the cake and put the (pieces/nieces) on a plate.
2. The blind man asked if he could (weave/leave) the city.
3. The spy was in danger, and this was his last (chance/glance) to get out of France.
4. The child (sneezed/squeezed) the tube of paste.
5. Grace asked her mum, 'Why do I have to (change/range) my coat?'

© 2000 H.A. Calder and Pascal Press 85

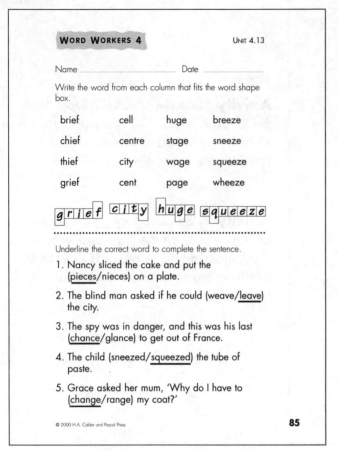

Activity 1: Students look at the columns of words. Tell them to put the word from each column that fits into the 'word shape' box below it.

Activity 2: Students read the sentences. They underline the word in brackets that best completes the sentence.

WORD WORKERS 4 UNIT 4.14

Name .... Date ....

Put each column in alphabetical order.

a		e		i	
waste	Clancy	tease	centre	find	child
place	place	cheese	cheese	child	find
Clancy	strange	gem	gem	splice	grind
wage	wage	centre	sleeve	vice	splice
strange	waste	sleeve	tease	grind	vice

o		u	
stroll	bolt	huge	bulge
gold	gold	bulge	huge
post	post	plunge	lunge
bolt	scold	lunge	plunge
scold	stroll		

86 © 2000 H.A. Calder and Pascal Press

Students place the words in each column in alphabetical order.

WORD WORKERS 4 UNIT 4.15

Name .... Date ....

Complete these crossword puzzles.

a: praise, tastes, place, strange, (down) taste, ... age
e: peace, fence, cent, freeze, tease
i: bind, blind, spice, ice, mild, spice
o: cool, colt, host, stroll, toll, hold
u: hunge, plunge, lunge, bulge, huge

 87

Students complete the crossword puzzles. They write the letter indicated in the blank spaces to make words that can be read going down or across the page.

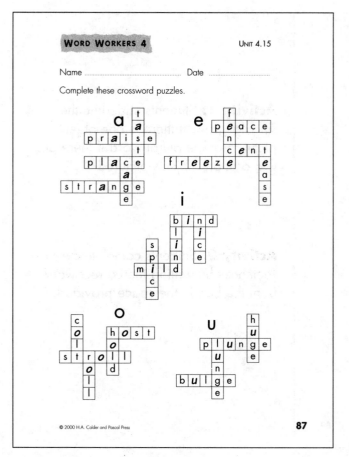

WORD WORKERS 4 UNIT 4.16

Name .... Date ....

Write the word with the correct spelling.

1. prinse prince prinze *prince*
2. strange strainge stranje *strange*
3. freaze freze freeze *freeze*
4. wild wield wilde *wild*
5. cheaf chief cheif *chief*

Fill in the missing letters to complete the word.

1. *d* ange *r*
2. *s* neezin *g*
3. *p* aste *d*
4. *n* icel *y*
5. *p* age *s*

pasted
pages
danger
sneezing
nicely

88

Activity 1: Students read the words going across the page, then write the word that is spelt correctly.

Activity 2: Students read the words in the box, then write the missing letters to complete the column of words on the left.

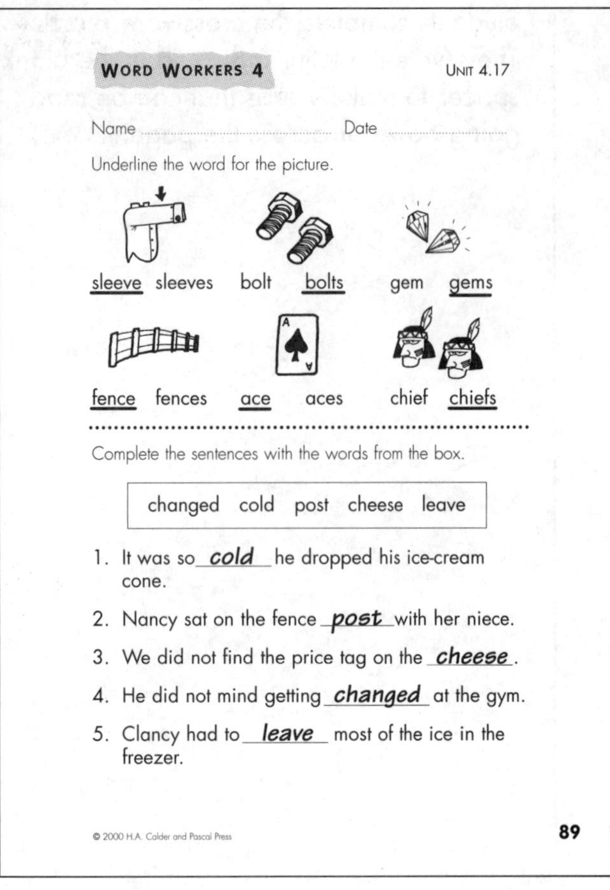

WORD WORKERS 4 UNIT 4.17

Name .... Date ....

Underline the word for the picture.

sleeve sleeves bolt bolts gem gems

fence fences ace aces chief chiefs

Complete the sentences with the words from the box.

changed cold post cheese leave

1. It was so *cold* he dropped his ice-cream cone.
2. Nancy sat on the fence *post* with her niece.
3. We did not find the price tag on the *cheese*.
4. He did not mind getting *changed* at the gym.
5. Clancy had to *leave* most of the ice in the freezer.

© 2000 H.A. Calder and Pascal Press 89

Activity 1: Students underline the singular word if there is one object pictured or the plural word if there are two or more objects pictured.

Activity 2: Students complete the sentences by writing the correct word from the box in the space provided.

WORD WORKERS 4 UNIT 4.18

Name .... Date ....

Draw a line from the picture to the matching word.

please / sneeze / cheese

since / prince / mince

race / place / grace

spice / twice / mice

Number the words in the box in alphabetical order, then answer the questions.

4 chance	*6* field	*2* breeze
1 bolt	*3* cage	*5* change

1. Which word comes *before* 'breeze'? *bolt*
2. Which word comes *after* 'cage'? *chance*
3. Which word comes *after* 'change'? *field*
4. Which word comes *after* 'chance'? *change*
5. Which word comes *before* 'cage'? *breeze*
6. Which word comes *after* 'breeze'? *cage*

90 © 2000 H.A. Calder and Pascal Press

Activity 1: Students say the word for the picture and then draw a line from the picture to the correct word beside it.

Activity 2: Students number the words in the box in alphabetical order, then use this information to answer the questions below.

For the following pages:

Students read the story. They read it several times until accuracy and fluency combine to improve comprehension.

Read the story.

Clancy's Colt

Clancy Page sat on the fence post while the three men led the colt into the ring. Its golden coat gleamed in the sun. The colt was wild. The men had to keep a strong hold on him. One of them was going to try to ride him.

The colt bucked fiercely. 'Take it easy!' the men yelled. They kept holding the rope. The colt reared up on his hind legs. Clancy Page could not keep still. 'Let me try,' he said. 'I can ride him!'

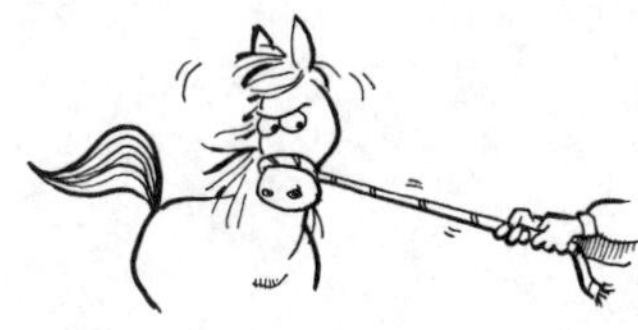

'Not a chance Clancy,' the men told him. 'Not at your age. You are just a child.' Clancy sat back on the fence post. One of the men jumped on the colt's back. He did not stay long. The colt was in a rage. He bucked wildly. The man shot off into the dust.

One by one the other men tried to ride the colt. One by one the wild colt left them with their faces in the dust. Clancy could not stand it. He went up to the boss. 'Let me try,' he said. 'I can ride that colt.'

Clancy's boss glanced down at him. He had a smile on his face. 'O.K. Clancy,' he said. 'Have a go at it. The others look like they are trying to fly!' Clancy did not waste time. He did not need to be told twice.

The colt was standing still now. His golden coat gleamed. He kept still as Clancy strolled up to him. 'Easy boy,' Clancy said. 'Keep nice and still.'

The men sat on the fence and looked at Clancy and the colt in the centre of the ring. 'The kid is in danger,' they said. The colt did not buck when Clancy patted him on the nose. That was strange — not one of them could do that. Had Clancy changed the colt?

And then Clancy was on the colt's back. The colt did not buck and rear wildly. He did not seem to mind Clancy on his back. Clancy Page was not in danger — not from the colt with the golden coat.

It did not take long for Clancy to train the colt. He was not wild when Clancy rode him. Clancy made up a name for the colt — Golden Chief. 'He is your colt now,' the boss told him. Then he looked at the other men. 'Not one of you could ride that colt,' he said. 'But Clancy Page did!' So off Clancy rode on his golden colt — the Golden Chief.

Students read the story. They read it several times until accuracy and fluency combine to improve comprehension.

Name .... Date ....

Write the letters 'a', 'b', 'c' and 'd' in the same order the pictures occurred in the story.

a b c d

1. *b* 2. *c* 3. *a* 4. *d*

Activity 1: Students sequence the events in the story by placing the pictures in their correct order.

Fill in the blank with the exact word from the story.

1. The men had to keep a strong *hold* on the colt.
2. 'Let me try,' Clancy said. 'I can *ride* him.'
3. The other men said that Clancy was just a *child* .
4. Clancy's boss said that the other men look like they are trying to *fly* .
5. The name Clancy made up for the colt was *Golden Chief* .

Activity 2: Students complete these sentences using the exact word from the story.

WORD WORKERS 4 UNIT 4.23

Name .... Date ....

Fill in the blanks with the correct word from the box.

One by one the other men tried to _ride_ the colt. One by one the wild colt left them with their _faces_ in the dust. Clancy could not stand it. He went up to the boss. 'Let me try,' he said. 'I can ride that colt.'

Clancy's boss _glanced_ down at him. He had a smile on his face. 'O.K. Clancy,' he said. 'Have a go at it. The others look like they are trying to _fly_ !' Clancy did not waste time. He did not need to be _told_ twice.

faces	ride	told	fly	glanced

Write the letters 'a', 'b', 'c' and 'd' beside the sentences in the same order they occurred in the story.

1. One of the men jumped on the colt's back. _b_
2. Clancy made up a name for the colt — Golden Chief. _d_
3. The colt reared up on his hind legs. _a_
4. The colt did not buck when Clancy patted him on the nose. _c_

 95

Activity 1: Students complete this cloze exercise using the words from the box.

Activity 2: Students sequence the events in the story by placing them in their correct order.

* Students complete *Word Workers Achievement Test 5* after completing this unit.

WORD WORKERS 4 UNIT 5.1

More work with words

Read these words.

1.	shack	sleeve	quite	due
2.	toe	huge	rope	rise
3.	wheel	trail	bench	fifth
4.	road	cute	clutch	bold
5.	raise	tree	mild	home
6.	brief	thank	when	swing
7.	wove	plunge	time	quest
8.	place	host	bunch	crash
9.	Pete	tie	slosh	lung
10.	stroll	cube	which	these
11.	gate	chest	quake	while
12.	soap	thump	chain	queen

96

For the following pages:

This unit consolidates the skills and phonic generalisations learned in the previous units.

Students read the words in the columns.

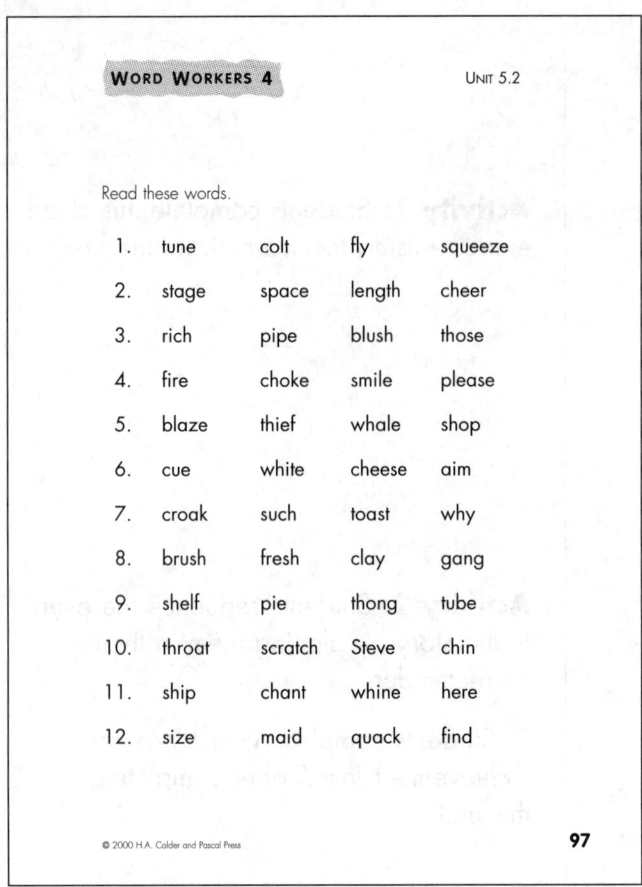

WORD WORKERS 4 UNIT 5.2

Read these words.

1.	tune	colt	fly	squeeze
2.	stage	space	length	cheer
3.	rich	pipe	blush	those
4.	fire	choke	smile	please
5.	blaze	thief	whale	shop
6.	cue	white	cheese	aim
7.	croak	such	toast	why
8.	brush	fresh	clay	gang
9.	shelf	pie	thong	tube
10.	throat	scratch	Steve	chin
11.	ship	chant	whine	here
12.	size	maid	quack	find

© 2000 H.A. Calder and Pascal Press 97

Students read the words in the columns.

WORD WORKERS 4 UNIT 5.3

Name .... Date ....

Write the words for the pictures.

1. *king* 2. *cake* 3. *queen*

4. *tree* 5. *fish* 6. *cry*

7. *toast* 8. *prince* 9. *chief*

10. *bone* 11. *chick* 12. *pipe*

98 © 2000 H.A. Calder and Pascal Press

Students write the words for the pictures. If necessary, they refer to the word lists to find the correct spelling.

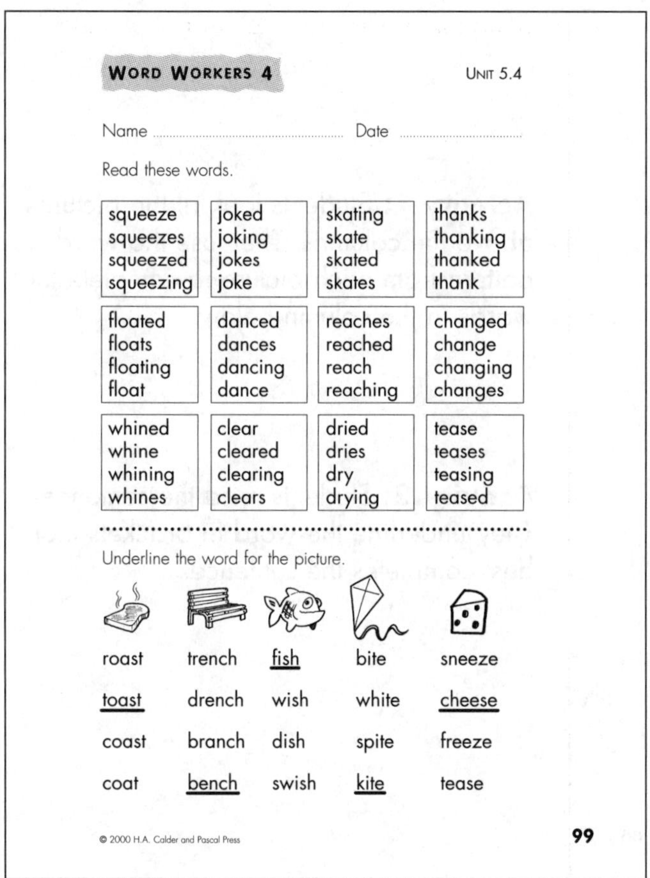

WORD WORKERS 4 UNIT 5.4

Name .... Date ....

Read these words.

squeeze squeezes squeezed squeezing	joked joking jokes joke	skating skate skated skates	thanks thanking thanked thank
floated floats floating float	danced dances dancing dance	reaches reached reach reaching	changed change changing changes
whined whine whining whines	clear cleared clearing clears	dried dries dry drying	tease teases teasing teased

Underline the word for the picture.

roast	trench	fish	bite	sneeze
toast	drench	wish	white	cheese
coast	branch	dish	spite	freeze
coat	bench	swish	kite	tease

© 2000 H.A. Calder and Pascal Press 99

Activity 1: Students read the words in the boxes. Tell them to add the endings to the smallest word or base word.

Activity 2: Students look at the columns of words. They underline the word in each column that matches the picture above it.

WORD WORKERS 4 UNIT 5.5

Name .... Date ....

Underline the nonsense word.

1. place	2. quest	3. beach	4. wove	5. breeze
thace	quit	teach	stove	squeeze
space	quick	neach	plove	streeze
trace	quimp	peach	drove	wheeze

Write the words for the pictures.

1. thongs 2. trees 3. cave

4. dice 5. snail 6. tie

7. fence 8. shell 9. roses

100 © 2000 H.A. Calder and Pascal Press

Activity 1: Students look at the columns of words. Tell them to underline the word in each column that is a nonsense word.

Activity 2: Students write the words for the pictures. Tell them to add the letter 's' if there is more than one. If necessary, they refer to the word lists to find the correct spelling.

WORD WORKERS 4 UNIT 5.6

Name .... Date ....

Complete these words with the word pattern from the picture.

pr _y_	p _ale_	b _oat_	h _ush_	st _one_
wh _y_	st _ale_	fl _oat_	bl _ush_	l _one_
sp _y_	t _ale_	g _oat_	cr _ush_	c _one_
fr _y_	m _ale_	thr _oat_	r _ush_	pr _one_

Underline the correct word to complete the sentence.

1. Dave had a milk (shake/flake) and a piece of cake.
2. Beth came home (state/late) from the beach.
3. All day long the men loaded the coal onto the (train/brain).
4. The gate squeaked as it swung in the strong (sneeze/breeze).
5. The old chief would not (leave/weave) his place in the shade.

© 2000 H.A. Calder and Pascal Press 101

Activity 1: Students look at the pictures above the columns. They use the word pattern from each picture to complete the words in the column below.

Activity 2: Students read the sentences. They underline the word in brackets that best completes the sentence.

WORD WORKERS 4 UNIT 5.7

Name .... Date ....

Read these words.

taste tastes tasted tasting	smoking smoked smokes smoke	gained gaining gains gain	scratch scratches scratching scratched
fierce fiercer fiercest	weaker weakest weak	whiter white whitest	strongest strong stronger
froze frozen	golden gold	shaken shake	thick thicken

Complete the words by writing the vowel sounds.

a	e	i	o	u
sh _a_ ke	squ _e_ ak	wh _i_ te	s _o_ ap	b _u_ lge
tr _a_ il	th _e_ se	f _i_ sh	ch _o_ ke	cl _u_ tch
b _a_ ng	l _e_ ngth	tr _i_ es	n _o_ tch	h _u_ ge
t _a_ ste	p _e_ ace	p _i_ nch	f _o_ ld	d _u_ e
ch _a_ nce	sl _e_ eve	tw _i_ ce	cr _o_ ak	c _u_ be

102 © 2000 H.A. Calder and Pascal Press

Activity 1: Students read the words in the boxes. Tell them to add the endings to the smallest word or base word.

Activity 2: Students complete the words by writing in the letter printed above each column.

WORD WORKERS 4 UNIT 5.8

Name .... Date ....

Draw a line to the word with the same word pattern.

shake	thong	cute	wise	dune	throat
hinge	queen	sheep	mute	host	queer
seen	cringe	rise	wheat	bite	most
niece	flake	lunge	steep	coat	tune
long	piece	cheat	plunge	cheer	white

Complete these sentences by writing the words for the pictures.

1. Nancy waited in the ___cave___ while the thunder crashed.
2. The queen blushed when the king gave her the golden ___ring___ .
3. Dean's mum told him to leave the ___cheese___ on the plate.
4. Dave chased the ___sheep___ out of the green field.
5. Ann did not hear the cheers while she danced on the ___stage___ .

 103

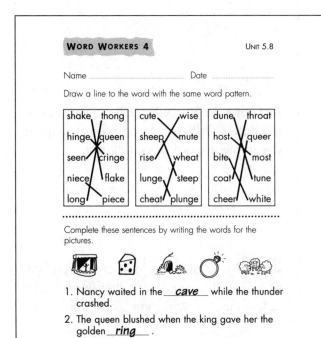

Activity 1: Students look at the two columns of words in each box. They draw a line from the word in the left-hand column to the word in the right-hand column that has the same word pattern.

Activity 2: Students look at the pictures and then complete the sentences below by writing the correct word for the picture in the space provided.

WORD WORKERS 4 UNIT 5.9

Name .... Date ....

Write the word for these jumbled letters.
The first letters are underlined.

ance<u>d</u>	***dance***	set<u>h</u>o	***those***	zae<u>b</u>l	***blaze***
<u>f</u>fee	***feet***	<u>s</u>hvea	***shave***	tie<u>w</u>h	***white***
ng<u>l</u>o	***long***	e<u>w</u>ave	***weave***	r<u>f</u>zoe	***froze***
<u>f</u>rie	***fire***	d<u>s</u>ol	***sold***	ge<u>h</u>u	***huge***

Underline the *two* words that have the same word pattern as the picture.

shape	<u>grace</u>	white	<u>space</u>
<u>sheet</u>	please	squeeze	<u>meet</u>
home	<u>those</u>	code	<u>chose</u>
<u>swipe</u>	shine	<u>ripe</u>	tide
page	<u>sail</u>	<u>mail</u>	praise

104

Activity 1: Students make a word from the jumbled letters. The first letter of each word is underlined. Students write the words in the spaces provided.

Activity 2: Students look at the pictures and the words on the lines beside them. They underline the two words in each line that have the same word pattern as the picture.

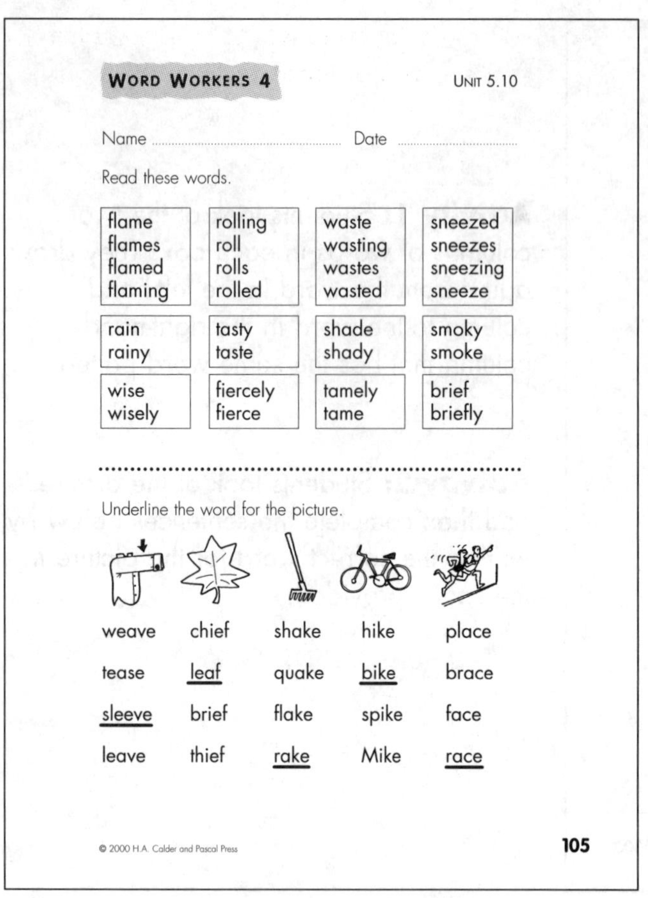

WORD WORKERS 4 UNIT 5.10

Name .... Date ....

Read these words.

flame flames flamed flaming	rolling roll rolls rolled	waste wasting wastes wasted	sneezed sneezes sneezing sneeze
rain rainy	tasty taste	shade shady	smoky smoke
wise wisely	fiercely fierce	tamely tame	brief briefly

Underline the word for the picture.

weave	chief	shake	hike	place
tease	<u>leaf</u>	quake	<u>bike</u>	brace
<u>sleeve</u>	brief	flake	spike	face
leave	thief	<u>rake</u>	Mike	<u>race</u>

© 2000 H.A. Calder and Pascal Press 105

Activity 1: Students read the words in the boxes. Tell them to add the endings to the smallest word or base word.

Activity 2: Students look at the columns of words. They underline the word in each column that matches the picture above it.

WORD WORKERS 4 UNIT 5.11

Name .... Date ....

Write the word from each column that fits the word shape box.

peach	niece	dune	soak
teach	fierce	huge	float
bleach	pierce	cube	road
reach	piece	cute	soap
reach	piece	huge	soap

Underline the correct word to complete the sentence.

1. Jake dropped the (mice/<u>ice</u>) cubes on the tray.
2. The thief (<u>stole</u>/pole) the gems that were locked in the safe.
3. The (<u>stranger</u>/danger) sat on the bench by the side of the road.
4. Jane broke a (peel/<u>wheel</u>) when she fell off her bike.
5. Mr and Mrs Smith went for a stroll on the (bath/<u>path</u>) by the lake.

106 © 2000 H.A. Calder and Pascal Press

Activity 1: Students look at the columns of words. Tell them to put the word from each column that fits into the 'word shape' box below it.

Activity 2: Students read the sentences. They underline the word in brackets that best completes the sentence.

WORD WORKERS 4 UNIT 5.12

Name .... Date ....

Put each column in alphabetical order.

a		e		i	
paste	*aim*	leave	*breeze*	white	*mind*
aim	*base*	cheek	*cheek*	tie	*size*
stray	*paste*	breeze	*leave*	size	*tie*
shave	*shave*	Pete	*Pete*	mind	*white*
base	*stray*	queen	*queen*	wild	*wild*

o		u	
froze	*coast*	huge	*bulge*
fold	*fold*	bulge	*cube*
post	*froze*	cube	*due*
toe	*post*	tune	*huge*
coast	*toe*	due	*tune*

© 2000 H.A. Calder and Pascal Press 107

Students place the words in each column in alphabetical order.

WORD WORKERS 4 UNIT 5.13

Name .... Date ....

Complete these crossword puzzles.

a: spray, shape, quakes, page, space

e: please, queer, trees, sneeze, rear

i: smiles, wild, fine, side, dice

o: coat, told, load, road, hoped

u: duke, huge, cube, cute, tune

108 © 2000 H.A. Calder and Pascal Press

Students complete the crossword puzzles. They write the letter indicated in the blank spaces to make words that can be read going down or across the page.

WORD WORKERS 4 UNIT 5.14

Name .... Date ....

Write the word with the correct spelling.

1. fancy fansy fancey *fancy*
2. stranje straneg strange *strange*
3. cheif chief cheef *chief*
4. quilt quillt qwilt *quilt*
5. squeaze squieze squeeze *squeeze*

Fill in the missing letters to complete the word.

1. *c* hangin *g*
2. *c* leare *d*
3. *s* tronges *t*
4. *f* roze *n*
5. *b* riefl *y*

strongest
changing
frozen
briefly
cleared

 109

Activity 1: Students read the words going across the page, then write the word that is spelt correctly.

Activity 2: Students read the words in the box, then write the missing letters to complete the column of words on the left.

WORD WORKERS 4 UNIT 5.15

Name .... Date ....

Underline the word for the picture.

cake cakes fish fishes snail snails

coat coats brush brushes tie ties

Complete the sentences with the words from the box.

train cake bath broken queen

1. Mr French ate a piece of the *cake* his wife baked.
2. The *queen* sat in the shade of the trees by the creek.
3. Mike changed the *broken* wheel on his bike.
4. My dad sloshes and splashes when he sings in the *bath*.
5. The man on the *train* gave his seat to Mrs Stone.

110

Activity 1: Students underline the singular word if there is one object pictured or the plural word if there are two or more objects pictured.

Activity 2: Students complete the sentences by writing the correct word from the box in the space provided.

WORD WORKERS 4 UNIT 5.16

Name .... Date ....

Draw a line from the picture to the matching word.

sleeve	bite
please	white
leave	kite

beach	glance
reach	dance
peach	prance

Number the words in the box in alphabetical order, then answer the questions.

1	maid	3	quick	5	raise
6	road	2	please	4	quit

1. Which word comes *after* 'raise'? *road*
2. Which word comes *before* 'quick'? *please*
3. Which word comes *after* 'please'? *quick*
4. Which word comes *after* 'quit'? *raise*
5. Which word comes *before* 'please'? *maid*
6. Which word comes *before* 'raise'? *quit*

 111

Activity 1: Students say the word for the picture and then draw a line from the picture to the correct word beside it.

Activity 2: Students number the words in the box in alphabetical order, then use this information to answer the questions below.

WORD WORKERS 4 UNIT 5.17

Read these words.

mad made	fed feed	cape cap	aim am	ride rid
ate at	wag wage	meet met	rod road	seat set
maid mad	pal pale	hop hope	beat bet	coast cost
steep step	cube cub	hug huge	pine pin	beast best
pad paid	bit bite	net neat	cute cut	pan pain

112

Students read the words in the boxes.

Students underline 'long' if the word has a long vowel sound or 'short' if it has a short vowel sound.

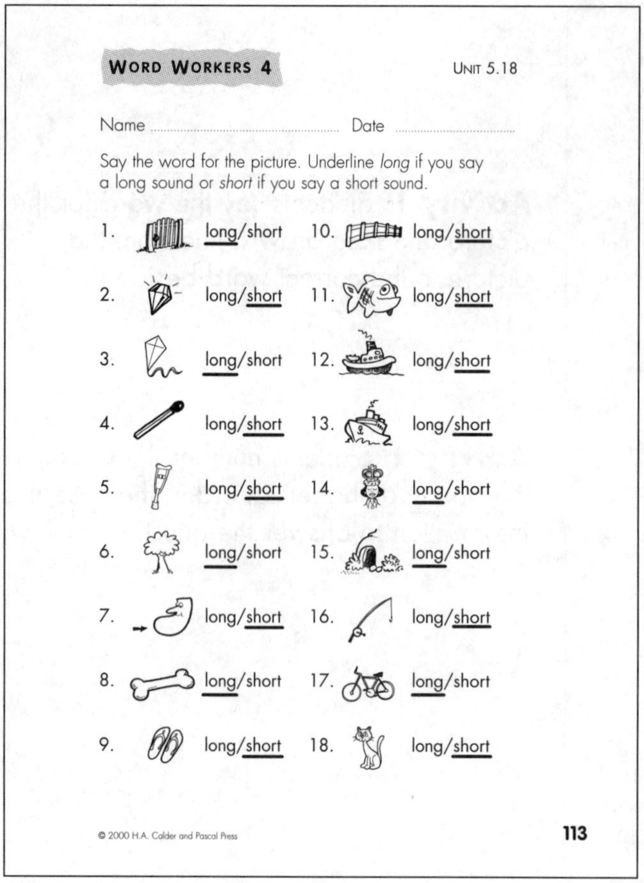

WORD WORKERS 4 UNIT 5.18

Name .... Date ....

Say the word for the picture. Underline *long* if you say a long sound or *short* if you say a short sound.

1. **long**/short
2. long/**short**
3. **long**/short
4. long/**short**
5. long/**short**
6. **long**/short
7. long/**short**
8. **long**/short
9. long/**short**
10. long/**short**
11. long/**short**
12. long/**short**
13. long/**short**
14. **long**/short
15. **long**/short
16. long/**short**
17. **long**/short
18. long/**short**

© 2000 H.A. Calder and Pascal Press 113

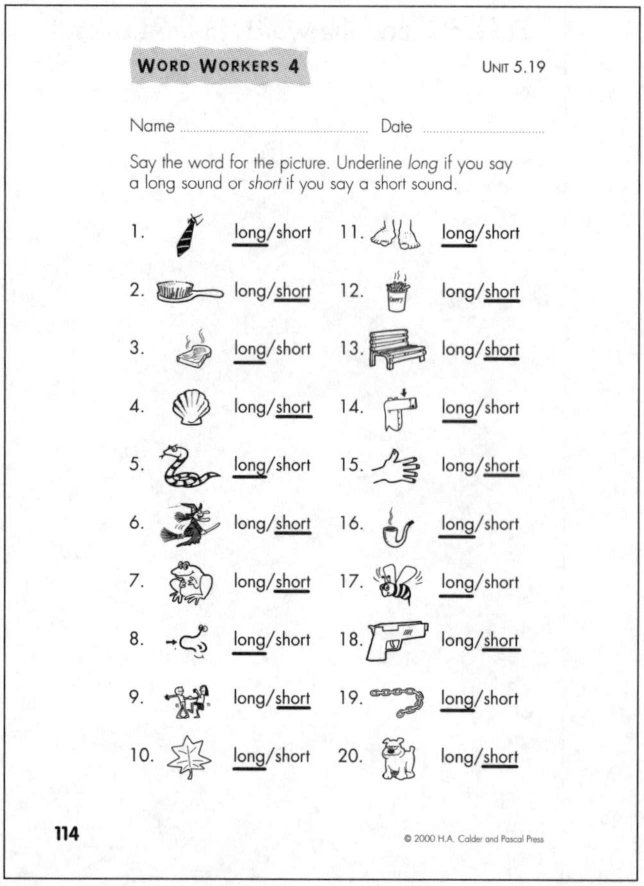

WORD WORKERS 4 UNIT 5.19

Name .... Date ....

Say the word for the picture. Underline *long* if you say a long sound or *short* if you say a short sound.

1. **long**/short
2. long/**short**
3. **long**/short
4. long/**short**
5. **long**/short
6. long/**short**
7. long/**short**
8. **long**/short
9. long/**short**
10. **long**/short
11. **long**/short
12. long/**short**
13. long/**short**
14. **long**/short
15. long/**short**
16. **long**/short
17. **long**/short
18. long/**short**
19. **long**/short
20. long/**short**

114 © 2000 H.A. Calder and Pascal Press

WORD WORKERS 4 UNIT 5.20

Name .... Date ....

Read these words.

tea tee	deer dear	cheep cheap	sea see	weak week
heal heel	bean been	read reed	creak creek	seem seam
rode road	plain plane	tail tale	made maid	sail sale
mail male	pale pail	main mane	gale Gail	here hear

Underline the correct word to complete the sentence.

1. Pete asked why the (plain/plane) was late taking off.
2. The queen told the maid to leave the (tea/tee) on the tray.
3. It can take a long time for a cut to (heel/heal).
4. Nancy steered the (sale/sail) boat into the breeze.
5. The teacher smiled when she asked the child to (read/reed).
6. Most of the (dear/deer) were hiding in the trees near the lake.

 115

Activity 1: Students read the words in the boxes.

Activity 2: Students read the sentences. They underline the word in brackets that best completes the sentence.

WORD WORKERS 4 UNIT 5.21

Read the story.

The Six Day Bike Race

It was a fine spring day. The sky was clear. It was the last day of the six day bike race. Jake Jones was the leading rider at this stage. His coach told him, 'All you have to do is stay on your bike and you will win.' So Jake stayed with the main bunch of riders for a while. He would wait till later in the day to try to take the lead.

The day got hotter and hotter. The sun beat down on Jake and the other riders. On and on they went. The road was flat and they made good time. It was easy for Jake to keep up. He was really pleased to be in the lead. This was his best chance to win a big race. He could hear the cheers from the side of the road. 'Come on Jake. Come on Jake Jones!'

116

For the following pages:

Students read the story. They read it several times until accuracy and fluency combine to improve comprehension.

WORD WORKERS 4 UNIT 5.22

Later in the day, it was time for Jake to try to take the lead. He pumped his legs up and down. The spokes in his wheels flashed. The line of riders stretched up the road. When Jake was getting closer to the leaders, the riders came to a bad stretch of road. It was bumpy with huge holes in it.

Just then a rider hit a hole. Down he went and off he came. There was no time for Jake to miss him. He did not have a chance. Down Jake went! He lay on the road with his bike on top of him. One wheel was spinning and clicking. The other wheel was broken.

When Jake tried to get up, he could feel a pain in his leg. It was bleeding from deep cuts and scrapes. His coach raced up with a wheel for the bike. He cleaned up Jake's cuts and scrapes while Jake changed the wheel. Jake had to make up the time he had lost. But could he do it?

Jake limped as he got back on his bike. He looked up the road. The riders who stayed on their bikes were a long way off. 'Go, Jake, go!' his coach told him. 'You can catch them!'

 117

WORD WORKERS 4 UNIT 5.23

Jake rode as fast as he could. He did not feel the scrapes on his legs. He had just one thing on his mind — he must catch up with the leaders. On and on he rode. In no time he was up with the main bunch. Quickly he shot past them.

Jake pumped his legs fiercely. There was not much time left. One by one he was catching the leaders till there was one rider left to catch. The line came closer and closer. And then Jake did it! He flashed past the other rider and beat him to the line.

Jake leaned back on his bike and waved. There was a wide smile on his face. He did not feel his cuts and scrapes now. Jake had got up after a bad crash to win the six day bike race — the biggest race of his life!

118

Students read the story. They read it several times until accuracy and fluency combine to improve comprehension.

WORD WORKERS 4 UNIT 5.24

Name .... Date ....

Write the letters 'a', 'b', 'c' and 'd' in the same order the pictures occurred in the story.

a b

c d

1. *a* 2. *c* 3. *b* 4. *d*

Fill in the blank with the exact word from the story.

1. Jake Jones was the *leading* rider on the last day of the race.
2. One of the other riders hit a huge *hole* in the road.
3. When Jake tried to get up, he could feel a *pain* in his leg.
4. The riders who stayed on their bikes were a *long* *way* *off*.
5. Jake had got up to win the biggest *race* of his *life*.

 119

Activity 1: Students sequence the events in the story by placing the pictures in their correct order.

Activity 2: Students complete these sentences using the exact word from the story.

WORD WORKERS 4 UNIT 5.25

Name .... Date ....

Fill in the blanks with the correct word from the box.

The day got hotter and hotter. The sun *beat* down on Jake and the other riders. On and on they went. The *road* was flat and they made good time. It was *easy* for Jake to keep up. He was really pleased to be in the lead. This was his best *chance* to win a big race. He could hear the *cheers* from the side of the road. 'Come on Jake. Come on Jake Jones!'

cheers	chance	beat	road	easy

Write the letters 'a', 'b', 'c' and 'd' beside the sentences in the same order they occurred in the story.

1. Jake limped as he got back on his bike. *c*
2. Jake leaned back on his bike and waved. *d*
3. Later in the day, it was time for Jake to try to take the lead. *b*
4. Jake stayed with the main bunch of riders for a while. *a*

120

Activity 1: Students complete this cloze exercise using the words from the box.

Activity 2: Students sequence the events in the story by placing them in their correct order.

Using Book 5

Word Workers Book 5 teaches students to read words containing diphthongs, digraphs, vowels before 'r', and silent letters. Below are some suggestions on how to use the book effectively. More detailed information on the teaching processes can be found in Chapter 2: 'Skills for successful teaching'. An activity-by-activity guide is provided with the answers.

- Read the section in the *Teacher Resource Book* that gives instructions on teaching the different rules and generalisations students need to know to be successful at this stage of their reading acquisition.
- Become familiar with the suggested lesson plan for Book 5 on the next page.

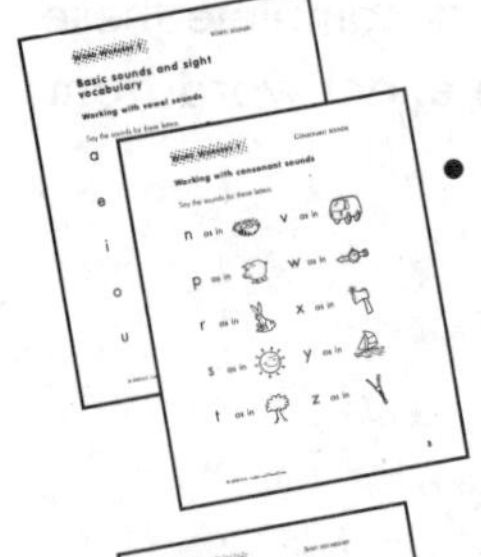

- Continue the drill with vowel and consonant sounds from the *Reading Freedom 2000* single letter–sound and common blends, digraphs and diphthongs wall charts. As new phonics rules and sounds are introduced, they can be incorporated into the drill at the beginning of each lesson.

- Students continue learning the *Reading Freedom* basic sight vocabulary lists.
- Introduce new sounds as students encounter them in each successive unit. Add them to the drill at the start of the lesson, using the *Reading Freedom 2000* wall charts or the page at the start of each unit.

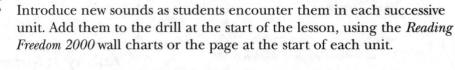

- Teach students how to recognise silent letters, especially the silent 'gh'. Use the wall chart on page 46 of the *Teacher Resource Book* to demonstrate the 'igh', 'eigh' and 'ough' sounds.
- Enlist parent support whenever possible. Parents are particularly helpful teaching sight vocabulary and reinforcing blending activities at home.

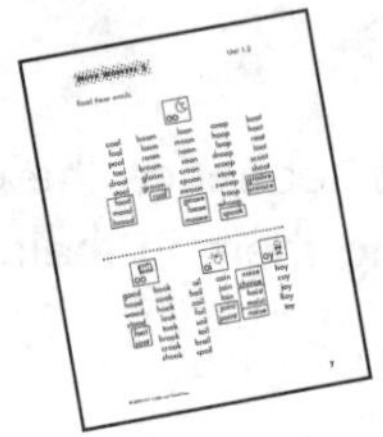

- Monitor students' progress while they read the word list at the beginning of each unit.
- When Units 1 and 2 of Book 5 are completed, record students' progress using *Word Workers* Achievement Test 6 and when Units 3 and 4 are completed, record students' progress using Test 7.

Book 5: Suggested lesson plan

Based on a lesson of approximately 30 minutes.

1 Students say a row of sounds from the three *Reading Freedom 2000* wall charts. For small groups, each student can say a row or column of sounds. If your class is large, select students to say a row or column until all the sounds have been repeated. As new sounds, rules and phonic generalisations are encountered in Book 5, incorporate them at the start of each lesson. For instance, after learning the diphthongs in Unit 1, add the diphthongs to the drill. This applies only to students who have been taught the skill or generalisation.

2 When teaching with small groups, each student reads a column of *Reading Freedom* basic sight vocabulary. When teaching the whole class, select students to read a column of sight words. Five or six columns is enough to start your lesson with. Be sure different students read the sight words each lesson.

3 Explain and demonstrate the sounds or phonic generalisations to be learned. Carefully explain the activities on the page or pages to be completed. Ensure that students understand the concepts involved and know what is required of them.

4 Assign activity pages to be completed (the number of pages depends on the teacher's professional judgment as well as the ability and enthusiasm of the student).

5 In Book 5, demonstrate and practise blending with each sound taught. Continue with this until the book is completed, learning new sounds as they are introduced. At this stage of instruction, blending skills are often firmly in place. The teacher's professional judgment and the ability of the student determines the need to continue with it.

6 Reward students for achievement on the activity pages or in learning sight vocabulary with stamps, stickers or gold stars. When they complete the activity book and finish the complementary Achievement Tests (found in *Word Workers Achievement Tests*) they receive a *Word Workers* Merit Certificate.

7 Assign any homework after demonstrating the activities. Ensure students understand the concept and what is to be done.

WORD WORKERS 5 SIGHT VOCABULARY

Reading Freedom sight vocabulary

Learn these sight words.

List one	
and	look
are	my
boy	of
can	play
come	red
funny	run
go	said
he	says
is	see
jump	the
like	this
little	to

List two	
at	man
away	me
big	not
blue	on
down	one
for	ran
good	saw
green	three
have	too
here	up
in	watch
it	you

1

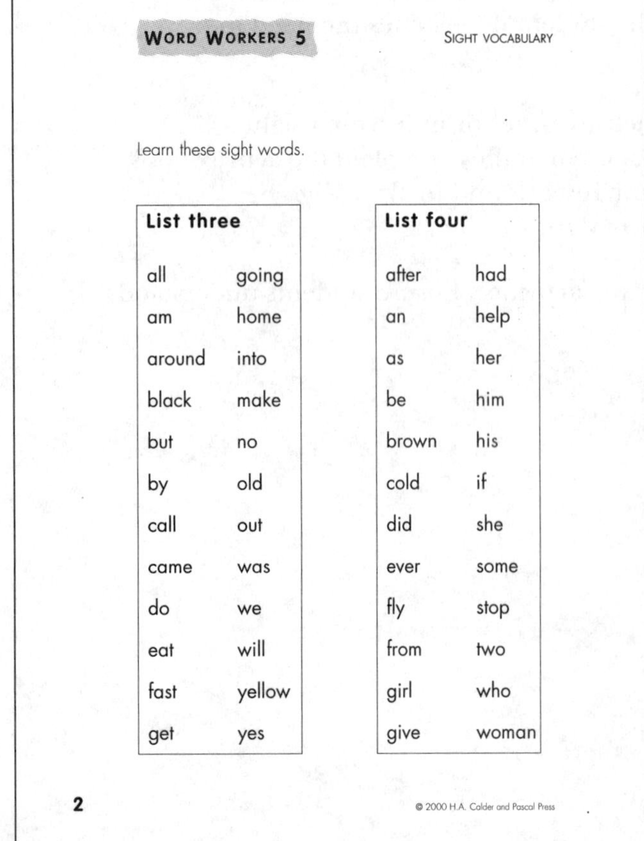

WORD WORKERS 5 SIGHT VOCABULARY

Learn these sight words.

List three	
all	going
am	home
around	into
black	make
but	no
by	old
call	out
came	was
do	we
eat	will
fast	yellow
get	yes

List four	
after	had
an	help
as	her
be	him
brown	his
cold	if
did	she
ever	some
fly	stop
from	two
girl	who
give	woman

2

For the following pages:

Students learn these sight words list by list. Reward successful acquisition of sight vocabulary with stars and stickers.

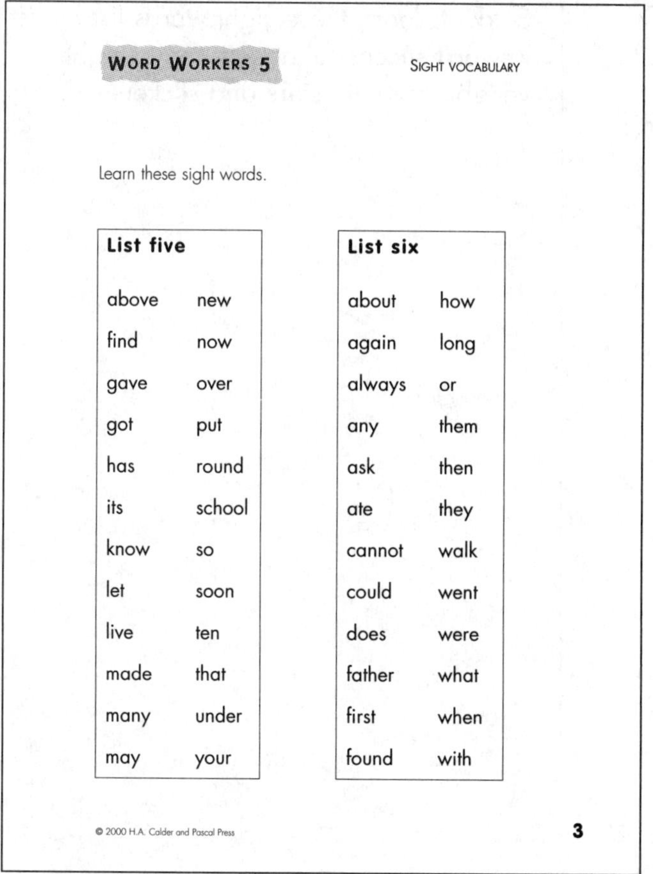
WORD WORKERS 5 SIGHT VOCABULARY

Learn these sight words.

List five	
above	new
find	now
gave	over
got	put
has	round
its	school
know	so
let	soon
live	ten
made	that
many	under
may	your

List six	
about	how
again	long
always	or
any	them
ask	then
ate	they
cannot	walk
could	went
does	were
father	what
first	when
found	with

© 2000 H.A. Calder and Pascal Press 3

WORD WORKERS 5 SIGHT VOCABULARY

Learn these sight words.

List seven	
because	once
been	open
before	our
bring	say
children	take
done	tell
every	there
goes	upon
mother	us
much	want
must	wish
never	would

List eight	
brother	pull
buy	show
draw	sit
drink	small
even	their
fall	these
grow	think
hold	those
hot	very
just	where
keep	which
only	work

4 © 2000 H.A. Calder and Pascal Press

Students learn these sight words list by list. Reward successful acquisition of sight vocabulary with stars and stickers.

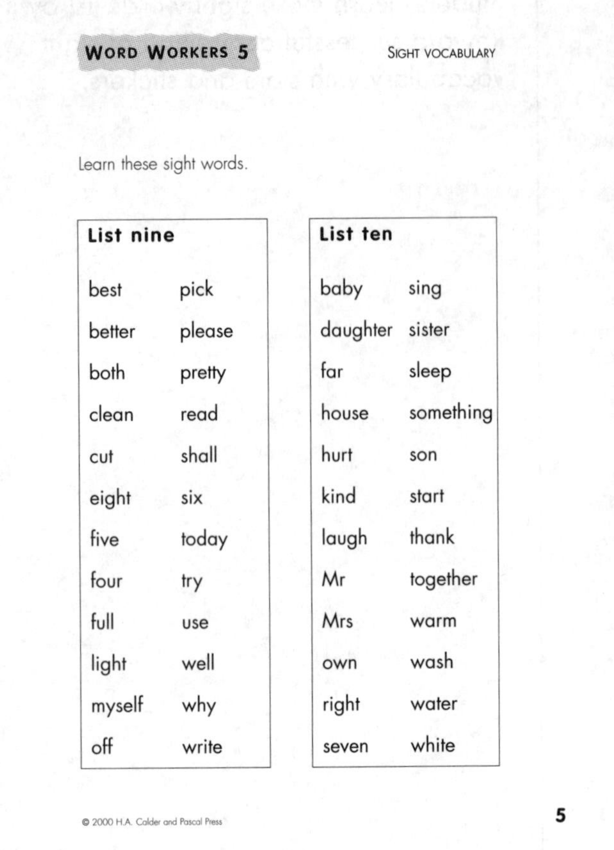

WORD WORKERS 5 SIGHT VOCABULARY

Learn these sight words.

List nine	
best	pick
better	please
both	pretty
clean	read
cut	shall
eight	six
five	today
four	try
full	use
light	well
myself	why
off	write

List ten	
baby	sing
daughter	sister
far	sleep
house	something
hurt	son
kind	start
laugh	thank
Mr	together
Mrs	warm
own	wash
right	water
seven	white

© 2000 H.A. Calder and Pascal Press 5

Students learn these sight words list by list. Reward successful acquisition of sight vocabulary with stars and stickers.

WORD WORKERS 5 UNIT 1.1

Working with 'oo', 'oi', 'oy', 'ou', 'ow', 'aw' and 'au' sounds

Say the sounds for these letters.

oo as in

oo as in

oi as in

oy as in

au as in

aw as in

ou as in

ow as in

ow as in

6 © 2000 H.A. Calder and Pascal Press

For the following pages:

This unit teaches students to read words containing diphthongs. Make sure each student knows them. Photocopy the introductory page for students to refer to. Encourage students to practise these sounds until they are learned satisfactorily.

From now on, incorporate repetition of the sounds of the diphthongs in the phonics drill at the start of each lesson.

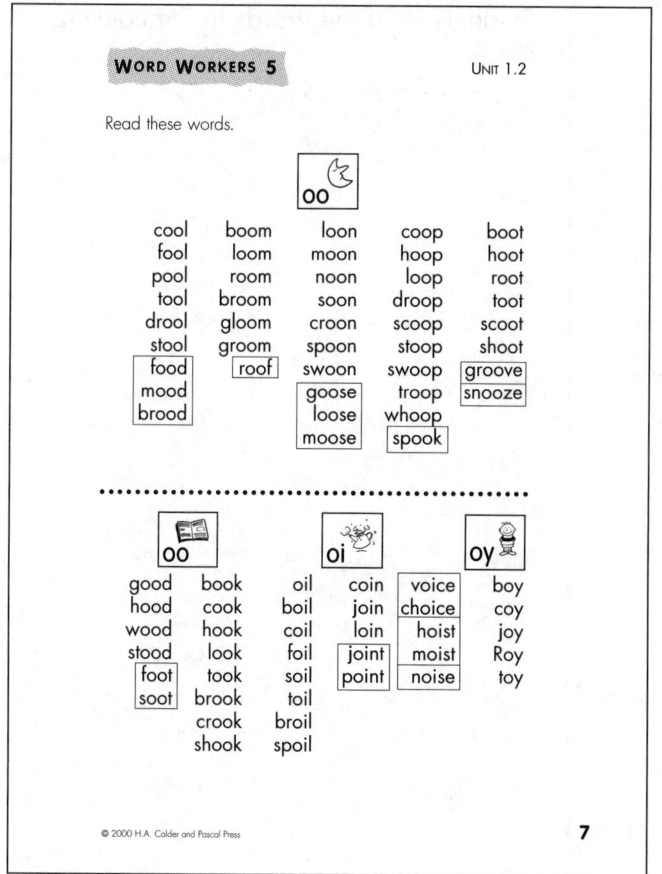

WORD WORKERS 5 UNIT 1.2

Read these words.

oo

cool	boom	loon	coop	boot
fool	loom	moon	hoop	hoot
pool	room	noon	loop	root
tool	broom	soon	droop	toot
drool	gloom	croon	scoop	scoot
stool	groom	spoon	stoop	shoot
food	roof	swoon	swoop	groove
mood		goose	troop	snooze
brood		loose	whoop	
		moose	spook	

oo		oi			oy
good	book	oil	coin	voice	boy
hood	cook	boil	join	choice	coy
wood	hook	coil	loin	hoist	joy
stood	look	foil	joint	moist	Roy
foot	took	soil	point	noise	toy
soot	brook	toil			
	crook	broil			
	shook	spoil			

© 2000 H.A. Calder and Pascal Press 7

Students read the words in the columns.

WORD WORKERS 5 UNIT 1.3

Name .... Date ....

Write the words for the pictures.

1. cook 2. boil 3. stool

4. foot 5. broom 6. roof

7. moon 8. boy 9. boot

10. goose 11. pool 12. book

8 © 2000 H.A. Calder and Pascal Press

Students write the words for the pictures. If necessary, they refer to the word lists to find the correct spelling.

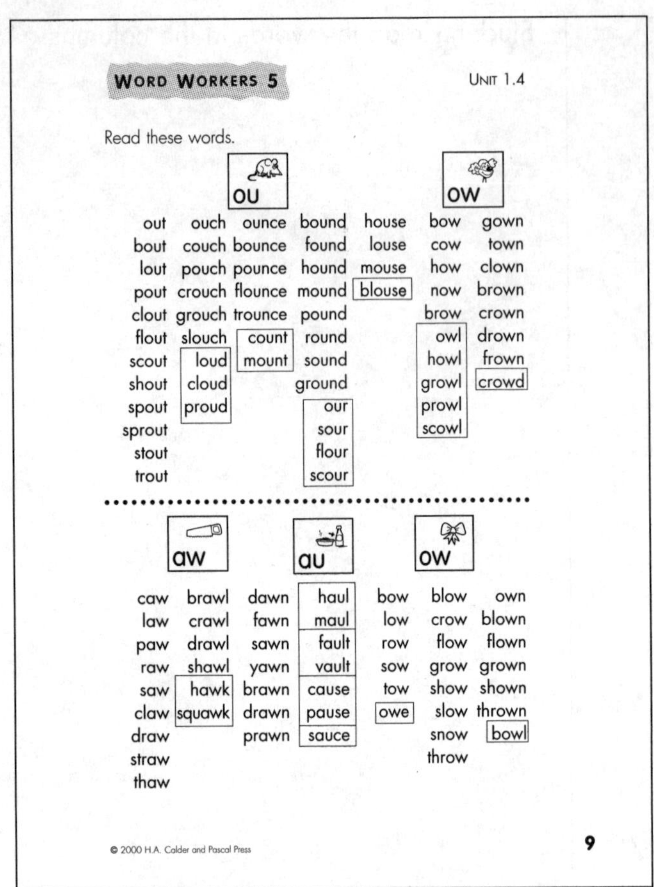

WORD WORKERS 5 UNIT 1.4

Read these words.

		ou			ow	
out	ouch	ounce	bound	house	bow	gown
bout	couch	bounce	found	louse	cow	town
lout	pouch	pounce	hound	mouse	how	clown
pout	crouch	flounce	mound	blouse	now	brown
clout	grouch	trounce	pound		brow	crown
flout	slouch	count	round		owl	drown
scout	loud	mount	sound		howl	frown
shout	cloud		ground		growl	crowd
spout	proud		our		prowl	
sprout			sour		scowl	
stout			flour			
trout			scour			

aw			au	ow		
caw	brawl	dawn	haul	bow	blow	own
law	crawl	fawn	maul	low	crow	blown
paw	drawl	sawn	fault	row	flow	flown
raw	shawl	yawn	vault	sow	grow	grown
saw	hawk	brawn	cause	tow	show	shown
claw	squawk	drawn	pause	owe	slow	thrown
draw		prawn	sauce		snow	bowl
straw					throw	
thaw						

© 2000 H.A. Calder and Pascal Press 9

Students read the words in the columns.

WORD WORKERS 5 UNIT 1.5

Name .... Date ....

Write the words for the pictures.

1. mouse 2. crown 3. owl

4. snow 5. house 6. row

7. saw 8. bow 9. sauce

10. crow 11. clouds 12. claw

10 © 2000 H.A. Calder and Pascal Press

Students write the words for the pictures. If necessary, they refer to the word lists to find the correct spelling.

WORD WORKERS 5 UNIT 1.6

Name .... Date ....

Read these words.

pound pounds pounded pounding	howled howl howling howls	crawling crawls crawl crawled	pauses pausing paused pause
cooking cook cooks cooked	stoop stooped stoops stooping	pointed pointing point points	shows showed show showing

Underline the word for the picture.

trout	mouse	cause	spoil	snooze
spout	grouch	haul	join	goose
flour	louse	sauce	point	groove
ground	house	fault	boil	shoot

 11

Activity 1: Students read the words in the boxes. Tell them to add the endings to the smallest word or base word.

Activity 2: Students look at the columns of words. They underline the word in each column that matches the picture above it.

WORD WORKERS 5 UNIT 1.7

Name .... Date ....

Underline the nonsense word.

1. spoon	2. point	3. hawk	4. pound	5. howl
broom	groil	yawn	crouch	crown
stool	spoil	strawn	pounce	yown
floop	noise	claw	spouch	growl

Write the word for the picture.

1. *clouds* 2. *boot* 3. *book*

4. *foot* 5. *bows* 6. *bowls*

7. *clowns* 8. *spoons* 9. *stool*

12

Activity 1: Students look at the columns of words. Tell them to underline the word in each column that is a nonsense word.

Activity 2: Students write the words for the pictures. Tell them to add the letter 's' if there is more than one. If necessary, they refer to the word lists to find the correct spelling.

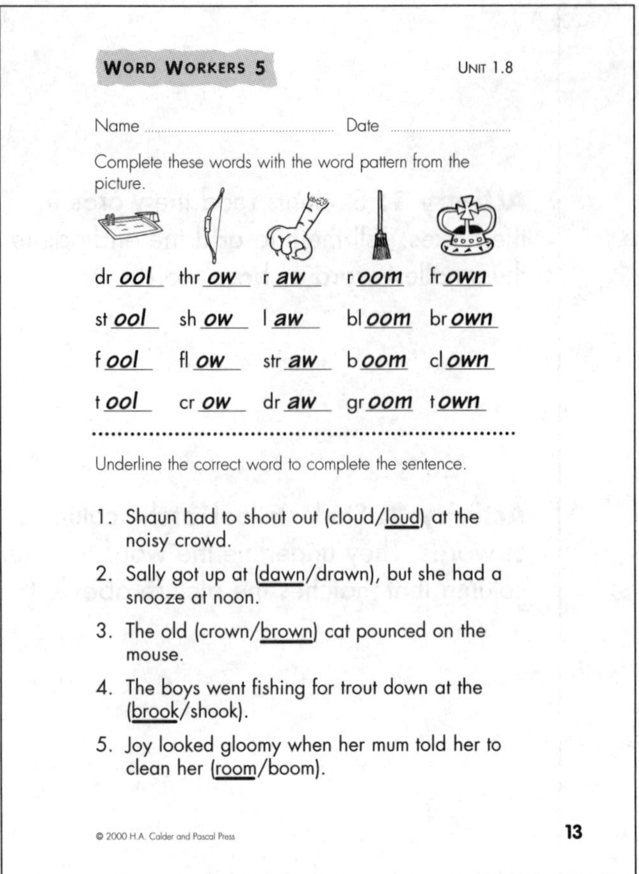

WORD WORKERS 5 UNIT 1.8

Name .... Date ....

Complete these words with the word pattern from the picture.

dr *ool*	thr *ow*	r *aw*	r *oom*	fr *own*
st *ool*	sh *ow*	l *aw*	bl *oom*	br *own*
f *ool*	fl *ow*	str *aw*	b *oom*	cl *own*
t *ool*	cr *ow*	dr *aw*	gr *oom*	t *own*

Underline the correct word to complete the sentence.

1. Shaun had to shout out (cloud/loud) at the noisy crowd.
2. Sally got up at (dawn/drawn), but she had a snooze at noon.
3. The old (crown/brown) cat pounced on the mouse.
4. The boys went fishing for trout down at the (brook/shook).
5. Joy looked gloomy when her mum told her to clean her (room/boom).

 13

Activity 1: Students look at the pictures above the columns. They use the word pattern from each picture to complete the words in the column below.

Activity 2: Students read the sentences. They underline the word in brackets that best completes the sentence.

WORD WORKERS 5 UNIT 1.9

Name .... Date ....

Read these words.

paw paws pawed pawing	mows mowed mowing mow	pounced pouncing pounce pounces	spoiling spoil spoiled spoils
slow slower slowest	louder loud loudest	loosest looser loose	browner brownest brown
wood wooden	loosen loose	wool woollen	

Complete the words by writing the vowel sounds.

aw	oi	ou	oo	ow
p *aw*	p *oi* nt	p *ou* ch	l *oo* se	m *ow*
dr *aw* n	sp *oi* l	h *ou* se	gr *oo* ve	thr *ow* n
sh *aw* l	v *oi* ce	sc *ou* t	r *oo* f	cr *ow*
h *aw* k	m *oi* st	b *ou* nce	p *oo* l	b *ow* l
th *aw*	n *oi* se	fl *ou* r	sh *oo* t	gr *ow* n

14

Activity 1: Students read the words in the boxes. Tell them to add the endings to the smallest word or base word.

Activity 2: Students complete the words by writing in the letters printed above each column.

WORD WORKERS 5 UNIT 1.10

Name .... Date ....

Draw a line to the word with the same word pattern.

howl	lawn	foot	scout	loud	choice
fault	crouch	soil	ground	hoop	proud
yawn	growl	loop	boil	cook	frown
own	vault	out	soot	voice	stoop
ouch	blown	found	troop	crown	shook

Complete these sentences by writing the words for the pictures.

1. Mr Brown frowned as he looked at the wood he had to ***saw***.
2. The cook spilled the ***bowl*** of sauce on Dawn's gown.
3. The owl hooted when the clouds hid the ***moon***.
4. The king said 'Ouch!' when his ***crown*** fell on his foot.
5. Paul found the tools when he stood on the ***stool***.

© 2000 H.A. Calder and Pascal Press 15

Activity 1: Students look at the two columns of words in each box. They draw a line from the word in the left-hand column to the word in the right-hand column that has the same word pattern.

Activity 2: Students look at the pictures and then complete the sentences below by writing the correct word for the picture in the space provided.

WORD WORKERS 5 UNIT 1.11

Name .... Date ....

Write the word for these jumbled letters. The first letters are underlined.

poosw ***swoop***	oyt ***toy***	rous ***sour***
choucr ***crouch***	wahk ***hawk***	ftoo ***foot***
nowt ***town***	drowc ***crowd***	loisp ***spoil***
oisen ***noise***	monut ***mount***	seuac ***sauce***

Underline the *two* words that have the same word pattern as the picture.

crook	soot	took	hood
grown	blow	bowl	throw
pool	hoop	tool	scoot
pout	proud	loud	pound
soon	roof	swoon	mood

16 © 2000 H.A. Calder and Pascal Press

Activity 1: Students make a word from the jumbled letters. The first letter of each word is underlined. Students write the words in the spaces provided.

Activity 2: Students look at the pictures and the words on the lines beside them. They underline the two words in each line that have the same word pattern as the picture.

WORD WORKERS 5 UNIT 1.12

Name .... Date ....

Read these words.

fool fools fooled fooling	owning owned own owns	growls growled growling growl	hauls haul hauling hauled
cloud cloudy	gloomy gloom	faulty fault	snow snowy
round roundly	loosely loose	slow slowly	moistly moist

Underline the word for the picture.

owe	cook	house	joy	bowl
own	shook	bounce	toy	low
crow	hood	mouse	boy	row
slow	soot	ground	coy	snow

© 2000 H.A. Calder and Pascal Press 17

Activity 1: Students read the words in the boxes. Tell them to add the endings to the smallest word or base word.

Activity 2: Students look at the columns of words. They underline the word in each column that matches the picture above it.

WORD WORKERS 5 UNIT 1.13

Name .... Date ....

Write the word from each column that fits the word shape box.

coin	room	shout	draw
point	roof	bounce	crawl
noise	food	blouse	squawk
moist	groove	crowd	fault

point food blouse draw

Underline the correct word to complete the sentence.

1. 'You have no (moist/choice),' Tom's dad told him. 'You must paint the house now!'
2. The hound growled when Mrs Hood came into the (room/broom).
3. Troy counted his (coins/joins) and took them to town.
4. The teacher asked the class to draw a clown's (south/mouth).
5. Roy said, 'I think the lawn is too moist to (mow/show) just now.'

18 © 2000 H.A. Calder and Pascal Press

Activity 1: Students look at the columns of words. Tell them to put the word from each column that fits into the 'word shape' box below it.

Activity 2: Students read the sentences. They underline the word in brackets that best completes the sentence.

WORD WORKERS 5 UNIT 1.14

Name .... Date ....

Put each column in alphabetical order.

au		aw		oi	
haul	*fault*	drawn	*brawl*	coil	*boil*
fault	*haul*	brawl	*brawn*	coin	*broil*
vault	*pause*	claw	*caw*	broil	*choice*
pause	*sauce*	brawn	*claw*	boil	*coil*
sauce	*vault*	caw	*drawn*	choice	*coin*

oo		ou		ow	
whoop	*scoop*	round	*pound*	snow	*shown*
snooze	*snooze*	trout	*round*	tow	*slow*
scoop	*toot*	pound	*spout*	shown	*snow*
troop	*troop*	spout	*trounce*	throw	*throw*
toot	*whoop*	trounce	*trout*	slow	*tow*

 19

Students place the words in each column in alphabetical order.

WORD WORKERS 5 UNIT 1.15

Name .... Date ....

Complete these crossword puzzles.

aw: clawed, paw, craw, drawn, shawl

oi: choice, hoist, coin, noise, spoil

oo: gloom, loose, mood, groove, sooner

ou: grouch, flour, slouch, ground, count

ow: grow, tow, clown, crow, drown

20

Students complete the crossword puzzles. They write the letters indicated in the blank spaces to make words that can be read going down or across the page.

WORD WORKERS 5 UNIT 1.16

Name .... Date ....

Write the word with the correct spelling.

1. loos loose loese *loose*
2. choice choyce choce *choice*
3. bownce bouns bounce *bounce*
4. yawn yaun yown *yawn*
5. mous mouse mowse *mouse*

Fill in the missing letters to complete the word.

1. *c* row *d*
2. *c* rawle *d*
3. *c* loud *y*
4. *h* aulin *g*
5. *c* ook *s*

crawled
cloudy
cooks
crowd
hauling

 21

Activity 1: Students read the words going across the page, then write the word that is spelt correctly.

Activity 2: Students read the words in the box, then write the missing letters to complete the column of words on the left.

WORD WORKERS 5 UNIT 1.17

Name .... Date ....

Underline the word for the picture.

cloud <u>clouds</u> <u>saw</u> saws <u>crown</u> crowns

boot <u>boots</u> broom <u>brooms</u> <u>cook</u> cooks

Complete the sentences with the words from the box.

loose	lawn	sour	wood	spoon

1. Mr Crouch mowed the *lawn* at noon.
2. The goose got *loose* and ran down to the brook.
3. Shaun looked gloomy when he saw the *wood* he had to chop.
4. The cook dropped the *spoon* in the boiling sauce.
5. The peach was *sour*, and Mrs Brown frowned when she tasted it.

22

Activity 1: Students underline the singular word if there is one object pictured or the plural word if there are two or more objects pictured.

Activity 2: Students complete the sentences by writing the correct word from the box in the space provided.

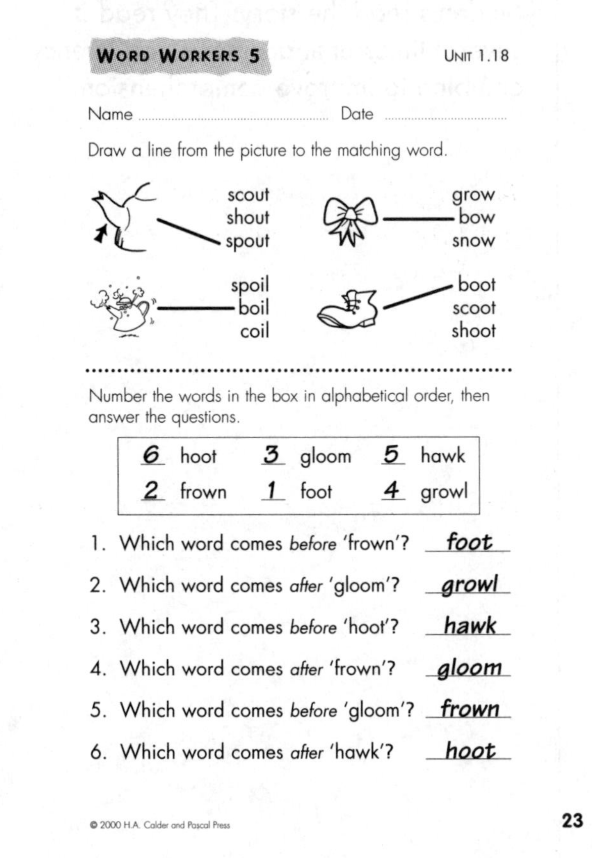

WORD WORKERS 5 UNIT 1.18

Name .... Date ....

Draw a line from the picture to the matching word.

scout
shout
spout

grow
bow
snow

spoil
boil
coil

boot
scoot
shoot

Number the words in the box in alphabetical order, then answer the questions.

6 hoot	3 gloom	5 hawk
2 frown	1 foot	4 growl

1. Which word comes *before* 'frown'? foot
2. Which word comes *after* 'gloom'? growl
3. Which word comes *before* 'hoot'? hawk
4. Which word comes *after* 'frown'? gloom
5. Which word comes *before* 'gloom'? frown
6. Which word comes *after* 'hawk'? hoot

© 2000 H.A. Calder and Pascal Press 23

Activity 1: Students say the word for the picture and then draw a line from the picture to the correct word beside it.

Activity 2: Students number the words in the box in alphabetical order, then use this information to answer the questions below.

WORD WORKERS 5 UNIT 1.19

Read the story.

The Grouch

Mr Brown was a grouch. The meanest and sourest grouch in town. He frowned when the boys down the block played in the street. His dog would growl at them. Mr Brown growled louder than his dog.

Mr Brown had grown the best lawn on the block. He would mow it and trim it and rake it. Mr Brown was proud of it. He said that it was the neatest and greenest lawn in town.

One day after he mowed his lawn, Mr Brown stood by his fence. His mouth went down when he saw two boys playing in the street. He growled and frowned at the boys. His dog growled too. But Mr Brown, the grouch, growled louder.

24 © 2000 H.A. Calder and Pascal Press

For the following pages:

Students read the story. They read it several times until accuracy and fluency combine to improve comprehension.

WORD WORKERS 5 UNIT 1.20

Then Mr Brown yawned and said, 'It is hot out here. I need a cool drink and then a snooze.' He went in his house with his dog. Mr Brown lay down on the couch and took a long snooze.

Shaun and Paul were still out on the street. Shaun was throwing a ball and Paul was hitting it. 'Whack!' Paul hit the ball with his bat. 'Look out!' he shouted. The ball took off. It sailed up and up. It seemed to come down very slowly. And then it landed on Mr Brown's roof! 'Bounce...bounce... bounce...' The ball landed on Mr Brown's back lawn and bounced into his pool.

 25

WORD WORKERS 5 UNIT 1.21

'Oh no. Not on grouchy Brown's house!' they said.

'It is your fault, Paul,' Shaun said. 'You hit the ball!'

'No, it is your fault, Shaun,' Paul said. 'It was a lousy throw.'

So the boys crept up to Mr Brown's house. They went round the back. They saw the ball in the pool. Mr Brown jumped off the couch when the ball bounced on his roof. He looked out and saw the boys by the pool. He ran out and shouted. His dog ran out too, with a loud growl. Shaun and Paul just stood there and pointed.

26

Students read the story. They read it several times until accuracy and fluency combine to improve comprehension.

Mr Brown looked where they were pointing. There, crouched by the tool shed, was a prowler. He was stooped down by Mr Brown's lawn mower. Then the prowler scooted off. Mr Brown's dog bounded after him with a loud growl. 'Owww...ouch!' the prowler shouted when the dog pounced on him.

Mr Brown grinned as he looked at his dog chasing the prowler down the street. 'That crook will not come back soon boys. Thanks for waking me. But you did not have to throw the ball on the roof to wake me up.'

Shaun looked at Paul. Then Paul looked at Shaun. They had fooled Mr Brown this time. But they would not fool the meanest grouch in town next time. So they took the ball out of the pool. After that they played way down the street.

Students read the story. They read it several times until accuracy and fluency combine to improve comprehension.

Name .... Date ....

Write the letters 'a', 'b', 'c' and 'd' in the same order the pictures occurred in the story.

a b c d

1. *a* 2. *c* 3. *b* 4. *d*

Answer the questions with the exact words from the story.

1. Mr Brown had the best *lawn* on the block.
2. *Paul* hit the ball on Mr Brown's roof.
3. The ball landed on the back *lawn* and bounced into the *pool* .
4. Mr Brown told the boys that they did not have to throw the ball on the *roof* to wake him.

Activity 1: Students sequence the events in the story by placing the pictures in their correct order.

Activity 2: Students complete these sentences using the exact word from the story.

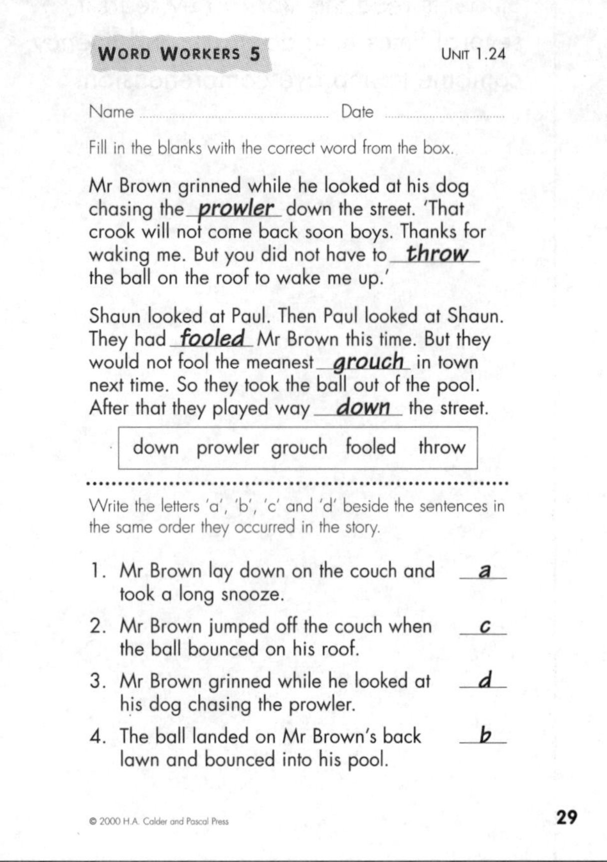

WORD WORKERS 5 UNIT 1.24

Name .... Date ....

Fill in the blanks with the correct word from the box.

Mr Brown grinned while he looked at his dog chasing the *prowler* down the street. 'That crook will not come back soon boys. Thanks for waking me. But you did not have to *throw* the ball on the roof to wake me up.'

Shaun looked at Paul. Then Paul looked at Shaun. They had *fooled* Mr Brown this time. But they would not fool the meanest *grouch* in town next time. So they took the ball out of the pool. After that they played way *down* the street.

down prowler grouch fooled throw

Write the letters 'a', 'b', 'c' and 'd' beside the sentences in the same order they occurred in the story.

1. Mr Brown lay down on the couch and took a long snooze. *a*
2. Mr Brown jumped off the couch when the ball bounced on his roof. *c*
3. Mr Brown grinned while he looked at his dog chasing the prowler. *d*
4. The ball landed on Mr Brown's back lawn and bounced into his pool. *b*

© 2000 H.A. Calder and Pascal Press 29

Activity 1: Students complete this cloze exercise using the words from the box.

Activity 2: Students sequence the events in the story by placing them in their correct order.

WORD WORKERS 5 UNIT 2.1

Working with vowels before 'r'

Say the sounds for these letters.

ar as in

er as in

ir as in

or as in

ur as in

30 © 2000 H.A. Calder and Pascal Press

For the following pages:

This unit teaches students to read words containing vowels before 'r'. Make sure each student knows them. Photocopy the introductory page for students to refer to. Encourage students to practise these sounds as they colour the page in.

From now on, incorporate repetition of vowels before 'r' sounds in the phonics drill at the start of each lesson.

Students read the words in the columns.

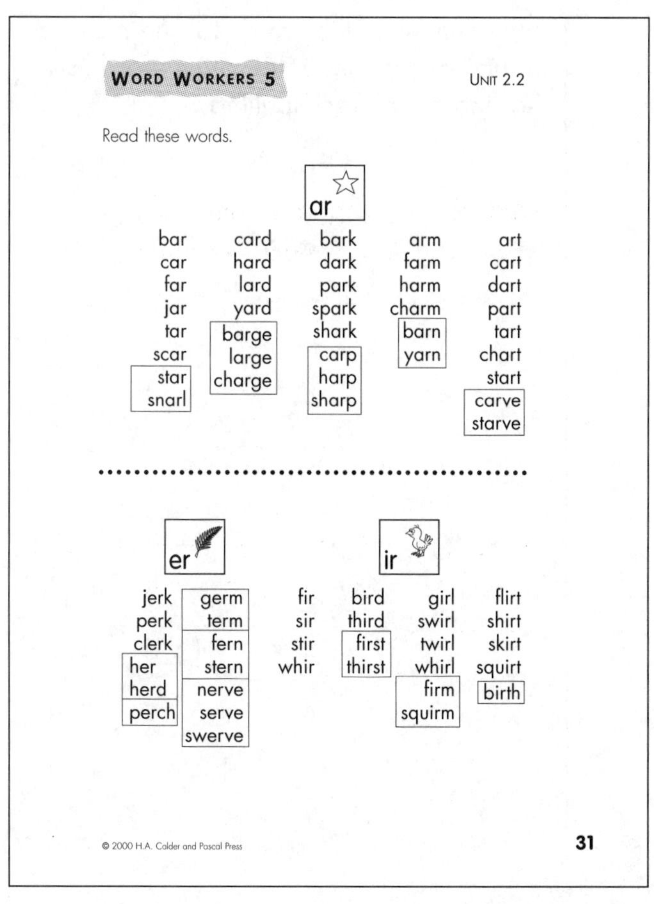

WORD WORKERS 5 UNIT 2.2

Read these words.

ar

bar	card	bark	arm	art
car	hard	dark	farm	cart
far	lard	park	harm	dart
jar	yard	spark	charm	part
tar	barge	shark	barn	tart
scar	large	carp	yarn	chart
star	charge	harp		start
snarl		sharp		carve
				starve

er

jerk	germ
perk	term
clerk	fern
her	stern
herd	nerve
perch	serve
	swerve

ir

fir	bird	girl	flirt
sir	third	swirl	shirt
stir	first	twirl	skirt
whir	thirst	whirl	squirt
		firm	birth
		squirm	

© 2000 H.A. Calder and Pascal Press 31

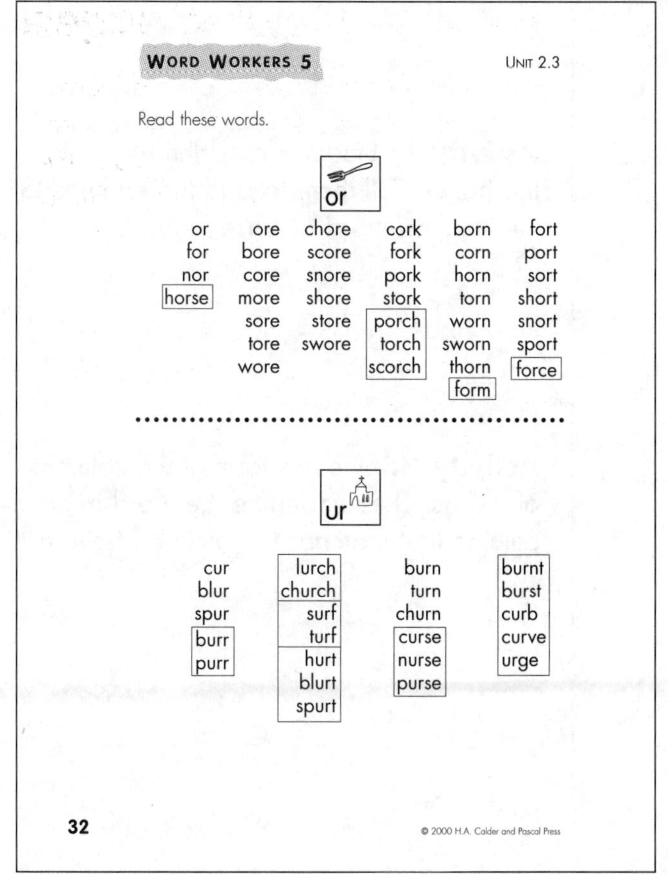

WORD WORKERS 5 UNIT 2.3

Read these words.

or

or	ore	chore	cork	born	fort
for	bore	score	fork	corn	port
nor	core	snore	pork	horn	sort
horse	more	shore	stork	torn	short
	sore	store	porch	worn	snort
	tore	swore	torch	sworn	sport
	wore		scorch	thorn	force
				form	

ur

cur	lurch	burn	burnt
blur	church	turn	burst
spur	surf	churn	curb
burr	turf	curse	curve
purr	hurt	nurse	urge
	blurt	purse	
	spurt		

32 © 2000 H.A. Calder and Pascal Press

Word Workers 5 Unit 2.4

Name .... Date ....

Write the words for the pictures.

1. shirt 2. dart 3. shorts

4. car 5. horse 6. church

7. snore 8. bird 9. first

10. fork 11. star 12. shark

 33

Students write the words for the pictures. If necessary, they refer to the word lists to find the correct spelling.

Word Workers 5 Unit 2.5

Name .... Date ....

Read these words.

score scores scored scoring	curling curls curled curl	perches perch perching perched	marched marching marches march
bores bore boring bored	stirring stirs stirred stir	charged charging charge charges	barked barks bark barking

Underline the word for the picture.

urge	swore	thorn	skirt	third
curb	shore	born	firm	girl
purr	cork	corn	birth	sir
spur	store	horn	twirl	first

34

Activity 1: Students read the words in the boxes. Tell them to add the endings to the smallest word or base word.

Activity 2: Students look at the columns of words. They underline the word in each column that matches the picture above it.

WORD WORKERS 5 UNIT 2.6

Name .... Date ....

Underline the nonsense word.

1. dart	2. chore	3. fern	4. burn	5. third
spark	torn	nerve	jurt	thirt
skart	sore	germ	purse	swirl
charm	blorn	sherve	burst	shirt

Write the word for the picture.

1. forks 2. arm 3. darts

4. horse 5. star 6. church

7. cars 8. bird 9. shark

 35

Activity 1: Students look at the columns of words. Tell them to underline the word in each column that is a nonsense word.

Activity 2: Students write the words for the pictures. Tell them to add the letter 's' if there is more than one. If necessary, they refer to the word lists to find the correct spelling.

WORD WORKERS 5 UNIT 2.7

Name .... Date ....

Complete these words with the word pattern from the picture.

ch art	p ark	sk irt	st ar	f orts
st art	sp ark	d irt	b ar	sp orts
p art	d ark	fl irt	sc ar	sn orts
c art	m ark	squ irt	j ar	s orts

Underline the correct word to complete the sentence.

1. The farmer loaded the (worn/corn) onto his cart.
2. The girl's skirt got dirty when she played in the (yard/hard).
3. Bert (sparked/parked) his car at the back of the store.
4. The army marched past the church in the rain (storm/form).
5. The dog snarled when the (third/herd) of deer charged past.

36

Activity 1: Students look at the pictures above the columns. They use the word pattern from each picture to complete the words in the column below.

Activity 2: Students read the sentences. They underline the word in brackets that best completes the sentence.

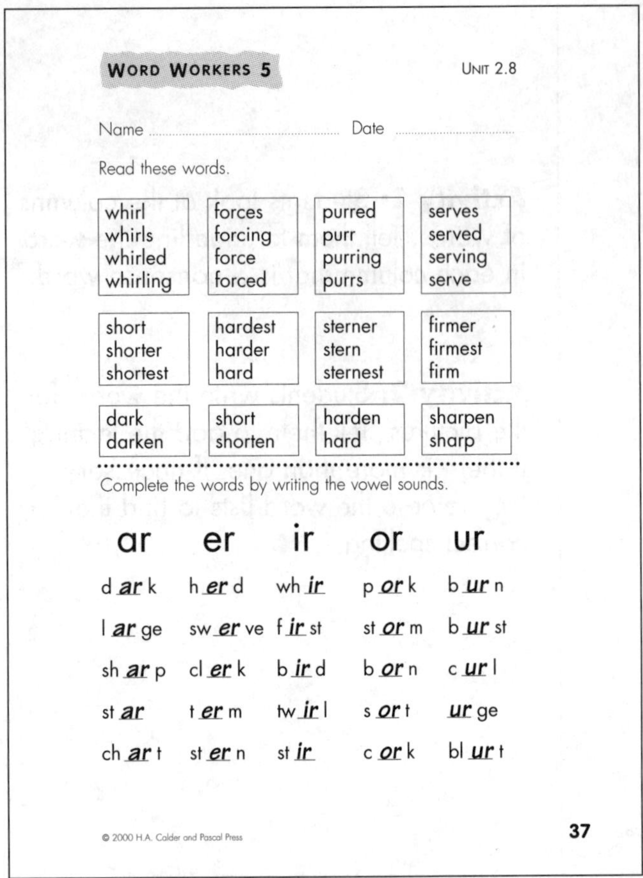

WORD WORKERS 5 UNIT 2.8

Name .... Date ....

Read these words.

whirl whirls whirled whirling	forces forcing force forced	purred purr purring purrs	serves served serving serve
short shorter shortest	hardest harder hard	sterner stern sternest	firmer firmest firm
dark darken	short shorten	harden hard	sharpen sharp

Complete the words by writing the vowel sounds.

ar	er	ir	or	ur
d ar k	h er d	wh ir	p or k	b ur n
l ar ge	sw er ve	f ir st	st or m	b ur st
sh ar p	cl er k	b ir d	b or n	c ur l
st ar	t er m	tw ir l	s or t	ur ge
ch ar t	st er n	st ir	c or k	bl ur t

 37

Activity 1: Students read the words in the boxes. Tell them to add the endings to the smallest word or base word.

Activity 2: Students complete the words by writing in the letters printed above each column.

WORD WORKERS 5 UNIT 2.9

Name .... Date ....

Draw a line to the word with the same word pattern.

turn	fort	fern	curse	shirt	yard
harm	serve	mark	stern	perk	born
sort	burn	core	spark	worn	churn
first	charm	bird	snore	hard	skirt
nerve	thirst	nurse	third	turn	clerk

Complete these sentences by writing the words for the pictures.

1. Norm hurt his arm when he tore his shirt.
2. Mrs Dark turned the car sharply into the corner.
3. The surfers raced to shore when they saw the shark .
4. Miss Turner wore her best skirt to the horse races.
5. While it sat on its perch, the dark bird sang and chirped.

38

Activity 1: Students look at the two columns of words in each box. They draw a line from the word in the left-hand column to the word in the right-hand column that has the same word pattern.

Activity 2: Students look at the pictures and then complete the sentences below by writing the correct word for the picture in the space provided.

WORD WORKERS 5 UNIT 2.10

Name .... Date ....

Write the word for these jumbled letters.
The first letters are underlined.

lrgea	large	lerck	clerk	mirf	firm
rewo	wore	stubr	burst	usern	nurse
norst	snort	thirb	birth	nefr	fern
larns	snarl	turps	spurt	soreh	horse

Underline the *two* words that have the same word pattern as the picture.

thorn force born for

third flirt whir squirt

snort tore wore horse

stork sort nor pork

nurse blur surf cur

© 2000 H.A. Calder and Pascal Press 39

Activity 1: Students make a word from the jumbled letters. The first letter of each word is underlined. Students write the words in the spaces provided.

Activity 2: Students look at the pictures and the words on the lines beside them. They underline the two words in each line that have the same word pattern as the picture.

WORD WORKERS 5 UNIT 2.11

Name .... Date ....

Read these words.

snarl snarls snarled snarling	squirts squirt squirting squirted	turning turned turn turns	sorted sorts sorting sort
chirp chirpy	thorny thorn	blur blurry	thirsty thirst
firm firmly	partly part	shortly short	hard hardly

Underline the word for the picture.

germ	lurch	scar	snore	charm
fern	blur	charge	score	card
swerve	churn	star	force	arm
herd	church	starve	form	snarl

40 © 2000 H.A. Calder and Pascal Press

Activity 1: Students read the words in the boxes. Tell them to add the endings to the smallest word or base word.

Activity 2: Students look at the columns of words. They underline the word in each column that matches the picture above it.

WORD WORKERS 5 UNIT 2.12

Name .... Date ....

Write the word from each column that fits the word shape box.

harm	stern	whirl	chore
barge	serve	flirt	stork
park	perch	birth	thorn
start	jerk	squirt	force

harm jerk birth chore

Underline the correct word to complete the sentence.

1. The first storm of the year came on the (bird/third) of March.
2. All morning long the (purse/nurse) said that her arm was sore.
3. The largest cat purred at the back of the (yarn/barn).
4. The farmer turned on the hose and squirted the thirsty (horse/force).
5. Martin found Mrs Parker's purse after she left it in the (marking/parking) lot.

 41

Activity 1: Students look at the columns of words. Tell them to put the word from each column that fits into the 'word shape' box below it.

Activity 2: Students read the sentences. They underline the word in brackets that best completes the sentence.

WORD WORKERS 5 UNIT 2.13

Name .... Date ....

Put each column in alphabetical order.

ar		er		ir	
chart	barge	germ	clerk	whirl	squirt
barge	card	fern	fern	squirt	stir
card	charge	herd	germ	stir	thirst
far	chart	clerk	herd	thirst	twirl
charge	far	jerk	jerk	twirl	whirl

or		ur	
chore	born	purse	purse
fort	chore	spurt	spur
born	force	turn	spurt
force	fort	surf	surf
horn	horn	spur	turn

42

Students place the words in each column in alphabetical order.

WORD WORKERS 5 UNIT 2.14

Name .... Date ....

Complete these crossword puzzles.

ar: bark, barge, snarled, starve, dart

er: germ, swerve, fern, nerve, perch

ir: birth, bird, firm, swirl, thirst

or: force, fort, horse, chores, cork

ur: urge, burning, blurt, church, spur

 43

Students complete the crossword puzzles. They write the letters indicated in the blank spaces to make words that can be read going down or across the page.

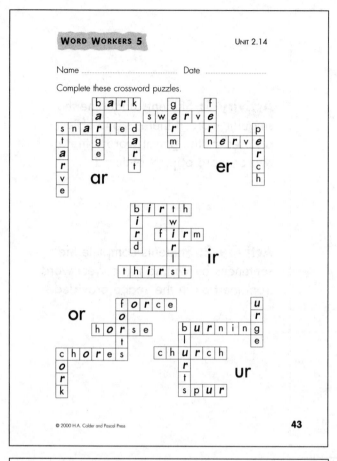

WORD WORKERS 5 UNIT 2.15

Name .... Date ....

Write the word with the correct spelling.

1.	charj	charge	charege	*charge*
2.	nerve	nerver	nerv	*nerve*
3.	squirt	skwirt	squert	*squirt*
4.	cherch	church	chirch	*church*
5.	force	fource	fourse	*force*

Fill in the missing letters to complete the word.

1. *s* harpe *n*
2. *l* arge *r*
3. *s* hortes *t*
4. *s* quirt *s*
5. *t* hirst *y*

shortest
squirts
thirsty
larger
sharpen

44

Activity 1: Students read the words going across the page, then write the word that is spelt correctly.

Activity 2: Students read the words in the box, then write the missing letters to complete the column of words on the left.

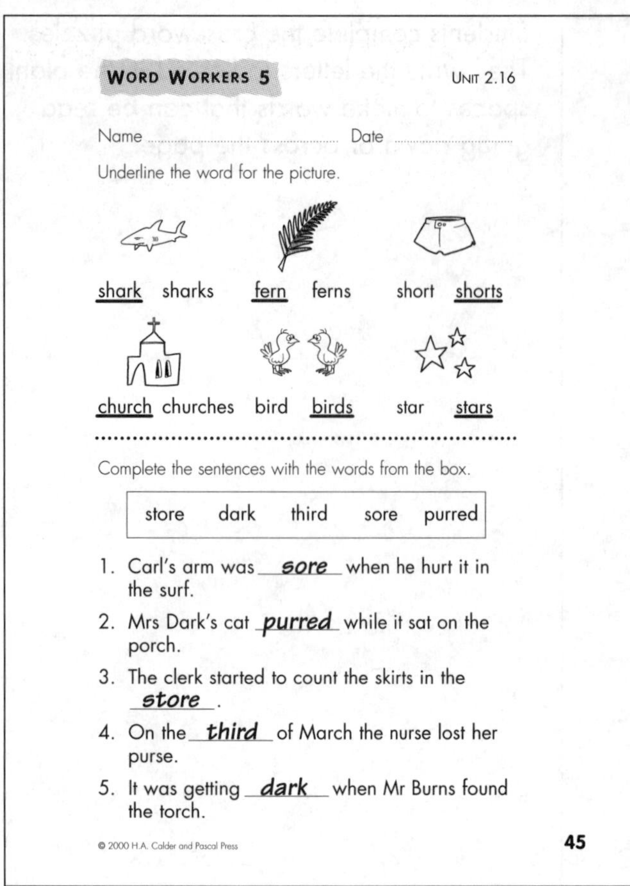

WORD WORKERS 5 UNIT 2.16

Name .... Date ....

Underline the word for the picture.

<u>shark</u> sharks <u>fern</u> ferns short <u>shorts</u>

<u>church</u> churches bird <u>birds</u> star <u>stars</u>

Complete the sentences with the words from the box.

store	dark	third	sore	purred

1. Carl's arm was *sore* when he hurt it in the surf.
2. Mrs Dark's cat *purred* while it sat on the porch.
3. The clerk started to count the skirts in the *store*.
4. On the *third* of March the nurse lost her purse.
5. It was getting *dark* when Mr Burns found the torch.

© 2000 H.A. Calder and Pascal Press 45

Activity 1: Students underline the singular word if there is one object pictured or the plural word if there are two or more objects pictured.

Activity 2: Students complete the sentences by writing the correct word from the box in the space provided.

WORD WORKERS 5 UNIT 2.17

Name .... Date ....

Draw a line from the picture to the matching word.

spur / blur / stir — start / dart / chart

lurch / perch / church — thirst / first / burst

Number the words in the box in alphabetical order, then answer the questions.

4 wore	*2* turn	*1* squirt
3 twirl	*5* worn	*6* yarn

1. Which word comes *before* 'turn'? *squirt*
2. Which word comes *after* 'worn'? *yarn*
3. Which word comes *after* 'wore'? *worn*
4. Which word comes *after* 'twirl'? *wore*
5. Which word comes *before* 'wore'? *twirl*
6. Which word comes *after* 'squirt'? *turn*

46 © 2000 H.A. Calder and Pascal Press

Activity 1: Students say the word for the picture and then draw a line from the picture to the correct word beside it.

Activity 2: Students number the words in the box in alphabetical order, then use this information to answer the questions below.

For the following pages:

Students read the story. They read it several times until accuracy and fluency combine to improve comprehension.

WORD WORKERS 5 UNIT 2.18

Read the story.

Shorty Thorn

Mark Thorn sat on his porch. He saw the big kids going down to the park to play. Mark jumped off the porch and jogged after them. The big boys snorted when they saw him. 'Not you, Shorty Thorn,' one of them said. 'You are too short and too little. You will get hurt!'

'I am not too short,' Mark blurted out. 'I can run faster than you can. I will not get hurt.' The biggest boy, Bart Clark, said, 'O.K. Shorty. Come with us. You can have a game.' Mark Thorn's chest nearly burst with pride. Off to the park he went. He was going to play with the big boys for the first time.

 47

WORD WORKERS 5 UNIT 2.19

When they got to the park, the boys charged onto the field. Bart Clark pointed to the bench. 'You stay there Shorty,' he said. 'Wait for a while.' Mark did not have to wait long. A player ran off with a sore arm. 'It is your turn Shorty,' he said. 'This is your big chance.'

Mark ran onto the field. A player on the other team snarled. 'Look at the short kid,' he said. 'He is so little, I bet the wind can blow him off his feet!' Mark kept his nerve and waited for his turn.

Just then Bart Clark gave him the ball and yelled, 'Go Shorty!' Mark took the ball and darted into a gap. A player on the other team lurched at him. Mark whirled and swerved, and ran past him. Another player grabbed his shirt but Mark got loose. He nearly ran into an arm, but he ducked just in time.

48

WORD WORKERS 5 UNIT 2.20

Mark's legs were a blur as he dived for the line. The ground was hard but the ball stayed in his arms. Mark Thorn scored in the corner. He had scored the first time he got his hands on the ball!

'Way to go Shorty,' Bart Clark shouted. But that was not the end of it. Mark scored three more times. After the game he was sore. His shirt was torn and dirty, but he had shown them what he could do. That day, Shorty Thorn was the biggest player at the park.

Now when they go to the park, the boys stop at Mark's porch. 'Come on Shorty Thorn,' they say. 'It is time for the game. We need the star of our team!'

 49

Students read the story. They read it several times until accuracy and fluency combine to improve comprehension.

WORD WORKERS 5 UNIT 2.21

Name .... Date ....

Write the letters 'a', 'b', 'c' and 'd' in the same order the pictures occurred in the story.

a  b 

c  d 

1. *b* 2. *d* 3. *a* 4. *c*

Answer the questions with the exact words from the story.

1. The big boys said Mark Thorn was too *short* and too *little*.
2. Mark's chest nearly *burst* with pride.
3. *Bart* *Clark* gave Mark the ball.
4. That day, Shorty Thorn was the *biggest* player at the park.

50

Activity 1: Students sequence the events in the story by placing the pictures in their correct order.

Activity 2: Students complete these sentences using the exact word from the story.

WORD WORKERS 5 UNIT 2.22

Name .... Date ....

Fill in the blanks with the correct word from the box.

Just then Bart Clark gave him the ball and yelled, 'Go Shorty!' Mark took the ball and *darted* into a gap. A player on the other team *lurched* at him. Mark whirled and *swerved*, and ran past him. Another player *grabbed* his shirt but Mark got loose. He nearly ran into an arm, but he *ducked* just in time.

ducked grabbed swerved lurched darted

Write the letters 'a', 'b', 'c' and 'd' beside the sentences in the same order they occurred in the story.

1. A player ran off with a sore arm. *b*
2. Mark Thorn's chest nearly burst with pride. *a*
3. Mark's legs were a blur as he dived for the line. *d*
4. Mark kept his nerve and waited for his turn. *c*

 51

Activity 1: Students complete this cloze exercise using the words from the box.

Activity 2: Students sequence the events in the story by placing them in their correct order.

* Students complete *Word Workers Achievement Test 6* after completing this unit.

WORD WORKERS 5 UNIT 3.1

Working with 'air', 'are', 'ear', 'ea', 'our', 'oar', 'all', 'al' and 'or' words

Say the sounds for these letters.

air as in 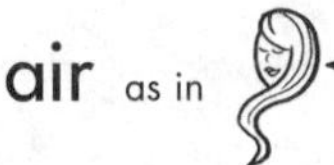 oar as in  

are as in  all as in 

ear as in  al as in 

ea as in  or as in 

our as in  ear as in 

52

For the following pages:

This unit teaches students to read words containing less regularly occurring digraphs. Make sure each student knows them. Photocopy the introductory page for students to refer to. Encourage students to practise these sounds as they colour the page in.

From now on, incorporate repetition of the sounds of the digraphs in the phonics drill at the start of each lesson.

Students read the words in the columns.

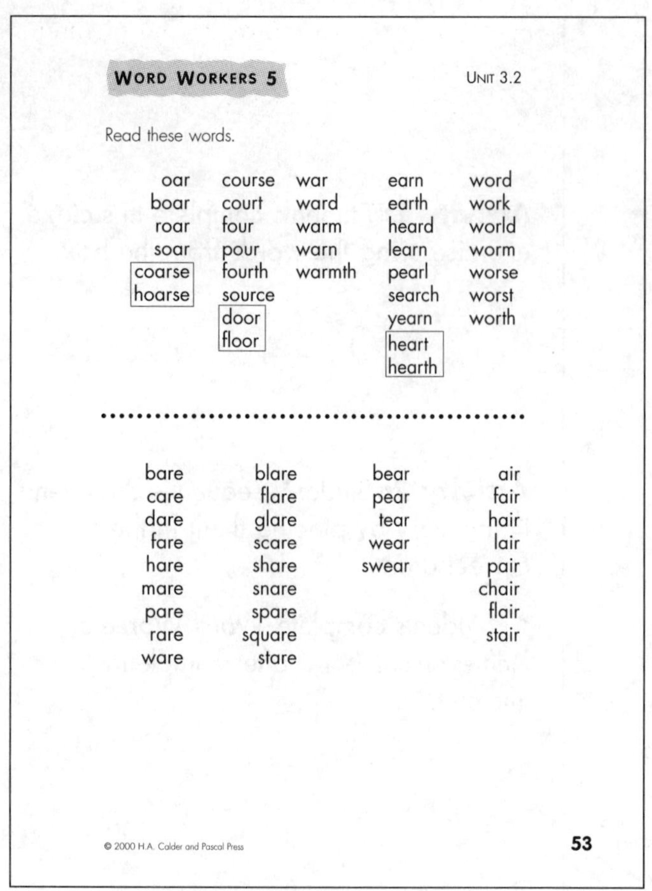

WORD WORKERS 5 UNIT 3.2

Read these words.

oar	course	war	earn	word
boar	court	ward	earth	work
roar	four	warm	heard	world
soar	pour	warn	learn	worm
coarse	fourth	warmth	pearl	worse
hoarse	source		search	worst
	door		yearn	worth
	floor		heart	
			hearth	

bare	blare	bear	air
care	flare	pear	fair
dare	glare	tear	hair
fare	scare	wear	lair
hare	share	swear	pair
mare	snare		chair
pare	spare		flair
rare	square		stair
ware	stare		

© 2000 H.A. Calder and Pascal Press

53

WORD WORKERS 5 UNIT 3.3

Read these words.

all	halt	dead	sweat	dove	bull
ball	malt	head	threat	love	full
call	salt	lead	meant	glove	pull
fall	bald	read	death	shove	
hall	scald	bread	breath	son	
mall	false	dread	health	won	
pall		tread	wealth	move	
tall		thread	stealth	prove	
wall		spread	give		
small		deaf	live		
stall					

blew	blue	new	cue
flew	true	few	due
drew	glue	dew	hue
grew		pew	
chew		spew	
crew		stew	
screw		news	
threw			

54

© 2000 H.A. Calder and Pascal Press

WORD WORKERS 5 UNIT 3.4

Name .... Date ....

Write the words for the pictures.

1. *bear* 2. *ball* 3. *heart*

4. *four* 5. *screw* 6. *worm*

7. *bull* 8. *pear* 9. *glue*

10. *chair* 11. *bread* 12. *hair*

 55

Students write the words for the pictures. If necessary, they refer to the word lists to find the correct spelling.

WORD WORKERS 5 UNIT 3.5

Name .... Date ....

Read these words.

earn earns earned earning	called calls calling call	threaded thread threading threads	chewing chew chews chewed
scared scaring scare scares	roar roared roars roaring	warns warned warning warn	scalded scalds scald scalding

Underline the word for the picture.

snare	scald	glove	blare	fair
rare	halt	love	share	chair
hare	false	shove	stare	stairs
flare	bald	dove	square	pair

56

Activity 1: Students read the words in the boxes. Tell them to add the endings to the smallest word or base word.

Activity 2: Students look at the columns of words. They underline the word in each column that matches the picture above it.

WORD WORKERS 5 UNIT 3.6

Name .... Date ....

Underline the nonsense word.

1. learn	2. halt	3. love	4. warn	5. glue
pearl	bald	spove	warmth	blue
pearn	false	glove	warm	splue
earth	smalt	shove	warsh	true

Write the word for the picture.

1. pears 2. glue 3. hearts

4. bread 5. screws 6. worm

7. balls 8. bull 9. glove

© 2000 H.A. Calder and Pascal Press 57

Activity 1: Students look at the columns of words. Tell them to underline the word in each column that is a nonsense word.

Activity 2: Students write the words for the pictures. Tell them to add the letter 's' if there is more than one. If necessary, they refer to the word lists to find the correct spelling.

WORD WORKERS 5 UNIT 3.7

Name .... Date ....

Complete these words with the word pattern from the picture.

sh are	f our th	h ead	st all	wor k
r are	p our	thr ead	f all	wor ld
bl are	c our t	spr ead	h all	wor th
d are	c our se	r ead	c all	wor se

Underline the correct word to complete the sentence.

1. Mrs Ward poured (four/court) cups of tea for the workers.
2. The clerk (word/heard) the door slam on the fourth floor.
3. The men sweated as they (shoved/loved) the blue chair up the stairs.
4. Mr Court said it was not (worst/worth) selling the pears he grew.
5. Mrs Hall stared as the dove (drew/flew) past.

58 © 2000 H.A. Calder and Pascal Press

Activity 1: Students look at the pictures above the columns. They use the word pattern from each picture to complete the words in the column below.

Activity 2: Students read the sentences. They underline the word in brackets that best completes the sentence.

WORD WORKERS 5 UNIT 3.8

Name .... Date ....

Read these words.

sweat sweats sweated sweating	stalled stall stalling stalls	glares glared glaring glare	pulling pulled pull pulls
small smaller smallest	fairer fair fairest	bluest blue bluer	rarer rarest rare
coarse coarsen	deaf deafen	fallen fall	worsen worse

Complete the words by writing the vowel sounds.

air	all	are	ea	or
ch ***air***	sm ***all***	gl ***are***	h ***ea*** lth	w ***or*** st
f ***air***	c ***all***	m ***are***	d ***ea*** f	w ***or*** d
st ***air***	w ***all***	st ***are***	thr ***ea*** t	w ***or*** th
fl ***air***	st ***all***	sh ***are***	m ***ea*** nt	w ***or*** k
p ***air***	t ***all***	r ***are***	w ***ea*** lth	w ***or*** m

 59

Activity 1: Students read the words in the boxes. Tell them to add the endings to the smallest word or base word.

Activity 2: Students complete the words by writing in the letters printed above each column.

WORD WORKERS 5 UNIT 3.9

Name .... Date ....

Draw a line to the word with the same word pattern.

door	salt	coarse	scald	hare	blue
tear	full	bald	call	flew	bare
halt	wear	sweat	hoarse	head	crew
give	floor	mall	pour	fair	bread
bull	live	four	threat	true	chair

Complete these sentences by writing the words for the pictures.

1. The bald man warned us that the ***bull*** was ready to charge.
2. The hunter was scared when he heard the ***bear*** roar.
3. Miss Drew left the pair of gloves she was wearing on the ***chair*** in the hall.
4. Tim ducked when the pitcher threw the ***ball*** at him.
5. Mr Small spread jam on the ***bread*** and shared it with his crew.

60

Activity 1: Students look at the two columns of words in each box. They draw a line from the word in the left-hand column to the word in the right-hand column that has the same word pattern.

Activity 2: Students look at the pictures and then complete the sentences below by writing the correct word for the picture in the space provided.

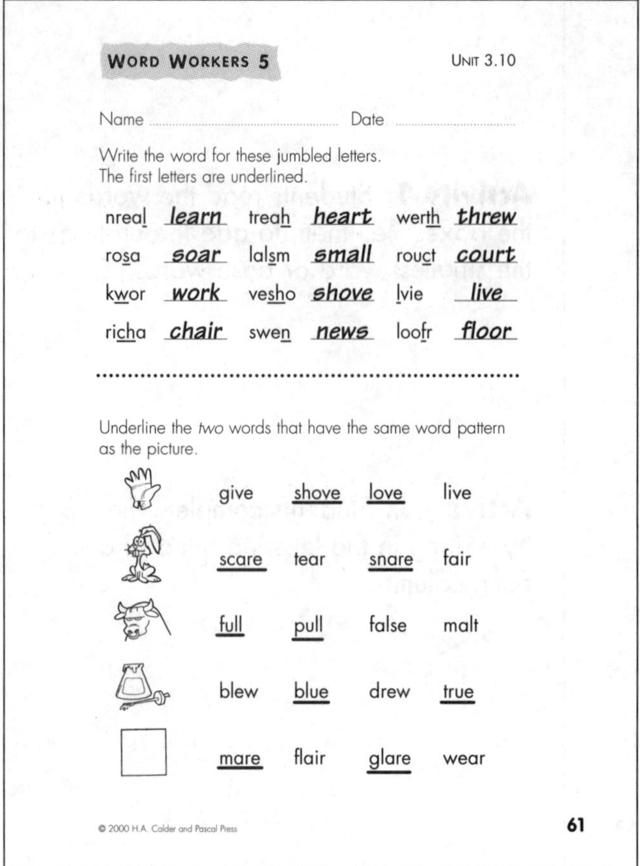

WORD WORKERS 5 UNIT 3.10

Name .... Date ....

Write the word for these jumbled letters.
The first letters are underlined.

nreal	*learn*	treah	*heart*	werth	*threw*
rosa	*soar*	lalsm	*small*	rouct	*court*
kwor	*work*	vesho	*shove*	lvie	*live*
richa	*chair*	swen	*news*	loofr	*floor*

Underline the *two* words that have the same word pattern as the picture.

give shove love live

scare tear snare fair

full pull false malt

blew blue drew true

mare flair glare wear

© 2000 H.A. Calder and Pascal Press 61

Activity 1: Students make a word from the jumbled letters. The first letter of each word is underlined. Students write the words in the spaces provided.

Activity 2: Students look at the pictures and the words on the lines beside them. They underline the two words in each line that have the same word pattern as the picture.

WORD WORKERS 5 UNIT 3.11

Name .... Date ....

Read these words.

work works worked working	stares staring stare stared	learning learns learned learn	shoved shoving shoves shove
chew chewy	pearly pearl	salt salty	sweaty sweat
warm warmly	truly true	falsely false	square squarely

Underline the word for the picture.

tear	wall	court	roar	flair
wear	fall	pour	boar	air
pear	small	course	oar	lair
bear	call	four	soar	hair

62 © 2000 H.A. Calder and Pascal Press

Activity 1: Students read the words in the boxes. Tell them to add the endings to the smallest word or base word.

Activity 2: Students look at the columns of words. They underline the word in each column that matches the picture above it.

WORD WORKERS 5 UNIT 3.12

Name .... Date ....

Write the word from each column that fits the word shape box.

work	flew	bread	heard
world	drew	thread	earth
worse	grew	dead	search
word	chew	spread	pearl

world drew bread pearl

Underline the correct word to complete the sentence.

1. Clare glared and said, 'Of course the news is (true/glue).'
2. The tallest runner was out of (breath/death) so he spoke in a hoarse voice.
3. They searched all morning for the (snare/spare) shaker of salt.
4. Mr Bull threw the book on the floor and said it was the worst book he had ever (read/dread).
5. Pearl worked all day and spent what she (earned/ learned) to get a haircut.

 63

Activity 1: Students look at the columns of words. Tell them to put the word from each column that fits into the 'word shape' box below it.

Activity 2: Students read the sentences. They underline the word in brackets that best completes the sentence.

WORD WORKERS 5 UNIT 3.13

Name .... Date ....

Put each column in alphabetical order.

are		air		ar	
dare	care	hair	chair	warm	war
snare	dare	flair	fair	ward	ward
care	glare	chair	flair	war	warm
glare	share	stair	hair	warmth	warmth
share	snare	fair	stair	warn	warn

all		ea		our	
tall	mall	sweat	meant	pour	course
wall	small	meant	stealth	four	court
stall	stall	threat	sweat	court	four
small	tall	wealth	threat	course	fourth
mall	wall	stealth	wealth	fourth	pour

64

Students place the words in each column in alphabetical order.

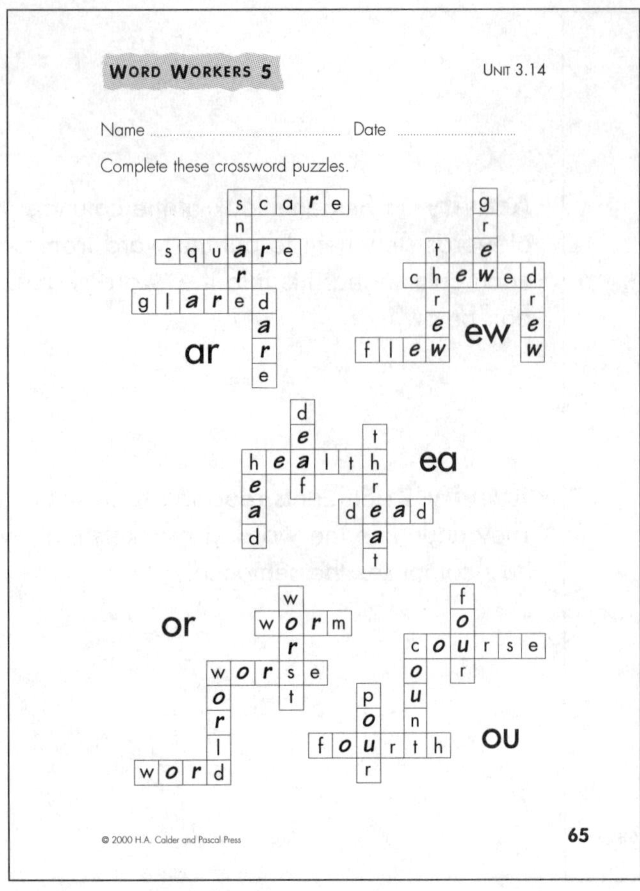
WORD WORKERS 5 UNIT 3.14

Name .... Date ....

Complete these crossword puzzles.

© 2000 H.A. Calder and Pascal Press 65

Students complete the crossword puzzles. They write the letters indicated in the blank spaces to make words that can be read going down or across the page.

WORD WORKERS 5 UNIT 3.15

Name .... Date ....

Write the word with the correct spelling.

1. scair scear scare ___*scare*___
2. breath breth brethe ___*breath*___
3. harte heart hearte ___*heart*___
4. worm werm wirm ___*worm*___
5. glov gluv glove ___*glove*___

Fill in the missing letters to complete the word.

1. _*c*_ hewin _*g*_
2. _*h*_ ealth _*y*_
3. _*w*_ arne _*d*_
4. _*t*_ hreate _*n*_
5. _*f*_ aire _*r*_

warned
chewing
healthy
fairer
threaten

66 © 2000 H.A. Calder and Pascal Press

Activity 1: Students read the words going across the page, then write the word that is spelt correctly.

Activity 2: Students read the words in the box, then write the missing letters to complete the column of words on the left.

WORD WORKERS 5 UNIT 3.16

Name .... Date ....

Underline the word for the picture.

ball <u>balls</u> pear <u>pears</u> <u>chair</u> chairs

<u>worm</u> worms heart <u>hearts</u> <u>glove</u> gloves

Complete the sentences with the words from the box.

chair	leather	true	warm	workers

1. Mrs Small said it was too *warm* to wear her coat.
2. 'It cannot be *true*!' Blair said when he heard the bad news.
3. The girl pulled the loose thread on her *leather* glove.
4. Bart got off the floor and read in his *chair*.
5. The *workers* sweated as they shoved the box up the stairs.

© 2000 H.A. Calder and Pascal Press 67

Activity 1: Students underline the singular word if there is one object pictured or the plural word if there are two or more objects pictured.

Activity 2: Students complete the sentences by writing the correct word from the box in the space provided.

WORD WORKERS 5 UNIT 3.17

Name .... Date ....

Draw a line from the picture to the matching word.

small / tall / fall — bald / scald / false

stair / chair / pair — true / blue / glue

Number the words in the box in alphabetical order, then answer the questions

3 course	*6* flare	*1* bare
4 deaf	*2* bread	*5* drew

1. Which word comes *before* 'bread'? *bare*
2. Which word comes *before* 'deaf'? *course*
3. Which word comes *after* 'bare'? *bread*
4. Which word comes *before* 'flare'? *drew*
5. Which word comes *after* 'drew'? *flare*
6. Which word comes *after* 'course'? *deaf*

68 © 2000 H.A. Calder and Pascal Press

Activity 1: Students say the word for the picture and then draw a line from the picture to the correct word beside it.

Activity 2: Students number the words in the box in alphabetical order, then use this information to answer the questions below.

WORD WORKERS 5 UNIT 3.18

Read the story.

The Snorer

Clair's dad was the worst snorer in the world. He was too bad to be true.

ZZZZZZZZZZZ!

Mr Earl's snores shook the walls of the house.

ZZZZZZZZZZZ!

Mr Earl sounded like a roaring bear.

ZZZZZZZZZZZ!

 69

WORD WORKERS 5 UNIT 3.19

Clair slept in her room down the hall. But she did not sleep long. The noise grew and grew. It shook her door. It lifted her chair off the floor. It scared the sleeping birds in the trees. The worms went deeper in the earth when they heard him snore.

'It is not fair,' cried Clair. 'I cannot sleep. Those snores will make me deaf.' Clair went up the stairs to her dad's room. The roar of his snores grew louder and louder. So loud that Mr Earl could not have heard the floor creak when Clair crept in.

'It is four in the morning,' Clair shouted. 'Be fair, I need some sleep.' She tried to give her dad a shove, but it was no good.

70

For the following pages:

Students read the story. They read it several times until accuracy and fluency combine to improve comprehension.

WORD WORKERS 5 UNIT 3.20

ZZZZZZZZZZZ!

The roaring snores went on and on. 'I give up,' Clair said. 'My dad must be the worst snorer in the world!' So she shut Mr Earl's door and went down the hall to her room. She got into bed and pulled the sheet over her head.

Soon it was morning. Mr Earl woke up and got ready for work. Clair sat in a chair and brushed her hair. Mr Earl looked at her. 'You look tired my dear,' he said in a cheery voice. 'You must try to get to bed early.'

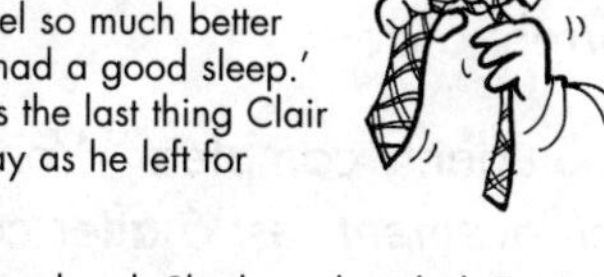

Clair stared at her dad. Then she glared at him. But Mr Earl went to the door and took a breath of fresh air. 'What a nice warm day it is. I feel so much better after I have had a good sleep.' And that was the last thing Clair heard him say as he left for work.

Clair shook her head. She loves her dad. But it is hard to live with the worst snorer in the world!

 71

Students read the story. They read it several times until accuracy and fluency combine to improve comprehension.

WORD WORKERS 5 UNIT 3.21

Name .... Date ....

Write the letters 'a', 'b', 'c' and 'd' in the same order the pictures occurred in the story.

a b

c d

1. *a* 2. *d* 3. *c* 4. *b*

Answer the questions with the exact words from the story.

1. Mr Earl sounded like a *roaring* *bear* .
2. The noise of Mr Earl's snores scared the *birds* in the trees.
3. Clair said her dad's snores were making her *deaf* .
4. Mr Earl said that Clair must try to get to bed *early*.
5. It is hard to live with the *worst* *snorer* *in* *the* *world* .

72

Activity 1: Students sequence the events in the story by placing the pictures in their correct order.

Activity 2: Students complete these sentences using the exact word from the story.

WORD WORKERS 5 UNIT 3.22

Name .... Date ....

Fill in the blanks with the correct word from the box.

Mr Earl sounded like a roaring *bear* .

ZZZZZZZZZZZ!

Clair slept in her room down the *hall* . But she did not sleep long. The noise grew and grew. It shook her *door* . It lifted her chair off the floor. It *scared* the sleeping birds in the trees. The worms went deeper in the *earth* when they heard him snore.

hall bear door earth scared

Write the letters 'a', 'b', 'c' and 'd' beside the sentences in the same order they occurred in the story.

1. Mr Earl woke up and got ready for work. *c*
2. Mr Earl went to the door and took a breath of fresh air. *d*
3. Mr Earl's snores shook the walls of his house. *a*
4. Clair went up the stairs to her dad's room. *b*

 73

Activity 1: Students complete the sentences by writing the correct word from the box in the space provided.

Activity 2: Students sequence the events in the story by placing them in their correct order.

* Students complete *Word Workers Achievement Test 6* after completing this unit.

WORD WORKERS 5 UNIT 4.1

Working with silent letters

The letters in these words are silent letters.

d as in

k as in

b as in

w as in

gh as in

t as in

l as in

74

For the following pages:

This unit teaches students to read words containing silent letters. Make sure each student knows them. Direct students' attention to the 'igh', 'eigh' and 'ough' wall chart from page 46 of the *Word Workers Teacher Resource Book* when they read words containing these silent letters. Encourage students to memorise these sounds until they are learned satisfactorily.

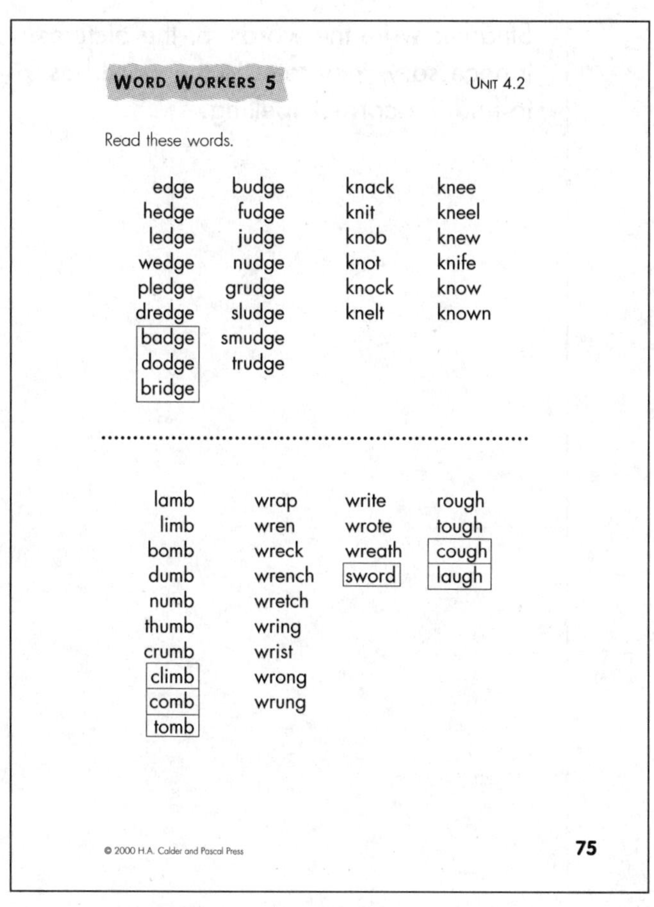

WORD WORKERS 5 UNIT 4.2

Read these words.

edge	budge	knack	knee
hedge	fudge	knit	kneel
ledge	judge	knob	knew
wedge	nudge	knot	knife
pledge	grudge	knock	know
dredge	sludge	knelt	known
badge	smudge		
dodge	trudge		
bridge			

lamb	wrap	write	rough
limb	wren	wrote	tough
bomb	wreck	wreath	cough
dumb	wrench	sword	laugh
numb	wretch		
thumb	wring		
crumb	wrist		
climb	wrong		
comb	wrung		
tomb			

© 2000 H.A. Calder and Pascal Press 75

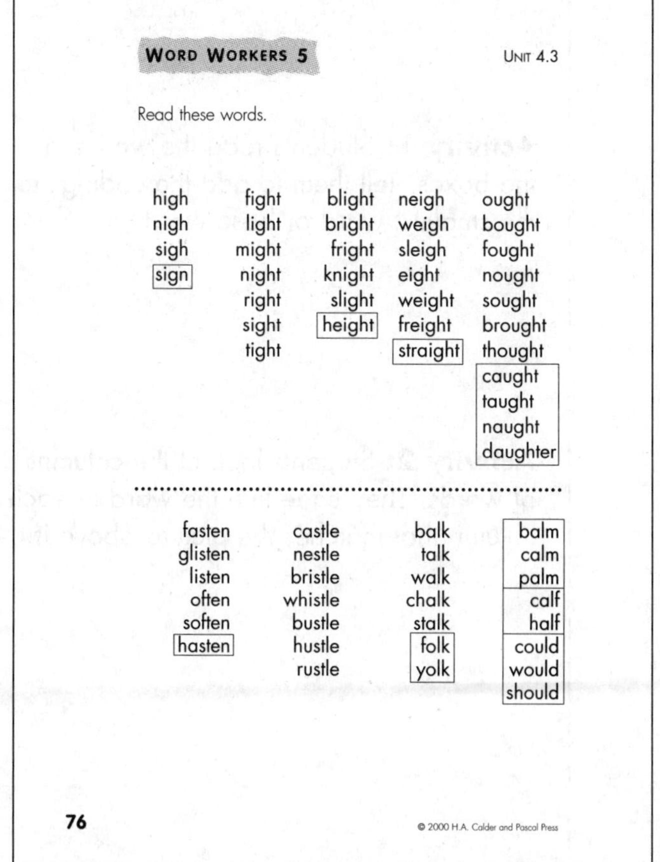

WORD WORKERS 5 UNIT 4.3

Read these words.

high	fight	blight	neigh	ought
nigh	light	bright	weigh	bought
sigh	might	fright	sleigh	fought
sign	night	knight	eight	nought
	right	slight	weight	sought
	sight	height	freight	brought
	tight		straight	thought
				caught
				taught
				naught
				daughter

fasten	castle	balk	balm
glisten	nestle	talk	calm
listen	bristle	walk	palm
often	whistle	chalk	calf
soften	bustle	stalk	half
hasten	hustle	folk	could
	rustle	yolk	would
			should

76 © 2000 H.A. Calder and Pascal Press

Students read the words in the columns.

WORD WORKERS 5 UNIT 4.4

Name .... Date ....

Write the words for the pictures.

1. *comb* 2. *castle* 3. *light*

4. *bridge* 5. *whistle* 6. *knife*

7. *bomb* 8. *palm* 9. *eight*

10. *knee* 11. *knight* 12. *wrench*

 77

Students write the words for the pictures. If necessary, they refer to the word lists to find the correct spelling.

WORD WORKERS 5 UNIT 4.5

Name .... Date ....

Read these words.

comb combs combed combing	knocking knocked knock knocks	judged judges judging judge	wraps wrap wrapping wrapped
glistens glistened glisten glistening	laughed laughing laughs laugh	calms calming calm calmed	weighed weigh weighing weighs

Underline the word for the picture.

stalk	wren	crumb	knit	weight
walk	<u>wrist</u>	lamb	knew	sleigh
<u>chalk</u>	wring	limb	<u>knob</u>	freight
balk	wreck	<u>thumb</u>	knock	<u>eight</u>

78

Activity 1: Students read the words in the boxes. Tell them to add the endings to the smallest word or base word.

Activity 2: Students look at the columns of words. They underline the word in each column that matches the picture above it.

WORD WORKERS 5 UNIT 4.6

Name .... Date ....

Underline the nonsense word.

1. wreck	2. calm	3. ought	4. weight	5. knot
wrong	half	blought	neigh	knamp
wrist	palk	brought	freight	knew
wrup	walk	taught	spleight	knife

Write the word for the picture.

1. knife 2. whistles 3. knob

4. combs 5. thumb 6. wrenches

7. badge 8. bombs 9. light

© 2000 H.A. Calder and Pascal Press 79

Activity 1: Students look at the columns of words. Tell them to underline the word in each column that is a nonsense word.

Activity 2: Students write the words for the pictures. Tell them to add the letter 's' if there is more than one. If necessary, they refer to the word lists to find the correct spelling.

WORD WORKERS 5 UNIT 4.7

Name .... Date ....

Complete these words with the word pattern from the picture.

sli gh t	he d ge	k nown	w rote	whis t le
mi gh t	gru d ge	k nit	w reck	nes t le
bri gh t	ju d ge	k nelt	w rung	bris t le
si gh t	le d ge	k nack	w retch	rus t le

Underline the correct word to complete the sentence.

1. Mrs Knight thought the child ought to be (caught/taught) to read.
2. They fastened the rope to the door (knob/knack) with a tight knot.
3. Jean cut her (numb/thumb) with the knife she had just bought.
4. Mr Lamb (weighed/neighed) the fish he caught.
5. Eighty knights crossed the bridge as they left the (rustle/castle).

80 © 2000 H.A. Calder and Pascal Press

Activity 1: Students look at the pictures above the columns. They use the word pattern from each picture to complete the words in the column below.

Activity 2: Students read the sentences. They underline the word in brackets that best completes the sentence.

WORD WORKERS 5 UNIT 4.8

Name .... Date ....

Read these words.

sigh sighs sighed sighing	knitting knitted knits knit	whistling whistle whistles whistled	fastened fastens fastening fasten
light lighter lightest	higher high highest	calmest calm calmer	brightest brighter bright
fright frighten	soften soft	height heighten	tighten tight

Complete the words by writing the silent letters.

b	d	gh	k	l	t
lam*b*	e*d*ge	bou*gh*t	*k*nee	wa*l*k	fas*t*en
clim*b*	ba*d*ge	thou*gh*t	*k*new	pa*l*m	cas*t*le
com*b*	tru*d*ge	ei*gh*t	*k*nife	ca*l*f	lis*t*en
tom*b*	he*d*ge	fi*gh*t	*k*not	yo*l*k	hus*t*le
thum*b*	bri*d*ge	cau*gh*t	*k*nelt	ha*l*f	sof*t*en

 81

Activity 1: Students read the words in the boxes. Tell them to add the endings to the smallest word or base word.

Activity 2: Students complete the words by writing in the letter(s) printed above each column.

WORD WORKERS 5 UNIT 4.9

Name .... Date ....

Draw a line to the word with the same word pattern.

caught	thumb	would	neigh	wedge	freight
numb	palm	bought	smudge	walk	pledge
listen	taught	weigh	flight	eight	stalk
hustle	glisten	budge	should	fought	tough
calm	rustle	tight	thought	rough	sought

Complete these sentences by writing the words for the pictures.

1. The wrestler could not write after he sprained his *wrist*.
2. The queen brought the kneeling knight the glistening *sword*.
3. She picked up the *chalk* and wrote eight words on the board.
4. They climbed onto the ledge of the *bridge* to see the freighter sail by.
5. Her frightened daughter turned on the brightest *light*.

82

Activity 1: Students look at the two columns of words in each box. They draw a line from the word in the left-hand column to the word in the right-hand column that has the same word pattern.

Activity 2: Students look at the pictures and then complete the sentences below by writing the correct word for the picture in the space provided.

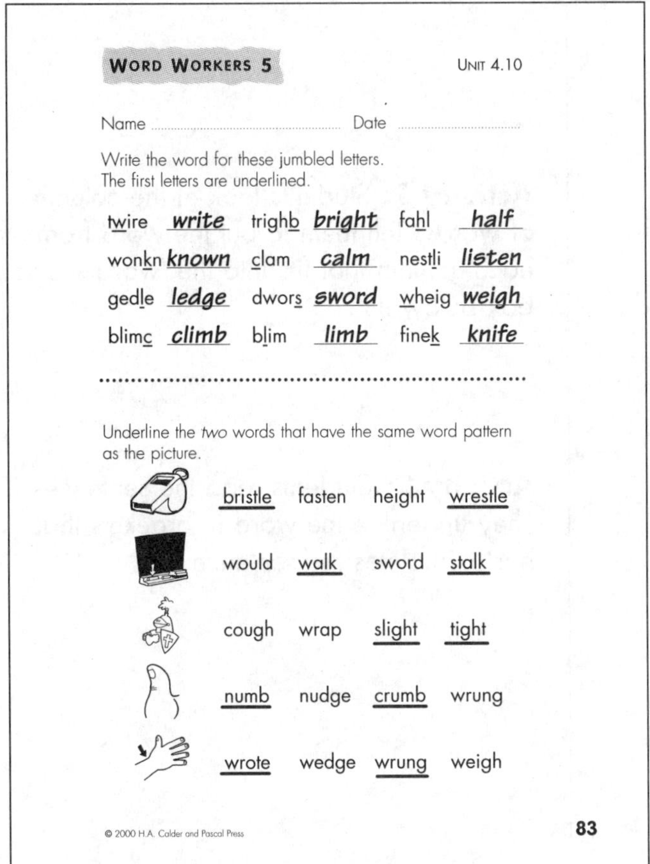

WORD WORKERS 5 UNIT 4.10

Name .... Date ....

Write the word for these jumbled letters.
The first letters are underlined.

twire	*write*	trighb	*bright*	fahl	*half*
wonkn	*known*	clam	*calm*	nestli	*listen*
gedle	*ledge*	dwors	*sword*	wheig	*weigh*
blimc	*climb*	blim	*limb*	finek	*knife*

Underline the *two* words that have the same word pattern as the picture.

bristle fasten height wrestle

would walk sword stalk

cough wrap slight tight

numb nudge crumb wrung

wrote wedge wrung weigh

© 2000 H.A. Calder and Pascal Press 83

Activity 1: Students make a word from the jumbled letters. The first letter of each word is underlined. Students write the words in the spaces provided.

Activity 2: Students look at the pictures and the words on the lines beside them. They underline the two words in each line that have the same word pattern as the picture.

WORD WORKERS 5 UNIT 4.11

Name .... Date ....

Read these words.

wrench wrenches wrenched wrenching	climb climbing climbed climbs	talking talk talks talked	soften softened softening softens
eight eighty	mighty might	balm balmy	weighty weight
tight tightly	calmly calm	wrong wrongly	dumbly dumb

Underline the word for the picture.

calm	wreck	dumb	castle	kneel
yolk	wrench	comb	hustle	knelt
half	wrap	bomb	nestle	knee
palm	write	numb	whistle	knot

84 © 2000 H.A. Calder and Pascal Press

Activity 1: Students read the words in the boxes. Tell them to add the endings to the smallest word or base word.

Activity 2: Students look at the columns of words. They underline the word in each column that matches the picture above it.

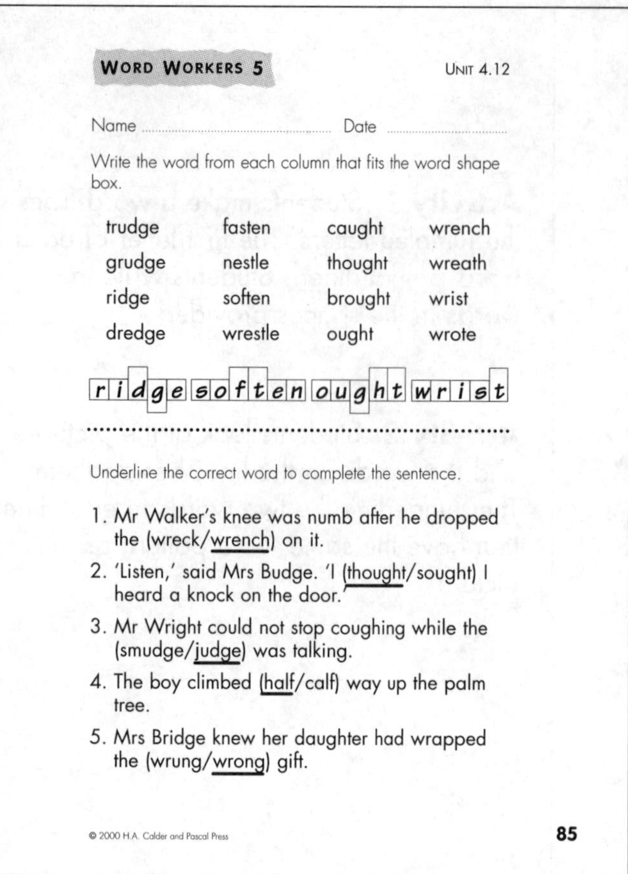

WORD WORKERS 5 UNIT 4.12

Name .... Date ....

Write the word from each column that fits the word shape box.

trudge	fasten	caught	wrench
grudge	nestle	thought	wreath
ridge	soften	brought	wrist
dredge	wrestle	ought	wrote

ridge soften ought wrist

Underline the correct word to complete the sentence.

1. Mr Walker's knee was numb after he dropped the (wreck/wrench) on it.
2. 'Listen,' said Mrs Budge. 'I (thought/sought) I heard a knock on the door.'
3. Mr Wright could not stop coughing while the (smudge/judge) was talking.
4. The boy climbed (half/calf) way up the palm tree.
5. Mrs Bridge knew her daughter had wrapped the (wrung/wrong) gift.

© 2000 H.A. Calder and Pascal Press 85

Activity 1: Students look at the columns of words. Tell them to put the word from each column that fits into the 'word shape' box below it.

Activity 2: Students read the sentences. They underline the word in brackets that best completes the sentence.

WORD WORKERS 5 UNIT 4.13

Name .... Date ....

Put each column in alphabetical order.

a		e		i	
chalk	castle	ledge	height	limb	knit
lamb	chalk	height	knelt	knit	limb
knack	knack	knelt	knew	listen	listen
castle	lamb	pledge	ledge	write	whistle
laugh	laugh	knew	pledge	whistle	write

o		u	
thought	sword	rustle	rustle
would	thought	wrung	sludge
sword	tough	sludge	smudge
wrote	would	thumb	thumb
tough	wrote	smudge	wrung

86 © 2000 H.A. Calder and Pascal Press

Students place the words in each column in alphabetical order.

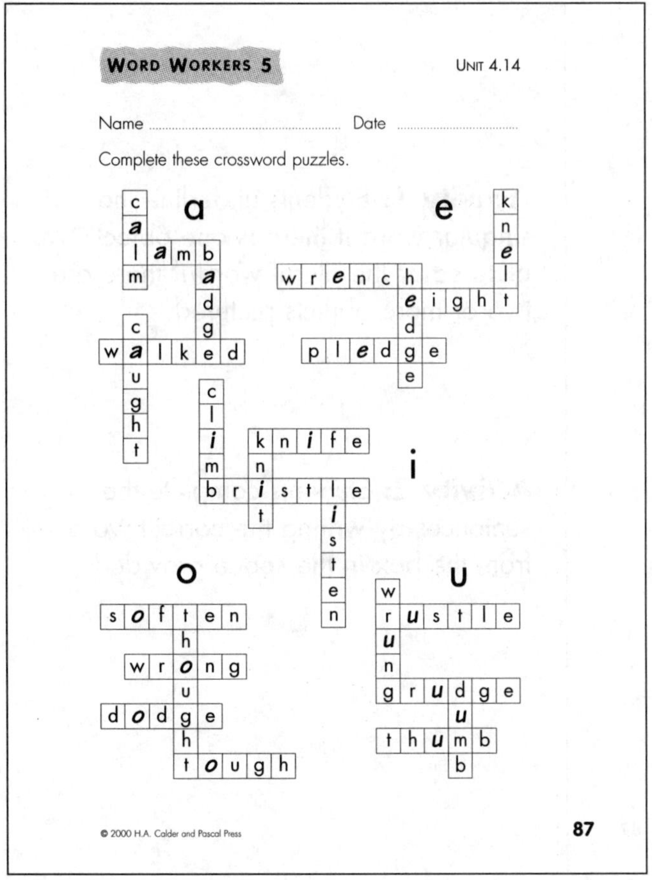

WORD WORKERS 5 UNIT 4.14

Name .... Date ....

Complete these crossword puzzles.

 87

Students complete the crossword puzzles. They write the letter indicated in the blank spaces to make words that can be read going down or across the page.

WORD WORKERS 5 UNIT 4.15

Name .... Date ....

Write the word with the correct spelling.

1.	budj	buge	budge	*budge*
2.	laugh	laff	luagh	*laugh*
3.	rite	right	rihte	*right*
4.	kneel	neel	kneal	*kneel*
5.	brawght	brought	brot	*brought*

Fill in the missing letters to complete the word.

1. *k* noc *k*
2. *w* rappe *d*
3. *h* ighes *t*
4. *s* ofte *n*
5. *t* hough *t*

wrapped
soften
knock
thought
highest

88

Activity 1: Students read the words going across the page, then write the word that is spelt correctly.

Activity 2: Students read the words in the box, then write the missing letters to complete the column of words on the left.

WORD WORKERS 5 UNIT 4.16

Name .... Date ....

Underline the word for the picture.

<u>sword</u> swords badge <u>badges</u> <u>knight</u> knights

bomb <u>bombs</u> comb <u>combs</u> <u>whistle</u> whistles

Complete the sentences with the words from the box.

sword	eight	weight	bridge	naughty

1. Mrs Wright sent her *naughty* daughter to her room.
2. The wrestler often thought he had put on too much *weight*.
3. The knight's *sword* glistened in the bright light.
4. Mr Bligh left *eight* pieces of fudge on the plate.
5. He caught the calf as it walked off the *bridge*.

 89

Activity 1: Students underline the singular word if there is one object pictured or the plural word if there are two or more objects pictured.

Activity 2: Students complete the sentences by writing the correct word from the box in the space provided.

WORD WORKERS 5 UNIT 4.17

Name .... Date ....

Draw a line from the picture to the matching word.

calm / palm / half — wrist / wring / wrote

knob / knot / knew — budge / badge / bridge

Number the words in the box in alphabetical order, then answer the questions.

1 hedge	4 knight	6 listen
3 knife	2 judge	5 limb

1. Which word comes *before* 'knight'? *knife*
2. Which word comes *after* 'hedge'? *judge*
3. Which word comes *before* 'judge'? *hedge*
4. Which word comes *after* 'knife'? *knight*
5. Which word comes *before* 'listen'? *limb*
6. Which word comes *after* 'limb'? *listen*

90

Activity 1: Students say the word for the picture and then draw a line from the picture to the correct word beside it.

Activity 2: Students number the words in the box in alphabetical order, then use this information to answer the questions below.

For the following pages:

Students read the story. They read it several times until accuracy and fluency combine to improve comprehension.

Read the story.

Tim Wright Gets it Wrong

This was Tim Wright's first day at his new school. He walked down the long hall and found his room. Tim knocked on the door. 'Come in please,' a voice said. He turned the knob and went in.

Tim was eight years old. His mum and dad had bought a new house. The school year was half over, so Tim had to start at this school. 'Starting school twice in the same year is too much,' Tim thought.

Tim's teacher was Mrs Bridges. She was talking to the class as Tim came in. She smiled at him and pointed to a desk. Tim sat down. Mrs Bridges wrote on the board with a piece of chalk. When she stopped writing she walked over to Tim's desk.

Tim looked at her in fright. He sat on the edge of his chair as she came closer. 'Oh no,' he thought. 'She will ask me to read. But I cannot read. I am eight years old and I ought to read by now. But the words come out all wrong. I am just plain dumb!'

Mrs Bridges knew what was wrong. She could tell by the look on Tim's face. 'Calm down Tim,' she said. 'Listen to me. I know it is hard for you to read. Lots of kids cannot read by the time they are eight, but that does not mean they are dumb.'

Mrs Bridges sighed as she spoke. 'I have taught lots of kids like you to read. You have to be taught the right way. Learning to read is a skill, Tim. You know how to ride a bike. Well, learning to ride a bike is a skill. My job is to teach you reading skills. So, I have to find a way to make reading easy for you.

WORD WORKERS 5 UNIT 4.20

After school that day Tim Wright whistled as he rode home on his bike. 'I got it wrong,' he said 'I am not dumb. I just do not have a skill. I *can* learn to read. I know I can. It is a skill — like learning to ride my bike. I just need to be shown the right way.' By the end of that year, Mrs Bridges had taught Tim to read. From then on he never thought he was dumb.

So Tim Wright got it wrong. He was not dumb. He just did not have a skill. And, like Tim, there are lots of kids who cannot read. But they are not dumb. They just do not have the skill.

 93

Students read the story. They read it several times until accuracy and fluency combine to improve comprehension.

WORD WORKERS 5 UNIT 4.21

Name .... Date ....

Write the letters 'a', 'b', 'c' and 'd' in the same order the pictures occurred in the story.

a 

b 

c 

d 

1. *c* 2. *d* 3. *a* 4. *b*

Answer the questions with the exact words from the story.

1. Tim Wright was *eight* years old.
2. Tim's teacher was *Mrs Bridges*.
3. Mrs Bridges *wrote* on the board with a piece of *chalk*.
4. Kids are not *dumb* when they cannot read, they just do not have the *skill*.

94

Activity 1: Students sequence the events in the story by placing the pictures in their correct order.

Activity 2: Students complete these sentences using the exact word from the story.

WORD WORKERS 5 UNIT 4.22

Name .... Date ....

Fill in the blanks with the correct word from the box.

Mrs Bridges _sighed_ as she spoke. 'I have taught lots of kids like you to read. You have to be _taught_ the right way. _Learning_ to read is a skill, Tim. You know how to ride a bike. Well, learning to ride a bike is a skill. My job is to _teach_ you reading skills. So, I have to find a way to make _reading_ easy for you.

reading	sighed	learning	taught	teach

Write the letters 'a', 'b', 'c' and 'd' beside the sentences in the same order they occurred in the story.

1. By the end of that year, Mrs Bridges had taught Tim to read. _d_
2. Mrs Bridges wrote on the board with a piece of chalk. _a_
3. After school that day Tim Wright whistled as he rode home. _c_
4. Mrs Bridges knew what was wrong. _b_

 95

Activity 1: Students complete this cloze exercise using the words from the box.

Activity 2: Students sequence the events in the story by placing them in their correct order.

* Students complete *Word Workers Achievement Test 7* after completing this unit.

WORD WORKERS 5 UNIT 5.1

More work with words

Read these words.

1.	boom	oar	lamb	snore
2.	fork	shook	door	pledge
3.	weigh	worn	choice	war
4.	learn	short	knot	toy
5.	spur	wrong	world	shout
6.	listen	rare	crown	burst
7.	bear	yawn	talk	star
8.	throw	chair	shark	laugh
9.	loose	wood	small	thought
10.	start	work	boil	false
11.	snooze	torch	care	wrench
12.	health	hawk	nurse	rough

96

For the following pages:

This unit consolidates the skills and phonic generalisations learned in the previous units.

Students read the words going across the page.

WORD WORKERS 5 UNIT 5.2

Read these words.

1.	bread	fight	perch	point
2.	fern	glove	boy	eight
3.	third	couch	give	caught
4.	brown	girl	knight	blew
5.	straw	cue	calm	horse
6.	shirt	blown	pew	whistle
7.	birth	write	sauce	true
8.	knife	farm	bald	shoot
9.	snarl	bull	haul	bridge
10.	halt	house	thumb	church
11.	ground	force	brought	four
12.	nerve	blue	grown	budge

 97

Students read the words going across the page.

WORD WORKERS 5 UNIT 5.3

Name .... Date ....

Write the words for the pictures.

1. *crown* 2. *ball* 3. *bird*

4. *knight* 5. *car* 6. *cook*

7. *hair* 8. *bomb* 9. *snore*

10. *row* 11. *bear* 12. *castle*

98

Students write the words for the pictures. If necessary, they refer to the word lists to find the correct spelling.

WORD WORKERS 5 UNIT 5.4

Name .... Date ....

Read these words.

pause pauses paused pausing	turns turned turning turn	worked works work working	knocking knock knocks knocked
charging charged charge charges	cooking cooks cooked cook	wrap wrapped wrapping wraps	shows show showing showed
chewing chew chews chewed	weigh weighed weighing weighs	pointing points point pointed	stirs stirred stir stirring

Underline the word for the picture.

store	rare	hawk	brown	palm
roar	wear	sauce	sour	chalk
shore	hair	fault	spout	could
pour	square	bald	shout	stalk

© 2000 H.A. Calder and Pascal Press 99

Activity 1: Students read the words in the boxes. Tell them to add the endings to the smallest word or base word.

Activity 2: Students look at the columns of words. They underline the word in each column that matches the picture above it.

WORD WORKERS 5 UNIT 5.5

Name .... Date ....

Underline the nonsense word.

1.	2.	3.	4.	5.
wreck	head	nurse	ploon	mouse
wring	sweat	purnt	shoot	flour
wrelf	health	burst	troop	slount
wrap	dreath	spurt	goose	spout

Write the word for the picture.

1. badges 2. bread 3. bowls

4. moon 5. stars 6. worm

7. bird 8. clouds 9. wrench

100 © 2000 H.A. Calder and Pascal Press

Activity 1: Students look at the columns of words. Tell them to underline the word in each column that is a nonsense word.

Activity 2: Students write the words for the pictures. Tell them to add the letter 's' if there is more than one. If necessary, they refer to the word lists to find the correct spelling.

WORD WORKERS 5 UNIT 5.6

Name .... Date ....

Complete these words with the word pattern from the picture.

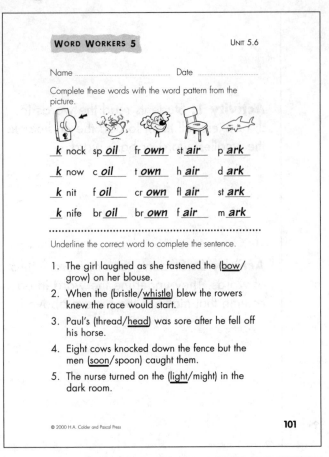

k nock	sp oil	fr own	st air	p ark
k now	c oil	t own	h air	d ark
k nit	f oil	cr own	fl air	st ark
k nife	br oil	br own	f air	m ark

Underline the correct word to complete the sentence.

1. The girl laughed as she fastened the (bow/grow) on her blouse.
2. When the (bristle/whistle) blew the rowers knew the race would start.
3. Paul's (thread/head) was sore after he fell off his horse.
4. Eight cows knocked down the fence but the men (soon/spoon) caught them.
5. The nurse turned on the (light/might) in the dark room.

 101

Activity 1: Students look at the pictures above the columns. They use the word pattern from each picture to complete the words in the column below.

Activity 2: Students read the sentences. They underline the word in brackets that best completes the sentence.

WORD WORKERS 5 UNIT 5.7

Name .... Date ....

Read these words.

haul hauls hauled hauling	marked marking marks mark	learning learns learn learned	fastening fastens fastened fasten
hard harder hardest	slowest slow slower	smaller smallest small	highest higher high
wood wooden	shorten short	deafen deaf	fright frighten

Complete the words by writing the vowel sounds.

a	e	i	o	u
sc a re	st e w	g i ve	l o ve	tr u e
l a mb	n e stle	wr i st	b o ught	j u dge
p a rk	g e rm	th i rd	w o rn	ch u rch
cr a wl	n e rve	cl i mb	v o ice	bl u e
w a rm	e ight	b i rth	cr o uch	sp u r

102

Activity 1: Students read the words in the boxes. Tell them to add the endings to the smallest word or base word.

Activity 2: Students complete the words by writing in the letter printed above each column.

WORD WORKERS 5 UNIT 5.8

Name .... Date ....

Draw a line to the word with the same word pattern.

blue	drawn
listen	glue
first	glisten
yawn	join
coin	thirst

harm	thumb
salt	toy
numb	halt
sour	charm
boy	flour

fought	thrown
large	mood
new	bought
grown	stew
food	charge

Complete these sentences by writing the words for the pictures.

1. The frightened ***crow*** flew off when the farmer ran out the door.
2. The cook carved half the goose with the sharpest ***knife***.
3. Late at night the boys heard the ***owl*** hooting in the woods.
4. Roy's knees shook when he saw the ***bull*** was ready to charge.
5. She was taught to write the words neatly in her ***book***.

© 2000 H.A. Calder and Pascal Press 103

Activity 1: Students look at the two columns of words in each box. They draw a line from the word in the left-hand column to the word in the right-hand column that has the same word pattern.

Activity 2: Students look at the pictures and then complete the sentences below by writing the correct word for the picture in the space provided.

WORD WORKERS 5 UNIT 5.9

Name .... Date ....

Write the word for these jumbled letters. The first letters are underlined.

mwor	***worm***	labd	***bald***	rodo	***door***
gabde	***badge***	thmub	***thumb***	kwon	***know***
lerck	***clerk***	ncrow	***crown***	coust	***scout***
noosp	***spoon***	mifr	***firm***	lasrn	***snarl***

Underline the *two* words that have the same word pattern as the picture.

listen <u>bristle</u> wrist <u>gristle</u>

<u>show</u> four <u>blow</u> bout

foot <u>noon</u> <u>soon</u> spoil

<u>blew</u> true growl <u>crew</u>

<u>wear</u> weigh <u>bear</u> bread

104 © 2000 H.A. Calder and Pascal Press

Activity 1: Students make a word from the jumbled letters. The first letter of each word is underlined. Students write the words in the spaces provided.

Activity 2: Students look at the pictures and the words on the lines beside them. They underline the two words in each line that have the same word pattern as the picture.

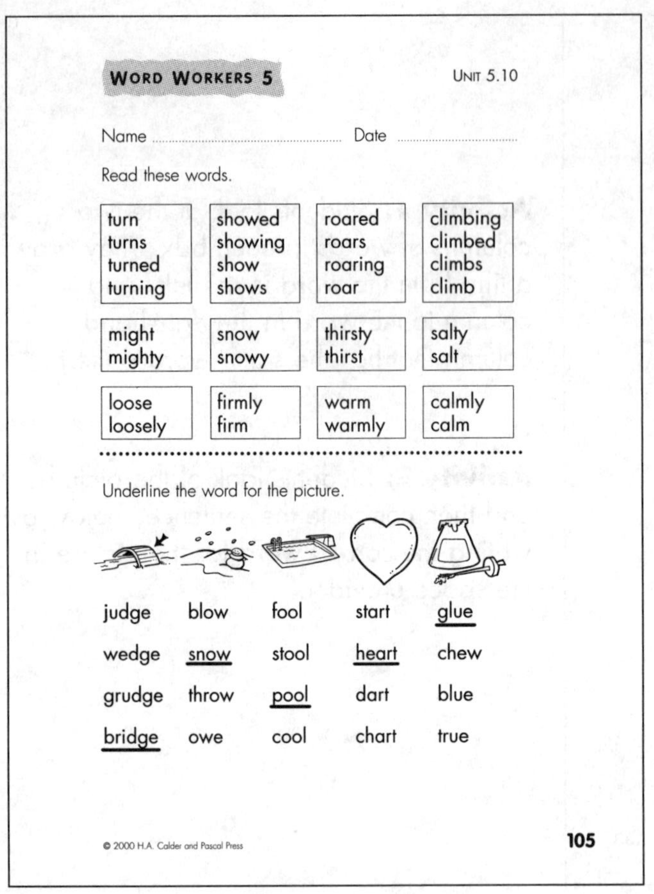

WORD WORKERS 5 UNIT 5.10

Name .... Date ....

Read these words.

turn turns turned turning	showed showing show shows	roared roars roaring roar	climbing climbed climbs climb
might mighty	snow snowy	thirsty thirst	salty salt
loose loosely	firmly firm	warm warmly	calmly calm

Underline the word for the picture.

judge	blow	fool	start	glue
wedge	snow	stool	heart	chew
grudge	throw	pool	dart	blue
bridge	owe	cool	chart	true

© 2000 H.A. Calder and Pascal Press 105

Activity 1: Students read the words in the boxes. Tell them to add the endings to the smallest word or base word.

Activity 2: Students look at the columns of words. They underline the word in each column that matches the picture above it.

WORD WORKERS 5 UNIT 5.11

Name .... Date ....

Write the word from each column that fits the word shape box.

work	weigh	foot	cause
world	freight	stood	fault
worm	sleigh	brook	sauce
worst	eight	soot	haul

worst weigh foot fault

Underline the correct word to complete the sentence.

1. Mrs Wright listened while she stood at the door of the (lurch/church).
2. Dawn thought she ought to (give/live) the gloves to the workers.
3. The (scorch/torch) burned brightly as they went down into the tomb.
4. He (earned/learned) that he had to start school on the fourth of March.
5. Bert took off his dirty (shirt/squirt) and dived into the pool.

106 © 2000 H.A. Calder and Pascal Press

Activity 1: Students look at the columns of words. Tell them to put the word from each column that fits into the 'word shape' box below it.

Activity 2: Students read the sentences. They underline the word in brackets that best completes the sentence.

WORD WORKERS 5 UNIT 5.12

Name .... Date ....

Put each column in alphabetical order.

a		e		i	
fair	*dare*	swerve	*pearl*	give	*bird*
dare	*draw*	term	*swerve*	bright	*bright*
harm	*fair*	weight	*term*	flirt	*fight*
draw	*fault*	pearl	*threw*	bird	*flirt*
fault	*harm*	threw	*weight*	fight	*give*

o		u	
coarse	*bomb*	nurse	*nurse*
bomb	*brought*	rustle	*purr*
brought	*coarse*	turn	*rustle*
door	*crown*	purr	*true*
crown	*door*	true	*turn*

 107

Students place the words in each column in alphabetical order.

WORD WORKERS 5 UNIT 5.13

Name .... Date ....

Complete these crossword puzzles.

a: small, walk, fasten, stealth, wrestle, drew, tear, fee, fen, each, wreath
e: wrestle, stealth, drew, fern, reach

i: listen, give, slight, knit, thirst

u: burnt, thumbs, true, rustle, burst

o: court, thought, roar, choice, coach

108

Students complete the crossword puzzles. They write the letter indicated in the blank spaces to make words that can be read going down or across the page.

WORD WORKERS 5 UNIT 5.14

Name .... Date ....

Write the word with the correct spelling.

1. hite hight height *height*
2. brought brawt braut *brought*
3. balld bald bawld *bald*
4. brown broun browne *brown*
5. therd thurd third *third*

Fill in the missing letters to complete the word.

1. *l* earnin *g*
2. *w* oode *n*
3. *w* ork *s*
4. *s* hootin *g*
5. *h* ardes *t*

works
learning
hardest
wooden
shooting

 109

Activity 1: Students read the words going across the page, then write the word that is spelt correctly.

Activity 2: Students read the words in the box, then write the missing letters to complete the column of words on the left.

WORD WORKERS 5 UNIT 5.15

Name .... Date ....

Underline the word for the picture.

bear bears car cars bowl bowls

knob knobs thumb thumbs wrench wrenches

Complete the sentences with the words from the box.

climb	write	crows	work	wrong

1. As soon as he walked in the door, Paul knew he was in the *wrong* room.
2. Clair spurred her horse to make it *climb* the steep hill.
3. The *crows* cawed and fought on the limb of the highest tree.
4. Mrs Bridge taught the class to read and *write* by the end of the year.
5. The whistle told Bert it was time to start *work* .

110

Activity 1: Students underline the singular word if there is one object pictured or the plural word if there are two or more objects pictured.

Activity 2: Students complete the sentences by writing the correct word from the box in the space provided.

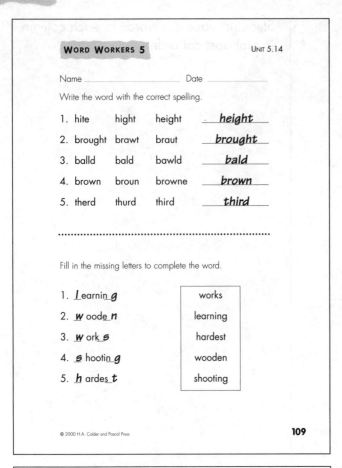

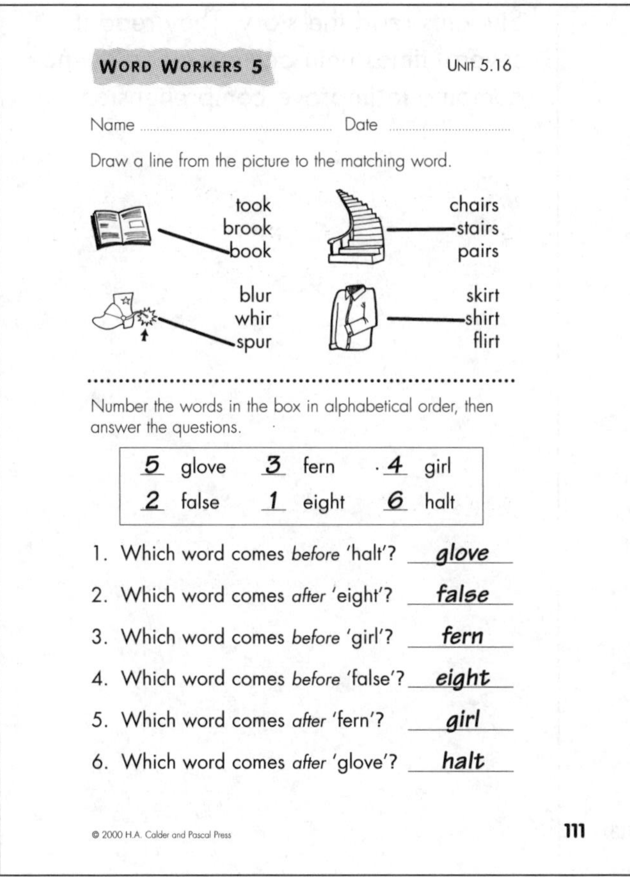

WORD WORKERS 5 UNIT 5.16

Name .... Date ....

Draw a line from the picture to the matching word.

took
brook
book

chairs
stairs
pairs

blur
whir
spur

skirt
shirt
flirt

Number the words in the box in alphabetical order, then answer the questions.

5 glove	3 fern	4 girl
2 false	1 eight	6 halt

1. Which word comes *before* 'halt'? glove
2. Which word comes *after* 'eight'? false
3. Which word comes *before* 'girl'? fern
4. Which word comes *before* 'false'? eight
5. Which word comes *after* 'fern'? girl
6. Which word comes *after* 'glove'? halt

© 2000 H.A. Calder and Pascal Press 111

Activity 1: Students say the word for the picture and then draw a line from the picture to the correct word beside it.

Activity 2: Students number the words in the box in alphabetical order, then use this information to answer the questions below.

WORD WORKERS 5 UNIT 5.17

Read the story.

On the High Board

Jack Bright sat in the sun at the edge of the pool. The older boys were diving off the high board. The board looked a long way up to him. Jack was a good diver but his coach said he was not ready for the high board.

One of the big boys came up to Jack. 'I hear you are a good diver,' he said, 'but just off the low board. Are you too scared to jump off the high board?' Jack shook his head. 'I am not scared,' he said. 'My coach says I am not ready for the high board.' The boy laughed. 'If you are not scared then let me see you dive off the high board.'

112 © 2000 H.A. Calder and Pascal Press

For the following pages:

Students read the story. They read it several times until accuracy and fluency combine to improve comprehension.

WORD WORKERS 5

UNIT 5.18

Jack Bright thought for a while. 'All right,' he said. 'I will do it — just to show I am not scared.' Jack stood up and walked to the ladder. Up and up he went. As he climbed the steps, Jack thought what he had to do. He was still thinking when he got to the top.

Jack looked down as he stood on the board. The blue square of water in the pool glistened. It looked small — too small! Jack's knees shook. He was glad the boy on the ground could not see how frightened he was. 'This is dumb,' Jack said. 'I should not be scared. If I can dive off the low board, I can dive off the high board.'

113

WORD WORKERS 5

UNIT 5.19

Jack stood straight and steady, he took a deep breath and counted his steps...one, two, three, four...and then he was in the air. Jack turned and twisted as he headed for the water. It was a neat, tight dive. Jack cut into the pool like a sharp knife. He hardly made a splash.

Jack swam to the edge of the pool and climbed out. He shook the water out of his hair. Jack glared at the older boy. 'Listen,' he said, 'Who is scared? Let me see you do better than that!' The bigger boy did not say a thing.

Jack's coach saw him dive. 'Where did you learn that?' he asked. Jack grinned at his coach. 'I did not need to learn how,' he said. 'If I can do it off the low board, I can do it off the high board!'

114

Students read the story. They read it several times until accuracy and fluency combine to improve comprehension.

WORD WORKERS 5 UNIT 5.20

Name .... Date ....

Write the letters 'a', 'b', 'c' and 'd' in the same order the pictures occurred in the story.

a b

c d

1. *a* 2. *c* 3. *b* 4. *d*

Answer the questions with the exact words from the story.

1. Jack's coach said he was not *ready* for the high board.
2. Jack was glad the other boy could not see how *frightened* he was.
3. Jack cut into the pool like a sharp *knife* .
4. Jack told his coach, 'if I can dive off the *low* board, I can dive off the *high* board.'

© 2000 H.A. Calder and Pascal Press 115

Activity 1: Students sequence the events in the story by placing the pictures in their correct order.

Activity 2: Students complete these sentences using the exact word from the story.

WORD WORKERS 5 UNIT 5.21

Name .... Date ....

Fill in the blanks with the correct word from the box.

One of the big *boys* came up to Jack. 'I hear you are a good diver,' he said, 'but just off the low *board* . Are you too scared to jump off the high board?' Jack *shook* his head. 'I am not scared,' he said. 'My coach says I am not *ready* for the high board.' The boy laughed. 'If you are not *scared* then let me see you dive off the high board.'

scared ready shook board boys

Write the letters 'a', 'b', 'c' and 'd' beside the sentences in the same order they occurred in the story.

1. Jack glared at the older boy. *d*
2. Jack was a good diver, but his coach said he was not ready for the high board. *a*
3. Jack stood up and walked to the ladder. *b*
4. Jack turned and twisted as he headed for the water. *c*

116 © 2000 H.A. Calder and Pascal Press

Activity 1: Students complete this cloze exercise using the words from the box.

Activity 2: Students sequence the events in the story by placing them in their correct order.

Using Book 6

Word Workers Book 6 teaches students the higher order phonics skills of recognising compound words and the techniques of syllabification which are necessary to become independent readers. Below are some suggestions on how to use the book effectively. More detailed information on the teaching processes can be found in Chapter 2: 'Skills for successful teaching'. An activity-by-activity guide is provided with the answers.

- Read the section in the *Teacher Resource Book* that gives instructions on teaching the different word attack skills students require to be successful at this stage of their reading acquisition.

- Become familiar with the suggested lesson plan for Book 6 on the next page.

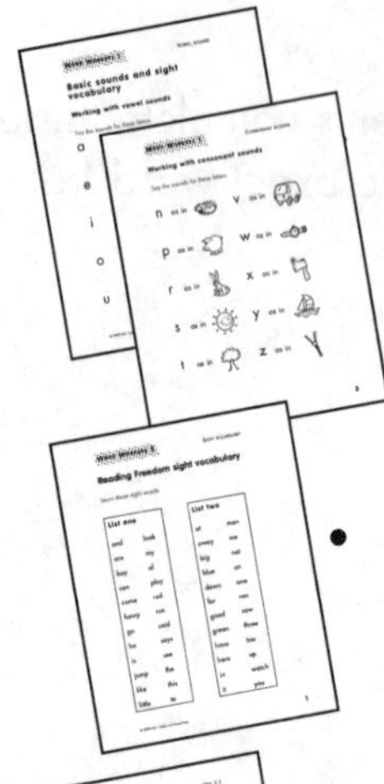

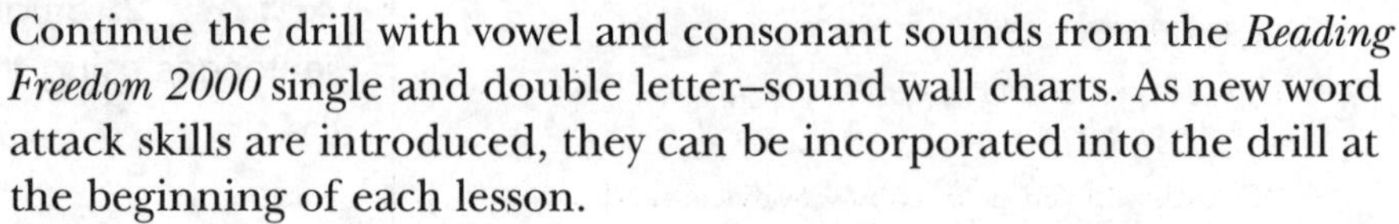

- Continue the drill with vowel and consonant sounds from the *Reading Freedom 2000* single and double letter–sound wall charts. As new word attack skills are introduced, they can be incorporated into the drill at the beginning of each lesson.

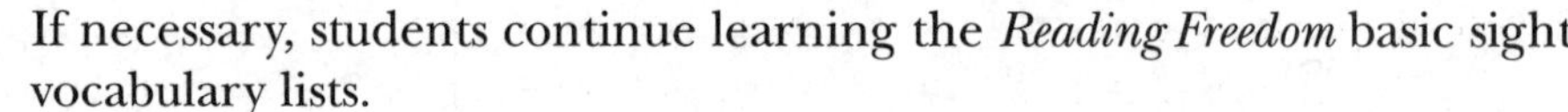

- If necessary, students continue learning the *Reading Freedom* basic sight vocabulary lists.

- Introduce the compound word recognition and syllabification skills as students encounter them in each successive unit.

- Enlist parent support whenever possible. Parents are particularly helpful teaching sight vocabulary and reinforcing sounds, rules and phonic generalisations at home.

- Monitor students' progress through regular oral reading.

- When Book 6 is completed, record students' progress using *Word Workers* Achievement Test 8.

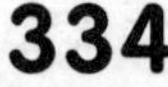

Book 6: Suggested lesson plan

Based on a lesson of approximately 30 minutes.

1 Students say a row of sounds from the three *Reading Freedom 2000* wall charts. For small groups, each student can say a row or column of sounds. If your class is large, select students to say a row or column until all the sounds have been repeated. As syllabification rules are encountered in Book 6, they can be incorporated at the start of each lesson.

2 When teaching with small groups, each student reads a column of *Reading Freedom* basic sight vocabulary. When teaching the whole class, select students to read a column of sight words. Five or six columns is enough to start your lesson with. Be sure different students read the sight words each lesson.

3 Explain and demonstrate the compound word and syllabification rules. Carefully explain the activities on the page or pages to be completed. Ensure that students understand the concepts involved and know what is required of them.

4 Assign activity pages to be completed (the number of pages depends on the teacher's professional judgment as well as the ability and enthusiasm of the student).

5 Reward students for achievement on the activity pages or in learning sight vocabulary with stamps, stickers or gold stars. When they complete the activity book and finish the complementary achievement test (found in *Word Workers Achievement Tests*) they receive a *Word Workers* Merit Certificate.

6 Assign any homework after demonstrating the activities. Ensure students understand the concept and what is to be done.

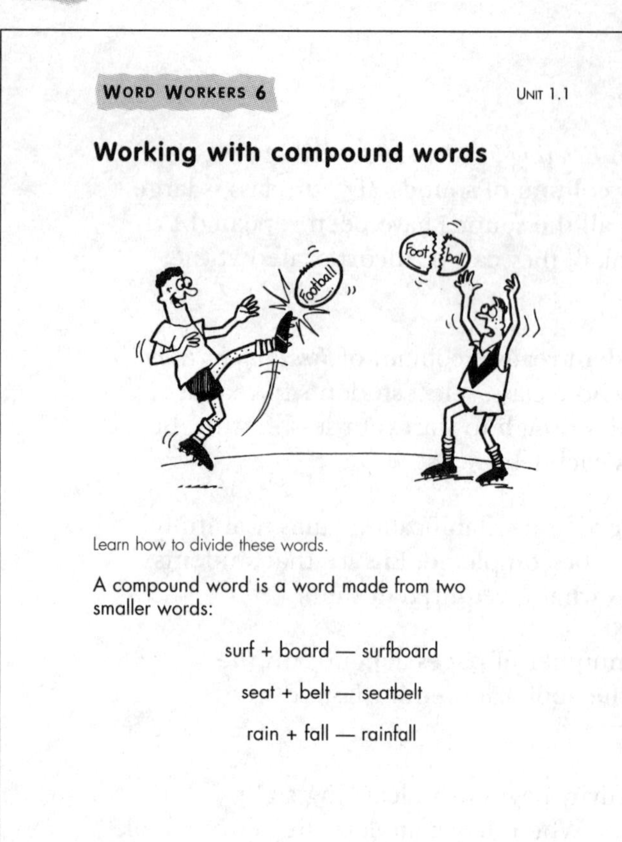

WORD WORKERS 6 UNIT 1.1

Working with compound words

Learn how to divide these words.

A compound word is a word made from two smaller words:

surf + board — surfboard

seat + belt — seatbelt

rain + fall — rainfall

© 2000 H.A. Calder and Pascal Press 1

For the following pages:

This unit teaches students how to read and divide compound words. Teach this skill carefully until students have mastered it.

From now on, incorporate knowledge of compound words in the phonics drill at the start of each lesson.

WORD WORKERS 6 UNIT 1.2

Name .... Date ....

Divide these compound words.

list 1			list 2		
1. footpath	*foot*	*path*	1. tugboat	*tug*	*boat*
2. oatmeal	*oat*	*meal*	2. stopsign	*stop*	*sign*
3. fireplace	*fire*	*place*	3. bookcase	*book*	*case*
4. windmill	*wind*	*mill*	4. sailboat	*sail*	*boat*
5. bedroom	*bed*	*room*	5. pitchfork	*pitch*	*fork*
6. skateboard	*skate*	*board*	6. handsome	*hand*	*some*
7. lighthouse	*light*	*house*	7. armchair	*arm*	*chair*
8. seatbelt	*seat*	*belt*	8. surfboard	*surf*	*board*
9. toothbrush	*tooth*	*brush*	9. rainbow	*rain*	*bow*
10. bathtub	*bath*	*tub*	10. peanut	*pea*	*nut*
11. tonight	*to*	*night*	11. scarecrow	*scare*	*crow*
12. doorknob	*door*	*knob*	12. hotdog	*hot*	*dog*
13. herself	*her*	*self*	13. cowboy	*cow*	*boy*
14. football	*foot*	*ball*	14. seagull	*sea*	*gull*
15. sunshine	*sun*	*shine*	15. snowflake	*snow*	*flake*

A compound word is made from two smaller words.

2 © 2000 H.A. Calder and Pascal Press

Students divide these words and write them in the spaces provided. Correct the work by having them read the word and then divide it.

WORD WORKERS 6 — UNIT 1.3

Name .... Date ....

Write the words for the pictures.

1. scarecrow
2. pitchfork
3. windmill
4. toothbrush
5. football
6. bathtub
7. seagull
8. stopsign
9. tugboat
10. skateboard
11. peanut
12. rainbow

 3

Students write the words for the pictures. If necessary, they refer to the word lists to find the correct spelling.

WORD WORKERS 6 — UNIT 1.4

Name .... Date ....

Divide these compound words.

list 3			list 4		
1. upstairs	up	stairs	1. farmhouse	farm	house
2. highway	high	way	2. something	some	thing
3. himself	him	self	3. maybe	may	be
4. today	to	day	4. airport	air	port
5. raincoat	rain	coat	5. driveway	drive	way
6. backyard	back	yard	6. without	with	out
7. racehorse	race	horse	7. teaspoon	tea	spoon
8. seaweed	sea	weed	8. meanwhile	mean	while
9. tiptoe	tip	toe	9. classroom	class	room
10. Sunday	sun	day	10. birthday	birth	day
11. weekend	week	end	11. forget	for	get
12. inside	in	side	12. postcard	post	card
13. barnyard	barn	yard	13. moonlight	moon	light
14. fireman	fire	man	14. outside	out	side
15. homework	home	work	15. playmate	play	mate

It is fun working with words.

4

Students divide these words and write them in the spaces provided. Correct the work by having them read the word and then divide it.

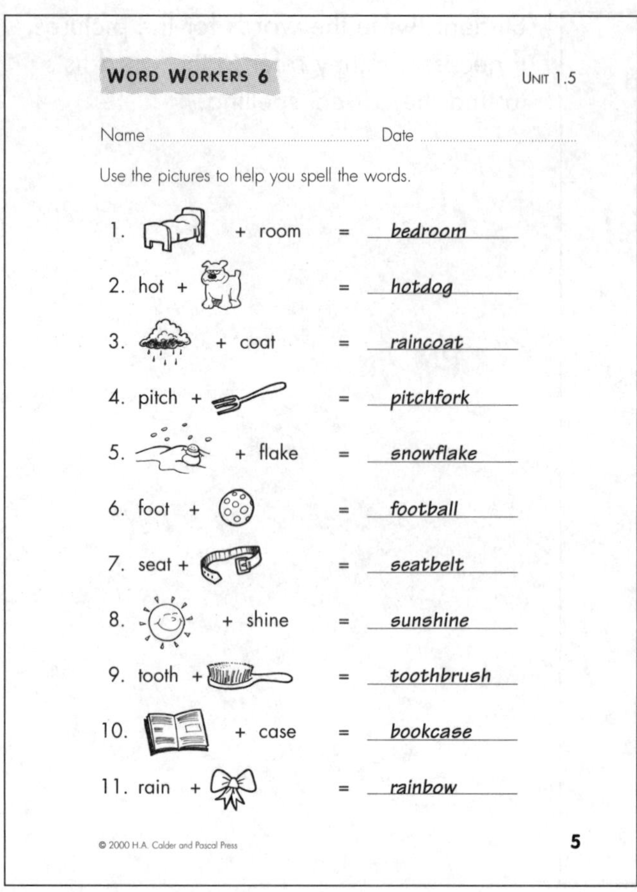

WORD WORKERS 6 UNIT 1.5

Name .... Date ....

Use the pictures to help you spell the words.

1. [picture] + room = *bedroom*
2. hot + [picture] = *hotdog*
3. [picture] + coat = *raincoat*
4. pitch + [picture] = *pitchfork*
5. [picture] + flake = *snowflake*
6. foot + [picture] = *football*
7. seat + [picture] = *seatbelt*
8. [picture] + shine = *sunshine*
9. tooth + [picture] = *toothbrush*
10. [picture] + case = *bookcase*
11. rain + [picture] = *rainbow*

© 2000 H.A. Calder and Pascal Press 5

Students spell these words using the picture as a clue. Tell them that the spelling for the picture may need to be changed in the complete word.

WORD WORKERS 6 UNIT 1.6

Name .... Date ....

I am a good word worker.

Underline the nonsense word.

1. rainfall	2. something	3. windmill	4. teadog
doorknob	barnport	maybe	lighthouse
tonight	classroom	forday	upstairs
upless	stopsign	armchair	himself

Complete these sentences by writing the words for the pictures.

1. The farmer stacked the hay with a *pitchfork*.
2. Mum told Tim he could ride his *skateboard* next weekend.
3. The *seagull* screeched at the man on the boat.
4. Jane smiled and said, 'Look at the lovely *rainbow*!'
5. Last Sunday the boys played *football* at the park.

6 © 2000 H.A. Calder and Pascal Press

Activity 1: Students look at the columns of words. Tell them to underline the word in each column that is a nonsense word.

Activity 2: Students look at the pictures and then complete the sentences below by writing the correct word for the picture in the space provided.

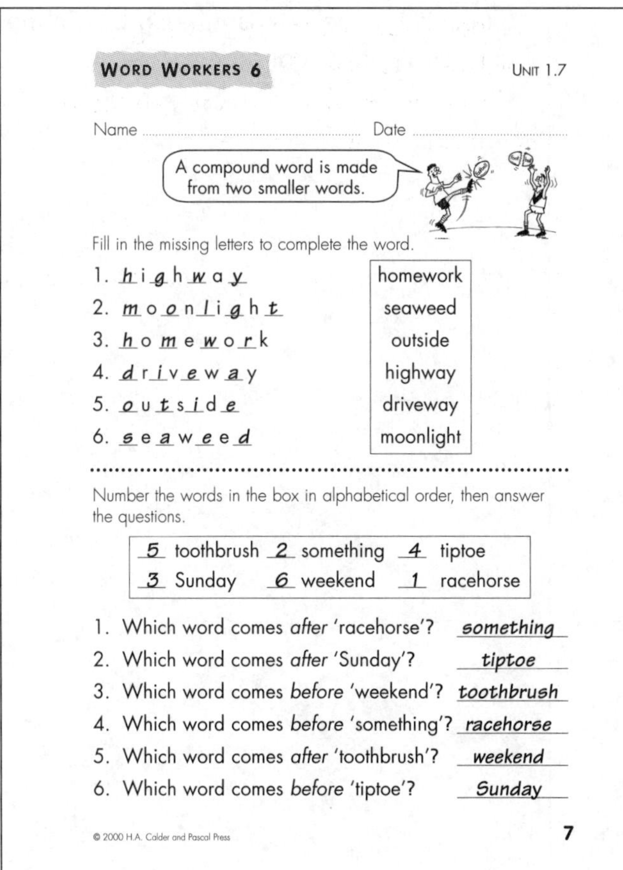

WORD WORKERS 6 UNIT 1.7

Name .... Date ....

A compound word is made from two smaller words.

Fill in the missing letters to complete the word.

1. highway	homework
2. moonlight	seaweed
3. homework	outside
4. driveway	highway
5. outside	driveway
6. seaweed	moonlight

Number the words in the box in alphabetical order, then answer the questions.

5 toothbrush	2 something	4 tiptoe
3 Sunday	6 weekend	1 racehorse

1. Which word comes *after* 'racehorse'? something
2. Which word comes *after* 'Sunday'? tiptoe
3. Which word comes *before* 'weekend'? toothbrush
4. Which word comes *before* 'something'? racehorse
5. Which word comes *after* 'toothbrush'? weekend
6. Which word comes *before* 'tiptoe'? Sunday

© 2000 H.A. Calder and Pascal Press 7

Activity 1: Students read the words in the box, then write the missing letters to complete the column of words on the left.

Activity 2: Students number the words in the box in alphabetical order, then use this information to answer the questions below.

WORD WORKERS 6 UNIT 1.8

Name .... Date ....

Underline the word for the picture.

STOP

inside	something	fireplace	fireman	cowboy
stopsign	racehorse	scarecrow	teaspoon	sailboat
maybe	backyard	classroom	peanut	doorknob
seaweed	tugboat	seatbelt	hotdog	rainfall

Underline the correct word to complete the sentence.

1. Mrs Mills waited for the plane to land at the (driveway/airport).
2. Steve stood in the hallway outside the (classroom/doorknob).
3. Mum told Jane, 'You must clean your bedroom (today/weekend).'
4. The sailboat floated on the bay near the (farmhouse/lighthouse).

8 © 2000 H.A. Calder and Pascal Press

Activity 1: Students look at the columns of words. They underline the word in each column that matches the picture above it.

Activity 2: Students read the sentences. They underline the word in brackets that best completes the sentence.

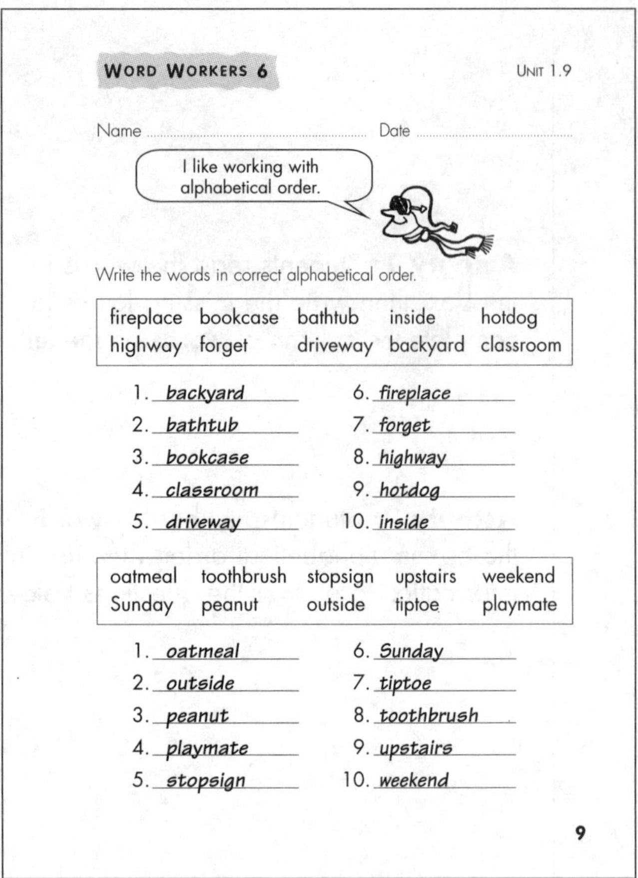

WORD WORKERS 6 UNIT 1.9

Name .... Date ....

I like working with
alphabetical order.

Write the words in correct alphabetical order.

fireplace	bookcase	bathtub	inside	hotdog
highway	forget	driveway	backyard	classroom

1. *backyard* 6. *fireplace*
2. *bathtub* 7. *forget*
3. *bookcase* 8. *highway*
4. *classroom* 9. *hotdog*
5. *driveway* 10. *inside*

oatmeal	toothbrush	stopsign	upstairs	weekend
Sunday	peanut	outside	tiptoe	playmate

1. *oatmeal* 6. *Sunday*
2. *outside* 7. *tiptoe*
3. *peanut* 8. *toothbrush*
4. *playmate* 9. *upstairs*
5. *stopsign* 10. *weekend*

9

Students put the words in each box in their correct alphabetical order.

WORD WORKERS 6 UNIT 1.10

Name .... Date ....

Write the word with the correct spelling.

1.	lighthose	lighthouse	ligthouse	*lighthouse*
2.	seagull	seegull	seagul	*seagull*
3.	fourget	foreget	forget	*forget*
4.	weekened	weekend	weakend	*weekend*
5.	homewerk	homwork	homework	*homework*

Complete these crossword puzzles.

scarecrow, *rainbow*, *windmill*, *tugboat*

toothbrush, *bathtub*, *skateboard*, *stopsign*

STOP

10

Activity 1: Students read the words going across the page, then write the word that is spelt correctly.

Activity 2: Students complete the crossword puzzles. They write the words for the pictures in the blank spaces.

WORD WORKERS 6 UNIT 1.11

Name .... Date ....

I like spelling.

Write six words from each list at the start of this chapter.

list 1

1. ____________
2. ____________
3. ____________
4. ____________
5. ____________
6. ____________

list 2

1. ____________
2. ____________
3. ____________
4. ____________
5. ____________
6. ____________

list 3

1. ____________
2. ____________
3. ____________
4. ____________
5. ____________
6. ____________

list 4

1. ____________
2. ____________
3. ____________
4. ____________
5. ____________
6. ____________

 11

Students are asked to spell six words from each of the lists indicated.

WORD WORKERS 6 UNIT 2.1

Working with VCCV words

traf | fic

cir | cus

Learn how to divide these words.

Dividing words is easy. When a word has a VCCV pattern, divide it between the two consonants:

object — ob – ject

happy — hap – py

umpire — um – pire

merchant — mer – chant

12

For the following pages:

This unit teaches students how to read and divide words containing the VCCV syllabification pattern. Teach the skill carefully until students have mastered it.

From now on, incorporate knowledge of the VCCV syllabification rules in the phonics drill at the start of each lesson.

Word Workers 6 Unit 2.2

Name .... Date ....

Read these VCCV words and then divide them.

list 1			list 2		
1. collar	col	lar	1. swimmer	swim	mer
2. kitten	kit	ten	2. army	ar	my
3. basket	bas	ket	3. arrow	ar	row
4. hammer	ham	mer	4. entire	en	tire
5. window	win	dow	5. bandit	ban	dit
6. igloo	ig	loo	6. button	but	ton
7. pencil	pen	cil	7. doctor	doc	tor
8. summer	sum	mer	8. fifty	fif	ty
9. corner	cor	ner	9. whisper	whis	per
10. surfer	sur	fer	10. picture	pic	ture
11. appear	ap	pear	11. dolphin	dol	phin
12. runner	run	ner	12. invite	in	vite
13. hunger	hun	ger	13. rabbit	rab	bit
14. ribbon	rib	bon	14. tennis	ten	nis
15. dismiss	dis	miss	15. sixty	six	ty

A syllable is the smallest part of a word that has a vowel in it.

 13

Students divide these words and write them in the spaces provided. Correct the work by having them read the word and then divide it.

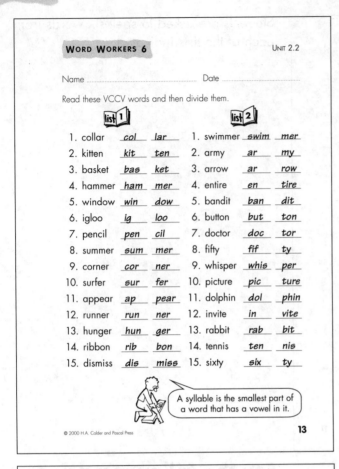

Word Workers 6 Unit 2.3

Name .... Date ....

Write the words for the pictures.

1. dolphin
2. basket
3. rabbit
4. fifty
5. hammer
6. window
7. button
8. swimmer
9. pencil
10. collar
11. arrow
12. igloo

14

Students write the words for the pictures. If necessary, they refer to the word lists to find the correct spelling.

WORD WORKERS 6 UNIT 2.4

Name .... Date ....

Read these VCCV words and then divide them.

list 3			list 4		
1. winter	win	ter	1. dollar	dol	lar
2. morning	mor	ning	2. happy	hap	py
3. arrive	ar	rive	3. rubbish	rub	bish
4. umpire	ump	ire	4. sister	sis	ter
5. sentence	sen	tence	5. market	mar	ket
6. perform	per	form	6. annoy	an	noy
7. rescue	res	cue	7. invent	in	vent
8. party	par	ty	8. kingdom	king	dom
9. yellow	yel	low	9. sloppy	slop	py
10. picnic	pic	nic	10. cartoon	car	toon
11. sunny	sun	ny	11. admit	ad	mit
12. traffic	traf	fic	12. selfish	sel	fish
13. problem	prob	lem	13. dentist	den	tist
14. circus	cir	cus	14. compete	com	pete
15. letter	let	ter	15. elbow	el	bow

When a word ends with a silent final 'e', the 'e' does not act as a vowel.

© 2000 H.A. Calder and Pascal Press 15

Students divide these words and write them in the spaces provided. Correct the work by having them read the word and then divide it.

WORD WORKERS 6 UNIT 2.5

Name .... Date ....

Use the pictures to help you spell the words.

1. ar + [picture] = arrow
2. [picture] + cil = pencil
3. 10 + nis = tennis
4. [picture] + toon = cartoon
5. [picture] + dom = kingdom
6. [picture] + ny = sunny
7. [picture] + er = corner
8. [picture] + ar = dollar
9. [picture] + y = army
10. sel + [picture] = selfish
11. 6 + ty = sixty

16 © 2000 H.A. Calder and Pascal Press

Students spell these words using the picture as a clue. Tell them that the spelling for the picture may need to be changed in the complete word.

WORD WORKERS 6 UNIT 2.6

Name .... Date ....

Underline the nonsense word.

1. bandit	2. arrow	3. surfer	4. cartence
runner	fiften	circus	kitten
market	perform	surtist	dollar
probter	rubbish	pencil	sunny

Complete these sentences by writing the words for the pictures.

1. The farmer chased the *rabbit* out of the garden.
2. James lost a *button* when he tore his shirt.
3. Mum took her *basket* when she went shopping at the market.
4. The *dolphin* played in the waves near the shore.
5. Beth dropped the *pencil* on the floor.

 17

Activity 1: Students look at the columns of words. Tell them to underline the word in each column that is a nonsense word.

Activity 2: Students look at the pictures and then complete the sentences below by writing the correct word for the picture in the space provided.

WORD WORKERS 6 UNIT 2.7

Name .... Date ....

When two letters go together to say one sound they count as one letter.

Fill in the missing letters to complete the word.

1. m o r n i n g
2. a n n o y
3. c o m p l e t e
4. r u b b i s h
5. r e s c u e
6. i n v i t e

rescue
complete
invite
morning
rubbish
annoy

Number the words in the box in alphabetical order, then answer the questions.

3 ribbon	5 sister	4 runner
1 perform	2 problem	6 tennis

1. Which word comes *before* 'problem'? *perform*
2. Which word comes *after* 'sister'? *tennis*
3. Which word comes *before* 'runner'? *ribbon*
4. Which word comes *before* 'tennis'? *sister*
5. Which word comes *after* 'perform'? *problem*
6. Which word comes *after* 'ribbon'? *runner*

18

Activity 1: Students read the words in the box, then write the missing letters to complete the column of words on the left.

Activity 2: Students number the words in the box in alphabetical order, then use this information to answer the questions below.

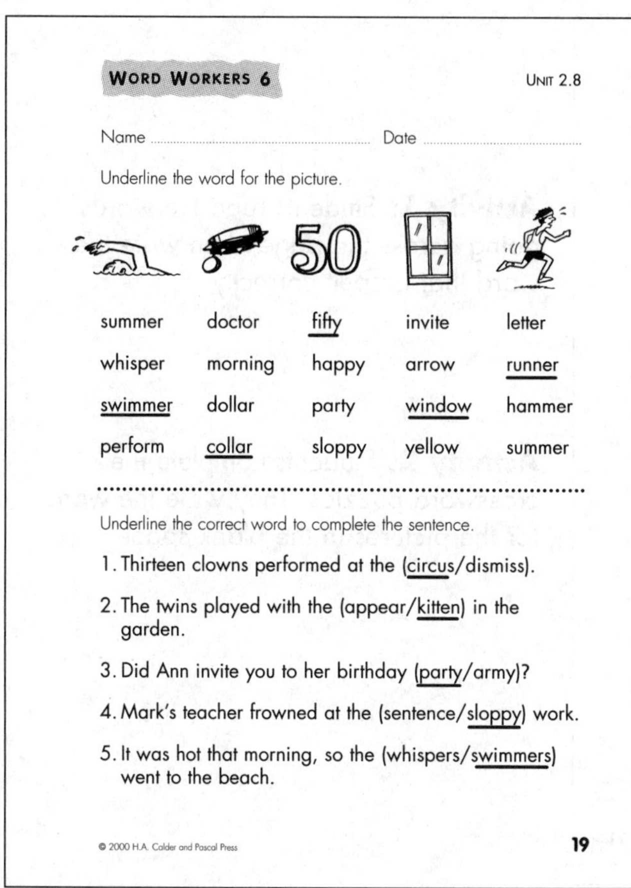

WORD WORKERS 6 UNIT 2.8

Name .... Date ....

Underline the word for the picture.

summer	doctor	fifty	invite	letter
whisper	morning	happy	arrow	runner
swimmer	dollar	party	window	hammer
perform	collar	sloppy	yellow	summer

Underline the correct word to complete the sentence.

1. Thirteen clowns performed at the (circus/dismiss).
2. The twins played with the (appear/kitten) in the garden.
3. Did Ann invite you to her birthday (party/army)?
4. Mark's teacher frowned at the (sentence/sloppy) work.
5. It was hot that morning, so the (whispers/swimmers) went to the beach.

© 2000 H.A. Calder and Pascal Press 19

Activity 1: Students look at the columns of words. Tell them to underline the word in each column that is a nonsense word.

Activity 2: Students read the sentences. They underline the word in brackets that best completes the sentence.

WORD WORKERS 6 UNIT 2.9

Name .... Date ....

I like working with alphabetical order.

Write the words in correct alphabetical order.

circus	kitten	entire	happy	appear
compete	dentist	army	collar	invite

1. *appear* 6. *dentist*
2. *army* 7. *entire*
3. *circus* 8. *happy*
4. *collar* 9. *invite*
5. *compete* 10. *kitten*

yellow	morning	winter	traffic	sentence
window	umpire	twenty	rescue	tennis

1. *morning* 6. *twenty*
2. *rescue* 7. *umpire*
3. *sentence* 8. *window*
4. *tennis* 9. *winter*
5. *traffic* 10. *yellow*

20 © 2000 H.A. Calder and Pascal Press

Students put the words in each box in their correct alphabetical order.

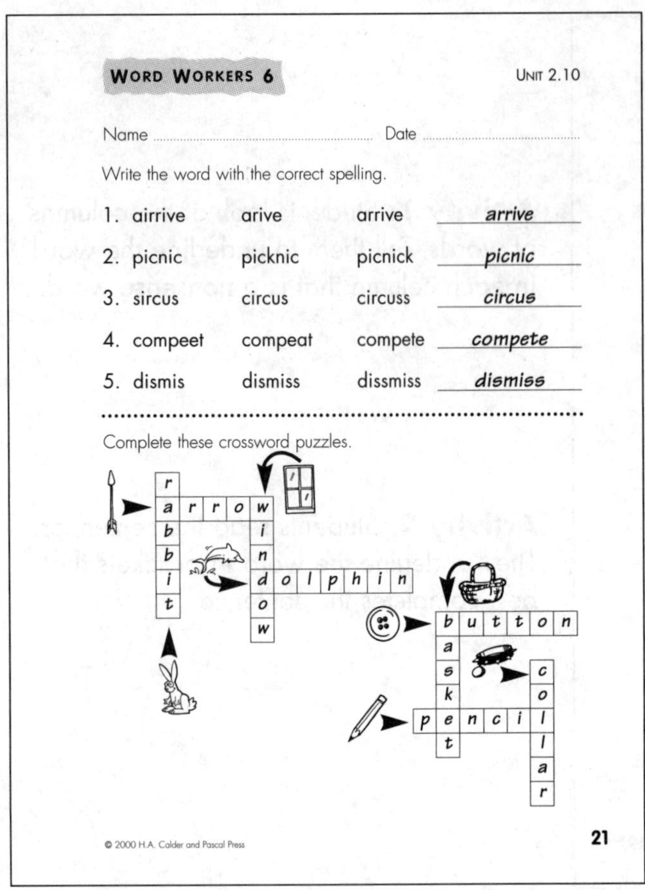

WORD WORKERS 6 UNIT 2.10

Name .... Date ....

Write the word with the correct spelling.

1. airrive arive arrive *arrive*
2. picnic picknic picnick *picnic*
3. sircus circus circuss *circus*
4. compeet compeat compete *compete*
5. dismis dismiss dissmiss *dismiss*

Complete these crossword puzzles.

© 2000 H.A. Calder and Pascal Press 21

Activity 1: Students read the words going across the page, then write the word that is spelt correctly.

Activity 2: Students complete the crossword puzzles. They write the words for the pictures in the blank spaces.

WORD WORKERS 6 UNIT 2.11

Name .... Date ....

I like spelling.

Write six words from each list at the start of this chapter.

list 1

1. ______
2. ______
3. ______
4. ______
5. ______
6. ______

list 2

1. ______
2. ______
3. ______
4. ______
5. ______
6. ______

list 3

1. ______
2. ______
3. ______
4. ______
5. ______
6. ______

list 4

1. ______
2. ______
3. ______
4. ______
5. ______
6. ______

22 © 2000 H.A. Calder and Pascal Press

Students are asked to spell six words from each of the lists indicated.

For the following pages:

This unit teaches students how to read and divide words containing the VCV syllabification pattern. Teach the skill carefully until students have mastered it.

From now on, incorporate knowledge of the VCV syllabification rules in the phonics drill at the start of each lesson.

WORD WORKERS 6 UNIT 3.1

Working with VCV words

Learn how to divide these words.

Dividing words is easy. When a word has a VCV pattern, divide it between the first vowel and the consonant.

oval — o – val

navy — na – vy

female — fe – male

speedy — spee – dy

© 2000 H.A. Calder and Pascal Press 23

Students divide these words and write them in the spaces provided. Correct the work by having them read the word and then divide it.

WORD WORKERS 6 UNIT 3.2

Name .... Date ....

Read these VCV words and then divide them.

list 1			list 2		
1. below	*be*	*low*	1. spider	*spi*	*der*
2. viking	*vi*	*king*	2. direct	*di*	*rect*
3. navy	*na*	*vy*	3. promote	*pro*	*mote*
4. diver	*di*	*ver*	4. baby	*ba*	*by*
5. pretend	*pre*	*tend*	5. easy	*ea*	*sy*
6. defeat	*de*	*feat*	6. pirate	*pi*	*rate*
7. minus	*mi*	*nus*	7. fever	*fe*	*ver*
8. elect	*e*	*lect*	8. tiger	*ti*	*ger*
9. bacon	*ba*	*con*	9. silence	*si*	*lence*
10. delight	*de*	*light*	10. Friday	*Fri*	*day*
11. pilot	*pi*	*lot*	11. halo	*ha*	*lo*
12. lady	*la*	*dy*	12. music	*mu*	*sic*
13. zero	*ze*	*ro*	13. major	*ma*	*jor*
14. decide	*de*	*cide*	14. miner	*mi*	*ner*
15. beneath	*be*	*neath*	15. robot	*ro*	*bot*

When the letter 'y' says a vowel sound it acts as a vowel.

24 © 2000 H.A. Calder and Pascal Press

WORD WORKERS 6 UNIT 3.3

Name .... Date ....

Write the words for the pictures.

1. spider	2. baby	3. minus
4. viking	5. zero	6. tiger
7. halo	8. robot	9. pirate
10. pilot	11. diver	12. bacon

© 2000 H.A. Calder and Pascal Press 25

Students write the words for the pictures. If necessary, they refer to the word lists to find the correct spelling.

WORD WORKERS 6 UNIT 3.4

Name .... Date ....

Read these VCV words and then divide them.

list 3			list 4		
1. virus	vi	rus	1. open	o	pen
2. sleepy	slee	py	2. recess	re	cess
3. before	be	fore	3. polite	po	lite
4. story	sto	ry	4. tulip	tu	lip
5. depart	de	part	5. behave	be	have
6. spicy	spi	cy	6. erupt	e	rupt
7. protest	pro	test	7. female	fe	male
8. season	sea	son	8. legal	le	gal
9. siren	si	ren	9. stupid	stu	pid
10. super	su	per	10. holy	ho	ly
11. pretend	pre	tend	11. career	ca	reer
12. digest	di	gest	12. police	po	lice
13. panic	pa	nic	13. motel	mo	tel
14. begin	be	gin	14. repair	re	pair
15. lazy	la	zy	15. finish	fi	nish

When two letters go together to say one sound they count as one letter.

26 © 2000 H.A. Calder and Pascal Press

Students divide these words and write them in the spaces provided. Correct the work by having them read the word and then divide it.

WORD WORKERS 6 UNIT 3.5

Name .... Date ....

Use the pictures to help you spell the words.

1. be + [4] = *before*
2. [bee] + gin = *begin*
3. [pan] + ic = *panic*
4. tu + [lips] = *tulips*
5. vi + [king] = *viking*
6. [hole] + ly = *holy*
7. de + [light] = *delight*
8. [tie] + ger = *tiger*
9. o + [pen] = *open*
10. [sleep] + y = *sleepy*
11. [car] + eer = *career*

© 2000 H.A. Calder and Pascal Press 27

Students spell these words using the picture as a clue. Tell them that the spelling for the picture may need to be changed in the complete word.

WORD WORKERS 6 UNIT 3.6

Name .... Date ....

It is fun working with words.

Underline the nonsense word.

1. major	2. spiren	3. virus	4. silence
open	lady	shazy	story
direct	detect	easy	fever
refore	season	label	betend

Complete these sentences by writing the words for the pictures.

1. The big black *spider* crawled out from under the rock.
2. The sleepy *baby* was put in its cot.
3. The *pilot* landed the plane safely on the runway at the airport.
4. Each night after the moon came out the *tiger* prowled near the creek.
5. On Friday morning mum cooked us *bacon* and eggs.

28 © 2000 H.A. Calder and Pascal Press

Activity 1: Students look at the columns of words. Tell them to underline the word in each column that is a nonsense word.

Activity 2: Students look at the pictures and then complete the sentences below by writing the correct word for the picture in the space provided.

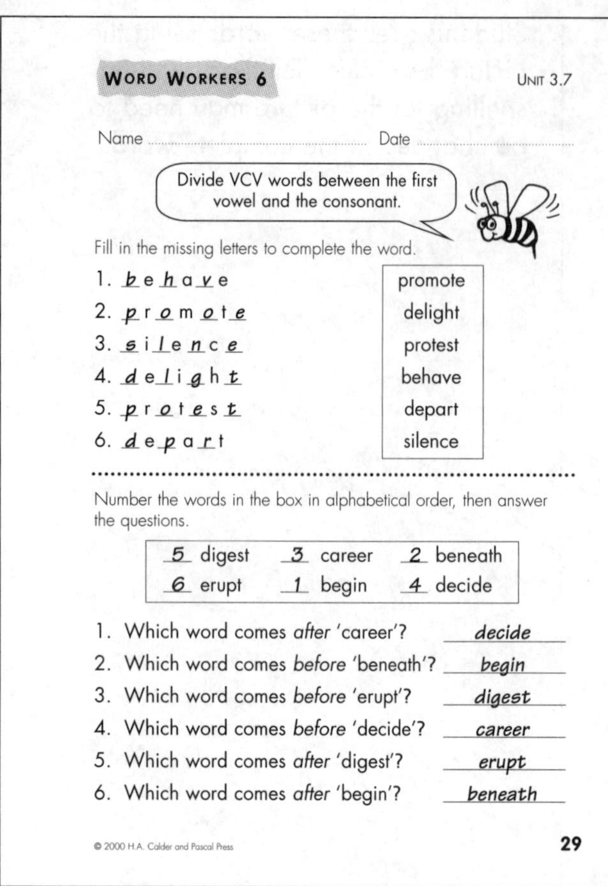

WORD WORKERS 6 UNIT 3.7

Name .... Date ....

Divide VCV words between the first vowel and the consonant.

Fill in the missing letters to complete the word.

1. b e h a v e		promote
2. p r o m o t e		delight
3. s i l e n c e		protest
4. d e l i g h t		behave
5. p r o t e s t		depart
6. d e p a r t		silence

Number the words in the box in alphabetical order, then answer the questions.

5 digest	3 career	2 beneath
6 erupt	1 begin	4 decide

1. Which word comes *after* 'career'? *decide*
2. Which word comes *before* 'beneath'? *begin*
3. Which word comes *before* 'erupt'? *digest*
4. Which word comes *before* 'decide'? *career*
5. Which word comes *after* 'digest'? *erupt*
6. Which word comes *after* 'begin'? *beneath*

© 2000 H.A. Calder and Pascal Press 29

Activity 1: Students read the words in the box, then write the missing letters to complete the column of words on the left.

Activity 2: Students number the words in the box in alphabetical order, then use this information to answer the questions below.

WORD WORKERS 6 UNIT 3.8

Name .... Date ....

Underline the word for the picture.

digest	begin	<u>robot</u>	elect	stupid
police	<u>zero</u>	direct	miner	<u>diver</u>
<u>pirate</u>	repair	student	direct	holy
behave	fever	lazy	<u>viking</u>	minus

Underline the correct word to complete the sentence.

1. The teacher made the (<u>lazy</u>/behave) students work at recess.
2. The (decide/<u>major</u>) had to order the troops to stop fighting.
3. The shop stayed (easy/<u>open</u>) till nine last night.
4. The crowd waited in silence for the (<u>music</u>/decide) to begin.
5. Mr King has to finish the work (<u>before</u>/below) next Friday.

30 © 2000 H.A. Calder and Pascal Press

Activity 1: Students look at the columns of words. They underline the word in each column that matches the picture above it.

Activity 2: Students read the sentences. They underline the word in brackets that best completes the sentence.

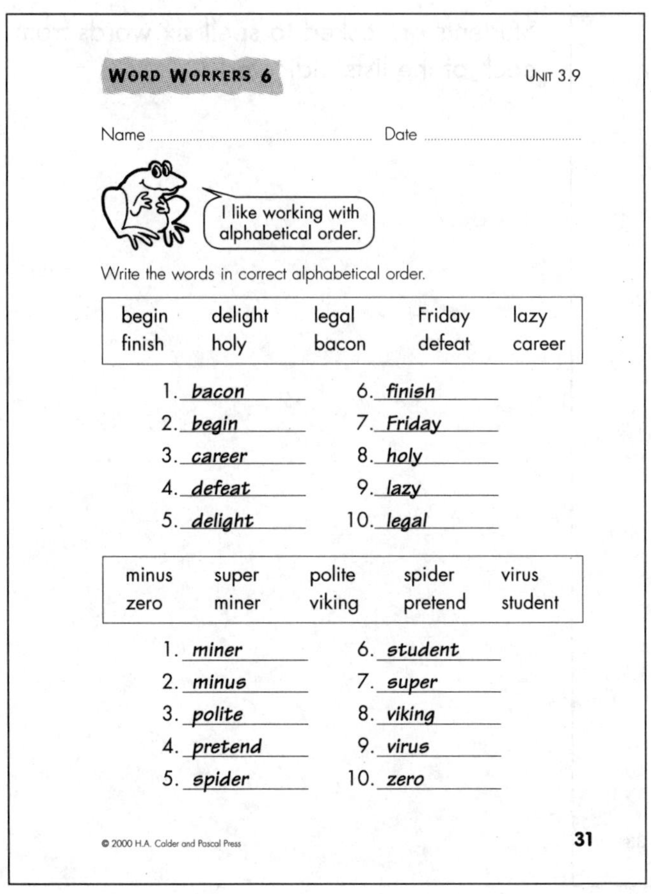

WORD WORKERS 6 UNIT 3.9

Name .... Date ....

I like working with alphabetical order.

Write the words in correct alphabetical order.

begin	delight	legal	Friday	lazy
finish	holy	bacon	defeat	career

1. *bacon*
2. *begin*
3. *career*
4. *defeat*
5. *delight*
6. *finish*
7. *Friday*
8. *holy*
9. *lazy*
10. *legal*

minus	super	polite	spider	virus
zero	miner	viking	pretend	student

1. *miner*
2. *minus*
3. *polite*
4. *pretend*
5. *spider*
6. *student*
7. *super*
8. *viking*
9. *virus*
10. *zero*

 31

Students put the words in each box in their correct alphabetical order.

WORD WORKERS 6 UNIT 3.10

Name .... Date ....

Write the word with the correct spelling.

1.	reces	recess	resess	*recess*
2.	diggest	dijest	digest	*digest*
3.	spicy	spicey	spiecy	*spicy*
4.	mayjor	major	maijor	*major*
5.	repare	repear	repair	*repair*

Complete these crossword puzzles.

s, p i r a t e, i, d i v e r, e, r o b o t

z e r o, b a c o, h a l o, v i k i n g

32

Activity 1: Students read the words going across the page, then write the word that is spelt correctly.

Activity 2: Students complete the crossword puzzles. They write the words for the pictures in the blank spaces.

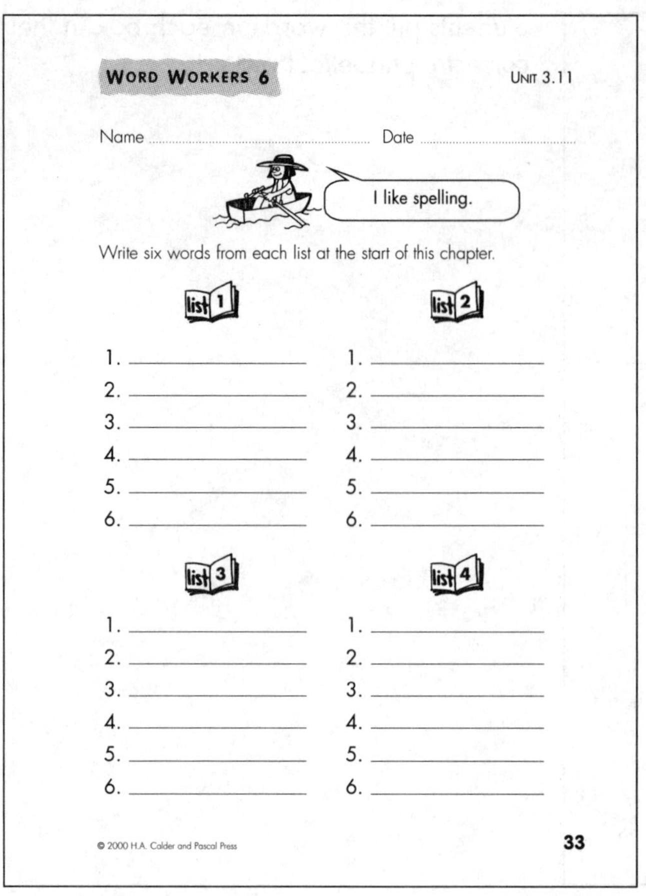

WORD WORKERS 6 UNIT 3.11

Name .... Date ....

Write six words from each list at the start of this chapter.

list 1	list 2
1. ______	1. ______
2. ______	2. ______
3. ______	3. ______
4. ______	4. ______
5. ______	5. ______
6. ______	6. ______

list 3	list 4
1. ______	1. ______
2. ______	2. ______
3. ______	3. ______
4. ______	4. ______
5. ______	5. ______
6. ______	6. ______

 33

Students are asked to spell six words from each of the lists indicated.

WORD WORKERS 6 UNIT 4.1

Working with VCCV and VCV words

Learn how to divide these words.

When a word has a VCCV pattern, divide it between the two consonants.

ob – ject

When a word has a VCV pattern, divide it between the first vowel and the consonant.

o – val

34

For the following pages:

This unit teaches students how to read and divide words containing the VCCV and VCV syllabification patterns. Teach the skill carefully until students have mastered it.

From now on, incorporate knowledge of the VCCV and VCV syllabification rules at the start of each lesson.

WORD WORKERS 6 UNIT 4.2

Name .... Date ....

Read these VCCV and VCV words, divide them and then write the pattern.

list 1

1.	arrow	ar	row	VCCV
2.	diver	di	ver	VCV
3.	music	mu	sic	VCV
4.	pencil	pen	cil	VCCV
5.	baby	ba	by	VCV
6.	kitten	kit	ten	VCCV
7.	dolphin	dol	phin	VCCV
8.	spider	spi	der	VCV
9.	surfer	sur	fer	VCCV
10.	zero	ze	ro	VCV
11.	miner	mi	ner	VCV
12.	collar	col	lar	VCCV
13.	sentence	sen	tence	VCCV
14.	before	be	fore	VCV
15.	spicy	spi	cy	VCV

When a word ends with a silent final 'e', the 'e' does not act as a vowel.

 35

Students divide these words and write the answers in the spaces provided, and then write the word pattern beside it.

WORD WORKERS 6 UNIT 4.3

Name .... Date ....

Write the words for the pictures.

1. dolphin 2. pirate 3. runner

4. pilot 5. pencil 6. spider

7. window 8. rabbit 9. tiger

10. halo 11. basket 12. viking

36

Students write the words for the pictures. If necessary, they refer to the word lists to find the correct spelling.

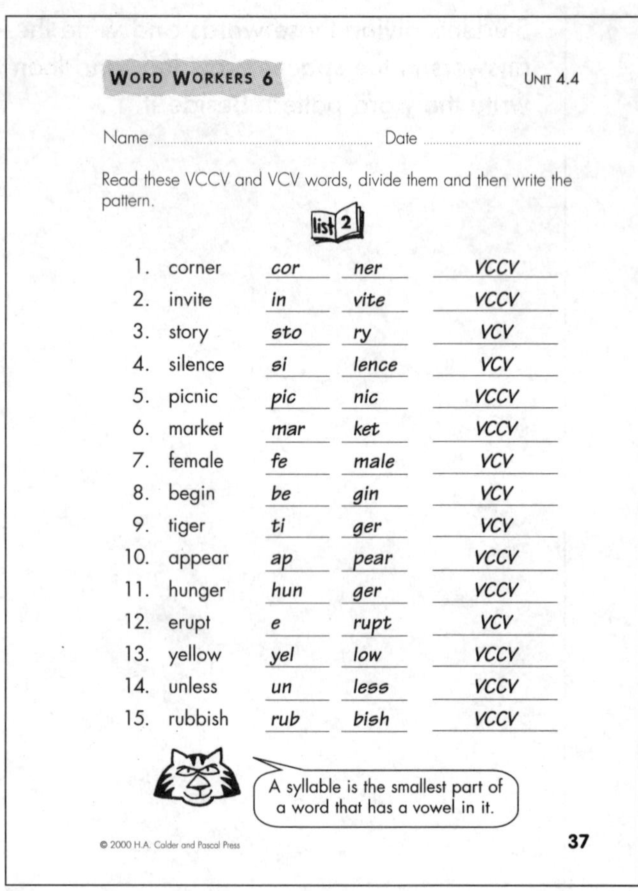

WORD WORKERS 6 UNIT 4.4

Name .... Date ....

Read these VCCV and VCV words, divide them and then write the pattern.

list 2

1.	corner	cor	ner	VCCV
2.	invite	in	vite	VCCV
3.	story	sto	ry	VCV
4.	silence	si	lence	VCV
5.	picnic	pic	nic	VCCV
6.	market	mar	ket	VCCV
7.	female	fe	male	VCV
8.	begin	be	gin	VCV
9.	tiger	ti	ger	VCV
10.	appear	ap	pear	VCCV
11.	hunger	hun	ger	VCCV
12.	erupt	e	rupt	VCV
13.	yellow	yel	low	VCCV
14.	unless	un	less	VCCV
15.	rubbish	rub	bish	VCCV

A syllable is the smallest part of a word that has a vowel in it.

© 2000 H.A. Calder and Pascal Press 37

Students divide these words and write the answers in the spaces provided, and then write the word pattern beside it.

WORD WORKERS 6 UNIT 4.5

Name .... Date ....

Use the pictures to help you spell the words.

1. + dom = kingdom
2. sel + = selfish
3. + toon = cartoon
4. o + = open
5. + ny = sunny
6. 10 + nis = tennis
7. tu + = tulips
8. + phin = dolphin
9. de + = delight
10. + ish = finish
11. el + = elbow

38 © 2000 H.A. Calder and Pascal Press

Students spell these words using the picture as a clue. Tell them that the spelling for the picture may need to be changed in the complete word.

WORD WORKERS 6 UNIT 4.6

Name .... Date ....

Read these VCCV and VCV words, divide them and then write the pattern.

list 3

1.	easy	*ea*	*sy*	*VCV*
2.	problem	*prob*	*lem*	*VCCV*
3.	behave	*be*	*have*	*VCV*
4.	pilot	*pi*	*lot*	*VCV*
5.	letter	*let*	*ter*	*VCCV*
6.	Friday	*Fri*	*day*	*VCV*
7.	viking	*vi*	*king*	*VCV*
8.	lesson	*les*	*son*	*VCCV*
9.	happy	*hap*	*py*	*VCCV*
10.	decide	*de*	*cide*	*VCV*
11.	traffic	*traf*	*fic*	*VCV*
12.	sleepy	*slee*	*py*	*VCV*
13.	cartoon	*car*	*toon*	*VCCV*
14.	open	*o*	*pen*	*VCV*
15.	winter	*win*	*ter*	*VCCV*

When two letters go together to say one sound they count as one letter.

 39

Students divide these words and write the answers in the spaces provided, and then write the word pattern beside it.

WORD WORKERS 6 UNIT 4.7

Name .... Date ....

When a word ends with a silent final 'e', the 'e' does not act as a vowel.

Underline the nonsense word.

1. surfer	2. appear	3. fiftil	4. window
fifty	marfit	sentence	cartist
suster	erupt	hunger	tennis
motel	collar	kitten	before

Complete these sentences by writing the words for the pictures.

50

1. After the race the *swimmer* was too tired to get out of the pool.
2. The student dropped her *pencil* on the floor of the classroom.
3. Scott broke the *window* when he threw the ball.
4. The *tiger* roared as he prowled in the dark night.
5. There were *fifty* runners in the last race.

40

Activity 1: Students look at the columns of words. Tell them to underline the word in each column that is a nonsense word.

Activity 2: Students look at the pictures and then complete the sentences below by writing the correct word for the picture in the space provided.

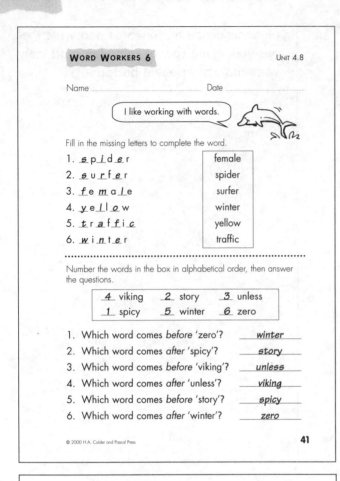

WORD WORKERS 6 UNIT 4.8

Name .... Date ....

I like working with words.

Fill in the missing letters to complete the word.

1. spider
2. surfer
3. female
4. yellow
5. traffic
6. winter

female
spider
surfer
winter
yellow
traffic

Number the words in the box in alphabetical order, then answer the questions.

4 viking	2 story	3 unless
1 spicy	5 winter	6 zero

1. Which word comes *before* 'zero'? winter
2. Which word comes *after* 'spicy'? story
3. Which word comes *before* 'viking'? unless
4. Which word comes *after* 'unless'? viking
5. Which word comes *before* 'story'? spicy
6. Which word comes *after* 'winter'? zero

 41

Activity 1: Students read the words in the box, then write the missing letters to complete the column of words on the left.

Activity 2: Students number the words in the box in alphabetical order, then use this information to answer the questions below.

WORD WORKERS 6 UNIT 4.9

Name .... Date ....

Underline the word for the picture.

window	music	whisper	lady	dismiss
arrow	miner	button	baby	morning
admit	minus	summer	navy	igloo
army	tulip	runner	lazy	ribbon

Underline the correct word to complete the sentence.

1. The miner asked for a (letter/hammer) and some nails.
2. The doctor will (arrive/rescue) later this morning.
3. Winter is the coldest (siren/season) of the year.
4. Did Pam (invite/entire) you to her birthday party?
5. 'This homework is too (elect/easy)!' Shaun told his teacher.

42

Activity 1: Students look at the columns of words. They underline the word in each column that matches the picture above it.

Activity 2: Students read the sentences. They underline the word in brackets that best completes the sentence.

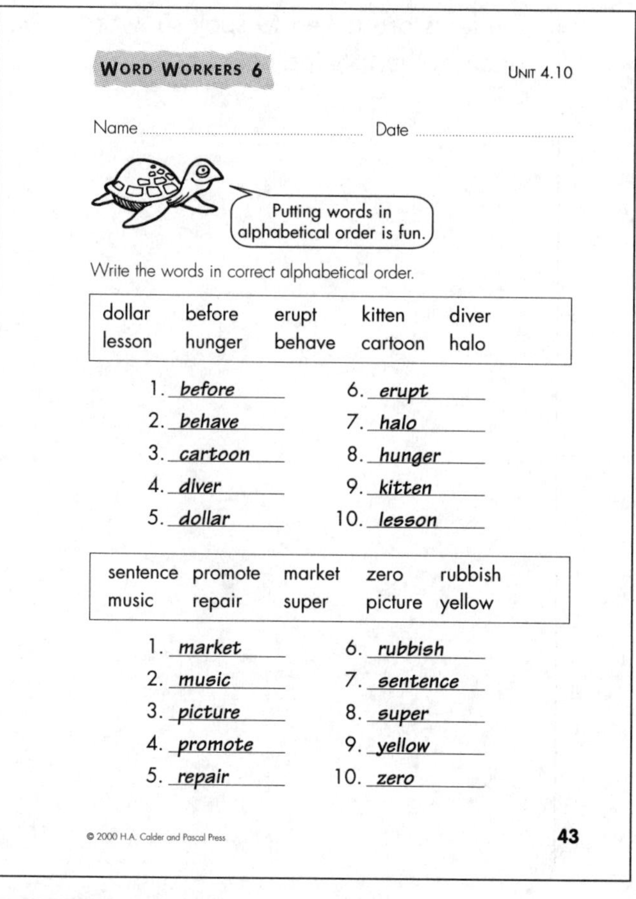

WORD WORKERS 6 UNIT 4.10

Name .... Date ....

Putting words in alphabetical order is fun.

Write the words in correct alphabetical order.

dollar	before	erupt	kitten	diver
lesson	hunger	behave	cartoon	halo

1. *before* 6. *erupt*
2. *behave* 7. *halo*
3. *cartoon* 8. *hunger*
4. *diver* 9. *kitten*
5. *dollar* 10. *lesson*

sentence	promote	market	zero	rubbish
music	repair	super	picture	yellow

1. *market* 6. *rubbish*
2. *music* 7. *sentence*
3. *picture* 8. *super*
4. *promote* 9. *yellow*
5. *repair* 10. *zero*

 43

Students put the words in each box in their correct alphabetical order.

WORD WORKERS 6 UNIT 4.11

Name .... Date ....

Write the word with the correct spelling.

1. appear	apear	appeer	*appear*
2. deside	decide	deciede	*decide*
3. pensil	pencill	pencil	*pencil*
4. unles	unless	unleess	*unless*
5. feamale	femail	female	*female*

Complete these crossword puzzles.

tiger, runner, swimmer, fifty, mint, pilot, pencil, button

50

44

Activity 1: Students read the words going across the page, then write the word that is spelt correctly.

Activity 2: Students complete the crossword puzzles. They write the words for the pictures in the blank spaces.

WORD WORKERS 6 UNIT 4.12

Name .... Date ....

Write six words from each list at the start of this chapter.

list 1

1. ____
2. ____
3. ____
4. ____
5. ____
6. ____

list 2

1. ____
2. ____
3. ____
4. ____
5. ____
6. ____

list 3

1. ____
2. ____
3. ____
4. ____
5. ____
6. ____

© 2000 H.A. Calder and Pascal Press 45

Students are asked to spell six words from each of the lists indicated.

WORD WORKERS 6 UNIT 5.1

Working with 'le' endings

sim ple ta ble

Learn how to divide these words.

When dividing 'le' words, join the consonant before the 'le' to make one syllable.

tumble — tum – ble

able — a – ble

eagle — ea – gle

chuckle — chu – ckle

whistle — whis – tle

46 © 2000 H.A. Calder and Pascal Press

For the following pages:

This unit teaches students how to read and divide words containing the 'le' ending syllabification pattern. Teach the skill carefully until students have mastered it.

From now on, incorporate knowledge of the 'le' ending syllabification rules at the start of each lesson.

WORD WORKERS 6 UNIT 5.2

Name .... Date ....

Read these 'le' ending words and then divide them.

list 1			list 2		
1. topple	top	ple	1. beetle	bee	tle
2. gentle	gen	tle	2. whistle	whi	stle
3. bottle	bot	tle	3. startle	star	tle
4. poodle	poo	dle	4. puzzle	puz	zle
5. needle	nee	dle	5. single	sin	gle
6. thimble	thim	ble	6. eagle	ea	gle
7. apple	ap	ple	7. nozzle	noz	zle
8. knuckle	knu	ckle	8. kettle	ket	tle
9. paddle	pad	dle	9. wrinkle	wrin	kle
10. castle	ca	stle	10. steeple	stee	ple
11. rifle	ri	fle	11. handle	han	dle
12. bugle	bu	gle	12. saddle	sad	dle
13. turtle	tur	tle	13. stumble	stum	ble
14. maple	ma	ple	14. table	ta	ble
15. rattle	rat	tle	15. candle	can	dle

I am a good word worker.

 47

Students divide these words into base word and suffix in the spaces provided. Correct the work by having them read the word and then divide it.

WORD WORKERS 6 UNIT 5.3

Name .... Date ....

Write the words for the pictures.

1. castle 2. bottle 3. saddle

4. apple 5. candle 6. kettle

7. nozzle 8. turtle 9. whistle

10. needle 11. table 12. paddle

48

Students write the words for the pictures. If necessary, they refer to the word lists to find the correct spelling.

WORD WORKERS 6 UNIT 5.4

Name .... Date ....

Read these 'le' ending words and then divide them.

list 3			list 4		
1. muffle	muf	fle	1. simple	sim	ple
2. twinkle	twin	kle	2. pebble	peb	ble
3. drizzle	driz	zle	3. nestle	ne	stle
4. nettle	net	tle	4. cradle	cra	dle
5. scramble	scram	ble	5. purple	pur	ple
6. cable	ca	ble	6. scribble	scrib	ble
7. bible	bi	ble	7. cattle	cat	tle
8. gamble	gam	ble	8. raffle	raf	fle
9. battle	bat	tle	9. puddle	pud	dle
10. ripple	rip	ple	10. tackle	ta	ckle
11. bubble	bub	ble	11. middle	mid	dle
12. buckle	bu	ckle	12. noodle	noo	dle
13. circle	cir	cle	13. little	lit	tle
14. juggle	jug	gle	14. feeble	fee	ble
15. fumble	fum	ble	15. fable	fa	ble

It is fun working with words.

 49

Students divide these words into base word and suffix in the spaces provided. Correct the work by having them read the word and then divide it.

WORD WORKERS 6 UNIT 5.5

Name .... Date ....

Use the pictures to help you spell the words.

1. + gle = juggle
2. + tle = startle
3. + tle = battle
4. + gle = wiggle
5. + tle = beetle
6. + tle = rattle
7. + le = single
8. + le = handle
9. + tle = nettle
10. + ple = topple
11. + tle = cattle

50

Students spell these words using the picture as a clue. Tell them that the spelling for the picture may need to be changed in the complete word.

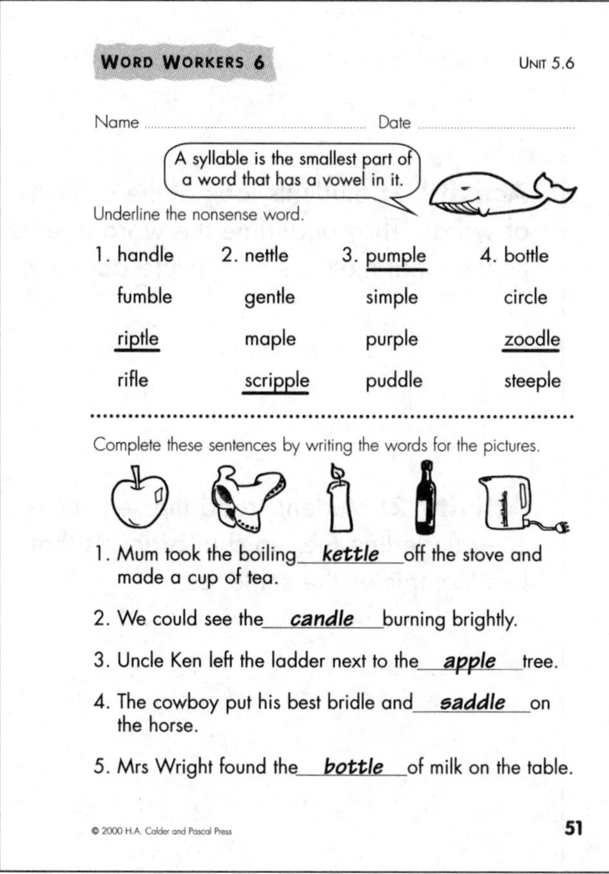

WORD WORKERS 6 UNIT 5.6

Name .... Date ....

A syllable is the smallest part of a word that has a vowel in it.

Underline the nonsense word.

1. handle	2. nettle	3. pumple	4. bottle
fumble	gentle	simple	circle
riptle	maple	purple	zoodle
rifle	scripple	puddle	steeple

Complete these sentences by writing the words for the pictures.

1. Mum took the boiling *kettle* off the stove and made a cup of tea.
2. We could see the *candle* burning brightly.
3. Uncle Ken left the ladder next to the *apple* tree.
4. The cowboy put his best bridle and *saddle* on the horse.
5. Mrs Wright found the *bottle* of milk on the table.

© 2000 H.A. Calder and Pascal Press 51

Activity 1: Students look at the columns of words. Tell them to underline the word in each column that is a nonsense word.

Activity 2: Students look at the pictures and then complete the sentences below by writing the correct word for the picture in the space provided.

WORD WORKERS 6 UNIT 5.7

Name .... Date ....

Dividing words is easy.

Fill in the missing letters to complete the word.

1. s t u m b l e
2. s c r a m b l e
3. w r i n k l e
4. g e n t l e
5. s c r i b b l e
6. c i r c l e

circle
wrinkle
gentle
stumble
scramble
scribble

Number the words in the box in alphabetical order, then answer the questions.

3 bottle	4 candle	1 apple
6 drizzle	2 bible	5 cradle

1. Which word comes *after* 'apple'? *bible*
2. Which word comes *before* 'drizzle'? *cradle*
3. Which word comes *after* 'bottle'? *candle*
4. Which word comes *before* 'candle'? *bottle*
5. Which word comes *after* 'cradle'? *drizzle*
6. Which word comes *before* 'bible'? *apple*

52 © 2000 H.A. Calder and Pascal Press

Activity 1: Students read the words in the box, then write the missing letters to complete the column of words on the left.

Activity 2: Students number the words in the box in alphabetical order, then use this information to answer the questions below.

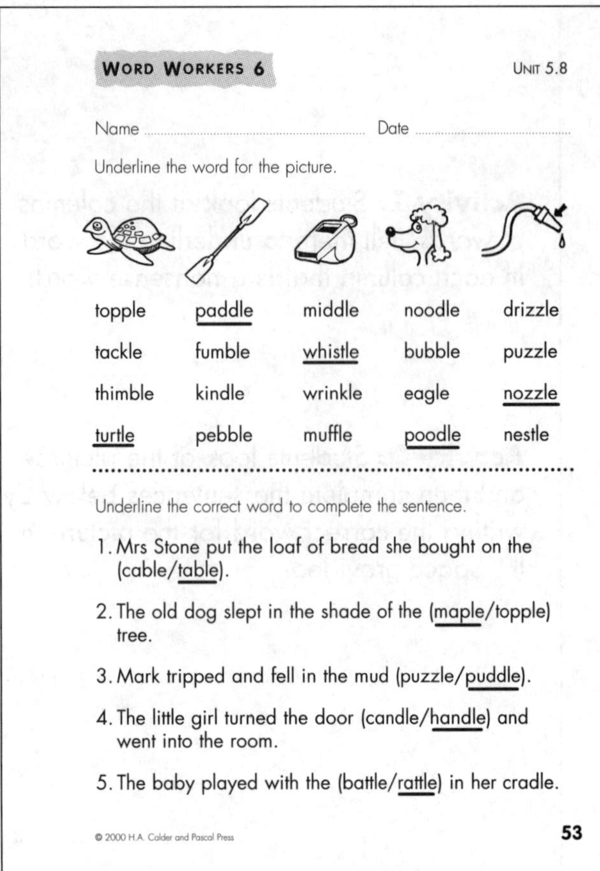

WORD WORKERS 6 UNIT 5.8

Name .... Date ....

Underline the word for the picture.

topple	paddle	middle	noodle	drizzle
tackle	fumble	whistle	bubble	puzzle
thimble	kindle	wrinkle	eagle	nozzle
turtle	pebble	muffle	poodle	nestle

Underline the correct word to complete the sentence.

1. Mrs Stone put the loaf of bread she bought on the (cable/table).
2. The old dog slept in the shade of the (maple/topple) tree.
3. Mark tripped and fell in the mud (puzzle/puddle).
4. The little girl turned the door (candle/handle) and went into the room.
5. The baby played with the (battle/rattle) in her cradle.

© 2000 H.A. Calder and Pascal Press 53

Activity 1: Students look at the columns of words. They underline the word in each column that matches the picture above it.

Activity 2: Students read the sentences. They underline the word in brackets that best completes the sentence.

WORD WORKERS 6 UNIT 5.9

Name .... Date ....

Putting words into alphabetical order is fun.

Write the words in correct alphabetical order.

gentle	cattle	bugle	feeble	apple
candle	fable	eagle	drizzle	bottle

1. *apple* 6. *drizzle*
2. *bottle* 7. *eagle*
3. *bugle* 8. *fable*
4. *candle* 9. *feeble*
5. *cattle* 10. *gentle*

single	needle	whistle	simple	turtle
wrinkle	raffle	nestle	scramble	rattle

1. *needle* 6. *simple*
2. *nestle* 7. *single*
3. *raffle* 8. *turtle*
4. *rattle* 9. *whistle*
5. *scramble* 10. *wrinkle*

54 © 2000 H.A. Calder and Pascal Press

Students put the words in each box in their correct alphabetical order.

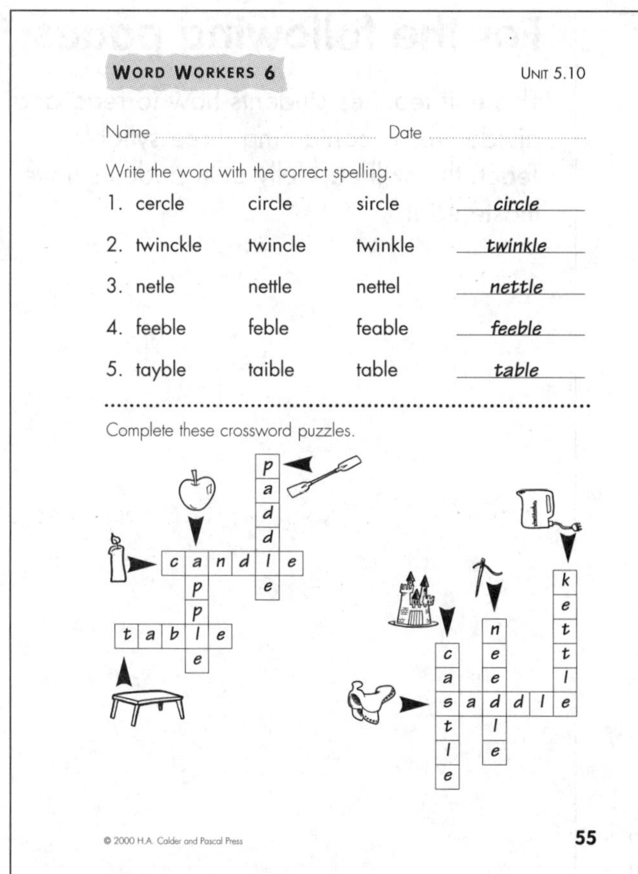
WORD WORKERS 6 UNIT 5.10

Name .... Date ....

Write the word with the correct spelling.

1.	cercle	circle	sircle	*circle*
2.	twinckle	twincle	twinkle	*twinkle*
3.	netle	nettle	nettel	*nettle*
4.	feeble	feble	feable	*feeble*
5.	tayble	taible	table	*table*

Complete these crossword puzzles.

© 2000 H.A. Calder and Pascal Press 55

Activity 1: Students read the words going across the page, then write the word that is spelt correctly.

Activity 2: Students complete the crossword puzzles. They write the words for the pictures in the blank spaces.

WORD WORKERS 6 UNIT 5.11

Name .... Date ....

Spelling is fun.

Write six words from each list at the start of this chapter.

list 1

1. ____
2. ____
3. ____
4. ____
5. ____
6. ____

list 2

1. ____
2. ____
3. ____
4. ____
5. ____
6. ____

list 3

1. ____
2. ____
3. ____
4. ____
5. ____
6. ____

list 4

1. ____
2. ____
3. ____
4. ____
5. ____
6. ____

56 © 2000 H.A. Calder and Pascal Press

Students are asked to spell six words from each of the lists indicated.

WORD WORKERS 6 UNIT 6.1

Working with long words

Learn how to divide these words.

Dividing long words is easy. Remember the two patterns are VCCV and VCV.

professor — pro – fes – sor

fantastic — fan – tas – tic

educate — e – du – cate

 57

For the following pages:

This unit teaches students how to read and divide words containing three syllables. Teach the skill carefully until students have mastered it.

WORD WORKERS 6 UNIT 6.2

Name .... Date ....

Read these long words and then divide them.

list 1		list 2	
1. carpenter	car pen ter	1. chimpanzee	chim pan zee
2. yesterday	yes ter day	2. romantic	ro man tic
3. dinosaur	di no saur	3. cucumber	cu cum ber
4. September	Sep tem ber	4. octopus	oc to pus
5. elephant	e le phant	5. volcano	vol ca no
6. fantastic	fan tas tic	6. dependent	de pen dent
7. computer	com pu ter	7. general	ge ner al
8. conductor	con duc tor	8. surrender	sur ren der
9. hamburger	ham bur ger	9. terrible	ter ri ble
10. remember	re mem ber	10. daffodil	daf fo dil
11. factory	fac tory	11. telephone	te le phone
12. submarine	sub mar ine	12. consonant	con so nant
13. professor	pro fes sor	13. crocodile	cro co dile
14. banana	ba na na	14. Saturday	Sa tur day
15. advertise	ad ver tise	15. gardener	gar de ner

A syllable is the smallest part of a word that has a vowel in it.

58

Students divide these words into prefix, base word and suffix in the spaces provided. Correct the work by having them read the word and then divide it.

WORD WORKERS 6 UNIT 6.3

Name .... Date ....

Write the words for the pictures.

1. crocodile 2. volcano 3. computer
4. general 5. submarine 6. telephone
7. octopus 8. carpenter 9. dinosaur
10. chimpanzee 11. elephant 12. hamburger

 59

Students write the words for the pictures. If necessary, they refer to the word lists to find the correct spelling.

WORD WORKERS 6 UNIT 6.4

Name .... Date ....

Read these long words and then divide them.

list 3		list 4	
1. argument	ar gu ment	1. performer	per for mer
2. balcony	bal co ny	2. interrupt	in ter rupt
3. horrible	hor ri ble	3. difficult	dif fi cult
4. elegant	e le gant	4. fortunate	for tu nate
5. Wednesday	Wed nes day	5. adventure	ad ven ture
6. entertain	en ter tain	6. medical	me di cal
7. passenger	pas sen ger	7. minister	mi nis ter
8. different	dif fe rent	8. important	im por tant
9. hospital	hos pi tal	9. animal	a ni mal
10. customer	cus to mer	10. reporter	re por ter
11. magazine	ma ga zine	11. horizon	ho ri zon
12. lemonade	le mo nade	12. advantage	ad van tage
13. principal	prin ci pal	13. alphabet	al pha bet
14. musical	mu si cal	14. October	Oc to ber
15. forgotten	for got ten	15. assemble	as sem ble

When the letter 'y' says a vowel sound, it acts as a vowel.

60

Students divide these words into prefix, base word and suffix in the spaces provided. Correct the work by having them read the word and then divide it.

WORD WORKERS 6 UNIT 6.5

Name .... Date ....

Use the pictures to help you spell the words.

1. + tastic = *fantastic*
2. ad + + tage = *advantage*
3. + penter = *carpenter*
4. con + + tor = *conductor*
5. forgot + 10 = *forgotten*
6. de + + dent = *dependent*
7. per + 4 + mer = *performer*
8. com + + y = *company*
9. conson + = *consonant*
10. + mantic = *romantic*
11. e + + ant = *elegant*

© 2000 H.A. Calder and Pascal Press 61

Students spell these words using the picture as a clue. Tell them that the spelling for the picture may need to be changed in the complete word.

WORD WORKERS 6 UNIT 6.6

Name .... Date ....

When two letters go together to say one sound, they count as one letter.

Underline the nonsense word.

1. daffodil	2. <u>chimpantic</u>	3. factory	4. romantic
<u>computest</u>	surrender	interest	crocodile
animal	general	<u>yesterdent</u>	remember
medical	telephone	principal	<u>fantastor</u>

Complete these sentences by writing the words for the pictures.

1. The *carpenter* forgot to fix the broken window.
2. The general picked up the ringing *telephone*.
3. The *chimpanzee* sat on a branch and ate a banana.
4. In the first week of October a *submarine* was seen floating off the coast.
5. The professor worked at his *computer* all morning.

62 © 2000 H.A. Calder and Pascal Press

Activity 1: Students look at the columns of words. Tell them to underline the word in each column that is a nonsense word.

Activity 2: Students look at the pictures and then complete the sentences below by writing the correct word for the picture in the space provided.

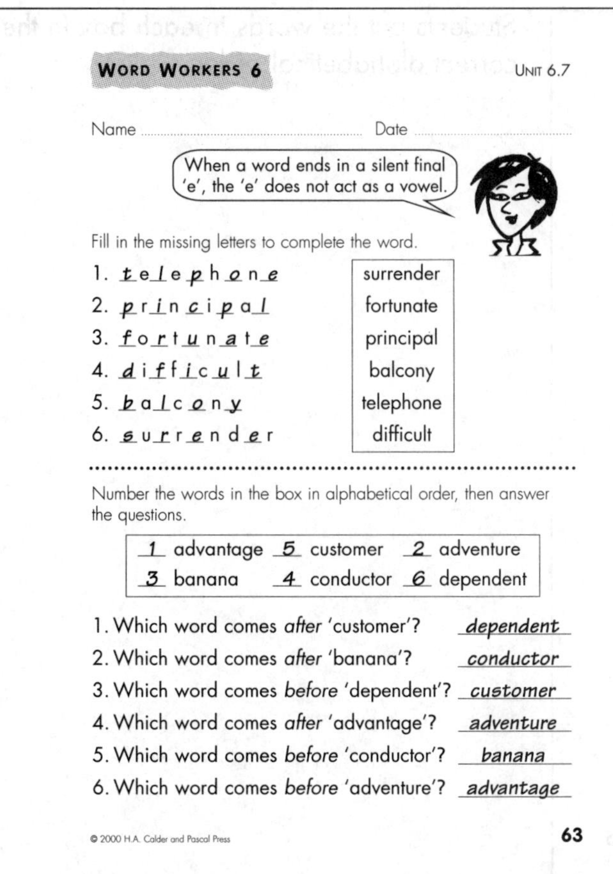
WORD WORKERS 6 UNIT 6.7

Name .... Date ....

When a word ends in a silent final 'e', the 'e' does not act as a vowel.

Fill in the missing letters to complete the word.

1. telephone
2. principal
3. fortunate
4. difficult
5. balcony
6. surrender

surrender
fortunate
principal
balcony
telephone
difficult

Number the words in the box in alphabetical order, then answer the questions.

1 advantage	5 customer	2 adventure
3 banana	4 conductor	6 dependent

1. Which word comes *after* 'customer'? *dependent*
2. Which word comes *after* 'banana'? *conductor*
3. Which word comes *before* 'dependent'? *customer*
4. Which word comes *after* 'advantage'? *adventure*
5. Which word comes *before* 'conductor'? *banana*
6. Which word comes *before* 'adventure'? *advantage*

© 2000 H.A. Calder and Pascal Press 63

Activity 1: Students read the words in the box, then write the missing letters to complete the column of words on the left.

Activity 2: Students number the words in the box in alphabetical order, then use this information to answer the questions below.

WORD WORKERS 6 UNIT 6.8

Name .... Date ....

Underline the word for the picture.

volcano	customer	gardener	horrible	dinosaur
conductor	medical	general	performer	adventure
entertain	important	minister	octopus	dependent
difficult	crocodile	passenger	yesterday	different

Underline the correct word to complete the sentence.

1. The (gardener/musical) picked a bunch of daffodils.
2. Last September the child spent a week in the (horizon/hospital).
3. Mrs Knight had a (terrible/remember) pain in her tooth so she went to see the dentist.
4. The principal asked the students if they knew the letters of the (advantage/alphabet).
5. Mr Lamb read each page in the (entertain/magazine) on Wednesday night.

64

Activity 1: Students look at the columns of words. They underline the word in each column that matches the picture above it.

Activity 2: Students read the sentences. They underline the word in brackets that best completes the sentence.

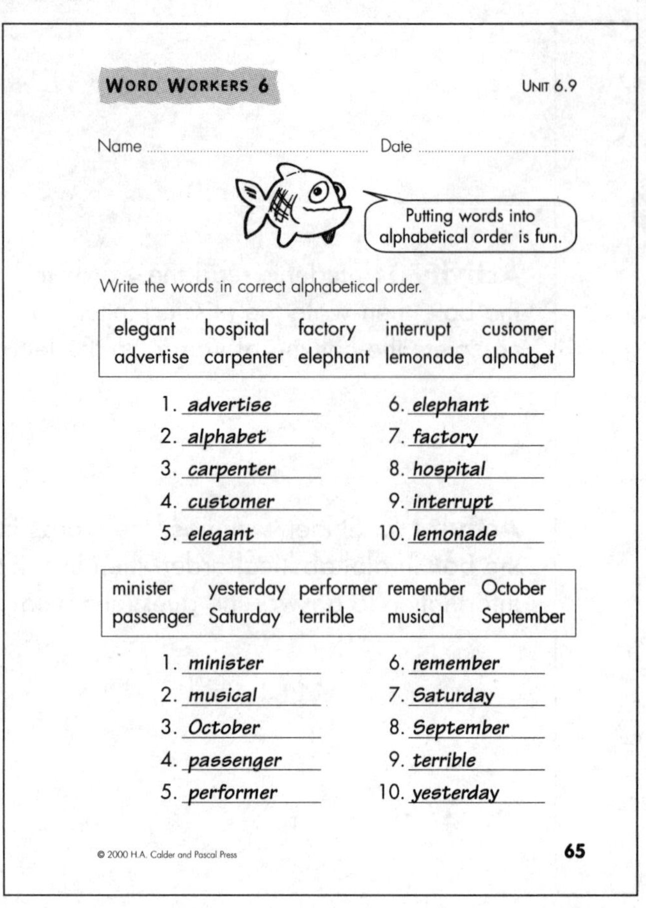
WORD WORKERS 6 UNIT 6.9

Name .... Date ....

Putting words into alphabetical order is fun.

Write the words in correct alphabetical order.

elegant	hospital	factory	interrupt	customer
advertise	carpenter	elephant	lemonade	alphabet

1. *advertise*
2. *alphabet*
3. *carpenter*
4. *customer*
5. *elegant*
6. *elephant*
7. *factory*
8. *hospital*
9. *interrupt*
10. *lemonade*

minister	yesterday	performer	remember	October
passenger	Saturday	terrible	musical	September

1. *minister*
2. *musical*
3. *October*
4. *passenger*
5. *performer*
6. *remember*
7. *Saturday*
8. *September*
9. *terrible*
10. *yesterday*

 65

Students put the words in each box in their correct alphabetical order.

WORD WORKERS 6 UNIT 6.10

Name .... Date ....

Write the word with the correct spelling.

1.	romantic	rowmanitc	romatic	*romantic*
2.	Wedensday	Wednesday	Wendesday	*Wednesday*
3.	principul	princibal	principal	*principal*
4.	interupt	interrupt	interput	*interrupt*
5.	entertane	entertrain	entertain	*entertain*

Complete these crossword puzzles.

volcano, *dinosaur*, *crocodile*, *general*

elephant, *octopus*, *submarine*, *carpenter*

66

Activity 1: Students read the words going across the page, then write the word that is spelt correctly.

Activity 2: Students complete the crossword puzzles. They write the words for the pictures in the blank spaces.

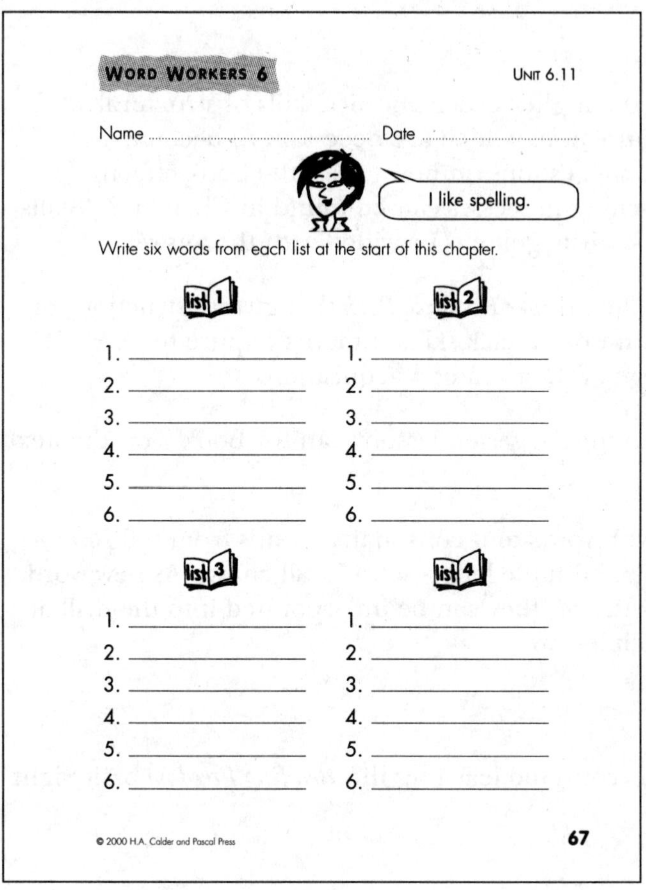
WORD WORKERS 6 UNIT 6.11

Name .... Date ....

Write six words from each list at the start of this chapter.

list 1

1. ____
2. ____
3. ____
4. ____
5. ____
6. ____

list 2

1. ____
2. ____
3. ____
4. ____
5. ____
6. ____

list 3

1. ____
2. ____
3. ____
4. ____
5. ____
6. ____

list 4

1. ____
2. ____
3. ____
4. ____
5. ____
6. ____

© 2000 H.A. Calder and Pascal Press 67

Students are asked to spell six words from each of the lists indicated.

* Students complete *Word Workers Achievement Test 8* after completing this unit.

Using Book 7

Word Workers Book 7 teaches students the higher order phonics skills of structural analysis and recognising common contractions, which are necessary to become independent readers. Below are some suggestions on how to use the book effectively. More detailed information on the teaching processes can be found in Chapter 2: 'Skills for successful teaching'. An activity-by-activity guide is provided with the answers.

- Read the section in the *Teacher Resource Book* that gives instructions on teaching the different word attack skills students require to be successful at this stage of their reading acquisition.

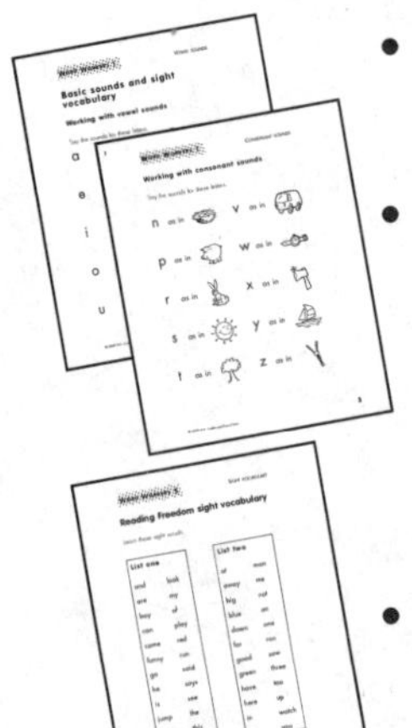

- Become familiar with the suggested lesson plan for Book 7 on the next page.
- Continue the drill with vowel and consonant sounds from the *Reading Freedom 2000* single and double letter–sound wall charts. As new word attack skills are introduced, they can be incorporated into the drill at the beginning of each lesson.

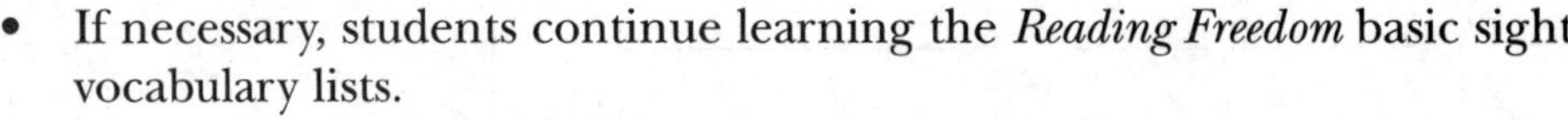

- If necessary, students continue learning the *Reading Freedom* basic sight vocabulary lists.

- Introduce the structural analysis skills as students encounter them in each successive unit.
- Enlist parent support whenever possible. Parents are particularly helpful teaching sight vocabulary and reinforcing sounds, rules and phonic generalisations at home.
- Monitor students' progress through regular oral reading.
- When Book 7 is completed, record students' progress using *Word Workers* Achievement Test 9.

Book 7: Suggested lesson plan

Based on a lesson of approximately 30 minutes.

1 Students say a row of sounds from the three *Reading Freedom 2000* wall charts. For small groups, each student can say a row or column of sounds. If your class is large, select students to say a row or column until all the sounds have been repeated. As new sounds and phonic generalisations are encountered in Book 7, they can be incorporated at the start of each lesson.

2 When teaching with small groups, each student reads a column of *Reading Freedom* basic sight vocabulary. When teaching the whole class, select students to read a column of sight words. Five or six columns is enough to start your lesson with. Be sure different students read the sight words each lesson.

3 Explain and demonstrate the structural analysis skills to be learned. Carefully explain the activities on the page or pages to be completed. Ensure that students understand the concepts involved and know what is required of them.

4 Assign activity pages to be completed (the number of pages depends on the teacher's professional judgment as well as the ability and enthusiasm of the student).

5 In Book 7, demonstrate and practise blending with each sound taught. Continue with this until the book is completed, learning new sounds as they are introduced. At this stage of instruction, blending skills are often firmly in place. The teacher's professional judgment and the ability of the student determines the need to continue with it.

6 Reward students for achievement on the activity pages or in learning sight vocabulary with stamps, stickers or gold stars. When they complete the activity book and finish the complementary achievement test (found in *Word Workers Achievement Tests*) they receive a *Word Workers* Merit Certificate.

7 Assign any homework after demonstrating the activities. Ensure students understand the concept and what is to be done.

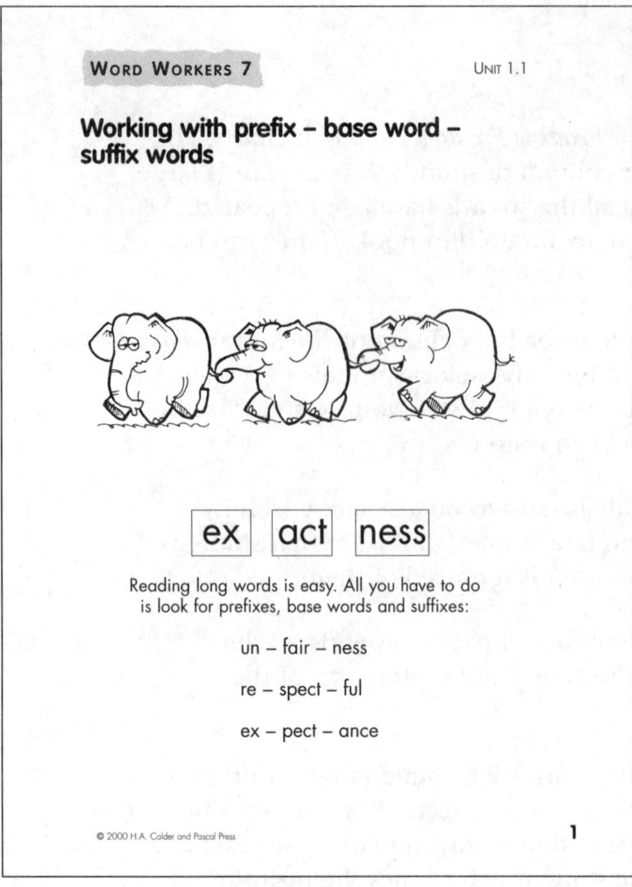

WORD WORKERS 7 — UNIT 1.1

Working with prefix – base word – suffix words

ex | act | ness

Reading long words is easy. All you have to do is look for prefixes, base words and suffixes:

un – fair – ness

re – spect – ful

ex – pect – ance

© 2000 H.A. Calder and Pascal Press — 1

For the following pages:

This unit teaches students how to read and divide words containing the prefix–base word–suffix pattern. Teach the skill carefully until students have mastered it.

From now on, incorporate knowledge of the prefix–base word–suffix pattern in the phonics drill at the start of each lesson.

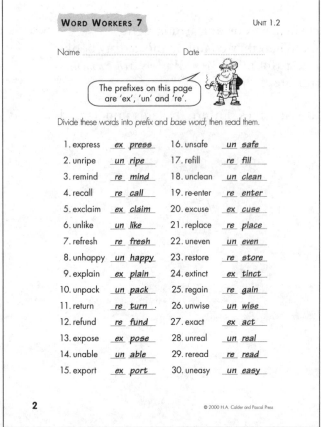

WORD WORKERS 7 — UNIT 1.2

Name .... Date ....

The prefixes on this page are 'ex', 'un' and 're'.

Divide these words into *prefix* and *base word*; then read them.

1. express	*ex press*	16. unsafe	*un safe*
2. unripe	*un ripe*	17. refill	*re fill*
3. remind	*re mind*	18. unclean	*un clean*
4. recall	*re call*	19. re-enter	*re enter*
5. exclaim	*ex claim*	20. excuse	*ex cuse*
6. unlike	*un like*	21. replace	*re place*
7. refresh	*re fresh*	22. uneven	*un even*
8. unhappy	*un happy*	23. restore	*re store*
9. explain	*ex plain*	24. extinct	*ex tinct*
10. unpack	*un pack*	25. regain	*re gain*
11. return	*re turn*	26. unwise	*un wise*
12. refund	*re fund*	27. exact	*ex act*
13. expose	*ex pose*	28. unreal	*un real*
14. unable	*un able*	29. reread	*re read*
15. export	*ex port*	30. uneasy	*un easy*

2 — © 2000 H.A. Calder and Pascal Press

Students divide these words into prefix and base word in the spaces provided. Correct the work by having them read the word and then divide it.

WORD WORKERS 7 UNIT 1.3

Name .... Date ....

A prefix comes at the beginning of a word to change the word's meaning.

Write the word from each column that fits the word shape box.

refresh	uneven	recall	export
exact	refill	unhappy	unripe
unwise	express	excuse	remind
return	regain	unreal	extinct
exact	regain	excuse	unripe

Underline the correct word to complete the sentence.

1. Mum had to (return/remind) Ann to do her homework.
2. The men were (unable/uneasy) to lift the largest crate onto the truck.
3. The teacher tried to (exclaim/explain) the problem to the students.
4. The (unlike/unripe) apples were hard and sour.
5. Mr Jones was asked to (regain/replace) the book on the top shelf.

3

Activity 1: Students look at the columns of words. Tell them to put the word from each column that fits into the 'word shape' box below it.

Activity 2: Students read the sentences. They underline the word in brackets that best completes the sentence.

WORD WORKERS 7 UNIT 1.4

Name .... Date ....

The suffixes on this page are 'ful', 'ness' and 'ance'.

Divide these words into *base word* and *suffix*; then read them.

Word	Base word	Suffix	Word	Base word	Suffix
1. cheerful	cheer	ful	16. careful	care	ful
2. brightness	bright	ness	17. darkness	dark	ness
3. distance	dist	ance	18. peaceful	peace	ful
4. sadness	sad	ness	19. importance	import	ance
5. clearance	clear	ance	20. dampness	damp	ness
6. handful	hand	ful	21. entrance	entr	ance
7. thickness	thick	ness	22. spoonful	spoon	ful
8. helpful	help	ful	23. illness	ill	ness
9. assistance	assist	ance	24. hopeful	hope	ful
10. sickness	sick	ness	25. fragrance	fragr	ance
11. painful	pain	ful	26. richness	rich	ness
12. appearance	appear	ance	27. wishful	wish	ful
13. stillness	still	ness	28. sweetness	sweet	ness
14. playful	play	ful	29. useful	use	ful
15. allowance	allow	ance	30. finance	fin	ance

4

Students divide these words into base word and suffix in the spaces provided. Correct the work by having them read the word and then divide it.

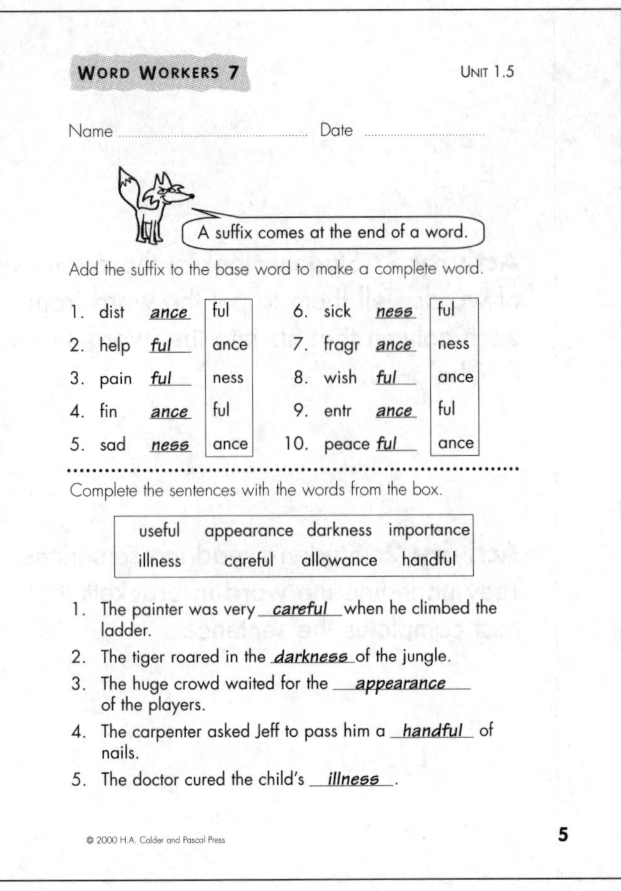

WORD WORKERS 7 UNIT 1.5

Name .... Date ....

A suffix comes at the end of a word.

Add the suffix to the base word to make a complete word.

1. dist *ance*	ful		6. sick *ness*	ful	
2. help *ful*	ance		7. fragr *ance*	ness	
3. pain *ful*	ness		8. wish *ful*	ance	
4. fin *ance*	ful		9. entr *ance*	ful	
5. sad *ness*	ance		10. peace *ful*	ance	

Complete the sentences with the words from the box.

useful	appearance	darkness	importance
illness	careful	allowance	handful

1. The painter was very *careful* when he climbed the ladder.
2. The tiger roared in the *darkness* of the jungle.
3. The huge crowd waited for the *appearance* of the players.
4. The carpenter asked Jeff to pass him a *handful* of nails.
5. The doctor cured the child's *illness*.

© 2000 H.A. Calder and Pascal Press 5

Activity 1: Students write the correct suffix beside the base word to make a complete word.

Activity 2: Students complete the sentences by writing the correct word from the box in the space provided.

WORD WORKERS 7 UNIT 1.6

Name .... Date ....

Many words can be divided by taking the prefix and suffix away from the base word.

Divide these words into *prefix*, *base word* and *suffix*; then read them.

1. unkindness	*un*	*kind*	*ness*
2. resistance	*re*	*sist*	*ance*
3. expectance	*ex*	*pect*	*ance*
4. respectful	*re*	*spect*	*ful*
5. unjustness	*un*	*just*	*ness*
6. reappearance	*re*	*appear*	*ance*
7. exactness	*ex*	*act*	*ness*
8. unfairness	*un*	*fair*	*ness*
9. reluctance	*re*	*luct*	*ance*
10. regretful	*re*	*gret*	*ful*
11. unfitness	*un*	*fit*	*ness*
12. unhelpful	*un*	*help*	*ful*
13. re-entrance	*re*	*entr*	*ance*
14. unhappiness	*un*	*happi*	*ness*
15. unlawful	*un*	*law*	*ful*

6 © 2000 H.A. Calder and Pascal Press

Students divide these words into prefix, base word and suffix in the spaces provided. Correct the work by having them read the word and then divide it.

WORD WORKERS 7 UNIT 1.7

Name .... Date ....

Write the base word beside the complete word.

1. reappearance	*appear*	expect
2. exactness	*exact*	resist
3. unhelpful	*help*	fair
4. respectful	*respect*	appear
5. unfairness	*fair*	happy
6. expectance	*expect*	help
7. unhappiness	*happy*	exact
8. resistance	*resist*	respect

Underline the correct word to complete the sentence.

1. Mrs Marsh said that the clerk in the shop was (unhelpful/unlawful).
2. Carly was (regretful/respectful) to the minister of her church.
3. The (resistance/reappearance) of the cat woke the sleeping dog.
4. Shaun's (reentrance/reluctance) to go to the dentist annoyed his mother.
5. The runner's (unfitness/unjustness) made him drop out of the race.

© 2000 H.A. Calder and Pascal Press 7

Activity 1: Students read the complete word and then, beside it, they write the base word from the right-hand column.

Activity 2: Students read the sentences. They underline the word in brackets that best completes the sentence.

WORD WORKERS 7 UNIT 1.8

Name .... Date ....

Underline the nonsense word.

1. reluctance	2. resistance	3. unjustness	4. regretful
unkindful	unlawful	exactness	explayful
unfitness	exsweetness	unhappiness	reentrance
expectance	reappearance	redarkance	unfairness

Write the word from the box beside its definition.

unreal	excuse	cheerful	respectful
peaceful	unclean	refresh	unhappiness

1. happy *c h e e r f u l*
2. not real *u n r e a l*
3. calm *p e a c e f u l*
4. dirty *u n c l e a n*
5. sadness *u n h a p p i n e s s*

A base word is not always a complete word.

8 © 2000 H.A. Calder and Pascal Press

Activity 1: Students look at the columns of words. Tell them to underline the word in each column that is a nonsense word.

Activity 2: Students write the word from the box beside its definition.

WORD WORKERS 7 UNIT 1.9

Name .... Date ....

Fill in the missing letters to complete the word.

1. u n e a s y
2. i m p o r t a n c e
3. r e g r e t f u l
4. e x p e c t a n c e
5. d a m p n e s s
6. e x t i n c t

expectance
regretful
extinct
dampness
uneasy
importance

Number the words in the box in alphabetical order, then answer the questions.

2 refund	5 sweetness	4 richness
1 peaceful	6 unfairness	3 respectful

1. Which word comes *after* 'respectful'? *richness*
2. Which word comes *before* 'refund'? *peaceful*
3. Which word comes *before* 'unfairness'? *sweetness*
4. Which word comes *after* 'peaceful'? *refund*
5. Which word comes *before* 'richness'? *respectful*
6. Which word comes *after* 'sweetness'? *unfairness*

© 2000 H.A. Calder and Pascal Press 9

Activity 1: Students read the words in the box, then write the missing letters to complete the column of words on the left.

Activity 2: Students number the words in the box in alphabetical order, then use this information to answer the questions below.

WORD WORKERS 7 UNIT 1.10

Name .... Date ....

I like putting words in alphabetical order.

Put the words in the boxes in alphabetical order.

explain	illness	exactness	careful	fragrance
allowance	finance	distance	hopeful	expectance

1. *allowance*
2. *careful*
3. *distance*
4. *exactness*
5. *expectance*
6. *explain*
7. *finance*
8. *fragrance*
9. *hopeful*
10. *illness*

refresh	unreal	sadness	unsafe	refill
peaceful	respectful	wishful	unlawful	unkindness

1. *peaceful*
2. *refill*
3. *refresh*
4. *respectful*
5. *sadness*
6. *unkindness*
7. *unlawful*
8. *unreal*
9. *unsafe*
10. *wishful*

10 © 2000 H.A. Calder and Pascal Press

Students put the words in each box in their correct alphabetical order.

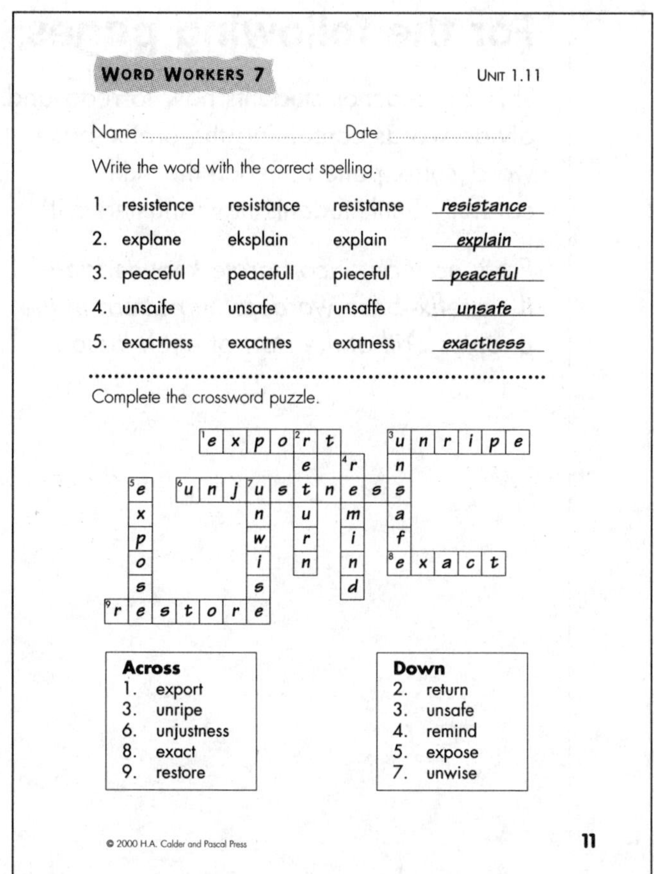

WORD WORKERS 7 UNIT 1.11

Name .... Date ....

Write the word with the correct spelling.

1.	resistence	resistance	resistanse	*resistance*
2.	explane	eksplain	explain	*explain*
3.	peaceful	peacefull	pieceful	*peaceful*
4.	unsaife	unsafe	unsaffe	*unsafe*
5.	exactness	exactnes	exatness	*exactness*

Complete the crossword puzzle.

Across
1. export
3. unripe
6. unjustness
8. exact
9. restore

Down
2. return
3. unsafe
4. remind
5. expose
7. unwise

© 2000 H.A. Calder and Pascal Press 11

Activity 1: Students read the words going across the page, then write the word that is spelt correctly.

Activity 2: Students complete the crossword puzzle by writing the answers in the correct spaces.

WORD WORKERS 7 UNIT 1.12

Name .... Date ....

Spelling words is fun.

Spell six words from each page.

page 2

1. ____
2. ____
3. ____
4. ____
5. ____
6. ____

page 4

1. ____
2. ____
3. ____
4. ____
5. ____
6. ____

page 6

1. ____
2. ____
3. ____
4. ____
5. ____
6. ____

12 © 2000 H.A. Calder and Pascal Press

Students are asked to spell six words from each of the lists indicated.

WORD WORKERS 7 — UNIT 2.1

Working with prefix – base word – suffix words

Reading long words is easy. All you have to do is look for prefixes, base words and suffixes:

com – pos – ition

en – joy – ment

de – cidu – ous

 13

For the following pages:

This unit teaches students how to read and divide words containing the prefix–base word–suffix pattern. Teach the skill carefully until students have mastered it.

From now on, incorporate knowledge of the prefix–base word–suffix pattern in the phonics drill at the start of each lesson.

WORD WORKERS 7 — UNIT2.2

Name .... Date ....

The prefixes on this page are 'de', 'com' and 'en'.

Divide these words into *prefix* and *base word*; then read them.

1. delight	*de light*	16. enforce	*en force*
2. combine	*com bine*	17. compare	*com pare*
3. enjoy	*en joy*	18. destroy	*de stroy*
4. defeat	*de feat*	19. endear	*en dear*
5. comfort	*com fort*	20. dethrone	*de throne*
6. deface	*de face*	21. common	*com mon*
7. entire	*en tire*	22. depress	*de press*
8. define	*de fine*	23. enrage	*en rage*
9. compute	*com pute*	24. degrade	*de grade*
10. engage	*en gage*	25. comment	*com ment*
11. complain	*com plain*	26. enquire	*en quire*
12. enlarge	*en large*	27. compose	*com pose*
13. defend	*de fend*	28. describe	*des cribe*
14. command	*com mand*	29. entrant	*en trant*
15. enrich	*en rich*	30. compete	*com pete*

14

Students divide these words into prefix and base word in the spaces provided. Correct the work by having them read the word and then divide it.

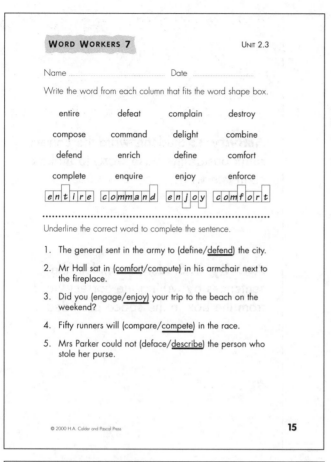

WORD WORKERS 7 UNIT 2.3

Name .... Date ....

Write the word from each column that fits the word shape box.

entire	defeat	complain	destroy
compose	command	delight	combine
defend	enrich	define	comfort
complete	enquire	enjoy	enforce
entire	command	enjoy	comfort

Underline the correct word to complete the sentence.

1. The general sent in the army to (define/defend) the city.
2. Mr Hall sat in (comfort/compute) in his armchair next to the fireplace.
3. Did you (engage/enjoy) your trip to the beach on the weekend?
4. Fifty runners will (compare/compete) in the race.
5. Mrs Parker could not (deface/describe) the person who stole her purse.

 15

Activity 1: Students look at the columns of words. Tell them to put the word from each column that fits into the 'word shape' box below it.

Activity 2: Students read the sentences. They underline the word in brackets that best completes the sentence.

WORD WORKERS 7 UNIT 2.4

Name .... Date ....

The suffixes on this page are 'ous', 'tion' and 'ment'.

Divide these words into *base word* and *suffix*; then read them.

1. joyous	joy	ous	16. placement	place	ment
2. pavement	pave	ment	17. nervous	nerv	ous
3. action	ac	tion	18. vacation	vaca	tion
4. famous	fam	ous	19. odorous	odor	ous
5. station	sta	tion	20. treatment	treat	ment
6. statement	state	ment	21. mention	men	tion
7. motion	mo	tion	22. jealous	jeal	ous
8. generous	gener	ous	23. shipment	ship	ment
9. agreement	agree	ment	24. position	posi	tion
10. dangerous	danger	ous	25. humorous	humor	ous
11. correction	correc	tion	26. nation	na	tion
12. payment	pay	ment	27. judgement	judge	ment
13. poisonous	poison	ous	28. collection	collec	tion
14. argument	argu	ment	29. glorious	glor	ious
15. section	sec	tion	30. settlement	settle	ment

16

Students divide these words into base word and suffix in the spaces provided. Correct the work by having them read the word and then divide it.

Refer students to the 'tion' wall chart on page 47 in the *Word Workers Teacher Resource Book* when they read words containing these suffixes. Display the chart prominently in the classroom.

WORD WORKERS 7 UNIT 2.5

Name .... Date ....

A suffix comes at the end of a word.

Add the suffix to the base word to make a complete word.

1. nerv *ous*	ment	6. vac *ation*	ous
2. state *ment*	ous	7. humor *ous*	ation
3. sta *tion*	ous	8. argu *ment*	ous
4. pay *ment*	tion	9. jeal *ous*	ition
5. gener *ous*	ment	10. pos *ition*	ment

Complete the sentences with the words from the box.

dangerous	vacation	betterment	station
generous	glorious	mention	pavement

1. The *generous* boy bought his sister an ice cream.
2. Kelly slipped on the wet *pavement* and twisted her ankle.
3. All winter long the students could hardly wait for their summer *vacation* .
4. The farmer grabbed his shotgun and killed the *dangerous* snake.
5. The passengers waited at the *station* for the last train to take them to the city.

 17

Activity 1: Students write the correct suffix beside the base word to make a complete word.

Activity 2: Students complete the sentences by writing the correct word from the box in the space provided.

WORD WORKERS 7 UNIT 2.6

Name .... Date ....

When the suffix 'tion' has an 'a' or an 'i' before it, add the letters to it like this: 'ation', 'ition'.

Divide these words into *prefix*, *base word* and *suffix*; then read them.

1. commandment	*com*	*mand*	*ment*
2. competition	*com*	*pet*	*ition*
3. engagement	*en*	*gage*	*ment*
4. compartment	*com*	*part*	*ment*
5. definition	*de*	*fin*	*ition*
6. enjoyment	*en*	*joy*	*ment*
7. composition	*com*	*pos*	*ition*
8. enforcement	*en*	*force*	*ment*
9. destruction	*de*	*struc*	*tion*
10. enrichment	*en*	*rich*	*ment*
11. commitment	*com*	*mit*	*ment*
12. description	*de*	*scrip*	*tion*
13. deciduous	*de*	*cidu*	*ous*
14. endearment	*en*	*dear*	*ment*
15. deformation	*de*	*form*	*ation*

18

Students divide these words into prefix, base word and suffix in the spaces provided. Correct the work by having them read the word and then divide it.

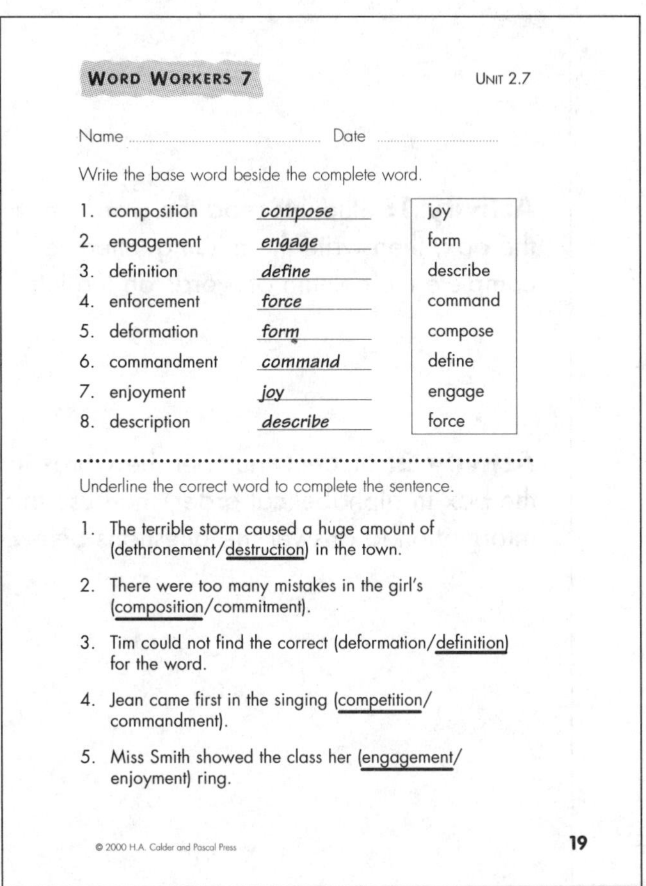

WORD WORKERS 7 UNIT 2.7

Name .... Date ....

Write the base word beside the complete word.

1.	composition	*compose*	joy
2.	engagement	*engage*	form
3.	definition	*define*	describe
4.	enforcement	*force*	command
5.	deformation	*form*	compose
6.	commandment	*command*	define
7.	enjoyment	*joy*	engage
8.	description	*describe*	force

Underline the correct word to complete the sentence.

1. The terrible storm caused a huge amount of (dethronement/destruction) in the town.
2. There were too many mistakes in the girl's (composition/commitment).
3. Tim could not find the correct (deformation/definition) for the word.
4. Jean came first in the singing (competition/commandment).
5. Miss Smith showed the class her (engagement/enjoyment) ring.

© 2000 H.A. Calder and Pascal Press 19

Activity 1: Students read the complete word and then, beside it, they write the base word from the right-hand column.

Activity 2: Students read the sentences. They underline the word in brackets that best completes the sentence.

WORD WORKERS 7 UNIT 2.8

Name .... Date ....

A base word is not always a complete word

Underline the nonsense word.

engagement	definition	compartment	competition
composition	commention	deformation	description
entrantous	enjoyment	endearment	comfortous
destruction	commitment	describement	enrichment

Write the word from the box beside its definition.

combine	mention	enrage	description
vacation	famous	definition	humorous

1. make very angry *e n r a g e*
2. join together *c o m b i n e*
3. well-known *f a m o u s*
4. funny *h u m o r o u s*
5. holiday *v a c a t i o n*

20 © 2000 H.A. Calder and Pascal Press

Activity 1: Students look at the columns of words. Tell them to underline the word in each column that is a nonsense word.

Activity 2: Students write the word from the box beside its definition.

WORD WORKERS 7 UNIT 2.9

Name .... Date ....

Fill in the missing letters to complete the word.

1. comment	entrant
2. poisonous	collection
3. entrant	comment
4. collection	endearment
5. endearment	compartment
6. compartment	poisonous

Number the words in the box in alphabetical order, then answer the questions.

3 destruction	6 famous	1 compartment
5 enjoy	4 enforce	2 dangerous

1. Which word comes *after* 'compartment'? *dangerous*
2. Which word comes *before* 'dangerous'? *compartment*
3. Which word comes *after* 'enjoy'? *famous*
4. Which word comes *before* 'famous'? *enjoy*
5. Which word comes *after* 'destruction'? *enforce*
6. Which word comes *before* 'enforce'? *destruction*

© 2000 H.A. Calder and Pascal Press 21

Activity 1: Students read the words in the box, then write the missing letters to complete the column of words on the left.

Activity 2: Students number the words in the box in alphabetical order, then use this information to answer the questions below.

WORD WORKERS 7 UNIT 2.10

Name .... Date ....

I like putting words in alphabetical order.

Put the words in the boxes in alphabetical order.

endearment	joyous	engage	argument	delightful
collection	action	defend	enforce	destruction

1. *action* 6. *destruction*
2. *argument* 7. *endearment*
3. *collection* 8. *enforce*
4. *defend* 9. *engage*
5. *delightful* 10. *joyous*

composition	odorous	command	statement	enlarge
deformation	deface	vacation	describe	section

1. *command* 6. *enlarge*
2. *composition* 7. *odorous*
3. *deface* 8. *section*
4. *deformation* 9. *statement*
5. *describe* 10. *vacation*

22

Students put the words in each box in their correct alphabetical order.

WORD WORKERS 7 UNIT 2.11

Name .... Date ....

Write the word with the correct spelling.

1. poisonus poysonous poisonous *poisonous*
2. destruction destruktion destrucshun *destruction*
3. entyre entire entier *entire*
4. arguement argumant argument *argument*
5. deepress depress depres *depress*

Complete the crossword puzzle.

		[1]c	o	m	[2]p	u	t	e						
					l									
	[3]c	o	m	m	a	n	d	m	[4]e	n	t			
[5]d					c				n					
e					e				g					[6]e
f					m		[7]c		[8]a	c	t	i	o	n
e					e		o		g					j
n					n		m		e					o
[9]d	e	f	e	a	t		p		m					y
							o		e					
							s		n					
						[10]s	e	c	t	i	o	n		

Across
1. compute
3. commandment
8. action
9. defeat
10. section

Down
2. placement
4. engagement
5. defend
6. enjoy
7. compose

 23

Activity 1: Students read the words going across the page, then write the word that is spelt correctly.

Activity 2: Students complete the crossword puzzle by writing the answers in the correct spaces.

WORD WORKERS 7 UNIT 2.12

Name .... Date ....

Spelling words is fun.

Spell six words from each page.

page 14

1. ____
2. ____
3. ____
4. ____
5. ____
6. ____

page 16

1. ____
2. ____
3. ____
4. ____
5. ____
6. ____

page 18

1. ____
2. ____
3. ____
4. ____
5. ____
6. ____

24

Students are asked to spell six words from each of the lists indicated.

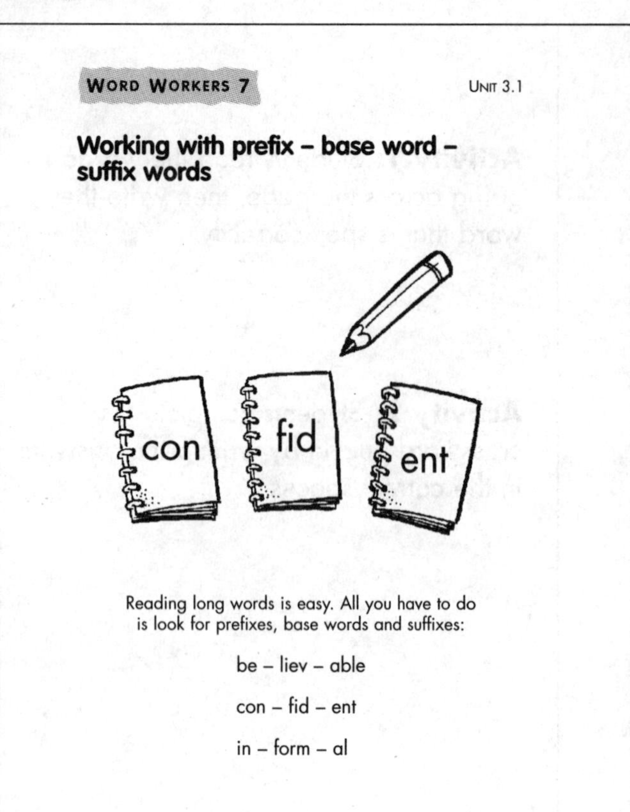

WORD WORKERS 7 UNIT 3.1

Working with prefix – base word – suffix words

Reading long words is easy. All you have to do is look for prefixes, base words and suffixes:

be – liev – able

con – fid – ent

in – form – al

 25

For the following pages:

This unit teaches students how to read and divide words containing the prefix–base word–suffix pattern. Teach the skill carefully until students have mastered it.

From now on, incorporate knowledge of the prefix–base word–suffix pattern in the phonics drill at the start of each lesson.

WORD WORKERS 7 UNIT 3.2

Name .... Date ....

The prefixes on this page are 'in', 'con', 'be' and 'pre'.

Divide these words into *prefix* and *base word*; then read them.

Word	Prefix	Base word	Word	Prefix	Base word
1. inform	*in*	*form*	16. enforce	*en*	*force*
2. contest	*con*	*test*	17. inject	*in*	*ject*
3. prefix	*pre*	*fix*	18. present	*pre*	*sent*
4. behave	*be*	*have*	19. beside	*be*	*side*
5. confirm	*con*	*firm*	20. prefer	*pre*	*fer*
6. inflame	*in*	*flame*	21. connect	*con*	*nect*
7. predict	*pre*	*dict*	22. preside	*pre*	*side*
8. confine	*con*	*fine*	23. inflate	*in*	*flate*
9. prevent	*pre*	*vent*	24. confide	*con*	*fide*
10. belong	*be*	*long*	25. preserve	*pre*	*serve*
11. increase	*in*	*crease*	26. insight	*in*	*sight*
12. prepare	*pre*	*pare*	27. believe	*be*	*lieve*
13. before	*be*	*fore*	28. intend	*in*	*tend*
14. pretend	*pre*	*tend*	29. betray	*be*	*tray*
15. consult	*con*	*sult*	30. control	*con*	*trol*

26

Students divide these words into prefix and base word in the spaces provided. Correct the work by having them read the word and then divide it.

WORD WORKERS 7 UNIT 3.3

Name .... Date ....

Write the word from each column that fits the word shape box.

present	beside	inflate	confide
inject	believe	contest	intend
confirm	insult	prepare	pretend
belong	contain	prefer	inflame

inject beside prepare intend

Underline the correct word to complete the sentence.

1. The plumber had to (confirm/connect) the pipes with a wrench.
2. Mrs Brown's daughter helped her (prepare/ prepaid) dinner last night.
3. Shaun was delighted with his birthday (present/ prevent).
4. The teacher told the naughty girl to (belong/behave) in the classroom.
5. A (preside/prefix) comes at the beginning of a word to change its meaning.

 27

Activity 1: Students look at the columns of words. Tell them to put the word from each column that fits into the 'word shape' box below it.

Activity 2: Students read the sentences. They underline the word in brackets that best completes the sentence.

WORD WORKERS 7 UNIT 3.4

Name .... Date ....

The suffixes on this page are 'al', 'ant', 'ent' and 'able'.

Divide these words into *base word* and *suffix*; then read them.

1. postal	post	al	16. pleasant	pleas	ant
2. claimant	claim	ant	17. teachable	teach	able
3. likable	lik	able	18. coastal	coast	al
4. formal	form	al	19. printable	print	able
5. trainable	train	able	20. musical	music	al
6. servant	serv	ant	21. laughable	laugh	able
7. workable	work	able	22. solvent	solv	ent
8. different	differ	ent	23. notable	not	able
9. central	centr	al	24. accident	accid	ent
10. normal	norm	al	25. trial	tri	al
11. readable	read	able	26. vacant	vac	ant
12. rental	rent	al	27. special	speci	al
13. passable	pass	able	28. agent	ag	ent
14. resident	resid	ent	29. general	gener	al
15. personal	person	al	30. thinkable	think	able

28

Students divide these words into base word and suffix in the spaces provided. Correct the work by having them read the word and then divide it.

WORD WORKERS 7 — UNIT 3.5

Name .... Date ....

A suffix comes at the end of a word.

Add the suffix to the base word to make a complete word.

1. person*al*	ent		6. think *able*	ant
2. differ *ent*	al		7. form *al*	able
3. teach *able*	ent		8. vac *ant*	al
4. pleas *ant*	able		9. solv *ent*	al
5. resid *ent*	ant		10. centr *al*	ent

Complete the sentences with the words from the box.

passable	solvent	different	pleasant
accident	personal	servant	vacant

1. Mrs Slade left her car in the *vacant* spot she found in the parking lot.
2. That morning Mr Clancy wore a *different* coat when he went to work.
3. It was lucky that no one was hurt in the *accident* .
4. We had a *pleasant* day in the park.
5. The *servant* who annoyed the king was ordered to leave the room.

 29

Activity 1: Students write the correct suffix beside the base word to make a complete word.

Activity 2: Students complete the sentences by writing the correct word from the box in the space provided.

WORD WORKERS 7 — UNIT 3.6

Name .... Date ....

Many words can be divided by taking the prefix and suffix away from the base word.

Divide these words into *prefix, base word* and *suffix;* then read them.

1. informal	*in*	*form*	*al*
2. consonant	*con*	*son*	*ant*
3. presentable	*pre*	*sent*	*able*
4. conformable	*con*	*form*	*able*
5. incurable	*in*	*cur*	*able*
6. preventable	*pre*	*vent*	*able*
7. contestant	*con*	*test*	*ant*
8. betrayal	*be*	*tray*	*al*
9. predictable	*pre*	*dict*	*able*
10. confident	*con*	*fid*	*ent*
11. inflammable	*in*	*flamm*	*able*
12. president	*pre*	*sid*	*ent*
13. believable	*be*	*liev*	*able*
14. preservable	*pre*	*serv*	*able*
15. insistent	*in*	*sist*	*ent*

30

Students divide these words into prefix, base word and suffix in the spaces provided. Correct the work by having them read the word and then divide it.

WORD WORKERS 7 UNIT 3.7

Name .... Date ....

Write the base word beside the complete word.

1.	incurable	*cure*	confide
2.	betrayal	*betray*	form
3.	preventable	*prevent*	serve
4.	contestant	*test*	preside
5.	preservable	*serve*	cure
6.	confident	*confide*	prevent
7.	president	*preside*	betray
8.	informal	*form*	test

Underline the correct word to complete the sentence.

1. Before the start of the race, James was (confident/consonant) that he would win.
2. The (presentable/president) spoke to the large crowd that waited to hear him.
3. We could not remember the name of the first (contestant/insistent) in the quiz show.
4. The doctor said that the man's illness was (conformable/incurable).
5. The judge said that the story the witness told was not (preventable/believable).

 31

Activity 1: Students read the complete word and then, beside it, they write the base word from the right-hand column.

Activity 2: Students read the sentences. They underline the word in brackets that best completes the sentence.

WORD WORKERS 7 UNIT 3.8

Name .... Date ....

A base word is not always a complete word.

Underline the nonsense word.

predictable	believable	conformable	prejectent
inflammable	contestant	inthinkant	confident
betrayal	beferal	president	incurable
consolvable	preventable	preservable	informal

Write the word from the box beside its definition.

inflame	likable	increase	connect
central	pretend	vacant	consonant

1. empty *v a c a n t*
2. set on fire *i n f l a m e*
3. make-believe *p r e t e n d*
4. join together *c o n n e c t*
5. letter of the alphabet *c o n s o n a n t*

32

Activity 1: Students look at the columns of words. Tell them to underline the word in each column that is a nonsense word.

Activity 2: Students write the word from the box beside its definition.

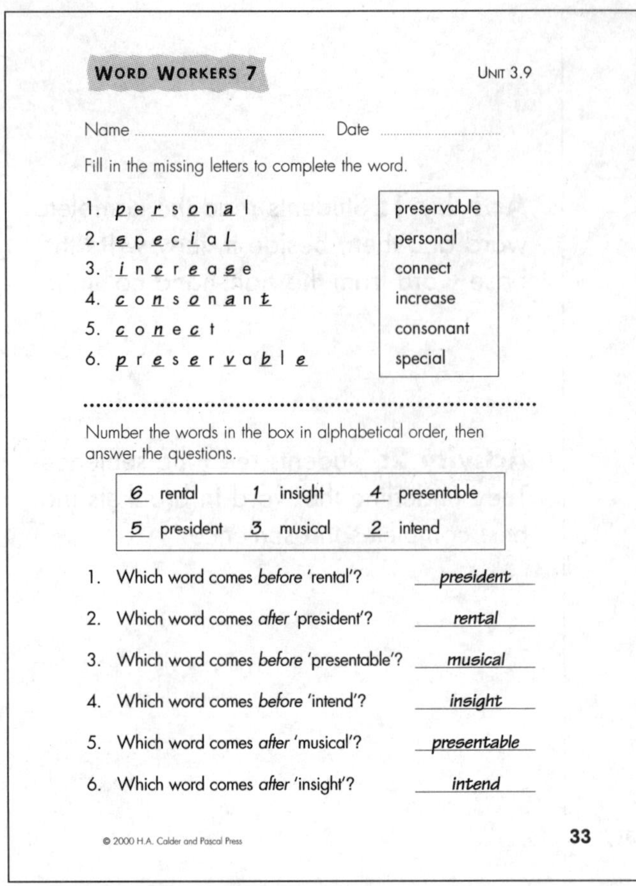

WORD WORKERS 7 UNIT 3.9

Name .... Date ....

Fill in the missing letters to complete the word.

1. p e r s o n a l
2. s p e c i a l
3. i n c r e a s e
4. c o n s o n a n t
5. c o n e c t
6. p r e s e r v a b l e

preservable
personal
connect
increase
consonant
special

Number the words in the box in alphabetical order, then answer the questions.

6 rental	1 insight	4 presentable
5 president	3 musical	2 intend

1. Which word comes *before* 'rental'? *president*
2. Which word comes *after* 'president'? *rental*
3. Which word comes *before* 'presentable'? *musical*
4. Which word comes *before* 'intend'? *insight*
5. Which word comes *after* 'musical'? *presentable*
6. Which word comes *after* 'insight'? *intend*

 33

Activity 1: Students read the words in the box, then write the missing letters to complete the column of words on the left.

Activity 2: Students number the words in the box in alphabetical order, then use this information to answer the questions below.

WORD WORKERS 7 UNIT 3.10

Name .... Date ....

I like putting words in alphabetical order.

Put the words in the boxes in alphabetical order.

beside	increase	belong	accident	contestant
agent	formal	general	confide	insistent

1. *accident*
2. *agent*
3. *belong*
4. *beside*
5. *confide*
6. *contestant*
7. *formal*
8. *general*
9. *increase*
10. *insistent*

preventable	vacant	likable	normal	workable
predictable	resident	informal	teachable	solvent

1. *informal*
2. *likable*
3. *normal*
4. *predictable*
5. *preventable*
6. *resident*
7. *solvent*
8. *teachable*
9. *vacant*
10. *workable*

34

Students put the words in each box in their correct alphabetical order.

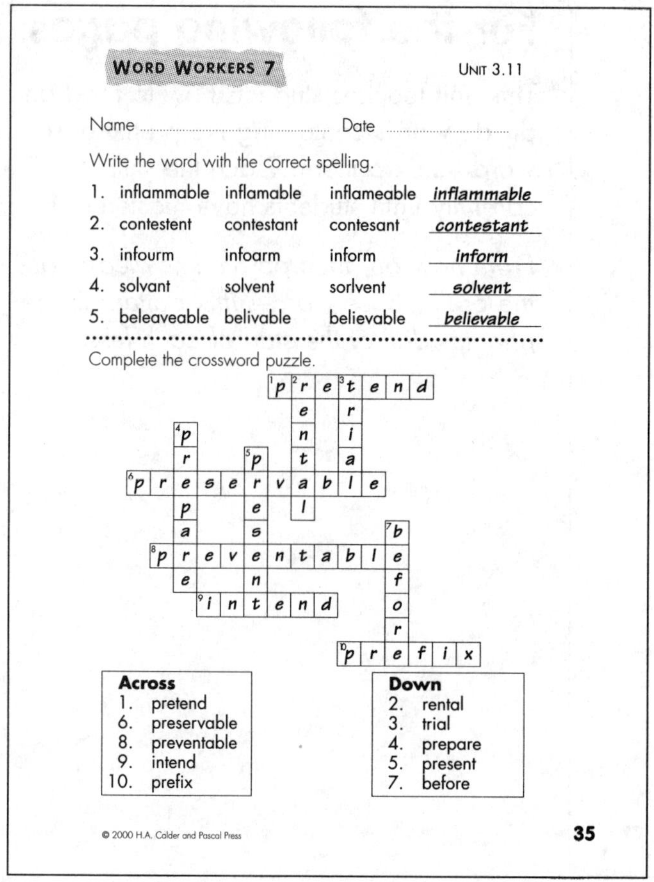
WORD WORKERS 7 UNIT 3.11

Name .... Date ....

Write the word with the correct spelling.

1.	inflammable	inflamable	inflameable	*inflammable*
2.	contestent	contestant	contesant	*contestant*
3.	infourm	infoarm	inform	*inform*
4.	solvant	solvent	sorlvent	*solvent*
5.	beleaveable	belivable	believable	*believable*

Complete the crossword puzzle.

Across
1. pretend
6. preservable
8. preventable
9. intend
10. prefix

Down
2. rental
3. trial
4. prepare
5. present
7. before

© 2000 H.A. Calder and Pascal Press 35

Activity 1: Students read the words going across the page, then write the word that is spelt correctly.

Activity 2: Students complete the crossword puzzle by writing the answers in the correct spaces.

WORD WORKERS 7 UNIT 3.12

Name .... Date ....

Spelling words is fun.

Spell six words from each page.

page 26

1. ____________
2. ____________
3. ____________
4. ____________
5. ____________
6. ____________

page 28

1. ____________
2. ____________
3. ____________
4. ____________
5. ____________
6. ____________

page 30

1. ____________
2. ____________
3. ____________
4. ____________
5. ____________
6. ____________

36 © 2000 H.A. Calder and Pascal Press

Students are asked to spell six words from each of the lists indicated.

Word Workers 7 Unit 4.1

Working with prefix – base word – suffix words

ad | vent | ure

Reading long words is easy. All you have to do is look for prefixes, base words and suffixes:

dis – tinct – ive

pro – ced – ure

ad – vant – age

© 2000 H.A. Calder and Pascal Press 37

For the following pages:

This unit teaches students how to read and divide words containing the prefix–base word–suffix pattern. Teach the skill carefully until students have mastered it.

From now on, incorporate knowledge of the prefix–base word–suffix pattern in the phonics drill at the start of each lesson.

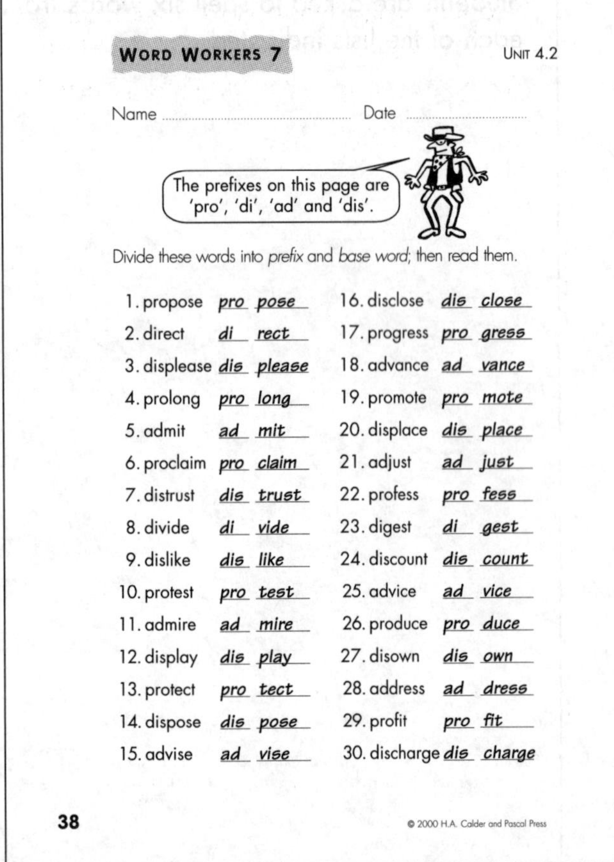

Word Workers 7 Unit 4.2

Name .... Date ....

The prefixes on this page are 'pro', 'di', 'ad' and 'dis'.

Divide these words into *prefix* and *base word*; then read them.

1. propose	*pro*	*pose*	16. disclose	*dis*	*close*
2. direct	*di*	*rect*	17. progress	*pro*	*gress*
3. displease	*dis*	*please*	18. advance	*ad*	*vance*
4. prolong	*pro*	*long*	19. promote	*pro*	*mote*
5. admit	*ad*	*mit*	20. displace	*dis*	*place*
6. proclaim	*pro*	*claim*	21. adjust	*ad*	*just*
7. distrust	*dis*	*trust*	22. profess	*pro*	*fess*
8. divide	*di*	*vide*	23. digest	*di*	*gest*
9. dislike	*dis*	*like*	24. discount	*dis*	*count*
10. protest	*pro*	*test*	25. advice	*ad*	*vice*
11. admire	*ad*	*mire*	26. produce	*pro*	*duce*
12. display	*dis*	*play*	27. disown	*dis*	*own*
13. protect	*pro*	*tect*	28. address	*ad*	*dress*
14. dispose	*dis*	*pose*	29. profit	*pro*	*fit*
15. advise	*ad*	*vise*	30. discharge	*dis*	*charge*

38 © 2000 H.A. Calder and Pascal Press

Students divide these words into prefix and base word in the spaces provided. Correct the work by having them read the word and then divide it.

WORD WORKERS 7

UNIT 4.3

Name .... Date ....

Write the word from each column that fits the word shape box.

admit	progress	admire	produce
display	divide	profess	displace
digest	protect	direct	address
profit	dispose	protest	displease

profit divide admire displace

Underline the correct word to complete the sentence.

1. Jill was in such a rush that she did not have time to sit down and (direct/digest) her lunch.
2. The postman had to admit that he left the letter at the wrong (address/adjust).
3. The mother bear ran to (protest/protect) her cubs.
4. We must take the time to (disclose/dispose) of our rubbish in the correct place.
5. Bob asked his mum to (divide/disown) his apple into four pieces

© 2000 H.A. Calder and Pascal Press 39

Activity 1: Students look at the columns of words. Tell them to put the word from each column that fits into the 'word shape' box below it.

Activity 2: Students read the sentences. They underline the word in brackets that best completes the sentence.

WORD WORKERS 7

UNIT 4.4

Name .... Date ....

The suffixes on this page are 'ive', 'ible', 'ure' and 'age'.

Divide these words into *base word* and *suffix*; then read them.

1. active	act	ive	16. bandage	band	age
2. sensible	sens	ible	17. closure	clos	ure
3. pleasure	pleas	ure	18. horrible	horr	ible
4. message	mess	age	19. massive	mass	ive
5. future	fut	ure	20. creature	creat	ure
6. terrible	terr	ible	21. package	pack	age
7. garbage	garb	age	22. festive	fest	ive
8. talkative	talkat	ive	23. manure	man	ure
9. possible	poss	ible	24. objective	object	ive
10. picture	pict	ure	25. credible	cred	ible
11. luggage	lugg	age	26. mature	mat	ure
12. attentive	attent	ive	27. baggage	bagg	age
13. pressure	press	ure	28. passive	pass	ive
14. effective	effect	ive	29. damage	dam	age
15. treasure	treas	ure	30. feature	feat	ure

40 © 2000 H.A. Calder and Pascal Press

Students divide these words into base word and suffix in the spaces provided. Correct the work by having them read the word and then divide it.

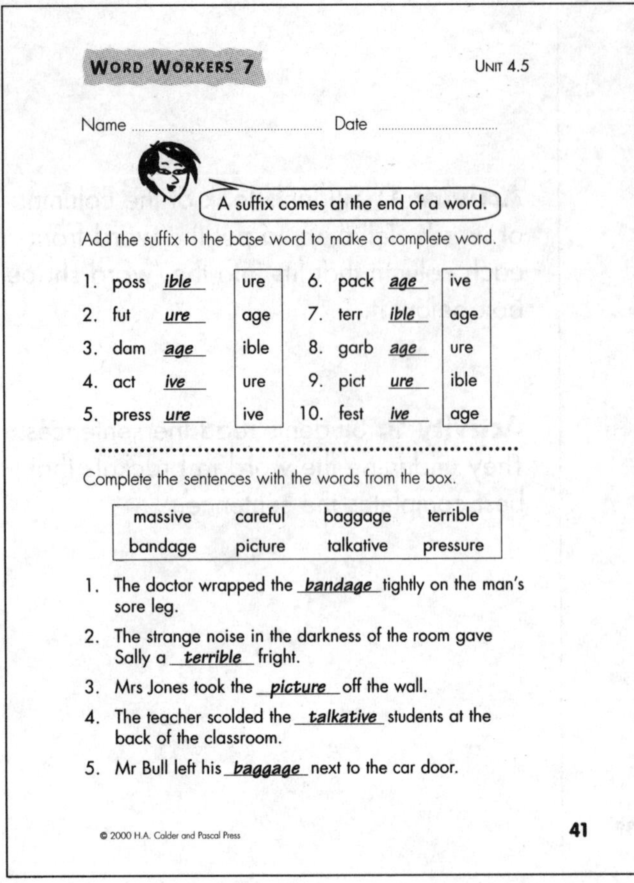

WORD WORKERS 7 UNIT 4.5

Name .... Date ....

A suffix comes at the end of a word.

Add the suffix to the base word to make a complete word.

1. poss *ible*	ure	6. pack *age*	ive
2. fut *ure*	age	7. terr *ible*	age
3. dam *age*	ible	8. garb *age*	ure
4. act *ive*	ure	9. pict *ure*	ible
5. press *ure*	ive	10. fest *ive*	age

Complete the sentences with the words from the box.

massive	careful	baggage	terrible
bandage	picture	talkative	pressure

1. The doctor wrapped the *bandage* tightly on the man's sore leg.
2. The strange noise in the darkness of the room gave Sally a *terrible* fright.
3. Mrs Jones took the *picture* off the wall.
4. The teacher scolded the *talkative* students at the back of the classroom.
5. Mr Bull left his *baggage* next to the car door.

© 2000 H.A. Calder and Pascal Press 41

Activity 1: Students write the correct suffix beside the base word to make a complete word.

Activity 2: Students complete the sentences by writing the correct word from the box in the space provided.

WORD WORKERS 7 UNIT 4.6

Name .... Date ....

Many words can be divided by taking the prefix and suffix away from the base word.

Divide these words into *prefix*, *base word* and *suffix*; then read them.

1. displeasure	*dis*	*pleas*	*ure*
2. progressive	*pro*	*gress*	*ive*
3. advantage	*ad*	*vant*	*age*
4. digestive	*di*	*gest*	*ive*
5. protective	*pro*	*tect*	*ive*
6. addictive	*ad*	*dict*	*ive*
7. productive	*pro*	*duct*	*ive*
8. dismissive	*dis*	*miss*	*ive*
9. directive	*di*	*rect*	*ive*
10. procedure	*pro*	*ced*	*ure*
11. distinctive	*dis*	*tinct*	*ive*
12. adventure	*ad*	*vent*	*ure*
13. prospective	*pro*	*spect*	*ive*
14. disclosure	*dis*	*clos*	*ure*
15. adjective	*ad*	*ject*	*ive*

42 © 2000 H.A. Calder and Pascal Press

Students divide these words into prefix, base word and suffix in the spaces provided. Correct the work by having them read the word and then divide it.

WORD WORKERS 7 UNIT 4.7

Name .... Date ....

Write the base word beside the complete word.

1. progressive	*progress*	prospect
2. digestive	*digest*	dismiss
3. displeasure	*please*	produce
4. protective	*protect*	progress
5. disclosure	*close*	protect
6. prospective	*prospect*	digest
7. dismissive	*dismiss*	close
8. productive	*produce*	please

Underline the correct word to complete the sentence.

1. If you expect to do well at school, it is an (advantage/adjective) to work hard.
2. Mrs Simpson told her class that smoking is harmful and (adventure/addictive).
3. The workers in the factory had a (procedure/productive) week.
4. The colours in our flag are very (directive/distinctive).
5. Craig had an (adventure/disclosure) last summer.

 43

Activity 1: Students read the complete word and then, beside it, they write the base word from the right-hand column.

Activity 2: Students read the sentences. They underline the word in brackets that best completes the sentence.

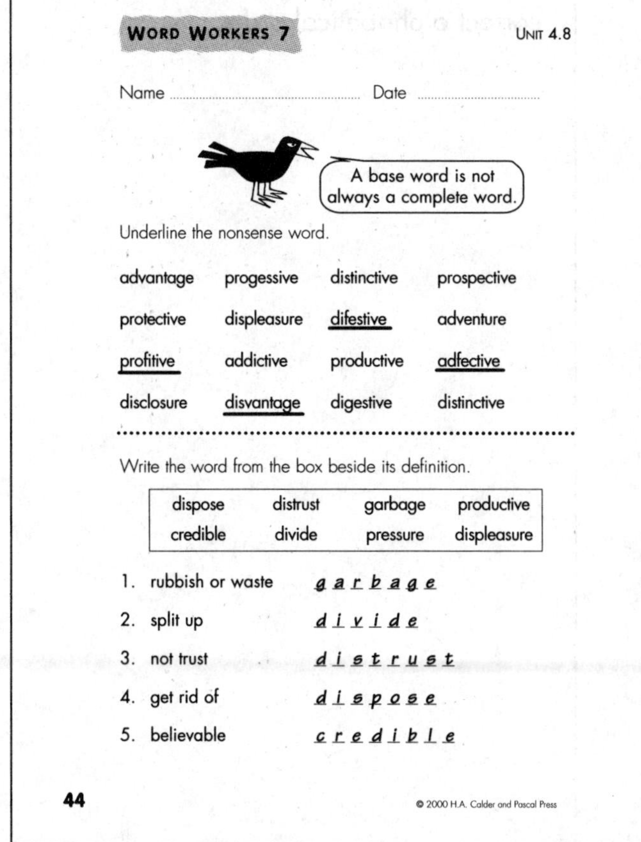

WORD WORKERS 7 UNIT 4.8

Name .... Date ....

A base word is not always a complete word.

Underline the nonsense word.

advantage	progessive	distinctive	prospective
protective	displeasure	difestive	adventure
profitive	addictive	productive	adfective
disclosure	disvantage	digestive	distinctive

Write the word from the box beside its definition.

dispose	distrust	garbage	productive
credible	divide	pressure	displeasure

1. rubbish or waste *garbage*
2. split up *divide*
3. not trust *distrust*
4. get rid of *dispose*
5. believable *credible*

44

Activity 1: Students look at the columns of words. Tell them to underline the word in each column that is a nonsense word.

Activity 2: Students write the word from the box beside its definition.

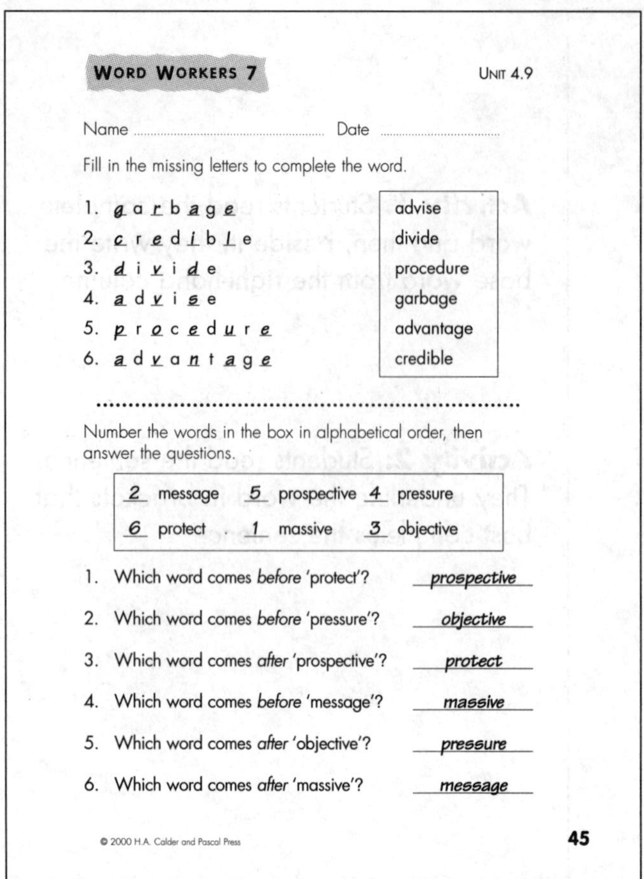

WORD WORKERS 7 UNIT 4.9

Name .... Date ....

Fill in the missing letters to complete the word.

1. g a r b a g e	advise
2. c r e d i b l e	divide
3. d i v i d e	procedure
4. a d v i s e	garbage
5. p r o c e d u r e	advantage
6. a d v a n t a g e	credible

Number the words in the box in alphabetical order, then answer the questions.

2 message	5 prospective	4 pressure
6 protect	1 massive	3 objective

1. Which word comes *before* 'protect'? *prospective*
2. Which word comes *before* 'pressure'? *objective*
3. Which word comes *after* 'prospective'? *protect*
4. Which word comes *before* 'message'? *massive*
5. Which word comes *after* 'objective'? *pressure*
6. Which word comes *after* 'massive'? *message*

© 2000 H.A. Calder and Pascal Press 45

Activity 1: Students read the words in the box, then write the missing letters to complete the column of words on the left.

Activity 2: Students number the words in the box in alphabetical order, then use this information to answer the questions below.

WORD WORKERS 7 UNIT 4.10

Name .... Date ....

I like putting words in alphabetical order.

Put the words in the boxes in alphabetical order.

horrible	credible	address	bandage	distinctive
direct	future	baggage	admit	digestive

1. *address* 6. *digestive*
2. *admit* 7. *direct*
3. *baggage* 8. *distinctive*
4. *bandage* 9. *future*
5. *credible* 10. *horrible*

package	treasure	progress	massive	procedure
propose	talkative	mature	terrible	productive

1. *massive* 6. *progress*
2. *mature* 7. *propose*
3. *package* 8. *talkative*
4. *procedure* 9. *terrible*
5. *productive* 10. *treasure*

46 © 2000 H.A. Calder and Pascal Press

Students put the words in each box in their correct alphabetical order.

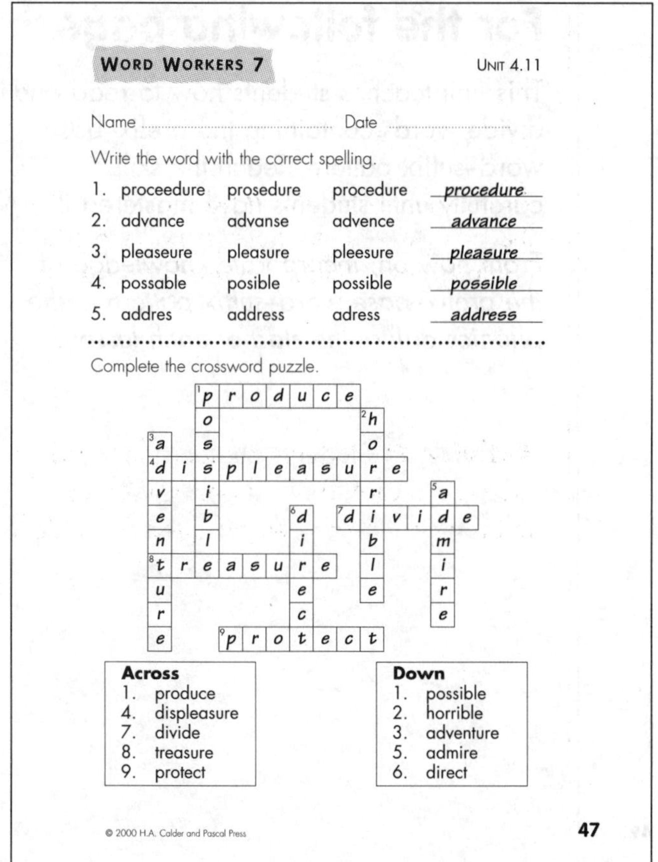

WORD WORKERS 7 UNIT 4.11

Name .... Date ....

Write the word with the correct spelling.

1.	proceedure	prosedure	procedure	*procedure*
2.	advance	advanse	advence	*advance*
3.	pleaseure	pleasure	pleesure	*pleasure*
4.	possable	posible	possible	*possible*
5.	addres	address	adress	*address*

Complete the crossword puzzle.

Across
1. produce
4. displeasure
7. divide
8. treasure
9. protect

Down
1. possible
2. horrible
3. adventure
5. admire
6. direct

© 2000 H.A. Calder and Pascal Press 47

Activity 1: Students read the words going across the page, then write the word that is spelt correctly.

Activity 2: Students complete the crossword puzzle by writing the answers in the correct spaces.

WORD WORKERS 7 UNIT 4.12

Name .... Date ....

Spelling words is fun.

Spell six words from each page.

page 38

1. ____________
2. ____________
3. ____________
4. ____________
5. ____________
6. ____________

page 40

1. ____________
2. ____________
3. ____________
4. ____________
5. ____________
6. ____________

page 42

1. ____________
2. ____________
3. ____________
4. ____________
5. ____________
6. ____________

48 © 2000 H.A. Calder and Pascal Press

Students are asked to spell six words from each of the lists indicated.

WORD WORKERS 7 UNIT 5.1

More prefix – base word – suffix words

de light ful

Reading long words is easy. All you have to do is look for prefixes, base words and suffixes:

un – fair – ness

di – gest – ive

in – spec – tion

© 2000 H.A. Calder and Pascal Press 49

For the following pages:

This unit teaches students how to read and divide words containing the prefix–base word–suffix pattern. Teach the skill carefully until students have mastered it.

From now on, incorporate knowledge of the prefix–base word–suffix pattern in the phonics drill at the start of each lesson.

WORD WORKERS 7 UNIT 5.2

Name .... Date ....

I am a good word worker.

Divide these words into *prefix, base word* and *suffix*; then read them.

1.	respectful	*re*	*spect*	*ful*
2.	exactness	*ex*	*act*	*ness*
3.	unkindness	*un*	*kind*	*ness*
4.	compartment	*com*	*part*	*ment*
5.	delightful	*de*	*light*	*ful*
6.	enjoyment	*en*	*joy*	*ment*
7.	composition	*com*	*pos*	*ition*
8.	unfairness	*un*	*fair*	*ness*
9.	commandment	*com*	*mand*	*ment*
10.	resistance	*re*	*sist*	*ance*
11.	enforcement	*en*	*force*	*ment*
12.	definition	*de*	*fin*	*ition*
13.	unhappiness	*un*	*happi*	*ness*
14.	destruction	*de*	*struct*	*ion*
15.	reluctance	*re*	*luct*	*ance*

50 © 2000 H.A. Calder and Pascal Press

Students divide these words into prefix, base word and suffix in the spaces provided. Correct the work by having them read the word and then divide it.

WORD WORKERS 7 UNIT 5.3

Name .... Date ....

Write the base word beside the complete word.

1. composition	*compose*	force
2. exactness	*exact*	resist
3. unfairness	*fair*	respect
4. commandment	*command*	compose
5. respectful	*respect*	define
6. enforcement	*force*	exact
7. definition	*define*	fair
8. resistance	*resist*	command

Underline the correct word to complete the sentence.

1. The (enforcement/endearment) of the law is the job of the police.
2. Jodie had a (respectful/delightful) time at the zoo.
3. Our team was unhappy with the umpire's (compartment/unfairness).
4. Dad and Dave had much (enjoyment/exactness) working on the farm.
5. Mrs Lake said the man's (unlawful/unkindness) to his dog was disgusting.

 51

Activity 1: Students read the complete word and then, beside it, they write the base word from the right-hand column.

Activity 2: Students read the sentences. They underline the word in brackets that best completes the sentence.

WORD WORKERS 7 UNIT 5.4

Name .... Date ....

It is fun working with words.

Divide these words into *prefix*, *base word* and *suffix*; then read them.

1. contestant	*con*	*test*	*ant*
2. believable	*be*	*liev*	*able*
3. adventure	*ad*	*vent*	*ure*
4. informal	*in*	*form*	*al*
5. displeasure	*dis*	*pleas*	*ure*
6. productive	*pro*	*duct*	*ive*
7. insistent	*in*	*sist*	*ent*
8. distinctive	*dis*	*tinct*	*ive*
9. betrayal	*be*	*tray*	*al*
10. president	*pre*	*sid*	*ent*
11. advantage	*ad*	*vant*	*age*
12. procedure	*pro*	*ced*	*ure*
13. confident	*con*	*fid*	*ent*
14. digestive	*di*	*gest*	*ive*
15. preservable	*pre*	*serv*	*able*

52

Students divide these words into prefix, base word and suffix in the spaces provided. Correct the work by having them read the word and then divide it.

WORD WORKERS 7 UNIT 5.5

Name .... Date ....

Write the base word beside the complete word.

1.	believable	*believe*	produce
2.	preservable	*preserve*	betray
3.	insistent	*insist*	test
4.	betrayal	*betray*	preside
5.	confident	*confide*	believe
6.	productive	*produce*	preserve
7.	contestant	*test*	confide
8.	president	*preside*	insist

Complete the sentences with the words from the box.

consonants	digestive	displeasure	procedure
president	advantage	protective	adjective

1. Mark showed his *displeasure* at having to go to bed early.
2. The carpenter had to wear a *protective* helmet when he worked in the factory.
3. Dawn used the correct *procedure* to solve the problem.
4. The letters 'b', 'c' and 'd' are *consonants*.
5. The *president* of the company praised the men for their hard work.

 53

Activity 1: Students read the complete word and then, beside it, they write the base word from the right-hand column.

Activity 2: Students complete the sentences by writing the correct word from the box in the space provided.

WORD WORKERS 7 UNIT 5.6

Name .... Date ....

Prefixes come at the beginning of words.
Suffixes come at the end of words.

Divide these words into *prefix*, *base word* and *suffix*; then read them.

1.	infection	*in*	*fect*	*ion*
2.	expensive	*ex*	*pens*	*ive*
3.	unmusical	*un*	*music*	*al*
4.	remarkable	*re*	*mark*	*able*
5.	premature	*pre*	*mat*	*ure*
6.	directness	*di*	*rect*	*ness*
7.	adventurous	*ad*	*ventur*	*ous*
8.	expectance	*ex*	*pect*	*ance*
9.	compatible	*com*	*pat*	*ible*
10.	confinement	*con*	*fine*	*ment*
11.	disgraceful	*dis*	*grace*	*ful*
12.	propellant	*pro*	*pell*	*ant*
13.	dependent	*de*	*pend*	*ent*
14.	disadvantage	*dis*	*advant*	*age*
15.	enclosure	*en*	*clos*	*ure*

54

Students divide these words into prefix, base word and suffix in the spaces provided. Correct the work by having them read the word and then divide it.

WORD WORKERS 7 UNIT 5.7

Name .... Date ....

Write the base word beside the complete word.

1. premature	*mature*	confine
2. dependent	*depend*	close
3. unmusical	*music*	infect
4. confinement	*confine*	remark
5. expensive	*expense*	depend
6. enclosure	*close*	music
7. remarkable	*remark*	expense
8. infection	*infect*	mature

Underline the correct word to complete the sentence.

1. Paul's mum said the bike he wanted was too (expectance/expensive).
2. Grace stepped on a nail and got an (infection/directness) in her foot.
3. The (adventurous/enclosure) puppy explored the back yard.
4. The teacher told Jade that she had done a (confinement/remarkable) job on her homework.
5. The (unmusical/compatible) man could not keep a tune.

 55

Activity 1: Students read the complete word and then, beside it, they write the base word from the right-hand column.

Activity 2: Students read the sentences. They underline the word in brackets that best completes the sentence.

WORD WORKERS 7 UNIT 5.8

Name .... Date ....

Prefixes come at the beginning of words.

Suffixes come at the end of words.

Divide these words into *prefix*, *base word* and *suffix*; then read them.

1. unharmful	*un*	*harm*	*ful*
2. reaction	*re*	*ac*	*tion*
3. disruption	*dis*	*rup*	*tion*
4. defensive	*de*	*fens*	*ive*
5. reservation	*re*	*serv*	*ation*
6. expedition	*ex*	*ped*	*ition*
7. unpleasant	*un*	*pleas*	*ant*
8. dismissal	*dis*	*miss*	*al*
9. considerable	*con*	*sider*	*able*
10. incredible	*in*	*cred*	*ible*
11. enjoyable	*en*	*joy*	*able*
12. replacement	*re*	*place*	*ment*
13. independent	*in*	*depend*	*ent*
14. uneasiness	*un*	*easi*	*ness*
15. investment	*in*	*vest*	*ment*

56

Students divide these words into prefix, base word and suffix in the spaces provided. Correct the work by having them read the word and then divide it.

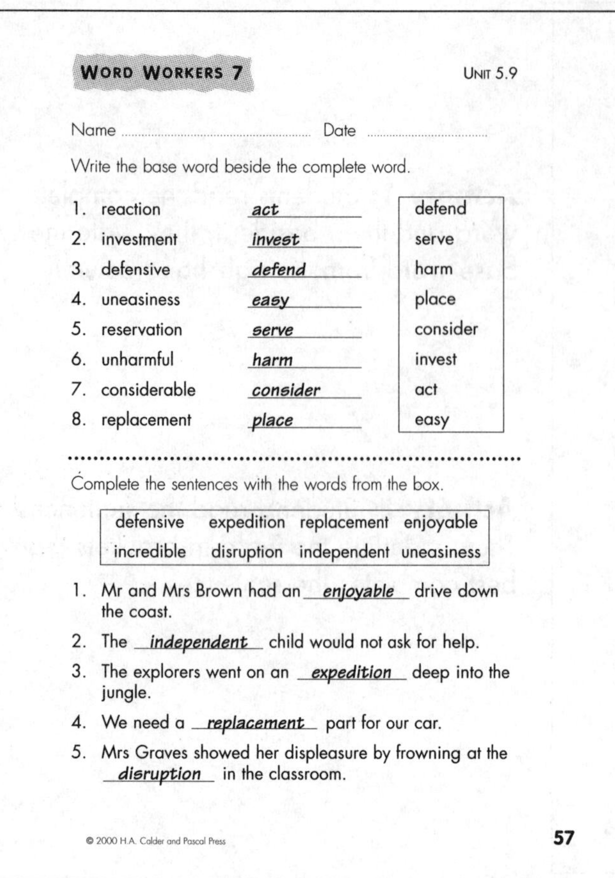

WORD WORKERS 7 — UNIT 5.9

Name .... Date ....

Write the base word beside the complete word.

1.	reaction	*act*	defend
2.	investment	*invest*	serve
3.	defensive	*defend*	harm
4.	uneasiness	*easy*	place
5.	reservation	*serve*	consider
6.	unharmful	*harm*	invest
7.	considerable	*consider*	act
8.	replacement	*place*	easy

Complete the sentences with the words from the box.

defensive	expedition	replacement	enjoyable
incredible	disruption	independent	uneasiness

1. Mr and Mrs Brown had an *enjoyable* drive down the coast.
2. The *independent* child would not ask for help.
3. The explorers went on an *expedition* deep into the jungle.
4. We need a *replacement* part for our car.
5. Mrs Graves showed her displeasure by frowning at the *disruption* in the classroom.

© 2000 H.A. Calder and Pascal Press 57

Activity 1: Students read the complete word and then, beside it, they write the base word from the right-hand column.

Activity 2: Students complete the sentences by writing the correct word from the box in the space provided.

WORD WORKERS 7 — UNIT 5.10

Name .... Date ....

Underline the nonsense word.

reluctance	contestant	<u>unmusicable</u>	infection
<u>exactment</u>	confident	digestive	premature
unkindness	<u>distinctable</u>	betrayal	enclosure
definition	informal	insistent	<u>compatance</u>

Write the word from the box beside its definition.

enclosure	expensive	compatible	premature
destruction	digestive	disgraceful	adventure

1. costly — *e x p e n s i v e*
2. shameful — *d i s g r a c e f u l*
3. demolition — *d e s t r u c t i o n*
4. too early — *p r e m a t u r e*
5. in agreement with — *c o m p a t i b l e*

58 © 2000 H.A. Calder and Pascal Press

Activity 1: Students look at the columns of words. Tell them to underline the word in each column that is a nonsense word.

Activity 2: Students write the word from the box beside its definition.

WORD WORKERS 7 UNIT 5.11

Name .... Date ....

Fill in the missing letters to complete the word.

1. r e l u c t a n c e	confident
2. d e f i n i t i o n	infection
3. c o n f i d e n t	preservable
4. d i s g r a c e f u l	reluctance
5. i n f e c t i o n	definition
6. p r e s e r v a b l e	disgraceful

Number the words in the box in alphabetical order, then answer the questions.

3 dependent	1 composition	6 expensive
5 exactness	4 digestive	2 delightful

1. Which word comes *before* 'delightful'? *composition*
2. Which word comes *after* 'exactness'? *expensive*
3. Which word comes *before* 'digestive'? *dependent*
4. Which word comes *after* 'composition'? *delightful*
5. Which word comes *before* 'expensive'? *exactness*
6. Which word comes *after* 'dependent'? *digestive*

 59

Activity 1: Students read the words in the box, then write the missing letters to complete the column of words on the left.

Activity 2: Students number the words in the box in alphabetical order, then use this information to answer the questions below.

WORD WORKERS 7 UNIT 5.12

Name .... Date ....

I like putting words in alphabetical order.

Put the words in the boxes in correct alphabetical order.

betrayal delightful advantage defensive exactness distinctive compartment enforcement destruction adventure

1. *advantage*	6. *delightful*
2. *adventure*	7. *destruction*
3. *betrayal*	8. *distinctive*
4. *compartment*	9. *enforcement*
5. *defensive*	10. *exactness*

unfairness resistance president uneasiness respectful procedure reservation reluctance premature productive

1. *premature*	6. *reservation*
2. *president*	7. *resistance*
3. *procedure*	8. *respectful*
4. *productive*	9. *uneasiness*
5. *reluctance*	10. *unfairness*

60

Students put the words in each box in their correct alphabetical order.

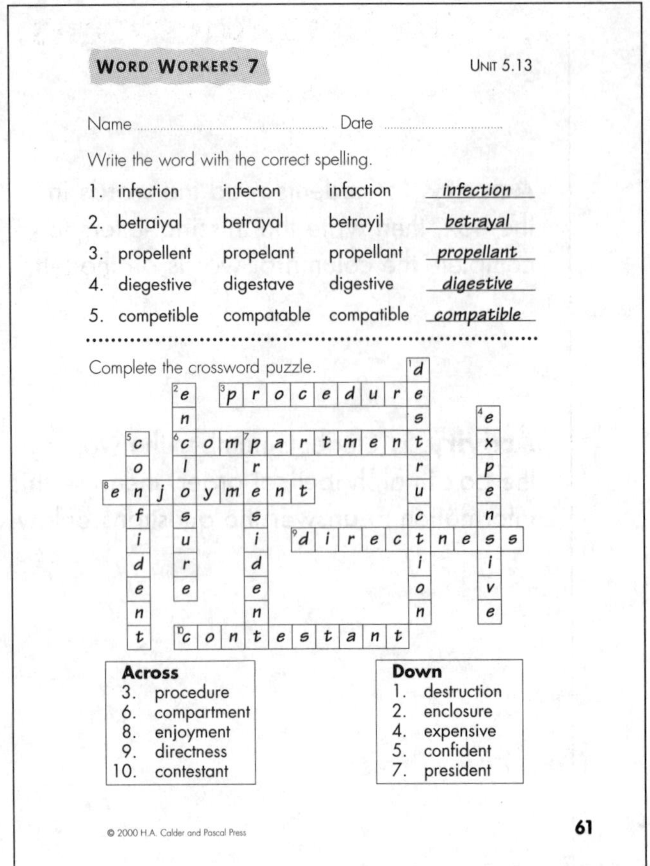

WORD WORKERS 7 UNIT 5.13

Name .... Date ....

Write the word with the correct spelling.

1.	infection	infecton	infaction	*infection*
2.	betraiyal	betrayal	betrayil	*betrayal*
3.	propellent	propelant	propellant	*propellant*
4.	diegestive	digestave	digestive	*digestive*
5.	competible	compatable	compatible	*compatible*

Complete the crossword puzzle.

Across	Down
3. procedure	1. destruction
6. compartment	2. enclosure
8. enjoyment	4. expensive
9. directness	5. confident
10. contestant	7. president

 61

Activity 1: Students read the words going across the page, then write the word that is spelt correctly.

Activity 2: Students complete the crossword puzzle by writing the answers in the correct spaces.

WORD WORKERS 7 UNIT 5.14

Name .... Date ....

Spelling words is fun.

Spell six words from each page.

page 50	page 52
1. ______	1. ______
2. ______	2. ______
3. ______	3. ______
4. ______	4. ______
5. ______	5. ______
6. ______	6. ______

page 54	page 56
1. ______	1. ______
2. ______	2. ______
3. ______	3. ______
4. ______	4. ______
5. ______	5. ______
6. ______	6. ______

62

Students are asked to spell six words from each of the lists indicated.

WORD WORKERS 7 UNIT 6.1

Working with contractions

When two words are joined together to make a shorter word, the new word is called a *contraction*. An *apostrophe* (') takes the place of the letters left out.

it is — it's
I have — I've
does not — doesn't
where did — where'd
will not — won't

cannot
no
can't

 63

For the following pages:

This unit teaches students how to work with commonly occurring contractions.

WORD WORKERS 7 UNIT 6.2

Name .... Date ....

I am a good word worker.

Write the correct contractions for these words.

1.	they are	*they're*	13.	could not	*couldn't*
2.	it will	*it'll*	14.	we have	*we've*
3.	is not	*isn't*	15.	who is	*who's*
4.	where is	*where's*	16.	I would	*I'd*
5.	had not	*hadn't*	17.	they had	*they'd*
6.	we are	*we're*	18.	cannot	*can't*
7.	did not	*didn't*	19.	what is	*what's*
8.	I will	*I'll*	20.	does not	*doesn't*
9.	that is	*that's*	21.	it is	*it's*
10.	would not	*wouldn't*	22.	will not	*won't*
11.	I have	*I've*	23.	they have	*they've*
12.	I am	*I'm*	24.	she will	*she'll*

64

Students write the contractions for the two words in the spaces provided.

WORD WORKERS 7 UNIT 6.3

Name .... Date ....

Write the correct contractions for the underlined words.

1. She will be home later today. *She'll*
2. What is your telephone number? *What's*
3. I am going to do my homework right now. *I'm*
4. We did not hear the knock on the door. *didn't*
5. I will not be suprised if she forgets to call. *won't*
6. They are going for a drive this weekend. *They're*
7. I could not finish the history test. *couldn't*
8. Where is the present I gave you? *Where's*
9. They had not seen the skateboard I lost. *hadn't*
10. 'It is time for bed,' Mum said. *It's*
11. I cannot remember where I left my bike. *can't*
12. They had better get in before it starts raining. *They'd*

 65

Students write the contractions for the two words in the spaces provided.

WORD WORKERS 7 UNIT 6.4

Name .... Date ....

A contraction is two words joined together to make a shorter word.

Write the correct words for these contractions.

1. couldn't	*could*	*not*	13. she's	*she*	*is*
2. let's	*let*	*us*	14. haven't	*have*	*not*
3. isn't	*is*	*not*	15. we're	*we*	*are*
4. they've	*they*	*have*	16. you've	*you*	*have*
5. who's	*who*	*is*	17. I'm	*I*	*am*
6. it'll	*it*	*will*	18. where's	*where*	*is*
7. he's	*he*	*is*	19. it's	*it*	*is*
8. weren't	*were*	*not*	20. shouldn't	*should*	*not*
9. what's	*what*	*is*	21. I'll	*I*	*will*
10. didn't	*did*	*not*	22. you'd	*you*	*had*
11. who'll	*who*	*will*	23. she'll	*she*	*will*
12. we'd	*we*	*had*	24. hadn't	*had*	*not*

66

Students write the two words that have been combined to make the contractions in the spaces provided.

WORD WORKERS 7 UNIT 6.5

Name .... Date ....

An apostrophe takes the place of the letters left out of a contraction.

Write the correct words for the underlined contractions.

1. Let's get going soon. *Let* *us*
2. He's the best player on the team. *He* *is*
3. I couldn't find my workbooks. *could* *not*
4. It's a good day to ride my bike. *It* *is*
5. She'll be late if she sleeps in again. *She* *will*
6. We hadn't heard that he left the school. *had* *not*
7. If it rains I won't play outside. *will* *not*
8. Where's the book I lent you? *where* *is*
9. Haven't they started their homework? *Have* *not*
10. Who's going to the beach with you? *Who* *is*
11. What's the reason you forgot to come? *What* *is*
12. She's going to a birthday party today. *She* *is*

 67

Students write the two words that have been combined to make the contractions in the spaces provided.

WORD WORKERS 7 UNIT 6.6

Name .... Date ....

Complete the crossword puzzles with the correct contractions.

Across
2. would not
5. have not
6. where is
8. you will
10. they are

Down
1. you are
3. do not
4. they have
7. had not
9. she is

Across
1. where did
4. we have
5. should not
7. that will
8. it will

Down
1. who is
2. does not
3. they had
5. she will
6. let us

68

Students complete the crossword puzzles by writing the answers in the correct spaces.

* Students complete *Word Workers Achievement Test 9* after completing this unit.

Using the Word Workers Achievement Tests

The *Word Workers Achievement Tests* are designed to monitor students' progress as they work their way through the activity books. Each activity book has a corresponding achievement test so teachers can evaluate their students' attainment of skills and determine those who need revision and re-teaching. At no time in any of the achievement tests do students encounter activities, words or sounds they have not encountered in the activity books they have completed.

When students finish an activity book, they then go on to complete the achievement test for that book. Before using the achievement tests, look through them carefully to become familiar with their structure and content. The activities in the test will be familiar to the students since they have encountered them in the activity books. Because of their familiarity with the material and the format of the exercises, there is no need for elaborate instructions about what is expected of students. Answers are provided for each test.

The test can be used with an entire class or an individual student. The procedure is virtually the same. Students complete the written parts of the tests individually and the teacher listens to each student read sight vocabulary and the mastery lists of the phonics skills tested. There is no need to complete both tasks on the same day. Students can complete the written work at their desks and then do the oral work with their teacher later. Alternatively, half the class may do the oral work while the other half does the written work, and then the process is alternated. Whatever the decision, students need to complete all components of the tests if their progress is to be monitored accurately.

The tests are to be administered as assessment tools, not teaching tools. If a student is having trouble decoding a word, allow her or him to move on to the next word or exercise after three attempts.

Suggested test administration

Allow approximately 30 minutes to complete the test.

1 Hand out tests and explain their purpose and structure. Reassure students that they have seen all the work before and that this is simply an exercise to see how well they have learned it. Maintain a positive, non-threatening environment while the test is being administered.

2 Students complete the written component of the test.

3 When students have completed the written work, the teacher can listen to them read the mastery and sight vocabulary pages individually.

4 Collect papers and mark them. Complete oral reading with students in subsequent lessons if necessary.

5 Give merit certificates for successful completion of the activity book and achievement test.

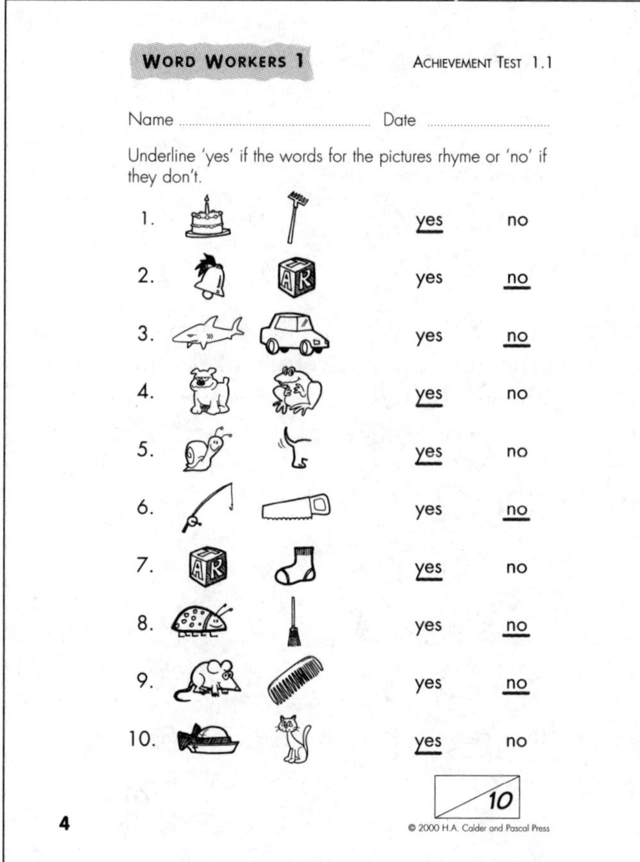

WORD WORKERS 1 ACHIEVEMENT TEST 1.1

Name .... Date ....

Underline 'yes' if the words for the pictures rhyme or 'no' if they don't.

1. yes no
2. yes no
3. yes no
4. yes no
5. yes no
6. yes no
7. yes no
8. yes no
9. yes no
10. yes no

10

4 © 2000 H.A. Calder and Pascal Press

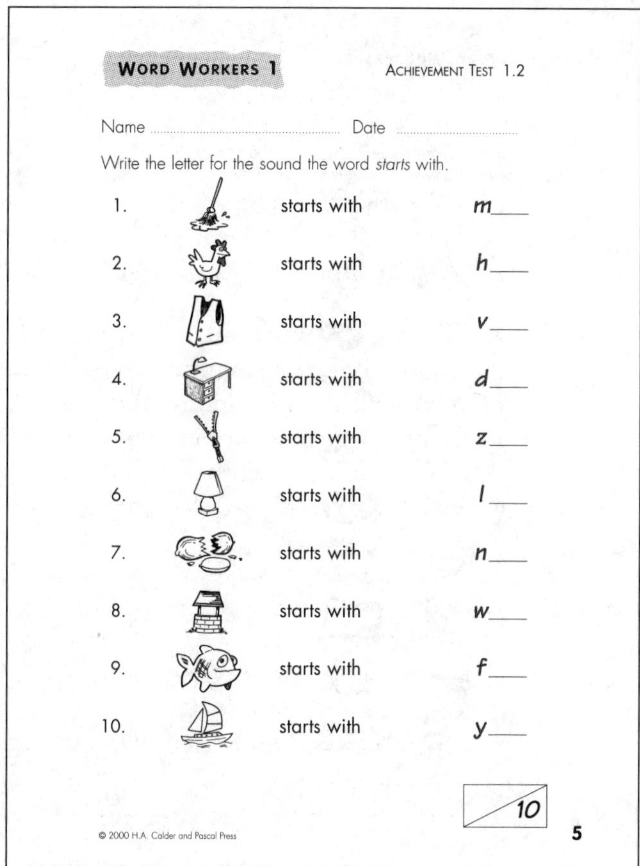

WORD WORKERS 1 ACHIEVEMENT TEST 1.2

Name .... Date ....

Write the letter for the sound the word *starts* with.

1. starts with m___
2. starts with h___
3. starts with v___
4. starts with d___
5. starts with z___
6. starts with l___
7. starts with n___
8. starts with w___
9. starts with f___
10. starts with y___

10

© 2000 H.A. Calder and Pascal Press 5

WORD WORKERS 1 ACHIEVEMENT TEST 1.3

Name .... Date ....

Write the letter for the sound the word *ends* with.

1. ends with g
2. ends with b
3. ends with x
4. ends with k
5. ends with n
6. ends with v
7. ends with p
8. ends with l
9. ends with s
10. ends with r

10

6 © 2000 H.A. Calder and Pascal Press

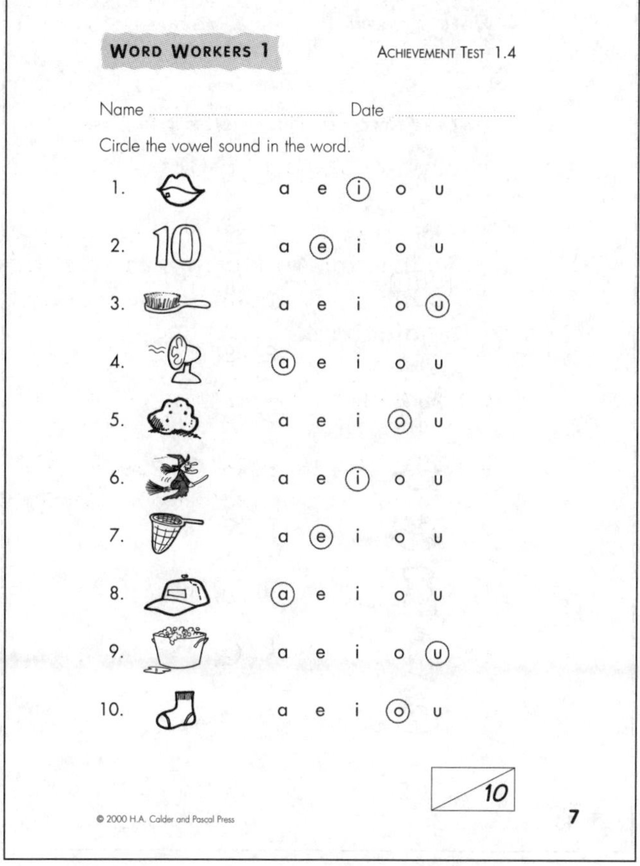

WORD WORKERS 1 ACHIEVEMENT TEST 1.4

Name .... Date ....

Circle the vowel sound in the word.

1. a e i o u
2. a e i o u
3. a e i o u
4. a e i o u
5. a e i o u
6. a e i o u
7. a e i o u
8. a e i o u
9. a e i o u
10. a e i o u

10

© 2000 H.A. Calder and Pascal Press 7

WORD WORKERS 1 ACHIEVEMENT TEST 1.5

Name .... Date ....

Circle 's' if the pictures *begin* with the *same* sound or 'd' if they *begin* with a *different* sound.

1. s (d)
2. s (d)
3. (s) d
4. (s) d
5. s (d)
6. (s) d
7. (s) d
8. s (d)
9. (s) d
10. s (d)

/10

8

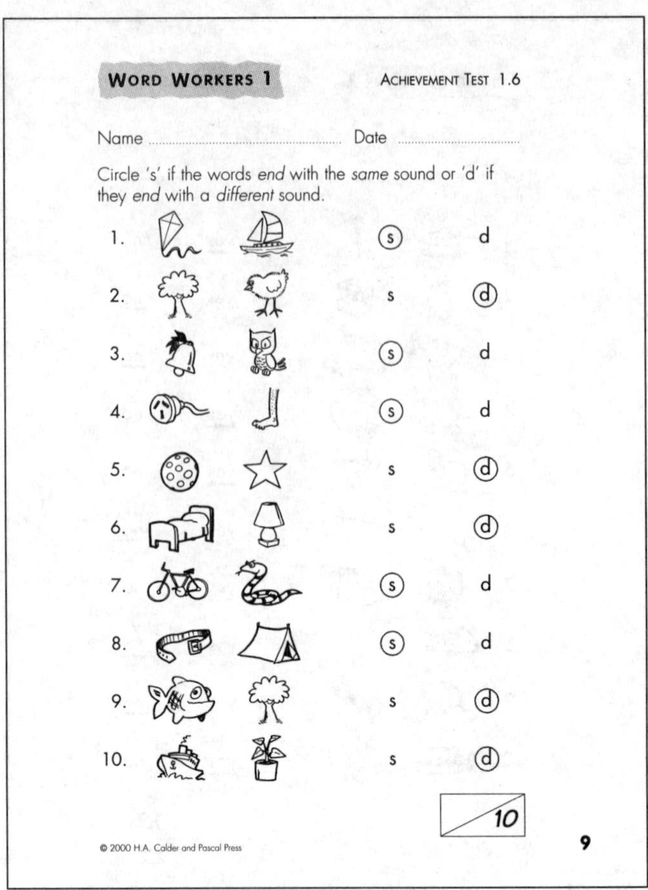

WORD WORKERS 1 ACHIEVEMENT TEST 1.6

Name .... Date ....

Circle 's' if the words *end* with the *same* sound or 'd' if they *end* with a *different* sound.

1. (s) d
2. s (d)
3. (s) d
4. (s) d
5. s (d)
6. s (d)
7. (s) d
8. (s) d
9. s (d)
10. s (d)

/10

9

WORD WORKERS 1 ACHIEVEMENT TEST 1.7

Name .... Date ....

Circle the letter for the sound you *do not* hear in the picture.

1. g i (l)
2. r (a) d
3. s u (t)
4. p (e) t
5. (e) t n
6. s p (t)
7. t (v) n
8. (d) b g
9. k (u) l
10. n w (t)

/10

10

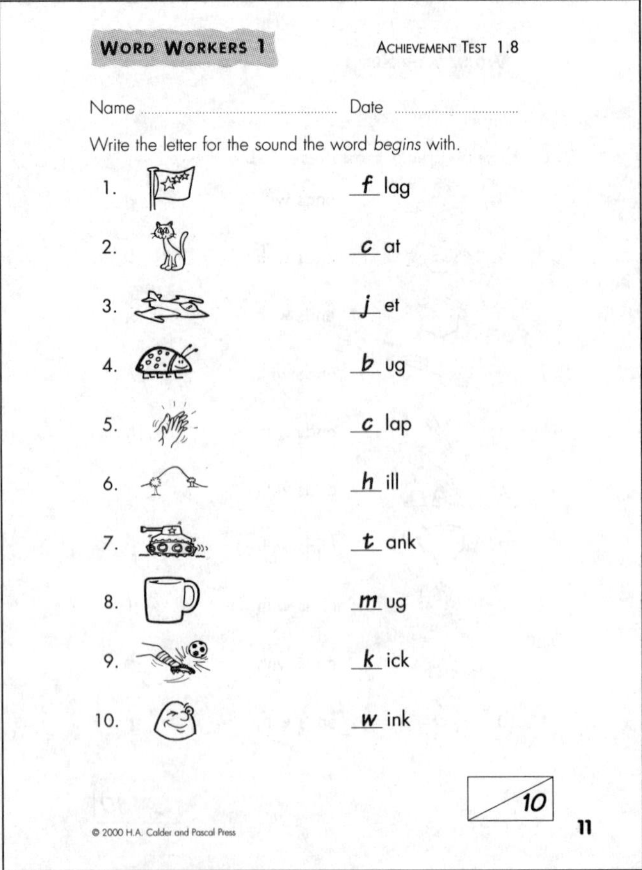

WORD WORKERS 1 ACHIEVEMENT TEST 1.8

Name .... Date ....

Write the letter for the sound the word *begins* with.

1. *f* lag
2. *c* at
3. *j* et
4. *b* ug
5. *c* lap
6. *h* ill
7. *t* ank
8. *m* ug
9. *k* ick
10. *w* ink

/10

11

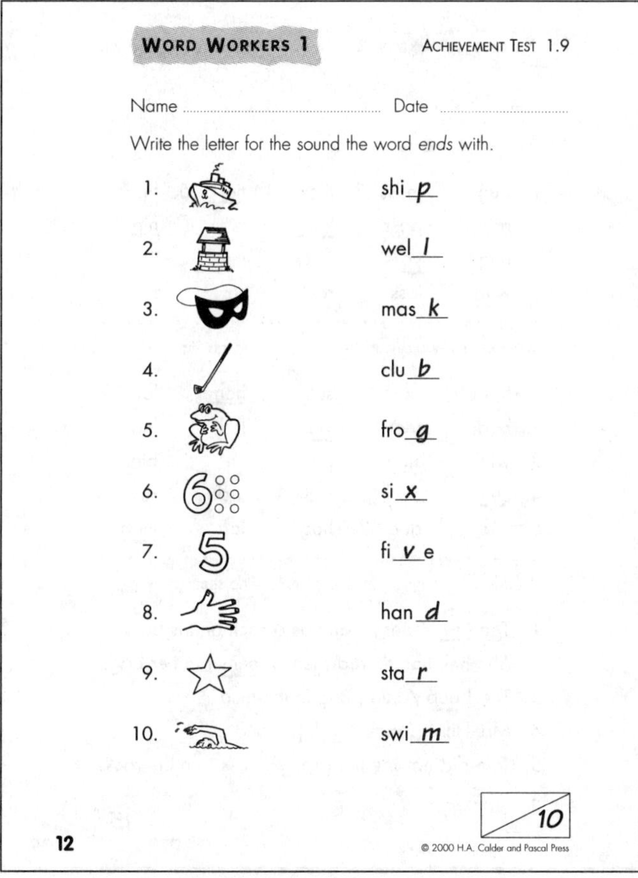

WORD WORKERS 1 ACHIEVEMENT TEST 1.9

Name .... Date ....

Write the letter for the sound the word *ends* with.

1. shi_p_
2. wel_l_
3. mas_k_
4. clu_b_
5. fro_g_
6. si_x_
7. fi_v_e
8. han_d_
9. sta_r_
10. swi_m_

10

12 © 2000 H.A. Calder and Pascal Press

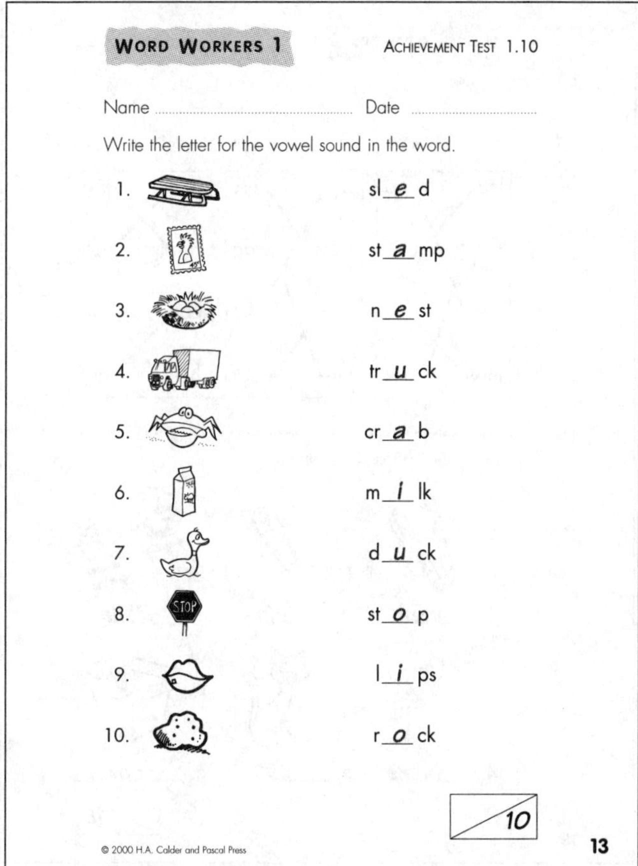

WORD WORKERS 1 ACHIEVEMENT TEST 1.10

Name .... Date ....

Write the letter for the vowel sound in the word.

1. sl_e_d
2. st_a_mp
3. n_e_st
4. tr_u_ck
5. cr_a_b
6. m_i_lk
7. d_u_ck
8. st_o_p
9. l_i_ps
10. r_o_ck

10

© 2000 H.A. Calder and Pascal Press 13

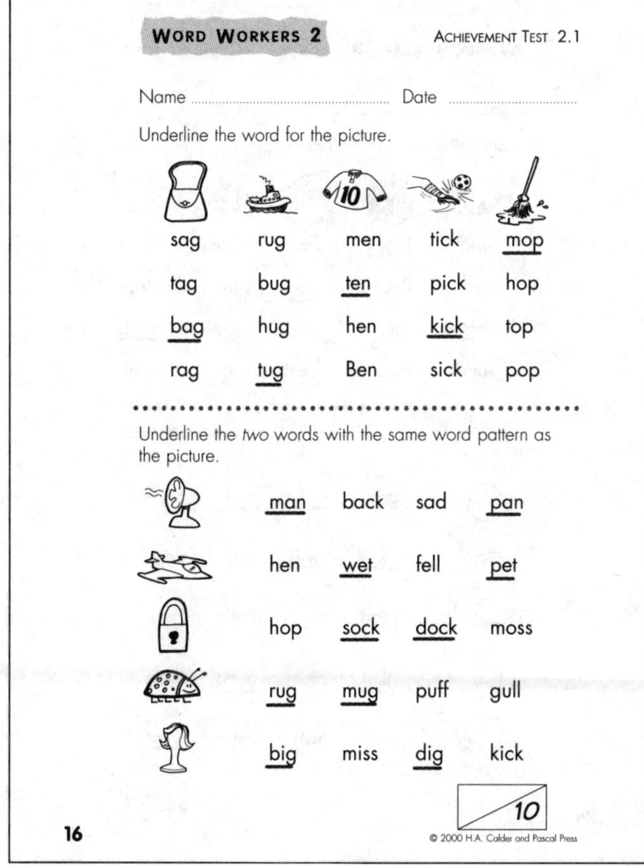

WORD WORKERS 2 ACHIEVEMENT TEST 2.1

Name .... Date ....

Underline the word for the picture.

sag	rug	men	tick	<u>mop</u>
tag	bug	<u>ten</u>	pick	hop
<u>bag</u>	hug	hen	<u>kick</u>	top
rag	<u>tug</u>	Ben	sick	pop

Underline the *two* words with the same word pattern as the picture.

<u>man</u>	back	sad	<u>pan</u>
hen	<u>wet</u>	fell	<u>pet</u>
hop	<u>sock</u>	<u>dock</u>	moss
<u>rug</u>	<u>mug</u>	puff	gull
<u>big</u>	miss	<u>dig</u>	kick

10

16 © 2000 H.A. Calder and Pascal Press

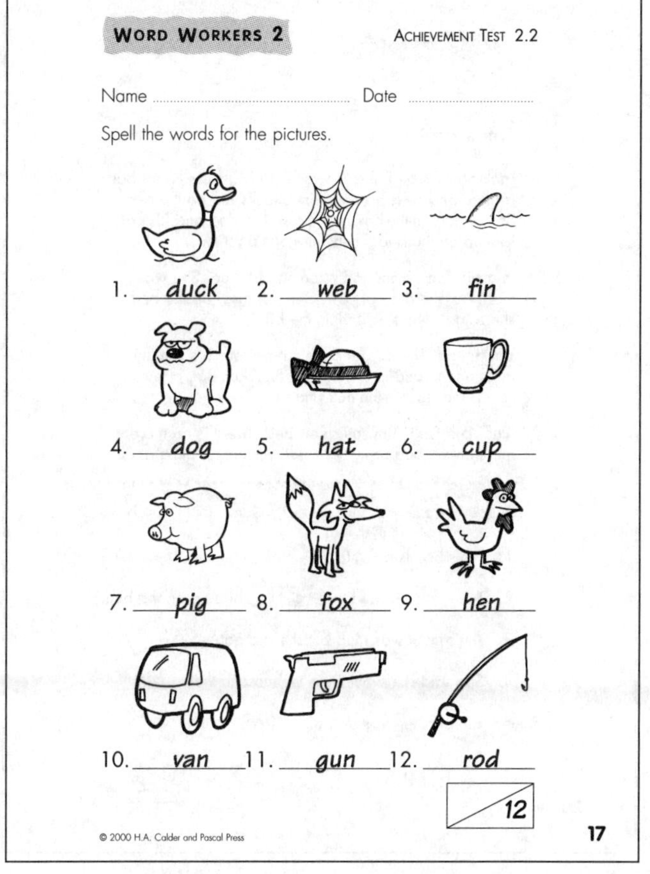

WORD WORKERS 2 ACHIEVEMENT TEST 2.2

Name .... Date ....

Spell the words for the pictures.

1. duck 2. web 3. fin

4. dog 5. hat 6. cup

7. pig 8. fox 9. hen

10. van 11. gun 12. rod

12

© 2000 H.A. Calder and Pascal Press 17

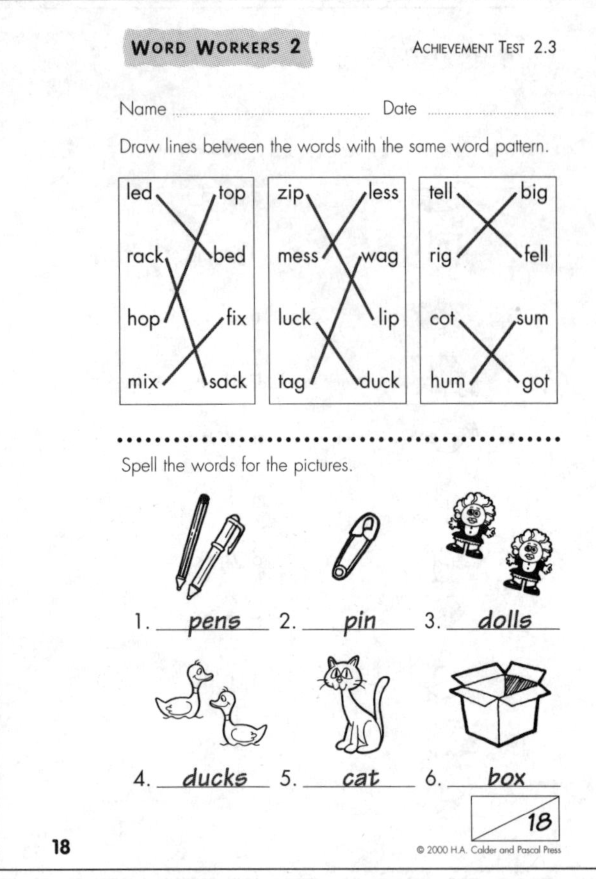

WORD WORKERS 2 ACHIEVEMENT TEST 2.3

Name .... Date ....

Draw lines between the words with the same word pattern.

led	top	zip	less	tell	big
rack	bed	mess	wag	rig	fell
hop	fix	luck	lip	cot	sum
mix	sack	tag	duck	hum	got

Spell the words for the pictures.

1. pens 2. pin 3. dolls

4. ducks 5. cat 6. box

18

18

© 2000 H.A. Calder and Pascal Press

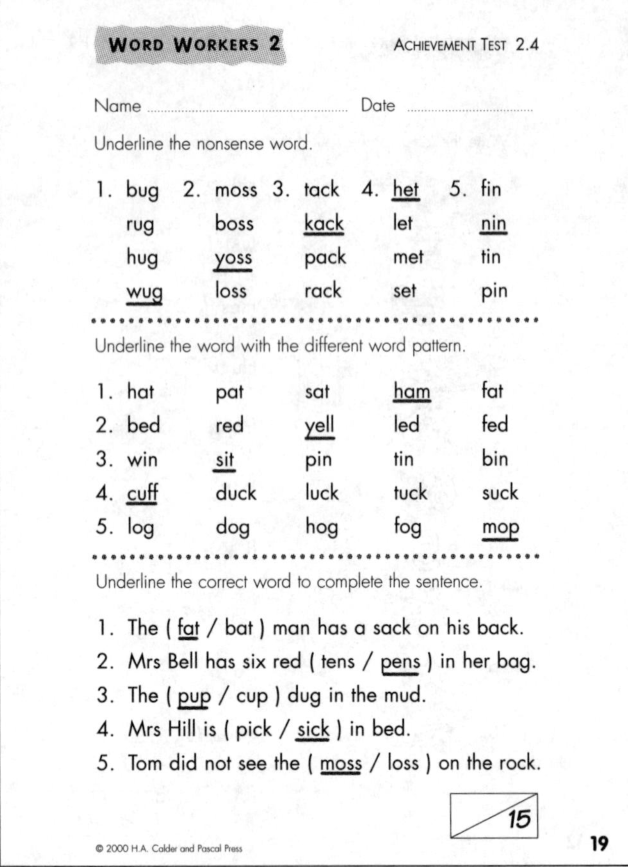

WORD WORKERS 2 ACHIEVEMENT TEST 2.4

Name .... Date ....

Underline the nonsense word.

1.	2.	3.	4.	5.
bug	moss	tack	het	fin
rug	boss	kack	let	nin
hug	yoss	pack	met	tin
wug	loss	rack	set	pin

Underline the word with the different word pattern.

1. hat pat sat ham fat
2. bed red yell led fed
3. win sit pin tin bin
4. cuff duck luck tuck suck
5. log dog hog fog mop

Underline the correct word to complete the sentence.

1. The (fat / bat) man has a sack on his back.
2. Mrs Bell has six red (tens / pens) in her bag.
3. The (pup / cup) dug in the mud.
4. Mrs Hill is (pick / sick) in bed.
5. Tom did not see the (moss / loss) on the rock.

15

© 2000 H.A. Calder and Pascal Press

19

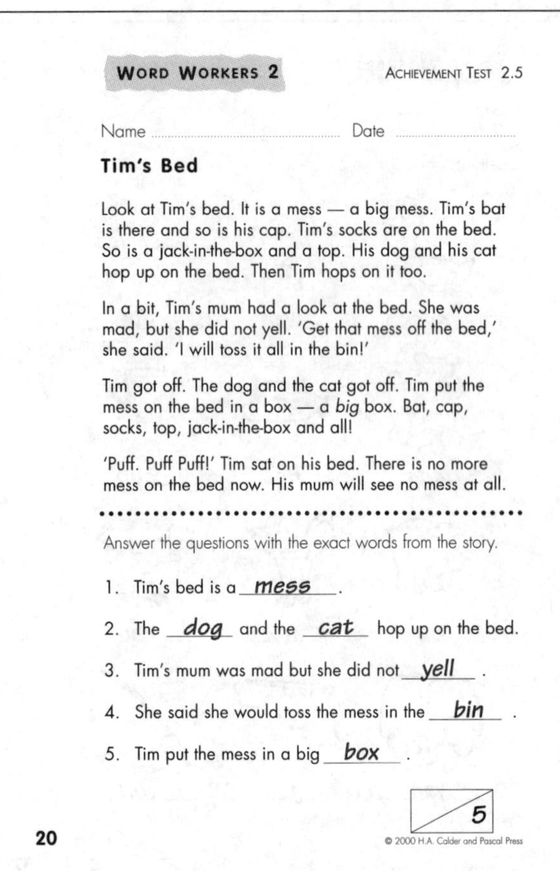

WORD WORKERS 2 ACHIEVEMENT TEST 2.5

Name .... Date ....

Tim's Bed

Look at Tim's bed. It is a mess — a big mess. Tim's bat is there and so is his cap. Tim's socks are on the bed. So is a jack-in-the-box and a top. His dog and his cat hop up on the bed. Then Tim hops on it too.

In a bit, Tim's mum had a look at the bed. She was mad, but she did not yell. 'Get that mess off the bed,' she said. 'I will toss it all in the bin!'

Tim got off. The dog and the cat got off. Tim put the mess on the bed in a box — a *big* box. Bat, cap, socks, top, jack-in-the-box and all!

'Puff. Puff Puff!' Tim sat on his bed. There is no more mess on the bed now. His mum will see no mess at all.

Answer the questions with the exact words from the story.

1. Tim's bed is a mess.
2. The dog and the cat hop up on the bed.
3. Tim's mum was mad but she did not yell.
4. She said she would toss the mess in the bin.
5. Tim put the mess in a big box.

5

20

© 2000 H.A. Calder and Pascal Press

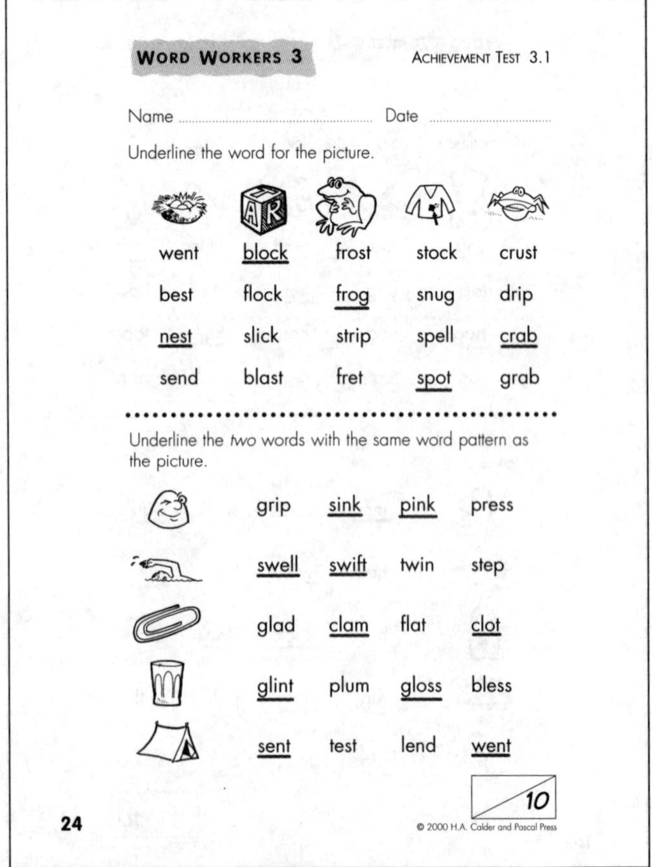

WORD WORKERS 3 ACHIEVEMENT TEST 3.1

Name .... Date ....

Underline the word for the picture.

went	block	frost	stock	crust
best	flock	frog	snug	drip
nest	slick	strip	spell	crab
send	blast	fret	spot	grab

Underline the *two* words with the same word pattern as the picture.

grip sink pink press

swell swift twin step

glad clam flat clot

glint plum gloss bless

sent test lend went

10

24

© 2000 H.A. Calder and Pascal Press

WORD WORKERS 3 ACHIEVEMENT TEST 3.2

Name .... Date ....

Spell the words for the pictures.

1. mask 2. plant 3. stump

4. sled 5. milk 6. cross

7. desk 8. drum 9. belt

10. club 11. skip 12. truck

12

© 2000 H.A. Calder and Pascal Press 25

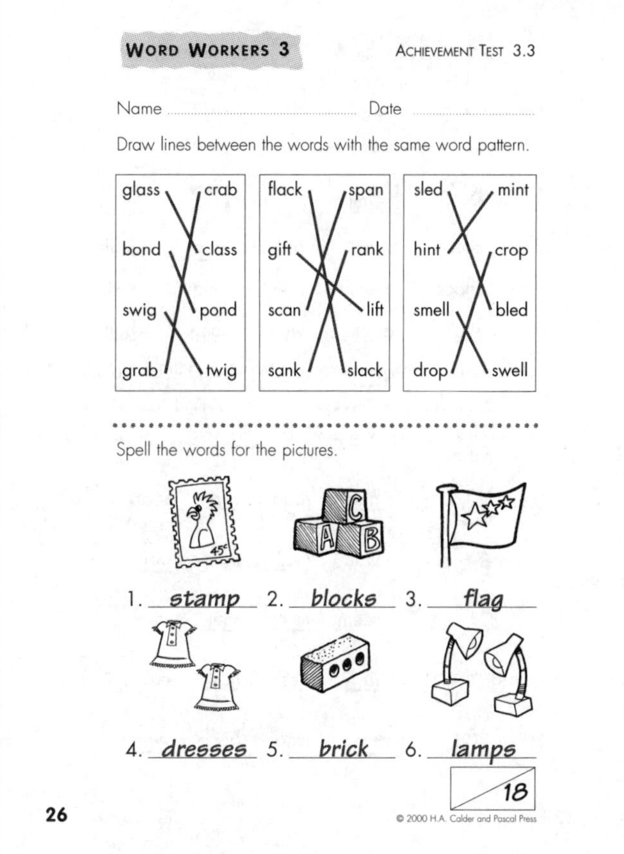

WORD WORKERS 3 ACHIEVEMENT TEST 3.3

Name .... Date ....

Draw lines between the words with the same word pattern.

glass	crab	flack	span	sled	mint
bond	class	gift	rank	hint	crop
swig	pond	scan	lift	smell	bled
grab	twig	sank	slack	drop	swell

Spell the words for the pictures.

1. stamp 2. blocks 3. flag

4. dresses 5. brick 6. lamps

18

26 © 2000 H.A. Calder and Pascal Press

WORD WORKERS 3 ACHIEVEMENT TEST 3.4

Name .... Date ....

Underline the nonsense word.

1.	2.	3.	4.	5.
crab	stuck	clip	hint	blink
crack	stug	slim	lump	crink
crust	snug	step	fint	sank
cruff	swam	blit	past	blank

Complete these words with the word pattern from the picture.

l and   pl ug   st ill   s ank   dr ag

b and   pl ant   st ick   bl ank   dr ift

Underline the correct word to complete the sentence.

1. Greg stacked the (tricks / bricks) on the truck.
2. Fran (swept / crept) the dust off the steps.
3. The dog sniffed the wet (slants / plants).
4. Mrs Bell left the (test / rest) on top of the desk.
5. The man's (belt / welt) fell off his pants.

15

© 2000 H.A. Calder and Pascal Press 27

WORD WORKERS 3 ACHIEVEMENT TEST 3.5

Name .... Date ....

The Pup and the Tent

Mum and dad had a camp next to the pond. The twins, Ben and Bob, helped set up the tent. Fred, the pup, sniffed the grass and the plants. When Dad held up the tent, the pup tugged at his pants.

'Stop it Fred', Dad said. 'That pup is a pest!' he said to Ben and Bob.

Just then a frog hopped past. Fred ran after it. One big jump and the frog landed on top of the tent. The pup jumped on a stump next to the tent. He yapped and yelped at the frog. Then ... one big jump and Fred landed on top of the tent too!

'Get off that tent!' Dad yelled. The twins yelled too. The tent fell on top of them. Fred, the pup, jumped off the tent and ran after the frog. Dad and the twins got out of the tent.

'Let me get my hands on that pup!' Dad said.
'Let us get our hands on that pup!' the twins said.
Mum just grinned and helped to lift the tent. And Fred the pup?
He yapped and yelped as he ran after the frog.

Answer the questions with the exact words from the story.

1. The pup tugged at Dad's pants.
2. A frog hopped past.
3. The frog landed on top of the tent.
4. The tent fell on top of Dad and the twins.
5. Dad said, 'Let me get my hands on that pup!'

5

28 © 2000 H.A. Calder and Pascal Press

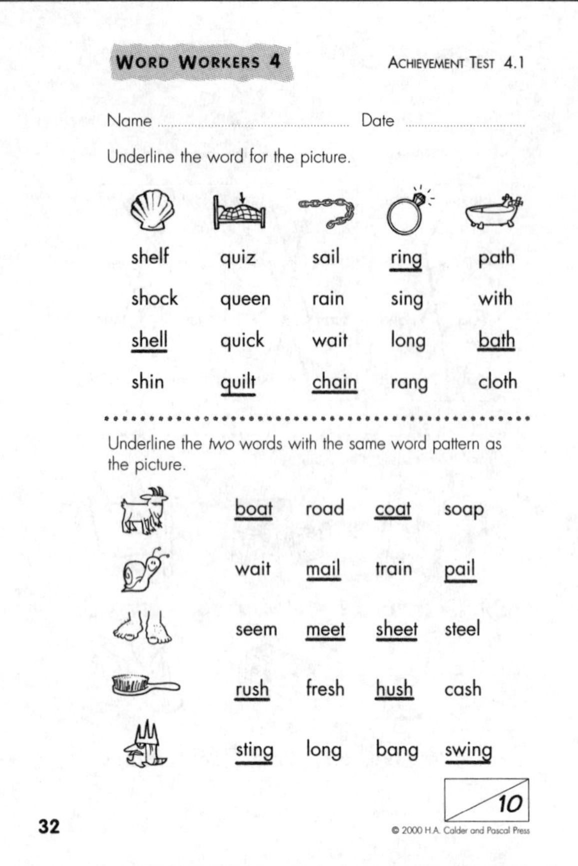

WORD WORKERS 4 — ACHIEVEMENT TEST 4.1

Name .... Date ....

Underline the word for the picture.

shelf	quiz	sail	<u>ring</u>	path
shock	queen	rain	sing	with
<u>shell</u>	quick	wait	long	<u>bath</u>
shin	<u>quilt</u>	<u>chain</u>	rang	cloth

Underline the *two* words with the same word pattern as the picture.

<u>boat</u>	road	<u>coat</u>	soap
wait	<u>mail</u>	train	<u>pail</u>
seem	<u>meet</u>	<u>sheet</u>	steel
<u>rush</u>	fresh	<u>hush</u>	cash
<u>sting</u>	long	bang	<u>swing</u>

/10

32

© 2000 H.A. Calder and Pascal Press

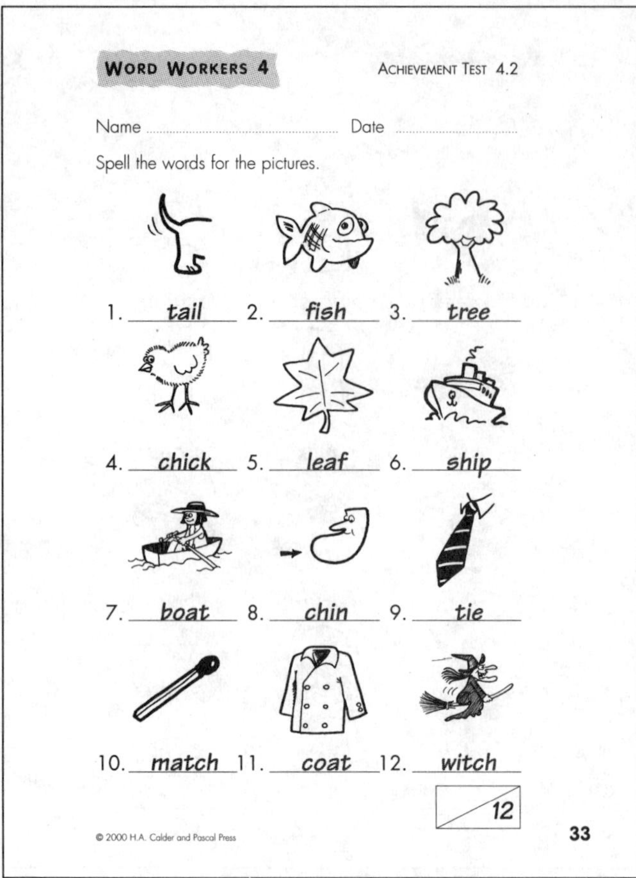

WORD WORKERS 4 — ACHIEVEMENT TEST 4.2

Name .... Date ....

Spell the words for the pictures.

1. tail 2. fish 3. tree
4. chick 5. leaf 6. ship
7. boat 8. chin 9. tie
10. match 11. coat 12. witch

/12

© 2000 H.A. Calder and Pascal Press

33

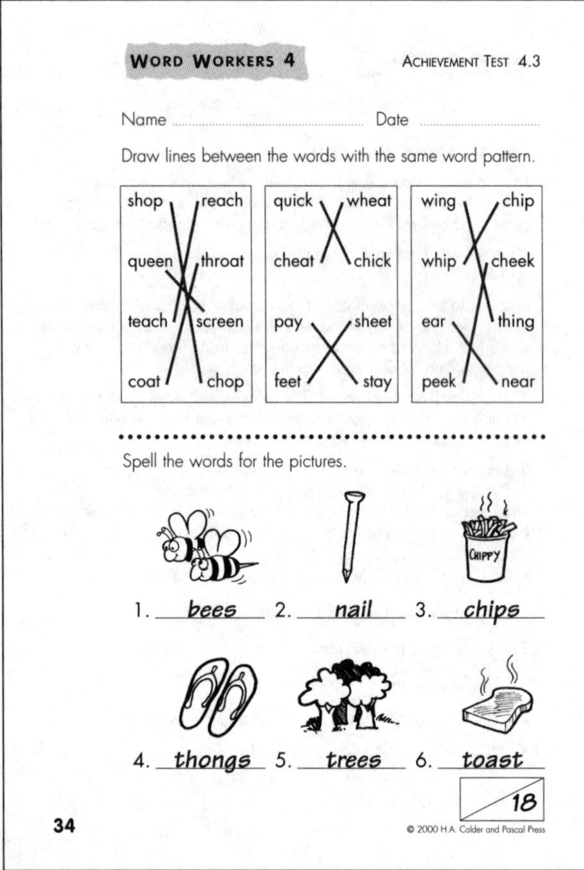

WORD WORKERS 4 — ACHIEVEMENT TEST 4.3

Name .... Date ....

Draw lines between the words with the same word pattern.

shop	reach	quick	wheat	wing	chip
queen	throat	cheat	chick	whip	cheek
teach	screen	pay	sheet	ear	thing
coat	chop	feet	stay	peek	near

Spell the words for the pictures.

1. bees 2. nail 3. chips
4. thongs 5. trees 6. toast

/18

34

© 2000 H.A. Calder and Pascal Press

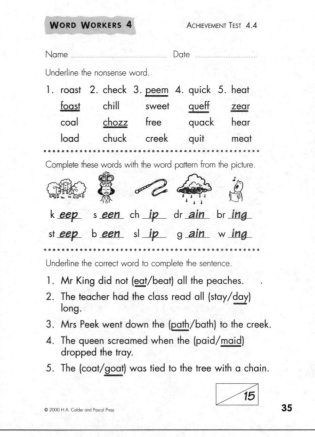

WORD WORKERS 4 — ACHIEVEMENT TEST 4.4

Name .... Date ....

Underline the nonsense word.

1.	2.	3.	4.	5.
roast	check	<u>peem</u>	quick	heat
<u>foast</u>	chill	sweet	<u>queff</u>	<u>zear</u>
coal	<u>chozz</u>	free	quack	hear
load	chuck	creek	quit	meat

Complete these words with the word pattern from the picture.

k eep s een ch ip dr ain br ing

st eep b een sl ip g ain w ing

Underline the correct word to complete the sentence.

1. Mr King did not (<u>eat</u>/beat) all the peaches.
2. The teacher had the class read all (stay/<u>day</u>) long.
3. Mrs Peek went down the (<u>path</u>/bath) to the creek.
4. The queen screamed when the (paid/<u>maid</u>) dropped the tray.
5. The (coat/<u>goat</u>) was tied to the tree with a chain.

/15

35

WORD WORKERS 4 ACHIEVEMENT TEST 4.5

Answer the questions with the exact words from the story.

1. There was no *cream* for the queen's tea.
2. '*Crash*!' went the pot of tea.
3. The king was eating a *peach*.
4. The queen stamped her feet and *sprained* her toe.
5. The maid said the queen was a *pain* in the neck.

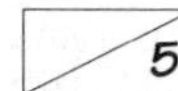

/5

 37

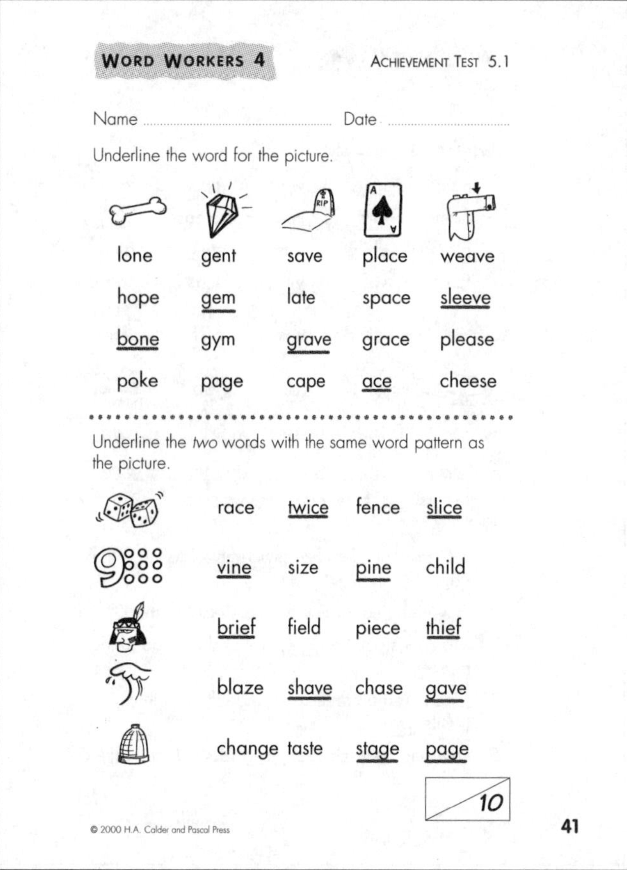

WORD WORKERS 4 ACHIEVEMENT TEST 5.1

Name .... Date ....

Underline the word for the picture.

lone	gent	save	place	weave
hope	gem	late	space	sleeve
bone	gym	grave	grace	please
poke	page	cape	ace	cheese

Underline the *two* words with the same word pattern as the picture.

race	twice	fence	slice
vine	size	pine	child
brief	field	piece	thief
blaze	shave	chase	gave
change	taste	stage	page

/10

 41

WORD WORKERS 4 ACHIEVEMENT TEST 5.2

Name .... Date ....

Spell the words for the pictures.

1. *cake* 2. *mice* 3. *bike*
4. *cry* 5. *snake* 6. *fence*
7. *five* 8. *stage* 9. *whale*
10. *nose* 11. *cave* 12. *rose*

/12

42

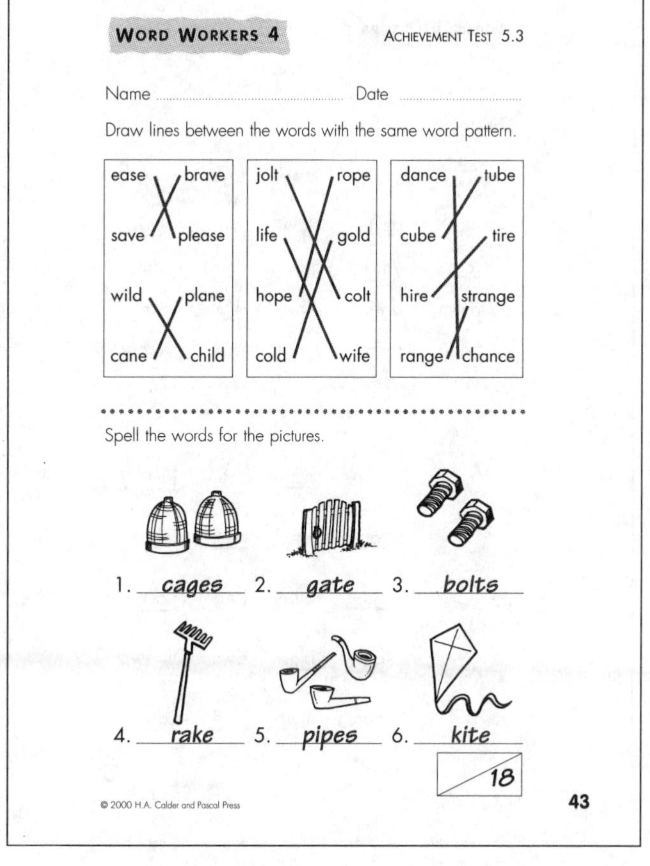

WORD WORKERS 4 ACHIEVEMENT TEST 5.3

Name .... Date ....

Draw lines between the words with the same word pattern.

ease	brave	jolt	rope	dance	tube
save	please	life	gold	cube	tire
wild	plane	hope	colt	hire	strange
cane	child	cold	wife	range	chance

Spell the words for the pictures.

1. *cages* 2. *gate* 3. *bolts*
4. *rake* 5. *pipes* 6. *kite*

/18

 43

WORD WORKERS 4 ACHIEVEMENT TEST 5.4

Name .... Date ....

Underline the nonsense word.

1. name	2. mild	3. white	4. ease	5. face
game	yild	kite	please	blace
plame	child	bite	mease	race
tame	wild	yite	tease	space

Complete these words with the word pattern from the picture.

tw ice   f ine   ch ose   sp y   st age

pr ice   w ine   p ose   cr y   c age

Underline the correct word to complete the sentence.

1. Mr Page told the child (twice/mice) to close the gate.
2. The thief tried to hide the stolen (cold/gold).
3. Mrs Jones put the (cake/wake) she made in the freezer.
4. Jane raked up the leaves and left them in a (while/pile).
5. Pete and Steve (faced/raced) down to the lake on their bikes.

15

44

WORD WORKERS 4 ACHIEVEMENT TEST 5.5

Nancy looked at the plate. Then she looked at Dave. She saw a grin on his face. 'You rat Dave,' she said. 'You ate *all* the cake mum made. I will tell her you told me a fib — a big, big fib. That cake was nice. It did not taste like old cheese. It did not taste like stale mince and not like fried mice!'

But Dave just smiled and rubbed his sides. 'I *really* like white cake,' he said, '... a nice piece of white cake.'

Answer the questions with the exact words from the story.

1. Nancy and Dave's mum left the cake on top of the stove .
2. Nancy said, 'I hate stale mince.'
3. Dave wiped his face with his sleeve.
4. Nancy said that Dave told her a big, big fib .
5. Dave said he really liked a nice piece of white cake .

5

46

WORD WORKERS 5 ACHIEVEMENT TEST 6.1

Name .... Date ....

Underline the word for the picture.

food	dart	blow	skirt	claw
roof	yard	grow	third	dawn
room	dark	bowl	first	saw
hoop	farm	crow	girl	crawl

Underline the *two* words with the same word pattern as the picture.

part	scar	snarl	jar
took	hood	look	foot
dark	barn	large	park
grow	blow	own	thrown
porch	more	stork	cork

10

50

WORD WORKERS 5 ACHIEVEMENT TEST 6.2

Name .... Date ....

Spell the words for the pictures.

1. foot 2. shirt 3. house

4. car 5. moon 6. snore

7. saw 8. arm 9. boil

10. church 11. crown 12. shorts

12

 51

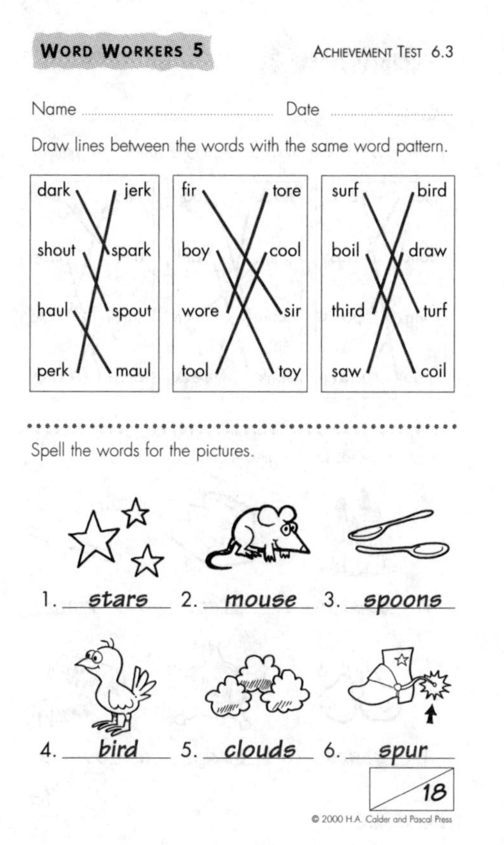
WORD WORKERS 5 ACHIEVEMENT TEST 6.3

Name .... Date ....

Draw lines between the words with the same word pattern.

dark	jerk	fir	tore	surf	bird
shout	spark	boy	cool	boil	draw
haul	spout	wore	sir	third	turf
perk	maul	tool	toy	saw	coil

Spell the words for the pictures.

1. stars 2. mouse 3. spoons

4. bird 5. clouds 6. spur

18

52 © 2000 H.A. Calder and Pascal Press

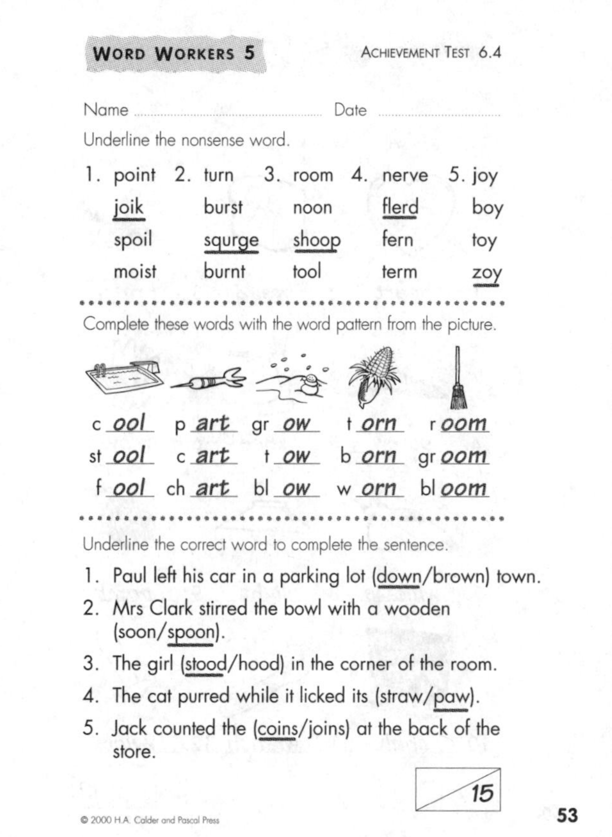
WORD WORKERS 5 ACHIEVEMENT TEST 6.4

Name .... Date ....

Underline the nonsense word.

1. point	2. turn	3. room	4. nerve	5. joy
joik	burst	noon	flerd	boy
spoil	squrge	shoop	fern	toy
moist	burnt	tool	term	zoy

Complete these words with the word pattern from the picture.

c ool	p art	gr ow	t orn	r oom
st ool	c art	t ow	b orn	gr oom
f ool	ch art	bl ow	w orn	bl oom

Underline the correct word to complete the sentence.

1. Paul left his car in a parking lot (down/brown) town.
2. Mrs Clark stirred the bowl with a wooden (soon/spoon).
3. The girl (stood/hood) in the corner of the room.
4. The cat purred while it licked its (straw/paw).
5. Jack counted the (coins/joins) at the back of the store.

15

© 2000 H.A. Calder and Pascal Press 53

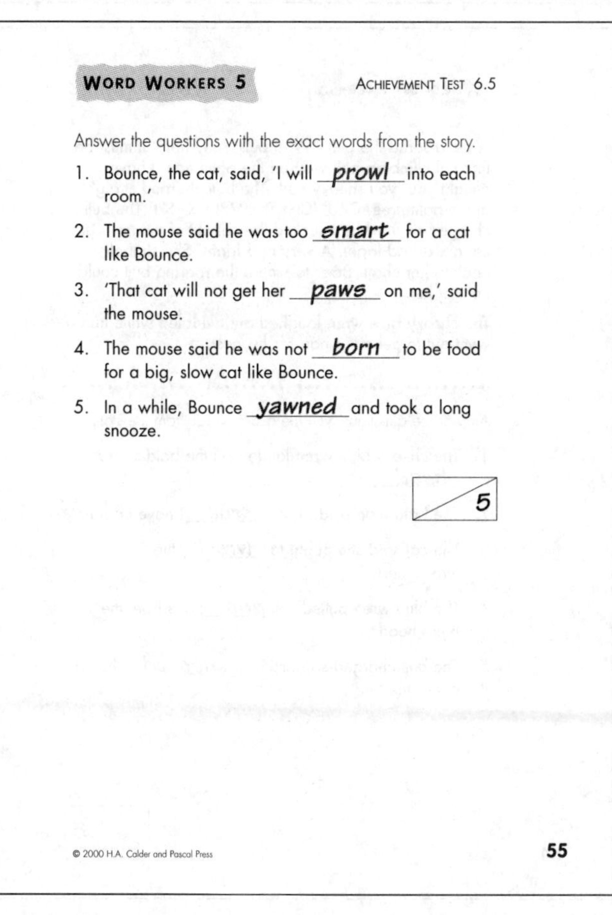
WORD WORKERS 5 ACHIEVEMENT TEST 6.5

Answer the questions with the exact words from the story.

1. Bounce, the cat, said, 'I will prowl into each room.'
2. The mouse said he was too smart for a cat like Bounce.
3. 'That cat will not get her paws on me,' said the mouse.
4. The mouse said he was not born to be food for a big, slow cat like Bounce.
5. In a while, Bounce yawned and took a long snooze.

5

© 2000 H.A. Calder and Pascal Press 55

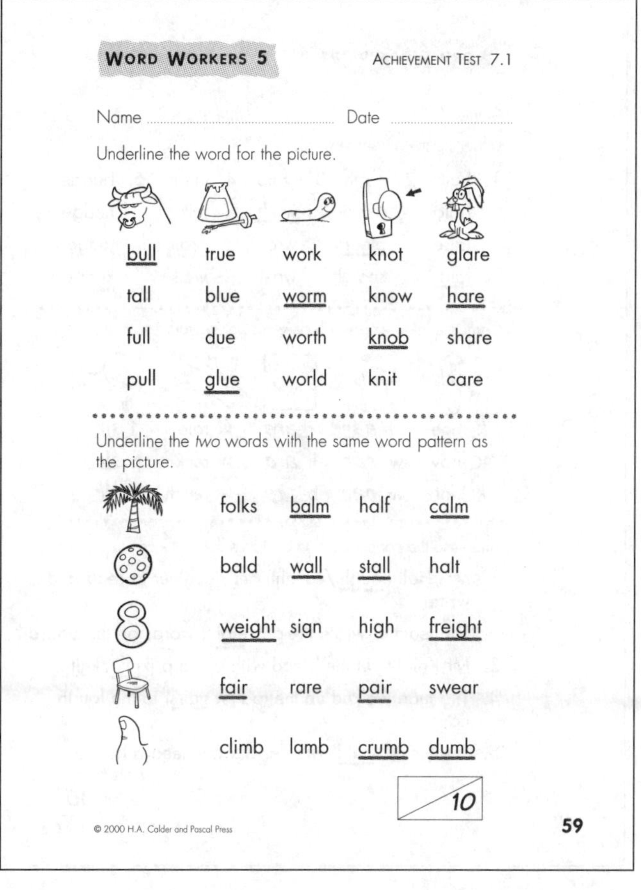
WORD WORKERS 5 ACHIEVEMENT TEST 7.1

Name .... Date ....

Underline the word for the picture.

bull	true	work	knot	glare
tall	blue	worm	know	hare
full	due	worth	knob	share
pull	glue	world	knit	care

Underline the *two* words with the same word pattern as the picture.

folks balm half calm

bald wall stall halt

8 weight sign high freight

fair rare pair swear

climb lamb crumb dumb

10

© 2000 H.A. Calder and Pascal Press 59

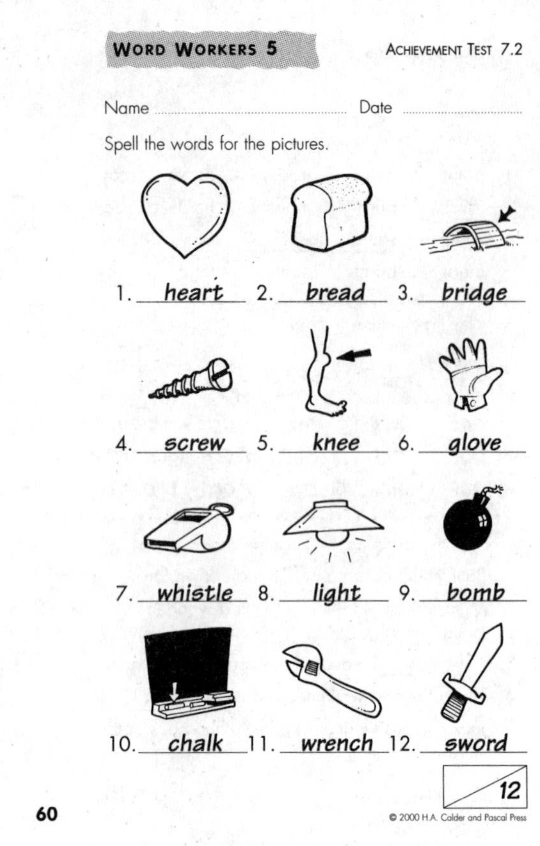

WORD WORKERS 5 ACHIEVEMENT TEST 7.2

Name .... Date ....

Spell the words for the pictures.

1. *heart* 2. *bread* 3. *bridge*

4. *screw* 5. *knee* 6. *glove*

7. *whistle* 8. *light* 9. *bomb*

10. *chalk* 11. *wrench* 12. *sword*

/12

60 © 2000 H.A. Calder and Pascal Press

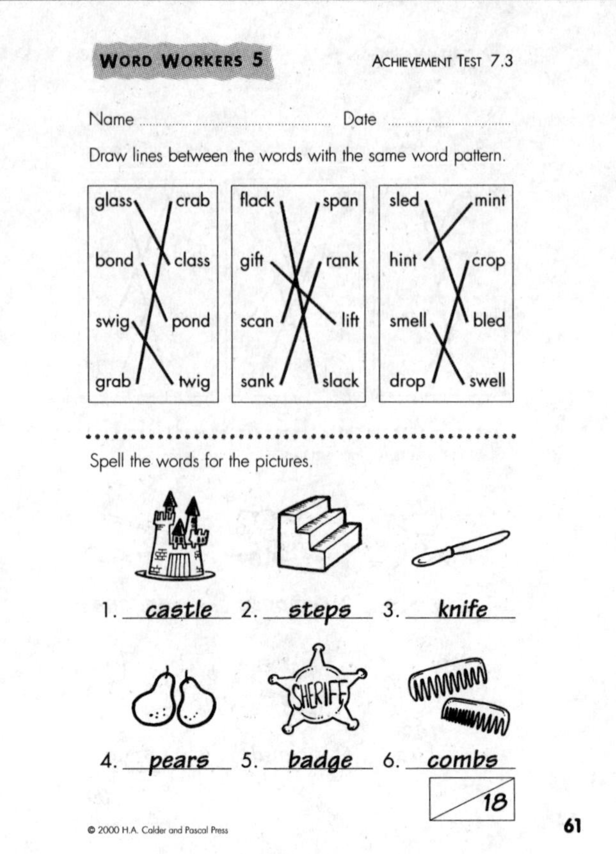

WORD WORKERS 5 ACHIEVEMENT TEST 7.3

Name .... Date ....

Draw lines between the words with the same word pattern.

glass	crab	flack	span	sled	mint
bond	class	gift	rank	hint	crop
swig	pond	scan	lift	smell	bled
grab	twig	sank	slack	drop	swell

Spell the words for the pictures.

1. *castle* 2. *steps* 3. *knife*

4. *pears* 5. *badge* 6. *combs*

/18

© 2000 H.A. Calder and Pascal Press 61

WORD WORKERS 5 ACHIEVEMENT TEST 7.4

Name .... Date ....

Underline the nonsense word.

1.	2.	3.	4.	5.
halt	earth	write	chalk	badge
bald	pearl	<u>wrelf</u>	talk	hedge
false	<u>bleam</u>	wrong	<u>pralk</u>	judge
<u>fald</u>	search	wrist	walk	<u>kudge</u>

Complete these words with the word pattern from the picture.

k nee	t *ear*	r *are*	*w* rote	f *air*
k now	sw *ear*	sh *are*	*w* reck	p *air*
k not	w *ear*	b *are*	*w* rench	ch *air*

Underline the correct word to complete the sentence.

1. Mrs Hall (<u>taught</u>/caught) her daughter to read and write.
2. The teacher wrote (freight/<u>eight</u>) words on the board.
3. Mr Knight cut the bread with a sharp (<u>knife</u>/knit).
4. The man walked up the (pairs/<u>stairs</u>) to the fourth floor.
5. The (scald/<u>bald</u>) wrestler did not need a hair cut.

/15

62 © 2000 H.A. Calder and Pascal Press

WORD WORKERS 5 ACHIEVEMENT TEST 7.5

'Yike,' roared the bull. 'Who pulled my hair? It must be that cat climbing half way up the palm tree. I have caught you, you sneaky cat!' The bull charged straight at the palm tree. CRUNCH! THUMP! CRASH! The bull charged so hard he knocked the cat out of the tree. The cat got a bad fright. A *very* bad fright! She shot off, back to her chair. Back to where the roaring bull could not get her.

The cheeky blue wren laughed and whistled while he went out to get more hair for his nest.

Answer the questions with the exact words from the story.

1. The cheeky blue wren landed on the bald man's *head* .
2. The bald man said, 'It is *true* I have no hair.'
3. The cat said she ought to *wreck* the wren's nest.
4. The blue wren pulled *eight* hairs from the bull's head.
5. The bull charged so hard he *knocked* the cat out of the tree.

/5

64 © 2000 H.A. Calder and Pascal Press

WORD WORKERS 6 ACHIEVEMENT TEST 8.1

Name .... Date ....

Divide these compound words.

1. sunshine	sun shine	8. highway	high way
2. cowboy	cow boy	9. weekend	week end
3. doorknob	door knob	10. barnyard	barn yard
4. armchair	arm chair	11. homework	home work
5. handsome	hand some	12. outside	out side
6. seagull	sea gull	13. fireman	fire man
7. fireplace	fire place	14. something	some thing

Use the pictures to help you spell these words.

1. (picture) + light = moonlight
2. farm + (picture) = farmhouse
3. race + (picture) = racehorse
4. 4 + get = forget
5. tea + (picture) = teaspoon
6. (picture) + chair = armchair

20

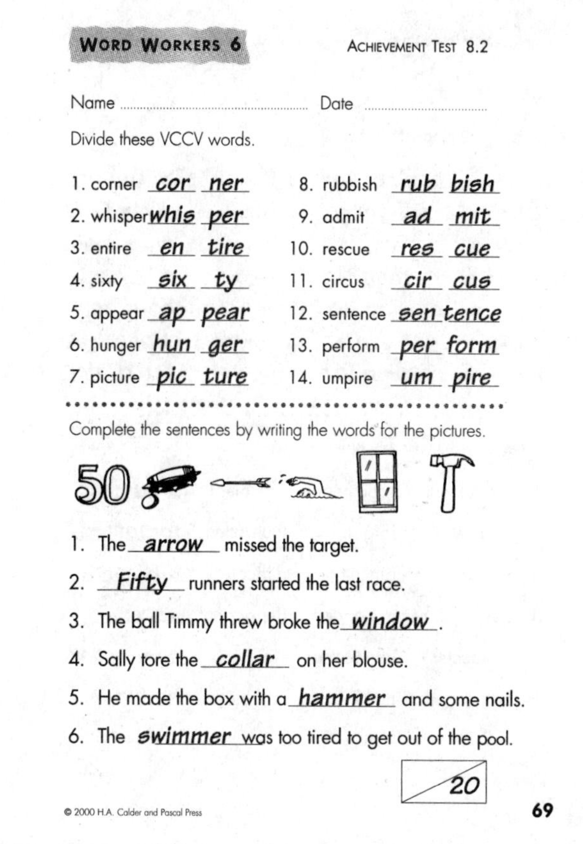

WORD WORKERS 6 ACHIEVEMENT TEST 8.2

Name .... Date ....

Divide these VCCV words.

1. corner	cor ner	8. rubbish	rub bish
2. whisper	whis per	9. admit	ad mit
3. entire	en tire	10. rescue	res cue
4. sixty	six ty	11. circus	cir cus
5. appear	ap pear	12. sentence	sen tence
6. hunger	hun ger	13. perform	per form
7. picture	pic ture	14. umpire	um pire

Complete the sentences by writing the words for the pictures.

50

1. The arrow missed the target.
2. Fifty runners started the last race.
3. The ball Timmy threw broke the window.
4. Sally tore the collar on her blouse.
5. He made the box with a hammer and some nails.
6. The swimmer was too tired to get out of the pool.

20

WORD WORKERS 6 ACHIEVEMENT TEST 8.3

Name .... Date ....

Divide these VCV words.

1. minus	mi nus	8. recess	re cess
2. decide	de cide	9. stupid	stu pid
3. fever	fe ver	10. finish	fi nish
4. promote	pro mote	11. season	sea son
5. defeat	de feat	12. before	be fore
6. direct	di rect	13. digest	di gest
7. music	mu sic	14. legal	le gal

Number the words in the box in alphabetical order, then answer the questions.

4 female	2 behave	5 halo
6 holy	3 delight	1 begin

1. Which word comes *before* 'holy'? halo
2. Which word comes *after* 'begin'? behave
3. Which word comes *before* 'female'? delight
4. Which word comes *before* 'behave'? begin
5. Which word comes *after* 'delight'? female
6. Which word comes *after* 'halo'? holy

20

WORD WORKERS 6 ACHIEVEMENT TEST 8.4

Name .... Date ....

Divide these –le ending words.

1. thimble	thim ble	8. drizzle	driz zle
2. single	sin gle	9. juggle	jug gle
3. gentle	gen tle	10. purple	pur ple
4. candle	can dle	11. twinkle	twin kle
5. puzzle	puz zle	12. gamble	gam ble
6. stumble	stum ble	13. fable	fa ble
7. castle	cas tle	14. buckle	buc kle

Complete these sentences with the words from the box.

table	circle	cradle
simple	maple	handle

1. We sat under the maple tree and ate our lunch.
2. Mum broke the handle off the kettle.
3. Each night I set the table before dinner.
4. The baby slept in its cradle .
5. Kate drew a circle on the paper.
6. Brad told his teacher that the test was too simple.

20

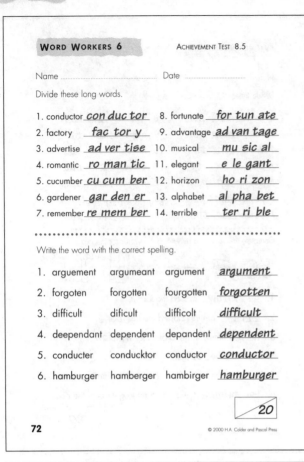

WORD WORKERS 6 — ACHIEVEMENT TEST 8.5

Name .... Date ....

Divide these long words.

1. conductor con duc tor
2. factory fac tor y
3. advertise ad ver tise
4. romantic ro man tic
5. cucumber cu cum ber
6. gardener gar den er
7. remember re mem ber
8. fortunate for tun ate
9. advantage ad van tage
10. musical mu sic al
11. elegant e le gant
12. horizon ho ri zon
13. alphabet al pha bet
14. terrible ter ri ble

Write the word with the correct spelling.

1.	arguement	argumeant	argument	argument
2.	forgoten	forgotten	fourgotten	forgotten
3.	difficult	dificult	difficolt	difficult
4.	deependant	dependent	depandent	dependent
5.	conducter	conducktor	conductor	conductor
6.	hamburger	hamberger	hambirger	hamburger

/20

72 © 2000 H.A. Calder and Pascal Press

WORD WORKERS 7 — ACHIEVEMENT TEST 9.1

Name .... Date ....

Divide these words into prefix and base word.

1.	remind	re	mind
2.	extinct	ex	tinct
3.	uneasy	un	easy
4.	replace	re	place
5.	exclaim	ex	claim

Divide these words into base word and suffix.

1.	peaceful	peace	ful
2.	assistance	assist	ance
3.	dampness	damp	ness
4.	importance	import	ance
5.	brightness	bright	ness

/10

© 2000 H.A. Calder and Pascal Press 75

WORD WORKERS 7 — ACHIEVEMENT TEST 9.2

Name .... Date ....

Divide these words into prefix, base word and suffix.

1.	reluctance	re	luct	ance
2.	regretful	re	gret	ful
3.	unfairness	un	fair	ness
4.	exactness	ex	act	ness
5.	resistance	re	sist	ance

Write the word with the correct spelling.

1.	dangerus	dangerous	dangrous	dangerous
2.	expectence	expactance	expectance	expectance
3.	cleerance	clearance	clearence	clearance
4.	wishful	wishfull	wisful	wishful
5.	uneazy	uneesy	uneasy	uneasy

/10

76 © 2000 H.A. Calder and Pascal Press

WORD WORKERS 7 — ACHIEVEMENT TEST 9.3

Name .... Date ....

Divide these words into prefix and base word.

1.	define	de	fine
2.	compare	com	pare
3.	enquire	en	quire
4.	destroy	de	stroy
5.	enlarge	en	large

Divide these words into base word and suffix.

1.	nervous	nerv	ous
2.	placement	place	ment
3.	action	ac	tion
4.	poisonous	poison	ous
5.	position	pos	ition

/10

© 2000 H.A. Calder and Pascal Press 77

WORD WORKERS 7 ACHIEVEMENT TEST 9.4

Name .... Date ....

Divide these words into prefix, base word and suffix.

1. destruction de struc tion
2. engagement en gage ment
3. commitment com mit ment
4. deformation de form ation
5. enjoyment en joy ment

Underline the correct word to complete the sentence.

1. Mum and dad took us away on a (station/vacation) last year.
2. Did you (enjoy/enforce) your trip to the beach?
3. Our teacher taught us how to find a word's (description/definition).
4. The (enrichment/enforcement) of the law is up to the police force.
5. The swimmers were very (glorious/nervous) before the start of the race.

10

78

WORD WORKERS 7 ACHIEVEMENT TEST 9.5

Name .... Date ....

Divide these words into prefix and base word.

1. prevent pre vent
2. believe be lieve
3. control con trol
4. increase in crease
5. prepare pre pare

Divide these words into base word and suffix.

1. central centr al
2. workable work able
3. vacant vac ant
4. different differ ent
5. special speci al

10

79

WORD WORKERS 7 ACHIEVEMENT TEST 9.6

Name .... Date ....

Divide these words into prefix, base word and suffix.

1. contestant con test ant
2. president pre sid ent
3. incurable in cur able
4. betrayal be tray al
5. predictable pre dict able

Number the words in the box in alphabetical order then answer the questions.

5 consonant 3 believable 4 claimant
1 accident 2 behave

1. Which word comes *before* 'behave'? accident
2. Which word comes *before* 'consonant'? claimant
3. Which word comes *after* 'accident'? behave
4. Which word comes *after* 'claimant'? consonant
5. Which word comes *after* 'behave'? believable

10

80

WORD WORKERS 7 ACHIEVEMENT TEST 9.7

Name .... Date ....

Divide these words into prefix and base word.

1. direct di rect
2. advance ad vance
3. displace dis place
4. promote pro mote
5. digest di gest

Divide these words into base word and suffix.

1. terrible terr ible
2. mature mat ure
3. attentive attent ive
4. damage dam age
5. pleasure pleas ure

10

81

WORD WORKERS 7 ACHIEVEMENT TEST 9.8

Name .... Date ....

Divide these words into prefix, base word and suffix.

1. productive *pro* *duct* *ive*
2. adventure *ad* *vent* *ure*
3. disclosure *dis* *clos* *ure*
4. directive *di* *rect* *ive*
5. advantage *ad* *vant* *age*

Complete the sentences with the words from the box.

profit	address	displeasure	damage
talkative	adjust	pressure	protective

1. The teacher frowned at the class to show her *displeasure*.
2. The men in the factory wore *protective* clothing.
3. The storm caused severe *damage* to our house.
4. The *talkative* students were kept in after class.
5. Did you write the correct *address* on the letter?

/10

82

WORD WORKERS 7 ACHIEVEMENT TEST 9.9

Name .... Date ....

Write the correct contractions for these words.

1. who would *who'd*
2. had not *hadn't*
3. I have *I've*
4. they are *they're*
5. they have *they've*

Write the correct contractions for these words.

1. Where did you put my work boots? *Where'd*
2. I am going to mow the lawn after school. *I'm*
3. We did not hear the car's horn. *didn't*
4. The black dog would not stop barking. *wouldn't*
5. They had better get home before dark. *They'd*

/10

83

WORD WORKERS 7 ACHIEVEMENT TEST 9.10

Name .... Date ....

Write the correct words for these contractions.

1. it'll *it* *will*
2. shouldn't *should* *not*
3. what's *what* *is*
4. they've *they* *have*
5. we're *we* *are*

Write the correct words for these contractions.

1. Who's coming to the beach with us? *Who* *is*
2. What's the score in the football match? *What* *is*
3. Mark isn't coming with us today. *is* *not*
4. It looks like it's going to rain soon. *it* *is*
5. Didn't you do your homework last night? *Did* *not*

/10

84